THE INSECTS

Readings from
SCIENTIFIC AMERICAN

THE INSECTS

Selected and Introduced by
Thomas Eisner
Cornell University

Edward O. Wilson
Harvard University

W. H. Freeman and Company
San Francisco

Cover: The fruit fly *Drosophila melanogaster.* Scanning electronmicrograph of a fly immobilized in flight by sudden freezing at $-160°C$. (By Thomas Eisner.)

Most of the *Scientific American* articles in THE INSECTS are available as separate Offprints. For a complete list of more than 1,000 articles now available as Offprints, write to W. H. Freeman and Company, 660 Market Street, San Francisco, CA 94104.

Library of Congress Cataloging in Publication Data

Main entry under title:

The Insects.

   Bibliography: p.
   Includes index.
   1. Insects—Addresses, essays, lectures.   I. Eisner, Thomas, 1929–   II. Wilson, Edward Osborne, 1929–
III. Scientific American.
QL463.I74   595.7′008   77–23843
ISBN 0–7167–0047–6
ISBN 0–7167–0046–8 pbk.

Printed in the United States of America

9 8 7 6 5 4 3 2 1

PREFACE

The time is overdue to recognize that insects are objects of importance to all biologists and not just to entomologists and agricultural experts. Our chief aim in preparing this anthology of *Scientific American* articles was to advance this recognition. Consider first that insects are the ecologically dominant animals on the land. Ornithologists cannot account for birds without reference to the insects the birds eat; and botanists cannot begin to understand terrestrial plants without an account of these little animals that constitute their most diversified and efficient herbivores. The coevolution of the more than one million insect species with their parasites, predators, symbionts, and prey is the most intricate and delicate among the land animals. Take away the insects and terrestrial ecosystems would become empty shells within a year.

An implicit but well-developed theme in fully half the articles in this collection is that insects are ideal model systems for most basic research. Many of their receptors are single-celled and sit exposed on the cuticular surface, so that microelectrodes may be inserted directly in the intact animal. The chemicals and chemoreceptors used in insect communication are far simpler than those in comparable vertebrate systems. The brains of insects have fewer cells by at least five orders of magnitude than those of vertebrates, yet their behavior patterns are in many cases equally complex. These patterns are also far more stereotyped and predictable and under the control of fewer cellular elements than in vertebrates, a favorable condition increasingly being exploited by neurobiologists and behaviorists. A total understanding of insect behavior, to the extent that such is theoretically possible, seems more nearly within our grasp than is the case for vertebrate behavior. Yet many of the underlying principles promise to be the same. Because insects go through rigid programs of development, often controlled by a surprisingly small number of stimuli from the external environment, many key questions in developmental biology—the nature of the biological clock, the control of cellular differentiation, the mechanisms of hormone action, and others—appear more tractable through experimental studies of insects.

We therefore recommend this collection of *Scientific American* articles to the widest possible audience of biologists and students of biology. Opportunities for fundamental research abound, and in the years to come a knowledge of entomology promises to be increasingly useful as a background for understanding the basic principles of biology.

Thomas Eisner

Edward O. Wilson

CONTENTS

General Introduction: The Conquerors of the Land   2

I   THE KEYS TO SUCCESS: ANATOMY AND PHYSIOLOGY

		Introduction 19
HINTON	1	Insect Eggshells 22
WILLIAMS	2	Insect Breathing 30
WEIS-FOGH	3	The Flight of Locusts 35
SMITH	4	The Flight Muscles of Insects 41
WIGGLESWORTH	5	Metamorphosis and Differentiation 50
WILLIAMS	6	The Juvenile Hormone 57
SAUNDERS	7	The Biological Clock of Insects 63
JONES	8	The Sexual Life of a Mosquito 71

II   THE KEYS TO SUCCESS: NEUROBIOLOGY AND BEHAVIOR

		Introduction 80
SCHNEIDER	9	The Sex-Attractant Receptor of Moths 84
WILSON	10	Pheromones 92
BENTLEY AND HOY	11	The Neurobiology of Cricket Song 102
VAN DER KLOOT	12	Brains and Cocoons 113
BENZER	13	Genetic Dissection of Behavior 118
WILSON	14	The Flight-Control System of the Locust 132
WEHNER	15	Polarized-Light Navigation by Insects 140
ROEDER	16	Moths and Ultrasound 150

III   PROCESSES OF EVOLUTION AND ECOLOGY

		Introduction 161
BISHOP AND COOK	17	Moths, Melanism, and Clean Air 164
TINBERGEN	18	Defense by Color 173
BENNET-CLARK AND EWING	19	The Love Song of the Fruit Fly 181
JOHNSON	20	The Aerial Migration of Insects 188
EHRLICH AND RAVEN	21	Butterflies and Plants 195
BATRA AND BATRA	22	The Fungus Gardens of Insects 203
HEINRICH	23	The Energetics of the Bumblebee 211

IV A DIVERSITY OF LIFE STYLES

			Introduction 220
ROTHSCHILD	24		Fleas 223
EVANS	25		Predatory Wasps 233
VON FRISCH	26		Dialects in the Language of the Bees 241
TOPOFF	27		The Social Behavior of Army Ants 247
WILSON	28		Slavery in Ants 257
HÖLLDOBLER	29		Communication Between Ants and Their Guests 263
LÜSCHER	30		Air-Conditioned Termite Nests 271

V INSECTS AND MANKIND

			Introduction 281
ALVARADO AND BRUCE-CHWATT	31		Malaria 284
SMITH AND ALLEN	32		Insect Control and the Balance of Nature 296
WILLIAMS	33		Third-Generation Pesticides 301
KNIPLING	34		The Eradication of the Screw-Worm Fly 306
WATERHOUSE	35		The Biological Control of Dung 315
			Bibliographies 323
			Index 329

Note on cross-references: References to articles included in this book are noted by the title of the article and the page on which it begins; references to articles that are available as Offprints, but are not included here, are noted by the article's title and Offprint number; references to articles published by SCIENTIFIC AMERICAN, but which are not available as Offprints, are noted by the title of the article and the month and year of its publication.

THE INSECTS

GENERAL INTRODUCTION: THE CONQUERORS OF THE LAND

GENERAL INTRODUCTION:
THE CONQUERORS OF THE LAND

Whether fully aware of it or not, we human beings are immersed in a world of insects. In every habitable part of the world, throughout the warm season, insects tirelessly flit past our heads, watch us from every bush and tree, and mine the earth beneath our feet. Their populations are so large as to defy imagination. The British entomologist C. B. Williams has estimated that 10^{18} (a billion billion, to the nearest order of magnitude) are alive at every instant. This means over 200 million for each human being and about 10 billion for every square kilometer of land surface. The insects are also more diverse than all of the rest of the Animal Kingdom combined (see Figure 1). Estimates of the numbers of species vary from one to 10 million. There is no way to make a more precise count, since most entomologists agree that the majority of species remain unknown to science. It always comes as a surprise to biology students to learn that Coleoptera are first among the foremost, as Figure 1 shows so clearly. The great British biologist J. B. S. Haldane was once asked his opinion of God's design as revealed by organic evolution. His answer: an inordinate fondness for beetles.

In a strictly ecological sense, insects all but own the land. They are above all the leading consumers of plants. We perceive this generalization from the simple circumstance that some insects are *the* pests of agriculture everywhere in the world. Other insects serve as the chief predators of the plant-eaters, while still others variously decompose the humus, turn the soil, and serve as food for vertebrates. To use a somewhat technical metaphor from ecology, insects fill most of the middle links of the trophic net. If man somehow had both the power and was so shortsighted as to extirpate these little animals, the world as we know it would cease to exist. Man himself would probably become extinct.

How did one class (Insecta) of one phylum (Arthropoda) achieve such eminence? The answer could well be that the insects were the first small animals to colonize the land with full success. The first plants formed low carpets over the ground by Silurian times, some 400 million years ago. By the Carboniferous period, 100 million years later, they had given evolutionary rise to the great coal forests. The amphibians and the first of their immediate descendants, the reptiles, were also flourishing by Carboniferous times. It was into this world, virtually a new planet ready for ecological conquest, that the first insects gained a secure foothold. By late Carboniferous times a wide diversity of insects were present, some of them already powerful fliers. The pace of their early evolution was prodigious. By the Permian period, closing the Paleozoic era, various groups had completed virtually every major step in their evolution that is still evident today: the origin of wings, the capacity to fold the wings over the body permitting travel through narrow spaces in

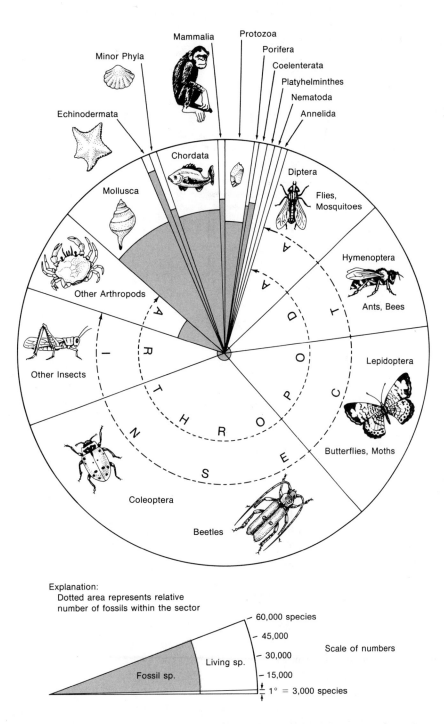

Mammalia
Minor Phyla
Echinodermata
Protozoa
Porifera
Coelenterata
Platyhelminthes
Nematoda
Annelida
Chordata
Mollusca
Diptera
Flies, Mosquitoes
Hymenoptera
Ants, Bees
Other Arthropods
Lepidoptera
Other Insects
Butterflies, Moths
Coleoptera
Beetles

A R T H R O P O D A   I N S E C T A

Explanation:
Dotted area represents relative
number of fossils within the sector

60,000 species
45,000
30,000
15,000
$\frac{1}{2}$ 1° = 3,000 species

Scale of numbers

Fossil sp.
Living sp.

Figure 1. Pie diagram of the relative numbers of living species belonging to the major taxonomic groups of animals. The diagram reveals the great diversity of insects, particularly of the beetles (Coleoptera), flies (Diptera), wasps and related forms (Hymenoptera), and moths and butterflies (Lepidoptera). Although the estimates of absolute numbers were made in 1953, and hence are somewhat out of date, the proportional representation of the major groups remains about the same. (From "The Relative Number of Living and Fossil Species of Animals," S. W. Muller and Alison Campbell, *Systematic Zoology,* 3(4):168-170.)

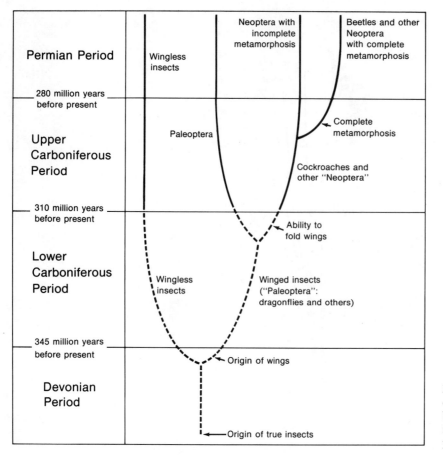

Figure 2. The most crucial events of insect evolution, represented in this diagram, had been completed by the end of the Carboniferous period, approximately 300 million years ago.

vegetation and the soil, and complete metamorphosis from egg to larva to pupa to adult (see Figure 2). Living orders of insects still display the various steps in this evolutionary sequence. Silverfish (Order Thysanura) are one of the few groups remaining in the primitive flightless condition. Dragonflies (Order Odonata) possess fully developed wings, but these appendages cannot be folded during rest and must be held in a permanently outstretched position —the state of the first winged insects of the Carboniferous (see Figure 3). Cockroaches (Order Blattodea) can fold their wings over their backs, allowing them to escape into holes and cracks; but while young they must grow the wings in external pads on the body surface, through a series of steps called incomplete (or gradual) metamorphosis. Finally, beetles (Order Coleoptera) not only can fold their wings, but they grow them internally and all within the single pupal stage.

Professor Frank M. Carpenter of Harvard University, a leading authority on insect evolution, has pointed out that all of the insect orders just listed were flourishing by the beginning of the Permian period, along with an array of other groups now extinct. The diversity of insects in those distant times, over 200 million years ago, was comparable to what it is today. Perhaps this unbroken history of success is not so surprising. Vertebrates have held sway on the land since Paleozoic times through dynastic successions of amphibians, reptiles, birds, and mammals. Insects have done the same, but their small size opened many more ecological niches to them and permitted a far greater diversification of major groups. They have taken over all niches where at most only a scattering of mollusks and annelids manage a weak coexistence and where coelenterates, bryozoans, echinoderms, and most of the other kinds of water-dwelling invertebrates have utterly failed to penetrate.

Figure 3. An Upper Carboniferous insect fossil of the extinct order Megasecoptera. The insect fauna of 300 million years ago was as diversified, and in most basic aspects as evolutionarily advanced, as the fauna of today. The creature shown here, *Mischoptera nigra*, was about as large as a modern, good-sized dragonfly. It possessed grasping forelegs and sucking mouthparts, but we can only guess at its food habits. (Courtesy Frank M. Carpenter, Harvard University.)

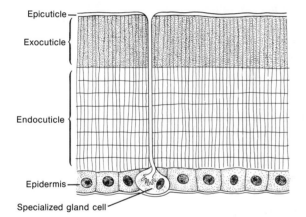

Epicuticle
Exocuticle
Endocuticle
Epidermis
Specialized gland cell

Figure 4. Diagram of a section through the insect integument. The waxy epicuticle provides much of the waterproofing. The exocuticle and endocuticle together comprise the so-called procuticle and are made up of chitin and protein. Strength is added to the integument as a whole when the protein of the exocuticle is hardened (and usually darkened) by the chemical process of tanning. The epidermis is responsible for secreting the cuticle. It commonly contains specialized gland cells that manufacture other products. Clusters of such cells form the integumental glands that secrete pheromones and defensive secretions. Not shown here are various types of sensory receptors, including mechanoreceptors and chemoreceptors, that are a characteristic part of the insect integument.

The early evolution of insects provides the perspective by which most of the facts of entomology can be gathered together and understood. We are aware that insects are exceptionally well adapted for terrestrial life. The question then arises as to the nature of this adaptation. What specific features of their anatomy, physiology, and behavior are the keys to their success? In the following discussion we will briefly characterize some of the most important and general of these traits.

The cuticle. The exoskeleton, comprised of an outer wall of cuticle and the underlying layer of epidermal cells that secrete the cuticle (Figure 4), is a necessary anatomical construction for life on the land. The reason follows a simple logic. Because insects are small they have a large surface-to-volume ratio. If the epidermis were exposed, the rate of water loss by the body (per gram of body weight) would be far greater than in vertebrates. The cuticle compensates for this difference. It forms a protective envelope that resists evaporation from the watery tissues within. The seal is further improved by the addition of a waxy outermost layer, the epicuticle.

Insects are able to move, often with amazing agility, because their exoskeleton is divided into segments that are joined by more flexible intersegmental membranes serving as hinges. In all insects, except a few that have been extremely modified by evolution, the segments are grouped into three major body parts. The head bears the mouthparts, the eyes, antennae, and some other sense organs, and it houses the chief processing center of the neural messages conveyed by the sense organs—the brain. The thorax is the loco-motory unit, bearing the three pairs of legs (each on its thoracic segment) and the wings, and containing the muscles that operate these appendages. The abdomen accommodates most of the viscera, including the reproductive organs, much of the digestive tract, and the excretory organs. Thus the typical insect has a more clearly linear body plan than the typical vertebrate. The orderly sequence of external body parts is the basis of the reference system used in studies of anatomy and classification (see Figure 5).

An exoskeleton also provides mechanical advantages for small animals such as insects. If insects had an endoskeleton like that of vertebrates, the bones of the appendages would be slender fragile rods that would easily snap from the intense strain placed on them by muscular contraction. A tubular casing provides an appendage with much greater rigidity than does an inner bone of equal weight.

The material that makes up much of the exoskeleton has remarkable chemical and mechanical properties of its own. This is chitin, a polysac-charide of high molecular weight, and the animal counterpart to cellulose. The chitin is infiltrated with a special protein called arthropodin. This sub-stance can be hardened and simultaneously darkened to variable degrees by tanning, a process of stabilization by the cross-linking of the protein molecules. It is quite common for the outer portion of the cuticle, the so-called exocuticle (see Figure 4), to be hardened and tanned. Resilin, another and more flexible protein, is found most frequently in hinges of the body where elasticity is a requirement.

The tracheae. Closely associated with the exoskeleton is the remarkable tracheal system by which the insect breathes. The insect does not inhale air into a single organ with a bellows-like movement of the body wall, in the vertebrate fashion. Instead, air flows into the body through a series of open-ings called spiracles, which lead inward into cuticle-lined tubes, or tracheae, that penetrate deeply into the tissues (see Figure 6). Each trachea divides and subdivides into branches whose microscopic terminal elements (called tracheoles) indent the individual cells to be serviced. Tracheae occur through-out the body but are most richly developed in wing muscles and wherever else oxygen is most in demand. Thus insects have opted for a direct system for delivering oxygen to the cells and do not rely on a fluid circulatory system to do the job, as vertebrates do. They were originally able to evolve in this direc-tion because their small body size permits a sufficiently rapid diffusional exchange of gases within the tracheae, and because the tracheae are so readily produced by a simple inward growth of the cuticular wall.

Metamorphosis. Not all of the features of an exoskeleton are advantageous. The growing insect is trapped like a knight in a suit of armor; it must somehow get out and obtain a larger suit in order to increase its size. Insects accomplish the change by the remarkable process of molting. As the time to molt ap-proaches, the individual becomes increasingly quiescent, its old cuticle is partially dissolved away from the inside, and a new, softer layer is deposited just underneath. When the dual process has been completed, the old "skin" is split and shed, and the insect expands within its more flexible new one. Full mobility is reattained when the new cuticle has been sufficiently hardened by tanning of the protein within it. In the great majority of insect species the molting process is repeated several times before individuals attain a mature size. Each episode requires temporary cessation of many basic activities, in-cluding feeding and the addition of dry weight. The molting insect is naturally

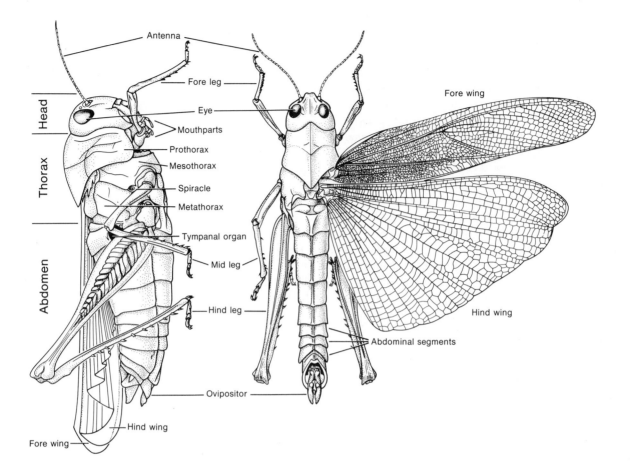

Figure 5. Major body parts of a grasshopper. The female, shown here, has an ovipositor at the rear of the abdomen. (After *The Insects of Australia*, D. F. Waterhouse, ed. Melbourne University Press, 1967).

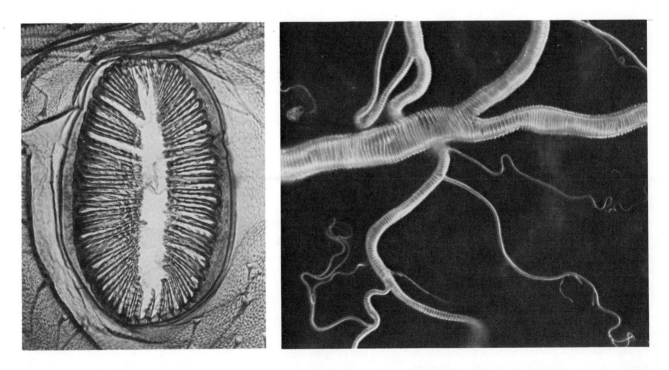

Figure 6. *Left:* Respiratory spiracle of a caterpillar. The opening is fringed with bristles that exclude unwanted particles and water. *Right:* Branched tracheae from the wall of the alimentary canal of a cockroach. (By T. Eisner, Cornell University.)

more vulnerable to predators during this time, and never so much as when it emerges soft and weak from its old exoskeleton (see Figure 7).

Cockroaches and other more primitive insects (those closer in anatomy to the Paleozoic ancestors) proceed from the egg to the adult stages by a succession of gradual changes achieved through a series of molts. Wings, for example, are grown in steps. The immature forms, or nymphs, have external wing pads that are neither long enough nor sufficiently muscled to serve in flight. At the final molt the wings attain their full length and the adult is ready to fly away. This process is called *incomplete metamorphosis*.

The great majority of insect species are programmed for the alternate, more advanced development called *complete metamorphosis*. Almost all growth occurs when the individual is a larva, such as a beetle grub, a fly maggot, or a moth caterpillar. The larva is a radically different creature from the sexually mature, usually winged adult. The metamorphosis between these two stages takes place entirely in the pupal stage. The pupa is simple in form and quiescent on the outside, but is intensely active biochemically on the inside, where larval tissues are dismantled and adult organs formed. It remains largely sealed off by an exceptionally rigid exoskeleton. Carbon dioxide continues to be replaced by oxygen through a functioning tracheal system, but there is no feeding and no elimination of wastes. Were the pupa to produce conventional nitrogenous wastes such as ammonia or urea, which are toxic and cannot be stored, it would inevitably die. But it produces uric acid, an insoluble waste that can be harmlessly stored in crystalline form until voided by the adult. Uric acid is the nitrogenous waste of insects generally, and not just of their pupae. In fact, the production of "dry urine," as it were, is to be viewed as a major adaptation to life on land, since it makes possible the elimination of nitrogenous wastes without loss of water.

Metamorphosis, whether complete or incomplete, contributes in an important way to the fitness of insects. The immature nymph (or larva) is an eating and growing machine. It lives wherever it can get the most food and does little else but feed. When it transforms into an adult it becomes more preoccupied with dispersal and reproduction—even, as in the case of mayflies and some moths, to the total exclusion of eating. Thus insects can live two lives, occupying two entirely different ecological niches. This last principle can be most clearly illustrated by an extreme example. The females of some parasitic wasp species drill through wood with their ovipositors to reach beetle larvae living inside. They then stab their ovipositors into the larvae and lay eggs. The eggs hatch into larvae that live as internal parasites, slowly consuming the tissues of their hosts. Finally, the young wasps pass through the pupal stage and hatch as adults. At this point they emerge from the permanent darkness of their tunnel homes to a wholly new world outside.

Wings. Most kinds of insects fly, most of the time, just in order to disperse. An observer looking out over a lawn or field on a warm day sees innumerable small insects flying up from the ground. They catch the wind and are carried along, often for long distances. These are aphids, leafhoppers, midges, beetles, and other small insects in the process of dispersing away from their birthplaces to search for new, richer grounds in which to breed. Other, usually larger forms also fly to capture prey. Virtually all kinds of insects, large and small, employ their wings to escape predators.

Paleopterous insects, such as dragonflies, which possess rigid, outstretched wings, are forced to remain in the open. A dragonfly can proceed only from perch to perch (see Figure 8). Its legs form a little basket for anchoring the body to twigs and grass blades as well as for enfolding insect prey. Neopterous insects, such as wasps and beetles, represent a more advanced evolutionary stage; they can fly as efficiently as the dragonfly but also alight on a tree or the ground, tightly fold their wings over their backs, and scuttle into holes and crevices (see Figure 8). The neopterous revolution was as profound in its

Figure 7. A cockroach nymph in the act of molting. The animal emerges soft and white from its old cuticle, which is still attached at its rear. (By T. Eisner, Cornell University.)

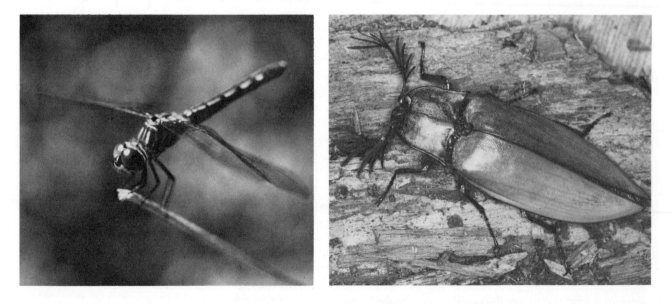

Figure 8. A paleopteran and a neopteran insect. The paleopteran dragonfly on the left can only hold its wings in an outstretched condition and is therefore forced to perch in the open. The neopteran elaterid beetle on the right can fold its wings over the abdomen and as a result is able to move about in narrower quarters. (By T. Eisner, Cornell University.)

effects as the invention of winged flight itself. The typical neopterous insect is a superb locomotory machine, as efficient in the air as on the land. Certain minute wasps are able to locomote on land and in water. In order to find the eggs of the aquatic insects they parasitize, they first fly down to the water surface, where they are able to walk about. They then plunge through the surface and swim by paddling movements of their wings.

Defense. Catching an insect by hand can be a hazardous proposition, as any naturalist knows. Insects can bite, sting, or eject noxious fluids, expedients which they employ with great effectiveness against predators. Were it not for the cuticular exoskeleton, such defenses might never have evolved in insects. The hard mandibles employed by many biting insects are essentially exoskeletal elaborations, as are the familiar stinging devices of bees and wasps. But even the common odoriferous or "stink" glands that insects use for discharge of repellents or irritants are cuticular derivatives. They are thin-walled sacs, produced by invagination of the body wall, and therefore are lined with an impervious cuticular membrane that provides appropriate insulation for the potent chemicals stored within the glands. Virtually every order of insect has some species with defensive glands of this sort, and their secretory capabilities are sometimes extraordinary. Ants commonly eject formic acid, a powerful irritant, which they produce at concentrations of 20 percent or higher. Certain Australian beetle larvae discharge a fluid that emits hydrogen cyanide, and some cockroaches, also from Australia, spray 2-ethyl acrolein, a tear gas. One of the most sophisticated defensive glands is possessed by certain beetles of the family Carabidae called "bombardiers." These animals discharge a spray containing quinones, which they can aim with great accuracy in virtually any direction (see Figure 9). The quinones are generated in an explosive oxidative reaction that occurs with considerable liberation of heat, so that the spray is ejected at the astonishingly high temperature of 100°C.

Aedeagus. Males in the winged orders of insects have an intromittant organ, essentially a penis, called the aedeagus. This seemingly ordinary device has the profound effect of freeing the species entirely from the water. Mating insects do not have to go to a pond or a stream just to release their eggs and spermatozoans. Nor do they have to engage in the elaborate procedure, practiced by primitive wingless insects, such as silverfish, and some other arthropods, of depositing the sperm in packets or spermotophores, which the females must then insert into their genital openings. The aedeagus makes it possible for insects to copulate and to transfer the sperm directly from male to female (see Figure 10). Insect copulation is sometimes completed in seconds, and may even be executed in flight. Thus, insects freed themselves from the aquatic environment by the same mating device that liberated reptiles, birds, and mammals. The aedeagus has been an important factor in allowing them to occupy all terrestrial habitats, from tundras to rain forests to deserts.

The aedeagi of male insects belonging to certain groups, including the wasps, moths, and flies, are often dismayingly complex in structure. They are furnished with strange arrays of spines, teeth, lobes, hooks, and hairs. Although entomologists exploit this peculiarity in a straightforward way by using the structures to distinguish and classify species, they have made little progress in understanding why such elaborate structures evolved in the first place. It is known that some of the organs are used as stimulating devices during courtship. In other species the grasping organs are used by the male to hold onto the female after insemination has been accomplished, a procedure that prevents other males from adding their sperm. Finally, entomologists are reasonably certain that the complex structures serve to isolate species from one another by acting as premating isolating mechanisms. If the aedeagus of a male can fit the aperture only of females of the same species, as a key might

When a bombardier beetle (*Stenaptinus insignis*) is pinched on a front leg by a pair of forceps, it discharges a hot (100°C) spray from the tip of the abdomen in that direction. A wire has been attached to the beetle's back with wax to hold it in place for photography. Defensive discharges are employed by many kinds of insects as an effective protection against predators. (By T. Eisner and D. J. Aneshansley, Cornell University.)

Figure 10. Copulating pair of grasshoppers (*Romalea microptera*). Intromission represents a major adaptation to life on land, since it provides for fertilization without exposure of sperm to air. (By T. Eisner, Cornell University.)

fit into a lock, this specificity alone will prevent cross-mating and the production of hybrids. It is also possible, therefore, that complex evolutionary changes in the male aedeagus serve as an important step in the formation of insect species. But the relative importance of this particular function, as opposed to that of the isolating role just cited, remains to be determined.

Mouthparts and feeding. The mouthparts of insects, like all of their body surface and many of their internal structures, are constructed of cuticle. As a result, these organs have the evolutionary potential of being projected outside the body and molded to serve one or another of a variety of feeding functions. Insects have realized virtually every conceivable possibility. Beetles have toothed jaws for cutting and shredding, mosquitoes slender stylets for piercing skin and sucking blood, assassin bugs dagger-like beaks for spearing and draining insect prey, butterflies delicate coiled tubes for siphoning nectar, and so on. No other group of organisms has developed such diversity in one organ as have the insects (see Figure 11). The adaptive radiation of the external mouthparts has been perhaps the single most important factor in the proliferation of insect species. The saturation by insects of virtually every possible feeding niche, going as far back as the Paleozoic era, must have been an important factor in the failure of other, water-dwelling groups to gain more than a foothold on the land. Ecologists define "closed communities" of species on a local scale as those so filled with various ecological representatives as to leave no room for other immigrants. The insects constitute a nearly closed community on a global scale.

Why are there so few marine insects? The dominance of insects on land is in sharp contrast to their mysterious near absence in the sea. The water strider *Halobates* is able to travel on water films far from land (see Figure 12). A variety of hemipterous bugs, beetles, and fly larvae have penetrated into the mud and pools of the intertidal zone. But not a single insect is to be found on the bottom in deeper water, in coral reefs, or among the underwater plankton of the open ocean. This nearly total ecological exclusion is a mystery to biologists. Insects are certainly capable of penetrating aquatic environments. Mayflies, caddisflies, midges, diving beetles, and many others dominate freshwater streams and ponds. So there is nothing inherent in the biology of insects that limits them to the dry land. Incompetence at salt excretion seems not to be a factor, because some insect larvae abound in salt lakes. The rougher water of the ocean might discourage insects. But even this limitation seems doubtful; many kinds of freshwater insect larvae have developed the ability to respire underwater and hence have no need to approach the more turbulent upper water layers during the larval stage.

Faced with the lack of any clearcut physiological explanation, some biologists have laid stress on an evolutionary hypothesis that complements the one developed to explain the preeminence of insects on land. This explanation holds that the marine invertebrates constitute a closed community in the sea. All of the major phyla of larger multicellular organisms, including the coelenterates, bryozoans, annelids, mollusks, arthropods (particularly the crustaceans), and echinoderms, were well developed by the Cambrian period 600 million years ago. By the time insects had been "invented" 200 million years later, the oceans had filled with life as diverse as that existing today, and the insects would have found no living space whatever in the sea. Whether this evolutionary explanation is correct, or whether some limiting physiological peculiarity of insects exists after all, remains an open subject for future research.

Figure 11. The success of insects is in large measure due to the diversification of their mouthparts and feeding habits. Some insects have chewing mouthparts, others suck fluids, and still others are adapted to pierce and suck. Four examples are shown here. *Upper left:* An ant (*Formica exsectoides*) is biting a sawfly larva with its powerful mandibles. *Upper right:* A butterfly (*Danaus chrysippus*) is imbibing nectar from a milkweed blossom with its long slender proboscis. *Lower left:* The pentatomid bug (*Stiretus anchora*) has impaled a chrysomelid beetle larva (*Chrysomela scripta*) on its beak, and is proceeding to suck out the body fluids of its prey. *Lower right:* The female horse fly (*Haematopota pluvialis*) is sucking human blood from a wound it made with its sharp dagger-like mandibles. (By T. Eisner, Cornell University.)

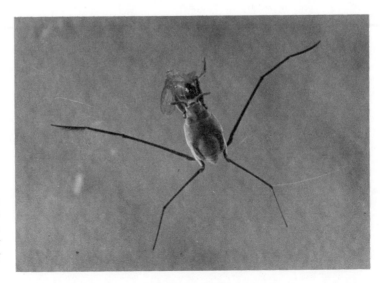

Figure 12. Waterstriders of the genus *Halobates* are among the few truly marine insects. This specimen, photographed in captivity, is feeding on a fruit fly. (Courtesy Larry D. Ford and Lanna Cheng, University of California, San Diego)

A simple classification of the Class Insecta (Phylum Arthropoda). Only the most abundant or evolutionarily important orders are listed (these are the groups given numbers). The Orders Ephemeroptera and Odonata are paleopterous; that is, they possess wings but cannot fold them over their backs. All other orders listed here are either primitively wingless or neopterous (wings can be folded over the back).

Subclass Apterygota (primitively wingless insects)
  1. Collembola (springtails; considered by many entomologists not to be true insects)
  2. Thysanura (silverfish and related forms)

Subclass Pterygota (winged and secondarily wingless insects)

Division Exopterygota (pterygote insects with gradual metamorphosis)
  3. Ephemeroptera (mayflies)
  4. Odonata (dragonflies and damselflies)
  5. Orthoptera (grasshoppers, crickets, and related forms)
  6. Blattodea (cockroaches)
  7. Isoptera (termites)
  8. Dermaptera (earwigs)
  9. Plecoptera (stoneflies)
  10. Psocoptera (booklice, barklice)
  11. Mallophaga (chewing lice)
  12. Anoplura (sucking lice)
  13. Thysanoptera (thrips)
  14. Hemiptera ("true" bugs: assassin bugs, water boatmen, water striders, stink bugs, and others)
  15. Homoptera (cicadas, whiteflies, aphids, scale insects, and related forms)

Division Endopterygota (pterygotes with complete metamorphosis)
  16. Neuroptera (antlions, lacewings, and related forms)
  17. Coleoptera (beetles)
  18. Mecoptera (scorpionflies)
  19. Trichoptera (caddisflies)
  20. Lepidoptera (butterflies and moths)
  21. Diptera (true flies)
  22. Siphonaptera (fleas)
  23. Hymenoptera (ants, bees, wasps)

SOME GENERAL BOOKS ON INSECTS

Borror, Donald J., Dwight M. DeLong, and Charles A. Triplehorn. 1976. *An Introduction to the Study of Insects,* fourth edition. Holt, Rinehart and Winston, New York. A comprehensive basic textbook of entomology. Includes good treatments of the various insect orders as represented by North American species.

Borror, Donald J., and Richard E. White. 1970. *A Field Guide to the Insects of America North of Mexico.* Houghton Mifflin, Boston. This book is up to the usual excellent standards of the Peterson Field Guide Series, which includes the familiar volumes on birds, and is worth owning by anyone with a naturalist's bent. It contains illustrations of many common insects, sometimes in stunning color, and the diagnostic characteristics for their identification.

Brues, Charles T., A. L. Melander, and Frank M. Carpenter. 1954. *Classification of Insects.* Bulletin of the Museum of Comparative Zoology, Vol. 108, Harvard University, Cambridge, Mass. Taxonomic keys to the living and extinct families of insects. A comprehensive monograph for the professional entomologist.

Chapman, R. F. 1969. *The Insects: Structure and Function.* American Elsevier, New York. Another basic entomology text. Stresses anatomy, physiology, and behavior.

Dethier, Vincent G. 1962. *To Know a Fly.* Holden-Day, San Francisco. A leading biologist tells about his years in the laboratory working on the physiology and behavior of flies. Gives a real feeling for the ways of the researcher. Delightful reading.

Evans, Howard Ensign. 1966. *Life on a Little-known Planet.* Dell, New York. A gem, worth owning and worth giving to one's friends. Teaches about insects and about research on insects, while making an impassioned plea for conservation and the love of nature. Knowledgeable, witty, and charming.

Oldroyd, Harold. 1958. *Collecting, Preserving, and Studying Insects.* Hutchinson, London. For the committed student of insects; a detailed and clear instruction manual.

Swan, Lester A., and Charles S. Papp. 1972. *The Common Insects of North America.* Harper and Row, New York. A most useful companion to the field guide by Borror and White. Provides illustrations and summaries of the biology of almost 1,500 species.

Waterhouse, Douglas F., ed. 1967. *The Insects of Australia.* Melbourne University Press, Australia. A superbly illustrated general treatise on insects. Deals primarily with Australian species, but the first nine chapters on the basic biology of insects constitute one of the best summaries of the subject to be found anywhere.

Wigglesworth, V. B. 1964. *The Life of Insects.* World Publishing, New York. A refreshingly original account of insects and their ways. Lucidly and informally written by one of the leading insects physiologists of our time.

THE KEYS TO SUCCESS: ANATOMY AND PHYSIOLOGY

THE KEYS TO SUCCESS: ANATOMY AND PHYSIOLOGY

I

INTRODUCTION

Our selection of *Scientific American* articles begins with a section devoted to the special anatomical and physiological adaptations of insects. Through the eyes of biologists who conducted the primary research the reader will witness some of the exquisite refinements in cuticle construction, respiration, flight, metamorphosis, and reproduction that gave mastery of the land to the insects. In the subsequent three sections various authors examine the more particularized adaptations achieved by insect species through behavior and symbiosis. Articles in the fifth and concluding section reveal how knowledge derived from pure research can lead to effective control of insect pests with a minimum amount of damage to the remainder of the environment.

Although it is not essential, we advise the reader to proceed through the articles in sequence. In each section we provide a brief synopsis and discussion of individual articles in order to help place them in the context of the collection. Technical points are also explained in the few cases where authors may have been too brief. In addition, a list of recommended books is provided for each section.

In the first article, "Insect Eggshells," H. E. Hinton shows how the insect egg provides a clearcut problem in biological engineering. If it is to survive in open air a severe problem must be overcome: the gas exchange necessary to life is accompanied by a steady and irreversible loss of water, which if carried too far will be fatal. Microscopic air ducts (the "aeropyles") and one or more layers of gas-filled meshwork have been built into the shell surface. These structures possess unusual geometrical properties that permit gas exchange at a much reduced rate of water evaporation. Curiously, eggs laid on land face a second, opposite hazard: when it rains they are often submerged under water. Here a special device called a plastron is called into play. The plastron is an extensive gas film held in place on the body surface by a system of water-repellent structures, across which gas exchange can occur with the surrounding water. Terrestrial eggs have evolved complex cuticular meshworks that increase the area of the plastron and hence the rate of underwater gas exchange. They are capable of surviving in a physical environment that is harsher and more capricious than that encountered in fresh water and the sea.

In his early but lucid and still useful introduction, "Insect Breathing," C. M. Williams gives the basic and often surprising facts about tracheal respiration. We learn that tracheae are both the essence of simplicity in design and highly efficient devices for moving air. Some kinds of insects can expire by contraction of their abdominal muscles; one breath can exchange half the total volume of the entire tracheal system. Tracheoles, the end branches of the tracheae, are equally impressive in performance. A study of a moth caterpillar (*Cossus*) has revealed that simple gas diffusion alone can supply the insect with 15 times the amount of oxygen it needs.

No creature, man least of all, can succeed at powered flight without machinery built according to exacting aerodynamic requirements. As the late Professor Torkel Weis-Fogh, one of the pioneers in the study of insect flight, shows in "The Flight of Locusts," the insect wing is as cleverly constructed and moved as the wing of a bird or the blade of a helicopter. When reading the article, keep in mind the advantages and disadvantages of the cuticular nature of the wing. Its strength, stiffness, and broad area are easily attained because of the physical qualities of cuticle, but the innate lack of flexibility and the difficulty of attaching muscles beyond its base limit the kind of movements it can make.

A midge hovers by beating its wings at an almost unbelievable 1,046 cycles per second. Some beetles and bees can cruise at speeds equal to those of many bird species. These maximum performers, which represent only a minority of the insect orders, have developed the ability to contract their wing muscles faster than nerve impulses arrive to stimulate them. "Weight for weight," David Smith tells us in "The Flight Muscles of Insects," "the flight muscles of such insects generate more energy than any other tissue in the animal kingdom." The capacity for such rapid action comes from the design of two sets of antagonistic muscles that fill much of the thorax. When the massive vertical muscles contract, they flatten the thorax slightly and twist the wings upward. When the equally massive horizontal muscles contract, and their vertical antagonists simultaneously relax, the thorax is narrowed and the wings are flicked downward. A single nerve impulse sets off a series of such oscillations; for this reason the muscles are called *asynchronous*. More conventional, synchronous flight muscles are found in other groups of insects. Refinements in the cell structure and biochemistry of both kinds of muscle help to bring flight in all kinds of insects to high levels.

The elementary facts concerning the development of insects are presented by Sir Vincent Wigglesworth in "Metamorphosis and differentiation." The overriding constraint in the life cycle of an insect is the need to molt. As noted in the introduction, the exoskeleton has to be shed periodically to permit growth, and therefore development proceeds by well-marked steps. Wigglesworth and his fellow insect physiologists have shown that the physiological events associated with this process are controlled by a delicate antagonism of hormones. One kind, originating in the brain and prothoracic gland, impels the transformation toward the adult state. The juvenile hormone, produced in the corpora allata, inhibits this action. When present in high enough concentrations it causes the insect to proceed through the molt with no significant change other than growth.

The pursuit of the juvenile hormone, the remarkable substance that holds the young insect in the immature condition by preventing it from changing into a reproductive adult, is one of the truly exciting detective stories of biology. This story is told by C. M. Williams in "The Juvenile Hormone," beginning with V. B. Wigglesworth's original experiment using the assassin bug *Rhodnius*, in which adult transformation was obtained simply by chopping off the head. We are then led through a series of experiments by Williams and others that pinpointed the source of the hormone in the paired endocrine glands called corpora allata, then to the methods by which the first enriched extracts were obtained. The final chapter of the story, the chemical identification and practical uses of juvenile hormone, is presented in Williams's article, "Third-Generation Pesticides," in the last section of this anthology.

Insects proceed through their repertory of physiological changes with amazingly precise timing. Each species has its own seasonal and daily schedule of activity. A female saturniid moth, for example, may emerge from the cocoon in early spring, mate within a span of an hour or two around midnight, and lay her eggs according to still another nocturnal schedule. Meanwhile, other moth species in the neighborhood simultaneously follow their own marching orders; each set of instructions appears to fit them to the demands of the particular environment in which they live. As D. S. Saunders stresses in his article "The Biological Clock of Insects," the timing mechanisms of insects present some of the most challenging and important physiological problems in modern biology. Although the internal clocks have not been isolated and described directly as molecular devices, rapid progress is being made in characterizing their modes of action. For example, the clock of certain species has been shown to act as though it consists of two oscillators, one entrained (set into motion) by the light of dawn and the other by the darkness of dusk. As the photoperiod (length of daylight in each 24-hour cycle) changes with the season, the oscillators are brought into greater or less coincidence, an interaction that then triggers the hormonal changes mediating such events as molting or diapause. Alternative models appear to fit other species. All are being extended and tested in what has become one of the "hottest" fields of basic entomology.

The seemingly humble topic of "The Sexual Life of a Mosquito," by Jack Colvard Jones, actually brings the preceding subjects together. In his article Jones describes the life cycle of a mosquito from the point of view of the insect itself. A mosquito must perform a complex set of physiological and behavioral feats in order to grow up and reproduce. All acts must be accomplished correctly and in the right sequence during a period of only days or weeks. The insect has no set of instructions beyond those tightly programmed in its brain. Especially noteworthy are the means by which the male finds the female, the method of intromission (illustrating the employment of a typical insect aedeagus), and the evidence of an internal clock in the subsequent timing of egg-laying.

RELATED BOOKS

Nachtigall, Werner. 1974. *Insects in Flight*. McGraw-Hill, New York. A readable account of the biophysics of insect flight, accompanied by clear diagrams and photographs.

Neville, A. C. 1975. *Biology of the Arthropod Cuticle*. Springer Verlag, New York. Discusses the structure, ultrastructure, chemistry, and physical properties of the arthropod cuticle. An outstanding monograph.

Rockstein, Morris (ed.). 1973–74. *The Physiology of Insecta*, Volumes I–VI, second edition. Academic Press, New York. The major subjects of insect physiology are reviewed by leading authorities in the field. An advanced, broadly encompassing reference work.

Sláma, K., M. Romanuk, and F. Sorm. 1974. *Insect Hormones and Bioanalogues*. Springer Verlag, New York. Stresses the chemistry and mode of action of insect hormones, and provides a review of the biology of the insect neuroendocrine system.

Smith, David S. 1968. *Insect Cells: Their Structure and Function*. Oliver and Boyd, Edinburgh. The intricate architecture of insect cells is illustrated by way of excellent electronmicrographs. Short essays put structural details into functional perspective.

Snodgrass, R. E. 1935. *Principles of Insect Morphology*. McGraw-Hill, New York. Although dated, this is still a classical reference work on the anatomy (particularly the external anatomy) of insects.

Wigglesworth, V. B. 1972. *Principles of Insect Physiology*, seventh edition. Chapman and Hall, London. The best first source of reference for facts on insect physiology. Authoritatively and clearly written.

1

Insect Eggshells

by H. E. Hinton
August 1970

The scanning electron microscope has revealed that insects' tiny eggs are structurally complex. Their peculiar architecture allows the free exchange of oxygen and carbon dioxide but minimizes the loss of water

On examining the apparently solid shell of a hen's egg, one may wonder how the egg can absorb the oxygen necessary to sustain the life and development of the embryo inside it. Obviously the shell must be permeable to oxygen; it must therefore have holes that are large enough to allow oxygen molecules to enter. But any holes large enough to allow oxygen molecules to enter will allow water to escape, because water molecules are smaller than oxygen molecules. This difference in the size of oxygen molecules and water molecules need not be hazardous to eggs laid in water or very moist places. But hen's eggs, and the eggs of many insects, are laid in dry places. The differences to be found in the respiratory arrangements of eggs of various kinds are obviously more or less successful attempts made during evolution to resolve the contradictory requirements imposed by dry environments simply because the oxygen molecule is larger than the water molecule.

The smaller an egg is, the greater is the ratio of surface area to volume. The problem of losing water by evaporation through the surface is correspondingly increased. A typical insect egg has about 50 square centimeters of surface area for each milliliter of volume. In a hen's egg this ratio is about 100 times more favorable, and accordingly a hen's egg can tolerate a much higher rate of evaporation. Most insect eggs laid on land have no means of replenishing their water supply. Insects have thus been forced to evolve eggshells that allow the exchange of gases with the air without the loss of too much water.

Many investigators have been drawn to the study of this intriguing phenomenon. Over the past decade I have explored the eggshells of a large variety of insects and have found that the shells of terrestrial eggs—those laid on land rather than in water—generally have a remarkably complex structure. The shell is made up of one or more layers of meshwork, each holding a layer of gas. Holes called aeropyles extend through the shell to the outside and connect its gas layers to the ambient air. In some insects (such as grasshoppers, water scorpions and certain beetles) the meshwork spaces fill with gas as the egg dries after it has been laid. In others (such as stick insects and flies) liquid is removed from the meshwork spaces and they are filled with gas while the egg is still immersed in the fluid of the oviduct. Presumably in these eggs liquid from the meshwork spaces must be actively absorbed. This would cause bubbles of gas to form. One can also conjecture that the appearance of gas in the shell may be assisted by the development of a water-repellent coat of fatty material on the struts of the meshwork, which would reduce adhesion between the meshwork and the contained fluid.

The aeropyles that mediate the transfer of gases between the egg and the atmosphere are from about one micron to a few microns wide, and the spaces in the meshwork are about the same width. These dimensions are many times the mean free path of the respiratory gases; the mean free path of oxygen at 23 degrees Celsius is a tenth of a micron. Hence diffusion of the gases and the ambient atmosphere is not significantly impeded. Nevertheless, the structure of the respiratory system of a terrestrial egg is such that comparatively little water is lost to the air as oxygen is taken in.

Among those eggs that have one or more layers of gas in the shell two rather different kinds of respiratory system have to be distinguished: those that function as a plastron, or physical gill, when the egg is immersed in water and those that do not. The plastron is simply a gas film of constant volume and an extensive water-air interface. Such a film is held in position by a system of water-repellent structures, and it resists wetting at the hydrostatic pressures to which it is normally subjected in nature. The plastron type of gill makes it possible for an egg to breathe under water indefinitely if there is plenty of oxygen dissolved in the water.

One might ask why a terrestrial egg should have a physical gill that can be used under water. Such eggs are normally glued or fastened in some way to leaves, stones or the earth, and when it rains heavily they necessarily remain submerged in water until it has stopped raining and the water has evaporated or flowed away. Thus in most climates the eggs of terrestrial insects are alternately dry and flooded. To be covered by water for several hours, or even days, a period that may exceed the duration of the egg stage, is no rare and isolated event but a normal hazard of the egg's environment. For this reason one should not be surprised to find that many terrestrial insects and their eggs are adapted for respiration in water quite as well as many aquatic insects. The main difference between the environment in which plastron-equipped aquatic insects flourish and that in which terrestrial insects do is that in the latter environment the flooded periods are shorter and less frequent.

If the respiratory system of the eggshell is to function as a plastron, the total water-air interface across the aeropyles, or across any superficial networks the eggshell may have, must be exten-

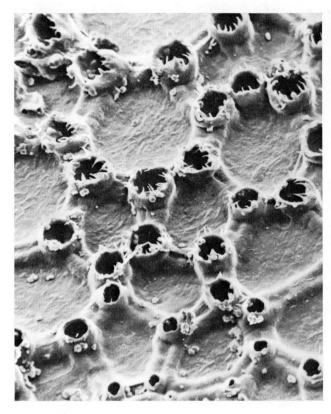

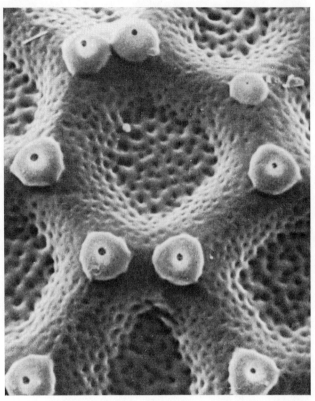

IRREGULAR SURFACE of an insect egg is seen in this scanning electron micrograph; it is the eggshell of the oak silkworm (*Antheraea pernyi*) enlarged 520 times. Ragged holes are outer ends of aeropyles, respiratory tubes leading to the inner layers. Irregularities, along with trapped air, comprise the eggshell's plastron.

AEROPYLES that jut up from the surface of this moth's egg are seen enlarged 4,300 times; they are much too small and scattered to comprise an efficient plastron. Air trapped by the plastron acts as a gill, allowing underwater respiration. Thus the eggs of this species (*Semiothisa signaria*) could not long survive submerged.

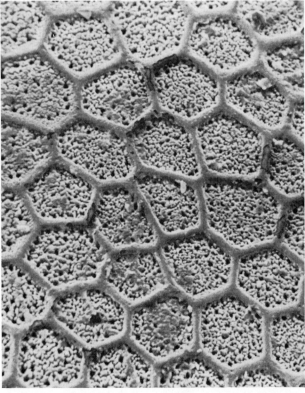

SHELL OF A BUG (*Piezodorus lituratus*) has tall aeropyles that rise from its surface like chimney rows; it is enlarged 340 times.

WATER-ADAPTED EGG, that of the giant Indian water bug (*Lethocerus indicus*), is enlarged 820 times to show plastron network.

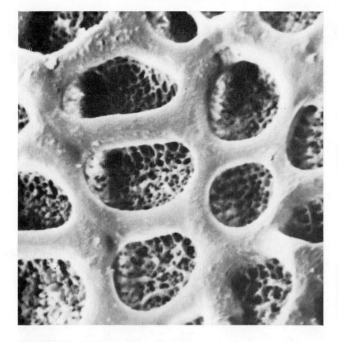

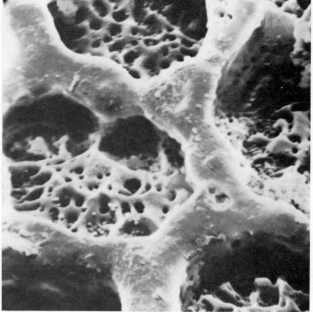

PLASTRON STRUCTURES, possessed by most insect eggs, show considerable variation in structure and location. Four examples are seen in these scanning electron micrographs, prepared during the author's investigation. At far left is an area of the front end of the egg of the long-horned grasshopper (*Plagiostira gilletti*); it is enlarged 2,200 times. Next is an area of the side of the egg of one

sive enough to satisfy a significant part of the oxygen demands of the developing embryo when the egg is in water. When the egg is dry, oxygen is taken in directly through the aeropyles. The plastron thus not only provides a large surface for the extraction of oxygen dissolved in the water but also, when the egg is dry, its network or aeropyles provide a means for the direct entry of oxygen from the air into the shell.

The plastron method of respiration was first discovered in adult aquatic insects, and it was thought that this type of respiration was confined to a few such insects. In 1959, however, I found that the eggs of the fruit fly *Drosophila* and some other terrestrial insects utilized plastron respiration when they were flooded. We now know that plastron respiration is much commoner in terrestrial

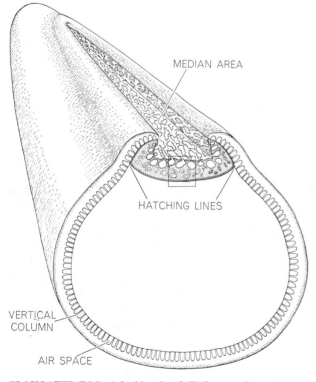

ELONGATED EGG of the blowfly (*Calliphora erythrocephala*) is one that confines the plastron structure to a median strip lying between the two hatching lines (*left*). A section of the structure (*color*) is enlarged (*right*) to show the plastron network and the air-filled outer layer underlying it, the meshwork of vertical columns comprising the inner layer, and the aeropyles between.

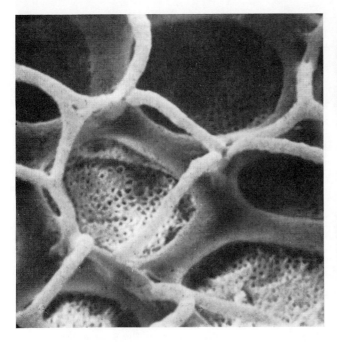 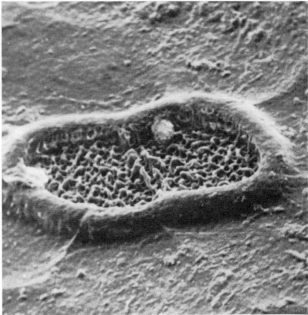

of the scorpion flies (*Panorpa anomala*); it is seen enlarged 3,000 times. Next is an area on the side of the egg of the fly *Fannia armata*, enlarged 7,500 times; the development of its lacy architec- ture is shown in the illustrations on page 27. At far right is one of the several plastron "craters" found on the side of the egg of the Australian bush fly (*Musca vetustissima*), enlarged 2,700 times.

insects than it is in aquatic ones. Moreover, it is present not only in the eggs but also in some of the other stages.

The plastron was evolved in response to two conditions: an environment that was alternately flooded and dry and an environment in which, when it was flooded, the water was rich in oxygen. Obviously if the water's oxygen pressure is lower than the oxygen pressure within the egg, the plastron will work in reverse and will extract oxygen from the egg rather than the ambient water. It is no accident that nearly all the aquatic insects with a plastron are found in waters where the oxygen content is maintained at a fairly high level: rapidly flowing streams, intertidal areas and the littoral of large lakes. The terrestrial insects equipped with plastrons are in much the same boat, so to speak. Their eggs can survive flooding only in oxygen-rich waters, and of course rainwater is rich in oxygen.

For eggs that depend on plastron respiration the problem of preventing loss of water under dry conditions is acute either because they have a great number of aeropyles or because they have an extensive open network. *Drosophila* and many other insects have evolved an answer to this problem in the form of respiratory horns that have a plastron over their surface. If the rest of the egg's surface is impermeable to water, the egg loses water only through the cross-sectional area of the base of the

horns, which is only a small part of the entire surface of the horns. When the egg is under water, the entire surface of the horns is available for the extraction of oxygen from the water. It is now known that at least 19 groups of insects have independently evolved respiratory horns with a plastron like that of *Drosophila*.

In eggs without respiratory horns the plastron may be an open network over the entire surface (as it is in the egg of the housefly), may be restricted to a certain area or may consist of discrete plastron craters scattered over the surface. In eggs where a large part of the surface is a plastron there is sometimes a membrane under the shell that has only small areas of permeability, so that under dry conditions the respiratory gases are funneled into and out of the egg with a minimum loss of water. When a relatively impermeable membrane is not present under the shell of such an egg, the egg cannot survive being dried. Indeed, many terrestrial eggs that have a plastron over their entire surface are liable to dry up. The egg of the housefly has a plastron over its entire surface but has no impermeable inner membrane; its embryo therefore survives only in terrestrial environments that are very moist.

If a plastron is to serve as an efficient respiratory structure, it must fulfill four requirements: (1) it must resist wetting at the hydrostatic pressures to which it is commonly subjected in water; (2) the

geometry of the plastron meshwork and the nature of its surface must be such that it is not wetted when the surface tension of the water is lowered by surface-active substances; (3) its total area must be large enough to satisfy the egg's need for oxygen, and (4) the drop in oxygen pressure along the length of the plastron should be small so that all the plastron can be effectively used. W. H. Thorpe and D. J. Crisp of the University of Cambridge established these criteria many years ago in their studies of adult aquatic insects. I have found that the same criteria apply to the plastrons of terrestrial insect eggs.

The first thing I had to find out about the resistance of egg plastrons to hydrostatic pressure was whether or not they could withstand the impact of falling raindrops. After all, many eggs are laid in places such as the surface of a leaf, where they are not protected from being hit by raindrops. One can calculate that the pressure a raindrop exerts in falling on a plastron is equivalent to a head of water about 1,000 times the diameter of the drop. Thus a large raindrop four millimeters in diameter would strike the plastron with a pressure amounting to about 31 centimeters of mercury. My observations in the field showed that eggs with plastrons were not wetted by raindrops. The reason was that a raindrop falling on the plastron exerts its high pressure for only about a millisecond; I found by experiment that even the plastrons least resistant to wetting

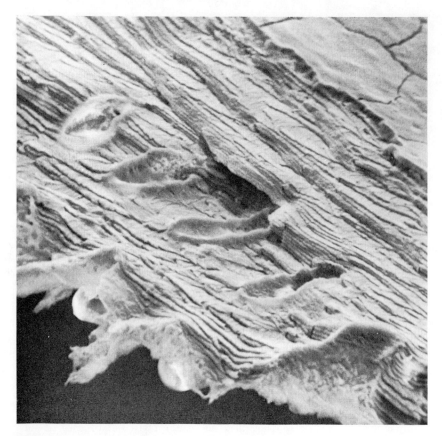

MULTIPLE LAYERS comprising the eggshell of the puss moth (*Cerura vinula*) are visible in this scanning electron micrograph. Broken edge of shell is seen enlarged 1,950 times.

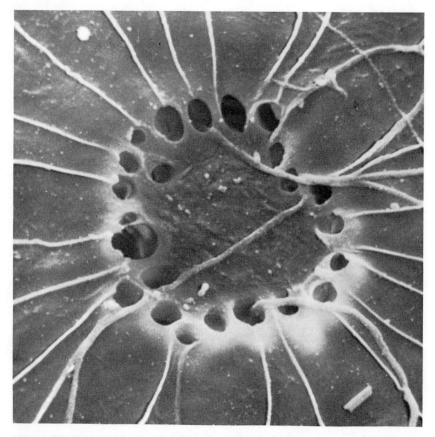

SMALL TUNNELS, or micropyles, in eggshells provide a way for the fertilizing sperm to reach the interior of the egg. These are micropyles in a puss-moth egg, enlarged 4,600 times.

could withstand such pressures for about 30 minutes.

Even in a heavy rainfall terrestrial eggs are not usually exposed to hydrostatic pressures such as insects living in streams have to tolerate. It was therefore a surprise to find that the plastrons of terrestrial eggs often showed a greater resistance to wetting by hydrostatic pressures than the plastron of the typical aquatic insect. For instance, the plastron of the terrestrial egg of *Drosophila funebris* was found to resist a pressure of 1.3 atmospheres above normal atmospheric pressure, whereas the plastron of the aquatic pupa of the fly *Antocha vitripennis* could resist only an excess pressure of a third of an atmosphere.

An explanation of this seeming paradox emerged when I looked into the effects of surface-active substances on the resistance of plastrons to wetting. In the clean waters of the streams where aquatic plastron-bearing insects live the surface tension of the water is high, usually between 70 and 72 dynes per centimeter. In contrast, terrestrial eggs, which are commonly laid on organic matter, are exposed to high concentrations of surface-active substances in the puddles of rainwater deposited on such matter. Surface-active substances lower the surface tension of the water, so that it more readily wets the plastron; the resistance of a plastron to wetting by excess pressures varies directly with the surface tension of the water. In response the plastron of many terrestrial eggs has undergone evolutionary changes in its geometry or in the nature of the surface of the meshwork struts that increase its resistance to wetting by surface-active substances. Such changes automatically increase the plastron's resistance to wetting by excess hydrostatic pressures in clean water. The consequence of such changes is that the resistance of the plastron of many terrestrial eggs to high pressures is appreciably greater than the resistance of the plastron of many aquatic insects.

Most of the terrestrial plastrons I tested were those of species that lay their eggs in cow dung or in decomposing vegetable or animal matter. These eggs could be placed in two distinct groups according to the resistance of their plastron to excess hydrostatic pressure. The first group included only those eggs found in cow dung. The plastron of these eggs was able to withstand excess pressures of up to 30 centimeters of mercury for about 30 minutes or more, but its resistance fell off rapidly at higher

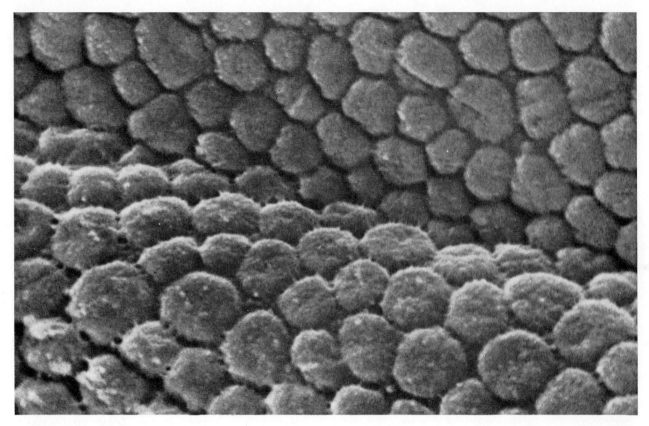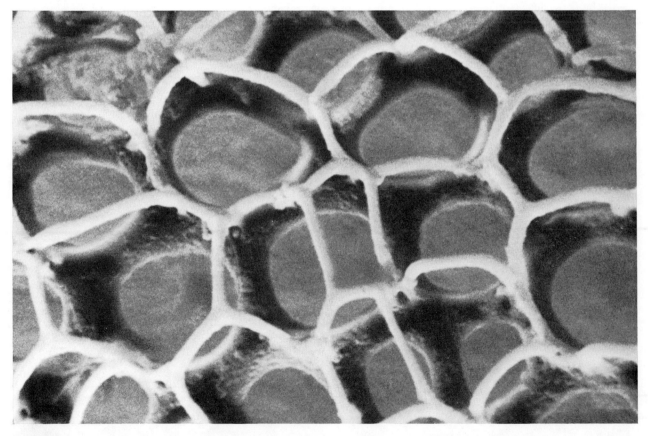

7

SURFACE CELLS of the ovarian follicles in the fly *Fannia arma-ta* are enlarged 1,500 times in this scanning electron micrograph.
These are the cells that secrete the eggshell; their distribution determines the pattern of the egg surface (*see illustration below*).

INCOMPLETE EGG, removed from the ovary of a fly of the same species, is seen enlarged 4,800 times. In most places the lacy
net of shell surface remains in contact with the follicular cells. The completed shell will look like the one at top left on page 25.

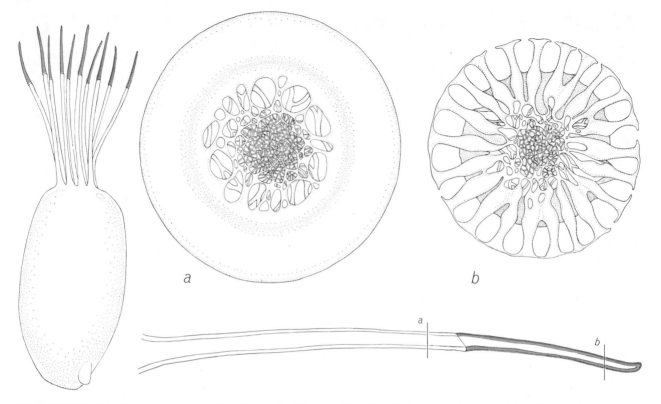

HORNED EGG of the European water scorpion (*Nepa rubra*) has its plastron structures confined to the tips of the horns (*left, color*).

Water loss during respiration is minimized because the impervious surface (*a*) is much greater in extent than the plastron area (*b*).

pressures. In the second group, represented by *Drosophila* and the blowflies, the plastron withstood considerably higher excess pressures (in the range of from 60 to 100 centimeters of mercury) for 30 minutes or more. This difference is of particular interest because when the surface tension of the rainwater puddles on cow dung was compared with the surface tension of water standing on decomposing flesh, it was found that the former was consistently higher (50 dynes per centimeter compared with 39 or 40 dynes per centimeter for water standing on flesh). The difference between the surface tension of water on cow dung and that of water on decomposing flesh or vegetable matter is understandable; liquefying flesh or vegetable matter, still containing most of its fats and proteins, would be expected to produce higher concentrations of organic acids and other surface-active substances than cow dung, which consists mainly of lignin

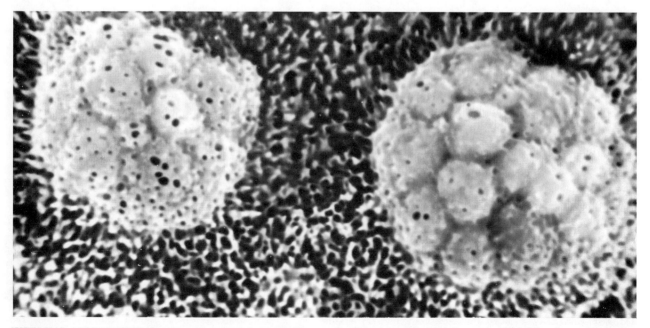

INTERNAL APPEARANCE of a plastron structure is revealed by a scanning electron micrograph. The surface of an egg of the stone

fly (*Pteronarcys dorsata*) is seen on the left-hand page. Shown is a part of the plastron area, enlarged 2,700 times. The same area is

and cellulose and decomposes slowly.

Many terrestrial eggs of butterflies and other insects do not have a plastron but nevertheless have a layer of gas in the inner part of the eggshell. Aeropyles extend from the gas film to the outer surface of the shell; it is through these aeropyles that gas is exchanged with the ambient air. Such eggs are distinguished from plastron eggs only because the number of their aeropyles is so small that when the egg is under water, the total water-air interface established across the outer openings of the aeropyles is not large enough to extract the amount of oxygen from the surrounding water necessary for the development of the embryo.

In eggs that do not have a plastron the aeropyles may be scattered evenly over the egg's surface or arrayed in bands, as they are in the eggs of some moths and beetles, or they may be clustered at the front end of the egg, as they are in the eggs of many bugs. In the eggs of some butterflies and other insects the aeropyles open on the crest of longitudinal ridges. The eggs of tortoiseshell butterflies and of some other insects have a particularly interesting defense against drowning, although they lack a plastron. These eggs are laid in masses. When it rains, a bubble of air is sometimes trapped over the front end of the mass. The bubble cannot resist pressure but, in the absence of a pressure difference that would collapse it, it functions as a temporary gill extracting oxygen from the surrounding water. The eggs extract much more oxygen from the bubble than it originally contained. As oxygen is withdrawn from the bubble, equilibrium tends to be restored by oxygen entering rather than by nitrogen leaving; nitrogen is much less soluble than oxygen and so passes through the air-water interface of the bubble much more slowly. Nevertheless, a little nitrogen is continually escaping and in time the bubble becomes too small to be effective as a gill.

Many terrestrial eggs, even some of those without a plastron, have their aeropyle openings on stalks that, like a diver's snorkel, give the egg access to the air. Thus the stalks can take in atmospheric oxygen while the rest of the egg is covered with water. In the eggs of some bugs these stalks are very long indeed, sometimes more than half as long as the egg itself. The stalk often serves not only to bring in air but also to deliver sperm to the egg by way of a special channel in the center of the stalk.

Many insects lay their eggs in water, but we would not expect to find elaborate respiratory systems in eggs that do not have the problem of losing water when breathing. In fact, I have not been able to find such systems in the eggshells of mayflies, caddis flies or most of the primitive two-winged flies. The eggs of these species have no layer of gas in the shell or any other distinct apparatus for respiration. Apparently they use the entire shell for this purpose, simply taking up dissolved oxygen from the water that bathes them. When the shell is examined with a light microscope or a low-resolution electron microscope, it appears to be solid. At high resolutions, however, the shell is seen to be composed of a meshwork of fibrils about 10 to 15 angstroms in diameter. The spaces between the fibrils are about 20 angstroms wide, quite wide enough to allow the diffusion of gases through the shell.

Some eggs are laid in shallow streams and other bodies of water that are liable to dry up, and among such eggs we might well expect to find the same kinds of elaborate respiratory system as those of terrestrial eggs. Indeed, the eggs of stone flies, of some bugs such as water scorpions and of many of the advanced two-winged flies have a highly developed plastron by means of which they extract oxygen from the water. Their elaborate respiratory structures also safeguard them against losing too much water while breathing when they are left high and dry, a hazard they often experience.

Some insects such as midges and caddis flies that lay their eggs in aquatic habitats that may dry up fairly suddenly embed their eggs in a hygroscopic jelly produced by the female. The jelly not only serves as a protection against small predators but also can tide the eggs over a short period of dryness, since the jelly gives up water slowly. It is intriguing that many midges and a few caddis flies also lay their eggs in a mass of jelly on leaves and other objects on land. The shell structure of these eggs resembles that of eggs laid under water, and they are in effect in a liquid or semiliquid medium even though they are terrestrial.

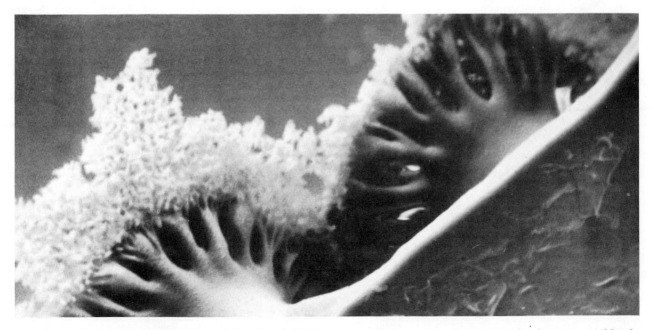

seen after tearing on the right-hand page; it is enlarged 2,800 times. The view is oblique, from the interior outward. Two of the many treelike structures that comprise the plastron are visible; the finely ramified tops intermesh to form the egg's water-air interface.

2

Insect Breathing

by Carroll M. Williams
February 1953

*Although these small creatures use oxygen, they have
no lungs. Each cell gets the gas from a private conduit,
a fact that is not only interesting but also important
to the welfare of man*

INSECTS, like men, must breathe. Indeed, to maintain their unparalleled rate of metabolism flying insects require more oxygen, ounce for ounce, than larger animals do. Insect evolution has met this demand by designing a respiratory system totally different from that of higher animals. Our "rhythmic sipping of the air" supplies oxygen to our body cells by the roundabout route of lungs and bloodstream. The insect respiratory system by-passes the blood and delivers oxygen directly to each and every one of the millions of cells buried deep in the various tissues and organs of the body. Each insect cell, in short, has its own private lung to keep the fire of its metabolism burning.

The insects and other tracheates (centipedes, millipedes, certain spiders, and so on) accomplish this by an amazingly efficient "tracheal system" of tubes and tubules. For practical as well as purely scientific reasons there is a growing interest in the tracheal system of respiration. Since the really serious enemies of the human race are all smaller than a horsefly, and since the life of such a creature as the mosquito depends upon the proper functioning of its tracheal system, entomologists have a favorite vision: a tracheal system filled, not with air, but with insecticide. Physiologists find equally good reasons for interesting themselves in the tracheal system. It embodies a refinement of biological engineering almost past belief. It also makes insects ideal animals for investigation of certain basic questions in biochemistry. By way of the tracheal system an investigator can introduce gaseous promoters and inhibitors of enzyme action into insect tissues and see them take effect promptly and directly.

In its ground plan the tracheal system is simplicity itself. During early embryonic development the skin of an insect pushes inward at certain points to form hollow tubes opening to the atmosphere. As these primary tracheae grow inward toward the tissues, they branch repeatedly. The branches spreading from the main trunks become progressively finer and their walls more delicate. The terminal twigs, called tracheoles, are so minute that the smallest capillaries in the human circulatory system would appear as large as pipelines in comparison. One or more tracheoles comes into intimate juncture with each cell in the insect and sometimes actually penetrates the cell. The insect is thus an intricate network of minute, air-filled tubes and tubules which convey the oxygen from the environment into immediate contact with the individual cells.

THE FACT that insects possess such an elaborate system of air-filled

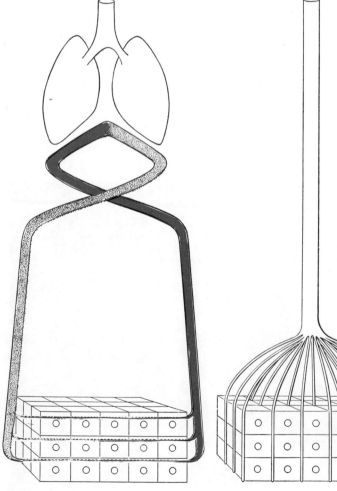

LUNG SYSTEM uses blood to move oxygen (*dark red*) to cells and carbon dioxide (*light red*) from them.

TRACHEAL SYSTEM consists of air-filled tubes which branch into others. Oxygen diffuses through air.

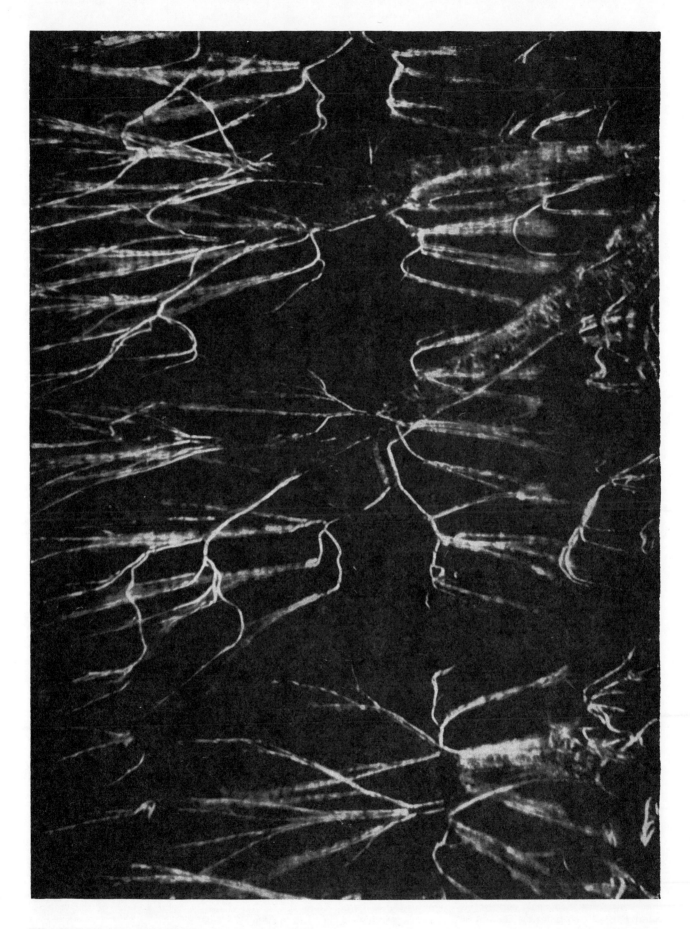

TRACHEAE AND TRACHEOLES are magnified 1,000 diameters in this dark-field photomicrograph of a living muscle fiber in the wing of a blowfly. The relatively large tracheae, the most conspicuous of which enter the picture from the upper right, branch into the fine tracheoles, each of which supplies a single cell.

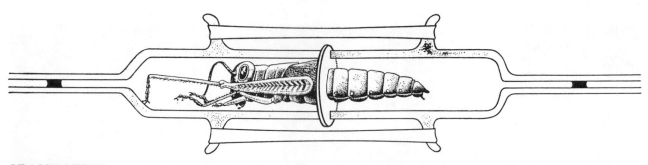

GRASSHOPPER was mounted in a glass chamber by Gottfried Fraenkel to determine the movement of air in the tracheal system of the insect. Around the middle of the grasshopper was a rubber diaphragm that divided the chamber into two parts. The oil drops at the far left and far right soon moved to the right, indicating that the grasshopper inhales through spiracles located in its thorax and exhales through those in its abdomen.

tubules was discovered in the 17th century by the versatile Italian biologist Marcello Malpighi. It was apparent that the tracheal system had something to do with respiration. But how could such tenuous tubules deliver enough oxygen to the cells?

The matter was settled early in this century by the Danish Nobel prize winner August Krogh. He was the first to appreciate the biological advantage inherent in the extreme agility with which a gas such as oxygen can diffuse through another gas. He showed that molecules of oxygen diffuse through air 300,000 times faster than through water and a million times faster than through living tissue. This, in a manner of speaking, was a measure of nature's good sense in equipping the tracheates with air-filled tubules instead of depending upon diffusion through tissues.

To prove that the tracheal system is in fact a respiratory system, Krogh had to carry the investigation a few steps further. Diffusion, like so many physical processes, is always downhill: a gas in diffusion always moves from a region of higher pressure to a region of lower pressure. The oxygen pressure in the atmosphere at sea level is three pounds per square inch. Given this limit on the pressure available to drive oxygen through the insect tracheal system into its tissues, Krogh had to show that the tracheal tubes are sufficiently short and their combined cross sections sufficiently great to deliver oxygen at the required rate. He did so in a series of simple and ingenious experiments of the type for which he was famous.

Krogh first measured the oxygen consumption of the caterpillar *Cossus*. Then, by a method which he developed himself, he made a wax cast of the insect's tracheal system. This involved injecting liquid wax into the tubes and dissolving the tissues away after the wax had hardened. Now Krogh was able to measure the dimensions of the tubes. The results were astonishing. He found that simple diffusion could supply the caterpillar with 15 times the amount of oxygen it needed.

Thus in small insects the act of respiration is reduced to a simple matter of pressure and automatic diffusion. As the tissues consume oxygen and reduce the local pressure, oxygen flows in through the tracheae from outside. The tissues can obtain more oxygen merely by using it. Since the tissues always have some positive pressure of oxygen which may be reduced to let in more oxygen, there is a clear margin of reserve which can be tapped as the occasion demands.

Besides admitting oxygen, a respiratory system has a second responsibility: getting rid of carbon dioxide. Krogh found that carbon dioxide, unlike oxygen, diffuses through water or living tissues with great ease. In insects a significant fraction diffuses out through the skin itself without ever entering the tracheae. Thus a diffusional system which is adequate to supply oxygen will always be more than adequate to excrete carbon dioxide.

T HE PASSIVE system of respiration demonstrated by August Krogh suffices, however, only for small insects. As an animal becomes larger, the volume of its oxygen-demanding tissue increases as the cube, but the supply of oxygen by diffusion can increase only in direct proportion to the linear increase in size, partly because the gas must travel farther through the tracheal tubes and partly because the cross-sectional area of the tubes cannot increase as fast as the insect's mass. Nature provides a partial solution by slowing down the pace of cellular metabolism as its creatures grow larger ("The Metabolism of Hummingbirds," SCIENTIFIC AMERICAN, January). Thus the rate of oxygen consumption increases approximately as the square rather than as the cube of linear size. Nonetheless, there remains a disproportion between the squared increase in the demand and the linear increase in possible supply. Beyond a certain size an insect would soon arrive at respiratory bankruptcy if it were to continue its passive dependence on diffusion. This is probably the main reason why insects are small animals.

The largest insects have had to evolve mechanisms for supplementing passive diffusion. They exert active respiratory movements which have the net effect of ventilating the larger tracheal trunks. The insect rhythmically compresses or flattens its abdominal segments by contraction and relaxation of the intersegmental muscles. The blood that fills the body cavity transmits the pressure of these contractions to the larger tracheal trunks. This, incidentally, is the sole contribution of blood to the respiration of most insects; not more than half a dozen genera of insects are furnished with hemoglobin or any other oxygen-carrying pigment.

In many insects the pressure is transmitted by way of thin-walled sacs placed at intervals along the larger tracheal trunks. In insects that lack such sacs, the trunks themselves, commonly oval in cross section, collapse in response to the pressure. Sometimes the trunk walls, of helical structure, are too strong to be compressed; in that case the trunks behave like spiral springs, shortening and expiring air when the blood pressure rises, and elongating and inspiring air when the pressure falls. Thus the larger tracheal trunks behave as hydraulic bellows, sucking and blowing air in and out with each respiratory movement.

The respiratory movements of insects, which expire air by contracting the abdominal muscles and inspire simply through the elastic recoil of the abdomen and tracheae, are just the reverse of those of mammals, where inspiration is active and expiration passive. The same result, however, is achieved in both cases. A current of air is moved to and fro in the larger air passages, and by this mechanical means the atmosphere is brought closer to the tissues. In insects the distance through which oxygen and carbon dioxide must diffuse is thereby reduced to the lengths of the smaller tracheal vessels which cannot be mechanically ventilated.

None of these adaptations was overlooked by Krogh. He even succeeded in measuring the magnitude of an insect's breath, and found that in one breath it could inspire a volume of air equal to half the total volume of the tracheal system.

Some insects have progressed a step beyond this to-and-fro ventilation. An example is the grasshopper. Gottfried

Fraenkel of the University of Illinois has studied its breathing. He placed a rubber diaphragm around the insect so that the abdomen could be enclosed in one chamber and the head and thorax in another chamber [*see drawing on the opposite page*]. The air pressure steadily decreased in the chamber enclosing the head and thorax and increased in the other. Obviously the air must have been sucked through the insect's longitudinal tracheae from thorax to abdomen. Closer inspection showed that the valves on the spiracles (openings to the air) open and close in such a sequence that inspiration must occur through the thoracic spiracles and expiration through the abdominal. By this maneuver the larger tracheal trunks are ventilated more efficiently than is possible by the to-and-fro method.

Both the respiratory movements and the opening and closing of the spiracle valves are under the control of respiratory centers within the central nervous system. There is a center in each body segment and apparently one in the thorax which coordinates the actions of the individual segments. The segmental centers are primarily sensitive to carbon dioxide; any increase in the carbon dioxide pressure augments the respiratory movements in a spectacular fashion. In contrast, the thoracic center seems to be especially sensitive to any decrease in oxygen pressure and, in this sense, is analogous to the aortic and carotid bodies which help govern the respiration of mammals. Even in the insect, nature has found it prudent to safeguard the organism against lack of oxygen and excess of carbon dioxide.

THE TRACHEAL system as described so far is clearly a mechanism adapted for life on land. It is an excellent piece of evidence that insects and their ancestors have always been primarily land-living animals. But an enormous number of insects desert the land to spend their immature phases in the water. After metamorphosis they usually give up their aquatic way of life and return to their ancestral home on land.

Although insects have been eminently successful in this secondary invasion of fresh water, the sea seems to present an insurmountable barrier to them. The truly marine species can be numbered on the fingers of one hand. Apparently it is not the sea's salt that bars insects, for some species are able to thrive even in salt lakes and the waters of brine pits. More probably their inability to adapt to the sea has something to do with the tracheal system; in the few marine insects the tubes are generally filled with fluid and have no function. An explanation of these facts awaits discovery.

The insects that have invaded fresh water have evolved an array of ingenious devices adapting the tracheal system to

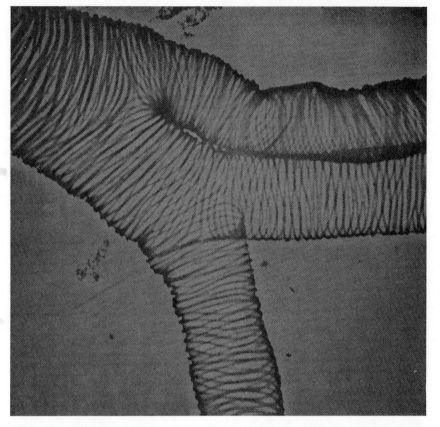

MOSQUITO TRACHEAE have a spiral construction which permits them to become longer or shorter. The mosquito is thus able to assist the flow of gases through its tracheae by alternately expanding and compressing them.

MOSQUITO TRACHEA is enlarged 6,000 diameters. This electron micrograph and the one above it were made by A. G. Richards of the University of Minnesota and T. F. Anderson of the University of Pennsylvania.

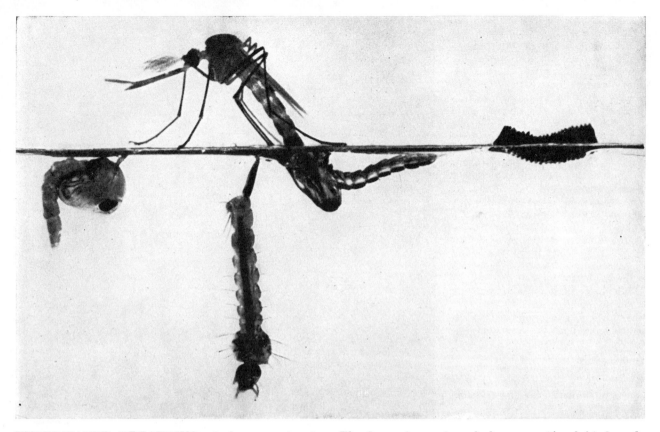

UNDERWATER BREATHING of the mosquito in the early stages of its life is illustrated in this photograph by the Australian entomologist A. J. Nicholson. The larva (*center*) and the pupa (*far left*) breathe through tubes that open at the surface. The adult mosquito at the top has just emerged from its pupal skin.

aquatic life. The devices include breathing tubes, diving bells and gills.

Enormous numbers of insects have applied to their underwater activities the principle of the "snorkel," such as is used in the latest submarines. Still dependent on the atmosphere for their supply of oxygen, they stick the snorkel above the surface from time to time for air. Some of them (*e.g.*, the rat-tailed maggot) even have a retractable breathing tube which they pull in when swimming under water.

The tip of the snorkel is generally equipped with two or more valvelike flaps. The mosquito larva's valves open automatically when it reaches the surface, for the simple reason that the outer surface of the flaps is wettable by water, whereas the inner surface is nonwettable. This superb little mechanism can be jammed, however, when the surface of the water is coated with oil or some other liquid able to wet the inner surface. The surfacing mosquito larva then inhales kerosene instead of air, as was first discovered by Aristotle. For the mosquito larva this is what the British biologist V. B. Wigglesworth has termed the "weak spot in the ecological armor" —a weak spot not without significance for the human race.

The diving-bell insects take oxygen along with them when they submerge. The "bell" consists of a bubble of air collected at the water's surface and held on one or more points of the body. During the dive the insect sucks oxygen from the bubble. Students of the phenomenon were long puzzled by the fact that the insect can stay under water long after it should have exhausted the bubble's oxygen content. The puzzle finally was unraveled by the Danish physiologist Richard Ege. He found that the bubble can serve as a veritable underwater lung. As the oxygen pressure in the air-filled bubble falls below that of the oxygen dissolved in the surrounding water, oxygen from the water diffuses into it. The insect can remain submerged until the nitrogen that keeps the bubble inflated diffuses into the surrounding water. So, strange as it may seem, the most important ingredient in the bubble of air which the insect picks up at the surface is nitrogen, not oxygen. The nitrogen, which makes it possible to use the bubble as a lung, allows the insect to be submerged 13 times as long as an equivalent bubble of oxygen would permit.

The third group of aquatic insects, equipped with gills, has managed to escape dependence on the atmosphere. Their gills are generally outfoldings of the body wall, richly supplied with tracheal tubes. By vibration or undulation of the gills, the insects equilibrate the gaseous content of their tracheae with the dissolved gases in the water. To reach the enclosed chambers of the tracheal system, oxygen must diffuse through the cuticle of the gill, through a thin layer of blood and finally through the walls of the tracheal tubes. But once a molecule of oxygen gets inside the tracheae, it can diffuse through the gases in the tubes and tubules about 300,000 times faster than through blood.

In a sense the gilled insects are not so different from the diving-bell types. In the bubble-breathers the bubble is external. In the gill-breathers the bubble is internal, contained within the tracheae of the gill. By this device the insect increases the surface area of the bubble, stringing it out through its tracheal system, and it also insures that its bubble will not collapse.

THE TRACHEAL system of respiration, different as it is from that of higher animals, proves to be one of evolution's most successful and versatile adaptations. It seems to have had the initial function of aiding and abetting the passive diffusion of oxygen and carbon dioxide between the atmosphere and the tissues. To the basic plan evolution gradually added ingenious new devices which permitted insects to increase in size, to fly and to live under water. In the tracheal system nature seems to have devised a method of breathing which, for small animals, is nearly perfect.

The Flight of Locusts

by Torkel Weis-Fogh
March 1956

*The tiny forces which a locust exerts in propelling
itself through the air have been measured in a series
of delicate experiments. The insect's muscle is
surprisingly efficient*

One of the distinguishing traits of the human species is an incurable curiosity about how other creatures manage to do things that we cannot do ourselves. Among nonhuman abilities none is more provocative than the flight of birds and insects. Our own ascent into the air on mechanical wings has not lessened the fascination of this age-old question. How, exactly, do birds and insects fly? In 20th-century terms, we are interested in the aerodynamic details—lift, drag, airfoils and so on. A biologist also has a special curiosity about the power plant. How a flying animal musters enough muscle power to fly, how it controls its flight, how efficiently it uses muscle energy—these are questions of general and fundamental interest on the frontier of biology.

In 1947 the late August Krogh, the Nobel prize-winning physiologist who had been interested in this subject for many years, Martin Jensen and I began an intensive study of insect flight in Krogh's private laboratory near Copenhagen. We wished to investigate the energetics of flapping flight. There is a vast literature on flying animals, but very little quantitative data on how they actually fly. We therefore set up a laboratory wind-tunnel apparatus where we could watch the details of winged flight closely and measure the forces involved. For the experimental animal we chose the big four-winged desert locust (*Schistocerca gregaria*), the celebrated pest which has recently caused great trouble in the Middle East and Africa. This insect was excellent for our purposes because it has an unparalleled ability to maintain steady flight for a long time.

The flapping flight of insects and small birds has some similarities to the flight of an airplane [see "Bird Aerodynamics," by John H. Storer; Scientific American Offprint 1115], but the operational differences are quite important. An airplane gets its lift and thrust from the combined action of two separate elements: rotating wings (the propellers) and fixed wings (the airfoils). A bird or insect, on the other hand, merges these functions in the same organ: its wings act both as propellers and as airfoils. The downstroke of the wings produces lift and thrust. On the upstroke the wings must move in such a way as to avoid canceling the lifting force of the downstroke. The pattern of wing motions is highly complex, and this was a focal point of our investigation.

In the experiments a tethered locust was placed in front of the mouth of a blower tube, and it flew against the windstream from the blower [see p. 24]. Its "tether," a slim metal rod attached to its body by a suction cup, allowed the insect free use of its wings, yet held the flying locust in one place in the windstream. It was suspended by this rod from a balance which measured its weight: as the locust flapped its wings, the amount of lift was measured by the reduction of weight on the balance. At the same time a pendulum hanging from the beam of the balance indicated the speed of the insect's flight: when its flying speed was the same as the speed of the air stream (*i.e.*, when its forward

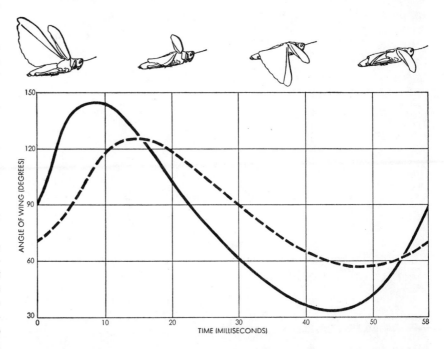

FLAPPING CYCLE of locusts' wings is remarkably constant over a wide range of flying conditions. The broken curve shows the angular up-and-down motion of the forewings; the solid curve, the motion of the hindwings. The angle of each wing at every point is measured between the downward vertical direction and the center line running the length of the wing.

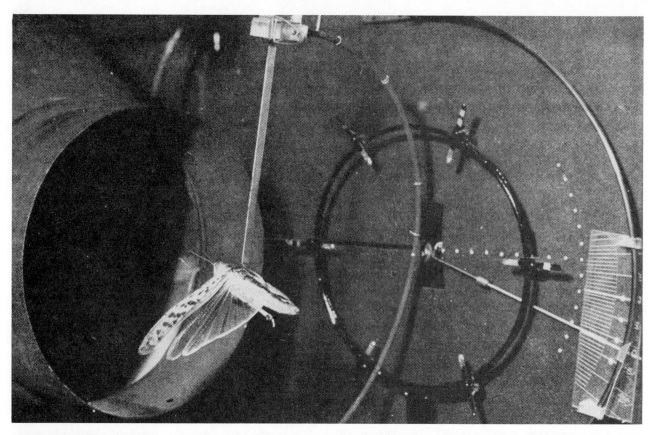

LOCUST IN WIND TUNNEL is suspended from a balance by means of the thin metal rod which passes under its wings and attaches to its body. At left is the mouth of the blower. At right is a scale which shows the insect's angle with respect to the air stream.

LOCUSTS ON MERRY-GO-ROUND flew for hours on end. The purpose of the experiment was to measure the fuel they consumed. This was done by comparing the fat and sugar in their bodies after the flight with the amount of these substances in resting insects.

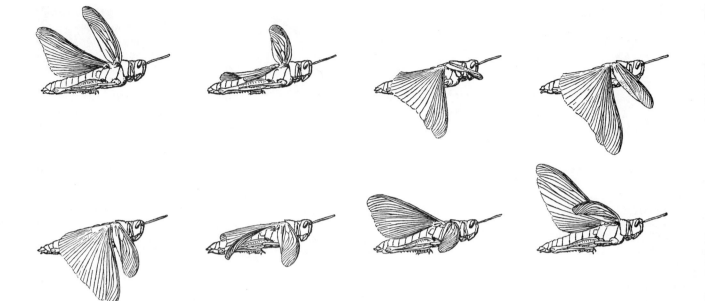

WING SHAPES must change continually as the locust adjusts to the varying speed and direction of the relative windstream. At the top are shown four positions during the downstroke in normal level flight. At the bottom are four positions during the upstroke.

thrust was equal to the drag of its body), the pendulum hung exactly vertical. Through a feedback servomechanism regulated by the pendulum, the locust controlled the speed of the windstream and thus set its own flying speed.

After studying many flights under these conditions, we were satisfied that the tethered locusts usually flew just about as they do in natural level flight. Their average flying speed was 12 feet per second, about the same as the average speed of a swarm in the field. Most often the insect's lift was equal to its body weight, as in free, level flight.

There was, however, considerable variation in the locusts' individual performances. Some loafed along at less than the minimum lift velocity (eight feet per second); some developed greater lift than their body weight and would have risen had they not been held in place by the suspension rod. Yet the remarkable fact was that the wing strokes on all the flights were found to be much the same, whatever the speed or lift. The up and down strokes were always at about the same beat (1,040 cycles per minute), covered the same distance from top to bottom and were inclined at the same angle to the insect's body.

This can mean only one thing: the main variable by which a locust controls its flight is the twisting of its wings. While it keeps the beat uniform, it constantly adjusts the angles of its airfoils to the air by turning the wings. In other words, the wings behave somewhat like a variable-pitch propeller. They "re-

volve" (flap) at a constant speed and in a fixed orbit, but during each cycle they alter the pitch of their surfaces so as to extract the maximum lift and thrust from the stream of air through which the insect is flying.

Having found, to our surprise and delight, that the variables were fewer than we had supposed, we were now in a position to calculate the energy a locust must put forth to fly. We could divide the work to be done into three different kinds.

The first is aerodynamic—the work of generating lift and thrust by its wing motions against the air. We made slow-motion pictures of the locust's wing strokes and closely examined the

changes in wing angle and shape throughout the cycle [see *drawings above*]. Let us take the forewings first. During the downstroke the leading edge of the wings bends downward. In the second half of the downstroke (when the wings are below the horizontal position), the trailing edge also bends downward, like the flap of an airplane wing. On the upstroke the twist is reversed; now the leading edge bends upward and the flap on the trailing edge straightens out. The twist varies, however, along the wing, being Z-shaped near the insect's body and relatively smooth out at the wing tip, which travels faster through the air.

In the hindwings the leading edge follows much the same cycle as the fore-

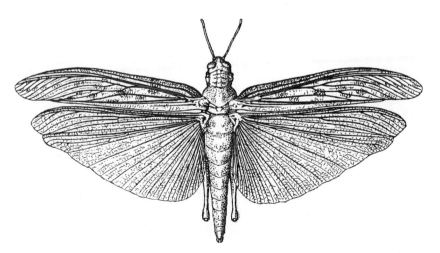

TOP VIEW OF LOCUST shows its wings in outline. The forewings are stiff throughout, and their shape is completely under the insect's control. The hindwings are stiff in their forward part, but their rear halves are flexible and their shape is molded by the air stream.

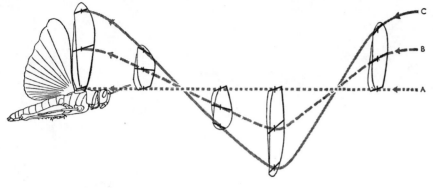

THEORETICAL WING TWIST required to maintain lift throughout a cycle is shown above. The solid curve indicates the relative wind direction against the wing tip; the broken curve indicates the wind against the midwing; the dotted curve, against the base. Straight-line markings on the wings show the angles of their surfaces some points in the cycle.

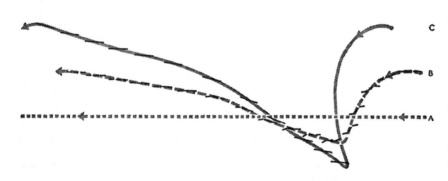

ACTUAL WING TWIST of the forewings of a flying locust was determined from slow-motion pictures. Solid curve shows the wind against the wing tip; broken curve, the wind against the midwing. The short, black line segments indicate the shape and angle of the wing's cross section. The upstroke turns out to be faster than theoretically predicted.

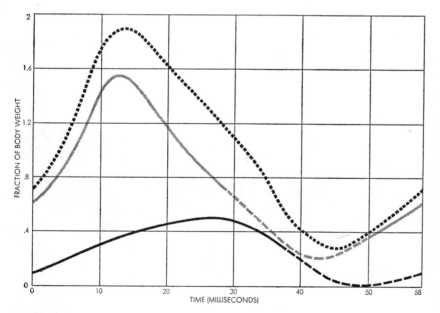

FORCES PRODUCED over the course of an average wing beat are summarized in this graph. The lower curve gives the contribution of the forewings; the middle curve, the contribution of the hindwings. Solid sections represent the downstroke; broken sections, the upstroke. Dotted curve at the top gives the total lift. About 70 per cent comes from the hindwings.

wings, but the trailing edge is flexible and is molded by the wind flow.

Now all this wing behavior is in accord with well-known aerodynamic principles. Throughout the stroke every part of the wing assumes an effective angle of attack toward the relative wind direction—a small angle which yields forces of lift and thrust. On the downstroke the relative wind is upward, so the wing twists downward to reduce the angle of attack; on the upstroke likewise it turns upward because the wind is downward. On the basis of theoretical considerations we plotted the angles that the wings should take toward the wind throughout the cycle [*top diagram at left*], and this schematic pattern was largely confirmed by observations. Martin Jensen worked out the sequence of wing angles in precise detail from an analysis of slow-motion films of actual locust flights [*middle diagram at left*].

Given the various angles of attack during the cycle, our problem now was to calculate how much work the insect had to do to push its wings through the air in generating lift for level flight. To do this it was necessary to compute the force exerted by the wings on the air throughout the cycle. The problem was exceedingly intricate, both because of the continual changes in angle of attack along the wing and because the wing speed varies considerably during the cycle (the upstroke, for example, is much faster than the downstroke).

Jensen went to work on this difficult task. He assumed that the sum of the forces exerted at successive instants during the stroke would give a true basis for computing the work done. The first step was to measure the forces on the wing at different positions in the cycle. For these measurements Jensen used detached locust wings. Exposing them to a controlled windstream, he twisted the wings into the configurations corresponding to successive stages of the stroke, measured the forces of lift and thrust at each position and from these measurements estimated the forces throughout the stroke. These estimates are plotted, for one full cycle, in the chart shown at left. It is an interesting fact, which could not have been predicted by theory, that the hindwings produce about 70 per cent of the total force.

After a couple of months of intense calculation, Jensen reduced his set of estimates of instantaneous forces to an average, estimating the forces of lift and thrust generated by the stroke as a whole. These figures proved to be very close to the actual lift and thrust developed by locusts flying in the wind tunnel, as measured by our instruments.

Thus we had a secure basis for estimating the aerodynamic work done by the locust. Jensen's plot of the variations in wind forces during the stroke gave us the information we needed for calculating the amount of this work.

We now turned to a second factor in the equation. When the locust moves its wings, it must spend energy not only to drive them against the resisting air but also to overcome the inertia of their mass. That is to say, work must be done to accelerate or decelerate the wing mass itself. During the locust's wing-flapping cycle it must stop its wings at the top and bottom of the stroke and accelerate them in the course of the stroke. Knowing the weight of the wings and their velocity at various stages of the stroke, we could calculate the work done against inertia.

Finally, we had to consider still another resisting force against which the locust must work in moving its wings. The wings are hinged to its body in such a way that the body changes shape when the wings flap. The body walls are elastic but rather stiff. Thus they act as a kind of spring which opposes the wing movements. We were able to estimate their opposing force in various positions of the wing stroke by removing the muscles and measuring the elastic pull of the walls on the wings by means of gauges.

Now we could proceed to estimate the total work done by a flying locust by combining the three quantities—aerodynamic, inertial and elastic [*charts on this page*]. The calculation showed that in level flight a locust uses 13.7 calories of energy per gram of body weight per hour. One calorie of energy is equivalent to the work of raising a three-pound weight about one foot. Thus in an hour's flying a two-gram locust expends enough energy to raise a three-pound weight to a height of more than 27 feet!

One might think that it should now be simple to compute the efficiency with which a locust uses its available muscular energy. By adding up its different forms of energy production or by measuring its rate of metabolism we can estimate that on the average a flying locust produces a total of about 70 calories of energy per gram of body weight per hour. Part of this energy goes into mechanical work, part into body heat and part into evaporating water. However, we cannot determine the muscles' mechanical efficiency simply by calculating the ratio of the work done to

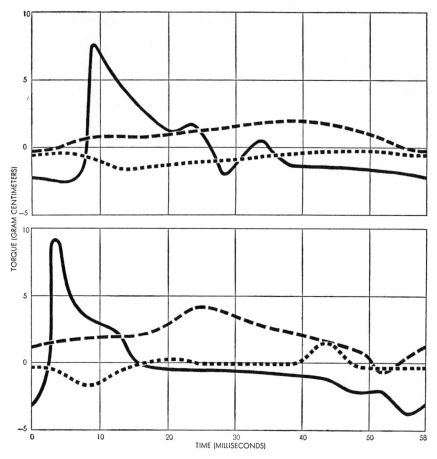

TURNING FORCE, or torque, must be produced by the locust's muscles to provide the aerodynamic forces of lift and thrust (*broken curves*), to overcome wing inertia (*solid curves*) and to change the shape of the insect's elastic body (*dotted curves*). The upper graph shows the forces developed in the forewings; lower graph, the forces in the hindwings. A positive torque tends to move the wings downward; a negative torque, upward.

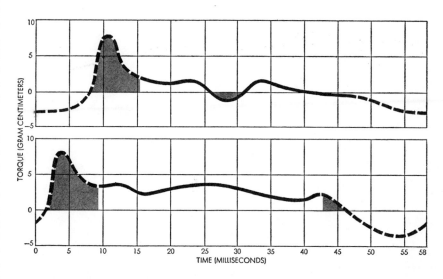

TOTAL TURNING FORCE required from the muscles is obtained by adding the curves in the graph at the top of the page. Upper curve gives forewing torque; lower curve, hindwing torque. Solid sections indicate downstroke; broken sections, upstroke. The shaded areas show the portions of the flapping cycle during which the muscles are doing negative work.

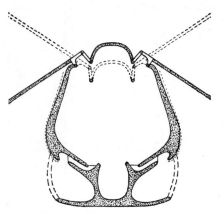

ATTACHMENT OF WINGS is diagrammed schematically. The view is a cross section through the insect. Each wing is a lever, pivoted at the top of the side wall of the body and fastened to the top, or back, wall. In flapping its wings the locust must use force to change the shape of its body walls.

the total energy produced. The difficulty is that in flapping its wings a locust does two kinds of work—positive and negative—and the efficiencies in the two kinds differ.

Negative work here means mainly the work done in slowing down the wings at the end of the upstroke or downstroke before they start in the opposite direction. This work is so considerable that the total inertial work may be greater than the aerodynamic work of producing lift. However, the inertial work is not so large a drain on the locust's energy as the aerodynamic, partly because negative work is less expensive than positive work; it is performed at a lower cost to metabolism. Human muscle, according to some studies, needs only about one fourth as much energy production for negative work as for positive work; that is, it is about four times as efficient in negative work.

Of the total power a locust uses in flying—13.7 calories per gram per hour—8.9 calories goes into positive work and 4.8 calories into negative. If the relative efficiencies for the two kinds of work are the same as in human muscle, the overall efficiency of a locust's flight muscles is about 14 per cent. If negative work is as expensive as positive work, then the locust's muscle efficiency is 20 per cent.

Either figure is astonishing. Some estimates have put the muscular efficiency of flying insects as low as 2 per cent. It appears now that the mechanical efficiency of the locust's muscles is as great as that of human leg muscles, although the insect's rate of metabolism is 10 to 20 times faster than man's. In other words, the muscles of a flying insect perform about 10 to 20 times more work, in proportion to size, than those of a human being working at top speed.

The Flight Muscles
of Insects

by David S. Smith
June 1965

The wings of some insects beat hundreds of times per second. The two kinds of muscle that power insect flight give clues to the operation of muscle throughout the animal kingdom

The voluntary muscles of almost all animals have an important feature in common: a single nerve impulse gives rise to a single response from a muscle. A significant exception is apparent in the flight of certain insects: their wings can beat many times faster than the most rapid rate at which a muscle responding to a series of nerve impulses can alternately contract and relax. Weight for weight the flight muscle of such insects generates more energy than any other tissue in the animal kingdom, and numerous investigators have attempted to find out how it does so. Before I relate some recent developments in the field the reader may find it helpful to have a few pertinent facts about the evolution of insects and about the study of muscle in general.

Some 350 million years ago—during the Devonian period or perhaps the early Carboniferous—the distant ancestors of today's insects made their first evolutionary experiments with flight. So far the fossil record has not revealed what type of insects these were nor what they looked like, but most students of the matter agree that the first advance was probably the appearance in some insects of stationary horizontal fins that enabled them to glide through the air. These gliding insects were superseded by the true winged insects, whose fins were larger and could be moved up and down around the point at which they joined the body.

Insects of course have an external skeleton, and they move by means of muscles that act on jointed parts of this more or less rigid shell. As insects evolved movable wings they also had to develop muscles to power them; it is believed that at first certain muscles of the legs and body wall were called into service. Insects, however, are highly diversified, and the various orders of flying insects exhibit many different mechanisms of flight. Everyone is familiar with the differences represented by the dancing flight of a butterfly, the hovering flight of a dragonfly and the remarkably maneuverable flight of the housefly and the honeybee.

It is insects of the last kind—the housefly and the honeybee—that are among those whose wings beat at a high rate. This can readily be perceived, but it was not until 1949 that the flight muscle of such insects was recognized as being physiologically unique. In that year J. W. S. Pringle, who was then at the University of Cambridge, was studying the main flight muscles of the blowfly. He observed that nerve impulses arrived in the muscles at a rate that was similar to the rate of nerve impulses arriving in other muscles, but that this rate was much slower than the rate at which the insect's wings beat. Earlier workers had found that cutting off portions of flies' wings had the effect of speeding up the beat; Pringle suggested that the rate of beat was determined not by the nerve impulses but by the load—in terms of wing area—imposed on a natural rhythm that was produced within the flight muscles themselves.

Later studies by Pringle, by Edward G. Boettiger of the University of Connecticut and by Kenneth D. Roeder of Tufts University showed that flight muscles of this kind are found in insects of only four of the 30 or so recognized insect orders: the beetles (Coleoptera); the wasps and bees (Hymenoptera); the flies, mosquitoes and similar forms (Diptera), and certain true bugs (Hemiptera), including the aphids. Because such muscle contracts and relaxes at a much higher rate than the nerve signals it receives it is called asynchronous muscle; the flight muscle of other insects contracts and relaxes in exact response

to nerve signals (as do the skeletal muscles of vertebrates) and is therefore called synchronous.

A few examples will make clear just how extraordinary the performance of asynchronous muscle is. O. Sotavalta of the University of Helsinki has measured the wingbeats of many insects; the wings of the swallowtail butterfly, for instance, oscillate through five cycles per second and those of the dragonfly through 35 cycles per second. Both insects have synchronous flight muscles; indeed, these frequencies are within the range of performance of vertebrate skeletal muscles. Among the insects with asynchronous flight muscles, beetles beat their wings at frequencies between 55 and 175 cycles per second, the honeybee at frequencies between 208 and 247 cycles and the mosquito at frequencies as high as 587 cycles. One midge (*Forcipomyia*) attains the almost incredible rate of 1,046 cycles per second. The special tissue that powers this sort of performance has been of great importance in the evolution of body shape and wing size in the insects that possess it; synchronous muscle can drive the large, lightly loaded wings of the butterfly but would be quite unable to lift the relatively bulky, small-winged body of a fly or bee.

Toward the end of the 19th century,

→

FLIGHT MUSCLE of a damselfly is shown enlarged 9,000 diameters in the electron micrograph on the following page. The cells are seen end on; the individual fibrils in which contraction takes place form a radial array (*light areas*). Between them are mitochondria (*dark areas*) that furnish the required power. Oblong fibrils are typical of primitive synchronous muscle, the less energetic of the two kinds of flight muscle.

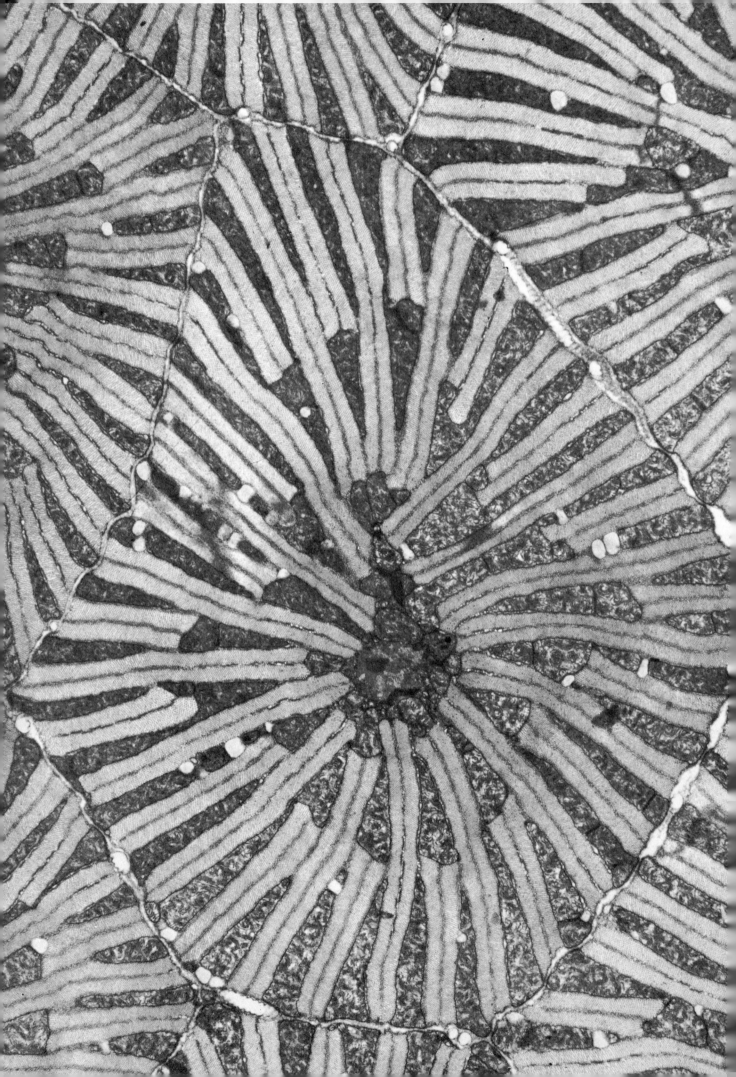

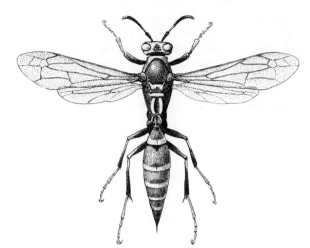

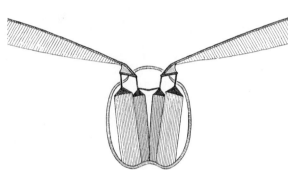

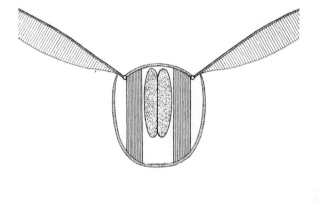

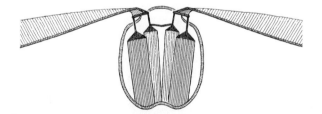

SYNCHRONOUS FLIGHT MUSCLE distinguishes all but four orders of insects; illustrated is a damselfly of the genus *Enallagma*.
As the first thorax section shows (*middle*), contraction of an inner
pair of muscles, applying force to a lever-like portion of the wing
base, raises the wings. Then a more robust outer pair of muscles
contracts to provide the downward power stroke (*bottom*). The
muscles are called synchronous because each contraction is in
response to a separate stimulus from the central nervous system.

ASYNCHRONOUS FLIGHT MUSCLE has evolved among bees
and wasps, flies and mosquitoes, beetles and some bugs; shown here
is a wasp of the genus *Polistes*. The muscle arrangement is antagonistic: the outer bundles contract vertically and the inner ones horizontally. Both do so alternately and in an oscillatory fashion. The
contractions deform the wasp's thorax so that the wings are driven
up (*middle*) and then down (*bottom*). This cycle is much faster
than the nerve-signal rate, hence the muscle is called asynchronous.

when ideas about the structure of muscle almost equaled the number of investigators interested in the matter, it
was realized that vertebrate skeletal
muscle, in contrast to "smooth" muscle
such as that of the vertebrate intestine,
is "striated." This is to say that each
of the many fibers, or cylindrical cells,
comprising such muscle appears regularly striped or banded when it is viewed
in the light microscope. These striations

are present whether the fiber is living
or has been fixed and sectioned; moreover, their pattern changes during the
cycle of contraction and relaxation.
There were various interpretations of
what the striations meant. Some investigators thought they were part of a contractile network embedded in a gelatinous ground substance; others held
that the ground substance alone was
able to contract.

At that time insect muscles were
widely examined in the microscope as a
convenient tissue for the study of muscle. The German anatomist Anton Kölliker showed in 1888 that the individual
cells of some insect flight muscles could
be teased apart into tiny fibrils, or cylindrical subunits, each with a diameter
of about two microns (.002 millimeter).
The fibrils too were banded; when they
were lined up side by side, they pre-

sented the characteristic striped appearance of the whole fiber. Kölliker also observed small spherical objects in the sarcoplasm: the fluid-filled space between the individual fibrils of the muscle cell. These spherical bodies, named sarcosomes, took up stains and dyes in the same way another cellular subunit did; this was the rodlike mitochondrion, which microscopists were then discovering in many types of cells. The two later proved to be identical.

These early observations with light microscopes go a fair way toward providing a basic model of striated muscle. Whether the muscle is vertebrate or invertebrate, each cell is a cylinder containing contractile fibrils in a sarcoplasmic matrix. In recent years, however—particularly during the past decade—biologists have been able to refine the model by using the electron microscope, which of course provides far higher magnification and resolution than the light microscope. Electron microscopy has made it possible to describe the structures within the muscle cell in considerable detail and has contributed much to modern theories of muscle contraction and relaxation and of the processes by which energy is supplied to the contractile mechanism.

On the basis of electron-micrograph studies H. E. Huxley of the University of Cambridge and Jean Hanson of King's College have developed the now generally accepted model of vertebrate muscle-fibril structure and function [see "The Contraction of Muscle," by H. E. Huxley: SCIENTIFIC AMERICAN Offprint 19]. They found that the fibril subunit was itself composed of subunits; cross-sectional micrographs looking, as it were, at the fibrils from the side reveal that each fibril is made up of two overlapping sets of filaments. The filaments of one set are thick and those of the other are thin; cross-sectional micrographs looking at the filaments from the end show that they lie together in a hexagonal array [see illustration on this page]. The thick filaments are made up of the protein myosin; the thin ones, of the protein actin. Huxley and Hanson propose that a muscle fibril contracts and relaxes not by any change in the length of its constituent filaments but by the fact that two sets of filaments slide past each other. The energy required for the sliding process is provided by adenosine triphosphate (ATP), and the utilization of this molecule within the fibrils during contraction requires the presence of calcium ions.

The contraction of a muscle cell is preceded by a chain of events, the first of which is the arrival of a nerve impulse at one or more localized regions where the endings of motor nerves are quite close to the muscle cell's thin surface membrane. A transmitter substance is released from the nerve ending into the narrow gap between the membranes of nerve and muscle; it initiates a wave of electrical activity—a loss of electrical polarity by the muscle membrane—that spreads over the whole fiber. A few milliseconds after the nerve impulse has arrived at the surface of the muscle cell the cell starts to contract.

This is only part of the story, and yet even this part presents an acute problem. Some 15 years ago A. V. Hill of the University of Cambridge pointed out a paradox: the response to electrical depolarization is so swift that even the fibrils farthest from the surface of the muscle cell begin to contract before it seems possible for any substance to have diffused inward from the depolarized surface membrane. The solution to this paradox was to remain unknown for more than a decade.

As I have indicated, in vertebrate muscle each nerve impulse gives rise to a single contractile event. In "fast" muscles (muscles that are able to contract and relax quickly) the event is a discrete twitch; in "slow" muscles successive impulses advance the contraction in a stepwise manner. A fast-muscle cell has only one junction with a nerve fiber; a slow-muscle cell has several junctions.

With these facts as background, the similarities and differences between vertebrate and insect muscle can now be examined. All insect muscle fibers resemble the "slow" fibers of vertebrates in having several nerve-muscle junctions rather than one. Electron micrographs of insect muscle show that the structure of these synapses between nerve and muscle is similar to that in vertebrates: the end of the axon—the elongated portion of the nerve cell—is in close contact with the membrane of the muscle cell and contains concentrations of vesicles, or minute sacs. Bernhard Katz of University College London and his co-workers have advanced the hypothesis that these synaptic vesicles hold "packets" of a transmitter substance that in the case of vertebrate synapses has been identified as acetylcholine. Although it is not definitely known what the insect transmitter substance is, it seems safe to infer that insect and vertebrate nerve endings have a common mechanism of transmitter-substance release.

The damselfly Enallagma—a familiar fluttering insect of streams and lakesides—provides an example of synchronous insect flight muscle in action. The insect's thorax, or mid-body, is divided into three segments; its flight apparatus consists of two pairs of wings, one pair mounted on the middle thoracic segment and the other on the rear segment. The segments are almost completely filled with the muscles that beat the wings [see illustration at left on preceding page]. Each muscle is made up of many separate fibers packed tightly together; each fiber is between 20 and 30 microns in diameter, a size common in vertebrate muscle. A low-power electron

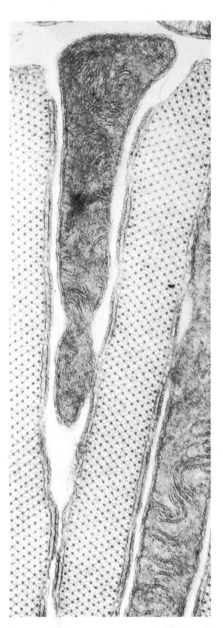

FIBRIL SUBUNITS lie in a geometric array; the large dots are filaments of the protein myosin, the small are actin. These fibrils, seen end on and enlarged 50,000 diameters, are from dragonfly flight muscle.

micrograph of these fibers in transverse section shows the striking arrangement of their contents: the sheetlike contractile fibrils form a radial array and alternate with dense mitochondria [*see illustration on page 42*]. At higher magnification the fibril structure is further resolved into its thick and thin filaments of myosin and actin, arranged in a hexagonal lattice. The radial arrangement of the sheetlike fibrils in damselfly flight muscle is typical of the leg and body muscles of insects in general, which are also synchronous.

There is a correlation between the metabolic activity of a muscle fiber and the number of mitochondria within it; these bodies house the enzymes that manufacture the ATP molecules necessary for muscular contraction [see "The Mitochondrion," by David E. Green; SCIENTIFIC AMERICAN, January, 1964]. One of the characteristic features of insect flight muscle, which is metabolically the most active insect tissue, is that it contains large numbers of mitochondria. As an example, although the damselfly has preserved in its flight muscle the primitive radial pattern of fibrils evolved in leg and body muscle, there is a great difference between the two kinds of tissue: to cope with higher metabolic demand the flight muscles have been much more abundantly endowed with mitochondria. Whether synchronous or asynchronous, however, most insect flight muscle has departed from the radial pattern of fibril organization; instead the contractile part of the fiber is divided into fibrils that are circular when seen in transverse section. Butterfly flight muscle, for example, contains cylindrical fibrils about which large mitochondria are wrapped [*see bottom illustration on page 47*].

One of the contrasts between insect and vertebrate muscle involves their provision for the supply of oxygen (and the removal of carbon dioxide). In vertebrates oxygen reaches all the organs in chemical combination with hemoglobin, the respiratory pigment of the red blood cells; in vertebrate muscles blood capillaries are located between the fibers. In insects the situation is different: the fluid hemolymph in the insect's body cavity contains no respiratory pigment. Instead atmospheric oxygen diffuses to the cells throughout the insect's body by way of a branching system of tubes—the tracheae—that are open to the exterior. The finest branches of this ramifying system are called tracheoles; they are present most abun-

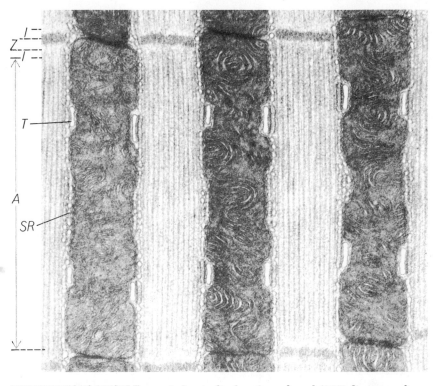

SYNCHRONOUS MUSCLE, seen in longitudinal section enlarged 40,000 diameters, shows the subunits of muscle cells along their long axes, bounded at each end by dark transverse "Z lines." These lines are flanked on both sides by narrow, light "I zones," whereas the bulk of each subunit is composed of a wide, medium-density "A band." One of the tubules comprising the "transverse" system of ducts is labeled T; SR identifies the chains of vesicles making up the sarcoplasmic reticulum that separates fibril from adjacent mitochondrion.

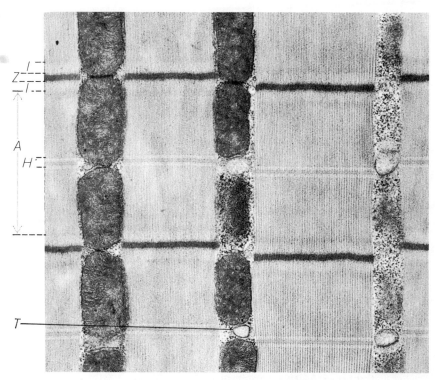

ASYNCHRONOUS MUSCLE, also in longitudinal section but enlarged only 16,000 diameters, contains subunits similarly bounded by dark Z lines flanked by narrow I zones. Each broad A band, however, is bisected by an "H zone" that is precisely aligned with the tubules of the transverse duct system (*most clearly visible among the mitochondria at center and right*). One major difference between this and synchronous flight muscle is the virtual absence of sarcoplasmic reticulum vesicles (*see illustration on following page*).

dantly in the organs that have the highest oxygen requirement—notably the flight muscles. Insect leg muscles (and flight muscles such as those of the damselfly, in which the diameter of the muscle fiber is rather small) are equipped with tracheoles that pass between the fibers as the capillaries in vertebrate muscle do; the oxygen simply diffuses inward from the surface of the fiber. In most insect flight muscles, however, the tracheolar system brings the oxygen much closer to the mitochondria by passing deep into the fibers, rather like fingers pushed into a toy balloon. (The tracheoles do not actually penetrate the muscle fiber; they are sheathed in the muscle cell's thin external membrane.) The result of this arrangement is that oxygen does not have to diffuse across the entire radius of the flight muscle

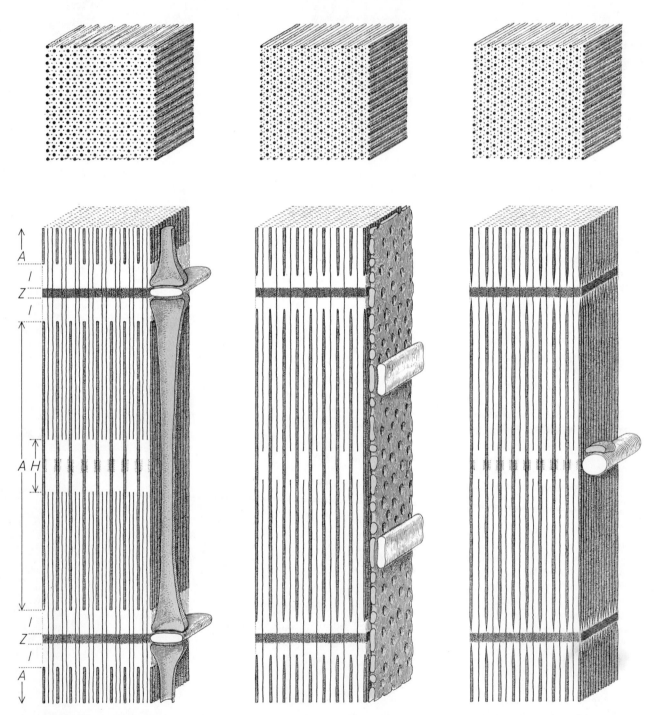

THREE KINDS OF MUSCLE are compared schematically at the level of fibril structure. At left is a vertebrate fibril; in center, an insect synchronous fibril; at right, an insect asynchronous fibril. The forward face of the cube above each of the longitudinal sections shows the hexagonal pattern formed by the filaments of myosin and actin when viewed in transverse section. The zones and lines that give muscle fiber its characteristic striated appearance are labeled at left. Asynchronous muscle is structurally different from the other kinds in two major respects. The tapering ends of its myosin filaments appear to reach almost to the Z line; actin filaments alone occupy the I zones bordering the Z line in other relaxed muscles. Although asynchronous muscle contains T-system tubules (*color*) as do other muscles, the membrane linked to fibril relaxation, the sarcoplasmic reticulum (*tint*), is greatly reduced.

fiber but only across a much shorter distance—on the average about five microns.

The existence of this network for oxygen supply hints at the solution to Hill's paradox concerning surface excitation and interior response. Could there not be some structure, similar to the structure for oxygen transport, that would channel excitatory signals deep into the muscle cell? If so, the signal would have to travel only a micron or so to influence the innermost fibrils. As has only recently been made clear, such a structure does exist. Called the *T* (for transverse) system, it extends deep into muscle fiber in association with a separate system of ducts and cavities known as the sarcoplasmic reticulum [see "The Sarcoplasmic Reticulum," by Keith R. Porter and Clara Franzini-Armstrong; SCIENTIFIC AMERICAN Offprint 1007].

Even after electron microscopy had revealed the *T* system of vertebrate muscle in detail, it was uncertain that its component tubules actually communicated with the exterior of the muscle cell. By means of a simple but elegant experiment Huxley has shown that the system is indeed open to the exterior. He soaked fibers of frog muscle in a solution of ferritin, a protein that contains iron particles .011 micron in diameter. These particles are readily recognized in electron micrographs, and in examining thin sections of soaked muscle Huxley found the iron in the tubules of the *T* system. The particles were never found in any of the cavities of the sarcoplasmic reticulum. Clearly the *T* system is an extension of extracellular space throughout the muscle cell. If very large molecules such as ferritin can diffuse freely through this system, it scarcely presents a barrier to the diffusion of ions and of molecules of a transmitter substance. Thus Hill's paradox is solved; a path is open so that excitation both at the surface and in the interior of the muscle fiber can be virtually simultaneous.

In insect muscle—except for asynchronous muscle—the organization of the *T* system is quite as clear-cut as it is in vertebrate muscle. The two systems are not identical, however. The striations of striated muscle consist of a repeating pattern of "Z lines" and "A bands." The light region between each Z line and A band is the "I zone"; the A band is also bisected by an "H zone." In vertebrate muscle the *T* system lies at right angles to the long axis of the muscle fiber, either in the plane of the Z

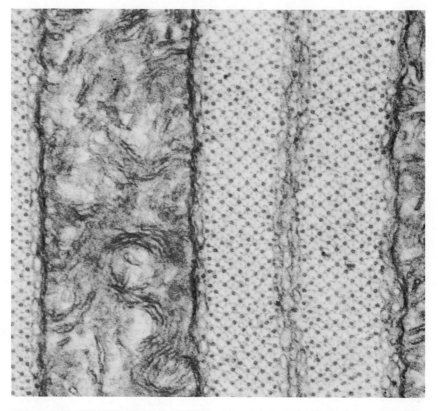

PRIMITIVE SYNCHRONOUS MUSCLE is characteristic of the dragonfly and damselfly; the platelike fibril structure is very much like that of insect leg and body muscle in general but the flight muscles are far more abundantly equipped with energy-supplying mitochondria. This is a transverse section of a damselfly flight muscle, enlarged 70,000 diameters.

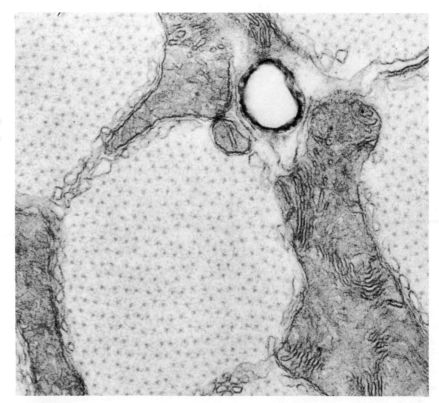

ADVANCED SYNCHRONOUS MUSCLE has its fibrils distributed in cylindrical rather than platelike structures; the mitochondria are wrapped around these cylinders. This is butterfly flight muscle in transverse section, enlarged 70,000 diameters. The tube at the top is a tracheole, part of the system that carries oxygen to and carbon dioxide from the tissues.

line or in the plane at the junction of the A band and the I zone [*see illustration on page 46*]. In insect muscle the T system lies instead in a plane midway between the Z line and the H zone. This arrangement is shown in longitudinal section in the top illustration on page 45 and in transverse section in the illustration on page 44.

The sarcoplasmic reticulum is at right angles to the T system; that is, it is oriented along the long axis of the muscle fiber. Its function is probably to provide regions of concentration for calcium ions in resting muscle fiber; the arrival of an excitation in the tubules of the T system evidently triggers the release of these ions from the sarcoplasmic reticulum, thus initiating the breakdown of ATP that powers the contraction of the fibrils. The sarcoplasmic reticulum then recaptures the activating ions, thereby halting the breakdown of ATP within the fibrils and allowing them to relax.

Although this picture of calcium ions being rapidly shuttled into and out of the fibrils has been put together on the strength of experiments with vertebrate muscle, the synchronous flight muscles of insects have an equally well-developed sarcoplasmic reticulum. In damselfly muscle fibers the sarcoplasmic reticulum almost fills the sarcoplasm between the elements of the T system; in butterfly muscle the sarcoplasmic reticulum is seen as chains of vesicles around transversely sectioned fibrils. Hence it appears that physiologically similar muscles in organisms as widely separated in the evolutionary scheme of things as insects and mammals are constructed on the same plan. The muscles contain not only the specialized array of protein filaments whose movements enable the muscle to do work but also the intricately related internal membranes that ensure that the muscle fibers give correctly timed responses to the directions issuing from the central nervous system.

In what ways has insect evolution modified normal synchronous striated muscle and enabled it to work in asynchronous fashion? The paper wasp *Polistes* will serve as an example of an insect whose wing mechanism is driven by these evolutionarily advanced fibers. Its bulky middle thoracic segment is almost filled with horizontal and vertical blocks of flight muscle. They serve to drive both pairs of wings, which are coupled together and work as one. The two sets of muscles, aligned at right

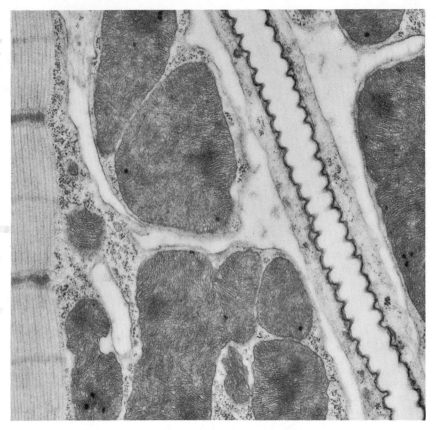

APHID FLIGHT MUSCLE, seen in longitudinal section and enlarged 16,000 diameters, is somewhat less regularly organized than the flight muscle of a wasp, although it is also asynchronous. The fibril (*left*) shows orderly banding, but the tubules of the T system (*light areas at top left, center and top right*) are neither uniform in shape nor aligned with the fibril bands. The indented diagonal structure is one of the tubes of the tracheolar system.

angles to each other, contract alternately; each action slightly deforms the shape of the thorax, and this in turn operates a delicate lever mechanism at the base of each wing. Contraction of the horizontal fibers lowers the wings and contraction of the vertical fibers raises them; they click up and down in time with the oscillatory shortening of the two antagonistic sets of muscles.

Electron micrographs immediately reveal one structural difference between asynchronous and synchronous muscle. This is in the way the myosin and actin filaments are fitted together at the ends of each repeating unit of striations. In relaxed synchronous muscle the I zones contain only filaments of actin; during contraction the ends of the myosin filaments are thought to slide into this region. In asynchronous muscle, however, the myosin filaments have tapered ends that seem to reach the central Z line. There they meet the actin filaments in a complicated arrangement; this has been shown by the work of J. Auber and R. Couteaux of the University of Paris.

When an asynchronous muscle con-

tracts, it shortens much less than a synchronous one, but this fact has shed no light on how the myosin filaments of asynchronous muscle move in the vicinity of the Z line. Although the sliding of overlapping filaments—along the lines of Huxley and Hanson's proposed model —may well occur here, there are still only a few hints as to how these muscles achieve their characteristic high-frequency oscillation. In any case it is certain that the fibrils of asynchronous muscle are able to utilize ATP. Experiments I have carried out in collaboration with Lois Tice of Columbia University show that a calcium-activated enzyme that splits ATP is present in the A bands of blowfly flight muscle and that the sites of this enzymatic activity are at the periphery of the myosin filaments.

The most striking difference of all between synchronous and asynchronous muscle fiber is found in the arrangement of the membranes situated between the fibrils. Electron micrographs make it clear that T-system tubules are present throughout asynchronous fiber just as they are in other muscle. In the wasp they are aligned with the *H* zone, in register with the middle of each repeating unit of striation [*see bottom illustration on page 45*]. Presumably the *T* system in asynchronous muscle fulfills the same role of transmitting excitatory signals that it does in other muscles. Although the frequency of oscillation in asynchronous muscle is much higher than the frequency of nerve impulses, a succession of excitations is necessary to maintain activity. In asynchronous muscle, however, there is almost no trace of the other membranous system so evident in synchronous muscle—the sarcoplasmic reticulum.

It is most interesting that the very structure that is believed to control the contraction-relaxation sequence in synchronous insect and vertebrate muscle is virtually absent from asynchronous muscle. Rather than alter our interpretation of the role of the sarcoplasmic reticulum, it is tempting to conclude that the flies, wasps, beetles and bugs have evolved a variety of muscle exceptional enough to prove the rule. Quite recently, however, Pringle and two of his colleagues at the University of Oxford, B. R. Jewell and J. C. Rüegg, have conducted experiments that may help to clarify at least one aspect of the function of asynchronous muscle. They took muscle cells of this type from two species of giant water bug and treated them with glycerine, a process that leaves the filaments of the fibrils intact but removes the sarcoplasm. When the treated muscle cells were placed in a medium containing calcium and ATP, they contracted and relaxed in an oscillatory fashion!

This result makes it clear that the mechanism that enables asynchronous muscle to oscillate resides within the contractile system of protein filaments that compose the fibrils. This being the case, perhaps it is no longer surprising to find that asynchronous muscle is poorly supplied with sarcoplasmic reticulum; the calcium ion give-and-take that operates synchronous muscle may not even occur in these specialized cells. In any case, when the details are fully elucidated of how the filaments in these muscles are organized, how they move with respect to one another and what chemical events are involved in their movement, we shall have not only an overall picture of the function of the most spectacularly active tissue that animals have evolved but also further insight into the mechanism of muscle in general.

5 Metamorphosis, Polymorphism, Differentiation

by V. B. Wigglesworth
February 1959

*The wondrous transformation of insects is explained
by two familiar growth processes. One accounts for
differences among individuals in a species; the other,
for differences among tissues in an organism*

I was five years of age when I made the most important scientific discovery of my life. A caterpillar I had imprisoned in a jam jar wrapped itself in silk and then, some days afterward, emerged under my close and astonished observation a butterfly!

Later on I learned that others, including Aristotle, had anticipated me in my discovery of insect metamorphosis. Natural philosophers and small boys apparently find the same amazement in the transformations of insects from caterpillar to chrysalis to butterfly, or from grub to pupa to bee. They have also usually arrived at the same explanation

for this peculiar departure from the common pattern of growth observed in other animals. According to Aristotle, the embryonic life of insects continues until the formation of the perfect insect, or imago. "The larva while it is yet in growth," he wrote, "is a soft egg." William Harvey, famous chiefly for his discovery of the circulation of the blood, surmised that the insect egg contains so little yolk that the embryo is obliged to emerge before completing its development. It then goes through a more or less prolonged larval stage during which it stores up quantities of food material—more yolk, as it were—before resuming the egg or pupa

form and completing its embryonic growth. Up to the end of the last century we still find authors writing of "those sorts of eggs that are called nymphs or pupae." And in current textbooks it is common to find the view expressed that metamorphosis is to be explained by the immaturity of the insect at the time of hatching from the egg.

But when metamorphosis is looked at more closely, this theory is not so satisfactory. Of course the development of the pupa has much in common with development of the embryo. Certain parts of the body, such as the wings, grow enormously, drawing upon reserves elsewhere in the body, just as the growing organs of the embryo draw upon the yolk. But that is no more than an analogy; it does not prove that the pupa, nor yet the larva, is an embryo. Instead of regarding the larva, the pupa and the adult as three stages in the progressive unfolding of a complex organism, it is possible to think of them as alternative forms which an already complex organism assumes at different periods in its development. In what follows we shall see that this view has the advantage of bringing metamorphosis into line with developmental patterns that are more universal in nature. Different individuals of a species, for example, frequently display variations in form that are no less extreme than those exhibited by an insect in different phases of its metamorphosis; such variation in form is called polymorphism. Similarly, different parts of many-celled organisms vary widely in form, though all of the tissues arise from the same single cell. Insect metamorphosis provides favorable opportunities for

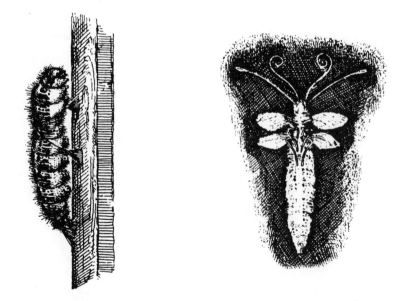

ADULT FORM CONCEALED in larva was discovered in 1669 by Jan Swammerdam, who dissected a caterpillar on the verge of spinning its cocoon. This demonstration of continuous growth of organs from existing structures helped dispel mystical views of metamorphosis.

observing this process of differentiation under experimental control.

In Harvey's conception of insect metamorphosis there was an element of the miraculous. Under the action of some mysterious influence the substance of the larva was rebuilt into an entirely new form. The Dutch naturalist Jan Swammerdam, in his *Historia Insectorum Generalis* published in 1669, strongly opposed this mysterious conception of metamorphosis. He had stripped away the skin of a caterpillar before it was due to be cast off and found the wings and other parts of the adult butterfly already in process of growth. From such observation he inferred that every structure arises by a process of continuous growth from an existing structure; that everything is already "preformed" in some state—some invisible state that we are unable to appreciate—from the earliest stages of growth.

At that time living cells were unknown, and genetics and evolution belonged to the future. Swammerdam's followers adopted the crude and exaggerated idea that all the future structures of the body were preformed in the egg, and that all growth and development consisted in the unfolding of these structures as successive covering shells were discarded. The height of absurdity was reached when observers claimed to have seen "homunculi," diminutive outlines of the human form, within the spermatozoon! Excesses such as this brought the reasonable views of Swammerdam into unfortunate disrepute.

With the advantage of current ideas on evolution and genetics and with the results of recent experiments in mind, we should be able to compose a truer picture of insect metamorphosis. The most obvious weakness of the "soft egg" theory lies in the fact that the larva of the more primitive insects, such as roaches, termites and grasshoppers, emerges from the egg in a form that more or less closely resembles the adult insect. The highest insects—the Coleoptera (beetles), the Lepidoptera (butterflies and moths), the Hymenoptera (bees and wasps) and the Diptera (flies)—offer the most striking examples of metamorphosis to be found. And yet the eggs of these insects are not notably deficient in yolk.

It can, of course, be argued that for some unknown reason these higher insects emerge from the egg at an early stage of embryonic development. But the resemblance of caterpillars or maggots to embryos is only superficial. When

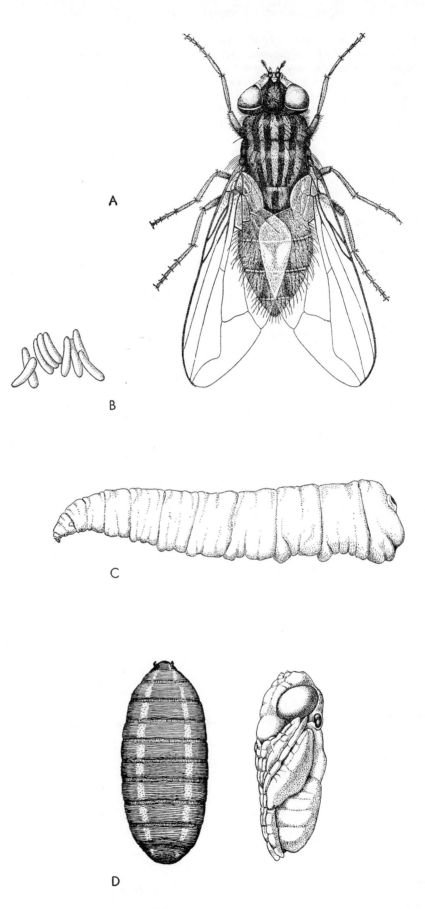

METAMORPHOSIS IN THE HOUSEFLY follows the classical pattern. From tiny embryo in egg (B) the creature grows to full-sized larva (C). The larval skin hardens and darkens to form the "puparium" that shelters the pupa (D). From pupa emerges the adult (A).

they are looked at closely they are seen to be most complex organisms, each highly adapted for its own mode of life.

At this point genetics and evolution enter decisively into the argument. Silkworm breeders long ago observed that there are many different genetic races of silkworms that can be distinguished as larvae but not as adults. Entomologists know of some species of insects that can be readily separated as larvae but only with difficulty or not at all as adults. The converse is also true. Clearly some genes affect only the structure of the larva, while others affect only the adult.

When the larva lives in conditions which differ from those in which the adult lives, it will be exposed to quite different selective pressures. In other words, it will become closely adapted to its special environment, while the pupal form and the adult form will evolve in

quite different directions according to the special requirements of their environments. Indeed, as soon as there are differences in the mode of life of the adult insect and its larva, the characteristics of the two forms will tend to diverge. Such divergence may continue until we reach the extremes that separate the maggot from the fly.

Variation in form is not, however, an exclusive distinction of insects. All animals are more or less polymorphic. Perhaps the most familiar are the male and female forms, which are often strikingly dissimilar within a single species. There is a large number of other variants. Now according to the view which holds metamorphosis to be a special example of polymorphism, the variations in form occur as successive stages in the development of an individual, instead of appearing in different individuals. But individuals of other species may undergo analogous transformation. A hen may be caused to change its plumage and become a functional cock by removal of its ovaries and implantation of a testis.

The sexual transformation of a fowl not only provides a close parallel to metamorphosis; it also raises an important aspect of the manner in which genetic inheritance is expressed in the in-

dividual. According to the simple tenets of classical Mendelism, the form of the animal is determined by the genes it carries in its cells. But in practice it does not always work out so simply, because other factors may control the manifestation or "penetrance" of some gene effects. Thus the change of sex hormones in the fowl causes its genetic constitution to find expression in an entirely new appearance and behavior.

Two genes in the fruit fly offer simpler demonstrations of the same principle. The main effect of one gene is to cause the antennae to fail to develop in the adult fly. But if the food of the larvae is rich in vitamin B-2, the genetically antennaless fly will develop normal antennae. The second mutant gene causes the modified hindwings—the little knobbed "halteres"—to develop into wings, so that these normally two-winged flies develop two pairs of wings. But this effect is greatly influenced by temperature. At 25 degrees centigrade the penetrance of this gene is 35 per cent; at 17 degrees it is only 1 per cent. Polymorphism in these cases is controlled indirectly by simple changes in nutrition and temperature.

Reversal of sex can also occur in insects. When certain solitary bees and

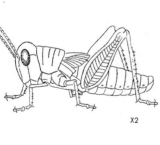

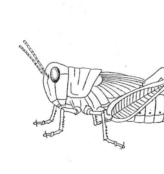

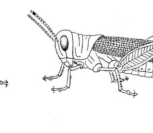

METAMORPHOSIS IN THE GRASSHOPPER presents far less dramatic changes than in the higher insects, and does not involve the resting pupal stage. The young grasshopper that emerges from the egg at upper left is wingless, but resembles adult except in proportion. The five nymphal (pre-adult) stages are shown same size to emphasize change in proportion. The magnification is given for each.

wasps are invaded during their larval life by the strange parasitic insect *Stylops*, male bees will develop the form and markings of females and female bees will acquire the characters of males. The cause of these changes seems to be nutritional; *Stylops* induces sex reversal only in those Hymenoptera which allocate a fixed ration to their larvae. If the larva is fed by its mother according to its needs, sex reversal does not occur. One must suppose that when the demands of the parasite deprive the growing organs of some essential factor in nutrition, the gene balance is upset and the latent genes of the opposite sex, which would normally be suppressed, are able to exert their action.

In some insects the whole outward form of the body may be transformed by a change in nutrition. The resulting insects may readily be mistaken for different species. The tiny parasitic wasp *Trichogramma semblidis* is an example. If its larva develops in the egg of various butterflies or moths, it arrives in the adult state as a normally winged insect. If it develops in the egg of the alder fly, however, the adult is devoid of wings, and the form of its legs and antennae is strikingly changed. Again one must suppose that some essential element in nutrition has influenced the penetrance of certain genes.

These examples of polymorphism provide all the elements of a satisfactory theory of metamorphosis. We simply picture the insect as having a larval, a pupal and an adult form. Each of these forms has evolved as an adaptation to life in a special environment, and each is controlled by its appropriate set of genes. What controls the activation, or penetrance, of these gene sets?

Twenty-five years ago it was shown by experiment that metamorphosis is controlled by a small gland known as the corpus allatum, which lies just behind the brain of an insect. During the larval stage this gland secretes a hormone, commonly called the juvenile hormone, or neotenin (the "youth substance"). Under the influence of the hormone the larval characters are retained. When the larva is fully grown, the corpus allatum no longer secretes the hormone; the adult characters are developed and metamorphosis occurs.

These facts were first established with the large South American blood-sucking bug *Rhodnius prolixus*, but they have been confirmed with almost all the other groups of insects. Furthermore, there is much evidence to suggest that in insects such as the Lepidoptera, which have a

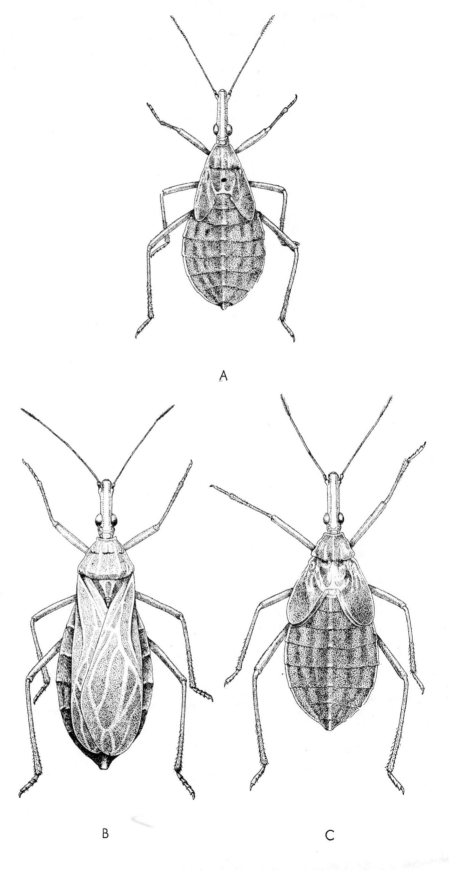

A

B

C

ARRESTED METAMORPHOSIS in the bloodsucking insect *Rhodnius* demonstrates the role of the juvenile hormone. At the end of the fifth stage of larval development (A) this insect normally molts to give rise to the winged adult (B). If the supply of juvenile hormone is artificially maintained by implantation of a corpus allatum gland from a young larva, however, the insect will emerge from the molting as a giant larva and without wings (C).

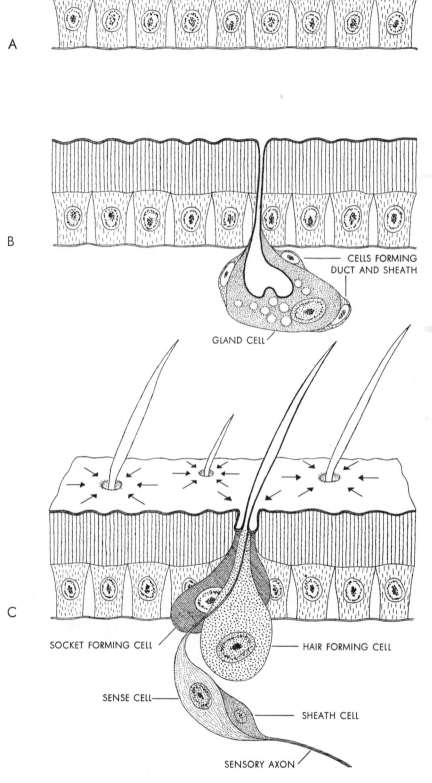

pupal stage, a large amount of hormone secretion is needed to produce the larval form, a very little is required to produce the pupa, while in the complete absence of hormone the adult form appears. Implantation of an active corpus allatum into a larva that is becoming full-grown causes the creature to retain its larval form and to grow into a giant larva [*see illustration on page 53*]. Conversely, removal of the gland causes the larva to undergo proc{o}cious metamorphosis and develop into a diminutive adult.

In the mature adult of many insects the corpus allatum begins once more to secrete the juvenile hormone, which may now be necessary for the proper development of the reproductive organs, notably for the deposition of yolk in the eggs. In the Cecropia silk moth, the hormone accumulates for some unknown reason in the abdomen of the male. This has made possible the preparation of active extracts of the hormone which reproduce all the effects previously obtained by the implantation of the corpus allatum.

The juvenile hormone must be a comparatively simple chemical substance, perhaps a sterol of the same general type as the sterol hormones of mammals. Indeed, Howard A. Schneiderman and Lawrence Gilbert of Cornell University have recently obtained a sterol from the adrenal gland of cattle which reproduces the effects of the juvenile hormone when injected into an insect. We have here a clear-cut example of a single chemical substance which determines whether the enzymes responsible for the development of larval characters shall be active or not. It is a reasonable assumption that the production of these enzymes is under the control of the appropriate genes. Thus when the juvenile hormone is present in quantity, the gene system of the larva is active; when little hormone is present, the gene system of the pupa asserts itself; when the hormone is absent, the gene system of the adult becomes ascendant. Just how a simple chemical substance leads to the activation of one set of genes or enzymes to the exclusion of another it is not yet possible to say. But the similarity of this phenomenon to other instances of polymorphism is obvious.

In the case of sex, as we have seen, differentiation can sometimes be reversed: one set of secondary sexual characteristics may give way to the other. This same reversal is possible also in metamorphosis. No one has succeeded in making whole insects revert from adult to larva. But when the juvenile hormone is applied to a restricted area of the abdomen of an adult *Rhodnius*, that area

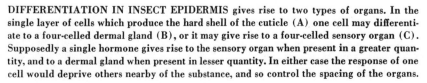

DIFFERENTIATION IN INSECT EPIDERMIS gives rise to two types of organs. In the single layer of cells which produce the hard shell of the cuticle (A) one cell may differentiate to a four-celled dermal gland (B), or it may give rise to a four-celled sensory organ (C). Supposedly a single hormone gives rise to the sensory organ when present in a greater quantity, and to a dermal gland when present in lesser quantity. In either case the response of one cell would deprive others nearby of the substance, and so control the spacing of the organs.

REVERSAL OF METAMORPHOSIS is demonstrated in *Rhodnius*. At left local application of the juvenile hormone has caused the cuticle of one segment in the abdomen to retain its juvenile characteristics. At right the author has traced his initials in larval cuticle.

at the next molt will lay down a cuticle with larval or partially larval characteristics [*see illustration above*]. Related effects have been reported in experiments with other insects. Clearly in some of the cells the enzyme system responsible for larval qualities is still present and capable of reactivation in the adult after metamorphosis.

We find, therefore, a close parallel between the "successive polymorphism," which we call metamorphosis, and the "alternative polymorphism," in which the different characters are developed by different individuals of a species. But there is yet another type of polymorphism which is even more familiar. I refer to the differentiation of the parts of a many-celled organism.

Such an organism begins its life as a single cell. As is well known, the process of cell division is so devised as to ensure an exact sharing of all the genetic material in the chromosomes in the daughter nuclei. It is therefore generally assumed that all the cells in the body have the same genetic constitution. But very soon after the egg cell has begun to divide,

the daughter cells become differentiated. Some go on to form the head, others the limbs, others the eyes.

We have here the most striking polymorphism of all. Since the nuclei appear to be genetically uniform throughout the organism, it is generally assumed that differentiation resides in the cytoplasm, that is, that part of the cell which is outside the nucleus. Presumably the different cytoplasms activate or inhibit the nuclei in such a way that different elements in the common gene system can exert their effects. Since the differences in the different cytoplasms are presumably chemical in nature, they must exert their effect on the gene system in the nucleus by chemical means.

Cell differentiation in the developing organism thus presents another close parallel with the other types of polymorphism. However, the factors responsible for bringing out differentiation do not spread freely throughout the body; the developing embryo is divided into "morphogenetic fields," in which the cytoplasm is committed or determined to form particular structures in the body.

We do not know how these fields be-

come different from one another in the embryo. One possible explanation is suggested, however, by the differentiation of cells in the epidermis of certain insects during metamorphosis. The insect epidermis consists of a single layer of cells which secrete the horny "cuticle," the only part of the insect which is normally visible. In the growing larva of *Rhodnius* the epidermal cells retain a certain capacity to differentiate and give rise to other organs. These organs are of two types. One is a dermal gland which secretes a thin protective covering on the outside of the cuticle. The other is a tactile sense organ which consists of an innervated hair arising from a socket at the center of a little dome of smooth cuticle. The essential parts of both organs are formed by four cells which are the daughters of a single epidermal cell [*see illustration on opposite page*].

Now the organs of each type are distributed in a regular way over the surface of the cuticle. Two of the sense organs, for example, are rarely found close together. On the other hand, if there is a wide space without a sense organ, a new one is sure to appear there at the next molt when a new cuticle is formed. If the epidermis is killed by applying a hot needle to a certain area of the abdomen, the surrounding cells multiply and grow inwards to repair the injury. The next time the larva molts this new epidermis lays down a cuticle without sense organs but with the normal distribution of dermal glands. At the following molt the sense organs reappear, spaced at the proper distance one from another.

What controls this regular distribution of organs? It is possible to suppose that the presence of a single chemical substance will induce an epidermal cell to give rise to a four-celled gland or sense organ. The hypothetical substance would be in limited supply, so that a developing organ would drain it away from the surrounding cells and thus prevent the appearance of another organ in the immedi-

ate vicinity. Beyond a certain distance, however, there would be sufficient substance to induce another cell to start differentiation. We may suppose that a larger amount is required for a sense organ than for a dermal gland. In normal development the two types of epidermal organ are quite distinct, but under certain conditions it is possible to obtain structures intermediate between the two. Admittedly no one has yet identified the controlling substance. But its postulated behavior is no more complicated than that of the juvenile hormone.

At the moment this is just a hypothesis. But it is worth pointing out that the distribution of human institutions is controlled in a similar fashion. An essential ingredient for the formation of a university, for example, is a supply of students. When a university is established,

it will drain off those students and will thereby inhibit the appearance of another university in the immediate neighborhood.

The integument of *Rhodnius* provides us with a model system for the differentiation of the body in general. We have a single layer of uniform and equipotent cells. During growth a single one of these cells divides and differentiates to form a complex organ of one type or another. If the hypothesis outlined above to account for the induction of these new structures bears any relation to the truth, it is clear that differentiation, polymorphism and metamorphosis may all be regarded as different aspects of a single phenomenon: the activation of specific gene systems latent in the nuclei by appropriate chemical stimuli furnished by hormones, inductors or specific nutritional factors.

6

The Juvenile Hormone

by Carroll M. Williams
February 1958

The larva of an insect makes a hormone which keeps it from changing into a pupa until it has reached its full growth. Recent experiments with this substance have produced both dwarf and giant adult insects

Twenty-five years ago the British biologist V. B. Wigglesworth performed an experiment which has given fascinating employment to a number of biologists ever since. The experiment in question was an operation on larvae of his favorite experimental animal, a blood-sucking bug known as *Rhodnius*. All he did was to chop off their heads (evidently it is not for nothing that Wigglesworth is known as the "Quick Professor of Biology" at the University of Cambridge). The results of the experiment were remarkable. A considerable number of the beheaded, immature larvae promptly metamorphosed into miniature adult Rhodniuses!

With little more to go on, Wigglesworth decided that he had discovered a "juvenile hormone" which blocks the metamorphosis of a larva until it has

FIVE PUPAE of the Polyphemus silkworm in this photograph received graded doses of juvenile hormone from the Cecropia silkworm. In each pupa the old pupal case has been shed. The pupa at far left received the largest dose; it has entered a second pupal stage. The pupa at far right received the smallest dose; it has turned into an adult moth, except for an island of pupal tissue at the bottom.

achieved its full growth. Since the hormone had been removed by decapitation of the insect, its source must be somewhere in the head. After a microscopic study of the heads of his bugs, Wigglesworth concluded that the hormone came from a tiny cluster of cells just behind the brain—a pair of glands called the "corpora allata."

The test of scientific genius is the ability to reason to correct conclusions from inadequate evidence. Each and every one of Wigglesworth's conclusions proved to be correct. There *is* a juvenile hormone, it *does* prevent metamorphosis, and it *is* secreted by the corpora allata. Furthermore, the corpora allata and the juvenile hormone have become fruitful subjects of investigation in many laboratories—in the U. S., France, Britain, Germany and Japan. Investigators have found corpora allata in the heads of all species of insects except a few ancient forms that do not metamorphose. The organs are so tiny that even in the largest insects they are scarcely visible without the aid of a microscope. But a Frenchman, Jean Bounhiol, developed a delicate operation which permitted him to remove the corpora allata from the head. He excised these organs from silkworms and got a clear-cut result: the little silkworms cut short their growth as caterpillars, spun miniature cocoons, changed into tiny pupae and finally emerged as midget adult moths. In short, the removal of the corpora allata caused the insect to abbreviate its childhood and play its life history as an end game.

The juvenile hormone itself remained a will-o'-the-wisp. Chemists tried to extract it from the corpora allata, mashing up glands dissected from hundreds of insects to get enough material, but their extracts uniformly failed to show any activity. Notwithstanding this failure, biologists were able to learn a great deal about the hormone by using the living factory that makes it—the corpora allata. They transplanted these glands from one insect to another and studied the effects.

Among other things, they learned that, just as removal of the corpora allata from a young larva would produce a dwarfed adult, so addition of these active organs to an older larva would produce a giant. As a larva (*i.e.*, caterpillar) reaches mature size, the corpora allata cease to make the juvenile hormone. The caterpillar then stops growing and metamorphoses. But experimenters found that if they implanted active corpora allata from a younger larva into a ma-

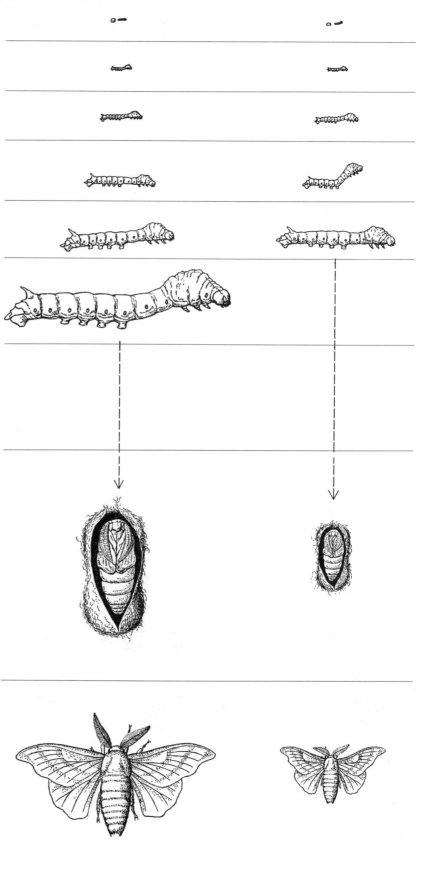

DWARF AND GIANT MOTHS were made by removing and implanting the corpora allata, a pair of glands in the head of an insect. The column at left outlines the normal development of the commercial silkworm *Bombyx mori*. At the top of the column is the egg of the insect and its newly hatched larva. Below them are five stages in the growth of the larva. Below these is the pupa in its cocoon, and below this is the adult moth. The second column

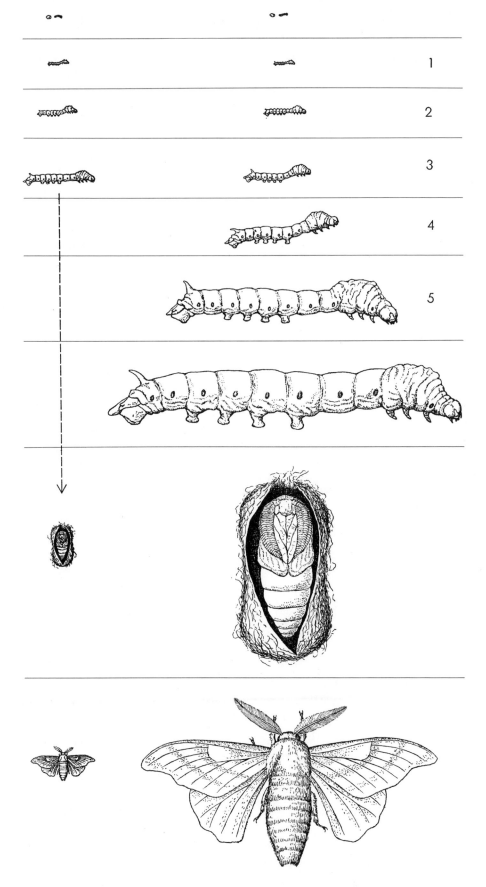

1

2

3

4

5

shows what happens when the corpora allata are removed at the fourth larval stage: the larva immediately changes into a dwarf pupa, and then into a dwarf moth. In the third column the corpora allata are removed at the third stage, resulting in an even smaller pupa and moth. In the fourth column the corpora allata of a young larva are implanted in a larva of the fifth stage. This larva continues to grow and then changes into a giant pupa and moth.

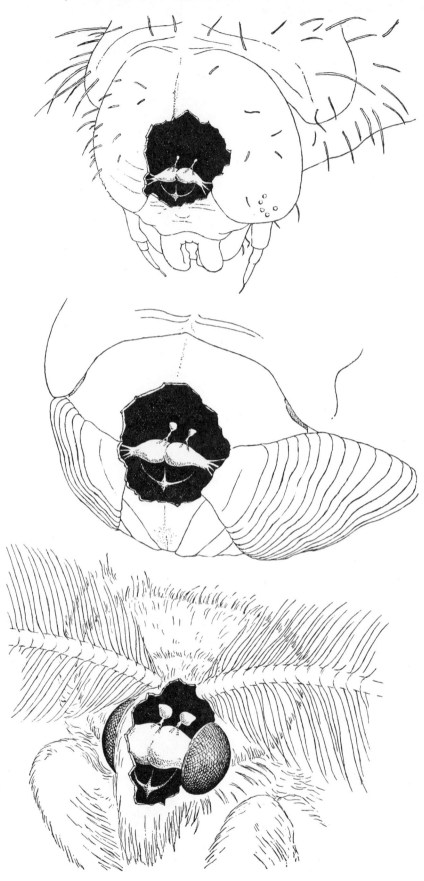

BRAIN AND CORPORA ALLATA of the Cecropia silkworm are shown in cutaway views of the head of the larva (*top*), the pupa (*middle*) and adult moth (*bottom*). The corpora allata are the two small bodies which project backward from the hemispheres of the brain.

turing one, the rejuvenated caterpillar would postpone its metamorphosis and eventually grow into a giant insect. Incidentally, this seems to be the only way that nature can make a very large insect, and we can begin to understand how it produced the enormous insect species, with three-foot wingspread, that lived in the Carboniferous Period some 200 million years ago. In those days the corpora allata must have continued to pour out juvenile hormone for a much longer period than is now fashionable among insects.

The whole idea of a juvenile hormone —a substance that can delay maturity or aging without interfering with growth as such—has haunted some of us for many years. It is such a powerful tool for biological experiments, and offers so many fascinating possibilities, that we have scarcely been able to put it out of our minds for more than a few minutes at a time. In our laboratory at Harvard University we turned our attention to the process of metamorphosis itself—the stage when the insect, having advanced from a larva to a pupa, is finally transformed into an adult. The juvenile hormone, we found, plays no part in this transformation: the corpora allata have stopped supplying it. Suppose we supplied the hormone to the pupa artificially. What would happen? We implanted active corpora allata from young silkworms in pupal insects, inserting the glands through a hole in the skin and sealing the hole with melted wax. The pupa turned into a monstrosity. We got a creature which was a mixture of pupa and adult moth, possessing parts or tissues of each. The higher the concentration of juvenile hormone, the more complete was the suppression of adult development.

This finding suggested a practical method for assaying the activity of the corpora allata at various stages of an insect's development. We found, indeed, that the glands' activity declined just before pupation and disappeared immediately afterward. During almost the whole period of the insect's development into a full-fledged moth, the glands remained totally inactive. But, curiously enough, just before it emerged as a moth the corpora allata became even more active than they had been in the young larva!

Here indeed is a puzzle. What possible function can the juvenile hormone perform in the adult moth? We have not yet found the answer. But the paradox did help us to run down and isolate the elusive juvenile hormone.

In other experiments, being pursued for reasons having nothing to do with juvenile hormone, we were grafting a pupa to a beheaded adult moth (of the well-known Cecropia species, our favorite experimental animal). When we performed the experiment with a male moth, we got a remarkable result. The headless male graft caused the pupa to go into a second pupal stage instead of metamorphosing into a moth, as it was supposed to do. That is to say, the pupa behaved as if it had received a rich dose of juvenile hormone. Where had the hormone come from? To make a long story short, we finally located the source in the abdomen of the headless adult moth. The abdomen proved to be full of juvenile hormone.

It was from this confusing state of affairs that we finally wrung forth the hormone itself. The abdomen cannot manufacture the hormone: it is secreted only by the corpora allata in the head. But the adult abdomen acts as a depot. When the corpora allata resume their production of the hormone in the adult moth, the abdomen receives and stores this output. Over a period of several weeks it caches away an enormous amount of the hormone. For some unknown reason only the male possesses this ability to take up the hormone in its abdominal tissues; the female abdomen has only a trace of it.

By a happy coincidence we succeeded in isolating our first extracts of juvenile hormone while visiting Wigglesworth's laboratory at Cambridge. We cut up the abdomens of adult male Cecropia moths and put them in ether to dissolve the soluble substances in the tissues. After evaporating the solvent, we had a beautiful golden oil, which proved to be extremely rich in juvenile hormone. A single insect's abdomen yields enough hormone to block the metamorphosis of 10 pupae. The extract from the Cecropia moth can act upon a great variety of other species and orders of insects. In each case it opposes metamorphosis and thus tends to preserve the *status quo*.

In collaboration, Howard Schneiderman and Lawrence Gilbert of Cornell University and I have now reduced the extract to a highly purified form of the hormone. Our best preparations are active at one part of hormone per million parts of insect. If all goes well, we hope we shall soon be able to write a chemical formula for the juvenile hormone. It ap-

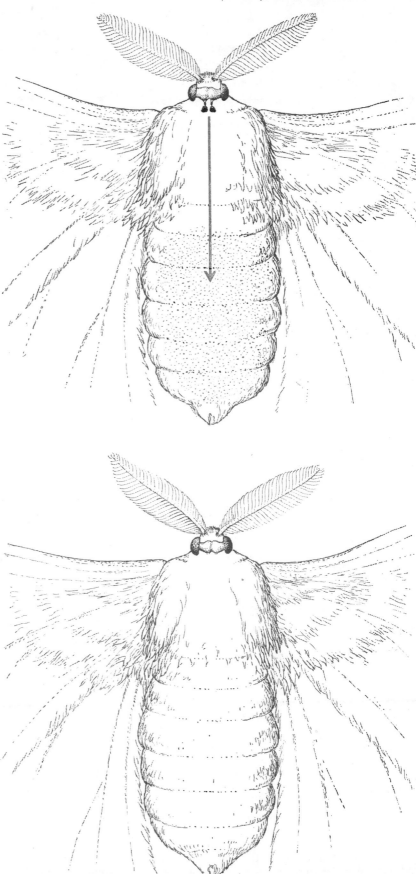

JUVENILE HORMONE IS STORED in the abdomen of the adult insect after it has been secreted by the corpora allata. In the drawing of the Cecropia moth at top the corpora allata are the small colored bodies; the stored hormone is represented by the colored stippling. In the drawing at bottom the corpora allata have been removed and no hormone is stored.

ANATOMY OF THE CECROPIA SILKWORM is shown in detail by these cutaway drawings. At top is the full-grown larva. At right center is the pupa. At bottom is the adult moth. The three stages are drawn to the same scale, but are about twice life size.

pears to be an extremely stable molecule—resistant to heat, dilute acids and bases. In fact, we have extracted active hormone from museum specimens of insects that have been dead as long as eight years.

One of our findings is that the hormone is effective even when it is merely applied to the surface of an insect's skin. Enough hormone gets into the body to foul up its metamorphosis. The animal soon dies, without completing its development. This suggests that we may be

able to use insect hormones as an insecticide—a truly perfect insecticide, for the insects could hardly evolve a resistance to their own hormones.

Cosmetic chemists apparently have sensed another use for the juvenile hormone. They want to put the hormone into their lotions, adding it to the "royal jelly" already incorporated in some of these preparations. We may look forward to a whole generation of non-aging queen bees.

From the standpoint of pure science

there seems little room to doubt that the juvenile hormone has much to tell us about the chemical engineering of growth. Here is an agent which somehow imposes a biochemical restraint on growing up without interfering with growth as such. It represents, at the insect level, a "Peter Pan hormone." Can there be such a thing in higher forms? Can we look forward to a chemotherapy for aging and senescence? Perhaps the juvenile hormone of insects may encourage a fresh look at this possibility.

7

The Biological Clock of Insects

by D. S. Saunders
February 1976

With the approach of winter, insects enter into a state of dormancy. This shift in metabolism implies that they have a clock to measure changes in the length of the day. What is the nature of the clock?

Organisms that have the ability to measure the passage of time are said to possess biological clocks. One kind of clock measures the length of the day or the night, thereby enabling the organism to distinguish between the long days of summer and the short days of winter. The organism may respond to these seasonal cycles with a change in its metabolism, and such a response is called photoperiodic.

Daily rhythms or oscillations control a wide range of activities in plants and animals, and because such rhythms have a period close to, but not exactly, 24 hours they are called circadian (from the Latin *circa dies*, "about a day"). In insects the usual response to the onset of short days is diapause, a period of dormancy between stages of active growth and development. Changes of as little as 10 to 15 minutes in the length of the day can shift the metabolic regime of a population of insects from growth and development to diapause. There has been much controversy about the nature of the clock in such insects: whether it is comparable to an hourglass or to an oscillator with a period of close to 24 hours. Recent experiments indicate that the distinction between the two mechanisms may not be quite as important as interested biologists once thought.

The selective advantage of diapause in the life cycle of an insect is twofold. It provides a mechanism for survival over periods when food is in short supply or when the climate is unfavorable, and it serves to synchronize the development of the individuals in a population so that all of them feed as larvae or emerge as adults at the appropriate time of year. Reliance on day length for determining the season also confers a selective advantage. Compared with seasonal changes in temperature or humidity,

changes in the length of the day are almost free of "noise," or irregularity. Furthermore, response to a certain day length well in advance of winter gives the insect's metabolism time to make the necessary adjustments for entering diapause. In anticipation of diapause the insect lays down reserves of fat, reduces the level of its metabolism and may form special layers of wax in order to resist dehydration.

The minimum requirements for a photoperiodic mechanism are (1) a receptor to detect the presence or absence of daylight, (2) a clock to measure the length of the day or the night and to integrate that information and (3) an effector system

to control such metabolic changes as entry into diapause. Most of the early investigations of photoperiodism in insects were concerned with the nature and location of the photoreceptors and the effector system; only recently has progress been made in determining the nature and the properties of the clock mechanism.

Studies of a wide variety of insects have shown that the receptors involved in the photoperiodic response are in the animal's brain. It has also been demonstrated that the insect's eye is not involved in its photoperiodic response. Indeed, the eyes can be surgically removed without impairing the response.

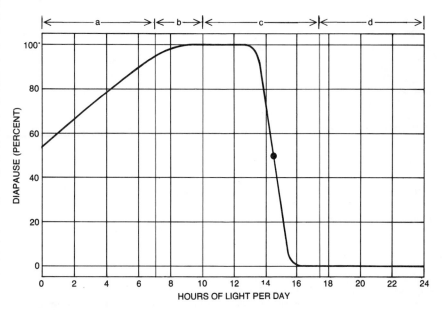

PHOTOPERIODIC RESPONSE CURVE for the fly *S. argyrostoma* shows the proportion of a population of larvae that produce diapausing pupae at various day lengths. The critical day length for the induction of diapause is 14½ hours. The photoperiods *a* and *d* do not occur naturally in the fly's normal environment. The photoperiods *b* occur during the winter, when the insects are in diapause, and photoperiods *c* occur during spring, summer and fall.

In 1934 V. B. Wigglesworth of the University of Cambridge suggested that insects enter diapause because of a temporary lack of certain hormones, "due sometimes, perhaps, to an inborn rhythm, sometimes, perhaps, to the indirect effects of environmental factors." His hormone-deficiency theory of diapause has since been verified experimentally for a wide variety of insects, and it is clear that the effector system controlling the onset of diapause involves glands in the insect's brain. It appears that when the brain is exposed to short days, the release of the hormones is inhibited, and that when the brain is exposed to long days, their release is promoted.

Since the photoreceptors and the hormone effector system are located in the insect's brain, it follows that the most likely site for the clock is also in the brain. Although there is some experimental evidence supporting this proposition, it is not conclusive. The central question, however, is the nature of the clock. How does it measure the length of the day or the night? How does it integrate successive long days or successive short days? And how does the clock translate the information that signals the effector system to either promote or inhibit the release of hormone by the brain?

Two models of how insects measure time have been put forward. One proposes that the length of the day or the night is measured by an interval timer, an hourglass type of mechanism. Such a mechanism could be started by dawn and stopped by dusk, or it could be started by dusk and stopped by dawn. The alternative model was suggested by Erwin Bünning of the University of Tübingen in 1936. He proposed that the measurement of the length of the day or the night was accomplished by an endogenous, or built-in, daily rhythm that consisted of two half-cycles, one photophilic ("light-loving") and the other scotophilic ("dark-loving"). He thought that the phase of the endogenous rhythm would be set by dawn. If the daily light period was long, the period of illumination would extend into the scotophilic part of the cycle, and the organism would exhibit its typical long-day responses. If the daily light period was short, the organism would exhibit short-day responses. In effect, Bünning was proposing that organisms measure time with an endogenous circadian oscillator.

At the time Bünning put forward his model there was little experimental evidence to support it. Its great contribution was that it focused attention on the possibility that all types of biological time measurement have a common mechanism. Although Bünning's hypothesis appears to be similar to Wigglesworth's suggestion that diapause in insects could be due to "an inborn rhythm," it is clear that Wigglesworth was thinking more of an inborn annual rhythm than of rhythms with a circadian period.

Unfortunately there is still no direct way to investigate the timing mechanisms of insects, and we are limited to treating the mechanism as a "black box." Accordingly most of the research has involved artificially varying the intervals of light and darkness and measuring the response of a population of insects to the various intervals in terms of the proportion of the population entering diapause. One successful technique is to expose the insects to repeated cycles of light and darkness, each consisting of a short period of light, say 12 hours, followed by an extended period of darkness, say 60 hours, with the dark period interrupted by brief pulses of light at a different time in the extended "night." Each experimental group of insects experiences the interrupting light pulse at a different time in the night. If the photoperiodic clock has something to do with a circadian rhythm, the diapause response should peak roughly at 24-hour intervals. If, on the other hand, the clock is like an hourglass, no such periodic effect should be observed.

A second technique is to alternate a fixed period of light with a fixed period of darkness and to expose different populations of the insect to different combinations of light and darkness. If the driving cycle (the light period plus the period of darkness) is close to 24 hours or to multiples of 24 hours, one would expect the diapause response to peak roughly at 24-hour intervals if the clock is a function of the circadian rhythm. This approach has been called the resonance technique because it shows that the circadian oscillator functions most effectively when it is driven close to its natural period, that is, in resonance with the normal 24-hour cycle of night and day.

These two techniques have been successfully used to demonstrate the circadian nature of the photoperiodic clock in plants and birds. Until recently the results with insects were largely inconclusive. The first demonstration that photoperiodic time measurement in insects is a circadian phenomenon has come from my experiments with the large flesh fly *Sarcophaga argyrostoma* and its parasite *Nasonia vitripennis*, a wasp.

S. argyrostoma is a fly common in northern Europe. The larvae of the fly, which are deposited on carrion, are sensitive to photoperiodic influences at all stages of their development, from the time they are embryos within the maternal uterus until they metamorphose into pupae. If the larvae are artificially exposed to short days (less than 14 hours of light), the pupae enter diapause rather than metamorphosing into adult flies. If the larvae are exposed to more than 14 hours of light, the pupae metamorphose into adult flies without interruption.

N. vitripennis is a small wasp that drills through the outer pupal case of *Sarcophaga* and other flesh-eating flies. It lays its eggs on the pupa, and when the wasp larvae hatch out, they feed

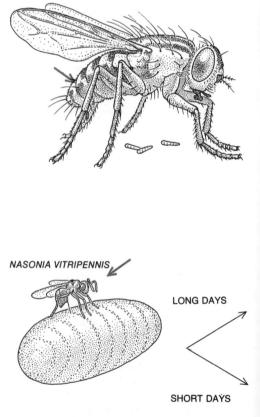

SARCOPHAGA ARGYROSTOMA

NASONIA VITRIPENNIS

LONG DAYS

SHORT DAYS

SENSITIVITY TO CHANGES in day length comes at different stages of development in the northern European flesh fly *Sarcophaga argyrostoma* and its parasite *Nasonia vitripennis*, a wasp. In the flesh fly sensitivity to

on the soft pupal tissues. They pupate within the host pupa and emerge as adults after biting a hole through its shell. The wasp larvae do not exhibit any photoperiodic response. The wasp's sensitive stage is the time when its eggs are still in the maternal ovaries.

If the female wasp is exposed to long days (more than 15¼ hours of light), the eggs will give rise to larvae that do not enter diapause. If the female wasp is exposed to shorter days, the larvae emerging from those eggs will go into diapause in the last stage of their development. I initially demonstrated that the photoperiodic response of this wasp was a circadian phenomenon by means of experiments where the female wasps were exposed to repeated cycles of a short period of light followed by a long period of darkness that was interrupted by brief pulses of light. Maximum diapause was observed when the brief interrupting pulses came at 19, 43 and 67 hours after the onset of the main photoperiod of the

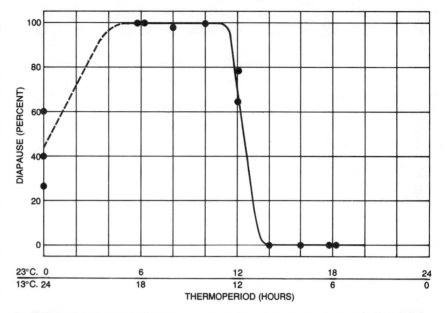

DAILY TEMPERATURE CYCLES can control diapause induction in *N. vitripennis* when the wasp is reared in complete darkness. Female wasps raised in a cycle that has more than 11 hours at 13 degrees Celsius give rise to progeny that go into diapause. The results show that the wasp's oscillators can be entrained by temperature cycles as well as by light cycles.

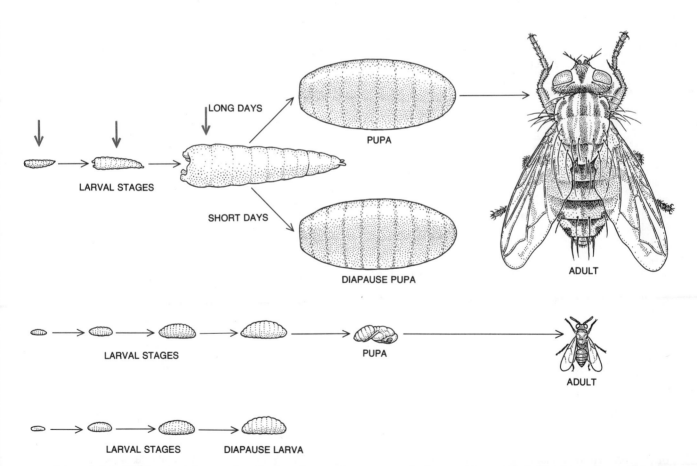

photoperiod (*colored arrows*) begins when the larvae are at the embryo stage in the maternal uterus and extends through three stages of larval development. Larvae exposed to more than 14 hours of light develop into adults without interruption, whereas larvae exposed to shorter days enter a period of diapause, or dormancy, as pupae. In the parasitic wasp the sensitivity to photoperiod comes while the eggs are in the maternal ovaries. The female wasp lays its eggs in the pupa of the flesh fly. Eggs exposed to more than 15¼ hours of light give rise to larvae that develop without diapause. Eggs exposed to shorter days give rise to larvae that go into diapause.

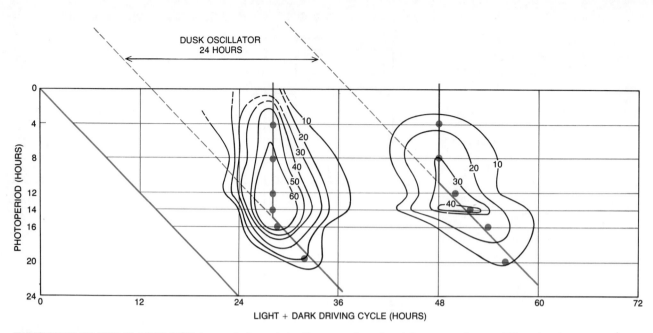

INDUCTION OF PUPAL DIAPAUSE in populations of the fly *S. argyrostoma* that were exposed to various cycles of light and dark is shown in the form of contour plots. The contours define the driving cycles of light and dark that induce diapause in the fly at the levels of 10, 20, 30, 40, 50 and 60 percent. The solid colored circles mark peaks of diapause induction. When the photoperiod is less than 12 hours, the diapause peaks come at the same time. When the photoperiod is more than 12 hours, the peaks form a slope that parallels the "light off" slope of the photoperiod, indicating that the oscillator now takes its principal time cue from beginning of dusk.

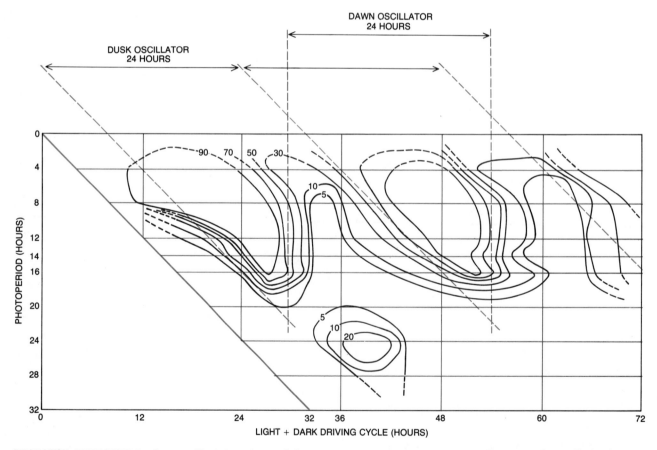

DIAPAUSE CONTOURS for the wasp *N. vitripennis* reveal three high-diapause plateaus at roughly 24-hour intervals. Diapause in the wasp is induced by exposing the females to short photoperiods while the eggs are still in the maternal ovaries. The contours define the driving cycles of light and dark that induce between 5 and 90 percent diapause in the wasp larvae. Each plateau has an ascending slope on its left side that is parallel to the "light off" slope of the photoperiod and a descending slope on its right side that is parallel to the vertical "light on" slope of the photoperiod. The slopes of the diapause plateaus are interpreted as being manifestations of two independent oscillators, one entrained, or set, by dusk and the other entrained by dawn. Each oscillator has a period of 24 hours.

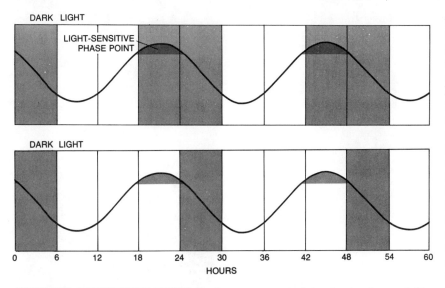

DARK LIGHT

LIGHT-SENSITIVE
PHASE POINT

DARK LIGHT

EXTERNAL-COINCIDENCE MODEL for the measurement of time by the photoperiodic clock, as proposed by Colin S. Pittendrigh of Stanford University, consists of a circadian oscillator with a light-sensitive phase point (*colored area*). When the day length is short, say 12 hours, the light-sensitive phase point is not illuminated and diapause occurs (*top*). When the days are long, the phase point is illuminated and diapause does not occur (*bottom*).

cycle (that is, at 24-hour intervals), and minimum diapause was observed when the interrupting pulses fell at intervening times.

In 1971 I spent a year at Stanford University working in the laboratory of Colin S. Pittendrigh. Pittendrigh has made intensive studies of the relation between photoperiodism and circadian rhythms, particularly in the fruit fly and the pink bollworm moth. He has extended Bünning's hypothesis with the proposal that the endogenous clock consists of two independent oscillators, one en-

trained, or set, by dawn and the other entrained by dusk. As the photoperiod changes, the phase relations of the two oscillations also change. In this internal-coincidence model, as it is now called, light has only one role: entrainment. Long days would shift one set of oscillations until it was in step with the other, and the combined effect of the two sets of oscillations would result in development without diapause, perhaps because any in-phase temporal relation between two cellular components would, for example, result in the synthesis of a third substance that is responsible for initiating development. Short days, on the other hand, would put the two sets of oscillations out of phase, and in the absence of the substance that promotes development, diapause would occur [*see bottom illustration on this page*]. A similar model was independently proposed by the Russian entomologist V. P. Tyshchenko in 1966.

In Pittendrigh's laboratory I conducted resonance experiments with both the fly *Sarcophaga argyrostoma* and its parasitic wasp *Nasonia vitripennis*. The results demonstrated that the photoperiodic response of both insects was circadian but that the details for the two species were quite dissimilar. In experimental populations of the parasitic wasp the results indicated the presence of independent "dawn" and "dusk" oscillations. In the flesh fly, however, the photoperiodic clock seemed to consist of a single oscillation that was entrained to the entire photoperiod when the photoperiod was less than 12 hours, but once the photoperiod exceeded 12 hours the oscillation obtained its principal time cue from dusk. The two species therefore showed the properties of the two current theoretical models for oscillatory photoperiodic clocks: respectively internal coincidence and external coincidence. The parasitic wasp displayed the properties of Pittendrigh's model with two oscillators, and the flesh fly displayed the properties of Bünning's model with a single oscillator.

If the photoperiodic clock of the parasitic wasp is of the internal-coincidence type, a simple test is available. It is known that a variety of circadian rhythms can be entrained by temperature. Since light has only the role of entrainment in this model, it should be possible to simulate the effects of photoperiodic entrainment with periods of higher and lower temperature in the complete absence of light.

Female wasps raised from the egg

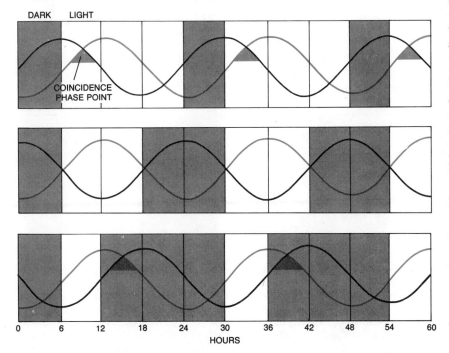

DARK LIGHT

COINCIDENCE
PHASE POINT

INTERNAL-COINCIDENCE MODEL, also proposed by Pittendrigh, consists of two circadian oscillators, the phase of one set by dawn (*colored curve*) and the phase of the other set by dusk (*black curve*). When the days are long, the two oscillations are partially in phase (*top*) and development proceeds without diapause. When the days are short, the oscillations are out of phase and diapause occurs (*middle*). Very short days (*bottom*) may produce some coincidence of the two oscillations, which would result in development without diapause.

stage in total darkness were exposed to various daily temperature cycles consisting of a period at 23 degrees Celsius followed by a period at 13 degrees C. Wasps raised in a cycle that had more than 13 hours at the higher temperature gave rise to progeny that did not go into diapause, and wasps raised in a cycle that had more than 11 hours at the lower temperature gave rise to progeny that did go into diapause [*see the top illustration on page 65*]. The results of the experiment not only show that temperature cycles can be substituted for light cycles in this wasp but also rule out for the wasp any model of a clock in which light induces, or starts, diapause or development by photobiological means other than mere entrainment.

The clock of the flesh fly, on the other hand, does suggest such an inductive property for environmental light. Pittendrigh has proposed an external-coincidence model in which light plays a dual role: entrainment and induction. That is, light can both entrain the oscillation and control induction. This model consists of a circadian oscillator that is entrained by light in such a way that a photoinducible phase of the oscillator is not illuminated in short days but is illuminated in long days. Illumination of the photoinducible phase results in long-day effects, or uninterrupted development, but when the photoinducible phase falls in the dark period, diapause supervenes.

Evidence supporting the external-coincidence model comes from Pittendrigh's intensive study of the emergence of fruit flies of the species *Drosophila pseudoobscura* from their pupae. The circadian rhythm of adult emergence is damped out by periods of light greater than 12 hours but resumes when the pupae are transferred to darkness. In a natural 24-hour light cycle with 12 hours or more of light the oscillation restarts each dusk and measures the length of the night as if it were an hourglass. Only when the night is extended to more than 24 hours is the oscillatory nature of the system revealed.

The resonance experiments with the fly *Sarcophaga argyrostoma* produced similar results and demonstrated the hourglass nature of the night-length measurement. Thus photoperiods greater than 12 hours had a damping effect on photoperiodic oscillation in *S. argyrostoma*. It therefore seems to be a reasonable working hypothesis that the clock of the fly is of the external-coincidence type.

Additional evidence for the existence of a dark-period hourglass in insects comes from studies of the aphid *Megoura viciae* by Anthony D. Lees of the Imperial College of Science and Technology. Lees found that the aphid's clock is set in motion at dusk and measures night length as an hourglass does. Moreover, the aphid, like the flesh fly, needs a photoperiod of a minimum length before the clock can act as an hourglass. When the aphid is subjected to extended nights, however, it does not display oscillatory properties. This suggests that the aphid's clock is an oscillator executing only a single cycle before it is extinguished. If that is the case, the dividing line between oscillators and hour-

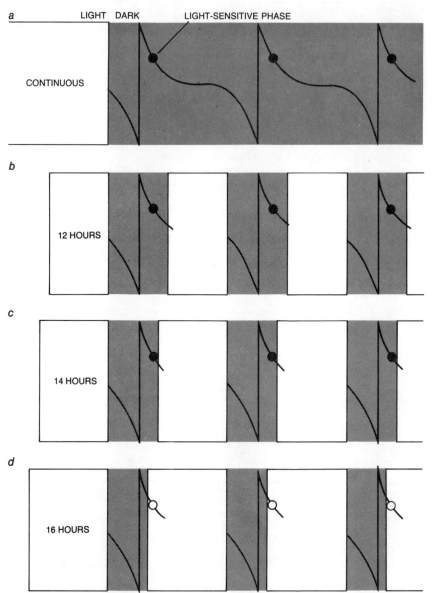

RHYTHM OF PUPAL EMERGENCE in the fruit fly *Drosophila pseudoobscura* shows the characteristics of the external-coincidence model for the photoperiodic clock. When pupae are transferred from continuous light to continuous darkness (*a*), the rhythm with which adult flies emerge from the pupa always starts at a fixed phase, called circadian time 12 because it is equivalent to the phase of the oscillation at the end of a 12-hour light period (*b*). The light-sensitive phase first occurs about nine hours later at circadian time 21, and in constant darkness it appears at about 24-hour intervals thereafter. With cycles of 12 hours of light and 12 of darkness (*b*) and 14 hours of light and 10 hours of darkness (*c*), the light-sensitive phase (*solid circles*) falls in the dark period, and since it is not illuminated, diapause occurs. When the cycle is 16 hours of light and eight hours of darkness (*d*), the light-sensitive phase is illuminated (*open circles*) and diapause does not occur. Since the rhythm always starts at dusk at the same circadian time, as the length of the light period increases dawn moves backward in relation to the oscillation. Since the oscillation is reset by each photoperiod, it measures the length of the night as though it were an hourglass.

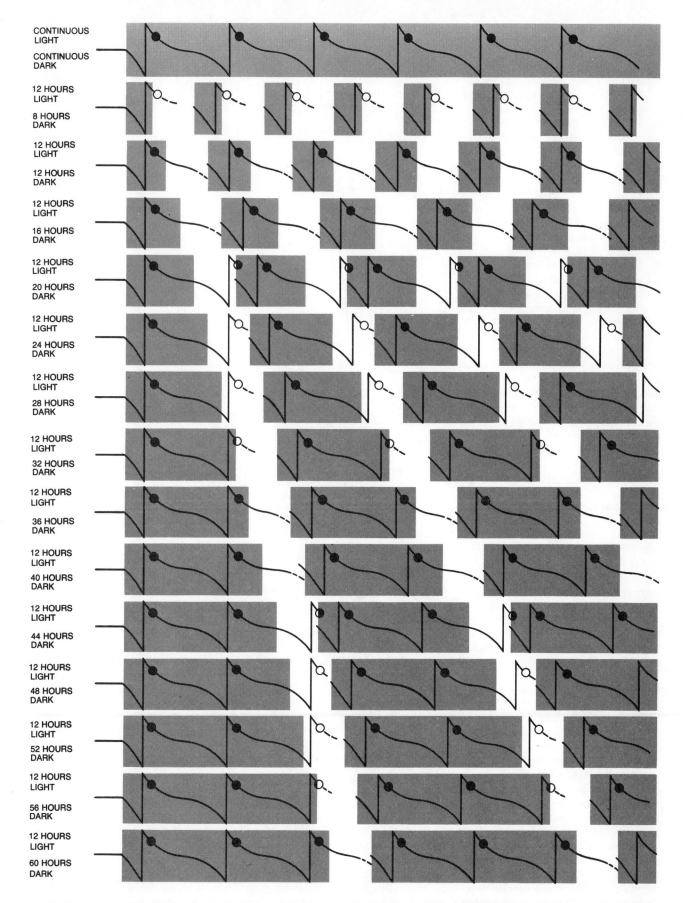

CONTINUOUS LIGHT
CONTINUOUS DARK

12 HOURS LIGHT
8 HOURS DARK

12 HOURS LIGHT
12 HOURS DARK

12 HOURS LIGHT
16 HOURS DARK

12 HOURS LIGHT
20 HOURS DARK

12 HOURS LIGHT
24 HOURS DARK

12 HOURS LIGHT
28 HOURS DARK

12 HOURS LIGHT
32 HOURS DARK

12 HOURS LIGHT
36 HOURS DARK

12 HOURS LIGHT
40 HOURS DARK

12 HOURS LIGHT
44 HOURS DARK

12 HOURS LIGHT
48 HOURS DARK

12 HOURS LIGHT
52 HOURS DARK

12 HOURS LIGHT
56 HOURS DARK

12 HOURS LIGHT
60 HOURS DARK

THEORETICAL APPLICATION of the external-coincidence model to resonance experiments involves using a 12-hour photoperiod and varying the periods of darkness. When the light-sensitive phase of the circadian oscillator falls in a dark period, diapause occurs (*solid circles*). When the light-sensitive phase is completely illuminated (*open circles*), diapause does not occur. Partial illumination of the sensitive phase results in a lower incidence of diapause. In all cases the oscillations take their time cue from onset of dusk.

glasses becomes very fine, perhaps even academic.

Bünning's single-oscillator model, the external-coincidence model and the two-oscillator internal-coincidence model have one thing in common: long days have a positive effect in that they give rise to development or prevent the insect from going into diapause, whereas short days are considered to be essentially neutral. All insects add up successive light periods before they display photoperiodic induction. It is therefore probable that long days lead to the production of a chemical substance, and the summation of long days is represented by the accumulation of that substance to a level where it stimulates the release of a brain hormone that initiates the chain of events in egg development, molting or metamorphosis.

In the flesh fly *Sarcophaga argyrostoma* and its parasitic wasp *Nasonia vitripennis*, however, the summation of short days has been shown to be virtually independent of temperature, and this temperature-compensated mechanism should probably be regarded as an integral part of the clock. The rate of development of the fly larvae or of the wasp eggs, however, is dependent on the temperature, like most other physiological processes. Therefore an interaction between on the one hand the temperature-dependent period when the insects are sensitive to photoperiod and on the other the temperature-insensitive number of short-day cycles required for the induction of diapause means that female wasps or fly larvae kept at higher temperatures show a lower diapause response than those kept at a lower temperature. The reason is that they are unable to summate a sufficient number of short-day cycles before the wasp eggs are deposited or the fly larvae pupate and the sensitive period comes to an end.

The conceptual difficulties with regard to whether long days have a positive inductive influence and short days are neutral are well illustrated in these responses. For example, the two insects clearly summate short days as well as long ones, so that short days are not neutral in the same sense that constant darkness is. In the flesh fly, however, these difficulties can be surmounted if we incorporate an additional component in the external-coincidence model of the insect's clock. That component measures the duration of the day. It has hourglass properties in that it requires at least six hours of light to register a short day and does not reset itself in extended periods of darkness.

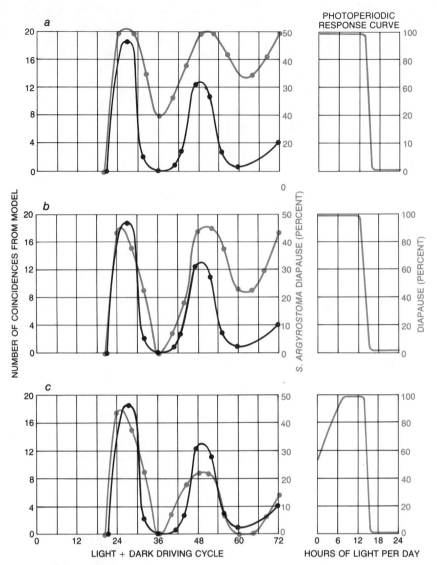

THREE EXTERNAL-COINCIDENCE MODELS are compared with the results of diapause experiments with the fly *S. argyrostoma*. The black curves show the number of inductive coincidences between the photoperiod and the light-sensitive phase in the external-coincidence model that is depicted on the preceding page. In the unmodified external-coincidence model (*a*) the data from the experiments with the fly (*colored curve*) do not correspond to the curve obtained from the model. Furthermore, the photoperiodic response curve (*right*) does not show the decrease in diapause at very short day lengths that was found experimentally. In the second version of the external-coincidence model (*b*) it is assumed that the diapause-promoting substance is synthesized when the photoperiod does not coincide with the light-sensitive phase and that the substance is destroyed when there is coincidence. The resulting curve (*color*) corresponds more closely to the theoretical model, but the photoperiodic response (*right*) lacks the characteristic drop at very short day lengths. The third version (*c*) incorporates a second component, an hourglass, that measures the length of the day. The two curves now correspond closely, and the photoperiodic response curve also matches the results that have been obtained experimentally for *S. argyrostoma*.

There are strong similarities between the two-component-clock model for the parasitic wasp and the actual properties shown by the photoperiodic clock of the flesh fly. The two-component clock accounts for the summation of short days as well as for the summation of long days, and it explains the decrease in diapause associated with very short periods of light. The principal value of

such a model lies in its predictive powers. If the model is valid, the experiments it suggests should bring us an important step closer to understanding the fundamental nature of biological timekeeping. Even as matters stand, it seems clear that the biological clock of an insect such as the flesh fly is not simply an hourglass or an oscillator. It is some subtle combination of both.

The Sexual Life of a Mosquito

by Jack Colvard Jones
April 1968

*Modern methods of insect control call for detailed
knowledge of an insect's physiology and behavior.
Reproduction in* Aedes aegypti, *the yellow-fever
mosquito, is surprisingly elaborate*

The spectacular success achieved in recent years in eradicating the screwworm fly by blocking its reproduction has encouraged hopes that a similar strategy might be effective against a much more serious insect pest —the mosquito. Mosquitoes, transmitting malaria, yellow fever, encephalitis and other grave diseases, have probably caused more human deaths than any other group of insects. The control or elimination of the mosquito, like the control or elimination of any insect pest, may call for an entire arsenal of judiciously chosen methods, and new methods are constantly being sought. Among the most attractive methods are biological ones: they are aimed at a specific pest and do not involve the use of chemicals that may be hazardous to other organisms. Biological methods of control, however, require an intimate knowledge of the target species' way of life.

The surest method of eradicating a species is to destroy its ability to reproduce. In the case of the screwworm fly this was accomplished by sterilizing males and releasing them into the wild population in saturating numbers. This tactic is now being studied with various species of mosquito, and it has proved highly effective in the laboratory. Unfortunately it has not met with much success under natural conditions. Clearly there is a need for more information about the sexual life and reproductive mechanisms of mosquitoes. The relatively small amount of information already available has suggested a number of approaches to preventing the reproduction of the insect and bringing about the autocide of disease-carrying species.

The sexual behavior of mosquitoes varies remarkably from species to species. The species for which the most de-

tailed information has been gathered is the yellow-fever mosquito *Aedes aegypti,* which has probably caused as much human illness and as many human deaths as any other man-biting mosquito. Here I shall describe what has been learned about the sexual life of this species by many investigators, including my colleagues and myself at the University of Maryland.

Every mosquito begins its life with the fertilization of the egg. Within the protective shell of the egg the embryo develops rapidly. When eggs containing fully developed embryos are placed in water that is poor in oxygen, they give rise to larvae. In about a week the larvae are mature. All mosquito larvae go through four distinct stages of growth, shedding their old skin before each new stage. Microscopic examination of the insect in its last larval stage shows that it has already formed the rudiments of the antennae, eyes, legs and wings of an adult mosquito. The antennae are enclosed within two small sacs in the larva's head. These sacs disclose the individual's sex: if they are large and well developed, the larva will give rise to a male; if they are small and poorly developed, the adult will emerge as a female.

After the transformation from the larval to the pupal state, the pupa (which to the unaided eye looks something like a comma) completes the development of the anatomical structures that will characterize the adult. In this development the alimentary tract is completely remodeled, the female forms its internal reproductive organs, the male develops mature sperm in its testes and many other changes hidden from surface view take place. The decaying larval tissues provide food for the synthesis of the adult tissues. In about two days the pupa sheds its skin and the insect emerges

as an adult mosquito. The female then differs from the male not only anatomically but also in behavior. For example, whereas the *Aedes aegypti* male feeds only on plant nectar and water, the female has a thirst, in addition, for animal blood—a thirst the male mosquito does not share because its proboscis lacks the necessary cutting tools.

The male is relatively small and is distinguished by large, hairy antennae. Shortly after the male's emergence into the winged state its rear end undergoes a remarkable rotation. The last two segments of the abdomen, pivoting on the membrane between the seventh and the eighth segment, begin to rotate (either clockwise or counterclockwise). In the first three hours this end portion turns 90 degrees, and by the 20th hour it has made a full turn of 180 degrees, so that the male's rear end is upside down from its original position. The change is permanent. Were it not for the 180-degree reversal of the abdominal tip, the male would be unable to copulate with the female—whose abdomen always retains its original position.

Similar rotations of the male abdomen are characteristic of all Diptera (two-winged insects). What kind of mechanism is responsible for this curious twist? The process is not fully understood. There is no indication that the muscles of the body wall cause the rotation. It appears that the twisting force may be applied by powerful rotational contractions of the hindgut, operating rather like a screwdriver. It has also been suggested that the membrane on which the end segments pivot may originally be plastic and then slowly harden during the rotation, thus fixing the rear end in the new position. The membrane itself shows no external

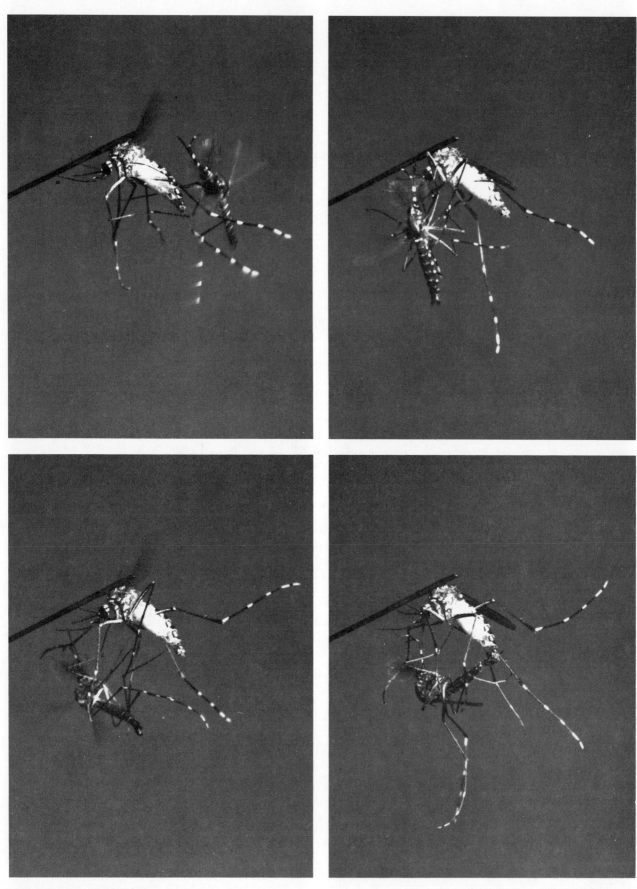

COPULATING MOSQUITOES belong to the yellow-fever species *Aedes aegypti*. The male mosquito is attracted to the female (tethered to a fine steel wire by rubber cement) by the sound of her moving wings (*top left*). With tiny hooks on his leg tips he grasps the female while swinging around to hang below her (*top right*). In this position he brings his genital organs into contact with those of the female (*bottom left and right*). These photographs and the others in this article were made by Thomas Eisner of Cornell University.

sign of having been twisted, but if the insect is dissected, the twist is clearly visible in internal organs such as the tracheae (air tubes), the nerve cord and the sperm ducts.

During the rotation of the male's rear end, spermatozoa from its two testes pass down thin-walled sperm ducts to fill two seminal vesicles at the end of the abdomen. The sperm, consisting of needle-like heads and long tails, all become precisely aligned inside the vesicles with the heads pointing toward the abdominal tip. On both sides of the seminal vesicles are large, pear-shaped accessory glands that secrete a major component of the seminal fluid. A small ejaculatory duct opens into the male's copulatory organ.

The genital apparatus is extremely complex [see *bottom illustration on page 74*]. The copulatory organ itself, deeply retracted in a fleshy pocket, is composed of a hinged pair of tiny, curved plates; these are intricately attached to a pair of large claspers positioned externally on the abdominal tip. A large anal cone between the two claspers obscures the copulatory organ. On both sides of the cone are hooks that serve as grasping accessories. The external genital structures of male mosquitoes are so intricate and distinctive that taxonomists use them to identify many mosquito species.

Whereas the male mosquito's reproductive system is complex on the outside and relatively simple on the inside, the female's is relatively simple on the outside and complex on the inside. Externally it consists of two paddle-like plates (called cerci) with long sensory hairs above the anus and a long tonguelike structure next to the retracted vagina below the anus. The vagina is S-shaped and contains three interlocking valves of different shapes, one of them with teeth along its tip. Four distinct internal structures open into the vagina: a sac called the bursa, which first receives sperm from the male; a tiny, globular accessory gland; three spherical organs called spermathecae to which the sperm migrate by way of a tiny funnel and long, twisted ducts, and a long oviduct through which the eggs pass from the ovaries.

In general female mosquitoes must feed on blood to develop eggs. Some species can develop the first batch of eggs without having had a blood meal, but even these require blood in order to lay subsequent batches. Some species must have more than one blood meal before

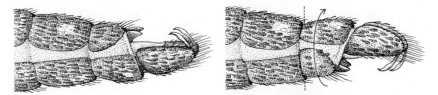

ROTATION of the tip of the male mosquito's abdomen takes place early in adult life. Before the 180-degree turn (which may be clockwise or counterclockwise) the clasper claw points up (*left*); it points down when the turn is completed about 20 hours later (*right*). With the tip reversed, copulation can occur (*see illustrations at bottom of next two pages*).

their eggs can mature. The blood meal initiates a chain of essential physiological events in the female. It is believed that her stomach, greatly distended by the drink of blood, presses on the nerve cord and causes it to send electrical signals to the brain. Within an hour the message excites certain cells in the upper part of the brain to secrete a hormone into the insect's circulating body fluid, and this in turn results within a few hours in the secretion of a secondary hormone from a pair of small glands in the female's neck. The latter hormone triggers a spectacular series of events in the ovaries. Submicroscopic pits (as many as 300,000 of them) appear on the surface of the egg. The eggs then begin to imbibe protein from the fluid in the ovary that collects in the surface pits; droplets of yolk form rapidly and soon fill the egg. The egg cell enlarges enormously and the egg nucleus, originally large, shrinks to a tiny mass of genetic material. A thin shell forms over the egg within the ovary.

A female mosquito that has fed on blood will produce and lay eggs even if she has not been fertilized. Fertilization, however, strikingly increases her egg production. Immediately after her blood meal the female is not very attractive to males, but at any other time she attracts them instantly merely by flying about. The males are drawn by the buzzing sound of the wings. The attractive

SPERM inside the seminal vesicle, the male's storage sac, are precisely aligned. The headpieces (*dark cigar-shaped areas*) all point in the same direction. The tails are wormlike. At right is the wall of the vesicle (*mottled area*). Magnification in this electron micrograph, made by Victor H. Zeve of the National Institutes of Health, is about 15,000 diameters.

FEEDING on human blood from an index finger, a female yellow-fever mosquito appears at left. The needle-like part of the proboscis is piercing the skin. At right the mosquito is seen with abdomen swollen from the blood meal. Only the female insect drinks blood.

sounds are in the range between 300 and 800 vibrations per second. Experiments conducted by Louis M. Roth, then at the U.S. Army Quartermaster Research and Development Center, show that a male mosquito will pursue a sound in this range regardless of the source—whether it is male or female, of its own or another mosquito species or even simply a tuning fork. (Mature females and males just emerged from the pupal state beat their wings at about the same rate and are pursued by older males; young, newly emerged females have a different beat and therefore are not pursued.) According to Roth, the male's hearing range is only about a foot. Roth has also demonstrated that the male is deaf to the flying female if his antennae are removed or prevented from vibrating.

The stimulating sound causes the male not only to pursue the source but also to seize it with his claspers. He will clasp the cloth walls of a cage if a tuning fork

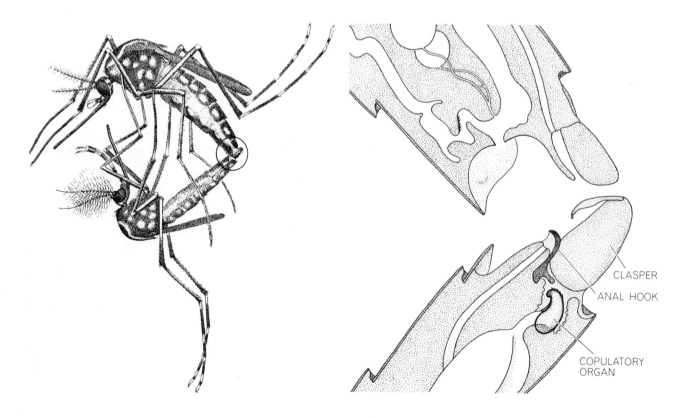

COPULATORY POSITION, bringing the male yellow-fever mosquito below the female, is shown at left. In the schematic diagram at right of the anatomy of the male and female insects, the organs are drawn as they appear before coital contact. The male's copulatory organ (here retracted), the anal hook and the clasper are rigid elements; in coitus they stretch and distort the female's more flexible tissues.

is sounded outside the walls, and indeed will seize anything that comes within his reach in the direction of a suitable vibrating source, including a male mosquito.

The process of copulation with a female is rapid but complex. On reaching the flying female the male first seizes her back with his legs, the tips of which are equipped with little grappling hooks. Then, with remarkable agility, he swiftly swings around until he is hanging face-to-face below his partner. The female, exhibiting no obvious response, may continue her flight, or the pair may fall to the floor of the cage. In either case the male quickly proceeds to bring his genitalia into contact with those of the female [*see illustrations at bottom of opposite page and below*]. His claspers grasp her cerci; this causes the tongue-like plate under her anus to move upward and expose the edges of the vagina. The male then uses his anal hooks to pull the female's genitalia toward him. He rapidly extends his previously retracted copulatory organ so that teeth at its tip mesh with the teeth on the dorsal valve in the vagina. The forceful entry everts the valve, and the hinged plates of the male's organ then spread out and widen

the vagina, enlarging the opening into the bursa. At that instant the male organ discharges a large quantity of seminal fluid, containing about 2,000 sperm, into the bursa. The pair then quickly separate, frequently with a parting kick against the male by the female's hind legs. The entire copulatory act takes from 14 to 20 seconds under natural circumstances, and about 30 seconds when a nonflying pair of mosquitoes are artificially induced to mate in the laboratory under a microscope.

Experiments in our laboratory have established that an *Aedes aegypti* male can be induced to mate mechanically if its rear end is placed in contact with the genitalia of an unfertilized female. The technique is quite simple. A male and a female are lightly anesthetized, a drop of glue is put on the head of a pin and the glue is applied to the abdomen of each insect. The mosquitoes are then rubbed together while being observed under the microscope. The technique makes possible a number of experiments that otherwise could not be done. With it we have demonstrated that the rear end of the male alone, immediately after being severed from the rest

of the body, is capable of copulating with and inseminating a female. A noteworthy and perhaps critically important finding is the fact that in such experiments only the rear end of an unfertilized female will cause the male to extend his copulatory organ and ejaculate. When a fertilized female is offered mechanically to a male under the microscope, he somehow recognizes instantly that she has been mated and he makes no attempt to copulate with her; indeed, he frequently draws away. A flying female, however, may induce the male to copulate even if she has been fertilized. Andrew Spielman and his colleagues at the Harvard School of Public Health have recently found that if these females are reinseminated, the mass of semen is rapidly ejected. Presumably the enticement of the female's buzzing overrides the male's recognition of her fertilized condition.

A male mosquito can inseminate five or six females in rapid succession. He may copulate with many more—as many as 30 within 30 minutes—but his supply of seminal fluid and sperm is exhausted after five or six matings. It takes about two days for the male to refill the seminal vesicles with a fresh supply of sperm and

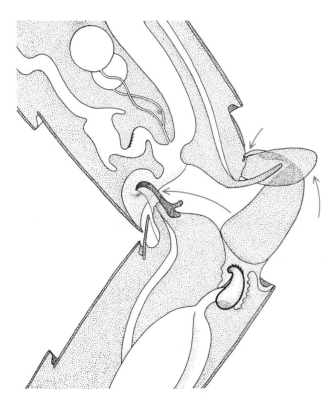

COPULATION begins as the male grasps the female with clasper and anal hook, thereby pulling her genitalia closer and enlarging the vagina entrance (*left*). The copulatory organ then thrusts for-

ward, engages the teeth of the dorsal valve and spreads to widen the entrance into the bursa (*right*). In this position the male ejaculates into the bursa sperm from the seminal vesicles (*colored arrows*).

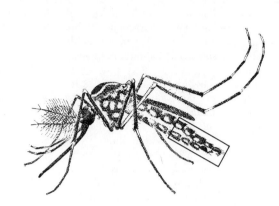

MALE AND FEMALE YELLOW-FEVER MOSQUITOES are shown 10 times actual size. The adult female (*left*) is larger than the adult male (*right*), and her antennae are less elaborate. The two rectangles outline the parts depicted in the cross sections below.

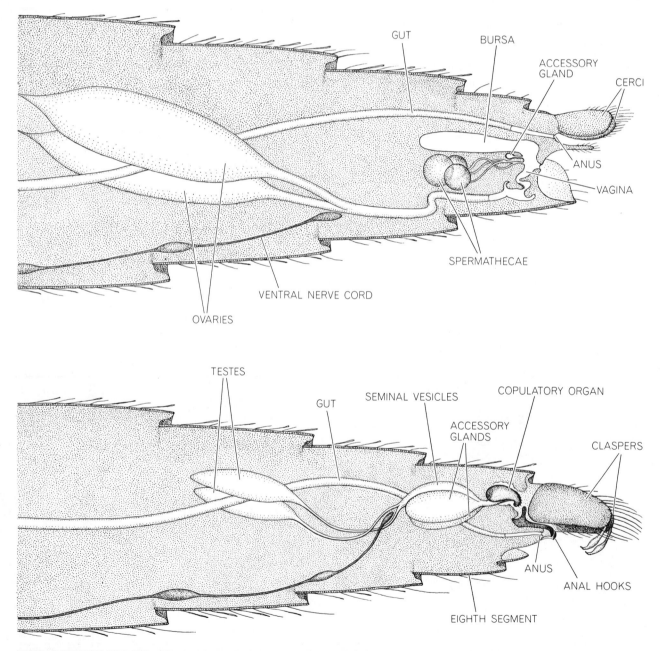

GUT

BURSA

ACCESSORY GLAND

CERCI

ANUS

VAGINA

SPERMATHECAE

VENTRAL NERVE CORD

OVARIES

TESTES

GUT

SEMINAL VESICLES

COPULATORY ORGAN

ACCESSORY GLANDS

CLASPERS

ANUS

ANAL HOOKS

EIGHTH SEGMENT

REPRODUCTIVE ORGANS of the female mosquito (*top*) and the male (*bottom*) appear in longitudinal section. The external struc-ture of the male's genital apparatus is more complex than that of the female; her internal structure is more complex than the male's.

regenerate the accessory-gland material.

Let us turn our attention now to the female. After her bursa has been filled with semen from the male the long, threadlike sperm swim toward the opening of the bursa and line up in dense bundles with their tails undulating rapidly. They remain there for 30 to 40 seconds. Then groups of the sperm abruptly make a sharp U-turn, swim to the funnel leading to the spermathecae and make their way up long, twisted ducts to those receiving organs. Generally they reach only two of the three spermathecae. Within less than five minutes the migrating sperm (perhaps 1,000 of them, probably together with seminal fluid) have filled the two reservoirs, and there the sperm swim rapidly in circles and remain active as long as the female lives. In short, once the female has been mated, she is fertilized for the rest of her lifetime.

The behavior of the sperm in the female's reproductive tract presents several puzzles. Why do the highly active sperm wait in the bursa for 30 to 40 seconds before starting their journey to the spermathecae? How do they make their way there without error, although neither the bursa nor the ducts provide contractions that might give them direction? Why do no sperm or so few sperm enter the third spermatheca? Curiously, our experiments have failed to develop any definite proof that the sperm can actually travel to the spermathecae without assistance. In fact, our efforts to fertilize females by artificially inseminating their bursae with highly active sperm and accessory gland material have generally been unsuccessful. We deduce from these facts that in some unknown way the female exercises a control of her own over fertilization.

At all events, the consequences of her fertilization are quite clear. The sperm that reach her spermathecae enable her to produce fertile eggs. And a fertilized female lays a great many more eggs than an unfertilized one, as a result of the slow absorption into her body of the seminal material (sperm and granular material from the male's accessory glands) that remains behind in her bursa after the migration of sperm to the spermathecae stops. It is not clear how the spermatozoa get out of the spermathecae to reach the egg. The sperm cell does, however, enter the egg through a specialized tiny opening at its front end just as it is laid.

The female lays her eggs one at a time. After finding a suitable water site for depositing them, she first lifts her

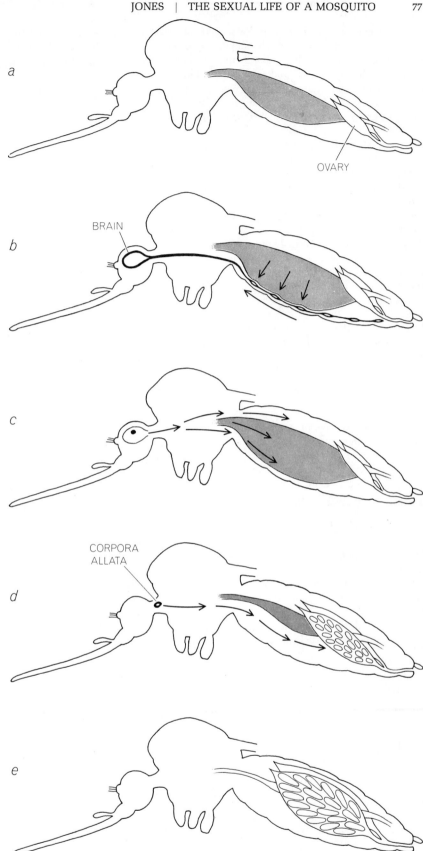

DEVELOPMENT OF EGGS begins after the female mosquito imbibes blood (*color*) and her gut distends (*a*). The gut then presses on the ventral nerve cord and signals are sent to the brain (*b*). In response certain brain cells secrete a hormone into the insect's circulating fluid (*c*), giving rise to the secretion of a second hormone by the corpora allata (glands in the neck). With the arrival of this hormone at the ovary (*d*), protein from the blood enters the ovary fluid and is taken up by the eggs. Yolk droplets form and eggs enlarge (*e*).

hind legs and fans them up and down. Then she wipes the tip of her abdomen with them and vigorously scrubs them together. The tip of the abdomen almost touches the water surface. Her cerci and the tonguelike plate below the anus are pressed close together and point down. As an egg descends from the ovary through the oviduct there is considerable contraction and twitching of the genital structures, particularly the edges of the vagina. In emerging from the vagina the large white egg pushes the cerci and subanal plate upward, everts the vaginal opening and then drops into the water. One egg follows another until the female has delivered her batch. Some species of mosquito array the eggs in rafts on the water. Some species lay their eggs while hovering over the water, the eggs dropping like little bombs. Others eject their eggs into water that has collected in the hollow of a tree. There is even a mosquito that lays her eggs on her hind legs and then dips her legs into the water to set the eggs free.

The female mosquito has a remarkable capacity for retaining eggs in her ovaries after the eggs have fully ripened. The majority of mosquitoes will not lay eggs unless they have located an appropriate site for them. We have been able to force such females to deposit their eggs under the microscope, however, by a shock treatment such as crushing the head or thorax or cutting off the head or abdomen. Within less than a minute after the injury eggs begin to emerge from the vaginal opening, and occasionally a considerable number will be laid.

We have also investigated the action of portions of the egg-delivering system. If the ovary itself is cut away from the body when it is greatly distended with ripe eggs and placed in a drop of saline solution on a glass slide, eggs will slide out through the open end. It appears, however, that in normal circumstances the main force for drawing eggs out of the ovary under natural conditions comes from vigorous rhythmic contractions of the internal oviducts (the exit ducts of the ovaries). Ordinarily the lateral oviducts are constricted, and this constriction may be responsible for the ovary's retention of ripe eggs until the female has found a suitable site in which to lay them.

The female mosquito invariably lays her eggs in daylight, principally in midafternoon between 2:00 and 3:00 P.M. It has been demonstrated by A. J. Haddow and J. D. Gillett of the East African Virus Research Institute in Uganda that light controls the egg-laying rhythm (perhaps by activating some hormone); these workers showed that the mosquito will lay her eggs in the nighttime hours and refrain in the daytime hours if the light cycle in her cage is reversed.

A female that is ready to lay eggs explores possible sites primarily with her feet. She flies about and alights on various water surfaces, setting all six legs down on the water. The hairs on her legs evidently possess a chemical sensitivity, particularly to salinity. It has been shown by Robert C. Wallis, who was then at the Johns Hopkins School of Medicine, that they can distinguish between distilled water and weak saline solutions. Most species of mosquito prefer fresh water for laying their eggs, but some favor brackish waters. On finding a favorable site the female walks to the edge of the water and lays her eggs there.

Soon after they are laid the white eggs swell and turn black. Normally the egg hatches into a larva in two days. If the conditions are not suitable, the larva, even though they are fully developed within the shell of the egg, can remain alive for a considerable time. Charles L. Judson of the University of California at Davis has shown that when such eggs are placed in water with a low oxygen content, the pharynx of the larvae suddenly becomes active. It makes rapid swallowing motions, apparently without actually imbibing fluid, and proceeds to break out of the shell. A small spine on top of its head presses against the shell along a preformed line and the top of the shell neatly snaps off.

The larva wriggles out quickly, air suddenly enters its breathing tubes, which take on the appearance of silvery capillaries, and its heart begins to beat. The insect at once starts to feed, and so a new cycle of mosquito life gets under way.

There are definite periods in the life cycle of mosquitoes in which reproduction can be profoundly affected by some specific treatment. William R. Horsfall and J. R. Anderson of the University of Illinois have demonstrated, for example, that the sex of larvae in certain strains of mosquito can be completely reversed by subjecting the larvae to a certain temperature at a certain period. Many other entomologists are examining similar phenomena in the sexual life of mosquitoes in the hope of finding some way of eliminating the insect when it is not wanted.

II

THE KEYS TO SUCCESS: NEUROBIOLOGY AND BEHAVIOR

II THE KEYS TO SUCCESS: NEUROBIOLOGY AND BEHAVIOR

INTRODUCTION

It is only a short step from the anatomical and physiological adaptations considered in the first section to those involving the nervous system and behavior. Brevity and simple-minded precision continue to be the ruling themes. The number of nerve cells in the insect brain is only on the order of 100 thousand, compared with 10 to 100 billion in the human brain. Many of the sensory cells leading to the central nervous system come directly from elements built into the cuticle, a circumstance that makes them easily accessible to experimental manipulation from the outside. Because of the relative simplicity of these combined systems, entomologists have made outstanding progress in analyzing elements of behavior and demonstrating their nervous control at the level of the cell. Moreover, the behavioral acts vary only slightly within species and are tightly programmed to occur only at certain times and in response to a small set of stimuli. As a consequence, they can be interpreted more securely as adaptive devices, that is, they can be demonstrated to have evolved to cope with particular challenges encountered by each insect species in its own environment. Behavioral phenomena can thus be studied in much the same way as anatomical and physiological phenomena. This circumstance has a general significance for science: there is a good chance that we will fully understand the behavior of certain insect species well before similar studies on vertebrates have progressed beyond an exploratory stage.

Many of the best questions concerning evolution are asked after biologists have found the answers. The following is an example: how do tens of thousands of insect species live together in the same habitats, many of them closely resembling each other in anatomy and behavior, without interbreeding to produce swarms of hybrids? Part of the answer has been presented in prospect by research on the sex attractants of insects. In particular, female moths have the remarkable capacity to lure males of their own species, often over considerable distances. As Dietrich Schneider shows in his article "The Sex-Attractant Receptor of Moths," the mechanism is the specific chemical attractants released by the female moths. The females of each species, or at least those of each closely related group of species, produce their own distinctive odorants, typically alcohols or esters containing between 10 and 20 carbon atoms. Additional exclusivity in communication is attained by restricting the release of the substances during specific short periods of the day. The sex attractant of the female silkworm moth is so potent that a single molecule can fire a nerve cell in the male's antenna. When only 200 cells are activated per second (the level of stimulation needed to overcome background noise in the antennal nerve) the male responds by fluttering its wings in the first step of the mating response. The male's antennae are feathery organs containing a total of about 34,000 sensory hairs, which respond only to the female sex attractant. This advanced form of chemical communication characterizes many (but by no means all) insect species. It helps to explain how such tiny creatures can find mates of their own kind unerringly and efficiently in the crowded world they inhabit.

E. O. Wilson's article "Pheromones" elaborates the subject of chemical communication, showing its ramifications in the evolution of molecular design. Wilson also discusses the possible categories of messages that can be most efficiently transmitted and the properties of the transmission itself. Pheromones have some marked advantages over other kinds of signals. In particular, they are energetically cheap to manufacture and broadcast; they can be disseminated over long distances and through long periods of time; and they can be made highly specific when privacy in communication is a requirement. Their disadvantages include a relative slowness of transmission and the difficulty of turning such signals off on those occasions when the insect needs to send another message or to stop signaling altogether.

Two chemical formulas given on page 99 have been shown to be erroneous. The structure presented for the sex attractant of the American cockroach (2,2-dimethyl-3-isopropylidenecyclopropylpropionate) has been synthesized and proven inactive. To this day the actual sex attractant of this insect remains unknown. The true structure for the sex attractant of the gypsy moth (gyplure), named disparlure, is now known, and has the following formula:

$$CH_3(CH_2)_{10}CH \underset{O}{\diagup} CH(CH_2)_4CH(CH_3)_2$$

cis-7,8-epoxy-2-methyloctadecane

"The Neurobiology of Cricket Song," by David Bentley and Ronald R. Hoy, complements the article on moth sex attractants by Schneider. It is an account of communication by sound (in crickets), as opposed to chemical communication. The interlocking of the sensory cells and the nerve cells in the brain controlling auditory communication is as complex and precise as that involved in chemical communication. A high point of the article is the description of the authors' remarkable experiments on hybridization of cricket species. Not only have Bentley and Hoy demonstrated the genetic basis of auditory communication in crickets, they have also made progress in determining the nature of the heredity mechanisms. For example, the intervals between trills in the male's song were shown to be influenced by genes located on the X, or sex, chromosome.

A cocoon, as William Van der Kloot points out in "Brains and Cocoons," is a three-dimensional map of the caterpillar's behavior. In a series of ingenious experiments conducted in collaboration with C. M. Williams, the author defined both the minimal set of movements that must be performed in order to create a cocoon and the sequence in which they must occur. This instinctive program is so rigid that each species of moth makes a cocoon that entomologists can identify at a glance. Because insects have such small brains, it is entirely possible that simple behaviors such as cocoon-weaving may someday be mapped onto specific nerve cells and, in this sense at least, the behavior will be fully understood.

In "Genetic Dissection of Behavior" the distinguished geneticist Seymour Benzer reports substantial progress toward the kind of complete characterization of behavior implicit in the previous articles. Using essentially the same techniques by which he earlier teased apart the ultimate genetic units in the bacterium *E. coli*, Benzer has set about mapping the exact relations between genes and behavioral acts in the fruit fly *Drosophila melanogaster*. The techniques are relatively simple, but the results rich and surprising. Behavioral mutants are first identified on the X chromosomes through conventional techniques. The link between the genes and the final behavioral anomalies are then explored by employing additional genetic techniques to create mosaics, which are patchworks of tissue on the same animal within which some patches express the mutant phenotype and others do not. Since mosaics form in early stages of embryonic development, it is possible to pinpoint the sites in the sensory and nervous systems that most affect the behavior. For example, in one case the site proves to be in the outer receptor of the eye, in another the ventral nerve cord, and in still another the wing muscles themselves. Thus in a quite literal sense the techniques of genetic analysis are being used to "dissect" the controls of behavior that form a chain from the gene to the outermost behavioral phenotype.

In "The Flight-Control System of the Locust" by Donald Wilson, whose early death by a drowning accident ended a brilliant career in neurobiology, we shift abruptly from sensory to motor systems. Wilson's notable achievement, along with Torkel Weis-Fogh and their co-workers, was the demonstration of a motor-control device in the flight of locusts comparable in simplicity to the sensory systems already elucidated in moths, sea hares, and other invertebrates. The prevailing idea of motor action up to the time of these experiments had been the peripheral-control hypothesis. This was the perfectly reasonable notion that input from the sense organs is processed by the central nervous system, which then decides on the motor commands to be sent out along the efferent nerves to the appropriate muscles. As muscle contraction takes place, new sensory information is generated. By means of proprioceptors (sense organs responding to pressure), the muscles themselves inform the central nervous system of the actions they have taken, while the change in the body's position causes new signals from the outside environment to reach the sensory system. The result is a feedback loop: a sequence of messages transmitted from sense organs to central nervous system to motor system to sense organs and on around again until the central nervous system "satisfies" itself that the correct action has been completed. Wilson and his associates obtained the surprising result that flight in locusts is partially independent of feedback control. When all the sources of sensory feedback are eliminated in experiments, the wings can continue to beat in a normal rhythm. Flight, in other words, is run by an internal motor that can be turned on or off by signals from the outside but does not require continued instructions to operate. Moreover, reiterating our theme of the simplified modes of invertebrate behavior, the muscles of each wing are activated by fewer than 20 motor nerve cells.

Many insects find it necessary to travel far from their nests on foraging trips and then to find their way back again. Honeybee workers can unerringly orient over distances of a kilometer or more, while *Cataglyphis* ants travel back and forth over thousands of square meters of almost featureless desert sand without losing their way. These insects orient by sun-compass orientation, in which they set their bearings by the position of the sun in the sky. But in all but the driest parts of the earth it is often covered by clouds. Nevertheless, so long as some parts of blue sky are showing, patterns of polarized light can be used to calculate the true position of the sun. In "Polarized-Light Navigation by Insects" Rüdiger Wehner first shows how a sophisticated physicist might figure out the rules for orientation by polarized light. Then he describes experiments that have revealed how the insects accomplish the same feat. Bees and ants, which are among the best "physicists" in the insect world, rely on reception in special sensitive spots in the ommatidia (individual facets) of the compound eye. They need only integrate information from as few as 10 facets to locate the hidden sun. How they then keep their position in mind while performing the many loops and twists of a typical foraging expedition is another, still largely unsolved problem.

Yet another case of the high achievement of a small group of nerve cells in an invertebrate is described by Kenneth Roeder in "Moths and Ultrasound." Only *two* nerve cells within each ear of the moth transmit all the information concerning sound in ultrahigh frequencies. Thanks to the ingenious field experiments conducted by Roeder and his associates, we also know the ecological significance of the two cells: they detect the sonar signals emitted by predatory bats and allow the moths to escape before being captured and eaten. No better documentation exists of the highly specific, idiosyncratic relationship between a particular behavior pattern, the nerve cells that mediate it, and the environmental pressure that caused it to evolve in the first place.

RELATED BOOKS

Alcock, John. 1975. *Animal Behavior.* Sinauer Associates, Sunderland, Massachusetts. A good first-level textbook, dealing with the behavior of all animals, including insects. Evolutionary in approach, well illustrated, and readable.

Dethier, V. G. 1976. *The Hungry Fly.* Harvard University Press, Cambridge, Massachusetts. A superb book on the neurobiology and behavior of feeding. Shows beautifully how experimental work with one species can lead to biological conclusions of broad implications. Highly recommended for the student of insect behavior.

Kuffler, Stephen W. and John G. Nicholls. 1976. *From Neuron to Brain.* Sinauer Associates, Sunderland, Massachusetts. Probably the best textbook for any student of insects wishing to obtain an up-to-date background on the basics of neurobiology.

Rockstein, Morris (ed.). 1973–74. *The Physiology of Insecta*, Volumes I–VI, second edition. Academic Press, New York. Includes several good chapters on insect behavior, sensory physiology, neural integration, and other topics related to the articles in Section II.

Roeder, Kenneth D. 1967. *Nerve Cells and Insect Behavior*, revised edition. Harvard University Press, Cambridge, Massachusetts. An outstanding, highly readable book. The author discusses his own ingenious experiments on moths, cockroaches, and preying mantids in a fashion that gives a real feeling for what is known and yet to be learned about the neurobiology of insects.

Shorey, H. H. 1976. *Animal Communication by Pheromones.* Academic Press, New York. A brief and excellent review of the principles of chemical communication, many of which were originally developed in studies of insects.

Treherne, J. E. (ed.). 1974. *Insect Neurobiology.* North Holland Publishing Company, Amsterdam. An advanced treatise, containing scholarly articles on major topics related to neuronal organization and function in insects.

Von Frisch, Karl. 1967. *The Dance Language and Orientation of Bees.* Belknap Press of Harvard University Press, Cambridge, Massachusetts. This monumental work, destined to become a classic of the scientific literature, summarizes the research carried out by von Frisch and his students over a period of 60 years on the waggle dance and other forms of honeybee communication. A *sine qua non* for anyone interested in insect behavior, and particularly for students contemplating a career in insect experimentation and wishing to gain some feeling for what constitutes excellence in the field.

9

The Sex-Attractant Receptor of Moths

by Dietrich Schneider
July 1974

*The sex attractant of the female silk moth is detected
by an array of receptors on the feathery antennae of
the male. A nerve impulse in a receptor cell can be
triggered by one molecule of attractant*

All sensory systems, each with its
specific peripheral receptor cells
and its integrating neurons in the
brain, are designed to form a biologically
relevant image of the outer environment
of the organism. In many animals chemical
signals play a major and often decisive
role as a means of communication.
The domesticated silk moth, for example,
cannot fly and therefore the male
cannot readily scout the terrain in search
of a mate. It does, however, have two
featherlike antennae that are finely tuned
to detect a certain chemical compound:
the scent emitted by the female. So sensitive
are the male's antennae that one
molecule of the vaporous sex attractant
will trigger a nerve impulse in a receptor
cell. When approximately 200 nerve impulses
have been generated in the span
of a second, a message is received in the
moth's brain and it moves upwind to
claim its mate.

Chemical compounds such as the sex
attractant of the silk moth, which are
secreted by an animal and elicit a specific
kind of behavior in animals of the
same species, are called pheromones [see
"Pheromones," by Edward O. Wilson,
beginning on page 92]. A major difficulty
in studying the olfactory system in
most animals is the enormous variety
of chemical compounds that elicit a
response. The situation is different in
the olfactory pheromone-receptor system
of the silk moth. Here we have found
a rather simple olfactory system where
many receptor cells respond identically
to only one compound.

In the past 20 years interest in pheromones
has grown steadily, and the number
of identified pheromones has rapidly
increased. This holds particularly for the
pheromones of insects because here the
investigator's curiosity is augmented by
the hope of putting pheromones to work
as lures in the control of insect pests

[see "Insect Attractants," by Martin
Jacobson and Morton Beroza; SCIENTIFIC
AMERICAN Offprint 189]. In most
cases sex-attractant pheromones are produced
and emitted by the female in
order to lure a mate. Sex attractants
are widespread in the insect world, but
they are also found in other animal
classes, as is well known to every owner
of a female cat or dog in heat.

The impressive attractiveness of a virgin
female moth to its male partners was
described as early as the 18th century by
naturalists such as René Antoine Ferchault
de Réaumur, F. Ch. Lesser and
August Johann Rösel von Rosenhof. At
the beginning of the 20th century the
psychiatrist and entomologist Auguste
Forel reported that when some wild European
female silk moths emerged from
the pupa in his studio in Lausanne, they
attracted large numbers of male moths to
the windows (along with a large number
of *Gassenbuben*, or street urchins, who
were attracted by the spectacular assembly
of moths).

Although most of the early observers of
the sexual attraction of male moths
to females agreed that an odorous signal
was involved, some were in doubt because
of certain puzzling facts. Not only
was the human nose unable to detect the
alluring odor but also it was hardly conceivable
that the amount of odorant that
could be produced by the female would
be able to lure the males from a distance
of at least a kilometer. The critical experiment
demonstrating that the attraction
was definitely based on odor was described
in 1879 by Jean Henri Fabre in
his famous *Souvenirs Entomologiques*.
When Fabre picked up a female moth
and put her under a glass hood, male
moths that flew into his house paid no
attention to her but went to the place
where she had been sitting a short time

earlier. Although Fabre realized that the
female's scent was guiding the male at
short range, he still believed unknown
radiations from the female lured and
guided the male from greater distances.

Other experiments with male moths
clearly showed that the presumed olfactory
faculty of these insects is localized
in the antennae, since the males did not
react to the "calling" female after their
antennae had been removed or covered
with varnish. This was the state of
knowledge about these moth sex attractants
until about 20 years ago. Then
advances in chemical, physiological and
histological methods led to the identification
of the chemical nature of the luring
substance and to the definite proof that
the receptors are on the male moth's antennae.

The first sex-attractant pheromone to
be chemically identified was the lure
substance of the female of the commercial
silk moth *Bombyx mori*. Adolf F. J.
Butenandt and his co-workers at the
Max Planck Institute for Biochemistry in
Tübingen (and later in Munich) reported
in 1959 that the attractant has a chain of
16 carbon atoms and is a doubly unsaturated
fatty alcohol (later identified
as *trans*-10-*cis*-12-hexadecadien-1-ol).
They named the compound bombykol.
Their success was the outcome of long
years of difficult analytical work, and
their choice of *Bombyx mori* was a wise
one. This moth is bred for silk production
in many parts of the world, so that
it is possible to obtain large quantities
of the female glands that manufacture
the compound. In order to extract 12
milligrams of pure bombykol the biochemists
needed the glands of half a million
moths.

In the early 1950's, when only enriched
extracts from female *Bombyx*
glands were available, I met with my
biochemical colleagues in Tübingen and

was challenged by the problems of olfactory perception in the silk moth. I thought that insight into the highly specific olfactory function in this animal might lead to a better understanding of the still unknown mechanisms of olfactory perception in general. My research began as a one-man enterprise but later involved my students and associates. Members of the silk moth research team in my laboratory at the Max Planck Institute for Behavioral Physiology in Seewiesen are the biologists K.-E. Kaissling, E. Kramer, E. Priesner and R. A. Steinbrecht and the chemist G. Kasang. My recent studies of the gypsy moth and the nun moth were done in collaboration with the biophysicist W. A. Kafka. In our research we hoped to approach an answer to questions about the threshold and the dose-response functions of the odor receptors, the specificity of the receptors, the mechanism of odor-molecule capture, the mechanism of stimulus transduction and the fate of the odor molecule after it has transferred its information.

The peripheral part of any sensory cell reacts to an adequate stimulus (chemicals, light, mechanical displacement or temperature) with a temporary change in the electric charge of its membrane. This response is called the receptor potential. It can be recorded from whole sense organs, provided that the sensory cells are lined up rather like an array of interconnected electric batteries. In a silk-moth antenna simultaneous receptor potentials of many olfactory cells can be recorded simply by mounting the antenna between two electrodes connected to an amplifier and a recording instrument [see illustration below]. The antenna is stimulated by putting an odor source into a glass tube and blowing air through the tube onto the antenna. We tested the response of the male silk-moth antenna to various concentrations of bombykol, of steric isomers of the compound and of homologous fatty alcohols. Although all these compounds generated a response of the olfactory cells, none was nearly as effective as the natural material. We also found that the dose-response curve of this olfactory system covers a wide range of stimulus intensities, as do the response curves of the visual and auditory systems [see bottom illustration on page 87]. Interestingly, the antenna of the female silk moth does not respond to bombykol.

Microelectrode probes revealed that only those receptor cells connected to the specialized long hairs of the antennae respond to bombykol and its isomers. The amplitude of the discharge of the receptor cells increases with increasing concentration of the stimulating compound. This receptor potential generates a series of nerve impulses that travel to the olfactory center of the brain. The frequency of these nerve impulses depends on the amplitude of the receptor potential.

We then asked the following key questions: How many bombykol molecules are required to elicit the male's behavior response and what is the minimum number of molecules a cell needs to generate a nerve impulse? Before we could deal with these questions, however, we had to collect information on the amount of bombykol in the stimulating airstream and on the number of molecules being adsorbed on the antenna and on the hairs. For this purpose we resynthetized the pheromone in a form that incorporated tritium, the radioactive isotope of hydrogen. The measurements we then made with the tritium-labeled bombykol yielded surprising results: more than 25 percent of the bombykol is

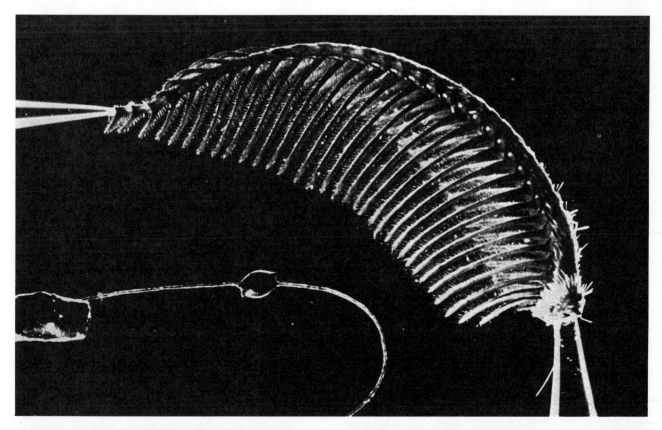

ANTENNA OF THE MALE SILK MOTH has some 17,000 long odor-receptor hairs on its branches. The electrophysiological response to an odor can be measured by mounting an isolated antenna between two glass-capillary electrodes (top left and bottom right) and passing over the antenna a stream of air containing the odor. The oscillographic record of the changes of electric potential in the antenna is called an electroantennogram. The wire loop at lower left holds a thermistor that measures the airflow past the antenna. The photograph was provided by K.-E. Kaissling of the Max Planck Institute for Behavioral Physiology in Seewiesen.

MALE SILK MOTH of the species *Bombyx mori* is seen from the front. The species is the commercial silk-producing one; it has been domesticated for some 4,000 years. Fifty percent of the odor-receptor cells in the male's antennae are tuned to respond to a single substance: bombykol, the sex attractant emitted by the female silk moth when it is ready to mate. The length of each of the male's antennae is six millimeters, or about a quarter of an inch.

TIP OF THE ABDOMEN of the female silk moth holds a pair of glands, the *sacculi laterales*, that contain about one microgram of the sex attractant bombykol. The glands shown here are in an expanded active state.

filtered out of the airstream when it hits the antenna.

We next conducted behavior tests and recorded electrophysiological signals from single odor-receptor cells in *Bombyx* males. When the male silk moth senses the sex attractant, it responds by fluttering its wings. A barely noticeable but nonetheless significant response is observed when the stimulating airstream contains about 1,000 bombykol molecules per cubic centimeter. Such a stimulus is produced by an odor source of only 3×10^{-6} microgram of bombykol. Within a second, which is somewhat more than the insect's reaction time, approximately 300 of the odor molecules are adsorbed on the 17,000 sensory hairs of the antenna. Each hair is innervated by the dendrites, or fiber endings, of two bombykol receptor cells. In this situation Poisson probability statistics, which mathematicians use to distinguish between different kinds of random events, enable us to predict that during that one second only two of the hairs receive double hits of bombykol molecules. The rest

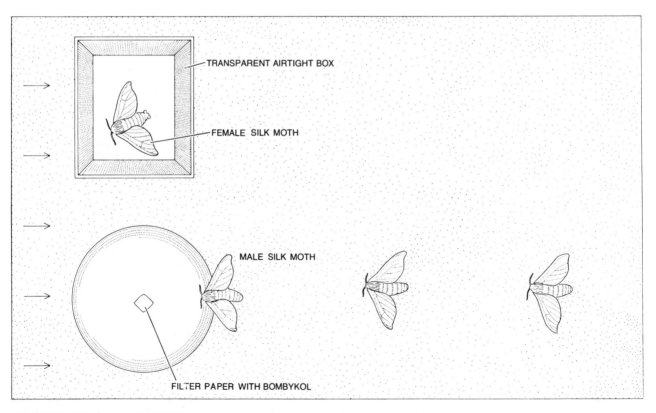

TRANSPARENT AIRTIGHT BOX

FEMALE SILK MOTH

MALE SILK MOTH

FILTER PAPER WITH BOMBYKOL

EXPERIMENTAL ARRANGEMENT for testing the sexual attractiveness of an odor is depicted. Male silk moths are placed downwind from a fan; the direction of the airflow is indicated by the arrows. The male moth cannot fly and is always sexually responsive. A female silk moth is placed in an airtight transparent box.

A small piece of filter paper soaked with bombykol is put on a glass dish near the female moth. When the males sense the sex attractant, they move upwind to the source of the odor and not to the visible female. Bending of the abdomen of the male moth is a copulatory movement regularly observed with strong stimulation.

receive single hits. This observation already made it highly probable that the receptor cells are activated by single bombykol molecules.

We now recorded olfactory-nerve impulses from hundreds of single bombykol receptor cells. The stimulating technique was essentially the same as the one we had used during the behavior tests, which enabled us to compare the two types of experiment. With a bombykol-source load of 10^{-4} microgram, one in three hairs adsorbs somewhat more than one molecule per second and fires about one impulse. Both of these values are averages.

How are the impulses distributed? After subtracting the spontaneous activity of the cells we plotted the experimental data against the Poisson curves. The responses were separately plotted for the cells that reacted with one impulse or more, two impulses or more and 10 impulses or more. The one-impulse curve and the two-impulse curve exactly fitted the "one hit" and "two hit" Poisson probability curves, whereas the 10-impulse curve did not correspond at all to the 10-hit probability curve [see illustration on page 91]. This shows that the small impulse numbers near the response threshold are randomly distributed, as one would expect to be the case with the stimulating molecules also. Behavior and single-cell responses therefore allow us to state that a single nerve impulse is generated when one molecule of bombykol hits a receptor and that two impulses are generated when two molecules hit. The transduction of hits into impulses is obviously more complex with higher hit rates per second.

One difficulty with the radioactivity measurements on which the calibrations of these experiments are based was the limited sensitivity of even the best measuring instruments available. The detection limit for tritium-labeled bombykol with these devices is 3×10^{-8} microgram, or about 10^8 molecules. That is enough for the measurement of the bombykol sources, but much smaller amounts are adsorbed on the antenna. Extrapolation is necessary to determine what the threshold amounts are. Our extrapolation is based on the assumption that the constant relation between the odor-source load and bombykol adsorption that is found in the range of the stronger stimuli holds true for the low rates near threshold.

We are now fairly certain that near the threshold level the receptors actually count the stimulating molecules. The cell can be said to be so sensitive

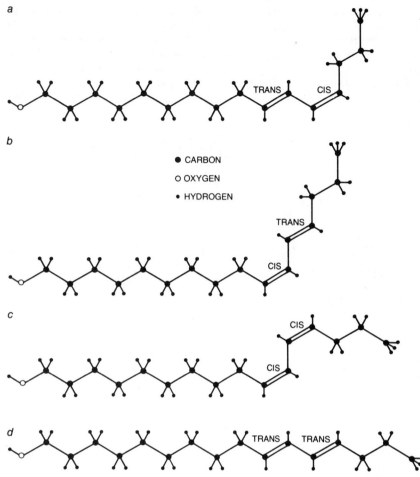

BOMBYKOL is an unsaturated fatty alcohol with the chemical designation *trans-10-cis-12-hexadecadien-1-ol* (*a*). It is the *trans-cis* isomer of the compound. The three other geometrical isomers, the *cis-trans* (*b*), the *cis-cis* (*c*) and the *trans-trans* (*d*) are much less effective.

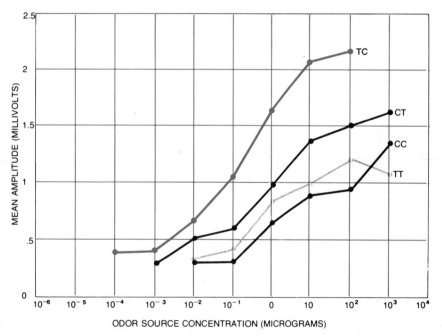

ELECTROANTENNOGRAM RESPONSE of the male silk moth to different concentrations of bombykol and its isomers is shown. When the concentration of the odor is less than .01 microgram, there is little or no difference in the antennal response to each isomer. At higher concentrations bombykol (*TC*) gives rise to a much greater response than the *cis-trans* (*CT*), *cis-cis* (*CC*) and *trans-trans* (*TT*) isomers do. In all cases the responses to very low odor concentrations are not significantly different from antennal responses to pure air.

that it reacts to single quanta of odor. A comparably high sensitivity has been found in the rod cells of the vertebrate retina, which respond to a single quantum of light.

If the receptor cells are already responding to a single pheromone molecule, why must 200 cells be activated to make the male moth respond with its typical vibrations? The answer is that all the bombykol receptor cells of the antenna spontaneously fire about 1,600 impulses per second in the resting state, and the threshold signal of 200 impulses is necessary to overcome this background noise. Information theory requires that a detectable signal be greater than three times the square root of the noise. Since here the noise is about 1,600 impulses per second, a meaningful signal must be greater than $3 \times \sqrt{1,600}$, which is equal to 120. The threshold signal of 200 impulses is well above the required minimum, so that the signal is sufficient to tell the moth's brain: "There is bombykol in the air."

The next questions we asked were: Why is the *Bombyx* antenna so effective in filtering the bombykol molecules out of the air? How do the molecules, after adsorption on the hair surface, find their way to the receptor-cell dendrite? Our thinking and experimentation on these lines have been strongly influenced and guided by Gerold Adam and Max Delbrück of the California Institute of Technology, who clearly outlined for us the physical principles that must govern these processes. Adam and Delbrück predicted that the antenna must be an optimal sieve for molecules because of the spacing and arrangement of the receptor hairs. The width of the mesh represented by the hairs is small enough so that the molecules of an odorant, because of their fast thermal movements, cannot pass through the hairs without coming in contact with them and being preferentially adsorbed. By measuring the adsorption of bombykol by the whole antenna and the adsorption by individual hairs that had been shaved from the antenna, we found that more than 80 percent of the molecules are adsorbed on the hairs. This result was significant because the total surface area of the hairs is less than 13 percent of the total surface area of the antenna.

If a receptor cell on a hair is to be activated by one or two molecules of bombykol, the molecules presumably need to diffuse to the receptor-cell dendrite from the surface of the hair. In order to demonstrate the validity of the assumption that there is such a two-dimensional diffusion of bombykol on the surface of the olfactory hair, it was necessary to analyze the structure of the hair. Such a hair, along with its olfactory receptor cells and auxiliary cells, is called a sensillum. The hair is part of the cuticle, which is the tough outer lining of the moth's body. The striking feature of the hairs is that they are perforated by pores connected to fine tubules. In some cases these tubules extend right down to the surface membrane of one of the receptor-cell dendrites. The pores and the tubules can be invaded by test

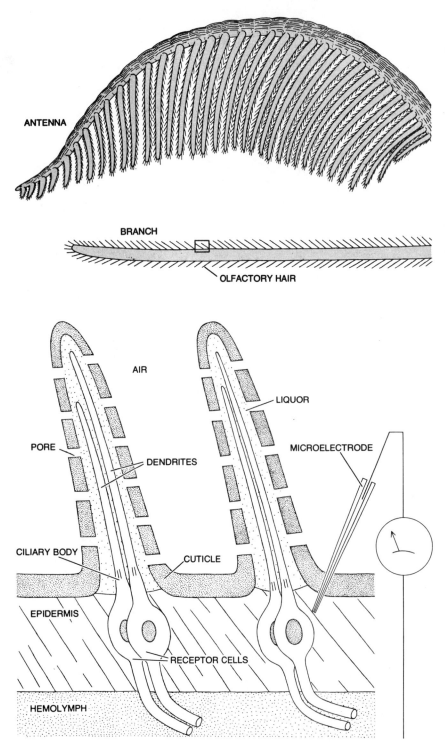

OLFACTORY RECEPTOR SYSTEM of the male silk moth is shown at increasing magnifications, first the entire antenna (*top*), then a single branch of the antenna (*middle*) and finally a schematic longitudinal section of two olfactory hairs (*bottom*). Each hair is innervated by dendrites of two receptor cells. Molecules of bombykol diffuse through the pore openings in the hair and give rise to an electrical change in the membrane of the receptor cell. Nerve impulses are recorded from a microelectrode inserted into the base of the hair.

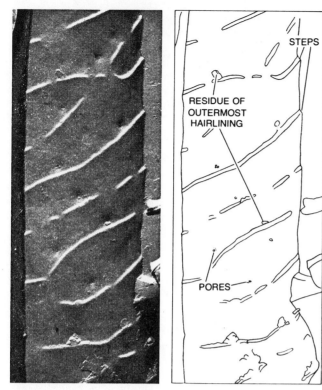
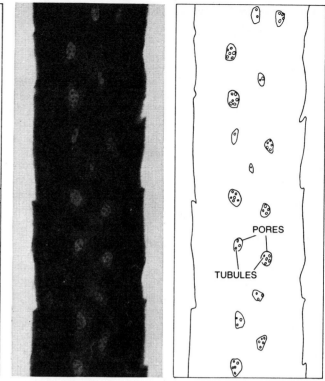

SURFACE OF RECEPTOR HAIR of a male silk moth is shown in replica after freeze etching in the electron micrograph at left. The tracing at right identifies the primary features that are visible. A tangential section of a receptor hair appears in the second micro-graph. The pores are shown in cross section. Inside the pores tubules that extend to the dendrite of the bombykol receptor cell can be seen. The electron micrographs were made by R. A. Steinbrecht of the Max Planck Institute for Behavioral Physiology.

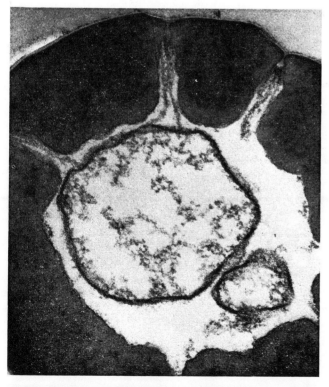
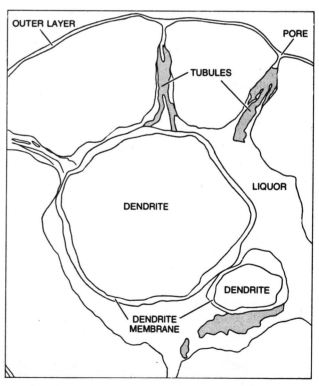

CROSS SECTION OF BOMBYKOL RECEPTOR HAIR is shown in this electron micrograph made by Steinbrecht. The cross section is through the apex of the hair. The tracing at right identifies certain of the hair's features. Some of the tubules in the pores reach to the outer membrane of the dendrite of the bombykol receptor cell. The outer pore openings are covered by several layers of a different electron density. Although the chemical composition of these layers is unknown, they are probably lipophilic, or fat-loving. Layers of such a composition would allow the fatty-alcohol molecules of bombykol to diffuse into the pore openings more readily.

substances from the outside, as K. D. Ernst has shown in our laboratory, but the content of the tubules is unknown [*see illustrations on preceding page*].

These observations enabled us to construct the following model: The odor molecules are adsorbed on the hair surface, diffuse to the pores and from there through the tubules to the receptor-cell dendrite, where they elicit the receptor potential. We calculated the diffusion time of bombykol on the hairs and found it to be well within the electrophysiologically determined response time. Although the adsorption of bombykol on the hair surface is an established fact and diffusion along the surface of the hair is highly probable, we have not yet been able to follow the pheromone into the pores and tubules. The spatial resolution of the currently available autoradiographic methods is not high enough to locate the bombykol molecule in these conduits.

The process by which stimulus energy is transduced into receptor excitation is only partly understood for any sensory receptor cell, but with some reasonable assumptions we can at least outline it for the *Bombyx* odor-receptor cell. Our working hypothesis is that the bombykol molecule interacts with an acceptor in the membrane of the receptor-cell dendrite. The acceptor could function as a gating device, controlling the flow of ions through the membrane and thus the distribution of electric charges inside and outside the cell. The gating might be achieved by conformational changes in the molecular structure of the acceptor when it adsorbs the bombykol molecule.

Although the gating mechanism of the acceptor is definitely speculative, we can make some predictions about the properties of the active site of the acceptor. Fortunately we have quantitative information on a number of compounds that are effective in stimulating odor-receptor cells in other insects. When we looked into the physical properties of those molecules that activate a given type of cell, we were led to the conclusion that what happens in the process is not chemical bonding but weak physical interaction. We assume that the binding site and its reaction partner, the odor molecule, are complementary. On this basis the molecular specificity of the binding site can be deduced from the relative effectiveness of various stimulating molecules. Our observation that even the synthetic steric isomers of bombykol were from 100 to 1,000 times less effective than the natural pheromone indicates that the selective binding capacity of the bombykol acceptors is very high. The answer to the often-raised question "What makes a molecule an odor?" is on this functional level "The binding properties of the acceptor."

What is the fate of the odor molecule after it is bonded to the acceptor site in the receptor-cell membrane? With such a sensitive system it is unlikely that after the information transfer the odor molecule has a chance to activate the cell again. On the other hand, the odor molecule should not stay on the receptor site for too long, because the cell must be freed to be able to respond to another stimulus. We do not know as yet how the odor molecule is removed. One possible mechanism would be that it is immediately metabolized after the interaction. We have found that there is such a mechanism available, but it is neither specific enough nor fast enough to be directly involved in the transduction process.

Three years ago Morton Beroza of the U.S. Department of Agriculture asked us if we would be interested in extending our investigations to the gypsy moth, *Porthetria dispar*. His group had just successfully identified the lure pheromone of the female of this insect. It is *cis*-7,8-epoxy-2-methyloctadecane, dubbed "disparlure." As a result of the work of Beroza and his colleagues the compound was available in synthetic form. They had also succeeded in synthesizing 50 related epoxides, some with a different carbon-chain length, a shifted epoxy bridge (an oxygen attached to two carbons in the chain) and/or a shifted methyl group (CH_3). Starting a fruitful collaboration, we first repeated the measurement of the antennal response that had been made by our American colleagues and the experiments they had conducted with gypsy moths in the field. We also recorded the responses of single pheromone-receptor cells.

Our experiments clearly showed that disparlure is a more potent sex lure than

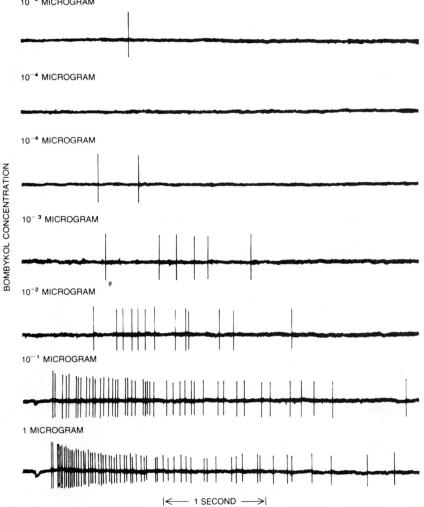

10⁻⁴ MICROGRAM

10⁻⁴ MICROGRAM

10⁻⁴ MICROGRAM

10⁻³ MICROGRAM

10⁻² MICROGRAM

10⁻¹ MICROGRAM

1 MICROGRAM

BOMBYKOL CONCENTRATION

|◄──── 1 SECOND ────►|

NERVE IMPULSES generated in a bombykol receptor cell increase in frequency as the concentration of odor increases. A concentration of 10⁻⁴ microgram of bombykol on odor source gives rise to one or two impulses or none. Recordings were made by E. Priesner.

any of the related compounds. The two compounds that elicited the next-largest responses are 20 and 100 times less effective. The male antennae of the gypsy moth and those of the silk moth are very much alike, so that there is little doubt that in principle the mechanisms by which the odor molecules are captured, are transferred and elicit electrical responses are identical in the two species. The details, however, have yet to be worked out.

The gypsy moth is a destructive forest pest in large parts of the eastern U.S. and in some parts of Europe (whence it was introduced to New England in 1869). The closest kin of this species is the nun moth, *Porthetria monacha*, which is found in the forests of central and northern Europe. We extended our studies to the nun moth, whose female sex attractant is not yet known. In our electrophysiological recordings we found that the nun moth had the same preference pattern for disparlure and related compounds as the gypsy moth has. The parallelism in their responses strongly suggests that the two species use the same compound as a sex attractant. Such a lack of species specificity in a sex attractant seems not to be an exception with species of the same genus but rather the rule.

Field experiments conducted earlier by H. Schönherr of the University of Freiburg, in which disparlure was successfully used to trap nun moths, also suggest that disparlure is probably the attractant for this species. In collaboration with R. Lange and F. Schwarz of the same institution, we have continued these studies by comparing disparlure as a bait with some of its related compounds. Again disparlure was by far the most effective attractant.

For two species to have the same attracting pheromone would not present any problem if the species were widely separated ecologically. For the nun moth and the gypsy moth, which live in close proximity in some parts of Europe, it could cause confusion. Possible mechanisms that would prevent uneconomical cross-attraction or even hybridization are differences in the rhythm of daily activity of the species, differences in general and sexual behavior and even a morphological incompatibility for copulation.

When Butenandt started the chemical analysis of the silk moth's sex attractant in the 1930's, he was not just interested in the composition of this enigmatic compound. He was already thinking of the possibility that such substances could be synthesized and used to lure pest in-

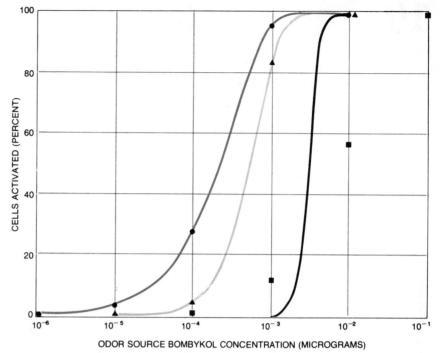

CELLS ACTIVATED (PERCENT)

ODOR SOURCE BOMBYKOL CONCENTRATION (MICROGRAMS)

NUMBER OF CELLS that responded with one or more impulses (*circles*), two or more impulses (*triangles*) and 10 or more impulses (*squares*) were plotted against the concentration of bombykol. The data for the one-impulse response exactly fitted the Poisson probability curve for a random one-hit process (*darker color*). The data for the two-impulse responses fitted the two-hit curve (*lighter color*). The data for 10 or more impulses did not fit the 10-hit probability curve (*black*). These results, together with measurements of the adsorption of radioactively labeled bombykol on antennae, indicate that single impulses are generated by single molecules of bombykol and double impulses by two molecules.

sects into traps with high specificity. He and others hoped that this stratagem could be used to avoid the dangerous side effects of the generalized chemical insecticides. Although the need for species-specific biological pest controls is now even more pressing than it was 40 years ago, the trapping of insects (or perhaps the confusion of insect sexual behavior) with pheromones does not appear to be the panacea. Nonetheless, in a number of cases the luring of pest insects with pheromone traps has proved to be useful in predicting the outbreak of a large infestation and thus in timing, calibrating and eventually reducing the application of generalized insecticides. The U.S. Department of Agriculture still hopes to be able to use the gypsy moth's sex attractant to prevent or even halt the insect's dangerous rate of expansion.

Successful pheromone research and promising field trapping has also been conducted with leaf-roller moths by Wendell L. Roelofs and his colleagues at the State Agricultural Experiment Station in Geneva, N.Y. They found that a mixture of pheromonal components will specifically attract several of these fruit tree pests. Another pheromone control method has been examined by H. H.

Shorey and his colleagues at the University of California at Riverside. They evaporated a synthetic sex attractant of the cabbage looper in cabbage fields and the attractant of the pink bollworm moth in cotton fields. Under favorable conditions and with high doses of the attractant they produced an impressive degree of confusion among the males and a high percentage of unfertilized females.

In the future pheromones will probably become a component of a concerted system of biological control methods against pests that threaten crops and human health. Biologists the world over are searching for the Achilles' heel in the life of many pest species. My own view is that in many of these investigations a detailed analysis of the physiology, behavior and ecology of the insect involved is neglected. To be sure, behavior and ecology are complex and not easily studied expressions of the phenomenon called life. They nonetheless deserve the best effort of investigators not only for economic reasons such as the control of insect pests but also for a more fundamental reason: to better learn how we humans can survive in an ecologically balanced world together with our fellow organisms.

10 Pheromones

by Edward O. Wilson
May 1963

A pheromone is a substance secreted by an animal that influences the behavior of other animals of the same species. Recent studies indicate that such chemical communication is surprisingly common

It is conceivable that somewhere on other worlds civilizations exist that communicate entirely by the exchange of chemical substances that are smelled or tasted. Unlikely as this may seem, the theoretical possibility cannot be ruled out. It is not difficult to design, on paper at least, a chemical communication system that can transmit a large amount of information with rather good efficiency. The notion of such a communication system is of course strange because our outlook is shaped so strongly by our own peculiar auditory and visual conventions. This limitation of outlook is found even among students of animal behavior; they have favored species whose communication methods are similar to our own and therefore more accessible to analysis. It is becoming increasingly clear, however, that chemical systems provide the dominant means of communication in many animal species, perhaps even in most. In the past several years animal behaviorists and organic chemists, working together, have made a start at deciphering some of these systems and have discovered a number of surprising new biological phenomena.

In earlier literature on the subject, chemicals used in communication were usually referred to as "ectohormones." Since 1959 the less awkward and etymologically more accurate term "pheromones" has been widely adopted. It is used to describe substances exchanged among members of the same animal species. Unlike true hormones, which are secreted internally to regulate the organism's own physiology, or internal environment, pheromones are secreted externally and help to regulate the organism's external environment by influencing other animals. The mode of influence can take either of two general forms. If the pheromone produces a more or less immediate and reversible change

in the behavior of the recipient, it is said to have a "releaser" effect. In this case the chemical substance seems to act directly on the recipient's central nervous system. If the principal function of the pheromone is to trigger a chain of physiological events in the recipient, it has what we have recently labeled a "primer" effect. The physiological changes, in turn, equip the organism with a new behavioral repertory, the components of which are thenceforth evoked by appropriate stimuli. In termites, for example, the reproductive and soldier castes prevent other termites from developing into

their own castes by secreting substances that are ingested and act through the *corpus allatum,* an endocrine gland controlling differentiation [see "The Termite and the Cell," by Martin Lüscher; Scientific American, May, 1953].

These indirect primer pheromones do not always act by physiological inhibition. They can have the opposite effect. Adult males of the migratory locust *Schistocerca gregaria* secrete a volatile substance from their skin surface that accelerates the growth of young locusts. When the nymphs detect this substance with their antennae, their hind legs,

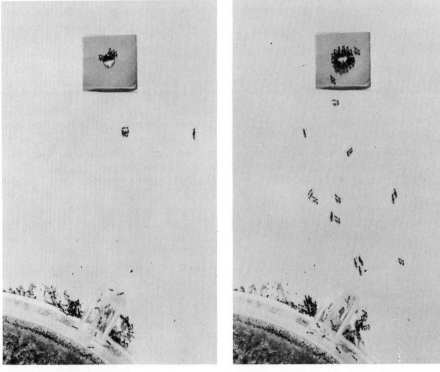

INVISIBLE ODOR TRAILS guide fire ant workers to a source of food: a drop of sugar solution. The trails consist of a pheromone laid down by workers returning to their nest after finding a source of food. Sometimes the chemical message is reinforced by the touching of antennae if a returning worker meets a wandering fellow along the way. This is hap-

some of their mouth parts and the antennae themselves vibrate. The secretion, in conjunction with tactile and visual signals, plays an important role in the formation of migratory locust swarms.

A striking feature of some primer pheromones is that they cause important physiological change without an immediate accompanying behavioral response, at least none that can be said to be peculiar to the pheromone. Beginning in 1955 with the work of S. van der Lee and L. M. Boot in the Netherlands, mammalian endocrinologists have discovered several unexpected effects on the female mouse that are produced by odors of other members of the same species. These changes are not marked by any immediate distinctive behavioral patterns. In the "Lee-Boot effect" females placed in groups of four show an increase in the percentage of pseudopregnancies. A completely normal reproductive pattern can be restored by removing the olfactory bulbs of the mice or by housing the mice separately. When more and more female mice are forced to live together, their oestrous cycles become highly irregular and in most of the mice the cycle stops completely for long periods. Recently W. K. Whitten of the Australian National University has discovered that the odor of a male mouse can initiate and

synchronize the oestrous cycles of female mice. The male odor also reduces the frequency of reproductive abnormalities arising when female mice are forced to live under crowded conditions.

A still more surprising primer effect has been found by Helen Bruce of the National Institute for Medical Research in London. She observed that the odor of a strange male mouse will block the pregnancy of a newly impregnated female mouse. The odor of the original stud male, of course, leaves pregnancy undisturbed. The mouse reproductive pheromones have not yet been identified chemically, and their mode of action is only partly understood. There is evidence that the odor of the strange male suppresses the secretion of the hormone prolactin, with the result that the *corpus luteum* (a ductless ovarian gland) fails to develop and normal oestrus is restored. The pheromones are probably part of the complex set of control mechanisms that regulate the population density of animals [see "Population Density and Social Pathology," by John B. Calhoun; SCIENTIFIC AMERICAN Offprint 506].

Pheromones that produce a simple releaser effect—a single specific response mediated directly by the central nervous system—are widespread in the

animal kingdom and serve a great many functions. Sex attractants constitute a large and important category. The chemical structures of six attractants are shown on page 101. Although two of the six—the mammalian scents muskone and civetone—have been known for some 40 years and are generally assumed to serve a sexual function, their exact role has never been rigorously established by experiments with living animals. In fact, mammals seem to employ musklike compounds, alone or in combination with other substances, to serve several functions: to mark home ranges, to assist in territorial defense and to identify the sexes.

The nature and role of the four insect sex attractants are much better understood. The identification of each represents a technical feat of considerable magnitude. To obtain 12 milligrams of esters of bombykol, the sex attractant of the female silkworm moth, Adolf F. J. Butenandt and his associates at the Max Planck Institute of Biochemistry in Munich had to extract material from 250,000 moths. Martin Jacobson, Morton Beroza and William Jones of the U.S. Department of Agriculture processed 500,000 female gypsy moths to get 20 milligrams of the gypsy-moth attractant gyplure. Each moth yielded only about .01 microgram (millionth of a gram) of

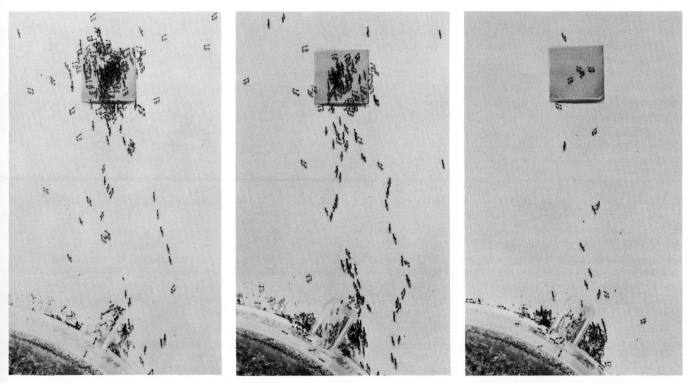

pening in the photograph at the far left. A few foraging workers have just found the sugar drop and a returning trail-layer is communicating the news to another ant. In the next two pictures the trail has been completed and workers stream from the nest in increasing numbers. In the fourth picture unrewarded workers return to the nest without laying trails and outward-bound traffic wanes. In the last picture most of the trails have evaporated completely and only a few stragglers remain at the site, eating the last bits of food.

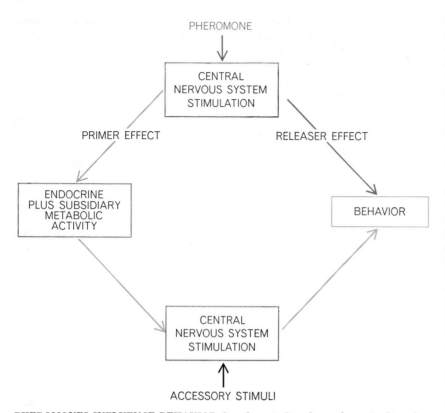

PHEROMONE

CENTRAL
NERVOUS SYSTEM
STIMULATION

PRIMER EFFECT

RELEASER EFFECT

ENDOCRINE
PLUS SUBSIDIARY
METABOLIC
ACTIVITY

BEHAVIOR

CENTRAL
NERVOUS SYSTEM
STIMULATION

ACCESSORY STIMULI

PHEROMONES INFLUENCE BEHAVIOR directly or indirectly, as shown in this schematic diagram. If a pheromone stimulates the recipient's central nervous system into producing an immediate change in behavior, it is said to have a "releaser" effect. If it alters a set of long-term physiological conditions so that the recipient's behavior can subsequently be influenced by specific accessory stimuli, the pheromone is said to have a "primer" effect.

French naturalist Jean Henri Fabre, speculating on sex attraction in insects, could not bring himself to believe that the female moth could communicate over such great distances by odor alone, since "one might as well expect to tint a lake with a drop of carmine." We now know that Fabre's conclusion was wrong but that his analogy was exact: to the male moth's powerful chemoreceptors the lake is indeed tinted.

One must now ask how the male moth, smelling the faintly tinted air, knows which way to fly to find the source of the tinting. He cannot simply fly in the direction of increasing scent; it can be shown mathematically that the attractant is distributed almost uniformly after it has drifted more than a few meters from the female. Recent experiments by Ilse Schwinck of the University of Munich have revealed what is probably the alternative procedure used. When male moths are activated by the pheromone, they simply fly upwind and thus inevitably move toward the female. If by accident they pass out of the active zone, they either abandon the search or fly about at random until they pick up the scent again. Eventually, as they approach the female, there is a slight increase in the concentration of the chemical attractant and this can serve as a guide for the remaining distance.

If one is looking for the most highly developed chemical communication systems in nature, it is reasonable to study the behavior of the social insects, particularly the social wasps, bees, termites and ants, all of which communicate mostly in the dark interiors of their nests and are known to have advanced chemoreceptive powers. In recent years experimental techniques have been developed to separate and identify the pheromones of these insects, and rapid progress has been made in deciphering the hitherto intractable codes, particularly those of the ants. The most successful procedure has been to dissect out single glandular reservoirs and see what effect their contents have on the behavior of the worker caste, which is the most numerous and presumably the most in need of continuing guidance. Other pheromones, not present in distinct reservoirs, are identified in chromatographic fractions of crude extracts.

Ants of all castes are constructed with an exceptionally well-developed exocrine glandular system. Many of the most prominent of these glands, whose function has long been a mystery to entomologists, have now been identified as the source of pheromones [*see illustra-*

gyplure, or less than a millionth of its body weight. Bombykol and gyplure were obtained by killing the insects and subjecting crude extracts of material to chromatography, the separation technique in which compounds move at different rates through a column packed with a suitable adsorbent substance. Another technique has been more recently developed by Robert T. Yamamoto of the U.S. Department of Agriculture, in collaboration with Jacobson and Beroza, to harvest the equally elusive sex attractant of the American cockroach. Virgin females were housed in metal cans and air was continuously drawn through the cans and passed through chilled containers to condense any vaporized materials. In this manner the equivalent of 10,000 females were "milked" over a nine-month period to yield 12.2 milligrams of what was considered to be the pure attractant.

The power of the insect attractants is almost unbelievable. If some 10,000 molecules of the most active form of bombykol are allowed to diffuse from a source one centimeter from the antennae of a male silkworm moth, a characteristic sexual response is obtained in most cases. If volatility and diffusion rate

are taken into account, it can be estimated that the threshold concentration is no more than a few hundred molecules per cubic centimeter, and the actual number required to stimulate the male is probably even smaller. From this one can calculate that .01 microgram of gyplure, the minimum average content of a single female moth, would be theoretically adequate, if distributed with maximum efficiency, to excite more than a billion male moths.

In nature the female uses her powerful pheromone to advertise her presence over a large area with a minimum expenditure of energy. With the aid of published data from field experiments and newly contrived mathematical models of the diffusion process, William H. Bossert, one of my associates in the Biological Laboratories at Harvard University, and I have deduced the shape and size of the ellipsoidal space within which male moths can be attracted under natural conditions [*see bottom illustration on opposite page*]. When a moderate wind is blowing, the active space has a long axis of thousands of meters and a transverse axis parallel to the ground of more than 200 meters at the widest point. The 19th-century

tion on page 97]. The analysis of the gland-pheromone complex has led to the beginnings of a new and deeper understanding of how ant societies are organized.

Consider the chemical trail. According to the traditional view, trail secretions served as only a limited guide for worker ants and had to be augmented by other kinds of signals exchanged inside the nest. Now it is known that the trail substance is extraordinarily versatile. In the fire ant (*Solenopsis saevissima*), for instance, it functions both to activate and to guide foraging workers in search of food and new nest sites. It also contributes as one of the alarm signals emitted by workers in distress. The trail of the fire ant consists of a substance secreted in minute amounts by Dufour's gland; the substance leaves the ant's body by way of the extruded sting, which is touched intermittently to the ground much like a moving pen dispensing ink. The trail pheromone, which has not yet been chemically identified, acts primarily to attract the fire ant workers. Upon encountering the attractant the workers move automatically up the gradient to the source of emission. When the substance is drawn out in a line, the workers run along the direction of the line away from the nest. This simple response brings them to the food source or new nest site from which the trail is laid. In our laboratory we have extracted the pheromone from the Dufour's glands of freshly killed workers and have used it to create artificial trails. Groups of workers will follow these trails away from the nest and along arbitrary routes (including circles leading back to the nest) for considerable periods of time. When the pheromone is presented to whole colonies in massive doses, a large portion of the colony, including the queen, can be drawn out in a close simulation of the emigration process.

The trail substance is rather volatile, and a natural trail laid by one worker diffuses to below the threshold concentration within two minutes. Consequently outward-bound workers are able to follow it only for the distance they can travel in this time, which is about 40 centimeters. Although this strictly limits the distance over which the ants can communicate, it provides at least two important compensatory advantages. The more obvious advantage is that old, useless trails do not linger to confuse the hunting workers. In addition, the intensity of the trail laid by many workers provides a sensitive index of the amount of food at a given site and the rate of its depletion. As workers move to and from

ANTENNAE OF GYPSY MOTHS differ radically in structure according to their function. In the male (*left*) they are broad and finely divided to detect minute quantities of sex attractant released by the female (*right*). The antennae of the female are much less developed.

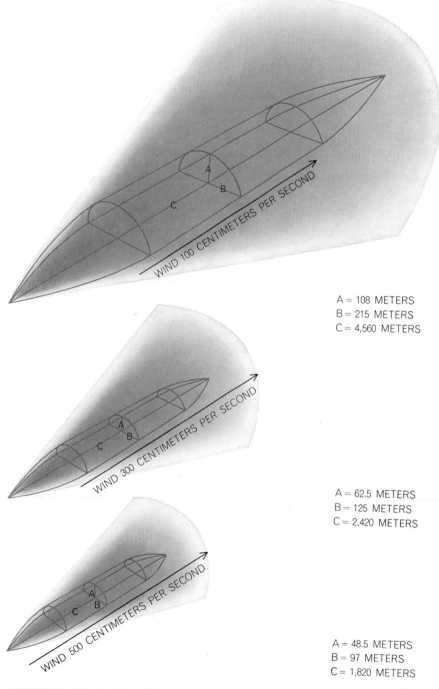

A = 108 METERS
B = 215 METERS
C = 4,560 METERS

A = 62.5 METERS
B = 125 METERS
C = 2,420 METERS

A = 48.5 METERS
B = 97 METERS
C = 1,820 METERS

ACTIVE SPACE of gyplure, the gypsy moth sex attractant, is the space within which this pheromone is sufficiently dense to attract males to a single, continuously emitting female. The actual dimensions, deduced from linear measurements and general gas-diffusion models, are given at right. Height (*A*) and width (*B*) are exaggerated in the drawing. As wind shifts from moderate to strong, increased turbulence contracts the active space.

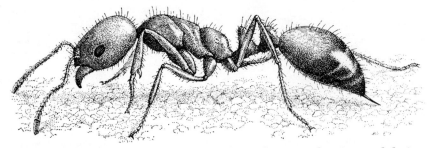

FIRE ANT WORKER lays an odor trail by exuding a pheromone along its extended sting. The sting is touched to the ground periodically, breaking the trail into a series of streaks.

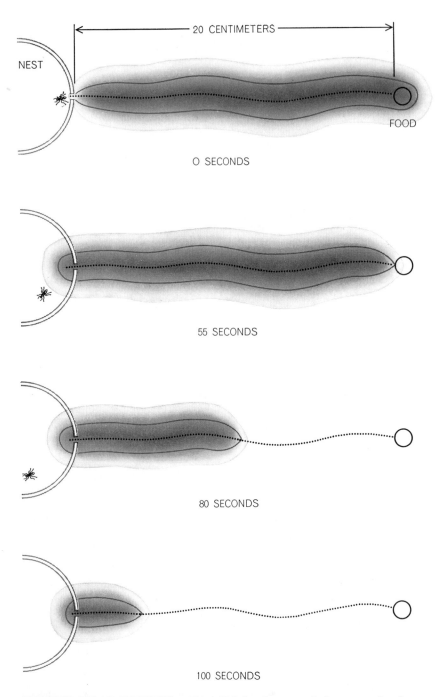

20 CENTIMETERS

NEST

FOOD

O SECONDS

55 SECONDS

80 SECONDS

100 SECONDS

ACTIVE SPACE OF ANT TRAIL, within which the pheromone is dense enough to be perceived by other workers, is narrow and nearly constant in shape with the maximum gradient situated near its outer surface. The rapidity with which the trail evaporates is indicated.

the food finds (consisting mostly of dead insects and sugar sources) they continuously add their own secretions to the trail produced by the original discoverers of the food. Only if an ant is rewarded by food does it lay a trail on its trip back to the nest; therefore the more food encountered at the end of the trail, the more workers that can be rewarded and the heavier the trail. The heavier the trail, the more workers that are drawn from the nest and arrive at the end of the trail. As the food is consumed, the number of workers laying trail substance drops, and the old trail fades by evaporation and diffusion, gradually constricting the outward flow of workers.

The fire ant odor trail shows other evidences of being efficiently designed. The active space within which the pheromone is dense enough to be perceived by workers remains narrow and nearly constant in shape over most of the length of the trail. It has been further deduced from diffusion models that the maximum gradient must be situated near the outer surface of the active space. Thus workers are informed of the space boundary in a highly efficient way. Together these features ensure that the following workers keep in close formation with a minimum chance of losing the trail.

The fire ant trail is one of the few animal communication systems whose information content can be measured with fair precision. Unlike many communicating animals, the ants have a distinct goal in space—the food find or nest site—the direction and distance of which must both be communicated. It is possible by a simple technique to measure how close trail-followers come to the trail end, and, by making use of a standard equation from information theory, one can translate the accuracy of their response into the "bits" of information received. A similar procedure can be applied (as first suggested by the British biologist J. B. S. Haldane) to the "waggle dance" of the honeybee, a radically different form of communication system from the ant trail [see "Dialects in the Language of the Bees," by Karl von Frisch, beginning on p. 241]. Surprisingly, it turns out that the two systems, although of wholly different evolutionary origin, transmit about the same amount of information with reference to distance (two bits) and direction (four bits in the honeybee, and four or possibly five in the ant). Four bits of information will direct an ant or a bee into one of 16 equally probable sectors of a circle and two bits will identify one of four equally probable distances.

It is conceivable that these information values represent the maximum that can be achieved with the insect brain and sensory apparatus.

Not all kinds of ants lay chemical trails. Among those that do, however, the pheromones are highly species-specific in their action. In experiments in which artificial trails extracted from one species were directed to living colonies of other species, the results have almost always been negative, even among related species. It is as if each species had its own private language. As a result there is little or no confusion when the trails of two or more species cross.

Another important class of ant pheromone is composed of alarm substances. A simple backyard experiment will show that if a worker ant is disturbed by a clean instrument, it will, for a short time, excite other workers with whom it comes in contact. Until recently most students of ant behavior thought that

the alarm was spread by touch, that one worker simply jostled another in its excitement or drummed on its neighbor with its antennae in some peculiar way. Now it is known that disturbed workers discharge chemicals, stored in special glandular reservoirs, that can produce all the characteristic alarm responses solely by themselves. The chemical structure of four alarm substances is shown on page 101. Nothing could illustrate more clearly the wide differences between the human perceptual world and that of chemically communicating animals. To the human nose the alarm substances are mild or even pleasant, but to the ant they represent an urgent tocsin that can propel a colony into violent and instant action.

As in the case of the trail substances, the employment of the alarm substances appears to be ideally designed for the purpose it serves. When the contents of the mandibular glands of a worker of the harvesting ant (*Pogonomyrmex badius*)

are discharged into still air, the volatile material forms a rapidly expanding sphere, which attains a radius of about six centimeters in 13 seconds. Then it contracts until the signal fades out completely some 35 seconds after the moment of discharge. The outer shell of the active space contains a low concentration of pheromone, which is actually attractive to harvester workers. This serves to draw them toward the point of disturbance. The central region of the active space, however, contains a concentration high enough to evoke the characteristic frenzy of alarm. The "alarm sphere" expands to a radius of about three centimeters in eight seconds and, as might be expected, fades out more quickly than the "attraction sphere."

The advantage to the ants of an alarm signal that is both local and short-lived becomes obvious when a *Pogonomyrmex* colony is observed under natural conditions. The ant nest is subject to almost innumerable minor disturbances. If the

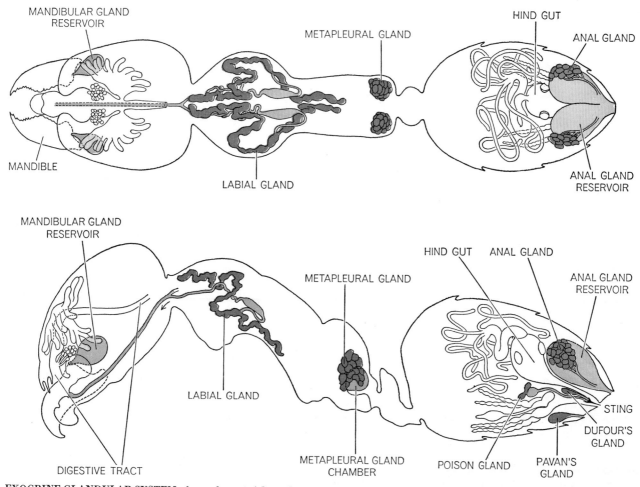

EXOCRINE GLANDULAR SYSTEM of a worker ant (*shown here in top and side cutaway views*) is specially adapted for the production of chemical communication substances. Some pheromones are stored in reservoirs and released in bursts only when needed; others are secreted continuously. Depending on the species, trail substances are produced by Dufour's gland, Pavan's gland or the poison glands; alarm substances are produced by the anal and mandibular glands. The glandular sources of other pheromones are unknown.

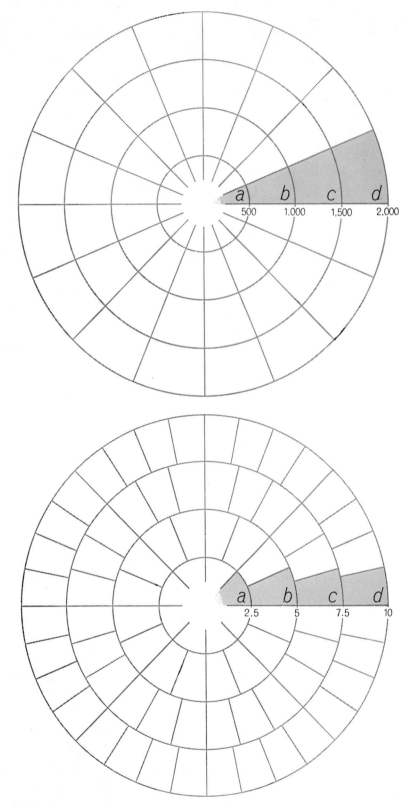

FORAGING INFORMATION conveyed by two different insect communication systems can be represented on two similar "compass" diagrams. The honeybee "waggle dance" (*top*) transmits about four bits of information with respect to direction, enabling a honeybee worker to pinpoint a target within one of 16 equally probable angular sectors. The number of "bits" in this case remains independent of distance, given in meters. The pheromone system used by trail-laying fire ants (*bottom*) is superior in that the amount of directional information increases with distance, given in centimeters. At distances *c* and *d*, the probable sector in which the target lies is smaller for ants than for bees. (For ants, directional information actually increases gradually and not by jumps.) Both insects transmit two bits of distance information, specifying one of four equally probable distance ranges.

alarm spheres generated by individual ant workers were much wider and more durable, the colony would be kept in ceaseless and futile turmoil. As it is, local disturbances such as intrusions by foreign insects are dealt with quickly and efficiently by small groups of workers, and the excitement soon dies away.

The trail and alarm substances are only part of the ants' chemical vocabulary. There is evidence for the existence of other secretions that induce gathering and settling of workers, acts of grooming, food exchange, and other operations fundamental to the care of the queen and immature ants. Even dead ants produce a pheromone of sorts. An ant that has just died will be groomed by other workers as if it were still alive. Its complete immobility and crumpled posture by themselves cause no new response. But in a day or two chemical decomposition products accumulate and stimulate the workers to bear the corpse to the refuse pile outside the nest. Only a few decomposition products trigger this funereal response; they include certain long-chain fatty acids and their esters. When other objects, including living workers, are experimentally daubed with these substances, they are dutifully carried to the refuse pile. After being dumped on the refuse the "living dead" scramble to their feet and promptly return to the nest, only to be carried out again. The hapless creatures are thrown back on the refuse pile time and again until most of the scent of death has been worn off their bodies by the ritual.

Our observation of ant colonies over long periods has led us to believe that as few as 10 pheromones, transmitted singly or in simple combinations, might suffice for the total organization of ant society. The task of separating and characterizing these substances, as well as judging the roles of other kinds of stimuli such as sound, is a job largely for the future.

Even in animal species where other kinds of communication devices are prominently developed, deeper investigation usually reveals the existence of pheromonal communication as well. I have mentioned the auxiliary roles of primer pheromones in the lives of mice and migratory locusts. A more striking example is the communication system of the honeybee. The insect is celebrated for its employment of the "round" and "waggle" dances (augmented, perhaps, by auditory signals) to designate the location of food and new nest sites. It is not so widely known that chemical signals play equally important roles in other aspects of honeybee life. The mother queen regulates the reproductive cycle of the colony by secreting from her mandibular glands a substance recently identified as 9-ketodecanoic acid. When this pheromone is ingested by the worker bees, it inhibits development of their ovaries and also their ability to manufacture the royal cells in which new queens are reared. The same pheromone serves as a sex attractant in the queen's nuptial flights.

Under certain conditions, including the discovery of new food sources, worker bees release geraniol, a pleasant-smelling alcohol, from the abdominal Nassanoff glands. As the geraniol diffuses through the air it attracts other workers and so supplements information contained in the waggle dance. When a worker stings an intruder, it discharges, in addition to the venom, tiny amounts of a secretion from clusters of unicellular

glands located next to the basal plates of the sting. This secretion is responsible for the tendency, well known to bee-keepers, of angry swarms of workers to sting at the same spot. One component, which acts as a simple attractant, has been identified as isoamyl acetate, a compound that has a banana-like odor. It is possible that the stinging response is evoked by at least one unidentified alarm substance secreted along with the attractant.

Knowledge of pheromones has advanced to the point where one can make some tentative generalizations about their chemistry. In the first place, there appear to be good reasons why sex attractants should be compounds that contain between 10 and 17 carbon atoms and that have molecular weights between about 180 and 300—the range actually observed in attractants so far identified. (For comparison, the weight of a single

carbon atom is 12.) Only compounds of roughly this size or greater can meet the two known requirements of a sex attractant: narrow specificity, so that only members of one species will respond to it, and high potency. Compounds that contain fewer than five or so carbon atoms and that have a molecular weight of less than about 100 cannot be assembled in enough different ways to provide a distinctive molecule for all the insects that want to advertise their presence.

It also seems to be a rule, at least with insects, that attraction potency increases with molecular weight. In one series of esters tested on flies, for instance, a doubling of molecular weight resulted in as much as a thousandfold increase in efficiency. On the other hand, the molecule cannot be too large and complex or it will be prohibitively difficult for the insect to synthesize. An equally important limitation on size is

BOMBYKOL (SILKWORM MOTH)

GYPLURE (GYPSY MOTH)

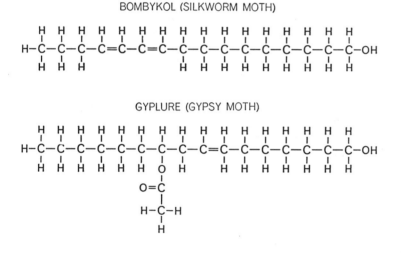

2,2-DIMETHYL-3-ISOPROPYLIDENECYCLOPROPYL PROPIONATE (AMERICAN COCKROACH)

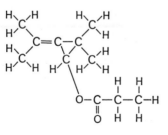

HONEYBEE QUEEN SUBSTANCE

CIVETONE (CIVET)

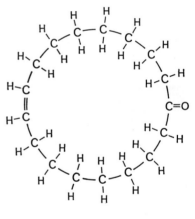

MUSKONE (MUSK DEER)

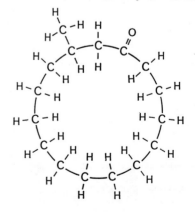

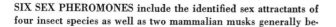

SIX SEX PHEROMONES include the identified sex attractants of four insect species as well as two mammalian musks generally believed to be sex attractants. The high molecular weight of most sex pheromones accounts for their narrow specificity and high potency.

the fact that volatility—and, as a result, diffusibility—declines with increasing molecular weight.

One can also predict from first principles that the molecular weight of alarm substances will tend to be less than those of the sex attractants. Among the ants there is little specificity; each species responds strongly to the alarm substances of other species. Furthermore, an alarm substance, which is used primarily within the confines of the nest, does not need the stimulative potency of a sex attractant, which must carry its message for long distances. For these reasons small molecules will suffice for alarm purposes. Of seven alarm substances known in the social insects, six have 10 or fewer carbon atoms and one (dendrolasin) has 15. It will be interesting to see if future discoveries bear out these early generalizations.

Do human pheromones exist? Primer pheromones might be difficult to detect, since they can affect the endocrine system without producing overt specific behavioral responses. About all that can be said at present is that striking sexual differences have been observed in the ability of humans to smell certain

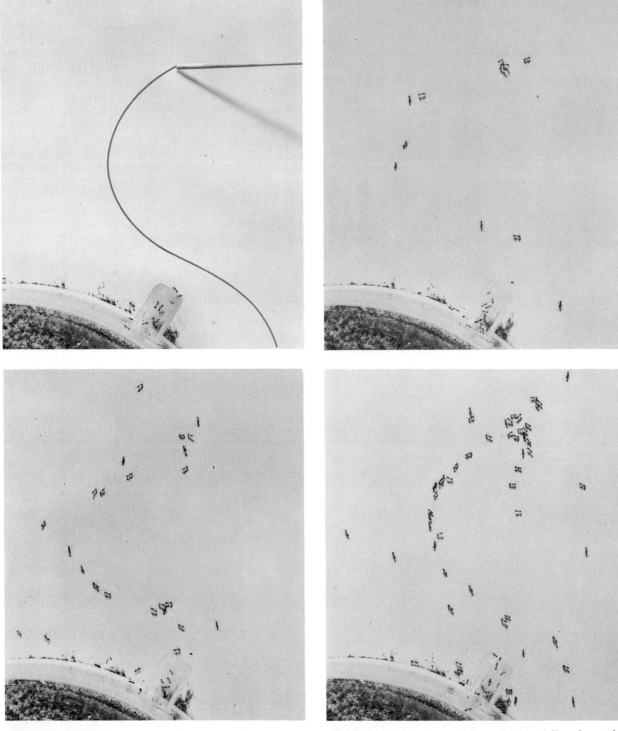

ARTIFICIAL TRAIL can be laid down by drawing a line (*colored curve in frame at top left*) with a stick that has been treated with the contents of a single Dufour's gland. In the remaining three frames, workers are attracted from the nest, follow the artificial route in close formation and mill about in confusion at its arbitrary terminus. Such a trail is not renewed by the unrewarded workers.

DENDROLASIN (*LASIUS FULIGINOSUS*)

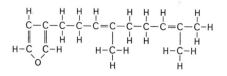

CITRAL (*ATTA SEXDENS*)

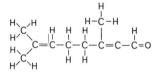

CITRONELLAL (*ACANTHOMYOPS CLAVIGER*)

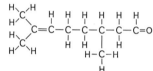

2-HEPTANONE (*IRIDOMYRMEX PRUINOSUS*)

FOUR ALARM PHEROMONES, given off by the workers of the ant species indicated, have so far been identified. Disturbing stimuli trigger the release of these substances from various glandular reservoirs.

substances. The French biologist J. Le-Magnen has reported that the odor of Exaltolide, the synthetic lactone of 14-hydroxytetradecanoic acid, is perceived clearly only by sexually mature females and is perceived most sharply at about the time of ovulation. Males and young girls were found to be relatively insensitive, but a male subject became more sensitive following an injection of estrogen. Exaltolide is used commercially as a perfume fixative. LeMagnen also reported that the ability of his subjects to detect the odor of certain steroids paralleled that of their ability to smell Exaltolide. These observations hardly represent a case for the existence of human pheromones, but they do suggest that the relation of odors to human physiology can bear further examination.

It is apparent that knowledge of chemical communication is still at an early stage. Students of the subject are in the position of linguists who have learned the meaning of a few words of a nearly indecipherable language. There is almost certainly a large chemical vocabulary still to be discovered. Conceiv-

ably some pheromone "languages" will be found to have a syntax. It may be found, in other words, that pheromones can be combined in mixtures to form new meanings for the animals employing them. One would also like to know if some animals can modulate the intensity or pulse frequency of pheromone emission to create new messages. The solution of these and other interesting problems will require new techniques in analytical organic chemistry combined with ever more perceptive studies of animal behavior.

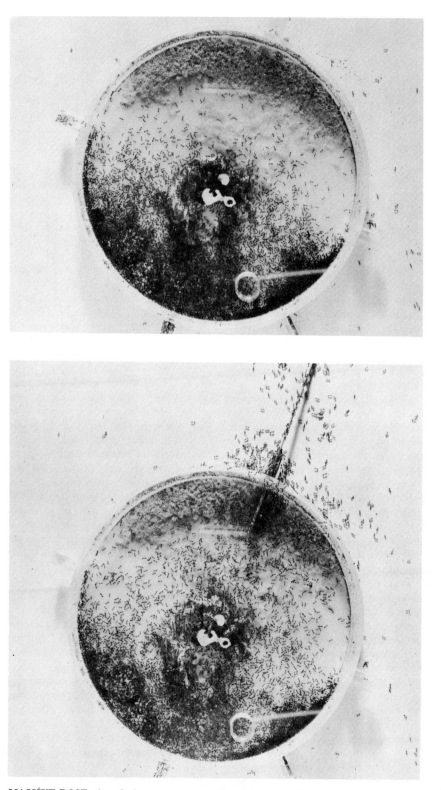

MASSIVE DOSE of trail pheromone causes the migration of a large portion of a fire ant colony from one side of a nest to another. The pheromone is administered on a stick that has been dipped in a solution extracted from the Dufour's glands of freshly killed workers.

11

The Neurobiology of Cricket Song

by David Bentley and Ronald R. Hoy
August 1974

The song pattern of each cricket species is stored in its genes. The songs are thus clues to the links among genetic information, development, the organization of the nervous system and behavior

Nowadays few people live where they can hear crickets singing on summer evenings, but makers of motion pictures know that nothing evokes a bucolic mood more effectively than the sound of crickets chirping in the background. Cricket song, which may seem like a random sequence of chirps and trills, is actually a communication system of considerable complexity. As Richard D. Alexander of the University of Michigan and others have shown, each species of cricket has a distinctive repertory of several songs that have evolved to transmit messages of behavioral importance.

From the work of many laboratories, including our own at the University of California at Berkeley and at Cornell University, it is known that the nerve networks needed for generating the songs of crickets are closely allied to those involved in flight. Both systems develop in stages as the cricket passes through its growth cycle from the larva to the adult. Through breeding experiments it has also been shown that the distinctive song patterns of various species are not learned behavior but are encoded in the insect's genes. Thus we have found that hybrids produced by mating different species exhibit song patterns that are intermediate between those of the parents. Progress is also being made in discovering the genes that control the song patterns and finding where they are located among the cricket's chromosomes. Ultimately it should be possible to piece together all the links in the chain from a sequence of chemical units in the DNA of the cricket's genes to the specification of a nerve network that leads to the production of a distinctive song. Cricket song is only one example of animal behavior that has a large genetically determined component.

The commonest cricket song is the calling song, which is sung by the males to guide sexually receptive females to the singer's burrow. The calling songs of different species that mature in the same area at the same time of year are always distinct. Confusion would result if all the males sang the same song. Once the male and the female have found each other, a new song, the courtship song, facilitates copulation. Following the transfer of the spermatophore, or sperm sac, the male may sing a postcopulatory song (known to French investigators as the "triumphal song"), which may help to maintain proximity between the partners. When a male cricket invades the territory of another male, a vigorous fight frequently results. (Cricket fights are even a traditional sport in the Far East.) Fighting is accompanied by the aggressive, or rivalry, song, which is sung by both combatants in an intense encounter and is nearly always sung by the winner. Thus the communication system consists of transmitters, which are always males, and receivers, which are both males and females, together with a variety of signals that convey information.

How is information encoded in the song? Each song is a sequence of sound pulses. The cricket generates a pulse by scissoring its fore wings once, drawing a scraper on one wing across a toothed file on the other [see *illustration on opposite page*]. This produces a remarkably pure tone. Features of the song theoretically capable of carrying information include the pitch, the relative amplitude of the pulses and their pattern in time. The temporal pattern has been shown to be the critical factor. Among different species the pattern varies from simple trills to complex sequences of chirps and trills with different intervals.

Fascinating as cricket communication may be to students of animal behavior, why should it interest the authors, who are neurobiologists? The answer is that one hopes the analysis of simple nerve networks associated with simple behavior will provide a foundation for the future understanding of more complex networks and more complex behavior, up to and including the behavior of our own species. Just as investigation of the bacterium *Escherichia coli* and the fruit fly *Drosophila* has been fundamental to current knowledge of molecular biology and genetics, we hope that through the study of cricket singing and similar simple behavioral systems some doors in neurobiology that have so far been closed will now be opened.

Throughout the animal kingdom neurons, or nerve cells, are basically similar in operation. Furthermore, both in vertebrates and in higher invertebrates some assemblies of neurons are organized in characteristic ways to facilitate the execution of sensory or motor tasks. The nervous systems of invertebrates are more amenable to analysis, however, because they generate simpler and more stereotyped behavior, because the neurons are fewer and larger and because many neurons are uniquely identifiable. The last feature means that individual neurons can be repeatedly "queried" by the investigator, whereas their vertebrate counterparts are nameless faces that can be polled once but then become lost in the crowd. Repeatability is so important to progress that investigation of invertebrate networks has proved a very powerful technique in analyzing nervous systems [see "Small Systems of Nerve Cells," by Donald Kennedy; SCIENTIFIC AMERICAN Offprint 1073]. The special appeal of crickets lies in the access they provide to a broad range of problems.

The cricket nervous system is a chain of 10 ganglia, or knots of neurons: two in the head, three in the thorax and five in the abdomen. Each ganglion consists of a cortex, or outer layer, of nerve-cell bodies that surrounds a dense feltwork of nerve fibers called the neuropile. The interactions between neurons that control behavior take place within the neuropile. These interactions produce trains of impulses that are conducted along axons either through connectives to other ganglia or through nerves that run to muscles and other peripheral structures. Information from sensory neurons lying in the peripheral parts of the cricket's body is conducted along axons through nerve trunks into the ganglia.

Where in this simple nervous system are the song patterns generated? Franz Huber, the founding father of cricket neurobiology, who is now at the Max Planck Institute for Behavioral Physiology at Seewiesen in Germany, demonstrated with the aid of his students Wolfram Kutsch, Ditmar Otto and Dieter Möss that only the two thoracic ganglia nearest the cricket's head ganglia are necessary for singing. This left open the question of what elements of the pattern are generated within the central nervous system and what elements rely on sensory feedback from the periphery. The experiments of the late Donald M. Wilson of Stanford University on locust flight suggested that virtually the entire pattern might be produced by neural circuits within the ganglia [see the article "The Flight-Control System of the Locust," by Donald M. Wilson, beginning on page 73]. This view was strongly supported by Huber's group in studies in which they observed the effect on the cricket's song patterns when the peripheral sensory system was either heavily loaded or acutely deprived. Neither condition had any significant effect on the song pattern.

One of us (Bentley) then began studying the song-production mechanism with the aid of microelectrodes implanted in various cells of the cricket's nervous system. This work was begun in Huber's laboratory and continued at Berkeley. In an early group of experiments the cricket's thoracic ganglia were completely isolated from sensory timing cues by the cutting of the peripheral nerves. Recordings from identified motor neurons showed that the cricket's nervous system could still produce a motor pattern practically indistinguishable from the normal calling-song pattern. This implied that the two anterior thoracic ganglia must

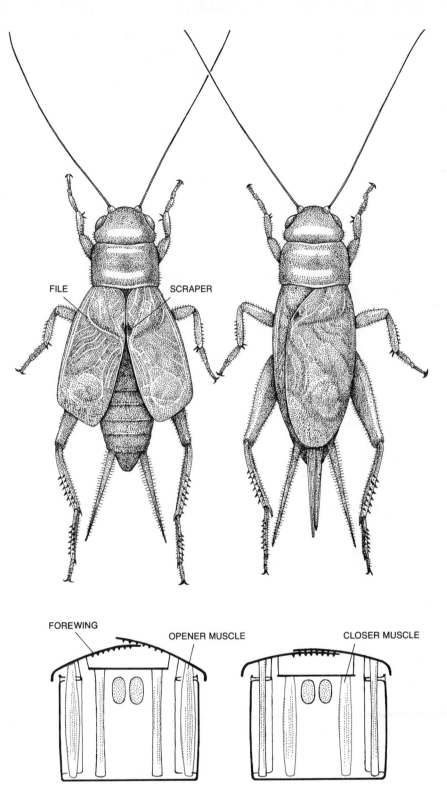

CRICKET SONG IS PRODUCED by specialized structures that are activated when the cricket closes its wings. The upper pair of diagrams show the wings moving from an open position (*left*) to a closed position (*right*). The lower pair of diagrams are simplified cross sections of the same positions as viewed from the front. When the wings are closing, a reinforced segment of cuticle (the scraper) on the edge of one wing bumps across a series of teeth, or ridges (the file), on the underside of the other wing. Both wings are similarly equipped, so that it does not matter which wing is on top and which on the bottom. The movement of the scraper across the file causes the wing to vibrate at about 5,000 cycles per second, producing a remarkably pure tone. Each closure of the wings produces a single sound pulse that lasts roughly 25 milliseconds, or about 125 cycles. The actual linkage between muscle contraction and wing movement involves a complex set of sclerites (small pieces of cuticle hinged to other pieces) that connect the wings to the thorax and muscles.

contain a network of nerve cells that are responsible for generating the calling-song pattern and that they are remarkably independent of sensory input.

The next task was to try to identify among the 1,000 or more nerve cells in each ganglion the neurons concerned with singing. During singing the wings of the cricket are operated by a small set of powerful "twitch" muscles. Each muscle is driven either by a single "fast" motor neuron or by up to five such neurons. The arrival of a nerve impulse at the bundle of muscle fibers that are innervated by a particular motor neuron results in a large action potential, or electrical impulse, in the muscle. Thus action potentials in a muscle unit are a direct one-to-one monitor of impulses in the corresponding motor neuron [*see illustration at left below*].

Fine insulated wire electrodes, which

will record these muscle action potentials, can be inserted through tiny holes drilled in the cricket's exoskeleton and implanted in each unit of any selected muscle. Many such electrodes can be implanted in an animal without interfering with its normal behavior. Therefore by successively implanting each muscle any behavior can be characterized in terms of which motor neurons are active, of the sequential impulse pattern in each neuron and of the relative timing of discharge in the different neurons. With this technique the motor neurons involved in the cricket's calling song were discovered and labeled according to the muscle units the neurons innervate.

Within the ganglion the same neurons can be found and identified with the aid of intracellular microelectrodes, ultrafine glass pipettes through which dye can be injected. The tip of the electrode is driv-

en into the neuron's cell body or one of its fibers. Once embedded the electrode can be used in either of two ways, passively or actively. When it is used passively, the electrode records the electrical activity of the cell and the synaptic inputs to the cell, either excitatory or inhibitory. When it is used actively, the electrode conveys current into the cell, making it possible to analyze the electrical activity within the cell and to stimulate the cell, revealing its effects on other cells [*see illustration at right below*]. When dye is injected into a cell through a micropipette, the dye permeates the cell body and all its fibers, revealing a structure that can be examined by either optical or electron microscopy.

With these techniques it has been possible to identify the activity patterns of the neurons involved in cricket singing, to learn their characteristic morphology

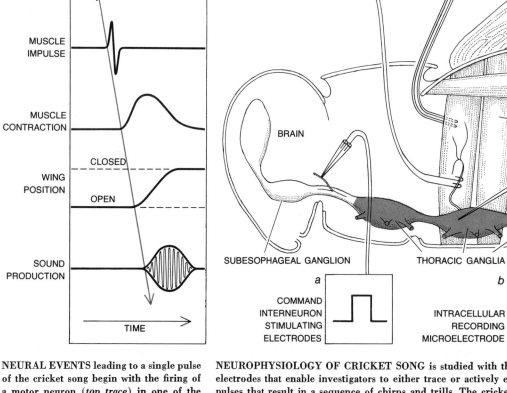

NEURAL EVENTS leading to a single pulse of the cricket song begin with the firing of a motor neuron (*top trace*) in one of the cricket's thoracic ganglia (*location "b" in illustration at right*). The arrival of the nerve impulse triggers a muscle impulse, or action potential (*location "d" at right*), that contracts one of the wing-closing muscles. The closing of the wing causes the scraper on one wing to rub across the file underneath the other wing, producing a sound pulse.

NEUROPHYSIOLOGY OF CRICKET SONG is studied with the aid of implanted microelectrodes that enable investigators to either trace or actively elicit the flow of nerve impulses that result in a sequence of chirps and trills. The cricket's central nervous system consists of a chain of 10 ganglia, of which only five, including the "brain" ganglion, are shown here. The two ganglia in color are sufficient for generating normal song. The song pattern can be elicited by stimulating specific "command" interneurons that lie in the nerve bundle connecting the two head ganglia to the thoracic ganglion (*a*). The command interneurons turn on the thoracic interneurons and motor neurons that generate song. Impulses from motor neurons are conducted along peripheral nerves to the song muscles. Vertical muscle fibers shown close the wings to produce a sound pulse and also to elevate the wings in flight. Horizontal muscle fibers open the wings in singing and depress the wings in flight.

and to discover how they are connected to other cells, particularly how motor neurons are connected to muscle units. In this way every fast motor neuron involved in singing was located, filled with dye and mapped within the ganglion.

What, then, are the characteristics and interconnections of the motor neurons that underlie the generation of cricket-song patterns? Are interneurons, or intermediate neurons, involved, and if so, what is their role? Like any motor pattern, the activity underlying the calling song requires a sequential timing of impulses in individual nerve cells and a coordinated timing of discharges in particular cell populations. The population of motor neurons involved in singing falls into two groups of synchronously firing cells that alternate with each other to open and close the wings. Intracellular recordings indicate that some synchronously firing motor neurons are coupled in such a way that an impulse in one greatly increases the probability of an impulse in its neighbor. The alternate firing of antagonistic motor neurons is established by the powerful inhibition of one group, the wing-closing motor neurons, during discharge of the other group, the wing-opening motor neurons. The wing-closing cells fire immediately after this inhibition, with the result that there is a characteristic spacing of impulses in the two groups [see lower two illustrations at right].

It has now been shown that interneurons help to establish the sequential timing of the song patterns. Even when crickets chirp normally, gaps appear in the song from time to time. The gaps do not, however, upset the established rhythm: the timing of the chirps continues as if there had been no gap [see second illustration from top at right]. This suggests that some internal oscillator, or "clock," within the ganglion has continued to run undisturbed in spite of the missing chirp. It has now been established that the motor neurons themselves are not part of the neuronal oscillator. During gaps not only do the motor neurons fail to fire but also the input signal that drives them is missing. Moreover, anomalous extra chirps that occur from time to time have no effect on the basic rhythm. One must conclude that the timing of the chirps is established by elements higher up in the cricket's nervous system, evidently interneurons whose output signal does not go directly to the motor neurons.

Although the interneuronal song oscillator is quite insensitive to influences

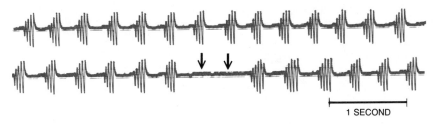

STIMULATION OF COMMAND INTERNEURONS (top trace) causes motor neurons to discharge (bottom trace) in a typical calling-song pattern. Stimulus site is labeled a and recording site c in illustration at right on the opposite page. Motor neurons fire as long as command interneurons are stimulated; arrow indicates several minutes of continuous firing.

CHIRP REGULARITY is shown in this sequence of 26 consecutive chirps, recorded inside a motor neuron in the second thoracic ganglion (site "b" in illustration at right on opposite page). Each chirp consists of four or five sound pulses, marked by oscillations of intracellular potential. Continuous record is here divided into two rows and aligned to show how rhythm persists in spite of two skipped chirps (arrows). Song resumes after the gap at exactly the right time, indicating existence of a "rhythm keeper" higher in the nervous system.

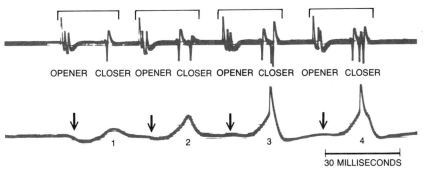

OPENER   CLOSER   OPENER   CLOSER   OPENER   CLOSER   OPENER   CLOSER

CHIRP CONSISTING OF FOUR RAPID SOUNDS is produced by alternate firing of wing-opening motor neurons and wing-closing motor neurons. The top trace shows nerve impulses arriving at their respective muscles (site "c" in illustration at right on opposite page). The bottom trace shows a recording from the larger of two closing motor neurons involved in producing the top trace. Immediately after the discharge of wing-opening motor neurons the closing motor neuron is inhibited from firing (arrows). Following inhibition the closing motor neuron is excited but first two excitations (1, 2) are below threshold.

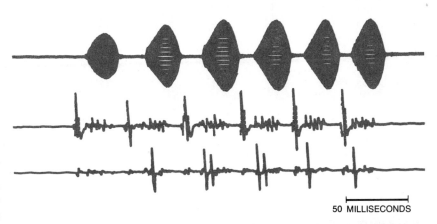

RELATION OF CHIRP SOUNDS TO MUSCLE IMPULSES is shown in simultaneous recordings. The top trace depicts the amplitude of the emitted sounds. The other two traces represent the impulses of a wing-opening muscle (middle trace) and of a wing-closing muscle (bottom trace). Muscle impulses were recorded at site d in illustration at right on opposite page. Simultaneous contraction of several wing-closing muscles produces sound pulse.

FLIGHT-MUSCLE SYSTEM can be studied by tethering crickets in a low-speed wind tunnel. Flight employs many of the same muscles and motor neurons used in singing. The neuronal system involved in song generation appears to be actively suppressed until the nymph, or young cricket, undergoes a final molt and reaches adulthood. This is not the case with flight behavior, which can be elicited and studied in the wind tunnel when nymphs are still four molts away from adulthood. Fine wire electrodes can be implanted in tethered insects.

They are bilaterally symmetrical, and when they are electrically stimulated at an appropriate frequency, they cause the song network to generate a perfectly normal calling-song pattern [see top illustration on preceding page]. One can show that a single command interneuron suffices to elicit the song pattern. There appear to be no conceptual or technical barriers to learning much more about how this hierarchically organized neural subsystem operates.

Many important questions are presented by the appearance in the adult cricket of a neuronal network that will generate a behavior pattern as precise as cricket song with such reliability. When are the neurons built? When do the cells become physiologically mature and what kind of electrical activity do they exhibit before reaching maturity? When are the functional connections that coordinate activity of the cells established? Is the network assembled before or after the cricket becomes an adult? If it is after, does perfection of the pattern depend on acoustical feedback, that is, on the cricket's hearing its first attempts at singing and then making corrections? Some answers to these questions have been found for singing and also for the closely related behavior of flight.

from outside the cricket's central nervous system, it can be manipulated internally. Huber and his colleagues have shown that singing behavior can be elicited either by electrical stimulation of the cricket's brain or by making small lesions in the brain. This indicates that interneurons running from the brain to the thoracic ganglia are capable of activating the song network. Cells of similar capability have been found in other simple nervous systems and are termed command interneurons.

At Berkeley one of us (Bentley) has been able to locate the axon of a command interneuron in the bundle of about 10,000 nerve fibers that runs between the cricket's brain and the first thoracic ganglion. The command interneurons are always found in the same location.

The development of the cricket proceeds without any dramatic metamorphosis. The female deposits her eggs singly in the soil. Following embryonic development the eggs hatch into miniature nymphs about the size of a fruit fly, which conspicuously lack wings, reproductive structures and associated behavior. During postembryonic development, which is several times as long as embryonic development, the nymphs pass through 10 instars, or developmental stages, separated by molts. With each successive molt the nymphs increase in size and resemblance to adults except for certain structures such as the wings and the ovipositor: the tube through which the female lays her eggs. These structures are not fully developed until the final molt to adulthood.

The male cricket normally begins to call about a week after its final molt. Nymphal crickets never attempt to sing, even if they are placed in a situation that would stimulate singing in the adult. For example, nymphs are strongly aggressive in competition for food, but they do not move their small wing pads in the pattern of aggressive song. Either the neural circuits that mediate singing are not yet laid down or, if they are, they must

FRUIT FLY AND NEWLY HATCHED CRICKET are about the same size. A common fruit fly, Drosophila melanogaster, is at left; a "wild type" (genetically typical) nymph of the species Teleogryllus oceanicus is in the middle. Mass screening of cricket nymphs for interesting mutations can be done immediately after hatching, before the first molt, when they are termed first instars. Nymphs molt 10 times on their way to adulthood. The first-instar nymph on the right is a mutant that lacks certain sensory hairs on rear-end antennae.

be actively suppressed. When we made lesions in the brain of last-instar nymphs in an area that would evoke singing in the adult, the wing pads finally moved in a pattern resembling song. To determine whether or not the motor pattern was the same as the one that gives rise to the calling song, we recorded muscle action potentials from identified motor units and compared the impulse pattern with the pattern the same unit would be expected to generate during the calling song of an adult [see bottom illustration at right].

Since the strength of the argument depends on the predictability of the adult motor pattern, this kind of analysis is possible only in animals, such as the cricket, that show highly stereotyped forms of behavior. Several conclusions can be drawn from this study: (1) the neuronal network for the calling song is completed in the nymph, (2) the assembly of the network does not depend on acoustical feedback and (3) song patterns are not prematurely activated in nymphs because of active inhibition originating in the brain.

We have not followed the maturation of the song networks in detail because the brains of the younger nymphs are so small that it is difficult to make the lesions required to elicit singing behavior. This is not the case, however, with the closely related behavior of flight. The highly invariant, rhythmic motor pattern of flight is similar to singing in that it involves the same set of muscles and the same motor neurons to operate the fore wings and also their homologues that operate the hind wings. The motor pattern consists in the alternate firing of elevator (upstroke) motor units and depressor (downstroke) motor units, with the hind-wing segments leading their fore-wing counterparts by about a third of a wing-stroke cycle.

In nymphs there does not seem to be any suppression of the neuronal network for flight. As a result one can induce nymphs of very early instars to attempt flying by suspending them in a small wind tunnel. Electrophysiological recordings are made from identified motor units, and their performance is evaluated by comparing their pattern with the pattern the same unit would make in the adult.

We find the first definite signs of the motor pattern of flight in nymphs of the seventh instar. Removing the nymph from contact with the ground and suspending it in a wind tunnel is sufficient to induce some flight motor neurons to discharge a few impulses at frequencies

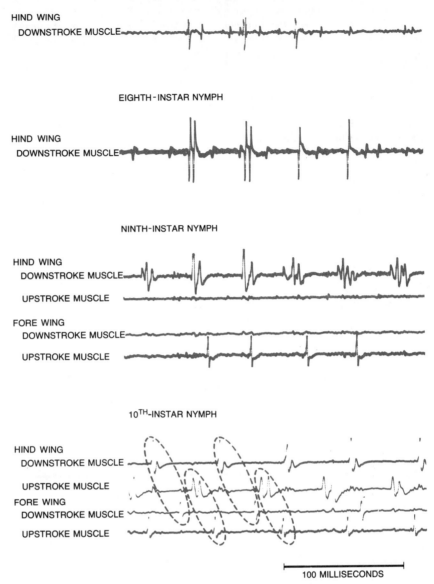

ASSEMBLY OF NERVE NETWORK FOR FLIGHT is completed during the last third of the cricket's larval life. The records show muscle-impulse patterns produced by tethered nymphs trying to fly in a wind tunnel. In seventh-instar nymphs the pattern is only fragmentary. In later instars new muscles come into play and the pattern becomes stronger. In the last stage before adulthood muscles are properly coordinated: upstroke and downstroke units alternate and the hind wing leads the fore wing (indicated by broken lines).

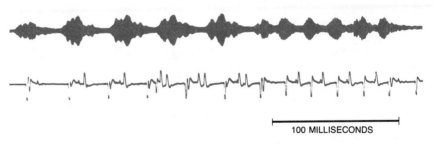

ASSEMBLY OF NERVE NETWORK FOR SINGING can be demonstrated by making lesions in the brain of 10th-instar cricket nymphs. Before the final molt to adulthood cricket nymphs do not attempt to sing. Certain lesions, however, that elicit singing in adult crickets also elicit the calling-song motor pattern in nymphs. The top trace is the calling-song sound-pulse pattern of an adult of the species T. commodus. The bottom trace shows the closely parallel activity of wing-opening muscles (downgoing impulses) and wing-closing muscles (upgoing impulses) elicited by brain lesions in a 10th-instar nymph of the same species.

approaching the normal rate of the wing stroke [*see top illustration on preceding page*]. During subsequent development the performance improves in several respects: first, there are more impulses per burst, corresponding to wing strokes of greater amplitude; second, there are more bursts per response, corresponding to more wing strokes and longer flights, and third, additional motor neurons are recruited into the pattern. As with singing, the neuronal network involved in flight seems to be fully assembled by the last instar, although the overall frequency of its oscillatory behavior does not reach normal speed until after the molt to adulthood.

How does the neuronal network develop structurally before its physiological activation begins? The information we have suggests that it develops as follows. Cell bodies and peripheral axons (long fibers, one from each cell body) arise while the cricket is still in the embryo stage. The richer growth of dendrites (short fibers) within the ganglia may come during the first third of postembryonic development. By filling identical neurons with dye one can show that by the sixth instar, halfway through postembryonic development, the major branching network has been completed. In the next instar the first signs of physiological activity in adult patterns can be

detected. During the last third of postembryonic development the sequential firing pattern steadily improves and precise coordination with other neurons is achieved. This last step may reflect the actual establishment of synapses, or connections, between neurons. By the last instar the neuronal network is fully assembled and potentially operative, although it may be suppressed by inhibition from the brain. Thus immediately after the molt to adulthood the nervous system of the cricket is ready to generate both flight and the calling song.

It is well established that in order to attract females of the same species

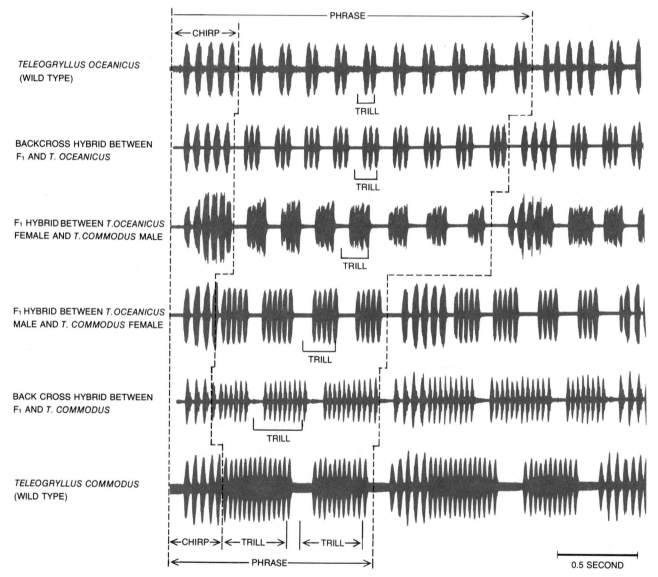

SONG PATTERNS OF HYBRID CRICKETS shift systematically in proportion to the ratios of the different wild-type genes inherited by the individual. These records show the song patterns of two cricket species and their hybrids. The records are aligned so that a complete phrase of the song starts at the left; each phrase consists of a chirp followed by two or more trills. The phrase of *T. oceanicus* (*top*) is not only much longer than the phrase of *T. com-* modus (*bottom*) but also distinctively different. In each of the last three patterns the first trill is fused to the chirp. The F_1, or first-generation, hybrids of these two species produced the third and fourth traces. Again they are quite different depending on which species served as the male parent and which as the female parent. The second and fifth traces were produced by backcrosses between the two different F_1 hybrids and members of the parental species.

successfully the male cricket must broadcast a very precise message. What is the source of the information underlying this precision? We have seen that neither motor practice of the songs nor acoustical feedback is required. The correct pattern arises from the neural properties and neural connections established during development. How do they become properly established? One hypothesis invokes the environmental information available to cricket nymphs during their development. For example, some songbirds have been shown to remember song patterns heard during their adolescence and to defer the use of the information until the following year in the songs they sing as adults. The main alternative hypothesis is that all the necessary information for cricket singing is stored genetically and is read out in the form of neuronal structures during the course of development.

These hypotheses can be tested by changing either the environmental input or the genetic one during development and observing the effects. We raised crickets under a variety of environmental conditions, including different regimes of population density, diet, temperature, cycles of light and darkness, and of course acoustical experience. Some crickets heard no songs, some heard only songs of their own species and some heard only songs of another species. In every case male crickets that had reached maturity produced the calling song characteristic of their own species. This indicates that environmental information is not utilized in the determination of the song pattern.

What would happen, however, if a wild-type (genetically "normal") male of one species were mated with a female of another? What song would the hybrid male offspring of such a union sing? Since these particular hybrids are fertile, we were able to backcross them with individuals of the parental species. From such genetic manipulations we learned that each genotype (that is, each hybrid, backcross or other mixture) gives rise to a unique calling song and that all individuals of each genotype sing the same song. Even more remarkable, the song patterns shift systematically according to the proportion of the wild-type genes carried by the male cricket [*see illustration on opposite page*]. One can only conclude that the information specifying song patterns is encoded in the genes.

In order to give rise to the song-generating neuronal network the information coded in the genes must be read out

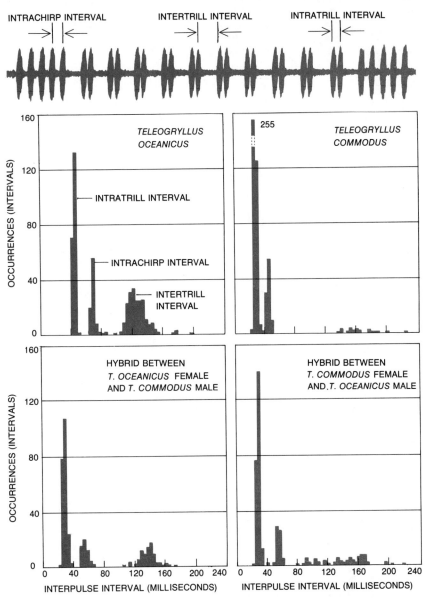

PRECISION OF SONG PATTERN becomes evident when the intervals between sound pulses in the calling song are measured for several hundred pulses. The two top histograms show the intervals in the calling songs of wild-type *T. oceanicus* (*left*) and *T. commodus* (*right*), which also appear in the illustration on the opposite page. When hybrids are made between these two species (*bottom*), their intertrill intervals resemble those of the species that served as the maternal parent: *T. oceanicus* on the left, *T. commodus* on the right. This shows that the genes influencing the intertrill interval are on the X, or sex, chromosome.

during development by a series of complex and subtle interactions between the cricket's environment and the genes of the cells involved. It seems, however, that the range of possible products of this interaction is stringently limited. If development is successful, the calling song of the adult is a very accurate reflection of the genotype.

How many genes are involved and where are they located on the cricket's 15 chromosomes? A start toward answering these questions can be made by examining the pattern of inheritance

of features of the calling song. If a particular feature (such as the number of chirps or the interval between chirps) were determined by a single gene that was dominant over the corresponding gene in another species, the feature should be transmitted unchanged to the first-generation (F_1) hybrids between the species.

When we examined 18 features in the calling songs of two cricket species (genus *Teleogryllus*) and their F_1 hybrids, we found no evidence that the features involved the dominance of single genes. If a character were controlled by a

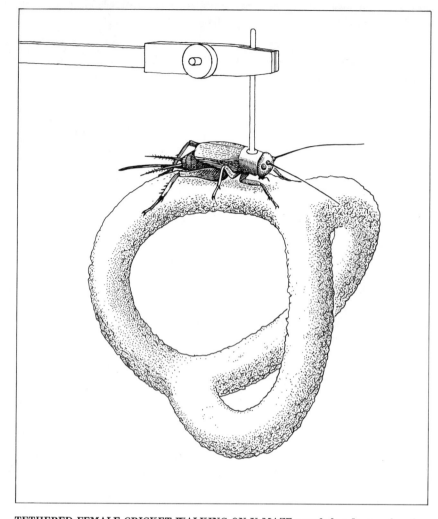

TETHERED FEMALE CRICKET WALKING ON Y MAZE reveals her degree of preference for calling songs of males of different species by the choice she makes when she comes to a fork in the Y. The cricket actually holds the featherweight Styrofoam maze as she travels along it. One loudspeaker is located on the left side of the cricket and another on the right side. In each test the cricket hears only one male calling song, played 40 times through one speaker or the other in random order. The frequency with which the cricket turns toward the song is taken as an index of its attractiveness (*see illustration on opposite page*).

the X chromosome and that other elements are not [*see illustration on preceding page*]. The genetic system that specifies the neuronal network accounting for cricket song is therefore a complex one, involving multiple chromosomes as well as multiple genes.

So far we have written exclusively about the transmitter in the cricket-song communication system. What about the receiver? A good deal has been learned about the way the female responds to the male's song. For example, Thomas J. Walker of the University of Florida and others have studied the selective responsiveness of females to song patterns. The female's orientation to a sound source and attraction to it have been investigated recently at Berkeley by Rodney K. Murphey and Malcolm Zaretsky. Zaretsky and John Stout in Huber's laboratory have begun to identify and characterize the sensory interneurons involved in responding to the song and "recognizing" it.

A fundamental problem common to the analysis of all animal communication systems is how the timing and the synchronous evolution of the transmitter and receiver are maintained. Found everywhere on the globe, crickets are classified into about 3,000 species whose song patterns have diverged widely in the course of evolution. How has it happened that in each case the receiver has changed along with the transmitter, so that the female still responds selectively to the call of a male of the same species?

One of us (Hoy), in collaboration with Robert Paul, has been studying this problem, first at the State University of New York at Stony Brook and recently at Cornell. Experiments were designed to quantify the ability of female crickets to detect and select calling songs of their own species, to determine the role of the genotype in that selectivity and to explore the relation between the genetic systems that control song transmission and song reception.

In these experiments a female cricket is suspended by her thorax and allowed to hold a hollow sphere of Styrofoam cut in the form of a continuous Y-shaped maze [*see illustration on this page*]. As she "walks" on the maze, which she is actually holding, she periodically comes to junctions that call for a decision to turn right or left. On each side of her there is a small loudspeaker through which different song patterns can be played. In each experiment the walking female is required to make 40 choices, 20 while the song is played through one speaker and 20 while it is played through

single nondominant gene, the crossing of an F_1 individual with a wild-type individual of the parental species should give rise to two distinct classes of backcross offspring, one like the parent and one like the F_1 individual. The more genes there are that influence a character, the broader and smoother is the distribution of types produced by backcrossing. Our analysis of many backcrosses has failed to reveal any examples of a simple bimodal distribution, which would indicate single-gene control of some characteristic of cricket song. Therefore we conclude that many genes are required to specify the neuronal network responsible for song production.

Genes that influence a particular characteristic or behavior, such as cricket song, can be localized on a specific chromosome, provided that they are on the X chromosome. Female crickets, like the females of many other species, have two X chromosomes (XX), whereas male crickets have only one X chromosome (and lack the Y chromosome found in many other animals). As a result two types of cross can be made between two species, one using males from species A and females from species B and the other using males from species B and females from species A. Male offspring from these crosses will be genetically alike except that they will have X chromosomes from different maternal parents. Thus differences in the songs of the two types of male can be attributed to genes located on the X chromosome. Analysis of hybrid calling songs reveals that certain elements of the song pattern (for example the interval between trills) do appear to be controlled by genes on

the other. The number of decisions made to turn toward the source of the sound divided by the total number of choices is taken as an index of the "attractiveness" of the song. Each female is tested only once and is presented with only one song. The tests clearly establish that female crickets prefer the calling song of the males of their own species.

The role of the genes in establishing this preference can be investigated by manipulating the genotype. In a typical study crickets of two different species are mated and the hybrid F_1 females are tested with songs of three types: the calling songs of the males of each parental species and the calling song produced by the females' F_1 hybrid brothers. Surprisingly, the hybrid females prove to be attracted to the songs of their brothers much more than to the songs of either parental species [see illustration below]. This result demonstrates that genetically shared information specifies the pattern of song recognition as well as the pattern or song production. Moreover, it suggests that similar genetic systems could be involved in encoding information for constructing either a neuronal network that will respond to a specific song pattern or a network that will produce a specific song pattern. Indeed, there is the fascinating possibility that some of the same genes are involved in both systems. Such an assemblage of genes would be a failsafe means of ensuring the synchronous evolution of the transmitter and the receiver.

The experiments described above firmly establish the link between genetically stored information and the cricket's nervous system, but how does the first control the design of the second? What kind of information about the structure, the physiology and the connectivity of neurons is stored, and how is it read out? Two quite different strategies for approaching the problem immediately suggest themselves and are currently being pursued by one of us (Bentley) at Berkeley. The first is to focus attention on single neurons and ask what features of the nervous system are actually under genetic control. The second is to concentrate on single genes and ask what a particular gene contributes to the design of the nervous system.

The first question can be tackled straightforwardly by crossing different species and hybrid individuals, thereby constructing cricket nervous systems according to different genetic blueprints. Then by examining identifiable homologous neurons in the different systems one can determine what is different about these neurons. The firing pattern during the calling song of two particular neurons in five different genotypes has now been examined: two wild types, the F_1 cross and two backcrosses. Not surprisingly, one finds that the song precisely reflects the firing pattern of the motor neurons, that neurons of each genotype fire in a distinctive pattern and finally that very small differences in pattern can be genetically specified. For example, motor neurons usually fire only once for each pulse of the trill sound. One wild-type cricket, Teleogryllus oceanicus, has trills consisting of two short pulses, whereas the backcross between the F_1 hybrid and T. oceanicus has three-pulse trills [see top illustration on next page]. This means that the actual difference in firing patterns of the responsible motor neurons in the two genotypes is only a single impulse. It is a remarkable example of fine genetic control.

Experiments are now in progress to discover why the neurons of the backcross fire three times rather than twice. One possibility is that there is a difference in how the neurons are excited by command interneurons. If one artificially stimulates the appropriate interneurons in the connective bundle between the cricket's brain and its thorax, one finds that only a slight increase in the rate of stimulation is needed to change the firing rate of the motor neurons involved in the calling song from a two-pulse pattern to a three-pulse one [see bottom illustration on next page]. This result suggests that the effect of the genetic change could be a similar increase in the firing rate of the command interneurons or perhaps an increased efficiency in the transmission of impulses at the synapses. There are many other possibilities, but these experiments at the very least show that it is possible to get at the heart of the pattern-generating mechanism and directly test the effect of genetic manipulation.

The alternative strategy of examining the role of single genes is also being investigated at Berkeley. One begins this process by accumulating a "stable" of organisms with mutations in a single gene. The mutations can be induced by exposing the organisms to X rays or to

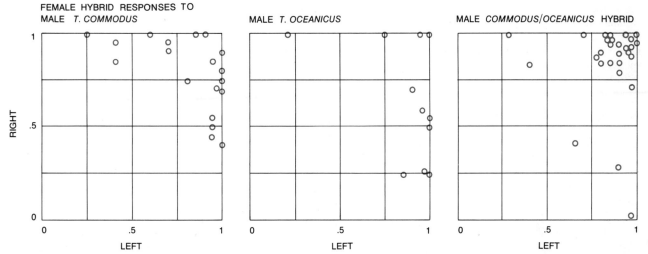

FEMALE HYBRID RESPONSES TO MALE *T. COMMODUS*

MALE *T. OCEANICUS*

MALE *COMMODUS/OCEANICUS* HYBRID

RIGHT

LEFT

LEFT

LEFT

FEMALES' PREFERENCE FOR MALE SONGS is plotted in scattergrams. Each female is required to make 40 choices while walking on a *Y* maze, 20 while the sound is played through one speaker and 20 while the sound is played through the other. Each open circle represents a 40-choice test. If the female always turned toward the song of a particular male whether played on her left or her right, the song would score 1 on both axes and an open circle would be placed in the extreme upper right corner. The females whose preferences are plotted here were all hybrid offspring of a *T. oceanicus* female and a *T. commodus* male. The three scattergrams show the females' relative preference for the song of a *T. commodus* male (*left*), the song of a *T. oceanicus* male (*middle*) and the song of a hybrid male whose genes closely resemble those of the females being tested (*right*). Females clearly prefer their "brother's" song.

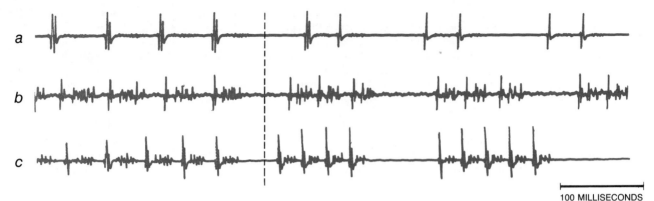

NEURAL ACTIVITY UNDERLYING CALLING SONG is patterned according to different genetic specifications, as illustrated by these three records of the firing of a particular identified motor neuron in three different crickets during the calling song. The crickets that produced the traces are of the same genetic type as those that produced the first three sound traces shown in the illustration on page 8: a wild-type *T. oceanicus* (*a*), the F_1 hybrid between a *T. oceanicus* female and a *T. commodus* male (*c*) and the backcross between the F_1 hybrid and *T. oceanicus* (*b*). The vertical broken line marks the end of a chirp and the start of a trill. It is evident that genetically stored information exerts extraordinary control over the output of the nervous system. Thus the backcross (*b*) has a three-pulse trill whereas its wild-type parent has a two-pulse trill and its F_1 hybrid parent has a trill of four or five pulses.

mutagenic chemical compounds. When crickets are raised at elevated temperatures (about 35 degrees Celsius, or 95 degrees Fahrenheit), they have a generation time of about six weeks. One female can produce as many as 2,000 eggs, and the resulting nymphs exhibit a wide diversity of behavioral characteristics. The mass screening of mutants for interesting behavior patterns can be done with first-instar nymphs that are no larger than fruit flies and are just as plentiful [*see bottom illustration on page 106*]. When an interesting mutant is found, it can be grown to an adult 1,000 times larger than a fruit fly in which single nerve cells are readily accessible for study.

The first behavior selected for screening is the evasive leap elicited by the stimulation of the cricket's cerci, which may be called rear-end antennae. The neuronal circuits involved in this response had previously been analyzed by John M. Palka and John Edwards of the University of Washington and by Murphey, working at the University of Iowa. In the screening program at Berkeley two mutants with an abnormal leap response have been isolated and established in breeding lines. In one case the mutant gene is a recessive gene on the X chromosome; in the other the gene is a dominant gene on one of the autosomal chromosomes (chromosomes other than the X sex chromosomes).

The mutants exhibit a selective loss of a single class of receptor hairs on the cerci. Each hair activates a single sensory neuron that has a direct synaptic connection with certain large, identified interneurons. The mutants are being studied to see whether or not the sensory neurons are also affected by the mutation and whether or not the structure of the interneurons has been changed by the lack of normal input from the sensory neurons. The ease with which such mutants can be isolated encourages hope that the single-gene strategy will ultimately be successful in the analysis of cricket song.

The promise of the approach we have taken in our study of cricket behavior lies in combining several levels of analysis in a single animal. This allows for a powerful infusion of techniques between levels, for example asking developmental questions by means of single-gene mutations or genetic questions by means of single-neuron recordings. An important feature of this approach is that it offers some relief from an affliction of neurobiology that has been called the chimera problem: the accumulation of volumes of data on different aspects of very different creatures. The cricket work links the several levels of analysis in a unitary system and provides a high degree of confidence on how biological integration is achieved. We view the cricket as a kind of decathlon performer in neurobiology: it may not excel at any one thing, but it can be counted on for a sound performance in every event.

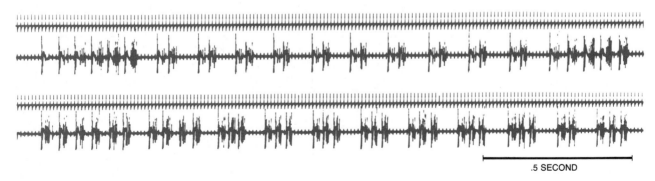

CHANGE FROM TWO-PULSE TO THREE-PULSE TRILL can be artificially evoked in the calling-song pattern of a wild-type *T. oceanicus* cricket by changing the firing rate of command interneurons. In each pair of records the top trace shows the stimulus applied to the commond interneuron and the bottom trace shows the impulse pattern of song motor neurons. In the bottom pair of traces the firing rate of the command interneuron has been increased about 10 percent, causing a shift in the motor pattern from the wild-type two-pulse trill to the three-pulse trill characteristic of the backcross whose trill appears in trace *b* in the illustration at the top of the page. Thus the command interneuron may be the neural element responsible for the difference in song patterns of the two genotypes.

Brains and Cocoons

by William G. Van der Kloot
April 1956

*The fluffy shroud of the silkworm represents a map of
its spinning movements. This pattern may be altered
by brain surgery, shedding light on the relationship
between the nervous system and behavior*

Every silkworm that is to become a moth must first spin itself a cocoon. This is an intricate process. Just how intricate can be seen by looking at the cross-sectioned cocoon in the photograph below. The caterpillar first spun a thin, tough, densely woven outer envelope. Then it laid down a loose cushion of silk. Inside this it enclosed itself in a second thin, tough envelope. There the caterpillar rests, metamor-

phosed to the pupal stage. In building the cocoon the caterpillar extruded more than a mile of silk.

The intricately woven cocoon gives us a three-dimensional map of the caterpillar's behavior. It thereby presents a visible record of the operations of the insect's nervous system. As such it serves as a convenient and relatively simple model for analyzing nervous systems in general. Beavers build dams, and men

may build cathedrals. Silkworm cocoons, beaver dams and cathedrals all arise basically from the action of units which are much the same in each case—the nerve cells. We know that all nerve cells function on the same elementary "all or nothing" principle. A nerve cell either fires an impulse or it remains dormant; the impulse either excites or inhibits a neighboring cell. It is the patterned firing of thousands and millions of nerve

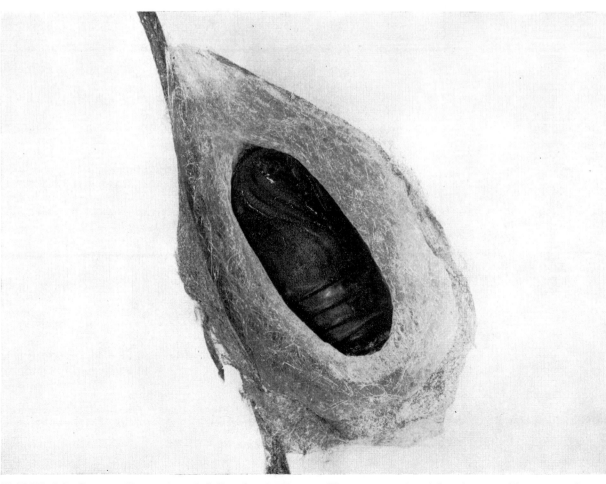

COCOON of the *Cecropia* silkworm is cut in half to show its inner construction. In the middle of the cocoon is the pupa of Cecropia.

The cocoon consists of three layers: a thin outer envelope, a thin inner envelope and a thick, loose cushion of silk between them.

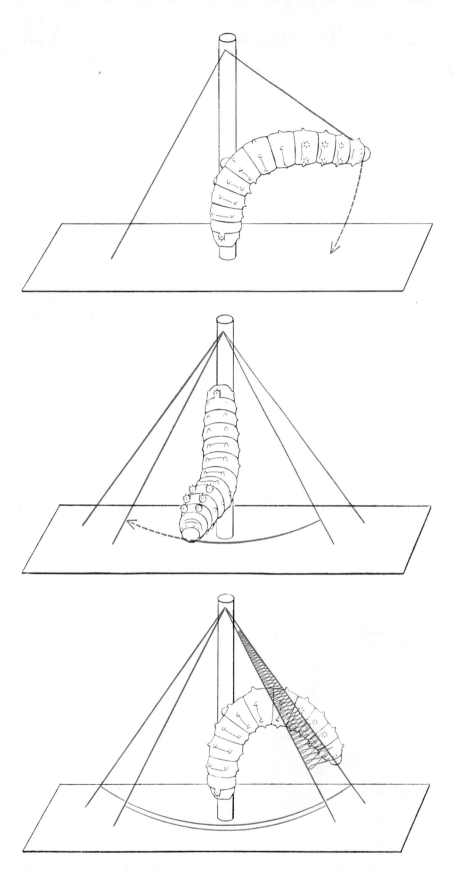

MOVEMENTS OF A SILKWORM spinning its cocoon are shown in these drawings. The movements are executed on a dowel mounted on a board in the laboratory. At first the silkworm climbs the dowel, fastens a thread to it and bends downward to attach the thread to the board (*top drawing*). Then the silkworm faces downward and spins the floor of the cocoon (*middle drawing*). When the floor and the framework of the cone are complete, the silkworm weaves a fabric between the threads of the framework with figure 8 movements (*bottom*). The silkworm is unable to make these movements near the apex of the cone.

cells that determines specific behavior. To understand how behavior is directed and controlled we must look into the circuitry by which a creature's nerve cells are hooked up in its central nervous system.

The building of cocoons provides an excellent approach to the investigation of nervous system circuitry. Although the silkworm's circuitry is sufficiently baffling, it is far simpler than the humblest vertebrate brain. Cocoon building is an inborn behavior pattern, dependably repeated by each individual without prior learning. The *Cecropia* silkworm invariably builds the same kind of cocoon; other caterpillars build other kinds. And the ways in which the silkworm's behavior may be modified by experiments are recorded visibly in its spinning patterns. These conveniences led Carroll M. Williams and me to select cocoon construction for study in the Biological Laboratories at Harvard.

We provide our silkworms with a spinning platform which consists of a dowel mounted perpendicularly in the center of a board. In this controlled situation they give us a uniform performance. Two patterns of movement shape the cocoon. The silkworm climbs up the dowel until its hind end is just above the board. In this position it stretches the forepart of its body upward and fastens the beginning of its silk thread to a point near the top of the dowel. Then it bends its forebody downward and to the side, paying out the line of silk as it moves, until its head touches the board. The caterpillar fastens the silk thread there, stretches upward again, glues the thread again to the dowel, and bends down to a different point on the board. The sequence of movements is repeated again and again. The silkworm gradually shrouds itself with a cone of silk.

Periodically during spinning its behavior changes. The silkworm reverses its position on the dowel so that its hind end is up and its head toward the board. It now swings the forebody first to one side and then to the other, spinning a relatively flat sheet of silk on the board. This will be the bottom of the cocoon. In nature the caterpillar rarely finds a flat surface beneath it, and the bottom is usually rounded. The shape of its cocoon, in short, is influenced by the environment: the silkworm must find points on a surface (or the webbing of its own silk) to attach the thread. If it does not make contact with some surface at the end of a movement, the silkworm will sway about until a contact is made. Where points of silk attachment are limited, the caterpillar goes through much wasted swaying motion.

When the silkworm has built the skeleton of its cocoon, it weaves the fabric of the envelopes with a third movement. Rocking its head back and forth in a figure 8 pattern, it connects the silk threads already laid down—adding, so to speak, the woof to the warp. At the apex of the cone, however, the space between the silk threads is too confined for figure 8 movements, and the top of the cocoon is therefore only loosely woven—so loosely that a pencil can be slipped through the fabric. This feature, though not the result of conscious foresight, is important in the life of the silkworm. It provides an escape hatch through which the mature moth will make its exit to the world outside.

Now these three movements, which normally produce a cocoon, will produce strange and distorted variants when the silkworm is restricted in some way in the laboratory. For example, we tried the experiment of tying the caterpillar to the dowel with its head toward the board, so that it could not reverse its body and face upward. The animal began by stretching its forebody to the farthest point on the board it could reach and fastening the thread there. Then it bent the forebody toward the dowel, but since it could not reach upward, it had to fasten the thread at a point below or alongside its body. The result was that, though the silkworm succeeded in spinning a cone, it was left outside its cocoon [*photograph above*].

The structure had the usual two layers, corresponding to the outer and inner envelopes of the normal cocoon. The question arises: What sort of stimulus causes the spinning of the second layer? Evidently it is not contact with the completed first layer, because the insect was not enclosed in it.

Normally the silkworm invests 60 per cent of its silk in the construction of the outer envelope. We wondered what a silkworm would construct if we could make it spend the initial 60 per cent of its silk in making a sheet instead of an envelope. To do this we had to provide the silkworm with a two-dimensional environment. Accordingly we inserted it in a large inflated balloon. In this endless two-dimensional world the insect could find no points in the third dimension for attachment of its silk. It had to spin the silk as a sheet spread out on the inner surface of the balloon. When a caterpillar had spun 60 per cent of its silk in this fashion, we restored it to the three-dimensional world. It proceeded

EXPERIMENT with one silkworm consisted in tying its tail to the dowel so that it could only face downward. The silkworm was able to spin the cocoon, but remained outside it.

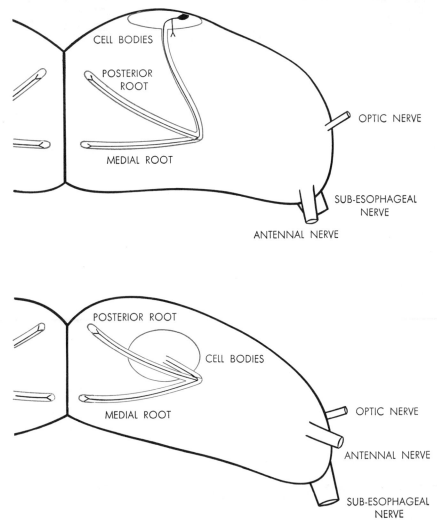

BRAIN of the silkworm is depicted in these schematic drawings. At the top the left hemisphere of the brain is seen from above. Its front faces down. At the bottom the hemisphere is seen from the front. The corpus pedunculatum, the message center of the brain, is in color.

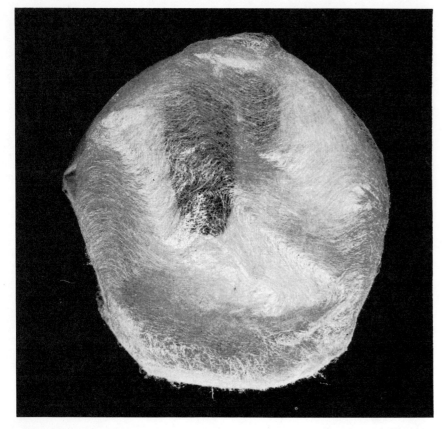

DAMAGED BRAIN caused another silkworm to spin its cocoon in this pattern. Placed in a cylindrical cardboard container, the silkworm covered the floor of the container with silk. Visible inside the silk sheet of the cocoon is the pupa and the shed skin of the silkworm.

as if it had made an outer envelope and built what corresponded to an inner one.

We concluded that the starting of the second layer must be controlled by sensory messages from the silk-forming gland, signaling when 60 per cent of the material has been spent. Further experiments showed that the silkworms actually measure the length of silk spun, "record" this information and finally act on the accumulated data.

Sensory messages from the spinning apparatus are important in other ways. By means of a simple device in our laboratory we are able to record the gross spinning movements of a silkworm even when it is not actually building a cocoon. When we plug the insect's silk outlet with paraffin, it performs the usual ordered pattern of movements—it "spins an imaginary cocoon." But when we remove the silk glands surgically, the movements become disorderly. Apparently control of the movements to build a cocoon depends on a constant background of messages from the silk gland to the central nervous system.

Our task now was to get inside the silkworm to see if we could find out how its central nervous system translates the inflowing sensory barrage into an outflow of coordinated motor signals. We conceived this to be essentially a geographical question: What areas of the central nervous system perform this sensory-to-motor translation?

A first look inside the head of a silkworm raises doubt whether its brain is capable of conducting such a sophisticated operation. One is reminded of the thesis of the 18th-century naturalist and classifier Carolus Linnaeus, who held that insects have no brains at all: "Organs of sense: tongue, eyes, antennae on the head, brain lacking, ears lacking, nostrils lacking." The silkworm does have a brain, but it is not much more than a millimeter across and weighs but one or two milligrams. The structure gets something of the appearance of a brain from a constriction down the middle which divides it into right and left hemispheres [see diagram on page 115]. Two nerves, one from each hemisphere, connect the brain to the rest of the central nervous system. They run downward around the esophagus and to a mass of nerve cells called the sub-esophageal ganglion. From here a pair of nerves extends down the length of the animal's abdomen. This is the ventral nerve cord, the insect's equivalent of the vertebrate spinal cord. Periodically the ventral

nerve cord branches off small packets of nerve cells. These ganglia send nerves to the body muscles and receive nerves from sense organs nearby.

Does the brain coordinate the spinning movements or can this function be performed by the ventral cord alone? To answer this question we cut the cord. We found that even when the cut is made close to the head, the muscles at the front end of the silkworm that are still commanded by the brain drag the rest of the body through the movements of spinning. As long as a small fraction of the body is directed by the brain, the silkworm tries gamely to shape a normal cocoon.

We get a very different result when we remove the brain. The caterpillar retains coordination; it can crawl or climb. But it does not attempt to spin a cocoon. This experiment showed that the brain must be the control center for cocoon construction.

In the next experiment we disconnected one of the hemispheres of the brain from the central nervous system by cutting the sub-esophageal nerve. The silkworms spun, but in a disorganized way. They crawled about laying down silk as a sheet over every surface they encountered [see photograph at left]. A similar derangement resulted when a hemisphere itself was cut through. Again the silkworms lined the inner surface of the container with a sheet of silk.

We went on to a more precise exploration of the brain. When a hemisphere was cut along a line close to the midline, the silkworms retained part of their normal behavior: they spun two layers of silk, one above the other, corresponding to the outer and inner envelopes of the normal cocoon. When we cut the brain through right on the midline, the animals spun perfect cocoons. Thus it was clear that nerve tracts which pass across the midline from hemisphere to hemisphere were not an essential part of the neural apparatus for spinning.

These results hinted that the control center could be located precisely somewhere in the hemispheres of the minute brain. To pinpoint that center, cuts through the brain, even with microscissors, were unavailing. We turned to burning tiny parts of the brain with high-frequency electric currents, which permitted us to destroy pieces of brain less than one twentieth of a millimeter in diameter.

We learned with this technique that more than half of the brain tissue was not involved in cocoon construction. The silkworm's spinning behavior was not affected by destruction of the receiving areas for nerves from the eyes and antennae or of regions containing tangles of association fibers. Eventually we located the critical areas around a pair of structures known as the corpora pedunculata. Even slight damage to these brain regions produced profound aberrations of spinning behavior.

The corpora pedunculata have long been familiar to insect neurologists. Félix Dujardin, a French zoologist, discovered these structures over a century ago in the course of an investigation which upset Linnaeus' contention that insects have no brains. He found that the structures attain maximum development in the social insects (bees and ants) and he called them "the seat of intellectual faculties."

There is a corpus pedunculatum ("body with stem") in each hemisphere of an insect brain; it can be seen even on external inspection. The "body" is a clump of nerve cells, and the "stem" is a cable which carries the cells' long filamentary axons to other centers in the brain. In the silkworm the structures are so small that it must be admitted the insect is an intellectual pauper. The stems follow a peculiar course. From the cell body, located at the rear near the top of the brain, each stem extends forward and downward into the hemisphere and later forks in a complex manner. Near the cell body each axon in the stem gives off one or more short branches, which make contact with axons coming from the sensory centers of the brain. A little further along, the stem forks into two roots, one running to the midline of the brain, the other running upward and back toward the cell body. At the end of the latter root, the axons carried by the stem make contact with motor pathways in the brain.

This circuitry suggests that the corpora pedunculata function as central message centers in the insect brain. Experiments strongly sustain the deduction. When the cell bodies of either corpus pedunculatum are destroyed, the caterpillar spins only one flat sheet. The same result in behavior occurs when we burn away the two roots running to the midline of the brain. If we leave these intact, however, and destroy only the roots going to the rear of the brain, caterpillars spin two layers. Thus it appears that the midline roots control the division of the silk into layers. The silkworms whose circuits were destroyed only at some points could perform all the motions of spinning, but they were unable to coordinate the individual motions into the building of a cocoon.

Anatomical studies suggest that the cells of the corpora pedunculata may be fired by sensory stimuli originating both inside and outside the body, and that the messages may interact, so that each pattern of stimulation causes a particular pattern of firing in the circuit. The resulting impulses pass down the stem and roots to excite the motor pathways and induce a patterned series of movements.

There is another possible circuit. Some of the axons that go to the roots do not connect with motor centers but instead return to the sensory centers. In the sensory center they may fire nerve fibers going to the input axons on the stem. This would provide a pathway by which some of the output of the circuit would be returned as input. We may deduce, in short, a feedback loop [*see diagram above right*]. It will be recalled

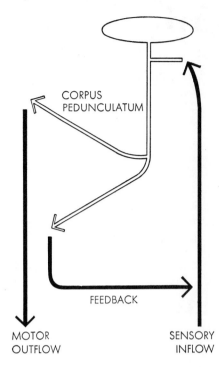

RELATIONSHIP between the corpus pedunculatum (*open lines*) and functions of the silkworm nervous system are outlined.

that feedback circuits of similar design are the essence of mechanical and electronic control mechanisms.

The circuitry of the silkworm brain appears to be an ideally simple testing ground for investigating animal coordination. In most nervous systems integration occurs in incredibly tangled masses of nerve cells. The corpus pedunculatum presents the experimenter with an accessible bundle of oriented fibers, now known to be essential for complex behavior.

13

Genetic Dissection of Behavior

by Seymour Benzer
December 1973

By working with fruit flies that are mosaics of normal and mutant parts it is possible to identify the genetic components of behavior, retrace their development and locate the sites where they operate

When the individual organism develops from a fertilized egg, the one-dimensional information arrayed in the linear sequence of the genes on the chromosomes controls the formation of a two-dimensional cell layer that folds to give rise to a precise three-dimensional arrangement of sense organs, central nervous system and muscles. Those elements interact to produce the organism's behavior, a phenomenon whose description requires four dimensions at least. Surely the genes, which so largely determine anatomical and biochemical characteristics, must also interact with the environment to determine behavior. But how? For two decades molecular biologists were engaged in tracking down the structure and coding of the gene, a task that was pursued to ever lower levels of organization [see "The Fine Structure of the Gene," by Seymour Benzer; SCIENTIFIC AMERICAN Offprint 120]. Some of us have since turned in the opposite direction, to higher integrative levels, to explore development, the nervous system and behavior. In our laboratory at the California Institute of Technology we have been applying tools of genetic analysis in an attempt to trace the emergence of multidimensional behavior from the one-dimensional gene.

Our objectives are to discern the genetic component of a behavior, to identify it with a particular gene and then to determine the actual site at which the gene influences behavior and learn how it does so. In brief, we keep the environment constant, change the genes and see what happens to behavior. Our choice of an experimental organism was constrained by the fact that the simpler an organism is, the less likely it is to exhibit interesting behavioral patterns that are relevant to man; the more complex it is, the more difficult it may be to analyze

and the longer it takes. The fruit fly *Drosophila melanogaster* represents a compromise. In mass, in number of nerve cells, in amount of DNA and in generation time it stands roughly halfway on a logarithmic scale between the colon bacillus *Escherichia coli* (which can be regarded as having a one-neuron nervous system) and man. Although the fly's nervous system is very different from the human system, both consist of neurons and synapses and utilize transmitter molecules, and the development of both is dictated by genes. A fly has highly developed senses of sight, hearing, taste, smell, gravity and time. It cannot do everything we do, but it does some things we cannot do, such as fly and stand on the ceiling. Its visual system can detect the movement of the minute hand on a clock. One must not underestimate the little creature, which is not an evolutionary antecedent of man but is itself high up on the invertebrate branch of the phylogenetic tree. Its nervous system is a miracle of microminiaturization, and some of its independently evolved behavior patterns are not unlike our own.

Jerry Hirsch, Theodosius Dobzhansky and many others have demonstrated that if one begins with a genetically heterogeneous population of fruit flies, various behavioral characters can be enhanced by selective breeding pursued over many generations. This kind of experiment demonstrates that behavior can be genetically modified, but it depends on the reassortment of many different genes, so that it is very difficult to distinguish the effect of each one. Also, unless the selective procedure is constantly maintained, the genes may reassort, causing loss of the special behavior. For analyzing the relation of specific genes to behavior, it is more effective to begin

with a highly inbred, genetically uniform strain of flies and change the genes one at a time. This is done by inducing a mutation: an abrupt gene change that is transmitted to all subsequent generations.

A population of flies exposed to a mutagen (radiation or certain chemicals) yields some progeny with anatomical anomalies such as white eyes or forked bristles, and it also yields progeny with behavioral abnormalities. Workers in many laboratories (including ours) have compiled a long list of such mutants, each of which can be produced by the alteration of a single gene. Some mutants are perturbed in sexual behavior, which in normal *Drosophila* involves an elaborate sequence of fixed action patterns. Margaret Bastock showed years ago that some mutant males do not court with normal vigor. Kulbir Gill discovered a mutant in which the males pursue one another as persistently as they do females. The mutant *stuck*, found by Carolyn Beckman, suffers from inability to disengage after the normal 20-minute copulation period. A converse example is *coitus interruptus*, a mutant Jeffrey C. Hall has been studying in our laboratory; mutant males disengage in about half the normal time and no offspring are produced. Obviously most such mutants would not stand a chance in the competitive natural environment, but they can be maintained and studied in the laboratory.

As for general locomotor activity, some mutants are *sluggish* and others, such as one found by William D. Kaplan at the City of Hope Medical Center, are *hyperkinetic*, consuming oxygen at an exaggerated rate and dying much earlier than normal flies. Whereas normal flies show strong negative geotaxis (a tendency to move upward against the force of gravity), *nonclimbing* mutants do not.

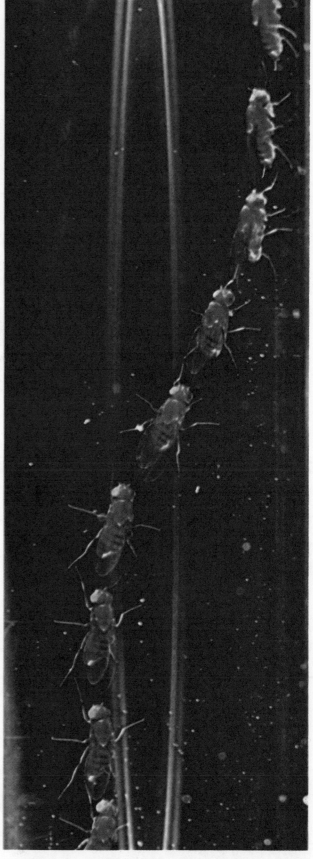

BEHAVIOR of a normal and of a mosaic fruit fly is demonstrated in an experiment photographed by F. W. Goro. Normal flies move toward light and upward against the force of gravity. A normal fly that is placed in a glass tube with a light at the top and photographed by successive stroboscopic flashes traces a line straight up the tube (*left*). A mosaic fly, with one good eye and one blind eye, also climbs straight up if there is no light, guided by its sense of gravity. If there is a light at the top of the tube, however, the mosaic fly traces a helical path (*right*), turning its bad eye toward the light in a vain effort to balance the light input to both eyes.

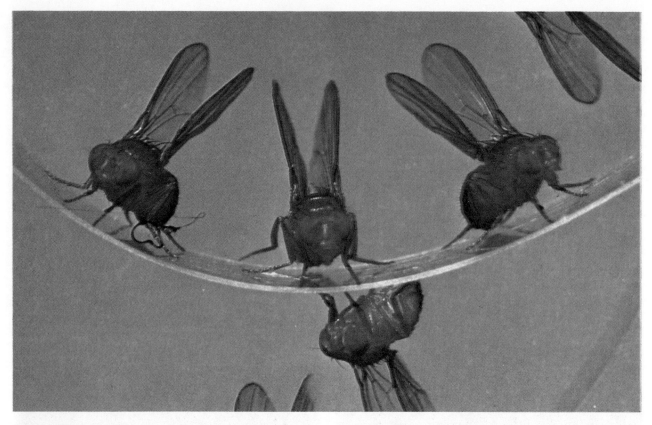

"WINGS-UP" FLIES are mutants that keep their wings straight up and cannot fly. Such behavior could be the result of flaws in wing structure, in musculature or in nerve function. Mosaic experiments in the author's laboratory have traced the defect to the muscle.

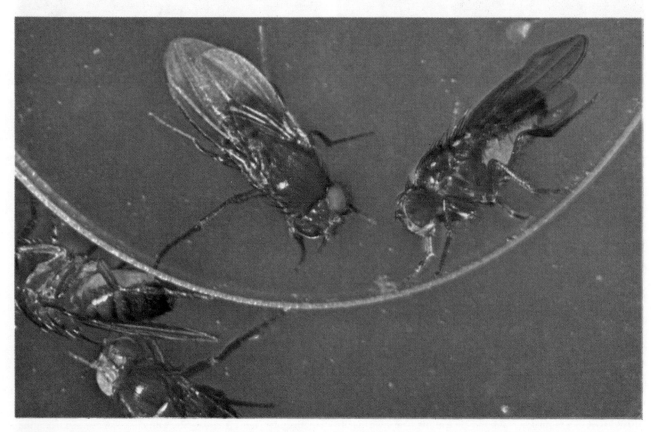

MOSAIC FLIES used for investigating behavior are gynandromorphs: partly male and partly female. The female parts are normal, the male parts mutant in one physical or behavioral trait or more. These flies have one normal red eye and one mutant white eye, and the male side of each fly also has the shorter wing that is normal for a male fly. The flies are about three millimeters long.

Flightless flies do not fly even though they may have perfectly well-developed wings and the male can raise his wing and vibrate it in approved fashion during courtship. Some individuals that appear to be quite normal may harbor hereditary idiosyncrasies that show up only under stress. Take the *easily shocked* mutants we have isolated, or the one called *tko,* found by Burke H. Judd and his collaborators at the University of Texas at Austin. When the mutant fly is subjected to a mechanical jolt, it has what looks like an epileptic seizure: it falls on its back, flails its legs and wings, coils its abdomen under and goes into a coma; after a few minutes it recovers and goes about its business as if nothing had happened. John R. Merriam and others working in our laboratory have found several different genes on the X chromosome that can produce this syndrome if they are mutated.

In many organisms mutations have been discovered that are temperature-sensitive, that is, the abnormal trait is displayed only above or below a certain temperature. David Suzuki and his associates at the University of British Columbia discovered a behavioral *Drosophila* mutant of this type called *paralyzed:* when the temperature goes above 28 degrees Celsius (82 degrees Fahrenheit), it collapses, although normal flies are unaffected; when the temperature is lowered, the mutant promptly stands up and moves about normally. We have found other mutants, involving different genes, that become similarly paralyzed at other specific temperatures. In one of these, *comatose,* recovery is not instantaneous but may take many minutes or hours, depending on how long the mutant was exposed to high temperatures. Recent experiments by Obaid Siddiqi in our laboratory have shown that action potentials in some of the motor nerves are blocked until the fly recovers.

An important feature of behavior in a wide range of organisms is an endogenous 24-hour cycle of activity. The fruit fly displays this "circadian" rhythm, and one can demonstrate the role of the genes in establishing it. A fly does well to emerge from the pupal stage around dawn, when the air is moist and cool and the creature has time to unfold its wings and harden its cuticle, or outer shell, before there is much risk of desiccation or from predators. (The name *Drosophila,* incidentally, means "lover of dew.") Eclosion from the pupa at the proper time is controlled by the circadian rhythm: most flies emerge during a few hours around dawn and those missing that interval tend to wait until dawn on the following day or on later days. This rhythm, which has been much studied by Colin S. Pittendrigh of Stanford University, persists even in constant darkness provided that the pupae have once been exposed to light; having been set, the internal clock keeps running. The clock continues to control the activity of the individual fly after eclosion, even if the fly is kept in the dark. By monitoring the fly's movement with a photocell sensitive to infrared radiation (which is invisible to the fly) one can observe that it begins to walk about at a certain time and does so for some 12 hours; then it becomes quiescent, as if it were asleep on its feet, for half a day. After that, at the same time as the first day's arousing or within an hour or so of it, activity begins anew. Ronald Konopka demonstrated the genetic control of this internal clock as a graduate student in our laboratory. By exposing normal flies to a mutagen he obtained mutants with abnormal rhythms or no rhythm at all. The *arrhythmic* flies may eclose at any time of day; if they are maintained in the dark

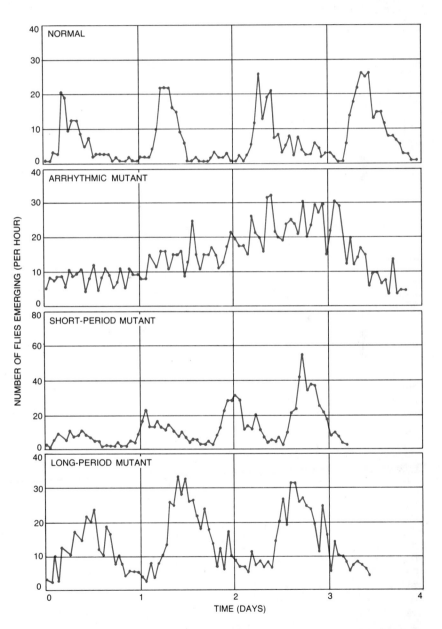

"BIOLOGICAL CLOCK" is an example of a behavioral mechanism that is genetically determined. It governs the periodicity of the time flies eclose from the pupa and also their daily cycle of activity as adults. The curves are for the eclosion of flies kept in total darkness. Normal flies emerge from the pupa at a time corresponding to dawn; those that miss dawn on one day emerge 24 hours later (*top*). Mutants include arrhythmic flies, which emerge at arbitrary times in the course of the day, and flies with 19-hour and 28-hour cycles.

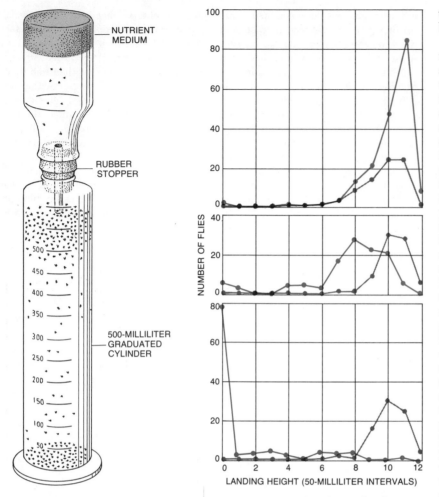

FLIGHT TESTER is a simple device for measuring the flying ability of normal and mutant flies. It is a 500-milliliter graduated cylinder, its inside wall coated with paraffin oil. Flies are dumped in at the top. They strike out horizontally as best they can, and so the level at which they hit the wall and become stuck in the oil film reflects their flying ability. The curves compare the performance of female control flies (*gray*) with that of males (*color*) that fly normally (*top*) or poorly (*middle*) and with male *flightless* mutants (*bottom*).

the dark, which suggests that they are blind.

My colleague Yoshiki Hotta, who is now at the University of Tokyo, and I studied the electrical response of the nonphototactic flies' eyes. Similar mutant isolation and electrical studies have also been carried out by William L. Pak and his associates at Purdue University and by Martin Heisenberg at the Max Planck Institute for Biology at Tübingen, so that many mutants are now available, involving a series of different genes. The stimulus of a flash of light causes the photoreceptor cells of a normal fly's eye to emit a negative wave, which in turn triggers a positive spike from the next cells in the visual pathway; an electroretinogram, a record of this response, can be made rather easily with a simple wick electrode placed on the surface of the eye. In some nonphototactic mutants the photoreceptor cells respond but fail to trigger the second-order neurons; in other cases the primary receptor cells are affected so that there is no detectable signal from them even though they are anatomically largely normal. These mutants may be useful in understanding the primary transduction mechanism in the photoreceptor cells. Mutant material provides perturbations, in other words, that enable one to analyze normal function. When Hotta and I examined the eyes of some of the nonphototactic mutants, we found that the photoreceptor cells are normal in the young adult but that they degenerate with age. There are genetic conditions that produce this result in humans, and it may be that the fly's eye can provide a model system for studying certain kinds of blindness.

Now, if one knows that a certain behavior (nonphototactic, say) is produced by a single-gene mutation and that it seems to be explained by an anatomical fault (the degenerated receptors), one still cannot say with certainty what is the primary "focus" of that genetic alteration, that is, the site in the body at which the mutant gene exerts its primary effect. The site may be far from the affected organ. Certain cases of retinal degeneration in man, for example, are due not to any defect in the eye but to ineffective absorption of vitamin A from food in the intestine, as Peter Gouras of the National Institute of Neurological Diseases and Blindness has demonstrated. In order to trace the path from gene to behavior one must find the true focus at which the gene acts in the developing organism. How? A good way to troubleshoot in an electronic system—a stereophonic set with two identical

after emergence, they are insomniacs, moving about during random periods throughout the day. The *short-period* mutant runs on a 19-hour cycle and the *long-period* mutant on a 28-hour cycle. (May there not be some analogy between such flies and humans who are either cheerful early birds or slow-to-awaken night owls?)

Let me now use a defect in visual behavior to illustrate in some detail how we analyze behavior. The first problem is to quantitate behavior and to detect and isolate behavioral mutants. It is possible to handle large populations of flies, treating each individual much as a molecule of behavior and fractionating the group into normal and abnormal types. We begin, using the technique devised by Edward B. Lewis at Cal Tech, by feeding male flies sugar water to which has been added the mutagen ethyl methane sulfonate, an alkylating agent that induces mutations in the chromosomes

of sperm cells. The progeny of mutagenized males are then fractionated by means of a kind of countercurrent distribution procedure [*see illustration on opposite page*], somewhat as one separates molecules into two liquid phases. Here the phases are light and darkness and the population is "chromatographed" in two dimensions on the basis of multiple trials for movement toward or away from light. Normal flies—and most of the progeny in our experiment—are phototactic, moving toward light but not away from it. Some mutants, however, do not move quickly in either direction; they are *sluggish* mutants. There are *runners,* which move vigorously both toward and away from light. A *negatively phototactic* mutant moves preferentially away from light. Finally, there are the *nonphototactic* mutants, which show a normal tendency to walk but no preference for light or darkness. They behave in light as normal flies behave in

channels, for example—is to interchange corresponding parts. That is in effect what we do with *Drosophila*. Rather than surgically transplanting organs from one fly to another, however, we use a genetic technique: we make mosaic flies, composite individuals in which some tissues are mutant and some have a normal genotype. Then we look to see just which part has to be mutant in order to account for the abnormal behavior.

One method of generating mosaics depends on a strain of flies in which there is an unstable ring-shaped X chromosome. Flies, like humans, have X and Y sex chromosomes; if a fertilized egg has two X chromosomes in its nucleus, it will normally develop into a female fly; an XY egg yields a male. In *Drosophila* it is the presence of two X chromosomes that makes a fly female; if there is only one X,

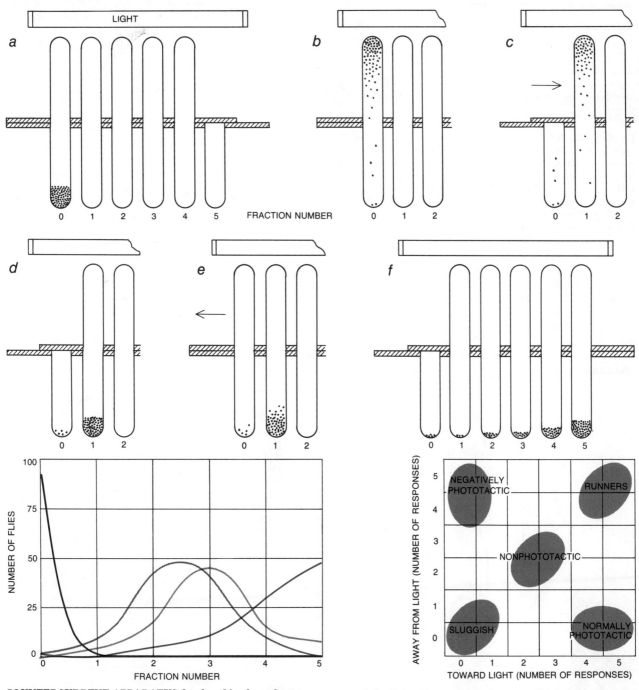

COUNTERCURRENT APPARATUS developed by the author can "fractionate" a population of flies as if they were molecules of behavior. The device consists of two sets of plastic tubes arranged in a plastic frame. Flies are put in Tube *0*; the device is held vertically and tapped to knock the flies to the bottom of the tube, and then the frame is laid flat and placed before a light at the far end of the tubes (*a*). Flies showing the phototactic response move toward the light, whereas others stay behind (*b*). After 15 seconds the top row of tubes is shifted to the right (*c*) and the responders are tapped down again (*d*), falling into Tube *1*. The upper frame is returned to the left (*e*), the frame is laid flat and again the responders move toward the light. The procedure is repeated five times in all. By then the best responders are in Tube 5, the next best in Tube 4 and so on (*f*). The curves (*bottom left*) show typical results. Phototactic flies show two very distinct peaks depending on whether the light was at the opposite end of the tubes from the starting point (*color*) or at the starting end (*black*). Nonphototactic flies, however, yield about the same curve (*light color or gray*) regardless of the position of the light. In order to distinguish variation in motor activity from phototaxis, the separation is carried out first toward light and then, processing the flies in each tube again, away from light, yielding a two-dimensional "chromatogram" (*bottom right*).

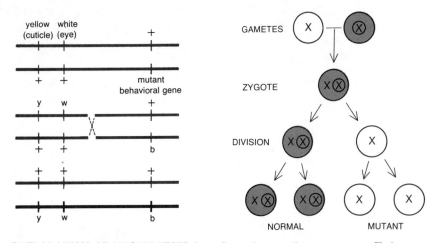

PREPARATION OF MOSAIC FLIES depends on the recombination on one *X* chromosome of genes for mutant "marker" traits and for a behavioral mutation. Recombination occurs through the crossing-over of segments of two homologous chromosomes, as shown at left. Males with an *X* chromosome carrying the desired recombination (*black*) are mated with females carrying an unstable ring-shaped *X* chromosome (*top row at right*). Among the resulting zygotes, or fertilized eggs, will be some carrying the mutation-loaded *X* and a ring *X*. In the course of nuclear division the ring *X* is sometimes lost. Tissues that stem from that nucleus are male, and mutant. In tissues that retain the ring *X*, however, the mutant genes are masked by the genes on the ring *X*, and these tissues are female and normal.

few times in a cluster and then migrate to the surface of the egg to form the early embryonic stage called a blastula: a single layer of cells surrounding the yolk [*see bottom illustration on this page*]. The nuclei tend to retain their proximity to their neighbors in the cluster, so that the female (*XX*) cells populate one part of the blastoderm (the surface of the blastula) and the male cells cover the rest. It is a feature of *Drosophila* that the axis of the crucial first nuclear division is oriented arbitrarily with respect to the axes of the egg. The dividing line between the *XX* and *X* cells can therefore cut the blastoderm in different ways. Once the blastoderm is formed the site occupied by a cell largely determines its fate in the developing embryo, and so the adult gynandromorph, a male-female mosaic, can have a wide variety of arrangements of male and female parts depending on how the dividing line falls in each particular embryo. The division of parts often follows the intersegmental boundaries and the longitudinal midline of the fly's exoskeleton. The reason is that the exoskeleton is an assembly of many parts, each of which was formed independently during metamorphosis from an imaginal disk in the larva that was in turn derived from a specific area of the blastoderm [*see illustrations on opposite page*].

the fly will be male. The ring *X* chromosome has the property that it may get lost during nuclear division in the developing egg. If we start with female eggs that have one normal *X* and one ring *X*, in a certain fraction of the embryos some of the nuclei formed on division lose the ring *X* and therefore have only one *X* chromosome left, and will therefore produce male tissues. This loss of the ring *X*, when it occurs, tends to happen at a very early stage in such a way as to produce about equal numbers of *XX* and *X* nuclei. The nuclei divide a

The reader will perceive that a mosaic fly is a system in which the effects of normal and of mutant genes can be distinguished in one animal. We use this system by arranging things so that both a behavioral gene and "marker" genes that produce anatomical anomalies are combined on the same *X* chromosome. This is done through the random workings of the phenomenon of recombination, in which segments of two chromosomes (in this case the *X*) "cross over" and exchange places with each other during cell division in the formation of the egg. In this way we can, for example, produce a strain of flies that are *nonphototactic* and also have white eyes (instead of the normal red) and a yellow body color. Then we breed males of this strain with females of the ring *X* strain. Some of the resulting embryos will have one ring *X* chromosome and one mutation-loaded *X* chromosome. In a fraction of these embryos the ring *X* (carrying normal genes) will be lost at an early nuclear division. The *XX* body parts of the resulting adult fly will have one *X* chromosome with normal genes and one with mutations; because both the behavioral and the anatomical genes in question are recessive (their effect is masked by the presence of a single nor-

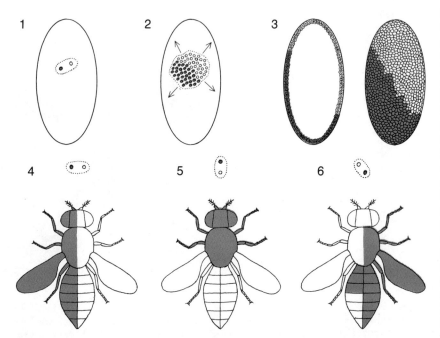

DEVELOPMENT OF A MOSAIC FLY proceeds from nuclear division (*shown in the illustration at top of page*), in which loss of the ring *X* occurs, producing an *XX* (*color*) nucleus and an *X* (*white*) nucleus (*1*). The nuclei divide a few times (*2*), then migrate to the surface of the egg and form a blastula: a single layer of cells, shown here in section and surface views (*3*). Note that female (*XX*) cells cover part of the surface and male (*X*) cells the other part. The arrangement of male (*white*) and female (*color*) parts in the adult fly depends on the way the boundary between the *XX* and *X* cells happened to cut the blastula, and that in turn depends on the orientation of the axis along which the original nucleus divides (*4–6*).

mal gene) the mutations will not be expressed in those parts. In the body parts having lost the ring *X*, however, the single *X* chromosome will be the one carrying the mutations. And because it is all alone the mutations will be expressed. Examination of the fly identifies the parts that have normal color and those in which the mutant genes have been uncovered. We can select from among the randomly divided gynandromorphs individuals in which the dividing line falls in various ways: a normal head on a mutant body, a mutant head on a normal body, a mutant eye and a normal one and so on. And then we can pose the question we originally had in mind: What parts must be mutant for the mutant behavior to be expressed?

When Hotta and I did that with certain visually defective mutants, for instance ones that produce no receptor potential, we found that the electroretinogram of the mutant eye was always completely abnormal, whereas the normal eye functioned properly. Even in gynandromorphs in which everything was normal except for one eye, that eye showed a defective electroretinogram. This makes it clear that the defects in those mutants are not of the vitamin A type I mentioned above; the defect must be autonomous within the eye itself.

The behavior of flies with one good eye and one bad eye is quite striking. A normal fly placed in a vertical tube in the dark climbs more or less straight up, with gravity as its cue. If there is a light at the top of the tube, the fly still climbs straight up because phototaxis (which the fly achieves by moving so as to keep the light intensities on both eyes equal) is consistent in direction with the negative geotaxis. A mosaic fly with one good eye also climbs straight up in the dark, since its sense of gravity is unimpaired. If a light is turned on at the top, however, the fly tends to trace a helical path, turning its defective eye toward the light in a futile attempt to balance input signals. If the right eye is the bad one, the fly traces a right-handed helix; if the left eye is bad, the helix is left-handed. (Sometimes it is difficult to resist the temptation, out of nostalgia for the old molecular-biology days, to put in two flies and let them generate a double helix.)

In these mutants the primary focus of the *phototactic* defect is in the affected organ itself. More frequently, however, the focus is elsewhere. A good way to see how this situation is dealt with is to consider a *hyperkinetic* mutant that

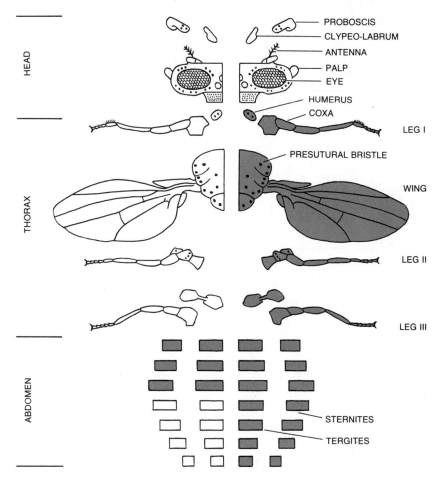

ADULT FLY is an assembly of a large number of external body parts, each of which was formed independently from a primordial group of cells of the blastula. In a mosaic fly the boundary between male and female tissues tends to follow lines of division between discrete body parts. Here the main external parts are named; black dots are the major bristles.

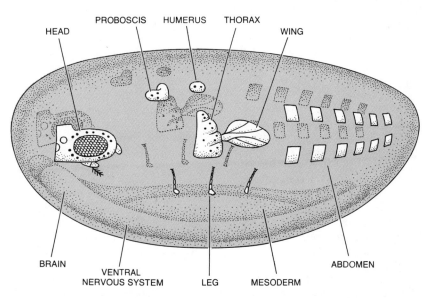

FANCIFUL DRAWING of the blastula shows how each adult body part came from a specific site on the blastula: left-side and right-side parts (or left and right halves of parts such as the head) from the left and right sides of the blastula respectively. The nervous system and the mesoderm (which gives rise to the muscles) have also been shown by embryologists to originate in specified regions of the blastula. It is clear that the probability that any two parts will have a different genotype (that is, that they will be on different sides of the mosaic boundary that cuts across the blastula) will depend on how far they are from each other on the blastoderm, the blastula surface. Conversely, the probability that two parts are of different genotypes should be a measure of their distance apart on the blastoderm.

was studied by Kaplan and Kazuo Ikeda. When such a fly is anesthetized with ether, it does not lie still but rather shakes all six of its legs vigorously. Kaplan and Ikeda found that flies that are mosaics for the gene shake some of their legs but not others and that the shaking usually correlates well with the leg's surface genotype as revealed by markers—but not always. (Suzuki and his colleagues found the same to be true of flies mosaic for the *paralyzed* mutation.) The point is that the markers are on the outside of the fly. The genotype of the surface is not necessarily the same as that of the underlying tissues, which arise from different regions of the embryo. And one might well expect that leg function would be controlled by nervous elements somewhere inside the fly's body that could have a different genotype from the leg surface. The problem is to find a way of relating internal behavioral foci to external landmarks. Hotta and I developed a method of mapping this relation by extending to behavior the idea of a "fate map," which was originally conceived by A. H. Sturtevant of Cal Tech.

Sturtevant was the genius who had earlier shown how to map the sequence of genes on the chromosome by measuring the frequency of recombination among genes. He had seen that the probability of crossing over would be greater the farther apart the genes were on the chromosome. In 1929 he proposed that one might map the blastoderm in an analogous way: the frequency with which any two parts of adult mosaics turned out to be of different genotypes could be related to the distance apart on the blastoderm of the sites that gave rise to those parts. One could look at a large group of mosaics, score structure *A* and structure *B* and record how often one was normal whereas the other was mutant, and vice versa. That frequency would represent the relative distance between their sites of origin on the blastoderm, and with enough such measurements one could in principle construct a two-dimensional map of the blastoderm. Sturtevant scored 379 mosaics of *Drosophila simulans*, put his data in a drawer and went on to something else. At Cal Tech 40 years later Merriam and Antonio Garcia-Bellido inherited those 379 yellowed sheets of paper, computed the information and found they could indeed make a self-consistent map.

When Hotta and I undertook to map behavior in *D. melanogaster*, we began by preparing our own fate map of the adult external body parts based on the scores for 703 mosaic flies [*see upper il-*

lustration on these two pages]. Distances on the map are in "sturts," a unit Merriam, Hotta and I have proposed in memory of Sturtevant. One sturt is equivalent to a probability of 1 percent that the two structures will be of different genotypes.

Now back to *hyperkinetic*. We produced 300 mosaic flies and scored each for a number of surface landmarks and for the coincidence of marker mutations at those landmarks with the shaking of each leg. We confirmed the observations of Ikeda and Kaplan that the behavior of each leg (whether it shakes or not) is independent of the behavior of the other legs and that the shaking behavior and the external genotype of a leg are frequently the same—but not always. The independent behavior of the legs indicated that each had a separate focus. For each leg we calculated the distance from the shaking focus to the leg itself and to a number of other landmarks [*see lower illustration on these two pages*] and thus determined a map location for each focus. They are near the corresponding legs but below them, in the region of the blastoderm that Donald F. Poulson of Yale University years ago identified by embryological studies as the origin of the ventral nervous system. This is consistent with electrophysiological evidence, obtained by Ikeda and Kaplan, that neurons in the thoracic ganglion of the ventral nervous system behave abnormally in these mutants.

Another degree of complexity is represented by a mutant we call *drop-dead*. These flies develop, walk, fly and otherwise behave normally for a day or two after eclosion. Suddenly, however, an individual fly becomes less active, walks in an uncoordinated manner, falls on its back and dies; the transition from apparently normal behavior to death takes only a few hours. The time of onset of the syndrome among a group of flies hatched together is quite variable; after the first two days the number of survivors in the group drops exponentially, with a half-life of about two days. It is as if some random event triggers a cataclysm. The gene has been identified as a recessive one on the *X* chromosome. Symptoms such as these could result from malfunction almost anywhere in the body of the fly, for example from a blockage of the gut, a general biochemical disturbance or a nerve disorder. In order to localize the focus we did an analysis of 403 mosaics in which the *XX* parts were normal and the *X* body parts expressed the *drop-dead* gene and surface-marker mutations, and we scored

for *drop-dead* behavior and various landmarks.

Drop-dead behavior, unlike shaking behavior, which could be scored separately for each leg, is an all-or-none property of the entire fly. First we did a rough analysis to determine whether the behavior was most closely related to the head, thorax or abdomen, considering only flies in which the surface of each of these structures was either completely mutant or completely normal. Among mosaics in which the entire head surface was normal almost all behaved

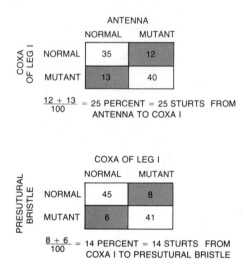

	ANTENNA	
	NORMAL	MUTANT
COXA OF LEG I — NORMAL	35	12
COXA OF LEG I — MUTANT	13	40

$$\frac{12 + 13}{100} = 25 \text{ PERCENT} = 25 \text{ STURTS FROM ANTENNA TO COXA I}$$

	COXA OF LEG I	
	NORMAL	MUTANT
PRESUTURAL BRISTLE — NORMAL	45	8
PRESUTURAL BRISTLE — MUTANT	6	41

$$\frac{8 + 6}{100} = 14 \text{ PERCENT} = 14 \text{ STURTS FROM COXA I TO PRESUTURAL BRISTLE}$$

FATE MAP, a two-dimensional map of the blastoderm, is constructed by calculating the distances between the sites that gave rise to various parts. This is done by observing a large number of adult flies and recording the number of times each of two parts is mu-

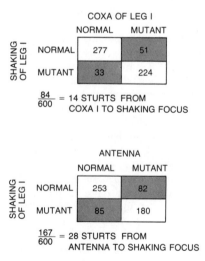

	COXA OF LEG I	
	NORMAL	MUTANT
SHAKING OF LEG I — NORMAL	277	51
SHAKING OF LEG I — MUTANT	33	224

$$\frac{84}{600} = 14 \text{ STURTS FROM COXA I TO SHAKING FOCUS}$$

	ANTENNA	
	NORMAL	MUTANT
SHAKING OF LEG I — NORMAL	253	82
SHAKING OF LEG I — MUTANT	85	180

$$\frac{167}{600} = 28 \text{ STURTS FROM ANTENNA TO SHAKING FOCUS}$$

BEHAVIORAL FOCI, the sites at which a mutant gene exerts its effect on behavior, are plotted in the same way. The behavior in this example (*left*) is abnormal shaking of

normally, but six flies out of 97 died in the *drop-dead* manner; in the reciprocal class eight flies of 80 with mutant head surfaces lived. In other words, the focus was shown to be close to, but distinct from, the blastoderm site of origin of the head surface. Comparable analysis showed that the focus was substantially farther away from the thorax and farther still from the abdomen. Next we considered individuals with mosaic heads. The reader will recall that in certain visual mutants the visual defect was always observed in the eye on the mutant

side of the head; flies with half-normal heads had normal vision in one eye. For *drop-dead*, on the other hand, of mosaics in which half of the head surface was mutant only about 17 percent dropped dead. All the rest survived.

Now, a given internal part should occur in normal or mutant form with equal probability, as the external parts in these mosaics did. On that reasoning, if there were a single focus inside the head of the fly, half of the bilateral-mosaic flies should have dropped dead. We formed the hypothesis, therefore, that there

must be two foci, one on each side, and that they must interact. Both of them must be mutant for the syndrome to appear. In other words, a mutant focus must be "submissive" to a normal one. In that case, if an individual exhibits *drop-dead* behavior, both foci must be mutant, and if a fly survives, one focus may be normal or both of them may be.

Mapping a bilateral pair of interacting foci calls for special analysis. By considering the various ways a mosaic dividing line could fall in relation to a pair of visible external landmarks (one on

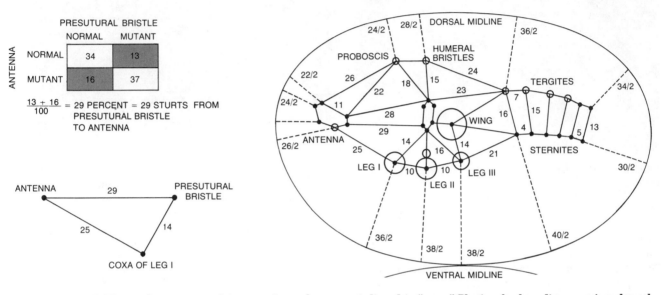

tant or normal. The numbers are entered in a matrix, as shown (*left*) for three pairs of parts. Instances in which one part is normal whereas the other part is mutant on the same fly (*colored boxes*) are totaled. That figure, divided by the total number of instances, gives the probability that the two parts are of different genotypes. And that probability is proportional to the distance between them, indicated in "sturts." Plotting the three distances triangulates the relative locations of the three sites. By thus scoring 703 mosaic flies for body parts, Yoshiki Hotta in the author's laboratory built up the fate map of external body parts (*right*). Broken lines represent distances to the blastula midlines, obtained by dividing by two the distances between homologous parts on opposite sides of the fly.

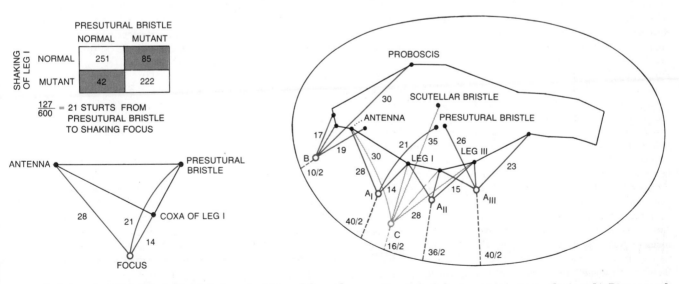

the legs under ether. The shaking is independent for each leg and here leg *I* has been scored for 300 flies—or 600 instances, since the data can be doubled to represent both sides of the fly. (The total of instances can be less than 600 because cases in which both the body part and the behavior are mosaic are eliminated.) Distances calculated (*colored lines*) triangulate the focus. In this way the foci for shaking behavior for each leg (*A*) are added to the map (*right*). Foci for *drop-dead* (*B*) and *wings-up* (*C*) behavior are also found.

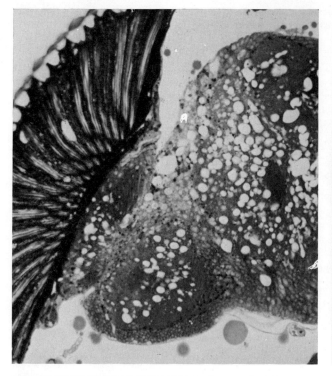

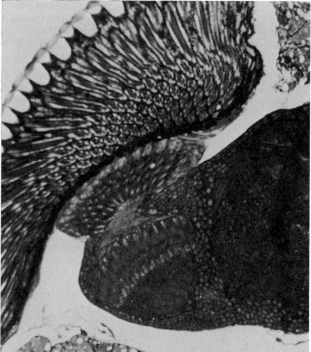

BRAINS OF DROP-DEAD MUTANTS that have reached the symptomatic stage show striking degeneration, as shown by photomicrograph (*left*) of a section of such a fly's head enlarged 300 diameters.

The brain and the optic ganglia are full of holes. Sections fixed before a mutant has shown any symptoms, on the other hand, show no more degeneration than a section of a normal brain does (*right*).

each side of the body) and a symmetrical pair of internal foci, one can set up equations based on the probability of each possible configuration. Using the observed data on how many mosaic flies showed the various combinations of mutant and normal external landmarks and mutant or normal behavior, it is possible to solve these equations for the map distance from each landmark to the corresponding focus and from one focus to the homologous focus on the other side of the embryo. The *drop-dead* foci turn out to be below the head-surface area of the blastoderm, in the area embryologists have assigned to the brain. Sure enough, when we examined the brain tissue of flies that had begun to exhibit the initial stages of *drop-dead* behavior, it showed striking signs of degeneration, whereas brain tissue fixed before the onset of symptoms appeared normal. As for mosaics whose head surfaces are half-normal, those that die show degeneration of the brain on both sides; the survivors' brains show no degeneration on either side, a finding consistent with the bilateral-submissive-focus hypothesis. It appears that the normal side of the brain supplies some factor that prevents the deterioration of the side with the mutant focus.

There is another kind of bilateral focus, "domineering" rather than submissive. An example is the mutant we call

wings-up. There are two different genes, *wup A* and *wup B*, which produce very similar overt behavior: shortly after emergence each of these flies raises its wings straight up and keeps them there. It cannot fly, but otherwise it behaves normally. Is *wings-up* the result of a defect in the wing itself, in its articulation or in the muscles or neuromuscular junctions that control the wing, or of some "psychological quirk" in the central nervous system? The study of mosaic flies shows that the behavior is more often associated with a mutant thorax than with a mutant head or abdomen. The focus cannot be in the wings themselves or anywhere on the surface of the thorax, however, because in some mosaics the wings and the thorax surface are normal and yet the wings are held up and in other mosaics the wings and thorax display all the mutant markers and yet the fly flies. These observations suggest that some structure inside the thorax could be responsible.

Once again we look at the bilateral mosaics, those with one side of the thorax carrying mutant markers and the other side appearing normal. Unlike the *drop-dead* bilateral mosaics, most of which were normal, these bilaterals are primarily mutant; well over half of them hold both wings up. Both wings seem to act together; either both are held up or both are in the normal position. This sug-

gests two interacting foci, one on each side, with the mutant focus domineering with respect to the normal one, that is, if either of the foci is mutant, or both are, then both wings will be up. Again we can set up equations based on the probability of the various mosaic configurations and solve to find the pertinent map distances. The focus comes out to be close to the ventral midline of the blastula. That is a region known to produce the mesoderm, the part of the developing embryo from which muscle tissue is derived, which suggested that a defect in the fly's thoracic muscle tissue could be responsible for *wings-up* behavior.

The abnormality became obvious when we dissected the thorax. In the fly the raising and lowering of the wings in normal flight is accomplished by changes in the shape of the thorax, changes brought about by the alternate action of sets of vertical and horizontal muscles. Under the phase-contrast microscope these indirect flight muscles are seen to be highly abnormal in both *wings-up* mutants. Developmental studies show that in *wup A* the muscles form properly at first, then degenerate after the fly emerges. In the *wup B* mutant, on the other hand, the myoblasts that normally produce the muscles fuse properly but the muscle fibrils fail to appear. In both mutants the other muscles, such as those of the leg, appear to be quite normal,

FLIGHT MUSCLE OF WINGS-UP MUTANTS shows degeneration that seems to account for their behavior. Normal flight muscle, enlarged 30,000 diameters in an electron micrograph, has bundles of filaments crossed by straight, dense bands: the *Z* lines (*left*). In the muscle of flies heterozygous for the gene *wup B*, which hold their wings normally but cannot fly, the *Z* lines are irregular (*right*).

and the flies walk and climb perfectly well. In flies that are heterozygous for *wup A* (nonmosaic flies with one mutated and one normal gene) the muscles and flight behavior are normal, that is, the gene is completely recessive. In *wup B* heterozygotes, on the other hand, the wings are held in the normal position but the flies cannot fly. Electron microscopy shows that even in these heterozygotes the indirect flight muscles are defective: the microscopic filaments that constitute each muscle fibril are arranged correctly, but the Z line, a dense region that should run straight across the fibril, is often crooked and forked. Examination of the muscles in bilateral mosaics confirmed the impression that the *wup* foci are domineering. In every mosaic that had shown *wings-up* behavior one or more muscle fibers were degenerated or missing; no fibers were seriously deficient in any flies that had displayed normal behavior. The natural shape of the thorax apparently corresponds to the *wings-up* position, and the presence of defective muscles on either side is enough to make it impossible to change the shape of the thorax, locking the wings in the vertical position.

The mutants so far mapped provide examples involving the main components of behavior: sensory receptors, the nervous system and the muscles. For some of the mutants microscopic examination has revealed a conspicuous lesion of some kind in tissue. The obvious question is whether or not fate mapping is necessary; why do we not just look directly for abnormal tissue? One answer is that for many mutants we do not know where to begin to look, and it is helpful to narrow down the relevant region. Furthermore, in many cases no lesion may be visible, even in the electron microscope. More important, and worth reiterating, is the fact that the site of a lesion is not necessarily the primary focus. For example, an anomaly of muscle tissue may result from a defect in the function of nerves supplying the muscle. This possibility has been a lively issue in the study of diseases such as muscular dystrophy. Recently, by taking nerve and muscle tissues from a dystrophic mutant of the mouse and from its normal counterpart and growing them in tissue culture in all four combinations, the British workers Belinda Gallup and V. Dubowitz were able to show that the nerves are indeed at fault.

The mosaic technique in effect does the same kind of experiment in the intact animal. In the case of the *wings-up* mutant the primary focus cannot be in the nerves, since if that were so the focus would map to the area of the blastoderm destined to produce the nervous system, not to the mesoderm, where muscle tissue is formed. The *wings-up* mutants clearly have defects that originate in the muscles themselves.

Another application of mosaics is in tagging cells with genetic labels to follow their development. The compound eye of *Drosophila* is a remarkable structure consisting of about 800 ommatidia: unit eyes containing eight receptor cells each. The arrangement of cells in an ommatidium is precise and repetitive; the eye is in effect a neurological crystal in which the unit cell contains eight neurons. Thomas E. Hanson, Donald F. Ready and I have been interested in how this structure is formed. Are the eight photoreceptor cells derived from one cell that undergoes three divisions to produce eight, or do cells come together to form the group irrespective of their lineage? This can be tested by examining the eyes of flies, mosaic for the *white* gene, in which the mosaic dividing line passes through the eye. By sectioning the eye and examining ommatidia near the border between white and red areas microscopically, it is possible to score the tiny pigment granules that are present in normal photoreceptor cells but absent in *white* mutant cells. The result is clear: A single ommatidium can contain a mixture of receptor cells of both genotypes. This proves that the eight cells cannot be derived from a single ancestral cell but have become associated in their special group of eight irrespective of lineage. The same conclusion applies to the other cells in each ommatidium, such as the normally heavily pigmented cells that surround the receptors.

Not all cells have such convenient pigment markers. It would obviously be valuable to have a way of labeling all the internal tissues as being either mutant or normal, much as yellow color labels a landmark on the surface. This can now be done for many tissues by utilizing mutants that lack a specific enzyme. If a recessive enzyme-deficient mutant gene is recombined on the X chromosome along with the *yellow, white* and behavioral genes and mosaics are produced in the usual way, the male tissues of the mosaic will lack the enzyme. By making a frozen section of the fly and staining it for enzyme activity one can identify normal and mutant cells.

In order to apply this method in the nervous system one needs to have an enzyme that is normally present there in a large enough concentration to show up in the staining procedure and a mutant that lacks the enzyme, and the lack should have a negligible effect on the behavior under study. Finally, the gene in question should be on the X chromosome. Douglas R. Kankel and Jeffrey Hall in our laboratory have developed several such mutants, including one with an acid-phosphatase-deficient gene found by Ross J. MacIntyre of Cornell University. By scoring the internal tissues they have constructed a fate map of the internal organs of the kind made earlier for surface structures. We are now adapting the staining method for electron microscopy in order to work at the level of the individual cell.

The staining procedure has demonstrated graphically that the photoreceptor cells of the eye come from a different area of the blastoderm than do the neurons of the lamina, to which they project. In the adult fly the two groups of cells are in close apposition, but the former arise in the eye whereas the latter come from the brain. The distance between them on the fate map, determined by Kankel, is about 12 sturts, so that a considerable number of mosaic flies have a normal retina and a mutant lamina or vice versa. This makes it possible to distinguish between presynaptic and postsynaptic defects in mutants with blocks in the visual pathway. In the nonphototactic mutants Hotta and I analyzed in mosaics, the defect in the electroretinogram was always associated with the eye. In contrast, a mutant with a similar electroretinogram abnormality that was studied by Linda Hall and Suzuki

MOSAIC EYE contains a patch of cells that carry the *white* gene and therefore lack the normal red pigment. The fly's compound eye is an array of hexagonal ommatidia, each containing eight photoreceptor cells (*circles*) and two primary pigment cells (*crescents*) and surrounded by six shared secondary pigment cells (*ovals*). The fact that a single ommatidium can have *white* and normal genotypes shows its cells are not necessarily descended from a common ancestral cell. Nor is the mirror-image symmetry about the equator (*heavy line*) the result of two cell lines: mutant cells appear on both sides. Drawing is based on observations by Donald Ready.

showed, in some mosaics, a normal trace for a mutant eye—and vice versa. Fate mapping placed the focus in precisely the region corresponding to the lamina. What appeared to be similar malfunctions in two mutants were thus shown to be different, due in one case to a presynaptic block and in the other case to a postsynaptic one.

Much of what has been done so far involves relatively simple aspects of behavior chosen to establish the general methodology of mutants and mosaic analysis. Can the methodology be applied to more elaborate and interesting behavior such as circadian rhythm, sexual courtship and learning? Some beginnings have been made on all of these. By making flies that are mutant for normal and mutant rhythms, Konopka has shown that the internal clock is most closely associated with the head. Looking at flies with mosaic heads, he found that some exhibited the normal rhythm and others the mutant rhythm but that a few flies exhibited a peculiar rhythm that appears to be a sum of the two, as if each side of the brain were producing its rhythm independently and the fly responded to both of them. By applying the available cell-staining techniques it may be possible to identify the cells that control the clock.

Sexual courtship is a higher form of behavior, since it consists of a series of fixed action patterns, each step of which makes the next step more likely. The sex mosaics we have generated lend themselves beautifully to the analysis of sexual behavior. A mosaic fly can be put with normal females and its ability to perform the typical male courtship steps can be observed. Hotta, Hall and I found that the first steps (orientation toward the female and vibrating of the wings) map to the brain. This is of particular interest because the wings are vibrated by motor-nerve impulses from the thoracic ganglion; even a female ganglion will produce the vibration "song" typical of the male if directed to do so by a male brain. It would appear that the thoracic ganglion in a female must "know" the male courtship song even though she does not normally emit it. This is consistent with recent experiments by Ronald Hoy and Robert Paul at the State University of New York at Stony Brook, in which they showed that hybrid cricket females responded better to the songs of hybrid males than to males of either of the two parental species.

Sexual behavior in *Drosophila,* although complex, is a stereotyped series of instinctive actions that are performed

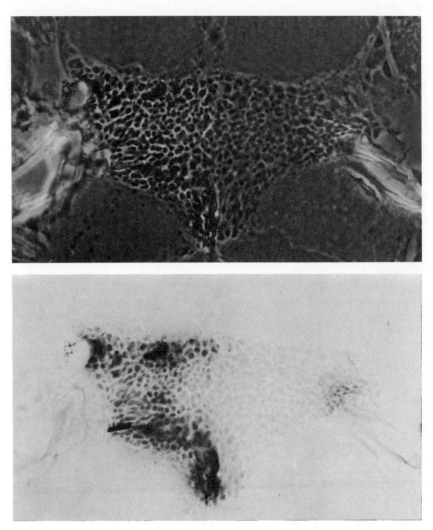

DIRECT SCORING OF NORMAL AND MUTANT CELLS within the nervous system is possible with a staining method developed by Douglas Kankel and Jeffrey Hall in the author's laboratory. Mosaics are produced in which mutant cells are deficient in the enzyme acid phosphatase. When the proper stain is applied to a section of nerve tissue, normal cells stain brown and mutant cells are unstained. Here a section of the thoracic ganglion, thus stained, is shown in phase-contrast (*top*) and bright-field (*bottom*) photomicrographs. In the bottom picture normal cells are marked by the stain, delineating the mosaic boundary.

correctly by a fly raised in isolation and without previous sexual experience. Other forms of behavior such as phototaxis also appear to be already programmed into the fly when it ecloses. Whether a fruit fly can learn has long been debated; various claims have been made and later shown to be incorrect. Recently William G. Quinn, Jr., and William A. Harris in our laboratory have shown in carefully controlled experiments that the fly can learn to avoid specific odors or colors of light that are associated with a negative reinforcement such as electric shock. This opens the door to genetic analysis of learning behavior through mutations that block it.

In tackling the complex problems of behavior the gene provides, in effect, a microsurgical tool with which to produce very specific blocks in a behavioral pathway. With temperature-dependent mutations the blocks can be turned on and off at will. Individual cells of the nervous system can be labeled genetically and their lineage can be followed during development. Genetic mosaics offer the equivalent of exquisitely fine grafting of normal and mutant parts, with the entire structure remaining intact. What we are doing in mosaic mapping is in effect "unrolling" the fantastically complex adult fly, in which sense organs, nerve cells and muscles are completely interwoven, backward in development, back in time to the blastoderm, a stage at which the different structures have not yet come together. Filling the gaps between the one-dimensional gene, the two-dimensional blastoderm, the three-dimensional organism and its multidimensional behavior is a challenge for the future.

14

The Flight-Control System of the Locust

by Donald M. Wilson
May 1968

Groups of nerve cells controlling such activities as locomotion are regulated not only by simplex reflex mechanisms but also by behavior patterns apparently coded genetically in the central nervous system

Physicists can properly be concerned with atoms and subatomic particles as being important in themselves, but biologists often study simple or primitive structures with the long-range hope of understanding the workings of the most complex organisms, including man. Studies of viruses and bacteria made it possible to understand the basic molecular mechanisms that we believe control the heredity of all living things. Adopting a similar approach, investigators concerned with the mechanisms of behavior have turned their attention to the nervous systems of lower animals, and to isolated parts of such systems, in the hope of discovering the physiological mechanisms by which behavior is controlled.

One way to approach the study of behavior mechanisms is to ask: Where does the information come from that is needed to coordinate the observable activities of the nervous system? We know that certain behavior patterns are inherited.

This means that some of the informational input must be directly coded in the genetic material and therefore has an origin that is remote in time. Nonetheless, probably all behavior patterns depend to some degree on information supplied directly by the environment by way of the sense organs. Behavior that is largely triggered and coordinated by the nervous input of the moment is commonly called reflex behavior. Much of neurophysiological research has been directed at the analysis of reflex behavior mechanisms. Recent work makes it clear, however, that whole programs for the control of patterns of animal activity can be stored within the central nervous system [see "Small Systems of Nerve Cells," by Donald Kennedy; SCIENTIFIC AMERICAN Offprint 1073]. Apparently these inherited nervous programs do not require much special input information for their expression.

I should point out here that whereas there is now general agreement among biologists that many aspects of animal behavior are under genetic control, it is not easy to show in particular cases that a kind of behavior is inherited and not learned. I believe, however, that this is a reasonable assumption for the cases to be discussed in this article, namely flight and walking by arthropods (insects, crustaceans and other animals with an external skeleton).

The studies I shall describe were begun as part of an effort to demonstrate how several reflexes could be coordinated into an entire behavior pattern. Until recently it was thought by most students of simple behavior such as locomotion that much of the patterning of the nervous command that sets the muscles into rhythmic movement flowed rather directly from information in the immediately preceding sensory input. Each phase of movement was assumed to be triggered by a particular pattern of input from various receptors. According to this hypothesis, known as the peripheral-

 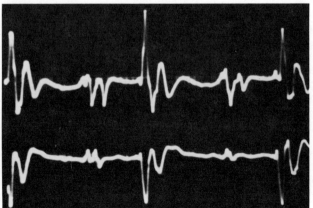

LOCUST WING position and wing-muscle action potentials were recorded in synchronous photographs. The flash that illuminates the locust (*left*) is triggered by the first muscle potential (*at left on oscilloscope trace*). The wing motion is traced by spots of white paint on each wing tip that reflect room light through the open shutter. The trace at the top shows three "doublet" firings of downstroke muscles controlling the forewing; the bottom trace shows similar firings for the hindwing. The smaller potentials visible between the large doublets are from elevator muscles more remote from the electrodes. The oscilloscope traces span 100 milliseconds.

control hypothesis, locomotion might begin because of a signal from external sense organs such as the eye or from brain centers, but thereafter a cyclic reflex process kept it properly timed.

This cyclic reflex could be imagined to operate as follows. An initiating input causes motor nerve impulses to travel to certain muscles, and the muscles cause a movement. The movement is sensed by position or movement receptors within the body (proprioceptors), which send impulses back to the central nervous system. This proprioceptive feedback initiates activity in another set of muscles, perhaps muscles that are antagonists of the first set. The sequence of motor outputs and feedbacks is connected so that it is closed on itself and cyclic activity results. Clearly such a system depends on a well-planned (probably inherited) set of connections among the many parts involved; thus both the central nervous system and its peripheral extensions (the

NERVE AND MUSCLE impulses were recorded during flight with this equipment. The locust is flying, suspended at the end of a pendulum, at the mouth of a wind tunnel. The scale at the right registers the insect's angle of pitch. The wires lead to amplifiers.

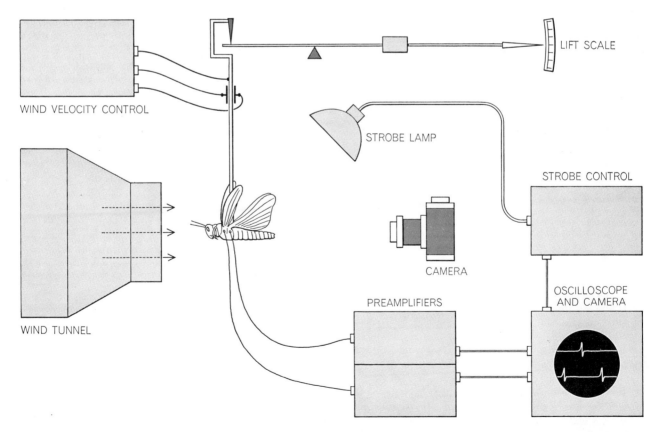

EXPERIMENTAL SETUP is diagrammed. The motion of the pendulum controls the wind-tunnel blower, so that the insect can fly at its desired wind speed. Muscle or nerve impulses are displayed on the oscilloscope, which in turn controls the stroboscopic flash lamp.

muscular and sensory structures) are crucial to the basic operation of the system.

An alternative hypothesis, known as the central-control hypothesis, suggests that the output pattern of motor nerve impulses controlling locomotion can be generated by the central nervous system alone, without proprioceptive feedback. This hypothesis has received much support from studies of embryological development. Only a few zoophysiologists have favored it, however, because the existence of proprioceptive reflexes had been clearly demonstrated. It seemed that if such reflexes exist, they must operate.

Proprioceptive reflexes certainly play an important role in the maintenance of posture. I suspect that this may be their basic and primitive function. In many animals—insects and man included—proprioceptive reflexes help to maintain a given body position against the force of gravity. A simple example was described by Gernot Wendler of the Max Planck Institute for the Physiology of Behavior in Germany. The stick insect, named for its appearance, stands so that its opposed legs form a flattened "M" [see illustration at right]. Sensory hairs are bent in proportion to the angle of the leg joints. The hairs send messages to the central nervous ganglia, concentrated groups of nerve cells and their fibrous branches that act as relay and coordinating centers. If too many impulses from the hairs are received, motor nerve cells are excited that cause muscles to contract, thereby moving the joint in the direction that decreases the sensory discharge. Thus the feedback is negative, and it results in the equilibration of a certain position.

If a weight is placed on the back of the insect, one would expect the greater force to bend the leg joints. Instead the proprioceptive feedback loop adjusts muscle tension to compensate for the extra load. The body position remains approximately constant, unless the weight is more than the muscles can bear. If the hair organs are destroyed, the feedback loop is opened and the body sags in relation to the weight, as one would expect in an uncontrolled system.

If the leg reflexes of arthropods are studied under dynamic rather than static conditions, one finds also that they are similar to the reflexes of vertebrates. When a leg of an animal is pushed and pulled rhythmically, the muscles respond reflexively with an output at the same frequency. At high frequencies of movement the reflex system cannot keep up and the output force developed by the muscles lags behind the input move-

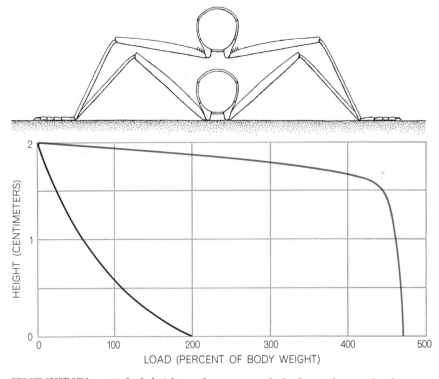

STICK INSECT keeps its body height nearly constant as the load on its leg muscles changes. Hairs at the first leg joint sense the angle of the joint and a reflex loop maintains the angle until the animal is overloaded (*colored curve*). If the sensory hairs are damaged, the reflex loop is opened and the body sags quickly as more weight is added to it (*black curve*).

ment. The peripheral-control hypothesis postulates an interaction of similar reflexes in each of the animal's legs. If one leg is commanded to lift, the others must bear more weight and postural reflexes presumably produce the increased muscle force that is needed. If any part oscillates, other parts oscillate too, perhaps in other phase relations. Although no such total system has been analyzed, one can imagine a sequence of reflex relationships that could coordinate all the legs into a smooth gait.

Against this background I shall describe the work on the nervous control of flight in locusts I began in the laboratory of Torkel Weis-Fogh at the University of Copenhagen in 1959. Weis-Fogh and his associates had already investigated many aspects of the mechanisms of insect flight, including the sense organs and their role in the initiation and maintenance of flight [see the article "The Flight of Locusts," by Torkel Weis-Fogh, beginning on page 35]. These studies, and the general climate of opinion among physiologists, tended to support a peripheral-control hypothesis based on reflexes. To test this hypothesis I set out to analyze the details of the reflex mechanisms.

An important consideration in the early phases of the work was how to study nervous activities in a small, rap-

idly moving animal. This was accomplished by having locusts fly in front of a wind tunnel while they were suspended on a pendulum that served as the arm of an extremely sensitive double-throw switch. The switch operated relays that controlled the blower of the tunnel, so that whenever the insect flew forward, the wind velocity increased and vice versa. Thus the insect chose its preferred wind speed, but it stood approximately still in space. Other devices measured aerodynamic lift and body and wing positions; wires that terminated in the muscles or on nerves conducted electrical impulses to amplifying and recording apparatus.

Early in the program of research we found that fewer than 20 motor nerve cells control the muscles of each wing, and that we could record from any of the motor units controlled by these cells during normal flight. We drew up a table showing when each motor unit was activated for various sets of aerodynamic conditions. The results of this rather tedious work were not very exciting but did provide a necessary base for further investigation. Moreover, I think we can say that these results constitute one of the first and most complete descriptions of the activity of a whole animal analyzed in terms of the activities of single motor nerve cells. In brief, we found that the output pattern consists of nearly synchronous impulses in two small populations of cooperating motor units, with activity alternating between antagonistic sets of muscles, the muscles that elevate the wings and the muscles that depress them. Each muscle unit normally receives one or two impulses per wingbeat or no impulse at all. The variation in the number of excitatory impulses sent to the different muscles serves to control flight power and direction.

We also found it possible to record from the sensory nerves that innervate, or carry signals to, the wings. These nerves conduct proprioceptive signals from receptors in the wing veins and in the wing hinge. The receptors in the

wing veins register the upward force, or lift, on the wing; the receptors in the wing hinge indicate wing position and movement in relation to the body. These sensory inputs occur at particular phases of the wing stroke. The lift receptors usually discharge during the middle of the downstroke; each wing-hinge proprioceptor is a stretch receptor that discharges one, two or several impulses toward the end of the upstroke [*see illustration on page 137*].

Everything I have described so far about the motor output and sensory input of an insect in flight is consistent with the peripheral-control hypothesis. Motor impulses cause the movements

the receptors register. According to the hypothesis the sensory feedback should trigger a new round of output. Does this actually happen?

A useful test of feedback-loop function is to open the loop. This we did simply by cutting or damaging the sense organs or sensory nerves that provide the feedback. Cutting the sensory nerve carrying the information about lift forces caused little change in the basic pattern of motor output, although it did affect the insect's ability to make certain maneuvers. On the other hand, burning the stretch receptors that measure wing position and angular velocity always resulted in a drastic reduction in wingbeat frequency. These proprioceptors provide the only input we could discover that had such an effect. Most important of all, we found that, even when we eliminated all sources of sensory feedback, the wings could be kept beating in a normal phase pattern, although at a somewhat reduced frequency, simply by stimulating the central nervous system with random electrical impulses.

From these studies we must conclude that the flight-control system of the locust is not adequately explained by the peripheral-control hypothesis and patterned feedback. Instead we find that the coordinated action of locust flight muscles depends on a pattern-generating system that is built into the central nervous system and can be turned on by an unpatterned input. This is a significant finding because it suggests that the networks within the nerve ganglia are endowed through genetic and developmental processes with the information needed to produce an important pattern of behavior and that proprioceptive reflexes are not major contributors of coordinating information.

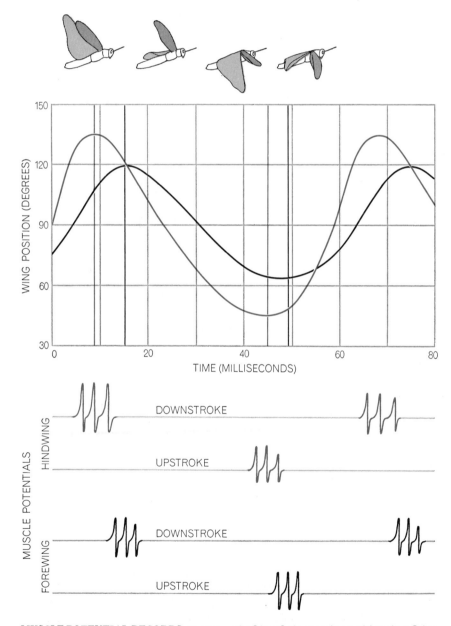

MUSCLE-POTENTIAL RECORDS are summarized in relation to wing positions in a flying locust. The curves (*top*) show the angular position (90 degrees is horizontal) of the hindwings (*color*) and forewings (*black*). The four simulated traces at the bottom show how the downstroke and upstroke muscles respectively fire at the high and low point for each wing.

Erik Gettrup and I were particularly curious to learn how the wing-hinge proprioceptor, a stretch receptor, helped to control the frequency of wingbeat. When Gettrup analyzed the response of this receptor to various wing movements, he found that to some degree it signaled to the central nervous system information on wing position, wingbeat amplitude and wingbeat frequency. We then cut out the four stretch receptors so that the wingbeat frequency was reduced to about half the normal frequency and artificially stimulated the stumps of the stretch receptors in an attempt to restore normal function. Under these conditions we found that electrical stimulation of the stumps could raise the frequency of wingbeat no matter what input pattern we used. Although the normal input

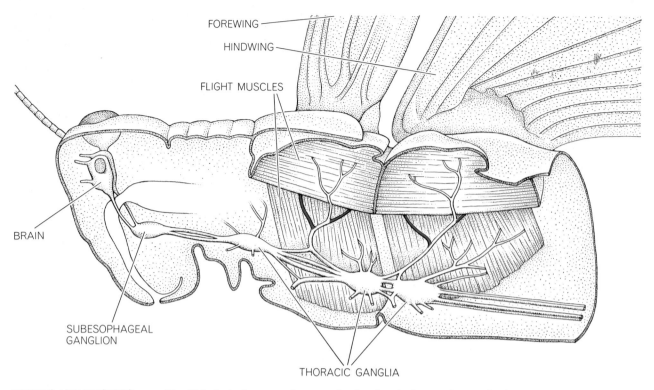

FOREWING

HINDWING

FLIGHT MUSCLES

BRAIN

SUBESOPHAGEAL
GANGLION

THORACIC GANGLIA

NERVES AND MUSCLES controlling flight in the locust are shown in simplified form. The central nervous system includes the brain and the various ganglia. From the thoracic ganglia, motor nerves lead to the wing's upstroke muscles (*vertical fibers*) and the downstroke muscles (*horizontal fibers*) above them. There are also sensory nerves (*color*) that sense wing position and aerodynamic forces.

from the stretch receptor arrives at a definite, regular time with respect to the wingbeat cycle, in our artificially stimulated preparations the effect was the same no matter what the phase of the input was.

We also found that the response to the input took quite a long time to develop. When the stimulator was turned on, the motor output frequency would increase gradually over about 20 to 40 wingbeat cycles. Hence it appears that the ganglion averages the input from the four stretch receptors (and other inputs too) over a rather long time interval compared with the wingbeat period, and that this averaged level of excitation controls wingbeat frequency. In establishing this average of the input most of the detailed information about wing position, frequency and amplitude is lost or discarded, with the result that no reflection of the detailed input pattern is found in the motor output pattern. We must therefore conclude that the input turns on a central pattern generator and regulates its average level of activity, but that it does not determine the main features of the pattern it produces. These features are apparently genetically programmed into the central network.

If that is so, why does the locust even have a stretch reflex to control wingbeat frequency? If the entire ordered pattern needed to activate flight muscles can be

coded within the ganglion, why not also include the code for wingbeat frequency? The answer to this dual question can probably be found in mechanical considerations. The wings, muscles and skeleton of the flight system of the locust form a mechanically resonant system— a system with a preferred frequency at which conversion of muscular work to aerodynamic power is most efficient. This frequency is a function of the insect's size. It seems likely that even insects with the same genetic makeup may reach different sizes because of different environmental conditions during egg production and development. Hence each adult insect must be able to measure its own size, as it were, to find the best wingbeat frequency. This measurement may be provided by the stretch reflex, automatically regulating the wingbeat frequency to the mechanically resonant one.

What kind of pattern-generating nerve network is contained in the ganglia? We do not know as yet. Nonetheless, a plausible model can be suggested. The arguments leading to this model are not rigorous and the evidence in its favor is not overwhelming, but it is always useful to have a working hypothesis as a guide in planning future experiments. Also, it seems worthwhile to present a hypothesis of how a simply

structured network might produce a special temporally patterned output when it is excited by an unpatterned input.

When neurophysiologists find a system in which there is alternating action between two sets of antagonistic muscles, they tend to visualize a controlling nerve network in which there is reciprocal inhibition between the two sets of nerve cells [*see top illustration on page 138*]. Such a network can turn on one or both sets at first, but one soon dominates and the other is silenced. When the dominant set finally slows down from fatigue, the inhibiting signal it sends to the silent set also decreases, with the result that the silent set turns on. It then inhibits the first set. This reciprocating action is analogous to the action of an electronic flip-flop circuit; timing cues are not needed in the input. The information required for the generation of the output pattern is contained largely in the structure of the network and not in the input, which only sets the average level of activity. A nerve network that acts in this way can consist of as few as two cells or be made up of two populations of cells in which there is some mechanism to keep the cooperating units working together.

In the locust flight-control system several tens of motor nerve cells work together in each of the two main sets. The individual nerve cells within each set seem to share some excitatory interconnections. These not only provide the coupling that keeps the set working efficiently but also have a further effect of some importance. Strong positive coupling between nerve cells can result in positive feedback "runaway"; the network, once it is activated, produces a heavy burst of near-maximum activity until it is fatigued [*see middle illustration on following page*] and then turns off altogether until it recovers. A network of this kind can also produce sustained oscillations consisting of successive bursts of activity alternating with periods of silence without any patterned input. Thus either reciprocal inhibition or mutual excitation can give rise to the general type of burst pattern seen in locust motor units. Both mechanisms have been demonstrated in various behavior-control systems. It is likely that both are working in the locust and that these two mechanisms, as well as others, converge to produce a pattern of greater stability than might otherwise be achieved.

In summary, the model suggests that each group of cooperating nerve cells is mutually excitatory, so that the units of each group tend to fire together and produce bursts of activity even when their input is steady. In addition the two sets are connected to each other by inhibitory linkages that set the two populations into alternation. Notice that in these hypothetical networks the temporal pattern of activity is due to the network structure, not to the pattern of the input. Even the silent network stores most of the information needed to produce the output pattern.

The locust flight-control system consists in large part of a particular kind of circuit built into the central ganglia. Some other locomotory systems seem much more influenced by reflex inputs. As an example of such a system I shall describe briefly the walking pattern of the tarantula spider. There is much variation in the relative timing of the eight legs of this animal, but on the average the legs exhibit what is called a diagonal rhythm. Opposite legs of one segment alternate and adjacent legs on one side alternate so that diagonal pairs of legs are in step [*see illustration on page 139*].

The tarantula can lose several of its legs and still walk. Suppose the first and third pairs of legs are amputated. If the spider's legs were coordinated by means of a simple preprogrammed circuit like the one controlling the locust's flight muscles, one would expect the spider to move the remaining two legs on one side

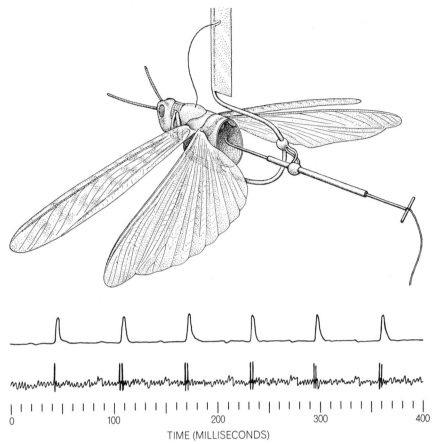

SENSORY DISCHARGES in nerves from the wing and wing hinge are recorded with wires manipulated into the largely eviscerated thoracic cavity of a locust. The top record is of downstroke muscle potentials, which are repeating at the wingbeat frequency. The bottom record is of a sensory (stretch) receptor from one wing, firing one or two times per wingbeat.

in step with each other and out of step with the legs on the other side. A four-legged spider that did this would fall over. In actuality the spider adjusts relations between the remaining legs to achieve the diagonal rhythm. Other combinations of amputations give rise to other adaptations that also maintain the mechanically more stable diagonal rhythm.

Thus it appears that the pattern of coordination does depend on input from the legs. One can advance a possible explanation. Each leg is either driven by a purely central nervous oscillator or each leg and its portion of ganglion forms an oscillating reflex feedback loop. Suppose the several oscillators are negatively coupled. A pair of matched negatively coupled oscillators will operate out of phase. If the nearest leg oscillators are negatively coupled more strongly than the ones farther apart, the normal diagonal rhythm will result. For example, if left leg 1 has a strong tendency to alternate with right leg 1 and right leg 1 alternates with right leg 2, then left leg 1 must operate synchronously with right leg 2, to which it is more weakly con-

nected. Now if some of the oscillators are turned off by amputating legs, so that either the postulated oscillatory feedback loop is broken or the postulated central oscillator receives insufficient excitatory input, new patterns of leg movements will appear that will always exhibit a diagonal rhythm.

The real nature of the oscillators involved in the leg rhythms is not known. These results and the postulated model nonetheless illustrate how sensory feedback could be used by the nervous system in such a way that the animal could adjust to genetically unpredictable conditions of the body or environment without recourse to learning mechanisms. Could this be the role of reflexes in general? We have seen that in the locust flight system much information for pattern generation is centrally stored—presumably having been provided genetically—and that the reflexes do seem to supply only information that could not have been known genetically.

A way to describe the two general models of muscle-control systems has been suggested by Graham Hoyle of the University of Oregon. He calls the cen-

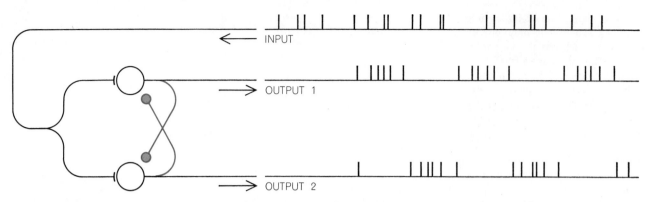

CROSS INHIBITION is one kind of interaction between nerve cells. The cells are connected in such a way that impulses from one inhibit the other (*color*). This can cause a pattern of alternating bursts, each cell firing (inhibiting the other) until fatigued. The hypothetical network shows how an unpatterned input can be transformed into a patterned output by structurally coded information.

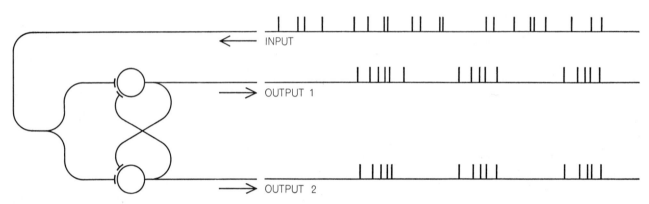

IN CROSS EXCITATION the output from each cell excites the other. This makes for approximate synchrony. There may also be a positive feedback "runaway" until fatigue causes deceleration or a pause; once rested, the network begins another accelerating burst.

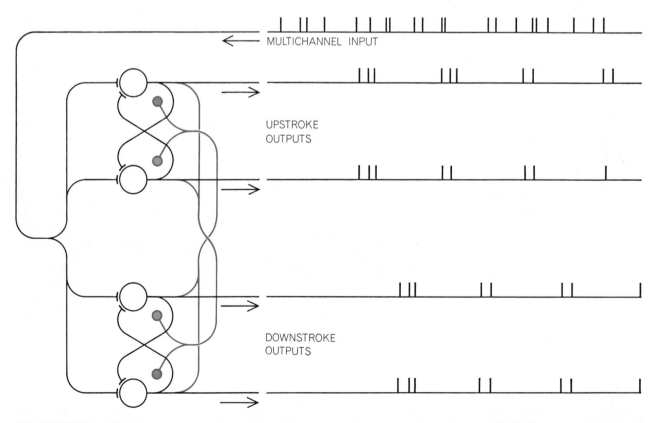

HYPOTHETICAL NETWORK of nerve cells in the locust might involve two cell populations, an upstroke group (*top*) and a downstroke group (*bottom*). Cells *within* a group excite one another but there are inhibitory connections *between* groups (*color*). The inhibition keeps the activity of one group out of phase with that of the other, so that upstroke and downstroke muscles alternate.

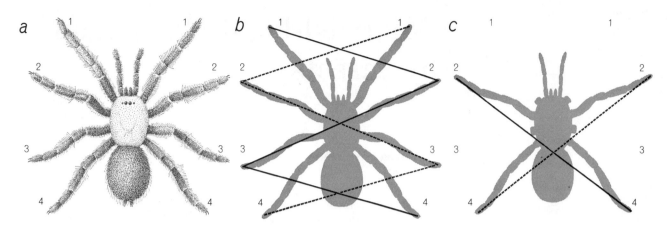

LEGS OF TARANTULA (*a*) move in diagonally arranged groups of four (*b*). The diagonal pattern persists if some legs are removed (*c*), suggesting that proprioceptive reflexes set the pattern or that changed input alters inherent central nervous system activity.

trally stored system of pattern generation a motor-tape system. In such a system a preprogrammed "motor score" plays in a stereotyped manner whenever it is excited. For a system in which reflexes significantly modify the behavioral sequences, Hoyle suggests the term "sensory tape" system. I prefer the term "sensory template." Such systems have a preprogrammed input requirement that can be achieved by various outputs. If the output at any moment results in an input that does not match the template, the mismatch results in a changed output pattern until the difference disappears. Such a goal-oriented feedback system can adapt to unexpected environments or to bodily damage. Spider and insect walking patterns show a kind of plasticity in which new movement patterns can compensate for the loss of limbs. In the past this kind of plasticity has often been interpreted as evidence for the reflex control of locomotory pattern. The locust flight-control system, on the other hand, certainly has a motor score that is not organized as a set of reflexes. Can a motor-score system show the plastic behavior usually associated with reflex, or sensory-template, systems?

For several years we thought that the locust flight-control system was relatively unplastic. We knew about the control of wingbeat frequency by the stretch reflex and about other reflexes, for example a reflex that tends to keep the body's angle of pitch constant. When I had made recordings of nerve impulses to some important control muscles before and after cutting out other muscles or whole wings, however, I had not found differences in the motor output. I therefore concluded that the flight-control system was not capable of a wide range of adaptive behavior. On this basis one

would predict that a damaged locust could not fly, or could fly only in circles.

The locust has four wings. Recently I cut whole wings from several locusts, threw the locusts into the air and found to my surprise that they flew quite well. The flying locust shows just as much ability to adapt to the loss of a limb as a walking insect or spider does. For the crippled locust to fly it must significantly change its motor output pattern. Why did the locust not show this change in the experiments in which I made recordings of nerve impulses to its muscles?

In all the laboratory experiments the locust was approximately fixed in space. If the insect made a motor error, it might sense the error proprioceptively, but it could not receive a feedback signal from the environment around it indicating that it was off course. The free-flying locust has at least two extraproprioceptive sources of feedback about its locomotory progress: signals from its visual system and signals from directionally sensitive hairs on its head that respond to the flow of air. Either or both of these extraproprioceptive sources can tell the locust that it is turning in flight. In the free-flying locust the signals are involved in a negative feedback control that tends to keep the animal flying straight in spite of functional or anatomical errors in the insect's basic motor system. When animals are studied in the laboratory under conditions that do allow motor output errors or anatomical damage to produce turning motions, then compensatory changes in the motor output pattern are observed provided only that the appropriate sensory structures are intact.

The locust flight-control system consists in part of a built-in motor score, but it also shows the adaptability expected of a reflex, or sensory-template, type of control. From these observations on plasticity in the locust flight system one

can see that there may be no such thing as a pure motor-tape or a pure sensory-template system. Many behavior systems probably have some features of each.

What we are striving for in studies such as the ones I have reported here is a way of understanding the functioning of networks of nerve cells that control animal behavior. Neurophysiologists have already acquired wide knowledge about single nerve cells—how their impulses code messages and how the synapses transmit and integrate the messages. Much is also known about the electrical behavior and chemistry of large masses of nerve cells in the brains of animals. The intermediate level, involving networks of tens or hundreds of nerve cells, remains little explored. This is an area in which many neurobiologists will probably be working in the next few years. I suspect that it is an area in which important problems are ripe for solution.

I shall conclude with a few remarks on the unraveling of the mechanisms of genetically coded behavior. As I see it, there are two major stages in the readout of genetically coded behavioral information. The first stage is the general process of development of bodily form, including the detailed form of the networks of the central nervous system and the form of peripheral body parts, such as muscles and sense organs that are involved in the reflexes. This stage of the genetic readout is not limited to neurobiology, of course. It is a stage that will probably be analyzed largely at the molecular level. The second stage involves a problem that is primarily neurobiological: How can information that is coded in the grosser level of nervous-system structure, in the shapes of whole nerve cells and networks of nerve cells, be translated into temporal sequences of behavior?

15

Polarized-Light Navigation by Insects

by Rüdiger Wehner
July 1976

Experiments demonstrate that bees and ants find their way home by the polarization of the light of the sky. The detection system insects have evolved for the purpose is remarkably sophisticated

The eyes of insects are sensitive to a natural phenomenon that man is blind to: the polarized light of the daytime sky. It is this capacity that underlies the remarkable navigational ability of many insect species. Exactly how can an insect navigate by polarized light? To ask this question is really to raise three separate questions: What makes the visual cell of an insect sensitive to polarized light? How do some minimum number of visual cells cooperate to determine the direction of polarization at one point in the sky? How much information from how many points in the sky does the insect need for unambiguous navigation?

The light radiated by the sun is unpolarized, that is, its waves vibrate in all directions at right angles to the line of sight. In traveling through the earth's atmosphere, however, it is scattered by molecules and other particles that are small with respect to the wavelength of light, so that at each point in the sky its waves tend to vibrate in a specific direction. This atmospheric polarization was first described by Lord Rayleigh in 1871, but it was not until 1950 that it was given a full theoretical analysis by S. Chandrasekhar of the University of Chicago. More recently a computer analysis has been developed by Zdenek Sekera and his colleagues at the University of California at Los Angeles. Their program makes it possible to specify both the directions and the degrees of polarization for all points in the sky, for different atmospheric conditions and for spectral wavelengths ranging from the infrared to the ultraviolet.

The pattern of polarization in the sky varies with the position of the sun or, more exactly, with the orientation of the plane of a triangle formed by the sun, the observer and the point observed [*see top illustration on page 143*]. At any point on the celestial sphere the direction of polarization is always perpendicular to the plane of such a triangle. By disregarding a few exceptions and applying this general rule to all points in the sky one can determine the entire pattern of polarization for any given position of the sun.

The general rule for the polarization of light by the atmosphere is easily demonstrated by making photographs of the sky with a 180-degree "fish-eye" lens fitted with a polarizing filter. Consider a pair of photographs that are taken just as the sun reaches the horizon [*see upper illustration on page 142*]. When the polarizing axis of the filter is parallel to the solar meridian (the arc connecting the sun and the zenith), a broad dark stripe runs across the celestial hemisphere at right angles to the solar meridian; the center of the stripe is 90 degrees away from the sun. When instead the polarizing axis of the filter is perpendicular to the solar meridian, no such stripe is evident. The presence of the stripe in the first instance is a function of the direction of skylight polarization at sunrise and sunset; the maximum polarization is found 90 degrees away from the sun. The pattern of polarization shifts around the celestial hemisphere as the sun moves across the sky; this too can be documented by successive fish-eye-lens photographs.

The ability of honeybees to navigate by the polarized light of the sky was first described some 25 years ago by Karl von Frisch. His finding came as a surprise; even though the polarization of skylight had been known since the 19th century, no one had really considered the possibility that the phenomenon could serve any navigational purpose. It has recently been learned, however, that about the year 1000 the Vikings were taking advantage of the polarization of skylight in their voyages west from

LONG-LEGGED ANT (*Cataglyphis bicolor*) of the North African desert was used by the author and his students in their studies of polarized-light navigation by insects. The ant forages until it finds food and then runs straight back to its nest. It can be trained for experimental purposes by rewarding it with a small piece of cheese. This ant holds cheese in its mandibles.

Iceland and Greenland to Newfoundland. The Danish archaeologist Thorkild Ramskou has pointed out that the "sunstones" described in the old sagas were nothing other than birefringent and dichroic crystals that could serve as polarization analyzers.

As I write this article I have on my table a small crystal of cordierite. When I look through it at any point in the sky, I can determine the direction of polarization by observing the changes of color and brightness as I rotate the crystal around the line of sight. Some years ago an airplane was steered with fair precision from Norway to Sondre Storm Fjord airfield in Greenland with a cordierite crystal as the only navigational aid. These crystals can be found as pebbles on the coast of Norway. Although it is unlikely that the Vikings knew anything about polarized light, they apparently perceived the relation between what they saw through a sunstone and the position of the sun (which was often hidden by clouds in those northern latitudes).

There are no polarizing crystals in the eye of insects. The eye of the members of another major group of arthropods—the now extinct marine trilobites—did have hundreds of lenses consisting of the highly birefringent crystal calcite, but the crystals were arranged in such a way that they could not have acted as polarization analyzers. Of course, that does not exclude the possibility that the trilobites were able to use the polarization of skylight for orientation in their marine habitat; Talbot H. Waterman of

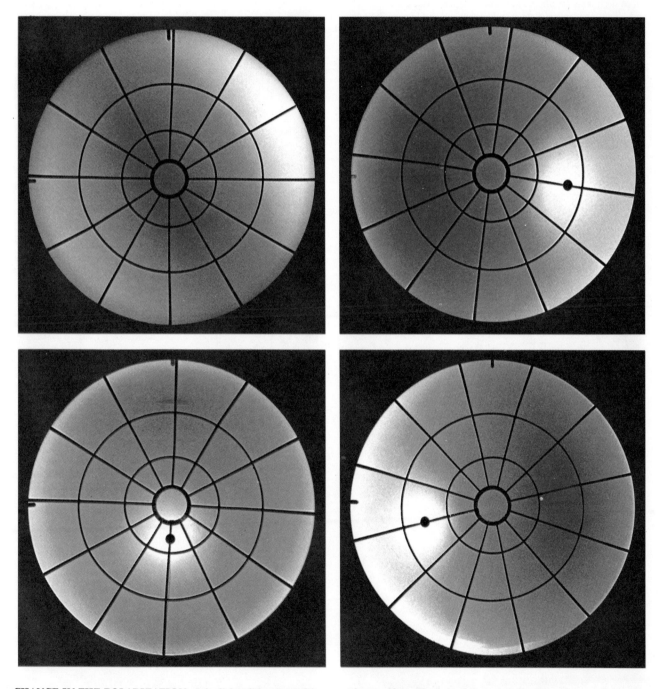

CHANGE IN THE POLARIZATION of the light of the sky at different times of the day is shown in this sequence of photographs made with a 180-degree "fish-eye" lens and a polarizing filter. The photographs, made on May 17, 1975, near Kairouan in Tunisia, were exposed at 5:15 A.M. (*top left*), 9:05 A.M. (*top right*), 12:30 P.M. (*bottom left*) and 3:40 P.M. (*bottom right*). A small black screen masks the sun in all the photographs but the first one; the screen also identifies the solar meridian. The axis of the polarizing filter was parallel to the solar meridian in all four photographs. At dawn maximum polarization (*dark region*), located 90 degrees from the sun, is centered in the sky. After sunrise the dark area shifts to the west. At the sun's maximum elevation in the southern sky the dark area shifts to the north; as the sun descends the dark area shifts around to the east. The two marks that appear on the horizon in the photograph indicate north and west.

Yale University has shown that the skylight visible to underwater organisms, like that visible to organisms that live above the water or on land, is polarized. It only means that the lenses were not analyzers located in front of the visual cells. The same is true of insects. Where, then, are the structures in insects that are sensitive to polarized light?

It is now generally agreed that the structures are located within the visual cells themselves. The ability of the visual cells to analyze the axial orientation of the polarized light is the result of a molecular oddity. In all animals, invertebrates and vertebrates alike, the visual pigment rhodopsin is pres-

ent in the photoreceptor membrane of the visual cells in the form of dipolar molecules, that is, molecules with a distinct axis. As a result the pigment absorbs a maximum of the incoming polarized-light energy when the direction of polarization is parallel to the dipole axis of the molecule.

In insects the photoreceptor membranes are bent into arrays of narrow tubes, the microvilli [see illustration on page 144]. Timothy H. Goldsmith of Yale and I have come to the conclusion, based on spectroscopic studies we conducted together at the Marine Biological Laboratory in Woods Hole, Mass., that the rhodopsin molecules

in the microvillar membrane are preferentially aligned parallel to the axis of the microvilli. Such an orientation would of course result in the maximum absorption of polarized light when, and only when, the axis of polarization coincided with the microvillar axis. (This, incidentally, is part of the reason the human eye is blind to polarized skylight. Among vertebrates, man included, the rhodopsin molecules are free to rotate in the photoreceptor membrane, so that their axial orientation is random. There is an equal chance that any pigment molecule will maximally absorb light with any direction of polarization, and so there is

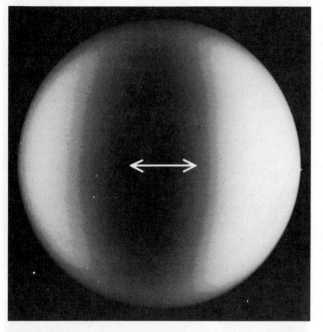

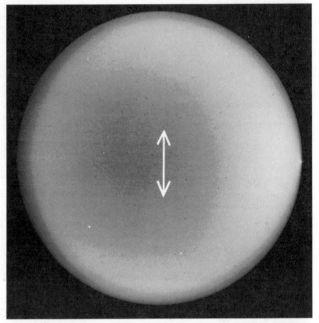

MAXIMUM POLARIZATION, demonstrated (left) with a fish-eye photograph of the dawn sky, is evident when the transmission axis of the polarizing filter is parallel to the solar meridian. When the axis is perpendicular (right), however, variation in intensity disappears.

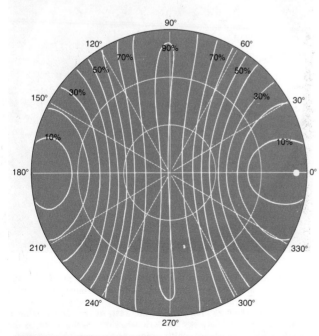

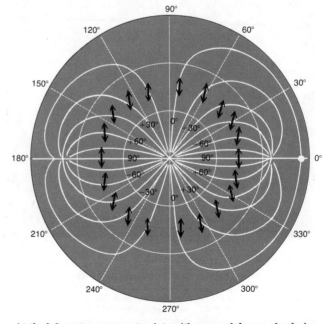

DEGREE OF POLARIZATION (left) and direction of polarization (right) at dawn are shown in these graphs of the celestial hemisphere. At the left contours connect points with an equal degree of polarization. At right arrows on contours indicate direction of polarization.

no particular sensitivity to the polarization of skylight.)

The common orientation of the rhodopsin molecules in the insect's photoreceptor membrane is not in itself enough to allow the analysis of skylight polarization, just as one kind of color receptor is not enough to allow color vision. Different kinds of receptors, each maximally sensitive to a different direction of polarization, must work together in order to enable the detecting system to provide unambiguous results for any direction of polarization. For example, the system must be proof against confusion arising from fluctuations in mean light intensity, degree of polarization and hue of color. But how many receptors are enough? Here we suspected that the principle of parsimony might apply. The number of receptors could be held to a minimum if only one type of color receptor was involved: the ultraviolet receptor, the blue receptor or the green receptor. If two of these types of receptor or all three contributed to polarized-light analysis, more receptors would have to cooperate and more neural circuitry would be needed. Hence natural selection should strongly favor a system that receives its input from only one type of color receptor. What, then, are the spectral wavelengths involved in the perception of polarized light? This question could be most conclusively answered by behavioral experiments.

Bees are only one of many kinds of insects that have been shown to navigate by the polarization of skylight. Ants also do so, and my students and I at the University of Zurich have used both bees and ants as experimental animals in our studies. In most of our experiments a desert ant native to North Africa, the species *Cataglyphis bicolor,* has been the preferred animal for several reasons. First of all, it is difficult enough to follow a flying bee over any great distance, but to keep a polarizer or any other optical equipment in place above a bee as it flies is impossible. The desert ant is a running forager, but it rarely runs faster than 20 meters a minute, which is less than a mile an hour. This enables the experimenter to record the ant's navigational courses in full detail and at the same time to continuously interpose between the animal and the sky almost any kind of optical equipment.

In addition the desert ant is a solitary hunter; it never forages en masse along a scout's scent trail as so many other ant species do. Its desert habitat is notably lacking in conspicuous landmarks, so that the ant must rely almost exclusively on skylight cues to guide it on its forays. A typical *Cataglyphis* excursion of the kind we have often recorded begins when the ant leaves its underground nest. The ant then meanders, covering a distance that may be equivalent to the length of a football field, until it captures prey. After that it runs straight back to the nest.

When I first observed these long-legged ants eight years ago, I was fascinated both by the extraordinary precision of their orientation and by their remarkable learning

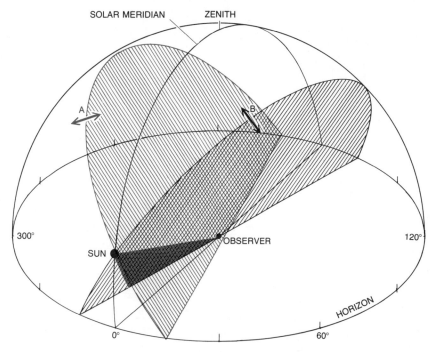

AXIS OF POLARIZATION (*short two-headed arrows*) of the light of the sky is always perpendicular to the plane of a triangle connecting the observer (*center*), the sun and the point in the sky being observed. The examples shown are for the points *A* and *B* on the celestial hemisphere. The planes of the great circles passing through the sun and each of the two points are hatched. Also shown is the solar meridian: the great circle passing through sun and the zenith.

capacity. Individual ants were easily trained to travel in a given direction for a given distance by rewarding them with a tiny piece of cheese. For experimental purposes we would transport the trained ants to a remote testing area, carrying them in individual lightproof flasks. The testing area, a hard sandy plain, was painted with a grid of fine white lines, a coordinate system that enabled us to record the ants' running courses on a reduced scale for later statistical analysis.

When each trained ant was released, it would set off in the home direction. It

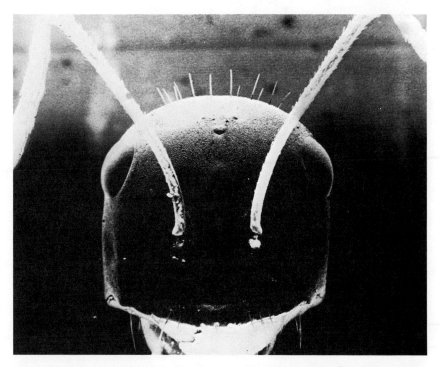

HEAD OF THE DESERT ANT is seen from the front in this scanning electron micrograph. Projecting upward from the front of the head are the antennae. At the left and right side of the head are the eyes. The fine pattern visible on the surface of the eyes is the ommatidia: the subunits into which the insect eye is divided. Each eye of desert ant is made up of 1,200 ommatidia.

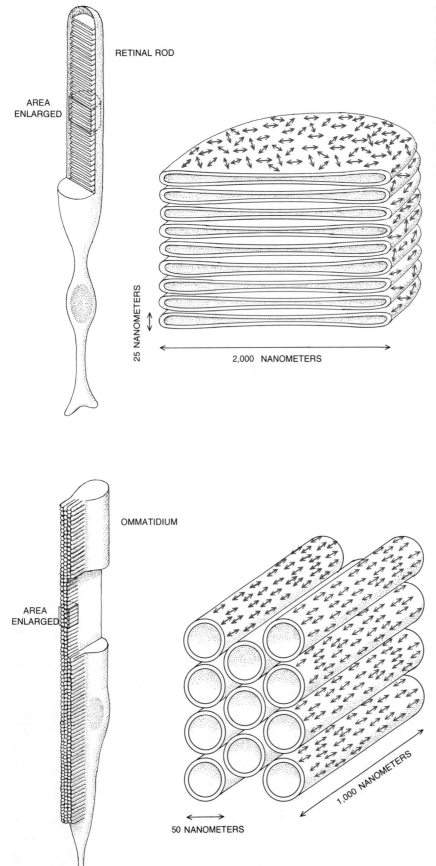

VISUAL CELLS of vertebrates (*top*) and invertebrates (*bottom*) differ in arrangement of photoreceptor membrane and orientation of molecules of visual pigment rhodopsin within membrane. In vertebrates axes of rhodopsin molecules (*color*) are randomly oriented; in insects they are parallel to long axis of tubelike microvilli. This maximizes absorption of polarized light.

RETINAL ROD

AREA ENLARGED

25 NANOMETERS

2,000 NANOMETERS

OMMATIDIUM

AREA ENLARGED

1,000 NANOMETERS

50 NANOMETERS

would travel the distance to which it had been trained and then start to circle at the place where the nest was supposed to be. (The actual nest might have been more than a mile away, where the ant had been trained.) On its journey back from the releasing point the ant was accompanied by a small vehicle loaded with optical equipment: neutral-density filters, spectral-cutoff filters, polarizers, depolarizers, retardation plates and so on. These and many similar open-field experiments could not have been accomplished without the enthusiastic cooperation of my graduate students. I am particularly indebted to Peter Duelli (who constructed the vehicle and developed considerable skill in piloting it), Immanuel Flatt, Res Burkhalter (who is now working at the Brain Research Institute in Zurich) and Reto Weiler of the University of Munich.

In order to discover what spectral wavelengths were utilized in skylight navigation we forced the running ants to view the sky through filters of various colors. We were surprised to find that their ability to detect polarized light disappeared completely at wavelengths greater than 410 nanometers; those wavelengths include the entire range of wavelengths visible to man. In light of that spectral range the ants ran in random directions. When we extended the spectral range only a little way into the ultraviolet, however, the ants' navigational accuracy was completely restored.

We concluded from this finding that only those visual cells in the ant's eye that are responsive to ultraviolet wavelengths are involved in the perception of polarized light. This can readily be confirmed by comparing the spectral-transmission functions of the filters with the spectral-sensitivity function of the ultraviolet receptor as measured electrophysiologically. Recently Otto von Helversen and Wolfgang Edrich of the University of Freiburg have shown that in bees too the ultraviolet receptors are the only ones involved in the detection of polarized light.

It is easy to understand why natural selection has made the ultraviolet receptors the input channel for an orientation signal. The use of only one type of receptor conforms with the principle of parsimony by holding the input channels down to three, which, as we shall see, is the minimum number. That the type of receptor selected was sensitive to ultraviolet instead of, say, green or blue can be regarded as an adaptation to a purely physical fact: it is in the ultraviolet range of wavelengths that the polarization of skylight is least affected by atmospheric disturbances and is therefore the most stable.

Let us now turn to the second question and consider the insect eye in somewhat more detail. How do the ultraviolet receptors cooperate in detecting polarized light? As is well known, insects have compound, multifaceted eyes. Each eye is composed of hundreds or thousands of the subunits known as ommatidia. Our desert ant's eye has 1,200 ommatidia; a worker bee's eye has 5,500. Each subunit has its own lens system, and underneath the lens are elongated visual cells that contain the densely packed tubular microvilli where the rhodopsin molecules are located. The microvilli are arranged so as to meet and form a central structure, the rhabdom, which functions as a light guide [see illustration below].

There are nine visual cells in each ommatidium. Eight of them are elongated and the ninth is foreshortened. Thus whereas the microvilli of the eight long cells contribute to the rhabdom along its total length, the contribution of the short ninth cell is confined to the lower end of the structure. From a number of independent electrophysiological and neuroanatomical studies one can draw the conclusion that in bees and ants three of the nine cells in each ommatidium are ultraviolet receptors: the

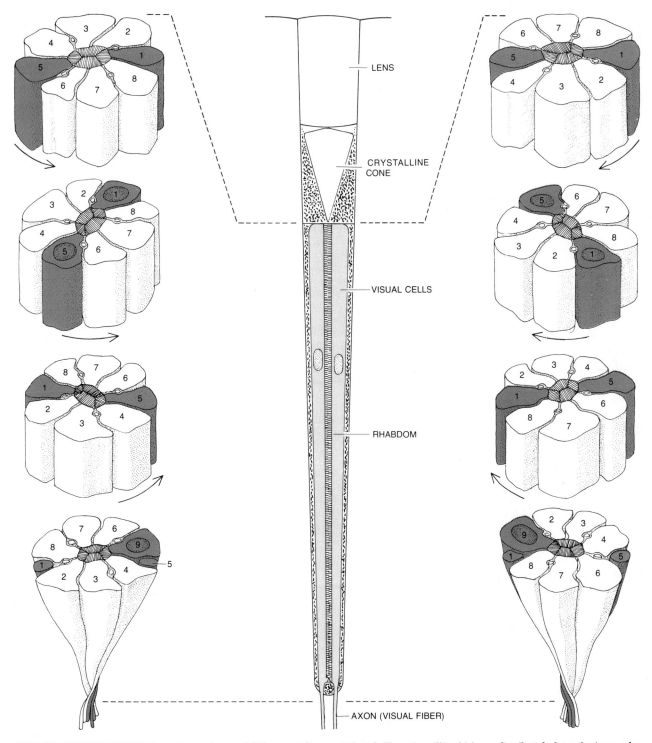

EYE OF THE HONEYBEE is made up of some 5,500 ommatidia, each consisting of nine visual cells and an overlying optical apparatus: a lens and a crystalline cone (center). Eight of the visual cells are elongated; the ninth is short and is confined to the base of the ommatidium. All nine of the cells are twisted. Half of the ommatidia in the bee's eye are twisted clockwise and half are twisted counterclockwise (left and right); the two kinds of ommatidium are randomly distributed. The microvilli, which are distributed along the inner edge of each cell, jointly form a central structure, the rhabdom; its membranes incorporate the rhodopsin molecules. Because two of the three visual cells that are sensitive to ultraviolet radiation (color) are twisted 180 degrees their preferential sensitivity to polarized light has been lost. The third cell, however, is the short cell; since it is twisted only about 40 degrees, it has retained sensitivity to polarized light.

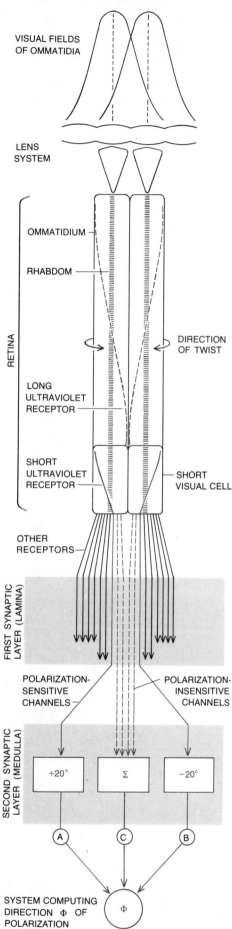

VISUAL FIELDS
OF OMMATIDIA

LENS
SYSTEM

OMMATIDIUM

RHABDOM

RETINA

DIRECTION
OF TWIST

LONG
ULTRAVIOLET
RECEPTOR

SHORT
ULTRAVIOLET
RECEPTOR

SHORT
VISUAL CELL

OTHER
RECEPTORS

FIRST SYNAPTIC
LAYER (LAMINA)

POLARIZATION-
SENSITIVE
CHANNELS

POLARIZATION-
INSENSITIVE
CHANNELS

SECOND SYNAPTIC
LAYER (MEDULLA)

+20°   Σ   −20°

A   C   B

SYSTEM COMPUTING
DIRECTION Φ OF
POLARIZATION

Φ

short receptor and two of the long ones. Among the workers who contributed to this conclusion are F. G. Gribakin of the U.S.S.R. Academy of Sciences, Randolf Menzel and Allan W. Snyder of the Australian National University, Hansjochem Autrum and Gertrud Kolb of the University of Munich and ourselves at the University of Zurich. Of particular note was Menzel's demonstration by intracellular recordings that the short visual cell of bees is an ultraviolet receptor.

We had started with the assumption that the most elegant system for the perception of polarized light would involve only one type of color receptor, most efficiently the ultraviolet receptor. It was satisfying to have this assumption confirmed. We were nonetheless startled by its implications, because we knew that at any given cross section of the ommatidium the microvillar orientation of the three ultraviolet receptors coincided. This meant that they could provide the analyzing system with only one input channel. Since more than one channel is needed for detecting polarization, more than one ommatidium must be involved. The question was: How many are involved?

At that time Kuno Kirschfeld of the Max Planck Institute for Biological Cybernetics in Tübingen had just proposed a theoretical model according to which three receptors with three different microvillar directions had to cooperate. When my student Esther Geiger and I looked at cross sections over fairly extensive areas of the bee's retina, however, we could not find the three necessary sets of ultraviolet receptors, which should be characterized by different microvillar directions. Furthermore, it had never

been proved beyond any doubt that the microvilli of one visual cell were really aligned parallel to one another along the entire length of the cell. The sensitivity of the cell to polarized light should nonetheless depend critically on such an alignment.

As we were working on a three-dimensional reconstruction of the ommatidia in the eye of the bee, a striking feature caught our attention and turned it in a new direction. It turns out that all rhabdoms are twisted. The twist extends the full length of the structure and amounts to about one degree per micrometer. In an elongated cell the twist totals 180 degrees from top to bottom. The twist is either clockwise or counterclockwise. Twists in each direction occur with equal frequency, and ommatidia enclosing rhabdoms twisted each way are randomly distributed in the insect's eye.

Recently Gary D. Bernard of the Yale Medical School and I conducted an optical analysis of the twisted rhabdoms. We discovered that the 180-degree twist deprives the two long ultraviolet-receptive visual cells of any sensitivity to polarized light. The short cell, however, is twisted only some 40 degrees, and so it is not severely deprived of its sensitivity to polarized light. Moreover, half of the short cells are twisted 40 degrees to the right and the other half 40 degrees to the left, so that their directions for maximum sensitivity do not coincide but are at an angle of 35 to 40 degrees. This means that any two short cells of opposite twist are perfectly designed to act as two independent polarization analyzers.

On the basis of these data we have constructed a simple theoretical model explaining how the eye of the insect analyzes the direction of skylight polarization. In brief, the model indicates that if two polarization

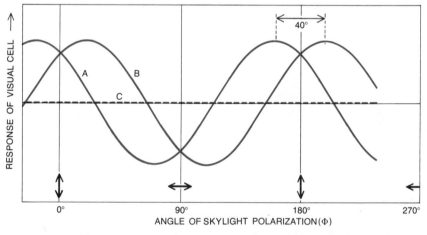

POLARIZATION-DETECTING SYSTEM of the honeybee is depicted schematically. The ultraviolet receptors of two adjacent ommatidia, one twisting clockwise and the other counterclockwise, are sufficient for the detection of any direction of polarization. Both ommatidia scan nearly the same small patch of the sky, less than five degrees in diameter. In the two ommatidia three types of ultraviolet receptors have to cooperate: polarization-insensitive cells (*signal C*) and two independent polarization-sensitive cells (*signals A and B*). This set of cells can unambiguously detect any direction of polarization (Φ). The directions of maximum sensitivity of the two polarization-sensitive cells differ by about 40 degrees, as is shown by the curves at the right. The nerve fibers extending from the ultraviolet receptors extend through the first of the insect's two visual ganglia (the lamina) to the second (the medulla). The nerve fibers extending from the receptors sensitive to green and blue light rather than to ultraviolet end in lamina.

analyzers of opposite twist work together with at least one long ultraviolet-sensitive cell that is insensitive to the polarization of skylight, then the orientation of the skylight polarization anywhere overhead can be determined unambiguously. Hence any two adjacent ommatidia of opposite twist are equipped with all three of the necessary cells and will provide the analyzing system with all three of the necessary signals: two independent signals that are modulated by polarized skylight and one signal that is not. The unmodulated signal is identical for all the long ultraviolet receptors of the two ommatidia.

The twist of the rhabdoms was surprising at first. After all, a straight alignment of the microvilli had always been considered a prerequisite for the analysis of polarized light. We have come to realize not only that analysis is possible in spite of the twist but also that the twist is exploited in the analytical process. On the one hand the twist ensures that the one long cell of the three is an input channel free of sensitivity to skylight polarization. On the other it ensures that the axes of the microvilli in the two polarization-sensitive input channels point in two different directions.

A skilled engineer could hardly design a simpler and more elegant system. Menzel and his colleague Margaret Blakers, working at the Technische Hochschule in Darmstadt, have found that the eye of a large hunting ant, the bulldog ant of Australia, has the same two kinds of oppositely twisted rhabdoms. Thus it appears that the eyes of ants as well as those of bees have a set of ultraviolet-receptive visual cells that are specially adapted to the strategy of detecting the polarization of skylight.

To recapitulate, any system that is capable of unambiguously analyzing polarized light with only one type of color receptor has to be fed by three independent receptors. That is because any state of partially polarized light as it is analyzed by an insect can be completely described by three independent numbers: direction of polarization, degree of polarization and mean intensity. If all three receptors are sensitive to polarized light, they have to show maximum sensitivity in different directions. In an insect's eye this would mean that three ultraviolet receptors with different microvillar directions would have to cooperate. In the bee, however, only two of these polarization-sensitive receptors function. Since their directions of maximum sensitivity are neither parallel nor crossed, they have only to cooperate with a polarization-insensitive receptor, a long twisted ultraviolet receptor cell, to get all the information on a given state of polarization. There are several reasons why the system with two polarization-sensitive receptors is more advantageous than the system with three. One reason, to which I shall return, is that the long twisted ultraviolet receptor can also contribute to color vision without introducing a polarization-sensitive signal into that system.

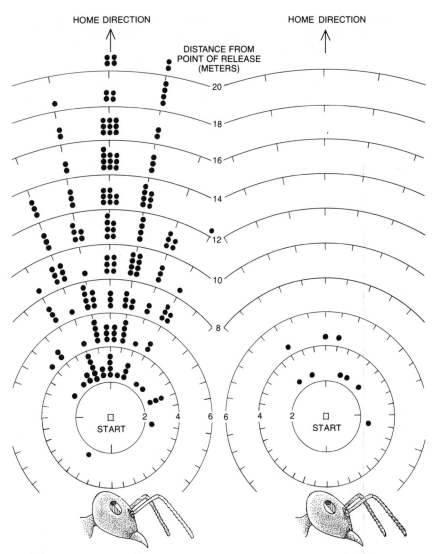

LOCATION OF OMMATIDIA in the desert ant's eye that perceive polarized ultraviolet radiation was confirmed experimentally by covering parts of ants' eyes with opaque paint. At the bottom are the heads of two experimental ants. The ommatidia that are sensitive to polarized ultraviolet radiation are at the upper front part of the eye (*small spot of color*). When the rear third of the eye was covered with paint (*hatching*), the ants' navigational ability was scarcely affected (*diagram at left*). Ants released at the starting point were found at various distances (*black dots*) along the way home. When the front third of the eye was covered, however, only a few of the ants went beyond the circle two meters from starting point, and none passed six-meter circle (*diagram at right*). Ants that remained within two-meter circle were not recorded.

The eyes of ants and bees, with their large number of ommatidia, simultaneously scan many different parts of the celestial hemisphere. And as we have seen, the light from the celestial hemisphere is differently polarized at different points in the sky. Neither insect, however, seems to have a nervous system complex enough to process signals from thousands of points in the sky. How many of these ultraviolet receptors are actually used for navigation, and which ones are they? We sought answers to these questions in two different ways. One was to cover specific regions of an ant's eyes with opaque paint and then observe its behavior. The other was to add a device to our tracking vehicle that enabled us to restrict the ant's view of the sky to one part or another of its normal visual field. Both approaches soon

demonstrated to our satisfaction that the part of the compound eye utilized by our desert ants for the detection of polarization is a small region near the upper edge of the eye. This specialized area is physically apparent from above the ant's eye as a small depression in the array of ommatidium lenses. Moreover, my former graduate student Paul L. Herrling has examined the structure of the visual cells of the ant and has found a completely different type of rhabdom near the upper edge of the eye.

The ant's dependence on the signals from this specialized area is dramatic. Insects can move their eyes only by moving their heads. When we blacked out the lower part of an ant's visual field (by inserting a screen in the device on our tracking vehicle), its behavior was unaffected until the blackout reached the lower edge of the area specialized for polarized-light perception. Then each upward shift of the screen was matched by a compensating upward tilt of the ant's head. As the screen was moved upward toward the zenith, a point was reached where the ant could not lift its head any higher; it would then turn a backward somersault, ending the experiment. By motion-picture analysis of the head positions we were able to plot the dimensions of that part of the eye which is concerned with the detection of polarized light.

In mapping the areas of the eye that play a role in skylight navigation we arrived at a further conclusion: In both ants and bees fewer than 10 ommatidia in the upper part of the eye are enough for the detection of polarization. So far our results do not allow us to judge whether the theoretical minimum predicted by our model—two adjacent ommatidia of opposite twist—might suffice or whether several pairs of ommatidia must cooperate to provide the precision necessary for navigation.

Here the last of the three questions arises. If an insect can unambiguously determine the direction of polarization at any point in the sky, does this ability in itself guarantee that the insect can navigate unambiguously? The answer is no. The one would unerringly lead to the other only if every point in the sky had its own exclusive direction of polarization. Such is not the case; any given direction of polarization is found at many different points in the sky.

How does the insect cope with this complicated and potentially ambiguous situation? It is hard to believe that the information about all the directions of polarization varying between different positions in the sky and different times of day are stored in

an insect's brain. Most likely the insect applies a general rule. What is that rule?

Let us consider some possibilities. There is one point in the sky the insect can always view regardless of whether it is moving north, south, east or west. That point is the zenith. According to the general rule of skylight polarization outlined above, the solar meridian (the arc through the sun and the zenith) extends at right angles to the direction of polarization in the zenith. Therefore, knowing that direction, the insect knows the position of the solar meridian in the sky. What it needs for an unambiguous decision is merely some means of deciding between both arcs of the solar meridian. Any additional cue that differs between both arcs of the solar meridian could suffice: the degree of polarization, the hue of color or the intensity of ultraviolet radiation in the sky.

Our desert ant, however, does not view the zenith with the region of the eye specialized for skylight navigation, so that a more general possibility has to be considered. If the degree of polarization is sufficiently high, the direction of polarization is parallel to the horizon at every point on the solar meridian. If one proceeds along a circle of given elevation from one arc of the solar meridian to the opposite arc, the direction of polarization first deviates increasingly from the horizontal and then approaches the horizontal again. Does the insect "know" this relation?

In collaboration with Martin Lindauer of the University of Würzburg and my student Samuel Rossel I have tested the hypothesis, using bees as the experimental animal. From a practical point of view it might appear more difficult to perform the appropriate experiments with bees than it is with our desert ants. This would be true if it were not for a behavioral characteristic of bees: the

workers communicate with their fellows, translating the course to be flown to a source of food into the direction of their "waggle dance" inside the hive. The direction of the bee's waggle dance on a horizontal honeycomb coincides with the direction of its foraging flight, provided that the bee can see the sky as it dances. Hence one can confine the bee's vision to certain parts of the sky and observe the effect of this limitation on its capacity to navigate, that is, to dance correctly.

For our experiments we placed a horizontal comb inside a planetarium dome where we could keep the bees from seeing any areas of the outside sky other than the selected ones. The bees had previously been trained to fly in a certain direction and to forage at a distant food source. Each bee was individually marked with a color code. In each test the patch of sky visible to the bee was so small—10 degrees in diameter— that only skylight with a single direction of polarization entered the planetarium.

Under such conditions the bees alternately danced in two directions: in the correct direction and in another direction they had never flown. This is exactly the result one would expect, because in general each direction of polarization is found twice in a circle of given elevation. Since in our experiment the bee was allowed to view only one point in the circle of given elevation, it could not decide between the two different navigational courses indicated by an identical direction of polarization.

Surprisingly, however, the wrong direction as danced by the bee did not coincide with the wrong direction as calculated by the actual distribution of polarization angles in the sky. The mismatch between the expected dance angle and the real dance angle was not accidental but consistent. Even more surprising, we were able to mislead the bees. With the aid of a polarizer we could change the direction of polarization in the point of the sky viewed by the dancing bee. When we changed it to those directions that did not occur in the natural sky at that elevation, the bees nonetheless showed a consistent orientation. What we had expected, of course, was a random orientation. This finding is exciting and may well lead to an overall solution of the insect-navigation problem. We do not yet have all the pieces needed to complete the jigsaw puzzle. All our evidence points, however, to the fact that the bee's brain incorporates a rather generalized and simple representation of the distribution of polarized light in the sky.

Recently Kirschfeld has proposed an elegant means by which the bee could navigate using the direction of polarization in any point of the sky and the elevation of the sun. So far, however, the bee's brain has turned out to be complex enough not to reveal its strategies to the human brain. The fact remains that both bees and ants do navigate successfully. Whereas our experiment demonstrated that ambiguity will disrupt a worker bee's navigation, the disruption

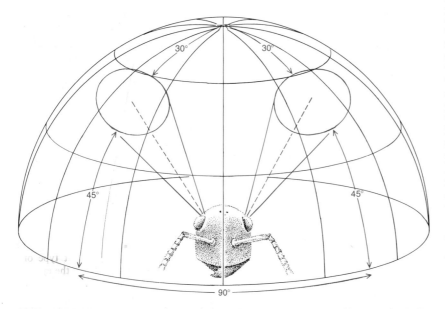

SPECIALIZED EYE REGIONS, consisting of only a few score of the 2,400 ommatidia in the desert ant's two eyes, scan a region of the sky from 45 to 60 degrees above the horizon when the ant is in a normal running position. Each of the specialized regions points in a different direction horizontally; the angle separating the two points of view is approximately 90 degrees.

took place only when the bee's access to skylight was confined to light with a single direction of polarization. This is a highly artificial situation a worker bee is unlikely to encounter with any frequency during its short life. As soon as a bee is able to detect polarized light from more than one point in the sky the situation becomes unambiguous. The bee dances in a single direction only: the correct one.

There is one point in the sky that by itself leads to unambiguity in navigation: the position occupied by the sun. This point lacks polarized light. It is also the brightest point in the sky. When we followed our desert ants after adapting the tracking vehicle so that the entire sky was depolarized, the navigational ability of the ants became very erratic. This happened in spite of the fact that the position occupied by the sun still remained the brightest part of the depolarized sky. One might conclude that whatever the ant's internal representation of the sky may be, the sun may be predominantly recognized as the point of least polarization.

In bees that point has become particularly meaningful. Because bees have developed the abstract language of the dance as a means of telling one another about navigation angles, each individual worker bee must be able to make use of a reference point that is common to all its fellow workers. Moreover, such a common reference point must be uniquely recognizable within the overall pattern of sky polarization. Therefore the position of the sun—the point of zero polarization—is the only point bees could select for unambiguous communication. The importance of the sun as a cue in bee navigation may well have resulted from its lack of polarization rather than from its relative brightness.

W hat choices, so to speak, had to be made in the evolution of the compound eyes of ants and bees for the ability for celestial orientation to develop? I cannot refrain from speculating on the potentialities and constraints inherent in this process. As an initial assumption, let us accept that the three visual cells of each ommatidium that are ultraviolet receptors evolved specifically to allow a navigational capability based on the polarization of skylight. How about the other six visual cells? In running or flying insects an optomotor, or motion-detecting, system monitors the movement of the environment across the entire visual field and serves to stabilize the animal's course. A number of investigators have demonstrated that in bees these systems that keep the insect on a straight course are almost exclusively triggered by the green receptors. Both in bees and in our desert ants the nerve fibers of the green receptors are relatively short, so that they terminate in the first of the insect's two visual ganglia, the lamina. The three ultraviolet receptors, however, have long nerve fibers; they project through the lamina to the second visual ganglion, the medulla. It seems to me most likely that these two separate subsystems,

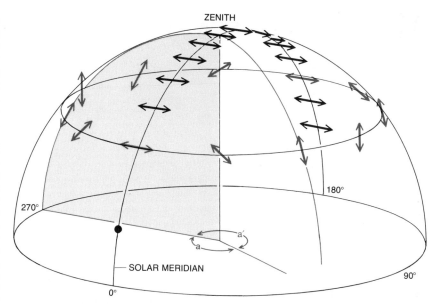

GENERAL PRINCIPLES OF THE POLARIZATION of the light of the sky are outlined. The arrows indicate the directions of polarization as they would be seen by an observer in the center of the hemisphere. Along the solar meridian (the arc through the sun and the zenith) the direction of polarization is parallel to the horizon. Along most circles of a given elevation the direction of polarization varies through all possible angles. Here the angles are plotted for the circle lying roughly halfway between the horizon and the zenith. In general each direction of polarization is found twice at each circle of elevation. (The angles *a* and *a'* denote the angular difference between the positions of identical polarization.) For this reason there is ambiguity in polarized-light navigational cues unless the insect can view more than one part of the sky.

each of which is incapable of detecting colors alone, are the ones that appeared earliest in the evolution of the insect eye. The ultraviolet system, dealing with celestial cues, has been designed to determine the direction of course in long-range orientation. The green system, on the other hand, became involved in the maintenance of course by exploiting the apparent movement of the floating environmental surround.

The green system also has to serve another function: the detection of visual objects in short-range orientation. It is likely that mechanisms for object detection have become increasingly important during the insects' evolutionary history. Whereas there is no need for color vision in celestial navigation and optomotor course control, color vision remarkably improves any mechanism that mediates the detection of objects. For bees the selective advantage of such an advance would probably have expressed itself from mid-Cretaceous times, some 100 million years ago, because it was then that the angiosperm plants, with their conspicuously colored flowers, first appeared. We can postulate an interactive evolutionary process that led on the one hand to the diversification of colors in flowers and on the other to the development of color vision in insects. For color vision to be possible, communication between the green and the ultraviolet channel had to be established. Indeed, the lamina of ants and bees is the site of synaptic connections between the two. In addition visual cells sensitive to light at blue wavelengths evolved, making the bee's color perception trichromatic. The

two blue receptors are most likely derived from two of the original six green receptors. Like the green receptors, the blue receptors have short nerve fibers that terminate in the lamina.

Different selection pressures have acted on the different visual subsystems. Sensitivity to polarized light, the sine qua non of navigation by skylight, is an entirely undesirable property when terrestrial cues need to be analyzed. That is because the polarization that results when light is reflected from terrestrial objects actually blurs the images of the objects, thereby decreasing visual acuity. As we have seen, the twisting of the rhabdom disposes of this disturbing effect for the long ultraviolet receptors; it does the same for the green and blue receptors, which are equally long. It is hard to imagine how evolution could have solved the problem of using a limited number of receptors for quite different sensory performances more efficiently. Color vision is insensitive to polarized light because the rhabdoms are twisted, and polarization vision is insensitive to the hue of color because it is confined to the ultraviolet receptors.

The insect's principal task in navigation is the retention of consecutive dead-reckoning summaries. For example, during an ant's foraging run its brain has to compute all the angles the animal has turned and all the distances it has traversed and to integrate all these vectors continuously. It is on the basis of such continuous integration that the brain is able to calculate the heading enabling the ant to return to its nest on a straight line from any point on its foraging course.

16 Moths and Ultrasound

by Kenneth D. Roeder
April 1965

Certain moths can hear the ultrasonic cries by which bats locate their prey. The news is sent from ear to central nervous system by only two fibers. These can be tapped and the message decoded

If an animal is to survive, it must be able to perceive and react to predators or prey. What nerve mechanisms are used when one animal reacts to the presence of another? Those animals that have a central nervous system perceive the outer world through an array of sense organs connected with the brain by many thousands of nerve fibers. Their reactions are expressed as critically timed sequences of nerve impulses traveling along motor nerve fibers to specific muscles. Exactly how the nervous system converts a particular pattern of sensory input into a specific pattern of motor output remains a subject of investigation in many branches of zoology, physiology and psychology.

Even with the best available techniques one can simultaneously follow the traffic of nerve impulses in only five or perhaps 10 of the many thousands of separate nerve fibers connecting a mammalian sense organ with the brain. Trying to learn how information is encoded and reported among all the fibers by following the activity of so few is akin to basing a public opinion poll on one or two interviews. (Following the activity of all the fibers would of course be like sampling public opinion by having the members of the population give their different answers in chorus.) Advances in technique may eventually make it possible to follow the traffic in thousands of fibers; in the meantime much can be learned by studying animals with less profusely innervated sense organs.

With several colleagues and students at Tufts University I have for some time been trying to decode the sensory patterns connecting the ear and central nervous system of certain nocturnal moths that have only two sense cells in each ear. Much of the behavior of these simple invertebrates is built in, not learned, and therefore is quite stereotyped and stable under experimental conditions. Working with these moths offers another advantage: because they depend on their ears to detect their principal predators, insect-eating bats, we are able to discern in a few cells the nervous mechanisms on which the moth's survival depends.

Insectivorous bats are able to find their prey while flying in complete darkness by emitting a series of ultrasonic cries and locating the direction and distance of sources of echoes. So highly sophisticated is this sonar that it enables the bats to find and capture flying insects smaller than mosquitoes. Some night-flying moths—notably members of the families Noctuidae, Geometridae and Arctiidae—have ears that can detect the bats' ultrasonic cries. When they hear the approach of a bat, these moths take evasive action, abandoning their usual cruising flight to go into sharp dives or erratic loops or to fly at top speed directly away from the source of ultrasound. Asher E. Treat of the College of the City of New York has demonstrated that moths taking evasive action on a bat's approach have a significantly higher chance of survival than those that continue on course.

A moth's ears are located on the sides of the rear part of its thorax and are directed outward and backward into the constriction that separates the thorax and the abdomen [*see top illustration on page 152*]. Each ear is externally visible as a small cavity, and within the cavity is a transparent eardrum. Behind the eardrum is the tympanic air sac; a fine strand of tissue containing the sensory apparatus extends across the air sac from the center of the eardrum to a skeletal support. Two acoustic cells, known as *A* cells, are located within this strand. Each *A* cell sends a fine sensory strand outward to the eardrum and a nerve fiber inward to the skeletal support. The two *A* fibers pass close to a large nonacoustic cell, the *B* cell, and are joined by its nerve fiber. The three fibers continue as the tympanic nerve into the central nervous system of the moth. From the two *A* fibers, then, it is possible—and well within our technical means—to obtain all the information about ultrasound that is transmitted from the moth's ear to its central nervous system.

Nerve impulses in single nerve fibers can be detected as "action potentials," or self-propagating electrical transients, that have a magnitude of a few millivolts and at any one point on the fiber last less than a millisecond. In the moth's *A* fibers action potentials travel from the sense cells to the central nervous system in less than two milliseconds. Action potentials are normally an all-or-nothing phenomenon; once initiated by the sense cell, they travel to the end of the nerve fiber. They can be detected on the outside of the fiber by means of fine electrodes, and they are displayed as "spikes" on the screen of an oscilloscope.

Tympanic-nerve signals are demonstrated in the following way. A moth, for example the adult insect of one of the common cutworms or armyworms, is immobilized on the stage of a microscope. Some of its muscles are dissected away to expose the tympanic nerves at a point outside the central nervous system. Fine silver hooks are placed under one or both nerves, and the pattern of passing action potentials is observed on the oscilloscope. With moths thus prepared we have spent much time in impromptu outdoor laboratories, where the cries of passing bats provided the necessary stimuli.

In order to make precise measurements we needed a controllable source of ultrasonic pulses for purposes of comparison. Such pulses can be generated by electronic gear to approximate natural bat cries in frequency and duration. The natural cries are frequency-modulated: their frequency drops from about 70 kilocycles per second at the beginning of each cry to some 35 kilocycles at the end. Their duration ranges from one to 10 milliseconds, and they are repeated from 10 to 100 times a second. Our artificial stimulus is a facsimile of an average series of bat cries; it is not frequency-modulated, but such modulation is not detected by the moth's ear. Our sound pulses can be accurately graded in intensity by decibel steps; in the sonic range a decibel is roughly equivalent to the barely noticeable difference to human ears in the intensity of two sounds.

By using electronic apparatus to elicit and follow the responses of the A cells we have been able to define the amount of acoustic information avail-

MOTH EVADED BAT by soaring upward just as the bat closed in to capture it. The bat entered the field at right; the path of its flight is the broad white streak across the photograph. The smaller white streak shows the flight of the moth. A tree is in background. The shutter of the camera was left open as contest began. Illumination came from continuous light source below field.

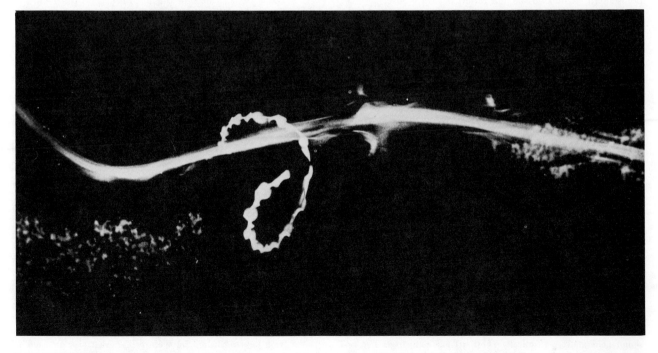

BAT CAPTURED MOTH at point where two white streaks intersect. Small streak shows the flight pattern of the moth. Broad streak shows the flight path of the bat. Both streak photographs were made by Frederic Webster of the Sensory Systems Laboratories.

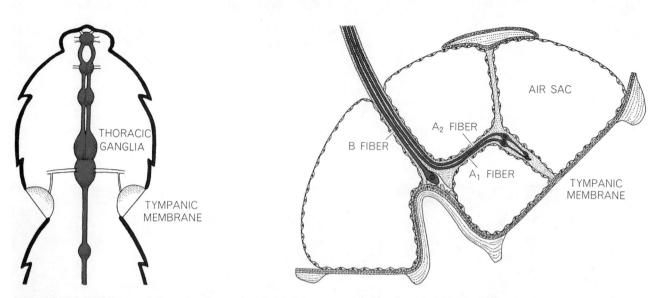

NERVES FROM EAR to central nervous system of moth are shown at two magnifications. Drawing at left indicates position of the tympanic organs on each side of the moth and the tympanic nerves connecting them with the thoracic ganglia. Central nervous system is colored. Drawing at right shows two nerve fibers of the acoustic cells joined by a nonacoustic fiber to form the tympanic nerve.

able to the moth by way of its tympanic nerve. It appears that the tympanic organ is not particularly sensitive; to elicit any response from the A cell requires ultrasound roughly 100 times more intense than sound that can just be heard by human ears. The ear of a moth can nonetheless pick up at distances of more than 100 feet ultrasonic bat cries we cannot hear at all. The reason it cannot detect frequency modulation is simply that it cannot discriminate one frequency from another; it is tone-deaf. It can, however, detect frequencies from 10 kilocycles to well over 100 kilocycles per second, which covers the range of bat cries. Its greatest talents are the detection of pulsed sound—short bursts of sound with intervening silence—and the discrimination of differences in the loudness of sound pulses.

When the ear of a moth is stimulated by the cry of a bat, real or artificial, spikes indicating the activity of the A cell appear on the oscilloscope in various configurations. As the stimulus increases in intensity several changes are apparent. First, the number of A spikes increases. Second, the time interval between the spikes decreases. Third, the spikes that had first appeared only on the record of one A fiber (the "A_1" fiber, which is about 20 decibels more sensitive than the A_2 fiber) now appear on the records of both fibers. Fourth, the greater the intensity of the stimulus, the sooner the A cell generates a spike in response.

The moth's ears transmit to the oscilloscope the same configuration of spikes they transmit normally to the central nervous system, and therein lies our interest. Which of the changes in auditory response to an increasingly in-

tense stimulus actually serve the moth as criteria for determining its behavior under natural conditions? Before we face up to this question let us speculate on the possible significance of these criteria from the viewpoint of the moth. For the moth to rely on the first kind of information—the number of A spikes—might lead it into a fatal error: the long, faint cry of a bat at a distance could be confused with the short, intense cry of a bat closing for the kill. This error could be avoided if the moth used the second kind of information—the interval between spikes—for estimating the loudness of the bat's cry. The third kind of information—the activity of the A_2 fiber—might serve to change an "early warning" message to a "take cover" message. The fourth kind of information—the length of time it takes for a spike to be generated—might provide the moth with

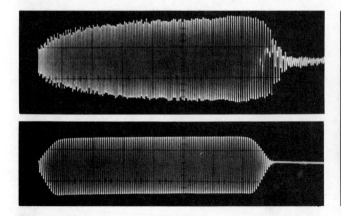

OSCILLOSCOPE TRACES of a real bat cry (top) and a pulse of sound generated electronically (bottom) are compared. The two ultrasonic pulses are of equal duration (length), 2.5 milliseconds, but differ in that the artificial pulse has a uniform frequency.

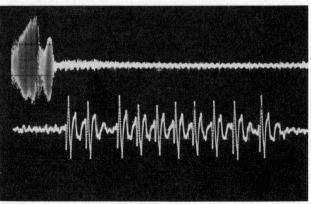

BAT CRY AND MOTH RESPONSE were traced on same oscilloscope from tape recording by Webster. The bat cry, detected by microphone, yielded the pattern at left in top trace. Reaction of the moth's acoustic cells produced the row of spikes at bottom.

the means for locating a cruising bat; for example, if the sound was louder in the moth's left ear than in its right, then A spikes would reach the left side of the central nervous system a fraction of a millisecond sooner than the right side.

Speculations of this sort are profitable only if they suggest experiments to prove or disprove them. Our tympanic-nerve studies led to field experiments designed to find out what moths do when they are exposed to batlike sounds from a loudspeaker. In the first such study moths were tracked by streak photography, a technique in which the shutter of a camera is left open as the subject passes by. As free-flying moths approached the area on which our camera was trained they were exposed to a series of ultrasonic pulses.

More than 1,000 tracks were recorded in this way. The moths were of many species; since they were free and going about their natural affairs most of them could not be captured and identified. This was an unavoidable disadvantage; earlier observations of moths captured, identified and then released in an enclosure revealed nothing. The moths were apparently "flying scared" from the beginning, and the ultrasound did not affect their behavior. Hence all comers were tracked in the field.

Because moths of some families lack ears, a certain percentage of the moths failed to react to the loudspeaker. The variety of maneuvers among the moths that did react was quite unpredictable and bewildering [see illustrations at top of next page]. Since the evasive behavior presumably evolved for the purpose of bewildering bats, it is hardly surprising that another mammal should find it confusing! The moths that flew close to the loudspeaker and encountered high-intensity ultrasound would maneuver toward the ground either by dropping passively with their wings closed, by power dives, by vertical and horizontal turns and loops or by various combinations of these evasive movements.

One important finding of this field work was that moths cruising at some distance from the loudspeaker would turn and fly at high speed directly away from it. This happened only if the sound the moths encountered was of low intensity. Moths closer to the loudspeaker could be induced to flee only if the signal was made weaker. Moths at about the height of the loudspeaker flew away in the horizontal plane; those above the loudspeaker were observed to turn directly upward

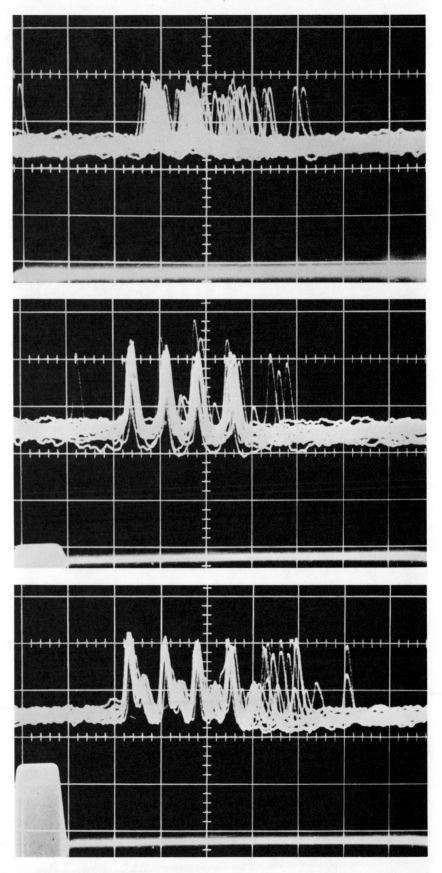

CHANGES ARE REPORTED by moth's tympanic nerve to the oscilloscope as pulses used to simulate bat cries gain intensity. Pulses (*lower trace in each frame*) were at five decibels (*top frame*), 20 (*middle*) and 35 (*bottom*). An increased number of tall spikes appear as intensity of stimulus rises. The time interval between spikes decreases slightly. Smaller spikes from the less sensitive nerve fiber appear at the higher intensities, and the higher the intensity of the stimulus, the sooner (*left on horizontal axis*) the first spike appears.

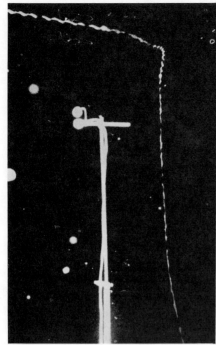

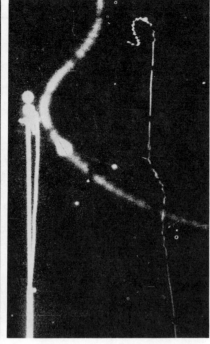

POWER DIVE is taken by moth on hearing simulated bat cry from loudspeaker mounted on thin tower (*left of moth's flight path*).

PASSIVE DROP was executed by another moth, which simply folded its wings. Blur at left and dots were made by other insects.

TURNING AWAY, an evasive action involving directional change, is illustrated. These streak photographs were made by author.

or at other sharp angles. To make such directional responses with only four sensory cells is quite a feat. A horizontal response could be explained on the basis that one ear of the moth detected the sound a bit earlier than the other. It is harder to account for a vertical response, although experiments I shall describe provide a hint.

O ur second series of field experiments was conducted in another outdoor laboratory—my backyard. They were designed to determine which of the criteria of intensity encoded in the pattern of A-fiber spikes play an important part in determining evasive behavior. The percentage of moths showing "no re-

action," "diving," "looping" and "turning away" was noted when a 50-kilocycle signal was pulsed at different rates and when it was produced as a continuous tone. The continuous tone delivers more A impulses in a given fraction of a second and therefore should be a more effective stimulus if the number of A impulses is important. On the other hand, because the A cells, like many other sensory cells, become progressively less sensitive with continued stimulation, the interspike interval lengthens rapidly as continuous-tone stimulation proceeds. When the sound is pulsed, the interspike interval remains short because the A cells have had time to regain their sensitivity during the

brief "off" periods. If the spike-generation time—which is associated with difference in the time at which the A spike arrives at the nerve centers for each ear—plays an important part in evasive behavior, then continuous tones should be less effective. The difference in arrival time would be detected only once at the beginning of the stimulus; with pulsed sound it would be reiterated with each pulse.

The second series of experiments occupied many lovely but mosquito-ridden summer nights in my garden and provided many thousands of observations. Tabulation of the figures showed that continuous ultrasonic tones were much less effective in producing evasive

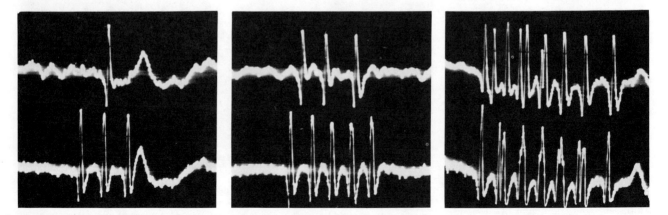

RESPONSE BY BOTH EARS of a moth to an approaching bat was recorded on the oscilloscope and photographed by the author. In trace at left the tympanic nerve from one ear transmits only one spike (*upper curve*) while the nerve from the other ear sends three. As the bat advances, the ratio becomes three to five (*middle*), then 10 to 10 (*right*), suggesting that the bat has flown overhead.

behavior than pulses. The number of nonreacting moths increased threefold, diving occurred only at higher sound intensities and turning away was essentially absent. Only looping seemed to increase slightly.

Ultrasound pulsed between 10 and 30 times a second proved to be more effective than ultrasound pulsed at higher or lower rates. This suggests that diving, and possibly other forms of non-directional evasive behavior, are triggered in the moth's central nervous system not so much by the number of A impulses delivered over a given period as by short intervals (less than 2.5 milliseconds) between consecutive A impulses. Turning away from the sound source when it is operating at low intensity levels seems to be set off by the reiterated difference in arrival time of the first A impulse in the right and left tympanic nerves.

These conclusions were broad but left unanswered the question: How can a moth equipped only with four A cells orient itself with respect to a sound source in planes that are both vertical and horizontal to its body axis? The search for an answer was undertaken by Roger Payne of Tufts University, assisted by Joshua Wallman, a Harvard undergraduate. They set out to plot the directional capacities of the tympanic organ by moving a loudspeaker at various angles with respect to a captive moth's body axis and registering (through the A_1 fiber) the organ's relative sensitivity to ultrasonic pulses coming from various directions. They took precautions to control acoustic shadows and reflections by mounting the moth and the recording electrodes on a thin steel tower in the center of an echo-free chamber; the effect of the moth's wings on the reception of sound was tested by systematically changing their position during the course of many experiments. A small loudspeaker emitted ultrasonic pulses 10 times a second at a distance of one meter. These sounds were presented to the moths from 36 latitude lines 10 degrees apart.

The response of the A fibers to the ultrasonic pulses was continuously recorded as the loudspeaker was moved. At the same time the intensity of ultrasound emitted by the loudspeaker was regulated so that at any angle it gave rise to the same response. Thus the intensity of the sound pulses was a measure of the moth's acoustic sensitivity. A pen recorder continuously graphed the changing intensity of the ultrasonic pulses against the angle from which

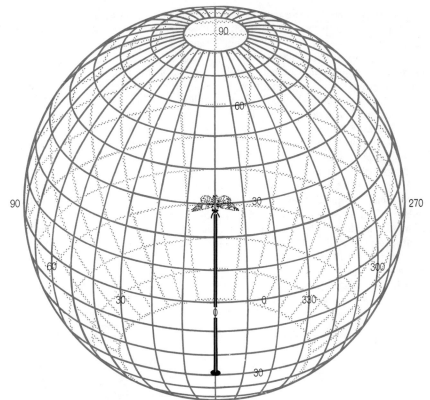

SPHERE OF SENSITIVITY, the range in which a moth with wings in a given position can hear ultrasound coming from various angles, was the subject of a study by Roger Payne of Tufts University and Joshua Wallman, a Harvard undergraduate. Moths with wings in given positions were mounted on a tower in an echo-free chamber. Data were compiled on the moths' sensitivity to ultrasound presented from 36 latitude lines 10 degrees apart.

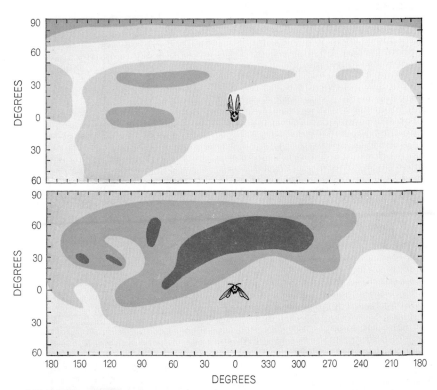

MERCATORIAL PROJECTIONS represent auditory environment of a moth with wings at end of upstroke (*top*) and near end of downstroke (*bottom*). Vertical scale shows rotation of loudspeaker around moth's body in vertical plane; horizontal scale shows rotation in horizontal plane. At top the loudspeaker is above moth; at far right and left, behind it. In Mercatorial projections, distortions are greatest at poles. The lighter the shading at a given angle of incidence, the more sensitive the moth to sound from that angle.

they were presented to the moth. Each chart provided a profile of sensitivity in a certain plane, and the data from it were assembled with those from others to provide a "sphere of sensitivity" for the moth at a given wing position.

This ingenious method made it possible to assemble a large amount of data in a short time. In the case of one moth it was possible to obtain the data for nine spheres of sensitivity (about 5,000 readings), each at a different wing position, before the tympanic nerve of the moth finally stopped transmitting impulses. Two of these spheres, taken from one moth at different wing positions, are presented as Mercatorial projections in the bottom illustration on the preceding page.

It is likely that much of the information contained in the fine detail of such projections is disregarded by a moth flapping its way through the night. Certain general patterns do seem related, however, to the moth's ability to escape a marauding bat. For instance, when the moth's wings are in the upper half of their beat, its acoustic sensitivity is 100 times less at a given point on its side facing away from the source of the sound than at the corresponding point on the side facing toward the source. When flight movements bring the wings below the horizontal plane, sound coming from each side above the moth is in acoustic shadow, and the left-right acoustic asymmetry largely disappears. Moths commonly flap their wings from 30 to 40 times a second. Therefore left-right acoustic asymmetry must alternate with up-down asymmetry at this frequency. A left-right difference in the

A-fiber discharge when the wings are up might give the moth a rough horizontal bearing on the position of a bat with respect to its own line of flight. The absence of a left-right difference and the presence of a similar fluctuation in both left and right tympanic nerves at wingbeat frequency might inform the moth that the bat was above it. If neither variation occurred at the regular wingbeat frequency, it would mean that the bat was below or behind the moth.

This analysis uses terms of precise directionality that idealize the natural situation. A moth certainly does not zoom along on an even keel and a straight course like an airliner. Its flapping progress—even when no threat is imminent—is marked by minor yawing and pitching; its overall course is rare-

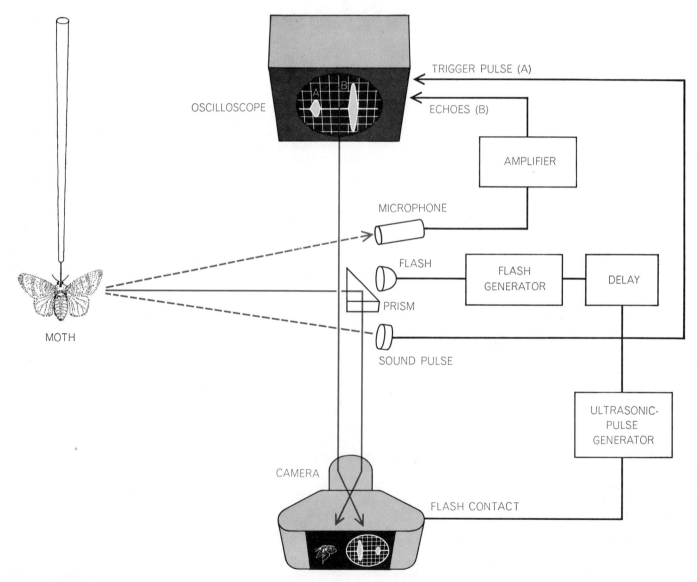

ARTIFICIAL BAT, the electronic device depicted schematically at right, was built by the author to determine at what position with respect to a bat a moth casts its greatest echo. As a moth supported by a wire flapped its wings in stationary flight, a film was made by means of a prism of its motions and of an oscilloscope that showed the pulse generated by the loudspeaker and the echo picked up by the microphone. Each frame of film thus resembled the composite picture of moth and two pulses shown inverted at bottom.

ly straight and commonly consists of large loops and figure eights. Even so, the localization experiments of Payne and Wallman suggest the ways in which a moth receives information that enables it to orient itself in three dimensions with respect to the source of an ultrasonic pulse.

The ability of a moth to perceive and react to a bat is not greatly superior or inferior to the ability of a bat to perceive and react to a moth. Proof of this lies in the evolutionary equality of their natural contest and in the observation of a number of bat-moth confrontations. Donald R. Griffin of Harvard University and Frederic Webster of the Sensory Systems Laboratories have studied in detail the almost unbelievable ability of bats to locate, track and intercept small flying targets, all on the basis of a string of echoes thrown back from ultrasonic cries. Speaking acoustically, what does a moth "look like" to a bat? Does the prey cast different echoes under different circumstances?

To answer this question I set up a crude artificial bat to pick up echoes from a live moth. The moth was attached to a wire support and induced to flap its wings in stationary flight. A movie camera was pointed at a prism so that half of each frame of film showed an image of the moth and the other half the screen of an oscilloscope. Mounted closely around the prism and directed at the moth from one meter away were a stroboscopic-flash lamp, an ultrasonic loudspeaker and a microphone. Each time the camera shutter opened and exposed a frame of film a short ultrasonic pulse was sent out by the loudspeaker and the oscilloscope began its sweep. The flash lamp was controlled through a delay circuit to go off the instant the ultrasonic pulse hit the moth, whose visible attitude was thereby frozen on the film. Meanwhile the echo thrown back by the moth while it was in this attitude was picked up by the microphone and finally displayed as a pulse of a certain height on the oscilloscope. All this took place before the camera shutter closed and the film moved on to the next frame. Thus each frame shows the optical and acoustic profiles of the moth from approximately the same angle and at the same instant of its flight. The camera was run at speeds close to the wingbeat frequency of the moth, so that the resulting film presents a regular series of wing positions and the echoes cast by them.

Films made of the same moth flying at different angles to the camera and the sound source show that by far the strongest echo is returned when the moth's wings are at right angles to the recording array [see illustrations at left]. The echo from a moth with its wings in this position is perhaps 100 times stronger than one from a moth with its wings at other angles. Apparently if a bat and a moth were flying horizontal courses at the same altitude, the moth would be in greatest danger of detection if it crossed the path of the approaching bat at right angles. From the bat's viewpoint at this instant the moth must appear to flicker acoustically at its wingbeat frequency. Since the rate at which the bat emits its ultrasonic cries is independent of the moth's wingbeat frequency, the actual sequence of echoes the bat receives must be complicated by the interaction of the two frequencies. Perhaps this enables the bat to discriminate a flapping target, likely to be prey, from inert objects floating in its acoustic field.

The moth has one advantage over the bat: it can detect the bat at a greater range than the bat can detect it. The bat, however, has the advantage of greater speed. This creates a nice problem for a moth that has picked up a bat's cries. If a moth immediately turns and flies directly away from a source of ultrasound, it has a good chance of disappearing from the sonar system of a still-distant bat. If the bat has also detected the moth, and is near enough to receive a continuous signal from its target, turning away on a straight course is a bad tactic because the moth is not likely to outdistance its pursuer. It is then to the moth's advantage to

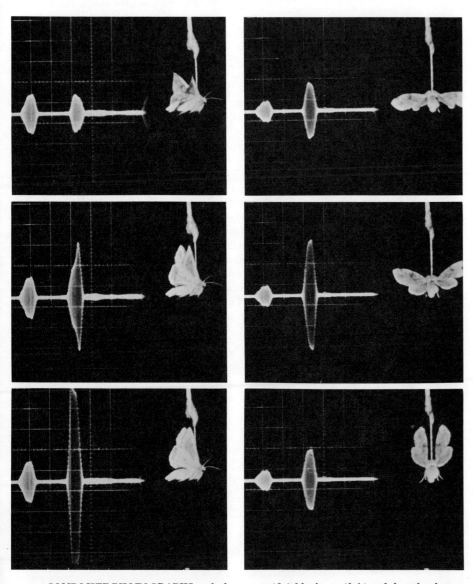

COMPOSITE PHOTOGRAPHS each show an artificial bat's cry (*left*) and the echo thrown back (*middle*) by a moth (*right*). The series of photographs at left is of a moth in stationary flight at right angles to the artificial bat. Those at right are of a moth oriented in flight parallel to the bat. The echo produced in the series of photographs at left is much the larger.

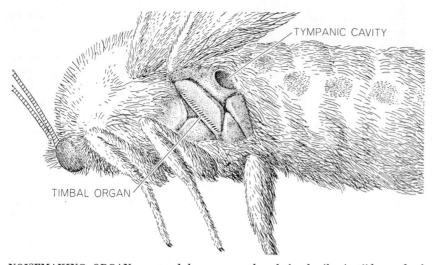

TYMPANIC CAVITY

TIMBAL ORGAN

NOISEMAKING ORGAN possessed by many moths of the family Arctiidae and of other families is a row of fine parallel ridges of cuticle that bend and unbend when a leg muscle contracts and relaxes. This produces a rapid sequence of high-pitched clicks.

go into tight turns, loops and dives, some of which may even take it toward the bat.

In this contest of hide-and-seek it seems much to a moth's advantage to remain as quiet as possible. The sensitive ears of a bat would soon locate a noisy target. It is therefore surprising to find that many members of the moth family Arctiidae (which includes the moths whose caterpillars are known as woolly bears) are capable of generating trains of ultrasonic clicks. David Blest and David Pye of University College London have demonstrated the working of the organ that arctiids use for this purpose.

In noisemaking arctiids the basal joint of the third pair of legs (which roughly corresponds to the hip) bulges outward and overlies an air-filled cavity. The stiff cuticle of this region has a series of fine parallel ridges [*see illustration above*]. Each ridge serves as a timbal that works rather like the familiar toy incorporating a thin strip of spring steel that clicks when it is pressed by the thumb. When one of the moth's leg muscles contracts and relaxes in rapid sequence, it bends and unbends the overlying cuticle, causing the row of timbals to produce rapid sequences of high-pitched clicks. Blest and Pye found that such moths would click when they were handled or poked, that the clicks occurred in short bursts of 1,000 or more per second and that each click contained ultrasonic frequencies within the range of hearing of bats.

My colleagues and I found that certain arctiids common in New England could also be induced to click if they were exposed to a string of ultrasonic pulses while they were suspended in stationary flight. In free flight these moths showed the evasive tactics I have already described. The clicking seems almost equivalent to telling the bat, "Here I am, come and get me." Since such altruism is not characteristic of the relation between predators and prey, there must be another answer.

Dorothy C. Dunning, a graduate student at Tufts, is at present trying to find it. She has already shown that partly tamed bats, trained to catch mealworms that are tossed into the air by a mechanical device, will commonly swerve away from their target if they hear tape-recorded arctiid clicks just before the moment of contact. Other ultrasounds, such as tape-recorded bat cries and "white" noise (noise of all frequencies), have relatively little effect on the bats' feeding behavior; the tossed mealworms are caught in midair and eaten. Thus the clicks made by arctiids seem to be heeded by bats as a warning rather than as an invitation. But a warning against what?

One of the pleasant things about scientific investigation is that the last logbook entry always ends with a question. In fact, the questions proliferate more rapidly than the answers and often carry one along unexpected paths. I suggested at the beginning of this article that it is my intention to trace the nervous mechanisms involved in the evasive behavior of moths. By defining the information conveyed by the acoustic cells I have only solved the least complex half of that broad problem. As I embark on the second half of the investigation, I hope it will lead up as many diverting side alleys as the study of the moth's acoustic system has.

III

PROCESSES OF EVOLUTION AND ECOLOGY

PROCESSES OF EVOLUTION AND ECOLOGY III

INTRODUCTION

As the articles in the first two sections showed, the simplicity of insects allows the rapid analysis of physiology and behavior at the level of the cell, an advantage that has put entomology in the forefront of many branches of experimental biology. Insects prove equally tractable in studies of evolutionary genetics and ecology. Some of the most secure case histories of evolution at the level of the gene have been worked out with *Drosophila*, moths, and butterflies. Other groups, especially those comprised of economically important species, have been the objects of pioneering studies on density-dependent population control, competition, predator–prey interaction, and other basic processes of ecology. The following six articles, which are typical of this genre, progress from a consideration of more general evolutionary phenomena to the complexities of coevolution, particularly the reciprocal genetic responses of predator and prey and of symbiotic partners as these interacting groups of species become increasingly well adjusted to one another.

For a hundred years, until about 1970, moth species living in the industrial areas of England (as well as other parts of Europe and North America) slowly grew dark in color. The change was due to the replacement of the "typical" genes, which induce a light, mottled wing color, by melanic genes that induce a dark color. In unpolluted localities lichens and algae lend a variegated, white-and-greenish coloration to much of the surface of tree trunks. Moths possessing the typical wing coloration blend in with the unpolluted surfaces when they alight, and predatory birds have difficulty finding them. But in the industrial areas soot darkens the trunk surfaces, so that the typical wing coloration stands out conspicuously—the melanic mutants, on the other hand, blend in nicely with the altered background. Experiments have shown that birds really do prey more heavily on the typical color form in sooty areas, and at a rate sufficient to cause the observed shift in favor of the melanic genes through decades of time. Now, thanks to pollution control, the trees of some English industrial areas are losing their soot. And, as the article "Moths, Melanism, and Clean Air" by J. A. Bishop and Lawrence M. Cook shows, the evolution has been reversed—the melanic genes are being replaced by the original, "typical" genes.

With the results of this article on industrial melanism in mind, consider next what happens when generations of birds and other predators pursue insects over literally millions of years, fixing one set of genes after another as generations of insects "invent" ever better ways to avoid being eaten. The result has been an astonishing array of techniques that either camouflage the body or else advertise the presence of poisonous weapons. The subject is reviewed in the article "Defense by Color" by Nikolaas Tinbergen, one of the three recipients of the 1973 Nobel Prize in Physiology and Medicine (the other two were Karl von Frisch and Konrad Lorenz) honored for their research on topics in animal behavior.

The fruit fly genus *Drosophila*, like so many comparable taxonomic groups of insects, consists of large numbers of species, many of which closely resemble one another and are packed into the same ecosystems. Biologists have made substantial progress in unraveling the processes by which the *Drosophila* species are formed and maintained as discrete entities. The crucial step of speciation is the acquisition of reproductive isolating mechanisms—the anatomical, physiological, or behavioral traits by which different species avoid cross-mating and hence the production of hybrids. In their article "The Love Song of the Fruit Fly," H. C. Bennet-Clark and A. C. Ewing show that one of the important reproductive isolating mechanisms in *Drosophila* is a patterned sound produced by the wingbeats of the courting male. The sound is functionally no different from bird song; it is used by males to lure potential mates into their spring territories. And, as in the birds, the males of each *Drosophila* species produces only the song that will stimulate a female belonging to the same species.

Most kinds of insects dwell in a capriciously changing world, where the rapid growth of their populations repeatedly outstrips their food supply. Insect ecologists have determined that most of the observed flight of insects is devoted to the search for newer, more productive habitats. Furthermore, the powered flight contributes only to a small part of the journey, as C. G. Johnson explains in the article "The Aerial Migration of Insects." A typical dispersal episode consists of use of the wings to get aloft, then dependence on the wind to travel for longer distances. Even the formidable migratory locusts, which have been known to cross half the Atlantic Ocean from Africa to the Azores, are carried mostly by the wind. Most migratory flights are conducted by freshly emerged adults, which are in the most opportune physiological condition to benefit from dispersal.

Plants that are eaten by insects have not simply sat around and taken this punishment for tens of millions of years. They have evolved many kinds of anatomical defenses to discourage their little enemies, including spines, thickened cuticles, and dense hair. But above all they depend on poisons to repel and kill the insects. The chemicals are not always toxic to human beings, and their true function has therefore in many instances only recently become apparent. Many of the substances are put to commercial use. For example, alkaloids such as cannabidiol, morphine, and cocaine are used by us as drugs; other chemicals, such as the essential components of cinnamon and mint, serve as spices. In this evolutionary battle insect species have fought back. Some have succeeded in specializing on the most poisonous plants by evolving the biochemical machinery required to neutralize the toxins. In a few remarkable cases they have even incorporated the chemicals into their bodies to use as a defense against their own predators. This mutual adjustment, described in "Butterflies and Plants" by Paul Ehrlich and Peter Raven, is one of the modes of coevolution that unites the members of plant and animal communities with a precision and fragility not dreamed possible by biologists 50 years ago.

Symbiosis is another realm of coevolution in which insects are extreme achievers. A wide range of forms have independently developed the ability to culture fungi as a source of food. The apex of this adaptation—and some would say the greatest single accomplishment in the social insects—has been attained by the macrotermitine termites and attine ants, which rear their symbionts on beds of decaying vegetable material kept in special chambers of their nests. A variety of insect–fungus relations are discussed in "The Fungus Gardens of Insects" by Suzanne and Lekh Batra.

The relation between flowering plants and their insect pollinators is a special form of symbiosis. It is to the advantage of the plants to be visited only by insects carrying pollen from other plants of the same species. It is of equal advantage to the insects to utilize only those plant species that can be discovered and drained of their nectar in an efficient manner. The two allies have worked out their joint problems with admirable efficiency. In "The Energetics of the Bumblebee" Bernd Heinrich examines the bumblebee, a large cold-climate insect whose size and ecology create special problems in energy management. It might be of interest to note that Professor Heinrich's expertise in the field of energetics is not limited to insects; he is also a student of the physiology of long-distance running and was a nationally ranked marathoner in 1975.

RELATED BOOKS

Cott, Hugh B. 1957. *Adaptive Coloration in Animals.* Methuen and Company, London. The prime reference source on the subject. Includes much fascinating information on how insects and other animals employ concealment, advertisement, and disguise as strategies for survival.

Edmonds, M. 1974. *Defense in Animals.* Longman, New York. Describes the numerous fascinating means whereby animals avoid being eaten by predators. Brings together much information on insects not to be found in compiled form elsewhere.

Ford, E. B. 1971. *Ecological Genetics,* third edition. Chapman and Hall, London. The ecological importance of genetic variability is discussed, with many insect examples, by a leading authority in the field.

Gilbert, Lawrence E., and Peter H. Raven (eds.). 1975. *Coevolution of Animals and Plants.* University of Texas Press, Austin. The subject of coevolution is of intense current interest to entomologists, who are attempting to interpret insect–plant interactions in the light of modern evolutionary and ecological theory. This anthology contains some provocative papers on the subject.

Johnson, C. G. 1969. *Migration and Dispersal of Insects by Flight.* Barnes and Noble, New York. Migratory flight may be the prime locomotory act of most winged insects. This remarkable subject, still very much open to experimentation, is nicely summarized and documented in this book.

Price, Peter W. 1975. *Insect Ecology.* Wiley, New York. A textbook dealing with trophic relations, population structure and dynamics, and problems of coexistence and competition. Excellent and up to date.

Ricklefs, Robert E. 1973. *Ecology.* Chiron Press, Newton, Massachusetts. This book, which presents many insect examples, ranges widely from the basic principles of ecology to evolutionary theory and biogeography.

Sondheimer, Ernest, and John B. Simeone (eds.). 1970. *Chemical Ecology.* Academic Press, New York. A series of papers on a subject of growing importance to entomology. Discusses chemical interactions between various insects, insects and predators, and insects and plants.

Wickler, Wolfgang. 1968. *Mimicry.* McGraw-Hill, New York. A very readable book. Familiar as well as lesser-known and bizarre cases of mimicry are beautifully depicted. Insect examples abound.

17 Moths, Melanism and Clean Air

by J. A. Bishop and Laurence M. Cook
January 1975

Some light species of moths that got dark in 19th-century England are reverting to light forms as air gets cleaner. A complex process of evolution is shaped by migration as well as by visual selection

Of more than 700 species of larger moths found throughout the British Isles, the peppered moth (*Biston betularia*) is surely the best-known to students of evolution. Light in color but with small dark markings, as its common name implies, this insect flies by night and rests by day on such surfaces as the lichen-clad bark of trees. There its mottled appearance provides camouflage. At least this is true of the peppered moths found in rural areas of Cornwall, Wales and Scotland. In smoky industrial England, however, some 90 percent of the peppered moths are not mottled but melanic, that is, they are almost coal black; only small numbers of the lighter form are found in the moth population. As H. B. D. Kettlewell demonstrated experimentally in the 1950's, the reason is the birds that are the natural predators of the species kill a high proportion of the moths that are poorly camouflaged. In unpolluted areas the melanic variety is the most conspicuous; in the industrial areas it is the light variety that is least likely to survive. Air pollution is the underlying cause of this evolutionary change, and so the phenomenon is called "industrial melanism" [see "Darwin's Missing Evidence," by H. B. D. Kettlewell; SCIENTIFIC AMERICAN Offprint 842].

The melanic mutation of the peppered moth is not the only example of industrial melanism, nor is the phenomenon confined to urban England. More than 70 other species of night-flying moths in Britain have exchanged light markings for dark ones, and the same is true of moths in industrial areas of continental Europe, Canada and the U.S. Today, as the control of air quality gets more effective, the environmental conditions that have until recently put light-colored moths at a disadvantage are changing, sometimes at a rapid pace.

One can predict that as selective predation decreasingly affects the light-colored moths but increasingly affects the dark ones, the evolutionary change should reverse itself. Our studies concern evidence that bears on this prediction. In reviewing the phenomenon of industrial melanism, however, it is prudent to emphasize the unknowns in what may at first seem to be an attractively clear-cut example of evolution in action.

Kettlewell's work is a classic of modern biology, and his experiments and observations have become a standard reference in texts on evolution and population genetics. Such brief accounts, however, often leave the reader unaware of the numerous qualifications Kettlewell expressed in his original papers. The fact is that many aspects of industrial melanism are still far from understood. For example, the process of change in gene frequencies has usually not reached the point where moth populations in polluted areas are made entirely of melanics even though the forces of natural selection have now been at work for at least a century. Instead the darker and lighter forms coexist in the state known to geneticists as polymorphism.

Industrial melanism is under active study both in Britain and in the U.S. In Britain, in recognition of its bearing on a general understanding of the environment, the work is partly supported by the Natural Environment Research Council. Two problems are of dominant interest to the investigators. The first is the question of why there is a difference in the proportion of melanics found among populations of various moth species that share the same environment. The second is the cause (or causes) of continuing polymorphism. For example, our own studies have examined the role of the migration of moths in the main-tenance of polymorphism. In collaboration with P. Harper of the National Medical School of Wales and J. Muggleton and R. R. Askew of the University of Manchester we have established the present pattern of frequency of the light and dark forms in populations of moths that inhabit two contrasting environments. The area we studied consisted of a region of intense urbanization and an adjacent but unpolluted rural region.

Historically the northwest of England was one of the earliest centers of the Industrial Revolution. One factor contributing to its development was the abundance of water from the rivers rising in the Pennines, a chain of mountains that extends for some 120 miles from the vicinity of Newcastle in the north to below Sheffield in the south. The mountain chain, with some crests that rise above 2,000 feet, is generally little more than 40 miles inland from the west coast of Britain and is the first high land encountered by the moisture-laden clouds that move eastward from the Atlantic. Both the rain-fed streams and the humid atmosphere were important assets in the spinning and weaving of yarn (wool at first but later cotton). The water was used as a source of power and also in the manufacturing processes; moreover, the humidity reduced the breakage of yarn.

Mill towns developed along the Pennine foothills: Bolton, Bury, Rochdale, Oldham, Ashton-under-Lyne, Stockport and many smaller centers. Manchester became not only a manufacturing city but also a distributing center and a hub of commerce. Liverpool, some 30 miles to the west, was the nearest seaport. Between the end of the 18th century, when industrial development began, and the middle of the 19th century the use of waterpower was gradually supplanted by steam. Coal, which was abundant in the region, was the fuel for the boilers.

It was also the fuel for household hearths, and the population was on the increase.

The inhabitants of Manchester numbered about 10,000 early in the 18th century. By the beginning of the 19th century the population of the city was 70,000; in 1850 it was 300,000. Before 1900 the population had risen to more than half a million. The novelist Elizabeth Gaskell, a local resident, witnessed much of the change. In one of her books, published in 1855, she describes the impressions of a family approaching Manchester for the first time. They were traveling by rail. "Quick they were whirled over long, straight, hopeless streets of regularly built houses, all small and of brick. Here and there a great oblong, many-windowed factory stood up, like a hen among her chickens, puffing out black 'unparliamentary' smoke, and sufficiently accounting for the cloud which Margaret had taken to foretell rain."

In a humid region subject to temperature inversions the daily release of great quantities of combustion products from homes and factories created an environment conducive to the rise of industrial melanism in several species of insects and other arthropods. Dark mutants appeared not only among moths other than the peppered moth but also among ladybird beetles and even spiders. Just as more than one factor contributed to the rise of industrialization, so the evolution of various industrial melanics cannot be attributed to the effects of coal smoke alone. As numerous studies have suggested, the effect of other pollutants was involved, acting either directly on the organisms that gave rise to mutants or indirectly on other organisms, such as algae and lichens. In addition the distribution of melanics has been shown to be strongly influenced by topographic and meteorological variations.

The time of the initial onset of industrial melanism is tantalizingly difficult

TWO PEPPERED MOTHS rest on the dark bark of an oak tree near Liverpool (*top*); the melanic, or black, form is better camouflaged than the typical light form. Until recently most trees near English industrial cities were like this oak. On a nearby beech tree that is more readily colonized by algae and the lichen *Lecanora conizaeoides* now that air quality is improving, the two forms of the moth are equally conspicuous (*middle*). On the light-colored, lichened bark of an oak tree in rural Wales the typical light peppered moth is almost invisible (*bottom*).

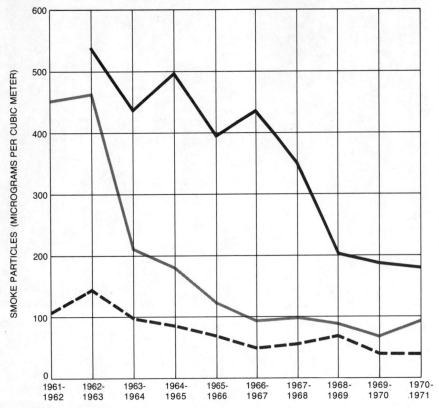

SMOKE POLLUTION has been reduced in English industrial cities by clean-air policies and redevelopment. The curves show the mean deposition of smoke particles during the winter in Salford, an industrial city near Manchester (*black curve*), in the Manchester suburb Withington (*gray curve*) and in Oxford, a city with modern industry (*broken curve*).

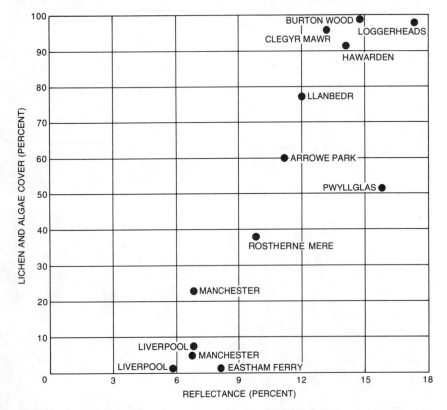

TREE TRUNKS ARE LIGHTER the more they are covered with lichens and algae. The cover increases with distance from industry. Here the reflectance of oak-tree trunks (as a percent of the reflectance of a standard white pigment) is plotted against the percent of the trunk, a meter and a half from the ground, that is covered with lichens and algae. Oaks are less favorable to the growth of such plants than some other species, such as beech.

to pin down. The first person in the area who is known to have captured a dark-colored peppered moth was an active lepidopterist, R. S. Edleston, who obtained a specimen in 1849. Edleston lived about a mile from the center of Manchester in the 1840's, and since he was an avid collector it seems safe to assume that the melanic mutants were rare in his day or else he would have captured more than one. In 1875 melanic peppered moths were still rare enough to merit frequent mention in the "readers' queries" section of the periodical *Entomologist*. J. Chappell, another collector, noted that melanic peppered moths had increased in proportion during his lifetime, so that by 1886 they were far commoner than nonmelanic moths.

In the same period the effect of air pollution on the lichens that colonized the bark of trees, beeches in particular, was recorded. In a description of the flora of Manchester published in 1859 it was noted that the quantity of lichens "had been much lessened of late years." By piecing together such scraps of information one can build up a picture of the change that was taking place. Evidently a rather short interval—the years between 1850 and 1890—was involved. The interval coincides precisely with the most rapid increase in the human population and the attendant rise in the amount of household coal consumed.

The effect of atmospheric pollution on human health had not gone unnoticed. By 1844 there was already legislation to control the smoke emitted by industrial furnaces in Manchester. It was not entirely effective; hence the "unparliamentary" blackness of the smoke described by Mrs. Gaskell. In 1866 the Medical Officer of Health in Manchester declared that the city's citizens were among the most unhealthy in Britain and related their condition to the state of the atmosphere. Only some 80 years later, following World War II, was anything significant done to improve the situation; before then commercial considerations had prevailed. Today the improvement in the quality of the air makes it possible to see vistas of Pennine scenery from Manchester that have been virtually invisible for more than a century.

The biological effects have also been noticeable. In particular there has been an increase in the quantities of algae and lichens growing on tree trunks in both Manchester and Liverpool. Whereas previously all the trees in the vicinity of the cities were uniformly blackened, the color of some of their surfaces has changed. English oaks, trees that are inhospitable to algae and lichens, remain dark, but the bark of the beech trees, some years earlier almost as blackened as the oaks, has become green as colonies of algae and lichens reappear. There is nonetheless a very long way to go before the region is restored to its preindustrial state.

The condition of tree trunks as resting sites for moths has been studied by E. R. Creed, J. G. Duckett and D. R. Lees of the University of Wales. With their methods we have recorded a striking increase in light reflectance and extent of colonization by pollution-sensitive lichens along a 30-mile corridor extending from industrial northwestern England into rural northern Wales [see bottom illustration on opposite page]. In this region of sharp transition the pro-

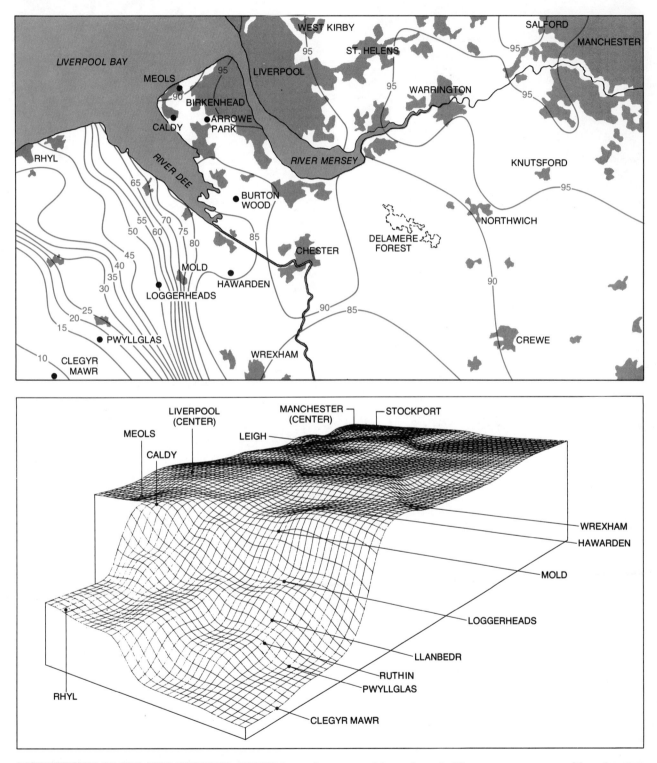

DISTRIBUTION OF MELANIC PEPPERED MOTHS in northwestern England and adjacent areas of Wales is shown on a contour map (top) and on a perspective diagram (bottom), both drawn by computer and based on samples of moths from more than 100 sites. The contours give the frequency of the melanic form as a percent of the total sample. The contours are converted into elevations in the lower diagram; the hills are areas where the melanic form is common. The surface is viewed from the southwest, from rural Wales. The frequency of the melanic form falls gradually as one moves away from cities, with a major decline evident in Wales.

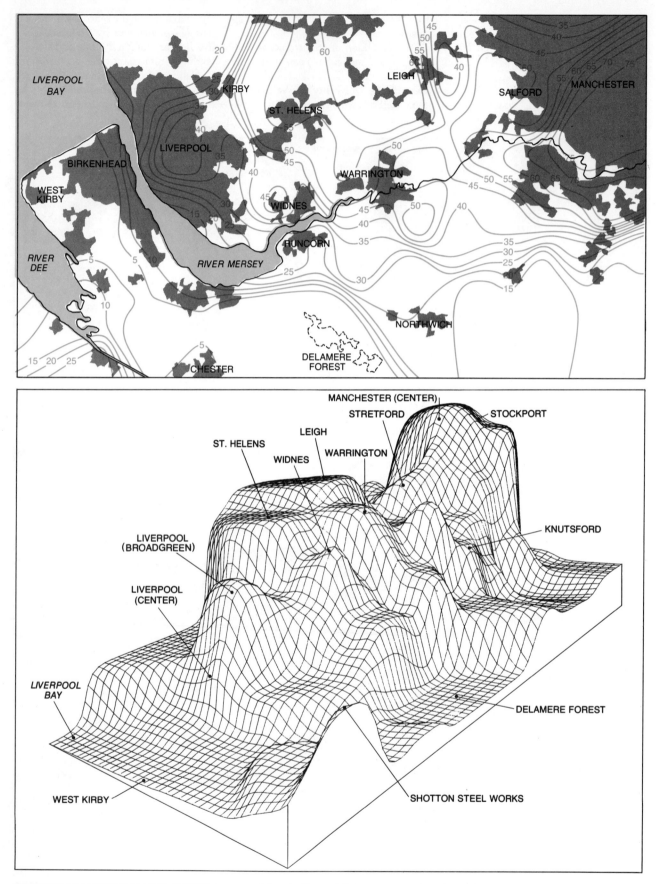

MELANIC SCALLOPED HAZEL MOTHS are mapped here in the same way that melanic peppered moths were mapped on the preceding page. The area covered is more restricted but again the perspective diagram is seen from the southwest. There are striking differences between these data and those for the peppered moth.

The frequency of scalloped hazel moth melanics falls sharply south of Manchester and more gradually west of the city. There is more variation (*hills and valleys*) in frequency, coinciding with industrial or rural environments. Melanic peppered moths remain at high frequency throughout the area covered by these diagrams.

portion of melanic moths in the local moth population is influenced both by natural selection on the spot and by the migration of moths from other areas where the effect of natural selection is not the same; a moth emerging from its cocoon in one area will often die in another area where the pollution level is quite different.

The corridor leading to Wales was first studied in this context by C. A. Clarke and P. M. Sheppard of the University of Liverpool; the peppered moth was the object of their study. We have investigated two other species of moth that also have populations made up of light and dark forms. Much of our work has been done within the corridor, but we also extended the study area as far east as the Pennines. The two species are the scalloped hazel moth (*Gonodontis bidentata*) and the pale brindled beauty moth (*Phigalia pilosaria*). Our initial objective was to determine the pattern of distribution of melanic moths in the region between Manchester and northern Wales, in the hope that the survey would provide a yardstick for measuring the reversal of the earlier evolutionary change.

We sampled the moth populations at more than 100 trap sites, luring the moths with mercury-vapor lamps or with females (which broadcast sex-attractant pheromones). The numbers of light-colored and dark-colored moths that were trapped were our raw data: the counts were weighted in terms of sample size and were converted by computer into contour maps and perspective views showing the proportion of melanic moths throughout the region [*see illustrations on page 167 and on opposite page*].

The graphic printouts showed that melanic moths were most numerous in populations sampled in urban areas where air pollution was the greatest. Away from towns and cities, particularly toward the southwest, the number of melanics fell rapidly. In the case of the scalloped hazel moth the drop in the number of melanics was most dramatic due south of Manchester. The gradients were just what one would have predicted on the basis of Kettlewell's studies.

Our data show a striking feature that is less readily understood: within the same areas there are obvious and major differences between the ratio of melanics found in each of the three species of moth. The proportion of melanics in a population of scalloped hazel moths is invariably lower than the comparable figure for a population of peppered moths. Where the data are available the

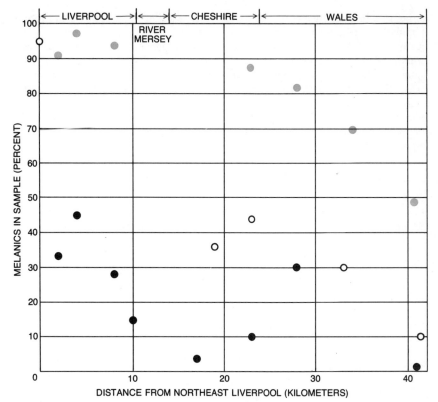

FREQUENCY OF MELANIC FORM is different in various species, as indicated by a comparison of the illustrations on the preceding two pages and as plotted here. In each species the proportion of melanic moths decreases with distance from Liverpool (*left*), but the frequency is generally higher for the peppered moth (*colored dots*) than for the scalloped hazel moth (*black dots*); data for the pale brindled beauty (*open circles*) fall in between.

proportion of melanics in populations of pale brindled beauty moths is intermediate [*see illustration above*]. The reason for these differences is only partly understood. Evidently they result from an interaction of some kind between, on the one hand, the expression of the gene for melanism and, on the other, the environment and unidentified aspects of species behavior and ecology.

Consider first the expression of the genes for melanism. Genes, of course, are carried on chromosomes. Since chromosomes come in pairs, each gene is represented twice: once on one chromosome and once, at the same position, on the other. In the three species of moth we are studying, the genes that determine melanism are dominant, so that the presence of one gene for the trait will mask the expression of the recessive gene that determines the typical, nonmelanic form. As a result there are two genetically distinct types of melanic moth. One is a heterozygote, with one melanic gene and one typical gene (Cc or cC). The other is a homozygote, with two melanic genes (CC).

A possible explanation for the differences in the numbers of melanics in the three moth species is that the heterozy-

gotes are "fitter," that is, they give rise to more surviving offspring, than either the dominant homozygote (CC) or the recessive homozygote (cc). This postulated superiority in fitness would not, of course, be evident in the dark coloring of the moths; in industrial areas the melanic homozygotes have the same visual advantage as the melanic heterozygotes. It would be some nonvisual disadvantage that reduces the fitness of the melanic homozygote compared with the heterozygote. Under these circumstances the differences in the number of melanics found in comparable populations of the three species would reflect a similarity in the melanics' visual advantage but a difference between homozygote and heterozygote with respect to nonvisual advantages.

The perspective displays of our data show variations between the moth species in their degree of local differentiation. For example, the "hills" and "valleys" in the display of the scalloped hazel moth are much more marked than those in the display of the peppered moth. This difference is readily explained as a consequence of the difference in the two species' population structures. In some areas scalloped-hazel populations are extraordinarily dense: as many as 50,000 to 100,000 moths per square kilometer per night. The corresponding figure for the peppered moth is as little as 10 per square kilometer.

The difference in density of population has one obvious consequence. A peppered moth is likely to have to travel a great deal farther to encounter a mate than a scalloped hazel moth. In capture-recapture experiments we released marked peppered moths in a parkland area of the Wirral peninsula; our traps were set at an even density at distances up to five kilometers from the release point. A significant proportion of the 1,433 moths we released flew one kilometer or farther before they were recaptured. Scalloped hazel moths, however, seldom flew more than 150 meters. Thus the scalloped hazels do not disperse their genes as far as the peppered moths. This gives rise to a much greater local differentiation of populations, thereby giving the scalloped-hazel display its rugged appearance. The rate of peppered-moth gene dispersal is greater, and so the three-dimensional display for this species is correspondingly smoother.

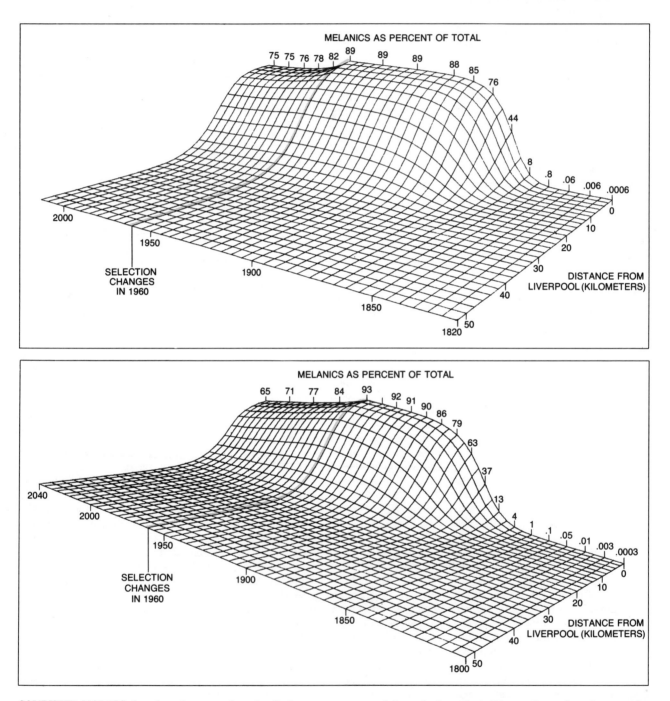

COMPUTER MODELS show how the proportion of melanic peppered moths may have developed, as a result of the interplay of natural selection and movement, over time and with distance from Liverpool. In the top diagram it is assumed that the melanic heterozygote has a 10 percent nonvisual selective advantage over the melanic homozygote. In the diagram at the bottom no heterozygous advantage is postulated. In both models it is assumed that the frequency of the melanic moths in Liverpool was about 1 percent in 1850 and that there has been no visual selective advantage for either the typical or the melanic form since 1960. The frequency of melanic moths increases more rapidly when the heterozygous advantage is assumed, but the values that are finally attained in 1960 are similar. When heterozygotes are at advantage, a new stable equilibrium is reached (at 75 percent) after environment changes.

As a further example of the greater homogeneity of populations in moths that range widely we cite the yellow underwing moth (*Triphaena pronuba*). C. E. M. Dale of the University of Manchester has investigated the mobility of this species, and he has found that it migrates considerably farther than the peppered moth. The yellow underwing moth is a polymorphic species, although none of its forms can be regarded as being an industrial melanic. It is significant that the proportion of the moth's various forms in local populations is almost invariant: the average difference in frequency between populations sampled in southern England and Scotland is less than 5 percent.

A third striking feature of the graphic displays of our data is the gradient with respect to melanism in peppered-moth populations as one moves away from Liverpool toward northern Wales. To assess the part that natural selection played in this phenomenon we undertook an experiment along lines first followed by Clarke and Sheppard. Natural selection is measured by assessing the comparative ability of two or more organisms that differ genetically to produce offspring in a given environment. In effect, will one live and breed longer than another? To make such an assessment one must compare each organism's "life table," that is, the probability that an individual will survive to a particular age, along with its age-specific birth rate, that is, the number of offspring produced by the females in each age category.

Our experimental procedure was to kill peppered moths, fix them in lifelike positions and glue them to trees chosen at random in each of seven areas of woodland between Liverpool and northern Wales. Equal numbers of melanic and nonmelanic moths were set out. After 24 hours of exposure the number and kind of moths that had been eaten by birds were noted and another series of moths was set out on a different group of trees. At the same time we estimated the number of eggs deposited by female moths of different ages.

Analysis of our figures showed a steady increase in the selective advantage enjoyed by nonmelanic moths, compared with melanic ones, as the distance from Liverpool increased. The estimated selective values correlated well with the change in the appearance of tree trunks that we had measured earlier.

Working with these natural-selection data and our information on moth migration, we constructed a computer

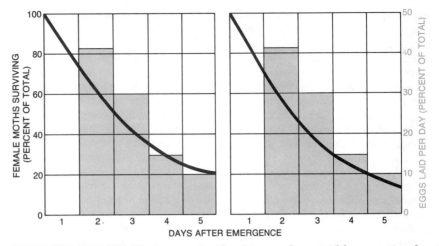

SELECTIVE ADVANTAGE of one or the other form was determined by comparing the day-by-day survival rate of female moths (*black curves and scale at left*) with the proportion of the total number of eggs laid per day (*colored bars and scale at right*). These data from a polluted locality near Liverpool showed that the melanic female (*left*) had a greater chance of surviving to reproduce in that environment than the typical female did (*right*). Away from Liverpool the situation was reversed: the typical form had a selective advantage.

model of how the observed gradient might have developed from its inception, assuming that the frequency of melanic moths in Manchester and Liverpool in 1850 was about 1 percent [*see illustration on opposite page*]. The computer model has not been a complete success: the synthetic gradient is considerably more displaced toward industrial Lancashire than the gradient observed in nature. The discrepancy may indicate that we are not correctly assessing the true nature of the resting sites of living moths when we are conducting experiments with dead ones. Alternatively, the assumption that natural selec-

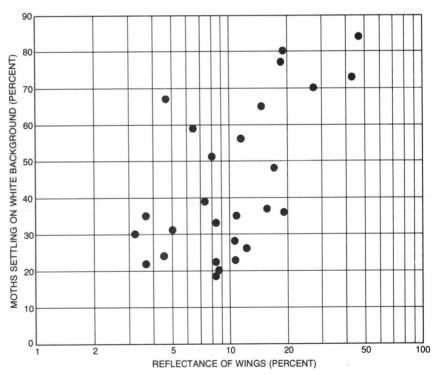

MOTHS TEND TO REST on backgrounds they resemble. Moths of 27 different species were provided with a surface containing equal areas of black and white. Here the proportion of each species that rested on the white surface is plotted against the average reflectance of its fore wings (as a percent of the reflectance of a standard white pigment). There is an obvious relation between lightness of wing color and preference for a white surface. The data were collected by Margaret Boardman, a student at the University of Manchester.

tion is entirely due to selective predation by birds may be mistaken. For example, in nature melanic moths remain common in areas where theoretically the birds should have exterminated them. Some factor may be counterbalancing the melanics' disadvantage, perhaps acting during the larval or pupal stages that make up most of the moths' life history. Complexities of this kind still remain to be investigated.

Is there any evidence that a reversal in frequency of industrial melanics has in fact begun? Changes in gene frequency progress slowly when the number of individuals possessing the favored mutation is low; hence we should not expect an immediate substantial response to the quite recent improvements in the quality of the air. Nevertheless, small but significant changes have already been observed. The first was noted by Clarke and Sheppard at a locality on the Wirral peninsula where they sample the moth populations each year. Between 1961 and 1964, following the introduction of local "smokeless" zones, they found that the frequency of nonmelanic peppered moths increased from 5.2 percent to 8.9. By 1974 the proportion had risen to 10.5 percent. In a less systematic investigation in Manchester we have found that, whereas there were no nonmelanic peppered moths in samples taken during the late 1950's and early 1960's, they now represent about 2.5 percent of the samples. Finally, Creed has reported an increase in Birmingham beginning in 1962 in the frequency of nonmelanic forms of the ladybird beetle (*Adalia bipunctata*), a species distasteful to birds that for some unknown reason also includes melanic mutants. It is therefore probably fair to conclude that

the reversal of industrial melanism is now under way.

The factor generally accepted as being responsible for the maintenance of polymorphism in industrial melanics is that a balance is achieved through the advantage of heterozygous animals. Some alternative possibilities nonetheless seem worth considering. For example, suppose that in some localities a polymorphic species of moth rests on tree bark on which colonies of lichens are distributed in patches. Suppose further that the individual moths settle and move onto the background where they are least conspicuous. Under those circumstances the melanics would have an advantage over the nonmelanics on bare bark, whereas the reverse would be true on patches of lichen. Provided that there was competition for resting sites, such a situation would maintain polymorphism in the species without any need to postulate that the heterozygote has an advantage over the homozygote.

When the frequency of one form or another diverged from the equilibrium level, the individual moths present in excess numbers would be forced to take up positions where they were conspicuous. Thus exposed to predation, they would tend to be eliminated, and so equilibrium would be restored. A mechanism of this kind could be at work among the populations of scalloped hazel moths, which are found in dense colonies and do not fly far.

A similar possibility may apply to the peppered moth. Sufficient migration between polluted and unpolluted localities may take place to maintain polymorphism in populations at both extremes. The evidence suggests this possibility;

peppered moths do migrate between areas where the degree of pollution and selective predation differs widely. For example, the proportional changes observed in the region including northwestern Cheshire and southwestern Lancashire could be attributed to this mechanism without invoking the heterozygotes' advantage.

An unexplained aspect of melanic polymorphism is the difference in gene frequency seen in the three moth species we have studied. It is, of course, possible that visual selection is of similar magnitude in all three species and that, as we have suggested, it is balanced by different degrees of nonvisual selection against homozygotes. Yet we know that moths vary greatly in their preferred resting sites [*see bottom illustration on page 171*]. Similarly the range of sites with a good match to the moths' wing patterns also varies. Therefore at least in theory the observed differences in equilibrium frequencies among the three species can also be accounted for by density-dependent selection working at varied resting sites.

These last comments are frankly speculative. If we are to fully understand industrial melanism, the nonvisual differences between melanic and nonmelanic moths must be studied more intensively. Such studies may well prove that the heterozygotes' advantage is established over a wide range of environmental conditions and is present in most or all polymorphic species. Nevertheless, the data now in hand are equally explicable by a system of density-dependent selection. It is clear that in future theoretical studies of the peppered moth the species' high migration rate and low population density cannot be ignored.

Defense by Color

by N. Tinbergen
October 1957

*It is generally assumed that the coloration of some
animals is for the purpose of deceiving predators.
Is this assumption true? An account of some
experimental efforts to answer the question*

Animals with the gift of "camouflage" have been a beguiling subject of debate ever since Charles Darwin's time. Is their coloring actually a disguise to deceive their enemies, or is it just an accident of nature? Anyone who has watched a flounder change color to match its background, or seen a "twig" suddenly start crawling along a branch, is not likely to be in much doubt about the answer. But it can be argued that this evidence is entirely subjective and circumstantial. After all, we see these animals with human eyes, and we cannot be sure that their predators see them exactly as we do; in fact, we know that the vision of many animals is quite different from ours. Furthermore, if we accept the idea of protective coloration, it is not easy to understand how the processes of evolution could have produced the exquisitely precise patterns of mimicry that some of these animals display.

The 19th-century naturalists looked for answers to these questions in the field; nowadays zoologists prefer to investigate them in the laboratory. This article is an account of experiments which have cleared up some of the questions and brought to light many fascinating new facts.

The English zoologist Hugh B. Cott, in his classic work called *Adaptive Coloration in Animals*, has described a number of ways in which color patterns can serve as defense. There are animals whose coloring gives concealment, by matching the background of their usual environment; there are evil-tasting animals whose coloring is bright and conspicuous, as if to advertise their distastefulness; there are animals that mimic these species, so that, although they are not distasteful themselves, predators avoid them; there are insects that display glaring "eye spots" which are thought to scare predators away; there are other insects with small eyelike spots on their wing tips which are believed to deceive predators into striking there instead of at the head.

Some of this may sound fanciful, but experiments have shown that the facts are stranger than fancy. Let us take the camouflage experiments first.

A classic series of experiments was performed by the late F. B. Sumner at the Scripps Institution of Oceanography [see "How Animals Change Color," by Lorus J. and Margery J. Milne; SCIENTIFIC AMERICAN, March, 1952]. He tested, among other things, the effectiveness of adaptive coloring in protecting fish against a predator. As subjects he used minnows of the genus called *Gambusia*, which turn dark when kept in a black tank and bleach out when kept in a white tank. Sumner put a large number of bleached and dark fish in a white tank and introduced a penguin to feed on them. Since the fish change color only slowly, the dark fish remained considerably more conspicuous in this tank than the bleached ones. The upshot of the experiment was that the penguin did in fact catch many more of the dark fish; conversely, in a dark tank the bleached fish suffered the heavier losses. Tests with other predators—herons and fish that prey on Gambusia—gave the same result.

Many other experiments have con-

LARVA OF THE PUSS MOTH (*Dicranura vinula*) illustrates the stratagem of countershading. The larva usually hangs upside down from a branch or twig; in that position its shading makes it appear flat. In this position the shading makes the larva conspicuous.

CONSPICUOUS CATERPILLARS advertise their distastefulness with yellow and black stripes. Birds that have tasted the cinnabar-moth larvae shown in this photograph learn to avoid them, and cease to prey upon other larvae which have a similar warning pattern.

firmed that camouflaged individuals come off far better against their predators than more conspicuous ones. Some of the camouflage patterns are quite remarkable: certain caterpillars look exactly like a twig [*see photograph on page 179*]; there is a peppered moth which matches tree bark almost perfectly [*see page 178*], and so on. One of the effective camouflage devices is countershading—a transition from a dark shade on the upper side of the animal to a lighter shade on the underside, which counteracts natural shading and makes the creature look like a flat spot instead of three-dimensional, at least to human eyes [*see photograph on the preceding page*].

Leen de Ruiter, one of my co-workers in the department of zoology at the University of Oxford, has demonstrated that countershading protects caterpillars against birds. He had to use killed caterpillars to eliminate the possibility of their giving themselves away by moving. (In nature all camouflaged animals freeze as soon as they spot a predator, and some of them hold a stationary position all day.) De Ruiter mounted countershaded caterpillars on twigs, half of them dark side up, the other half, light side up. He then distributed these objects in a naturally planted aviary occupied by European jays. The birds ate many more of the inverted (light-side-up) caterpillars than of the others. De Ruiter was able to prove that the loss of countershading was responsible for their readier detection. By tests with models he established further that shading creates an illusion of three-dimensionality for birds, as it does for us in a painting.

De Ruiter next tested the birds on caterpillars that resemble twigs. The very first experiment yielded a result almost too good to be true. Over the floor of the aviary he scattered some birch twigs and caterpillars of a species that looks like these twigs. When jays were admitted to the cage, they began to hop about looking for food. For the first 20 minutes or so they ignored the twigs and the motionless caterpillars. Then one of the birds happened to step on a caterpillar, and this made the animal wriggle. The jay snapped it up and immediately began to pick up, indiscriminately, other caterpillars and twigs as well! Clearly the bird confused twigs with caterpillars, and *vice versa*. Much the same thing happened in repetitions of the test with other jays and with chaffinches. When caterpillars outnumbered twigs, the birds took the disappointments in stride

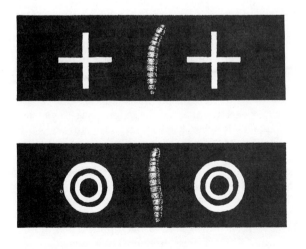

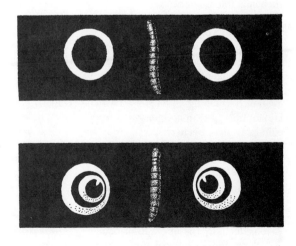

EFFECTIVENESS OF FRIGHTENING PATTERNS at bottom was tested by flashing a light in the box at top just as a bird approached a mealworm, so that the patterns appeared suddenly on either side of the worm. The birds were frightened most by the eye spots at lower right, which closely resemble the "warning spots" on the wings of certain moths (*see photographs on next two pages*).

EYED HAWK MOTH (*Smerinthus ocellata*) in the photographs on these two pages shows how a species with eye spots on its wings uses them to frighten birds. In its usual position (*photograph at left*) the moth's eye spots are concealed. It will remain in this

and went on hunting for caterpillars. But if they picked up more twigs than caterpillars, they became discouraged and gave up searching. This suggests that in nature it is important for stick caterpillars not to become as numerous as their inedible models.

The tests illustrated another interesting point. The detection of the first caterpillar apparently affected the bird's nervous system in some way: in anthropomorphic language, it suddenly began to "expect" stick caterpillars. This phenomenon of developing a "set" for a particular stimulus—a searching image of a specific prey—has been observed in many animals. The German physiologist Erich von Holst has noted similar effects at lower integration levels of the nervous system, and he has proposed a theory to explain such "stimulus expectation."

Consider now the opposite of camouflage—the showy coloring that announces distastefulness. A good example is the caterpillar stage of the European cinnabar moth. This larva is boldly col-

ored with yellow and black stripes, and its characteristic swarms on ragwort can be seen a long way off [*see photograph on page 174*]. Birds and other caterpillar-eaters sometimes try the creature, but after one taste they let it strictly alone. The German zoologist Wilhelm Windecker made a systematic analysis to find out what part of the cinnabar caterpillar was distasteful to birds, offering them various portions of its body in a mixture with mealworms. He found that the unpalatable part was the caterpillar's hairs.

Windecker also discovered that once a bird has tasted this unpleasantness, it will avoid all animals colored like the cinnabar caterpillar. Other experimenters have demonstrated the same phenomenon. For example, Georg Mostler of Germany found that a bird will not attack wasps after one or two disagreeable experiences with them; furthermore, it will not even take certain flies with the same yellow and black pattern as wasps, although it has previously eaten these flies with relish. The mem-

ory of a bird for unpleasant experiences is very good indeed; one of Mostler's birds refused wasps eight months after its last encounter with one. Another experimenter who has looked into the matter of color-pattern conditioning is Hans Mühlmann of Germany. He painted red rings around mealworms, dipped them in a distasteful substance and then offered them to his birds. The birds thereafter shied away from mealworms with red wings or any roughly similar markings.

Possibly the strangest form of visual armor is the frightening "eye spots" possessed by certain moths and butterflies. These species have no bad taste or other weapon: their only defense is a pair of big, bold eyelike markings on their underwings which they display suddenly when touched by a predator [*see photograph on next page*]. My colleague A. D. Blest proved that this bluff scares birds off. He presented peacock butterflies, a species that has these markings, to his birds. When the butterflies, on being pecked, displayed their eye

position until it is touched or pecked at by a bird. When this happens it will display its eye spots (*photograph at right*). The spots are called false warning colors because they are capable of frightening a bird even though the moth poses no real threat.

spots, the birds jumped back. Sometimes the birds tried again later and ate the butterflies, but in most cases they let the creatures alone. Testing the birds on peacock butterflies whose eye spots had been rubbed off, Blest found them much less inhibited about attacking these.

He went on to compare the effects of various patterns. For these experiments he constructed a simple box with slides bearing patterns—a pair of crosses, a pair of rings, etc. The pattern was displayed by switching on a light in the box [*see illustrations on page 175*]. Blest laid a mealworm on top of the box to attract the bird and switched on the display suddenly just as the bird pecked. Its frightening effect was measured by how frequently it put birds to flight. Each pattern evoked very consistent responses from the various birds tested, some of which had been raised in cages, others caught in the wild. The birds were somewhat troubled by a pair of crosses or parallel bars; a pair of single rings was more frightening; double rings still more frightening; and the pattern that drove

the birds off most effectively was a pair of eyelike designs exactly like the eye spots on insects' wings.

Finally, Blest tested the theory that small spots on the extremities of some insects serve as deceptions to deflect predators from a vulnerable part of the animal. Using mealworms for his experiments, he painted a small spot on either the head or tail end. The birds then usually picked up the end that had the spot, whether it was at the head or the tail, although they normally show a slight bias for the head end. The experiments gave support to the idea that the natural spots found on the wing tips of insects may serve as deceptive targets for birds.

We have overwhelming evidence, then, that the protective colors and markings of animals cannot be mere accidents. An enormous number of animal forms have patterns of the kinds I have been discussing. Moreover, the behavior of the animal is generally calculated to make the most of its deceptive markings.

For instance, a countershaded animal always keeps its dark side up: indeed, there is a fish (*Synodontis batensoda*) whose bottom side is darker than its top, and this fish habitually swims upside down! Countershaded animals vary considerably in the mechanisms responsible for their color scheme (in some it is due to the skin, in others to the skin and blood, etc.), and they differ in the method of determining which side is up (some responding to light, others to gravity), but in every case the net result is the same: all of them keep the darker side turned up. This can only mean that the phenomenon is a true adaptation.

If protective coloration is not an accident but an adaptive product of evolution, how does the crude process of natural selection produce the highly special and intricate patterns that these animals display? In the case of the insects we have been considering, birds must act as the selectors. Now birds are notoriously undiscriminating in some ways: for instance, a male robin will posture at the sight of a dummy made

PEPPERED MOTH (*Biston betularia*) is almost invisible against the varicolored background of a mossy tree trunk. The reader will find the moth just above and to the right of the center of this photograph. This kind of camouflage is called disruptive coloration.

of red feathers, as if it were a rival male robin. What reason is there to suppose, then, that birds can act as fine-grain selectors, destroying, say, caterpillars that differ slightly from twigs, so that only the very "best" stick insects survive? De Ruiter's and Blest's experiments give direct information on this point.

De Ruiter strewed various kinds of twigs in a cage, along with caterpillars that mimicked one of the twig types. He found that birds confused a caterpillar only with a twig that it resembled closely. For instance, when a bird discovered the caterpillar resembling a birch twig (by accidentally stepping on it), the bird proceeded to pick up birch twigs but not other kinds. This discrimination suggests that a bird is capable of distinguishing between a twig and a caterpillar that does not quite match the twig.

Blest's experiments with the various patterns on his slides likewise demonstrated that birds have fairly good powers of discrimination. His birds were markedly less frightened by a doubling-ring pattern than by a drawing which included shading and a highlight so that it looked more like an eye.

The same set of experiments suggests an answer to another key question about the evolution of protective patterns: How did such adaptations start? It is quite unlikely that mutation suddenly produced a butterfly with spots on its wings that looked like eyes. The eye spots must have evolved from much cruder beginnings. Let us imagine some ancient ancestor of this butterfly which had only a weak tendency to fly. When pecked by a bird, it merely flapped its wings. This would be a poor defense against the bird, but if a mutant of the butterfly turned up with spots on its wings, the deterrent would be stronger. As Blest's experiments showed, even a pair of crosses suddenly displayed to a bird has a slightly frightening effect upon it. So wing spots which appeared suddenly when a butterfly spread its wings would give it a slightly improved chance of survival; in the course of time evolution would favor the descendants whose spots came more and more to resemble an eye. Thus the insect, armed only with this phony but effective threat, would remain a viable species in spite of its stationary habits.

Of course we have no direct proof of such a theory, but we can at least say that the results of the experiments performed so far are consistent with it. Indeed, it is hard to think of any other reasonable explanation of the experimental findings and the amazingly artful color defenses of these animals in nature.

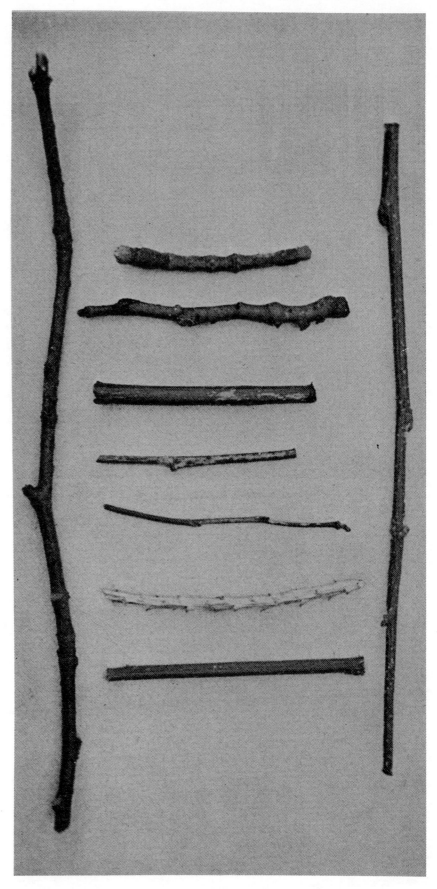

MIMICRY OF A TWIG (*second from top*) by a caterpillar (*at top*) is shown in this photograph. The mimicked twig came from the species of birch that this caterpillar normally inhabits. The rest of the twigs came from other trees. In experiments predatory birds confused the caterpillars only with twigs from the caterpillars' host trees.

SERENADING MALE FLY stands close to the female and, with right wing extended, prepares to go through the motions that make a sound characteristic of all the males of his species. If the female fly belongs to another species, she will be unreceptive to his song.

The Love Song of the Fruit Fly

by H. C. Bennet-Clark and A. W. Ewing
July 1970

*Most species of Drosophila have overlapping ranges,
yet hybrid fruit flies are rare. One reason is that in
courtship the females respond to a unique signal
that is emitted only by males of the same species*

Unlike the strident proclamations of the cricket and the cicada, the love song of the tiny fruit fly is a quiet and private affair. The courting male approaches to within two millimeters of the female and engages in a wing display. He extends one wing or both and assumes a posture that is identical among all males of the species; the wing vibrations that follow generate a characteristic sound. The female senses this sound through her aristae: feathery projections of the antennae. If the female is receptive mating ensues. If she is unreceptive (which is to say that she is immature, already mated or of a different species), she produces her own song, a buzz with a fundamental frequency near 300 cycles per second. The sound causes the male to turn away and stop courting. Recording the love songs of fruit flies in our laboratory at the University of Edinburgh, we have found that, whereas the female's repulsion signal is essentially the same among all the species we have observed, the male's song differs from species to species.

The genus *Drosophila* includes some 2,000 species of flies. The flies are not easy to tell apart. Some are light and some dark, some are short-winged and some long-winged, but even viewed side by side they look rather alike. Some species are cosmopolitan; *D. melanogaster, D. repleta* and *D. simulans,* for example, are found on all continents. Few species have a geographical range that is not shared with several other species. (In the Hawaiian Islands alone there are more than 1,000 species.) The various species have nonetheless managed to remain genetically isolated. A few species can be interbred in the laboratory, but the offspring are often partially or wholly sterile. All of this suggests that the unique love song of each species constitutes a powerful isolation mechanism that acts as a barrier to interbreeding and thus maintains the genetic integrity of each species.

As is well known, geneticists have long favored *Drosophila* as an experimental animal. The flies are easy to maintain, their life cycle is short and comparisons can readily be made between changes in the morphology or biochemistry of the individual fly on the one hand and changes in its chromosomes on the other. Thanks both to these studies and to taxonomic investigations, so much is now known about the evolutionary history of the genus that fruit flies are becoming important for studies of the genetics underlying the evolution of behavior. We have sought answers to two such questions: How did the love song of the fruit fly evolve? What is the significance of the song?

It is not hard to demonstrate the key role that the love song plays in mating. Remove the male fly's wings and he will court with the same persistence as before, but his courtship is seldom successful. It is apparent that the male's wing display, at least, is a prerequisite to mating. Indeed, one species (*D. obscura*) sings no song and courts only by means of a silent wing display. This, however, is one of the few fruit fly species that will not mate in the dark. Since most species breed successfully at night, one must conclude that visual display alone is not enough to win female acceptance. The importance of sound to the female is also easy to demonstrate. Our colleague A. W. G. Manning has shown that when the antennae of a sexually responsive female are immobilized with glue, she ceases to be receptive.

Sound appears to be the major element in mating. Contact chemical stimuli are also evident. In the species *D. melanogaster,* for example, the male taps the female with his forelegs to "taste" her before beginning his wing display. If tasting reveals that the female is of another species, the male normally breaks off contact. The specific scent of the female does not develop, however, until about two days after she reaches the adult stage of development. Before then males will court foreign females, and differences in song may be the only clue for discriminating between species. Moreover, the male tastes the female only at the onset of courtship. Once the male is sexually aroused, he may, in a mixed population of flies, switch his attention from a female of his own species to a female of another. In such circumstances the female would again be able to distinguish a male of the same species from an alien suitor by means of the love song.

Our first step in studying the fruit flies' love songs was to record the sounds produced by males of various species. This presented difficulties because the song is so quiet. We have calculated (on the basis of amplitude of wing movement and the thrust produced in free flight) that in terms of power output the signal does not exceed a ten-billionth of a watt. This minuscule output can easily be drowned out by other sounds in the environment. In order to record the songs we had to install a sensitive crystal microphone, which fed into a low-noise amplifier, in an elaborately sound-proofed box. We then placed the flies directly on the microphone diaphragm. Even under these circumstances we found it best to record the songs in the middle of the night or on the weekend, when the rest of the laboratory was quiet.

We discovered that a song usually

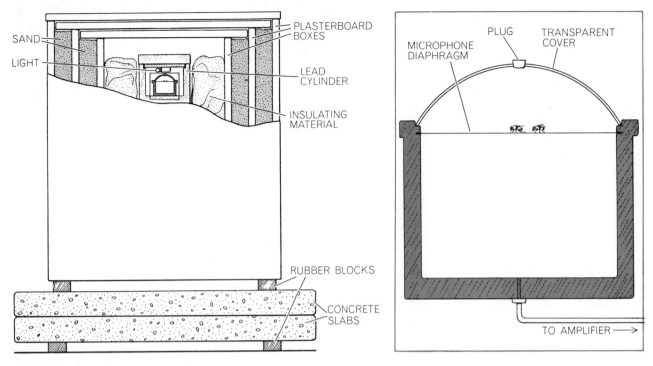

EXPERIMENTAL ENCLOSURE for recording the fruit flies' songs consists of a series of nesting boxes, each insulated from its neighbor by sand (*left*). The innermost box contains a cylindrical lead casting that houses a microphone and a small illuminating lamp. The female fly and the courting male are confined in a small cell that is placed directly on the diaphragm of the microphone (*right*).

---

consists of a train of sound pulses, with each short pulse normally followed by a period of silence. The intervals are usually the same throughout the song, but the pattern of sound and silence varies considerably from species to species. At one extreme is the song pulse of *D. melanogaster*, which consists of a single cycle that lasts only three thousandths of a second. At the other extreme is the pulse of *D. micromelanica*: a continuous buzz that may last as long as 10 seconds. Between these extremes are song pulses that continue for two to four cycles (*D. ananassae* and *D. athabasca*) or for three to seven cycles (*D. pseudoobscura* and *D. persimilis*).

Of the 22 species whose songs we have recorded, six had song pulses that consisted of a single cycle: *D. melanogaster*, *D. paulistorum* and four others. In all the single-cycle singers the pulse is of about the same duration, three thousandths of a second, and the tone is roughly 330 cycles per second. The flies with multiple-cycle songs, however, produce sound pulses with a variety of tones. The highest tone is generated by *D. bipectinata* and has a frequency of 575 c.p.s. The tone of *D. athabasca* is 440 c.p.s. and the tone of *D. algonquin* is 225 c.p.s.

The love songs of the fruit flies that are continuous buzzers are not monotonous, to use that word in its pure sense.

The song of *D. paramelanica*, for example, is one of those that continue for several seconds. For the first tenth of a second the tone of the buzz is 440 c.p.s. The tone then shifts to 265 c.p.s. for a slightly longer interval; the two tones are then repeated at the same intervals until the song ends. The 10-second song of *D. micromelanica*, another continuous buzzer, is basically a soft 440 c.p.s., combined with an intermittent louder and lower 385 c.p.s.

In addition to possessing variations in duration and tone, the love songs of fruit flies also vary with respect to the interval between sound pulses. The briefest interval, eight thousandths of a second, is found in *D. bipectinata*. *D. melanogaster* repeats its song 30 times a second, and its near relative *D. simulans* does so 20 times a second. At the far end of the range is *D. melanica*; nearly four tenths of a second may pass before it repeats its song.

With such a wide range of variation the possible number of fruit fly songs is very large. We could not judge which of the many variables were significant in terms of signal content without acquiring some knowledge of the mechanisms that produce the songs and of the physiology of the female receptor organ. We began by examining the mechanics of song production. We had already re-

corded the buzz produced by *D. melanogaster* in flight, and we also knew that the shape of the sound pulses produced by the courting fly was similar to the shape of a portion of the flight buzz. This suggested to us how the love song might be generated.

By making a series of multiple-flash photographs of *D. melanogaster* in flight we were able to establish its normal wingbeat cycle. We next used the sounds produced in flight to trigger the multiple flashes. The resulting photographs showed that the flight sound resembling the love song is produced by the upstroke of the wing, whereas the downstroke is fairly noiseless.

We then made multiple-flash photographs of a male during courtship, using a prearranged time interval between flashes. These photographs showed that the courting male lifts his extended wing for a single beat about every three hundredths of a second; the upstroke lasts for only three thousandths of a second, whereas the downstroke lasts for more than four thousandths of a second. Since our courtship recordings had already revealed that the love song of *D. melanogaster* was a single pulse with a duration of three thousandths of a second, it was probable that the wing upstroke in courtship produces the song pulse just as the same upstroke in flight produces the characteristic buzz. The activation of the system responsible for the sound, however, differs in the two instances. In flight it is a resonant oscillation of the fly's thoracic mechanism that produces the continuous train of sound pulses. In courtship the pulses are not produced continuously but intermittently.

Using the same technique, we went on to examine the courtship wingbeat of *D. persimilis*, whose song consists of a five-cycle pulse with a tone of about 540 c.p.s. [*see upper illustration at right*]. During courtship this fly's wings beat about 270 times per second. Because the wingbeat frequency is only half the frequency of the pulse tone we concluded that in this fly's courtship display the wing movement produces sound on both the upstroke and the downstroke and that a short burst of movement is involved. This means that its thorax is activated in a way different from the activation of the thorax in *D. melanogaster*.

Since the oscillation that produces the love song is mechanically similar to the oscillation in flight, it appears that courtship for the fruit fly means using in a special way a mechanism that already exists. This also appears to be true in the case of the female's receptor organ. Studies of other kinds of fly have shown that the primary function of the insects' antennae is to monitor and control the act of flying. Using very loud sounds, we have excited the antennae of fruit flies and have found that the frequencies that cause the aristae to resonate are much the same as the frequency of the flies' wingbeat. The aristae's secondary function as a receptor of the male love song evidently arose from this coincidence.

Having learned something about the ways songs are generated and about the organs that receive them, we thought it would be instructive to test the effects of synthetic songs that we could vary with respect to length of pulse and interval between pulses. As we have noted, wingless males court with the same perseverance as winged ones, but the females rarely accept their advances. This meant that we could assess the efficacy of an artificial song by observing whether or not it contributed to a wingless male's success in courtship. The species of fly studied in the experiment was *D. melanogaster*.

We used a sine-wave oscillator driven by a pulse generator to obtain single sinusoidal voltage pulses, but it was harder to reproduce the pulses than to generate them. Each pulse consists of a harmonic series of frequencies, and if

the transducer is to be accurate, it must have a "flat" output for all frequencies in the series. We solved the problem by modifying a high-fidelity loudspeaker, making its diaphragm rigid and aiming it into a pipe containing the cell that housed the flies. The sound pulses we reproduced in this way were faithful imitations of the real thing.

Our first test involved spacing the song pulses at different intervals. We

not only used the interval between pulses that is normal for the species—three hundredths of a second—but also piped to the flies sound pulses separated by intervals half or twice that long. Only the song with the normal interval induced receptivity in the female flies. This result interested us because many simple animal "clocks" and "counters" can be deceived by presenting signals that are half or double the normal value. The fe-

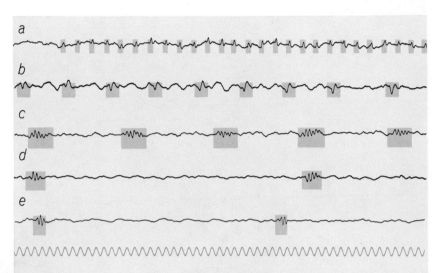

SIMPLE SONGS of five species produce quite different oscilloscope records. The first (*a*), the song of *Drosophila bipectinata*, consists of rapidly repeated pulses, each made up of a single cycle of tone (*colored area*). The interval between pulses is .0085 second. The song of *D. affinis* (*b*) consists of less frequent pulses, spaced .028 second apart and having a double cycle of tone. The pulses of the next three songs may have from three to seven cycles of tone. *D. persimilis* (*c*) and *D. pseudoobscura* (*d*) are New World species with overlapping natural ranges; interbreeding is evidently prevented by the three-to-one difference in their song intervals. The difference in interval between *D. pseudoobscura* and *D. ambigua* (*e*) is slight, but the chance of interbreeding in the wild is remote because *D. ambigua* is an Old World species. The frequency used for calibration (*color*) is 200 cycles per second.

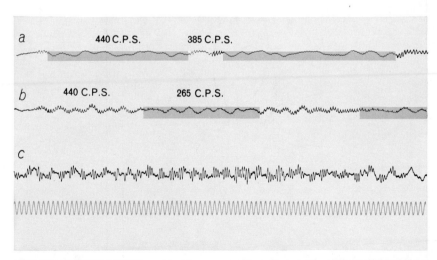

MORE COMPLEX SONGS at first appear to be almost continuous tones. In the case of *D. micromelanica* (*a*) a quiet song (*colored area*) is irregularly interrupted by a loud buzz. In the song of *D. paramelanica* (*b*) the quiet song regularly gives way to a louder portion. The song of *D. athabasca* (*c*) shows amplitude variations but a steady frequency of 440 c.p.s.

male fly's success in discrimination suggests that her analysis of the courtship signal is a fairly complex process. We also presented pulses separated by an interval of nearly five hundredths of a second, which is the normal interval for the song of a closely related species, *D.* *simulans.* This song too failed to induce receptivity in the female flies, leading us to the conclusion that the difference in interval is one effective isolating mechanism between these two species.

We next tested the effects of pulses of longer and shorter duration than normal. The pulse of the *D. melanogaster* love song lasts for three thousandths of a second. We presented the flies with pulses half or twice that long; the females proved equally responsive to all three signals. Since any one of the three will excite a single damped vibration of

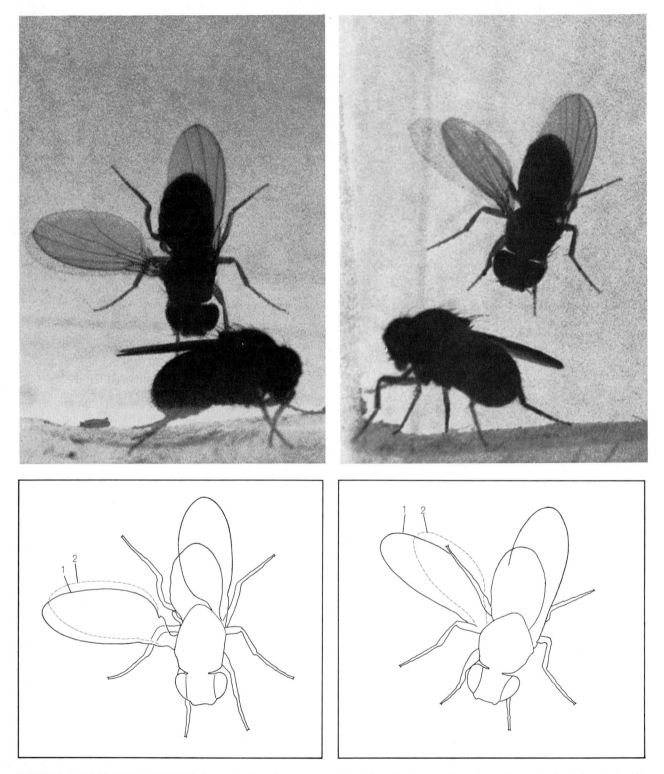

MULTIPLE-FLASH PHOTOGRAPHS of courting *D. melanogaster* males reveal the wing motions responsible for the flies' courtship song. In the first of the four photographs a dim flash is followed three thousandths of a second later by a brighter flash. The drawing below the photograph outlines changes in the right wing's position: it has been lifted up and to the rear. The single sound pulse characteristic of the species' song is produced by the movement. In the second photograph the flashes are two thousandths of a second

the female's aristae, we did not find the result surprising. In the case of love songs that continue the pulse for more than one cycle, however, the possibility exists that the female is perceiving not only the interval between pulses but also the frequency of the tone and the number of cycles in the pulse. If so, the vocabulary of the love song is elaborate and the range of meaningful song variation between species is great.

We found that the sound pressure needed to stimulate the female was about 115 decibels, which in human terms is roughly equivalent to the climax of Tchaikovsky's "1812 Overture." This led us to the calculation that when both the male and the female fly are standing on a flat surface, the male must approach within two millimeters of the female if his song is to deliver that much sound

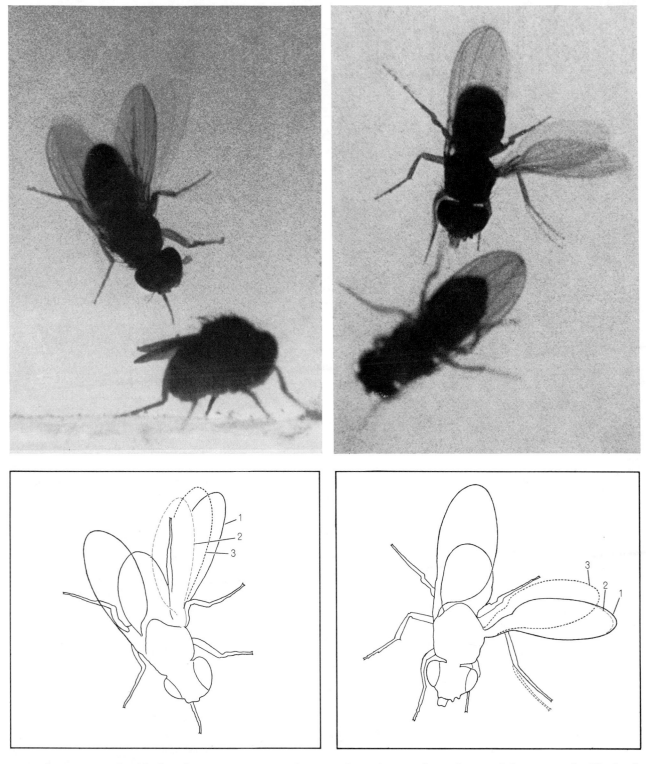

apart; the same upward and backward wing movement is evident. The male's left wing is extended in the third photograph; its motion is recorded by a sequence of dim, bright and dim flashes three thousandths of a second apart. The last of the flashes shows the wing as it moves down after completing an upstroke. The fourth photograph was also made with three flashes at the same interval; the instant recorded is evidently the interval between upstrokes. It is not until the third flash that the male's wing rises again.

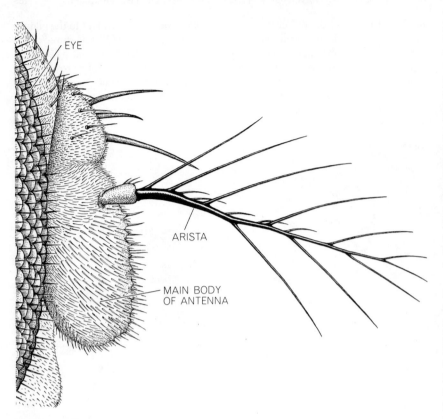

EYE

ARISTA

MAIN BODY
OF ANTENNA

FEMALE ORGAN that is vibrated by the song of the male fruit fly is the arista, a feathery extension of the fly's antenna. The organ is shown here 360 times larger than natural size.

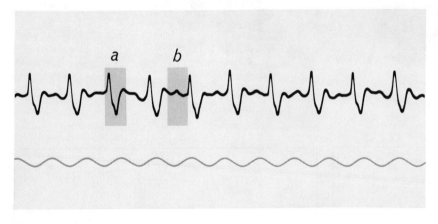

a　　*b*

FLIGHT SOUND of *D. melanogaster* is caused by resonant oscillations of the fly's thoracic mechanism associated with wing motion. The upstroke (*a*) is loud, the downstroke (*b*) quiet.

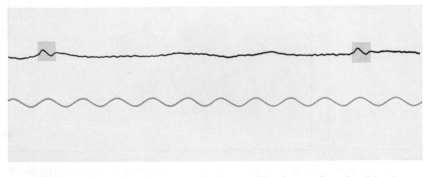

COURTSHIP SONG of *D. melanogaster* closely resembles the sound produced by the upstroke of the insect's wings in flight. The pulses (*colored areas*) are .034 second apart.

pressure to her aristae. By getting that close two flies can meet and identify each other even in noisy surroundings.

Good circumstantial evidence supports our conclusion that courtship songs are important in maintaining sexual isolation between various fruit fly species. The closely related species *D. pseudoobscura* and *D. persimilis* can scarcely be told apart on morphological grounds, but it is simple to separate them on the basis of their completely different love songs. The same is true of the closely similar species *D. algonquin* and *D. affinis*. On the other hand, *D. ananassae* and *D. athabasca*, species that are only distantly related, have songs that are quite alike.

Two closely related species of fruit fly have similar songs; they are *D. pseudoobscura* and *D. ambigua*. A real possibility of hybridization might exist here, but a meeting of the species outside the laboratory is extremely unlikely. In nature *D. pseudoobscura* is confined to North America and *D. ambigua* to the Old World. All of this suggests that different song patterns evolve only when there is a possibility that the integrity of the species might break down.

How did the various song patterns evolve? One of us (Ewing) has examined this question, working with flies of closely related races within the superspecies *D. paulistorum*. This is a group that has been studied from the genetic standpoint by Theodosius Dobzhansky and his co-workers; it is believed to be in the process of splitting into several true species. There are six distinct races of *D. paulistorum*, and until recently the species *D. pavlovskiana* was also included in the superspecies. Crosses between the races are partially sterile. The races also show some behavioral isolation: in mixed populations the individual flies mate preferentially with members of their own race.

The songs of the group follow the pattern of *D. melanogaster*: each pulse consists of a single cycle of a single tone. The intervals between pulses, however, are variable. The songs of five of the *D. paulistorum* races are quite similar but the song of the sixth is unique. *D. pavlovskiana* also has a unique song. Judging by other criteria, the race with the unique song is also the most distinctive of the six. Taking all seven populations into consideration, it is evident that the most distinctive are the ones with the unique songs. This suggests that the original barrier to interbreeding of the races is not a difference in song but rather a mechanism that evolved in some other way. The unique songs evidently evolve later as a secondary mechanism reinforcing an existing sexual isolation.

Once the song patterns have evolved, how are they inherited? One of us (Ewing) was able to examine this question by hybridizing *D. persimilis* and *D. pseudoobscura* in the laboratory. The hybrid males are sterile but they still court, so that it is possible to record their songs. The hybrid females fortunately are fertile and so can be backcrossed with either parent species.

The songs of the two species are not at all alike. *D. pseudoobscura* begins its song by emitting a series of widely spaced pulses with a tone of 540 c.p.s. The interval between pulses is nearly two tenths of a second. When the part of the song with the low repetition rate is concluded, there follows a part with a high repetition rate: now the pulse tone is 260 c.p.s. and the interval between pulses is four hundredths of a second. In contrast, the song of *D. persimilis* seldom includes a part with a low repetition rate; when on occasion it does, the pulses are few in number and together last for no more than half a second. Usually the song consists only of a signal with a high repetition rate; the pulse tone is 540 c.p.s. and the interval between pulses is about two hundredths of a second.

The type of song the hybrids inherited proved to be the type of the maternal species. Furthermore, when first-generation females are backcrossed to males of either species, half of the male progeny perform songs of the first species and half perform songs of the second. It follows that the inheritance of song type is sex-linked and that the genes are borne on the X chromosome rather than on the Y chromosome. The inheritance of pulse interval is more complex and may be partly controlled by genes on chromosomes other than sex chromosomes (the X and Y chromosomes).

The outcome of the hybridization experiment suggests an answer to one of the knottier evolutionary questions that is raised by the very existence of elaborate, species-specific signals. How, one wonders, have the signals been able to change with the passage of time? Any change that occurred in the signal or the receiver would obviously be disadvantageous. This is borne out by the fact, established by our studies, that the songs of a single fruit fly species are extremely durable, showing no measurable variability even when the populations of the species are geographically isolated. We have recorded *D. melanogaster* males that were native to Edinburgh, to San Francisco and to the Amazon basin; all have identical songs.

The fact that inheritance of song type is sex-linked suggests a means for new songs to evolve. The first-generation hybrid females from the crossbreeding of *D. pseudoobscura* and *D. persimilis* were receptive to males of both species. The same could well be true in the case of a gene change that affected the qualitative aspect of a song. The result would be first-generation males that performed a new song pattern and first-generation females that were receptive to it. Selection for sex-linked characteristics is much more rigorous than selection for non-sex-linked ones. Under suitable circumstances such a genetic change would rapidly become fixed in a population.

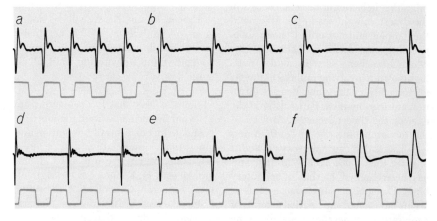

ARTIFICIAL SONGS were played to *D. melanogaster* females to determine if the interval between pulses was a key factor in song recognition. The interval normal to the species is .034 second (*b*); the females were responsive to this signal. When pulses were presented at twice the rate (*a*) and half the rate (*c*), the females did not respond. The normal duration of each song pulse is .003 second (*e*). Artificial pulses of half the duration (*d*) and twice the duration (*f*) but retaining the normal interval between pulses were played to the females; they responded to all three signals. The calibration frequency (*color*) is 50 c.p.s.

20

The Aerial Migration of Insects

by C. G. Johnson
December 1963

A few insects migrate seasonally over great distances rather like birds. Recently it has been learned that most other species also migrate by simply beating their wings while the wind carries them

The literature of entomology, beginning with the Bible, records many astonishing accounts of the migration behavior of insects. Locusts in the desert, mosquitoes in the Arctic and the Tropics and butterflies, moths, beetles, bugs and dragonflies almost everywhere have been seen in sudden mass flights, often involving millions of insects all traveling in the same general direction at the same time. Particularly in the case of the desert locust of Africa and the monarch butterfly of North America—insects that can make seasonal flights of more than 2,000 miles—this behavior has been likened to that of migratory birds. The spectacular character of these flights has invited explanation in terms of a migration instinct that would cause the individual insects to congregate in response to overcrowding or to some other unfavorable change in the environment, and has inspired speculation about sensory mechanisms that would enable the individuals to orient themselves in space, navigate and hold course toward distant destinations. Migratory flight thus more or less elaborately defined became one hallmark of a few species and much controversy has flamed from efforts to distinguish "true" migrators from mere drifters whose populations were dispersed by the wind.

It was closer acquaintance with the desert locust—established with the aid of photographic film interpreted by R. C. Rainey and Z. V. Waloff of the Anti-Locust Research Centre in London—that helped to set modern studies of insect migration on an entirely new and more fruitful course. Locusts are insect migrants par excellence. Vigorous fliers, they give an observer the strong subjective impression of concerted, purposeful progress in a direction under their own control. The camera too will show whole groups of insects headed in one direc-

tion. In successive images registered on the same film, however, individuals headed in one direction are seen to be carried in another direction by the wind. Within a swarm there will be many groups of similarly oriented insects flying in different directions, but the swarm as a whole will move with the wind, albeit more slowly.

The discovery that locust swarms are wind-borne eliminated the need to postulate mechanisms of orientation and navigation as essential features of insect migration. What is common to all migrants, as J. D. Kennedy of the Agricultural Research Council in Cambridge, England, has insisted, is an intense "locomotory drive" that sets the insect off on a relatively prolonged and undistracted flight compared with other kinds of flight associated with egg-laying or feeding. The drive arises from the internal physiology of the individual in a way not yet understood, but it is associated somehow, at least in females, with sexual immaturity. With the behavior of individuals synchronized by the simultaneity of their development, the migratory flight seems to have evolved as an adaptation designed primarily to relinquish habitats destined to become unsuitable and to secure new ones. This often leads to dispersal of the species. In this view migratory behavior appears as a key phase in the life history not of merely a few species of insects but of a large proportion of winged species. To the universal cycle of birth, reproduction and death must be added the process of migration or dispersal, with the winged adult as the essential, mobile element in the system.

For an understanding of migratory behavior in a generalized form, the lowly plant-sucking aphid provides a most typical and instructive example. Aphids

move on the wind. In spring and summer some species called the migratory aphids feed and deposit their larvae on herbs (these aphids are viviparous, delivering small larvae rather than eggs), and in fall and winter they transfer their activities to woody shrubs. These insects have been under intensive study by our group at the Rothamsted Experimental Station and by other workers at the Agricultural Research Council in Cambridge.

At the end of the larval stage the aphid molts into either a wingless or a winged adult [*see top illustration on page 190*]. The wingless form stays where it is, but every new winged adult, after waiting for some hours until its cuticle hardens, takes off on a strong vertical flight, attracted by the blue light of the sky. It is caught by the wind and, still flying actively, may be carried hundreds or thousands of feet aloft and often many miles overland. Typically the locomotory drive begins to fail within an hour or two and the aphid starts its fortuitous descent. If the plant on which it lands is one to which it is adapted, the insect feeds for the first time since leaving its birthplace. Then it may begin to deposit larvae. If the flight has been short or if the plant is unsuitable, the aphid may take off again. It may make several flights and cover many miles in the few days before it is finally grounded by the dissolution of its wing muscles. The migratory flight thus spreads the species to new habitats and effects the seasonal transfer of the population from green herbs to woody shrubs, even though the direction and distance of travel depend in part on the wind.

All other migrants share some elements of this behavioral routine with the aphid. Characteristically, most insects make their migratory flight soon after completion of their metamorphosis and

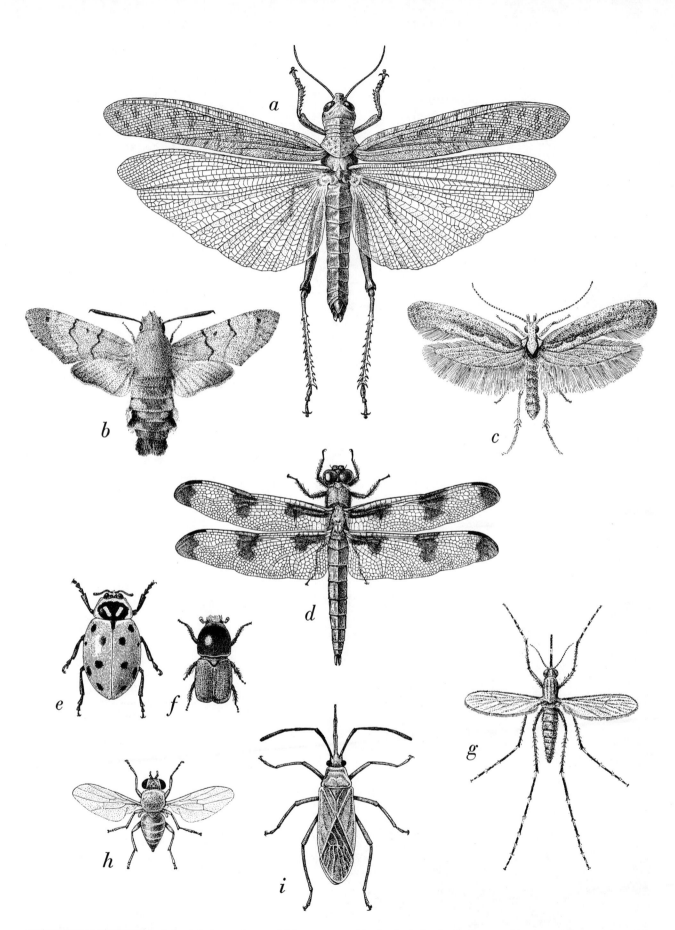

MIGRATORY INSECTS include (*a*) desert locust, *Schistocerca gregaria*, (*b*) hummingbird hawk moth, *Macroglossa stellatarum*, (*c*) diamondback moth, *Plutella maculipennis*, (*d*) dragonfly, *Libellula pulchella*, (*e*) ladybird beetle, *Hippodamia convergens*, (*f*) elm bark beetle, *Scolytus multistriatus*, (*g*) mosquito, *Aëdes taeniorhynchus*, (*h*) frit fly, *Oscinella frit*, and (*i*) tropical cotton stainer, *Dysdercus suturellus*. Although these insects are not drawn to exact scale, they are shown in their approximate relative sizes.

APHIS FABAE, a migratory species of aphid, occurs in many forms during a year. The five shown here are the fundatrix (*top*), which hatches in spring from an overwintering egg and founds a new line; a wingless female that gives live birth to new larvae (*center left*); a winged female that migrates and gives live birth (*center right*); a male (*bottom left*) that mates with an egg-laying female (*bottom right*). Species changes host plants with season.

DESERT LOCUSTS in this swarm covered 400 square miles of Ethiopia in October, 1958. Locusts are a form of grasshopper. They travel in swarms and decimate vegetation as they go.

before they enter the reproductive phase of their life history. The mosquito *Aëdes taeniorhynchus,* studied in Florida by Maurice W. Provost, E. T. Nielsen and James S. Haeger, begins its migration with its first flight after emergence and may travel up to 20 miles in a direction strongly influenced by the wind. The butterfly *Ascia monuste,* also observed in Florida, makes a few preliminary feeding flights, but these gradually lengthen into a prolonged migratory flight along the coast in the shelter of the dunes. Although the individual insect normally migrates only during the first 24 hours of adult life, it may travel nearly 100 miles. Thereafter it settles down and makes many short local feeding and egg-depositing flights. The literature contains numerous reports of early migratory flights in other orders, including dragonflies and beetles. Of equal importance, species not usually regarded as migrants have been observed to do the same thing. Winged ants and termites make an intense first flight in the adult form. Although short in duration, these flights enable them to establish new colonies at some distance from their natal habitat.

Other insects, such as some scolytid beetles, hibernate after they emerge and, still sexually immature, migrate months later. Many insects, including some moths, thrips and beetles, migrate first to sites where they hibernate and then migrate again at the end of hibernation. Most adult insects live for less than a year, some for only a few days, but certain ladybird beetles live up to two or three years. They are believed to undertake several migratory or dispersal flights during their lifetime and not simply one flight after emergence. These are some of the insects that have attracted attention by their habit of migrating simultaneously and massing together during hibernation and therefore prior to remigration.

In their migratory flight aphids do not excite as much wonder as the same behavior does in the case of larger insects. They appear against the sky as tiny elements in the aerial plankton, part of the busy swarm of "gnats" that may lend visual discomfort to the heat of a summer's day. At Rothamsted we have developed suction traps to plot the diurnal rise and fall of the aphid population in the air. Suspended at measured heights from steel towers or from barrage balloons, these traps suck in the air and collect the insects in a tube. Disks are dropped into the collecting tube at preset intervals in order to divide the catch

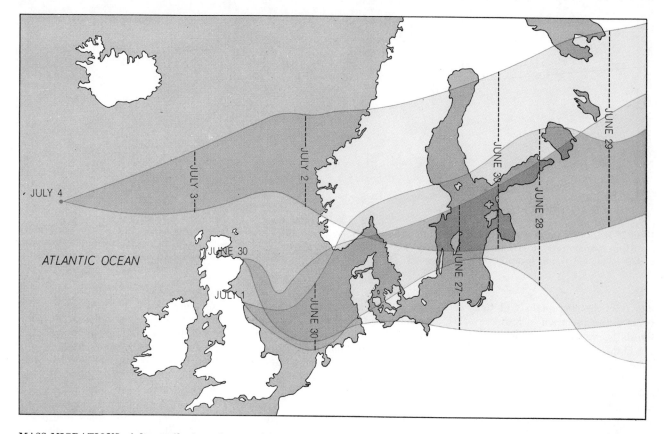

MASS MIGRATIONS of diamondback moth were observed June 30 and July 1, 1958, at two points on the northern coast of Britain, and on July 4, 1958, by a weather ship at sea, when thousands of tiny moths appeared on the bridge. The colored shading marks the air masses that carried the migrating moths. Dates indicate approxi- mate positions of these air masses on days before observations of migrations. Presumably the moths came from the region where the three air masses overlap. Moths observed at sea had evidently traveled 1,000 miles from the coast of Norway, beating their wings all the time. If they reached America, they flew for two more days.

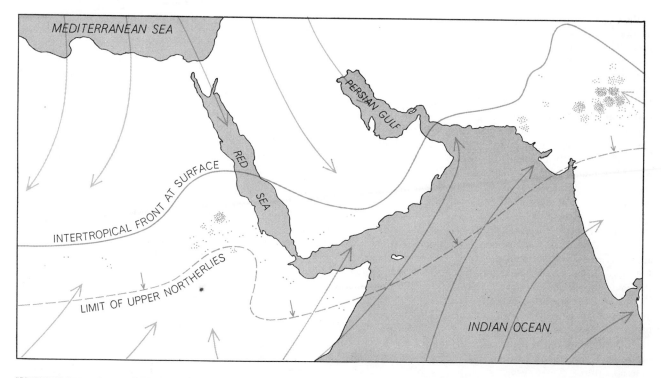

INTERTROPICAL CONVERGENCE ZONE, where winds from north meet those from south (colored arrows), producing rain, pro- vides moisture that enables locusts to breed. The rain also brings growth of vegetation, on which locust larvae can feed. Thus, travel with the wind serves ecological needs. Each colored dot denotes a report of a locust swarm between July 12 and July 31, 1950.

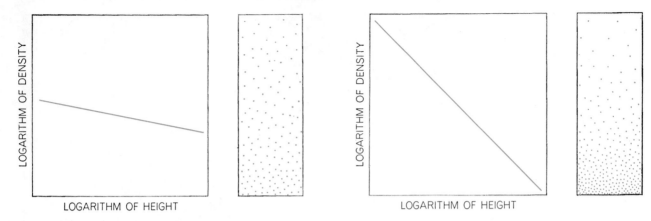

INSECT DENSITY varies with height according to turbulence of air. Rising currents carry insects up and slope of graph of logarithm of density plotted against logarithm of height is small (*left*). Still air produces a steep slope (*right*) because the insects remain near the ground. The colored dots in the accompanying panels represent insects and illustrate the density associated with each graph.

into fractions over periods of time. A count of the insects on each disk reveals the shifts and changes in the concentration of the air-borne population of aphids (and other insects) throughout the day.

By this technique we have found that aphid flights have a daily rhythm that frequently shows two peaks. We have also established the underlying mechanism of this cycle and thereby the explanation of the massing of the aphids in their migratory flight. The aphids that molt from the larval stage during the night are inhibited from flying by the cold and darkness. When the light and temperature rise above flight thresholds in the morning, the new adults that have accumulated all take off at the same time. Their exodus is recorded by our suction traps as a midmorning peak. Meanwhile the individuals whose maturation has been slowed by the low temperatures of the last hours before dawn mature more quickly as the day grows warmer. Their simultaneous departure yields another peak of migration in the early afternoon. By evening the fall in temperature and intensity of light from the sky brings a corresponding drop in the number of air-borne aphids. Since the temperature threshold for maturation is lower than that for flight, however, the next morning's crop of aphids now begins to accumulate. Trevor Lewis of Rothamsted has found that the mass migrations of another insect, the thrip, also occur in the warmup after a period of low temperature. Thus many mass insect flights must be regarded as gushes of newly emerged and waiting winged adults, released by a rise in temperature.

These observations can be matched to the recorded behavior of many classical and well-recognized migrants. As long ago as 1880 S. B. J. Skertchly noted an early-morning emergence of thousands of painted butterflies (*Vanessa cardui*); within an hour they all flew off together in the same direction. It is now known that such migrants as locusts, monarch butterflies, *Aëdes* and *Ascia* similarly emerge together at their breeding sites and then depart on the simultaneous flight that is featured in the literature on insect migration. The analogy so often drawn with bird migration in these cases fails to take into account the fact that all the individuals are of the same age; in contrast, flocks of birds may contain adults of all ages, and they may have congregated, unlike insects, from different places.

The strength and direction of the wind play an important but not necessarily crucial role in determining how far wind-borne migrants will go. The contribution of the insect—the duration of its locomotory drive—constitutes an equally important variable, for most insects must beat their wings if they are not to fall out of the air. The desert locust, geared to travel great distances, refueling as it goes, spends most of its adult life migrating, after which it lays eggs and dies. In contrast, termites migrate for only a few minutes but spend months reproducing. The travel of aphids (at least of those with temporary wing muscles) is limited by their initial fuel (fat) supply; they cannot refuel during migration.

In laboratory studies of flight capacity some insects turn in extraordinary performances. For example, although aphids are weak fliers, A. J. Cockburn of Rothamsted has shown that some can continue to beat their wings for 16 hours nonstop, until all their fuel is exhausted. These intrinsic performances, however, bear little relation to distances traveled in nature. An analysis of daily flight rhythms of aphids at different altitudes at Cardington in England shows that the average flight lasts for only one to three hours. In elegant flight-chamber experiments by J. S. Kennedy, aphids permitted to fly freely stay up for about the same length of time. Height-density studies of aphids and other insects reveal that the general aerial population, at least over Britain, resembles a daily explosion, with millions of insects thrown up, often to great heights, followed by an almost complete settling-out by nightfall.

In contrast with the short, daylight-only flights of the insects in the aerial plankton over Britain, desert locusts have been known to travel across the sea for 24 to 60 hours, going as many as 1,400 miles in one hop. This greatly exceeds their records for tethered flights in the laboratory. R. A. French and J. H. White have reported an observation by a ship 1,000 miles at sea of millions of tiny diamondback moths. Apparently they had been going for at least two days nonstop [*see top illustration on preceding page*], carried irresistibly by the wind at 20 miles per hour, beating their wings all the time in order to stay up.

The distance traveled overland does not necessarily reflect the duration of the insects' flight for another reason: the air currents may carry them upward as well as horizontally. In vigorous convection currents locusts form towering cumuliform swarms thousands of feet high. When convection is low, the swarms become flat and remain near the ground. As would be expected, smaller insects are even more sensitive to air currents. In still, stable air crowds concentrate near the ground; this accounts for dense swarms observed at eye level on quiet summer evenings. In rising currents they go up for thousands of feet. There is an approximately linear inverse relation between the logarithms of the density of the air-borne population and altitude, as would be expected in plotting the turbulent diffusion of small particles. The slope of the curve, when density is plotted against height, correlates well with the degree of atmospheric stability [see preceding page] and makes it possible to calculate from measurements of air currents the density of insects in particular altitude zones. These calculations show, for example, that in Britain in the middle of a typical summer day half of the population of frit flies (*Oscinella frit,* a cereal pest hitherto thought to fly only near the crop) is above 1,300 feet!

Travel in air currents is haphazard and many insects are lost in unfavorable places. Perhaps only a few reach a good site, but these are enough to perpetuate the species. Even this seemingly fortuitous system of movement can be highly adapted for survival, as Rainey has shown for the desert locust. Their migrations are associated with the movement of the convective air currents of the intertropical convergence zone, a region in which winds from the north and from the south converge, tend to ascend and so produce rain. As this zone moves across Africa and the Middle East with the change of seasons, the winds coming into it from the desert carry locusts from dry areas into wet areas [see bottom illustration on page 191]. Locust eggs must have moisture to survive and the larvae need vegetation when they hatch. Thus the apparent haphazard movements of the swarms are geared to their basic ecological requirements.

In all other species it can be anticipated that migratory behavior will prove to be correspondingly adapted to placing them in the right habitat at the right time in their life cycles. Some insects, such as the monarch butterfly, migrate long distances to overwintering sites and so escape adverse seasonal changes in climate and food. The migratory aphid, by moving a short distance from herbs to woody plants as the season changes, is doing the same thing. Adults of other species merely scatter in successive generations, without a regular change of host or complete change of habitat. In every case, however, the species engages in migration or adaptive dispersal (sometimes in both, since some classical migrants disperse en route) in order to relinquish a habitat that would eventually become untenable. T. R. E. Southwood of the Imperial College of Science

and Technology in London has recently shown that species occurring in relatively temporary habitats produce more migrant adults than species living in more permanent situations. Many migratory dragonflies, for example, live in ponds that dry up periodically, whereas nonmigratory species tend to inhabit rivers. Agricultural pests are wide-ranging and mobile because nearly all crops are temporary, annual plants. Hence pests are here today, gone tomorrow and where they come from often seems to be a mystery. It is not so mysterious, however, when one realizes that millions of individual insects of the aerial plankton rain down almost everywhere on the earth day after day.

Whereas adaptive advantages of migration are found in study of the eco-

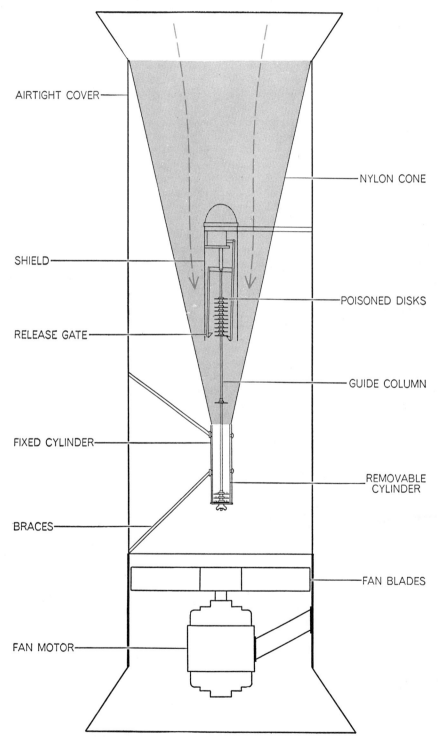

AIRTIGHT COVER

NYLON CONE

SHIELD

POISONED DISKS

RELEASE GATE

GUIDE COLUMN

FIXED CYLINDER

REMOVABLE CYLINDER

BRACES

FAN BLADES

FAN MOTOR

SEGREGATING SUCTION TRAP pulls in air and insects (*arrows*). At preset intervals, poisoned disks drop, dividing catch. This gives a direct measure of aerial density of insects at a given time. Various types of trap are suspended from posts, towers and balloons.

logical relations of each species, the cause of the behavior must be sought in the individual insects. In some cases a currently unfavorable environment induces the insects to leave; froghoppers have been known to move from cut vegetation and locusts have been thought to respond to dryness. Nevertheless, most mass migrations do not seem to be in direct response to any current adversity. Monarch butterflies, ladybird beetles, hover flies, noctuid moths and other species that go into winter quarters begin to migrate long before cold weather sets in. Neither food shortage nor "intolerable overcrowding" are evident to the human observer at the time of departure of aphids, *Ascia* and many others. The migration, therefore, usually comes in advance of any obvious change for the worse in living conditions.

The recognition that many mass migrations are made by fresh adults soon after emergence suggests that the cause be sought in the physiology and developmental history of the individual. It is well known that many insects are polymorphic: the adults of the same species differ in appearance either because of difference in sex (sexual polymorphism) or in structure, as in the various castes in a colony of termites or ants. Locusts reared in crowds produce adults of the phase *gregaria*, which are migrants and differ structurally to some extent from individuals reared in isolation, the phase *solitaria*. In migratory aphids the polymorphism takes the form of winged or wingless adults (alary polymorphism).

It has been observed that a small aphid population produces few winged adults, but as the population becomes large and dense the proportion with wings increases. This may be caused in some unknown manner by the increase in amount of direct contact between in-dividuals or by other factors. Perhaps change in the quantity or quality of food influences development one way or the other. Be this as it may, winged aphids all migrate; as far as is known, none stay behind. Migration is obligatory once the winged form appears.

Many insects, however, produce only winged adults; then it is the proportion that migrates that varies from year to year, and some generations may have no migrants. This has been another mystery of migration. Yet perhaps the mystery is no deeper than that associated with aphid migrations. It is certainly not unreasonable to assume that if aphids produced winged individuals in response to the environmental pressures that induce migration, the insects that always produce winged adults can generate some individuals with a "behavioral polymorphism" that endows them with the locomotory drive necessary to migration. These polymorphs would appear when the ecological situation of the species demanded it, just as the winged aphids appear.

The principal physiological clue to the triggering of the locomotory drive is the finding that it is associated with delay in the development of ovaries and of the endocrines that control ovary development. Most migratory flights are made by sexually immature females. Among migratory insects it is always the females that engage in migration, because it is they that spread the species. Males present different and distinct problems since even in some migratory species the males never migrate.

It is known that several factors, such as crowding, a short day or poor food (particularly protein deficiency) all delay development of the ovaries. It is also known that many insects cease migrating when ovaries mature. It should be possible, therefore, to make experimental tests of whether or not changes in such factors as length of day, food and temperature produce the postulated behavioral polymorphism. If they do, this would bring us back to the old idea that migration and adaptive dispersal are induced by overcrowding, changing seasons or poor food, but that the mechanism is in the biochemical rather than the sensory responses of the individual insect.

Still awaiting investigation by entomologists are some of the real puzzles of nature that surround such highly specialized migrants as the monarch butterfly. How, for example, do vast numbers of different species make their way seasonally along well-defined routes, often in mountain passes? What are the factors that determine the orientation of migrants that fly at a certain height when it is relatively calm and so control their own direction?

It will be difficult to find the means of attacking such problems. On the other hand, recent progress in the study of migratory behavior in insects has opened up equally interesting new questions to investigation. It remains to be determined, for example, if there is any general connection between the length of the period before egg-laying begins and the tendency to undistracted migration in different species. We must study the effect of length of day, larval crowding and quantity and quality of food on the length of the migratory period and also find out how these factors relate to the attraction of the sky that takes the migrating insect into the windy air. Finally, we should like to know how many species are in the aerial plankton by accident and how many by adaptation. I suspect that far more are there by adaptation than is commonly believed.

Butterflies and Plants

21

June 1967

The hungry larvae of butterflies are selective in choosing the plants they eat. This reflects the fact that the evolution of both plants and the animals that feed on them is a counterpoint of attack and defense

Anyone who has been close to nature or has wandered about in the nonurban areas of the earth is aware that animal life sometimes raises havoc with plant life. Familiar examples are the sudden defoliation of forests by hordes of caterpillars or swarms of locusts and the less abrupt but nonetheless thorough denudation of large areas by grazing animals. A visitor to the Wankie National Park of Rhodesia can see a particularly spectacular scene of herbivore devastation. There herds of elephants have thinned the forest over hundreds of square miles and left a litter of fallen trees as if a hurricane had passed through.

Raids such as these are rare, and the fertile regions of the earth manage to remain rather green. This leads most people, including many biologists, to underestimate the importance of the perennial onslaught of animals on plants. Detailed studies of the matter in recent years have shown that herbivores are a major factor in determining the evolution and distribution of plants, and the plants in turn play an important part in shaping the behavior and evolution of herbivores.

The influence of herbivores on plants is usually far from obvious, even when it is most profound. In Australia huge areas in Queensland used to be infested with the spiny prickly-pear cactus, which covered thousands of square miles of the area and made it unusable for grazing herds. Today the plant is rare in these areas. It was all but wiped out by the introduction of a cactus moth from South America, which interestingly enough is now hardly in evidence. When one searches scattered remaining clumps of the cactus, one usually fails to find any sign of the insect. The plant survives only as a fugitive species; as soon as a clump of the cactus is discovered by the moth it is devoured, and the population of moths that has flourished on it then dies away. A similar situation is found in the Fiji Islands. There a plant pest of the genus *Clidemia* was largely destroyed by a species of thrips brought in from tropical America, and the parasitic insect, as well as the plant, has now become rare in Fiji.

The interplay of plant and animal populations takes many forms—some direct, some indirect, some obvious, some obscure. In California the live oak is disappearing from many areas because cattle graze on the young seedlings. In Australia a native pine that was decimated by rabbits has made a dramatic comeback since the rabbit population was brought under control by the myxomatosis virus. Australia also furnishes a striking example of how the evolution of a plant can be influenced by the presence or absence of certain animals. The plant involved is the well-known acacia. In Africa and tropical America, where grazing mammals abound, the acacia species are protected by thorns that are often fearsomely developed. Until recently there were comparatively few grazing mammals in Australia, and most of the acacia plants there are thornless, apparently having lost these weapons of their relatives on other continents.

By far the most important terrestrial herbivores are, of course, the insects. They have evolved remarkably efficient organs for eating plants: a great variety of mouthparts with which to pierce, suck or chew plant material. They eat leaves from the outside and the inside, bore through stems and roots and devour flowers, fruits and seeds. In view of the abundance, variety and appetites of the insects, one may well wonder how it is that any plants are left on the earth. The answer, of course, is that the plants have not taken the onslaught of the herbivores lying down. Some of their defenses are quite obvious: the sharp spines of the cactus, the sharp-toothed leaves of the holly plant, the toxins of poison ivy and the oleander leaf, the odors and pungent tastes of spices. The effectiveness of these weapons against animal predators has been demonstrated by laboratory experiments. For example, it has been shown that certain leaf-edge-eating caterpillars normally do not feed on holly leaves but will devour the leaves when the sharp points are cut away.

The plant world's main line of defense consists in chemical weapons. Very widespread among the plants are certain chemicals that apparently perform no physiological function for the plants themselves but do act as potent insecticides or insect repellents. Among these are alkaloids, quinones, essential oils, glycosides, flavonoids and raphides (crystals of calcium oxalate). Long before man learned to synthesize insecticides he found that an extract from chrysanthemums, pyrethrin, which is harmless to mammals, is a powerful killer of insects.

Particularly interesting are the alkaloids, a heterogeneous group of nitrogenous compounds found mainly in flowering plants. They include nicotine, caffeine, quinine, marijuana, opium and peyote. Considering the hallucinogenic properties of the last three drugs, it is amusing to speculate that the plants bearing them may practice "chemopsychological warfare" against their enemies! Does an insect that has fed on a fungus containing lysergic acid diethylamide (LSD) mistake a spider for its mate? Does a zebra that has eaten a

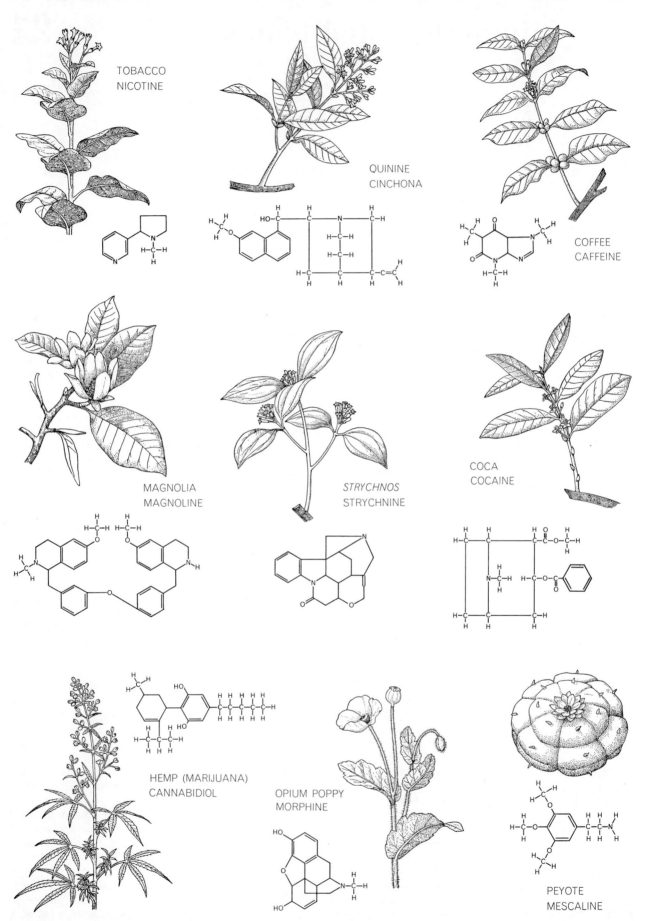

TOBACCO
NICOTINE

QUININE
CINCHONA

COFFEE
CAFFEINE

MAGNOLIA
MAGNOLINE

STRYCHNOS
STRYCHNINE

COCA
COCAINE

HEMP (MARIJUANA)
CANNABIDIOL

OPIUM POPPY
MORPHINE

PEYOTE
MESCALINE

ALKALOIDS give the plants that contain them protection from predators; nine such plants are illustrated. The authors note that plant alkaloids can disturb a herbivore's physiology and that hallucinogenic alkaloids may be "chemopsychological" weapons.

plant rich in alkaloids become so intoxicated that it loses its fear of lions? At all events, there is good reason to believe eating plant alkaloids produces a profound disturbance of animals' physiology.

Of all the herbivores, the group whose eating habits have been studied most intensively is the butterflies—that is to say, butterflies in the larval, or caterpillar, stage, which constitutes the major part of a butterfly's lifetime. Around the world upward of 15,000 species of butterflies, divided taxonomically into five families, have been identified. The five families are the Nymphalidae (four-footed butterflies), the Lycaenidae (blues, metalmarks and others), the Pieridae (whites and yellows), the Papilionidae (including the swallowtails, the huge bird-wings of the Tropics and their relatives) and the Libytheidae (a tiny family of snout butterflies). The Nymphalidae and Lycaenidae account for most (three-fourths) of the known genera and species.

A caterpillar is a formidable eating machine: by the time it metamorphoses into a butterfly it has consumed up to 20 times its dry weight in plant material. The numerous species vary greatly in their choice of food. Some are highly selective, feeding only on a single plant family; others are much more catholic in their tastes, but none feeds on all plants indiscriminately. Let us examine the food preferences of various groups and then consider the evolutionary consequences.

One group that is far-ranging in its taste for plants is the Nymphalinae, a subfamily of the Nymphalidae that comprises at least 2,500 species and is widespread around the world. The plants that members of this group feed on include one or more genera of the figwort, sunflower, maple, pigweed, barberry, beech, borage, honeysuckle, stonecrop, oak, heather, mallow, melastome, myrtle, olive, buttercup, rose, willow and saxifrage families. Another group that eats a wide variety of plants is the Lycaeninae, a subfamily of the Lycaenidae that consists of thousands of species of usually tiny but often beautifully colored butterflies. The Lycaeninae in general are catholic in their tastes, and among their many food plants are members of the pineapple, borage, pea, buckwheat, rose, heather, mistletoe, mint, buckthorn, chickweed, goosefoot, morning glory, gentian, oxalis, pittosporum and zygophyllum families.

What determines the caterpillars'

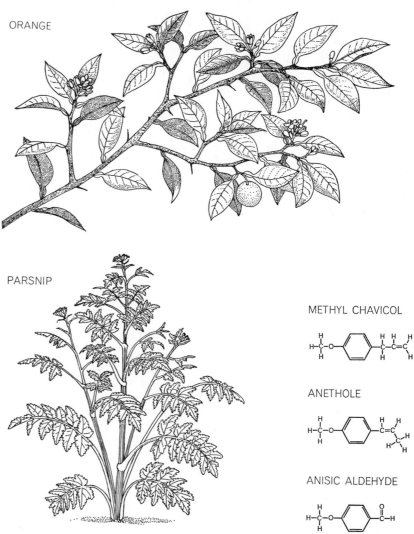

ORANGE

PARSNIP

METHYL CHAVICOL

ANETHOLE

ANISIC ALDEHYDE

PLANTS OF TWO FAMILIES, citrus (*top*) and parsley (*bottom*), produce the same three essential oils attractive to the larvae of black swallowtail butterflies. The chemical kinship between these plant families suggests a closer ancestral tie than had been suspected.

food preferences? We learn a great deal about this subject by examining the diets of those butterfly species that are particularly selective in their choice of plants. One large group of swallowtails, for example, confines its diet mainly to plants of the Dutchman's-pipe family. Another feeds only on the "woody Ranales," a group of primitive angiosperms that includes the magnolias, the laurels and many tropical and subtropical plants. A third group of swallowtails is partial to plants of the citrus and parsley families; the striped caterpillars of these butterflies, which extrude two bright orange scent horns when they are disturbed, are familiar to gardeners, who often see them feeding on parsley, dill, fennel and celery plants. The caterpillars of the white butterfly group (a subfamily of the Pieridae) feed primarily on caper plants in the Tropics and on plants of the mustard family in temperate re-

gions. Similarly, the monarch butterfly and its relatives (a subfamily of the Nymphalidae) confine their diet primarily to plants of the milkweed and dogbane families.

Analysis of the plant selections by the butterfly groups has made it clear that their choices have a chemical basis, just as parasitic fungi choose hosts that meet their chemical needs. Vincent G. Dethier, then at Johns Hopkins University, noted some years ago that plants of the citrus and parsley families, although apparently unrelated, have in common certain essential oils (such as methyl chavicol, anethole and anisic aldehyde) that presumably account for their attractiveness to the group of swallowtails that feeds on them. Dethier found that caterpillars of the black swallowtail would even attempt to feed on filter paper soaked in these substances. The

same caterpillars could also be induced to feed on plants of the sunflower family (for example goldenrod and cosmos), which contain these oils but are not normally eaten by the caterpillars in nature.

The chemical finding, incidentally, raises an interesting question about the evolutionary relationship of plants. The sunflower, citrus and parsley families have been considered to be very different from one another, but their common possession of the same group of substances suggests that there may be a chemical kinship after all, at least between the citrus and the parsley family. Chemistry may therefore become a basis for reconsideration of the present classification system for plants.

In the case of the cabbage white butterfly larva the attractive chemical has been shown to be mustard oil. The pungent mustard oils are characteristic of plants of the caper and mustard families (the latter family includes many familiar food plants, such as cabbages, Brussels sprouts, horseradish, radishes and watercress). The whites' larvae also feed occasionally on plants of other families that contain mustard oils, including the garden nasturtium. The Dutch botanist E. Verschaeffelt found early in this century that these larvae would eat flour, starch or even filter paper if it was smeared with juice from mustard plants. More recently the Canadian biologist A. J. Thorsteinson showed that the larvae would eat the leaves of plants on which they normally do not feed when the plants were treated with mustard oil glucosides.

In contrast to the attractive plants, there are plant families on which butterfly larvae do not feed (although other insects may). One of these is the coffee family. Although this family, with some 10,000 species, is probably the fourth largest family of flowering plants in the world and is found mainly in the Tropics, as the butterflies themselves are, butterfly larvae rarely, if ever, feed on these plants. A plausible explanation is that plants of the coffee family are rich in alkaloids. Quinine is one example. Other plant families that butterflies generally avoid eating are the cucurbits (rich in bitter terpenes), the grape family (containing raphides) and the spiny cactus family.

One of the most interesting findings is that butterflies that are distasteful to predators (and that are identified by conspicuous coloring) are generally narrow specialists in their choice of food. They tend to select plants on which oth-

FIVE BUTTERFLIES protected by their unpalatability are illustrated with their preferred plants. They are *Thyridia themisto* and one of the nightshades (*a*), *Battus philenor* and Dutchman's-pipe (*b*), *Danaus plexippus* and milkweed (*c*), *Heliconius charitonius* and passion flower (*d*) and *Pardopsis punctatissima* and a representative of the violet family (*e*).

er butterfly groups do not feed, notably plants that are rich in alkaloids. It seems highly probable that their use of these plants for food has a double basis: it provides them with a feeding niche in which they have relatively little competition, and it may supply them with the substances, or precursors of substances, that make them unpalatable to predators. The distasteful groups of butterflies apparently have evolved changes in physiology that render them immune to the toxic or repellent plant substances and thus enable them to turn the plants' chemical defenses to their own advantage. Curiously, the butterfly species that mimic the coloring of the distasteful ones are in general more catholic in their feeding habits; evidently their warning coloration alone is sufficient to protect them.

The fact that some butterflies' diets are indeed responsible for their unpalatability has been demonstrated recently by Lincoln P. Brower of Amherst College and his co-workers. They worked with the monarch butterfly, whose larvae normally feed on plants of the milkweed family. Such plants are rich in cardiac glycosides, powerful poisons that are used in minute quantities to treat heart disease in man. When adult butterflies of this species are offered to hand-reared birds (with no previous experience with butterflies), the butterflies are tasted and then promptly rejected, as are further offerings of either the monarch or its close mimic, the viceroy. Recently Brower succeeded in spite of great difficulties in rearing a generation of monarch butterflies on cabbage and found that the resulting adults were perfectly acceptable to the birds, although they were refused by birds that had had previous experience with milkweed-fed monarchs.

The concept of warfare between the plants and the butterflies leads to much enlightenment on the details of evolutionary development on both sides. On the plants' side, we can liken their problem to that of the farmer, who is obliged to defend his crops from attack by a variety of organisms. The plants must deploy their limited resources to protect themselves as best they can. They may confine their growing season to part of the year (limiting their availability to predators); they may be equipped with certain mechanical or chemical defenses; some develop a nutrient-poor sap or nutritional imbalances that make them an inefficient or inadequate source of food. The herbivorous insects, for their part, reply with specializations to cope with the special defenses, as a hunter uses a high-powered rifle to hit deer or bear, a shotgun to hit birds or a hook to catch fish. No butterfly larva (or other herbivore) possesses the varieties of physical equipment that would allow it to feed on all plants; in order to feed at all it must specialize to some degree. Some of the specializations are extremely narrow; certain sap-sucking insects, for example, have developed filtering mechanisms that trap the food elements in nutrient-poor sap, and some of the caterpillars possess detoxifying systems that enable them to feed on plants containing toxic substances.

By such devices herbivores of one kind or another have managed to breach the chemical defenses of nearly every group of plants. We have already noted several examples. The mustard oils of the mustard and caper plant families,

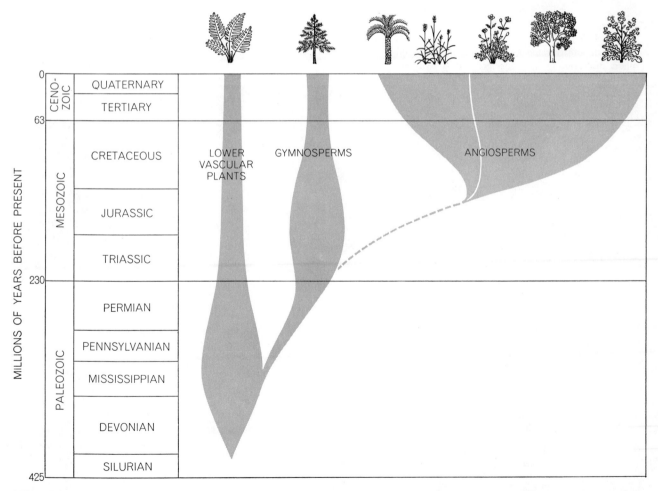

RECORD OF EVOLUTION within the plant kingdom shows that among the vascular plants the gymnosperms (*center*) declined as the angiosperms (*right*) became abundant. The authors attribute this to the acquisition of chemical defenses by the angiosperms.

BUTTERFLY EGGS (*top*) stand upright on a leaf of clover, the egg-laying site selected by the gravid female. Clover is the food plant preferred by this species: *Colias philodice*, the clouded sulphur. After hatching (*bottom*), growing clouded sulphur larvae feed on the plant preselected for them by the parent. When they metamorphose, they too will seek out clover as an egg-laying site.

for instance, serve to make these plants unpalatable to most herbivores, but the white butterflies and certain other insects have become so adapted to this defense mechanism that the mustard oils actually are a feeding stimulus for them. O. L. Chambliss and C. M. Jones, then at Purdue University, showed that a bitter, toxic substance in fruits of the squash family that repels honeybees and yellow jackets is attractive to the spotted cucumber beetle. Incidentally, this substance has been bred out of the cultivated watermelon, as any picnicker who has had to wave yellow jackets away from the watermelon can testify. By selecting against this bitter taste man has destroyed one of the natural protective mechanisms of the plant and must contend with a much wider variety of predators on it than the watermelon had to in the wild.

An important aspect of the insects' chemical adaptability is the recent finding that insects that feed on toxic plants are often immune to man-made insecticides. They evidently possess a generalized detoxifying mechanism. H. T. Gordon of the University of California at Berkeley has pointed out that this is commonly true of insects that are in the habit of feeding on a wide variety of plants. He suggests that through evolutionary selection such insects have evolved a high tolerance to biochemical stresses.

What can we deduce, in the light of the present mutual interrelations of butterflies and plants, about the evolutionary history of the insects and flowering plants? We have little information about their ancient history to guide us, but a few general points seem reasonably clear.

First, we can surmise that the great success of the angiosperm plants (plants with enclosed seeds), which now dominate the plant world since most of the more primitive gymnosperm lines have disappeared, is probably due in large measure to the angiosperms' early acquisition of chemical defenses. One important group of protective secondary plant substances, the alkaloids, is found almost exclusively in this class of plants and is well represented in those groups of angiosperms that are considered most primitive. Whereas other plants were poorly equipped for chemical warfare, the angiosperms were able to diversify behind a biochemical shield that gave them considerable protection from herbivores.

As the flowering plants diversified, the insect world also underwent a tremendous diversification with them. The intimate present relation between butterflies and plants leaves no doubt that the two groups evolved together, each

MODEL   MIMETIC FORM   NONMIMETIC FORM

a   *b*   *c*

d   *e*

f   *g*   *h*

UNPALATABLE BUTTERFLIES, whose disagreeable taste originates with the plants they ate as larvae, are often boldly marked and predators soon learn to avoid them. The three "models," so called because unrelated species mimic them, are the monarch, *Danaus* (*a*), another Danaine, *D. chrysippus* (*d*) and a third Danaine, *Amauris* (*f*). Their imitators are the viceroy, *Limenitis* (*b*), one form of *Papilio dardanus* (*e*) and another form of *P. dardanus* (*g*). Mimicry is not a genus-wide phenomenon: *L. astyanax* (*c*), a relative of the viceroy, is nonmimetic. So is a third form of *P. dardanus* (*h*), whose cousins (*e, g*) mimic two of the Danaine models.

influencing the development of the other. In all probability the butterflies, which doubtless descended from the primarily nocturnal moths, owe their success largely to the decisive step of taking to daytime feeding. By virtue of their choice of food plants all butterflies are somewhat distasteful, and Charles L. Remington of Yale University has suggested that this is primarily what enabled them to establish themselves and flourish in the world of daylight. The butterflies and their larvae did not, of course, overwhelm the plant world; on the contrary, in company with the other herbivores they helped to accelerate the evolution of the plants into a great variety of new and more resistant forms.

From what little we know about the relationships between other herbivore groups and their associated plants, we can assume that the butterfly-plant association is typical of most herbivore-plant pairings. This information gives us an excellent starting point for understanding the phenomenon that we might call "communal evolution," or coevolution. It can help, for example, to account for the great diversity of plant and insect species in the Tropics compared with the much smaller number of species in the temperate zones. The abundance of plant-eating insects in the Tropics, interacting with the plants, unquestionably has been an important factor, perhaps the most important one, in promoting the species diversity of both plants and animals in those regions. Indeed, the interaction of plants and herbivores may be the primary mechanism responsible for generating the diversity of living forms in most of the earth's environments.

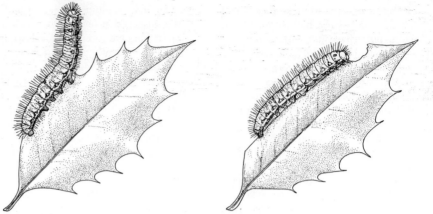

TOOTHED EDGE of the holly (*left*) normally protects it from leaf-edge eaters, such as the tent caterpillar. After the leaf's teeth are trimmed (*right*) the insect readily devours it.

Since the welfare, and even the survival, of mankind depend so heavily on the food supply and on finding ways to deal with insects without dangerous contamination of the environment with insecticides, great benefits might be derived from more intensive study of plant-herbivore associations. With detailed knowledge of these associations, plants can be bred for resistance to insects. Crop plants might be endowed with bred-in repellents, and strains of plants containing strong attractants for pests might be planted next to the crops to divert the insects and facilitate their destruction. New methods of eliminating insects without danger to man might be developed. Carroll M. Williams of Harvard University and his co-workers have discovered, for example, that substances analogous to the juvenile hormone of some insects are present in tissues of the American balsam fir. Since the juvenile

hormone acts to delay metamorphosis in insects, plants bred for such substances might be used to interfere with insect development. It is even possible that insects could be fought with tumor-inducing substances: at least one plant alkaloid, nicotine, is known to be a powerful carcinogen in vertebrates.

Such methods, together with techniques of biological control of insects already in use and under development, could greatly reduce the present reliance on hazardous insecticides. The insects have shown that they cannot be conquered permanently by the brand of chemical warfare we have been using up to now. After all, they had become battle-hardened from fighting the insecticide warfare of the plants for more than 100 million years. By learning from the plants and sharpening their natural weapons we should be able to find effective ways of poisoning our insect competitors without poisoning ourselves.

22

The Fungus Gardens of Insects

by Suzanne W. T. Batra and Lekh R. Batra
November 1967

*Several kinds of insects live only in association with
one kind of fungus, and vice versa. In some instances
the insect actively cultivates the fungus, browsing on it
and controlling its growth*

Anyone with at least a passing interest in biology is aware that fungi, being plants that lack chlorophyll and cannot conduct photosynthesis, live on other organisms or on decaying organic matter. It is less well known that many insects are similarly dependent on fungi. Indeed, there are insects that tend elaborate gardens of a fungus, controlling the growth of the plant according to their own specialized needs.

Some insect species are always found in association with a certain fungus, and some fungi only with a certain insect. Such complete interdependence is called mutualism. The mutualistic partners of insects are not limited to fungi; they include other microbial forms such as bacteria and protozoa. In some cases the insect feeds on its partner or on the partner's own partly digested food. In others the partner lives in the insect's alimentary tract and digests food the insect cannot digest for itself; frequently the partner supplies an essential constituent that is deficient in the insect's diet, such as nitrogen or a vitamin. Some mutualistic partners serve more than one of these functions.

The insects that are mutualistic with microbial organisms are divided into two groups. In one group the fungus, bacterium or protozoon lives inside the insect, either in the alimentary tract or in specialized cells. In the other group a fungus lives in the insect's nest. Here we shall discuss the relations between fungi and insects in the latter group, leading up to those insects that actively cultivate fungus gardens. Such relations have been studied for more than a century, but they offer many new possibilities for investigation. One wants to know more about the physiology of the relations, about how the partners interact at the molecular level. A deeper knowledge of the physiological mecha-

nisms would undoubtedly clarify how the mutualistic partnership came to be established in the course of evolution. It might also have important by-products. For example, much work has been done on the possibility of using fungi that are harmful to insects as a means of selectively controlling insect pests; such work might be advanced by knowing more about the relation between insects and beneficial fungi. As a second example, those insects that control the growth of fungi in gardens may do so by means of antibiotic substances that might well be useful to man.

The first kind of insect-fungus relation we shall take up centers on the tumor-like galls that sometimes appear on the bud, leaf or stem of a plant. These galls develop when certain insects deposit their eggs in the plant and somehow cause it to form an abnormal tissue which then nourishes the larva that emerges from the egg [see "Insects and Plant Galls," by William Hovanitz; SCIENTIFIC AMERICAN, November, 1959]. The galls caused by the mosquito-like midges of the family Itonididae also contain fungi. Growing parasitically on the gall tissue, these fungi usually form a thick layer on the inside of the gall. They appear at an early stage of the gall's development, and a single species of fungus is consistently found in association with larvae of each midge species. Many of these fungi, however, also grow independently of the insect. How fungus and insect come to be together in the gall is not known, but some workers believe the female midge deposits spores of fungus at the time she lays her eggs. Many of the fungus galls are caused by insects that feed by sucking plant sap, and except for a few cases it is unlikely that the fungus acts directly as a source of

food. It may be that the fungus assists the insect indirectly by partly breaking down the gall tissue so that the insect can digest it.

Many plants bear insect-fungus galls but only a few of the fungi have been identified. Some galls we have studied in our laboratory at the University of Kansas are leaf-blister galls on several kinds of goldenrod and aster caused by at least nine species of the midge *Asteromyia* (all of them associated with the fungus *Sclerotium asteris* in the U.S.), and flower-bud galls of the broom (*Cytisus*) caused by the midge *Asphondylia cytisii* (associated with the fungus *Diplodia* in the U.S. and Europe).

In contrast to the casual association between insects and fungi in plant galls, several species of the fungus *Septobasidium* and various scale insects (family Coccidae) that inhabit the fungal tissue coexist in a manner that is clearly mutualistic. *Septobasidium* resembles a thick lichen: it clings tightly to the leaves or branches of trees. The scale insects that inhabit this fungus in some way modify its growth in their vicinity, giving it a different texture or color; as a result some colonies of *Septobasidium* have a mottled surface.

The relation between this fungus and the insects that colonize it has been described by John N. Couch of the University of North Carolina. The insect, which feeds on sap, is attached to the tree by its sucking tube. The mycelium of the fungus—its thick mat of fine threads—shelters the insect from the weather and shields it from birds and parasitic wasps. In turn a few of the insects are penetrated by specialized threads, called haustoria, that extract nourishment from the insects' blood. Scale insects characteristically ingest more sap than they need; the fungus may take advantage of this fact by uti-

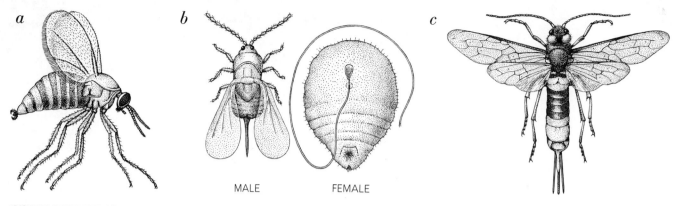

INSECT GARDENERS comprise unrelated species. Depicted here are representatives of six groups of insects that nest with a fungus. At left is a gall midge of the genus *Lasioptera*; its larvae probably feed on plant material that a fungus has partly digested. The scale insect *Aspidiotus osborni* (*b*) lives on trees under a protective canopy of fungus. The wood wasp *Sirex gigas* (*c*) deposits eggs cov-

lizing such nutrients while they are still circulating in the insect's body.

Septobasidium is distributed by scale insects as well as nourished by them; it does not live independently in nature. When the insects are young, some of them crawl on the surface of the fungus and become covered with spores. A few of the contaminated insects migrate to new areas on the tree, where they insert their sucking tube. Shielded by new mycelium, they survive. They are

also invaded, however, by haustoria from the developing spores, and as a result they do not attain maturity and reproduce. The new mutualistic colony is nonetheless able to continue because uncontaminated insects now find shelter in the mycelium. In some species of *Septobasidium* the entire process has apparently been made more efficient by the development of hollow "insect houses" that attract and hold the migrating scale insects. Thus the fungus

furnishes a shelter for the insects and the insects provide both a food supply and a means of dispersal for the fungus. Some insects are sacrificed for the benefit of the colóny as a whole; both fungus and insect benefit at the expense of the tree.

A different kind of mutualism has been observed involving on the one hand the wood wasps of the genera *Sirex*, *Tremex* and *Urocerus* and on the other the fungi *Stereum* and *Daedalea*.

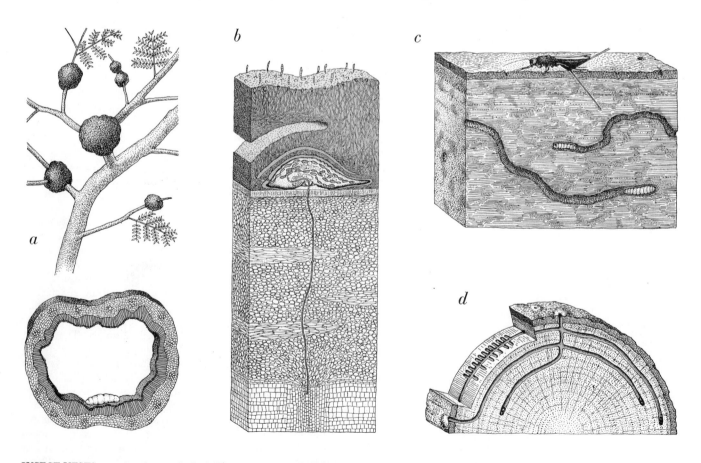

INSECT NESTS contain a fungus (*color*). The nests were made by the insects at the top of these two pages, or by an insect of the same group. The plant gall that encloses larvae of the midge is lined with a fungus parasitic on the plant (*a*). *Septobasidium* fungus sends threads into some of the insects it shelters and extracts nourishment from their blood (*b*). The burrows of wood

d   *e*   *f*

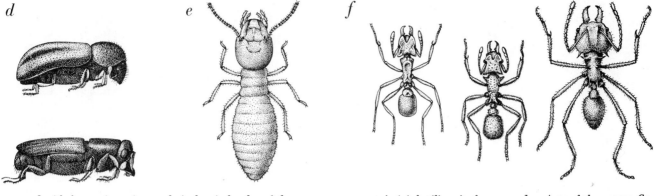

ered with fungus in moist wood. Ambrosia beetles of the genera *Trypodendron* (*d, top*) and *Crossotarsus* (*d, bottom*) carry spores from which grow their fungus. The termite *Odontotermes gurda-*

spurensis (*e*) fertilizes its fungus garden. Ants of the genera *Cyphomyrmex, Trachymyrmex* and *Atta* (*f, left to right*) actively cultivate fungus gardens. The insects are not drawn to the same scale.

These common fungi sometimes build a semicircular "bracket" out from a tree. The adult female wood wasp deposits her eggs in moist wood by means of a long, slender ovipositor, and at the base of this organ are tiny pouches that contain fungus cells called oidia. When the egg is deposited, oidia cling to it. Then the mycelium of the fungus grows into the wood, and when the wasp larva emerges from the egg it follows the path of the mycelium. The fungus partly di-

gests the wood before it is eaten by the larva. In the laboratory wood wasp larvae have been reared on a diet consisting only of *Stereum*, but whether the fungus is essential to the insect's nutrition is not known. Both in nature and in the laboratory the fungus grows well without the help of any insect.

The wood wasp nonetheless acts as an agent for the dissemination of *Stereum*. A larva that later develops into a female has organs that ensure the pres-

ervation of the fungus. These organs are tiny pits hidden in folds between the wasp's first and second abdominal segments; in them bits of fungus are trapped in a waxy material. Here an inoculum of fungus remains viable, whereas fungus in wood is inactivated when the wood eventually dries out. When the larva metamorphoses into a pupa, the organs that hold the fungus are discarded. Then, when the adult female wasp emerges from the pupal skin, tiny flakes

e

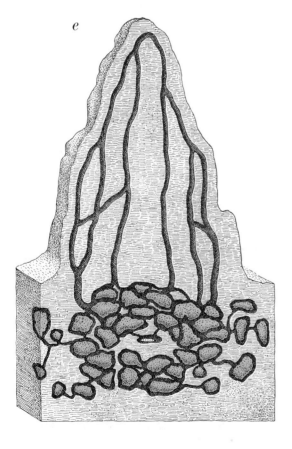

f

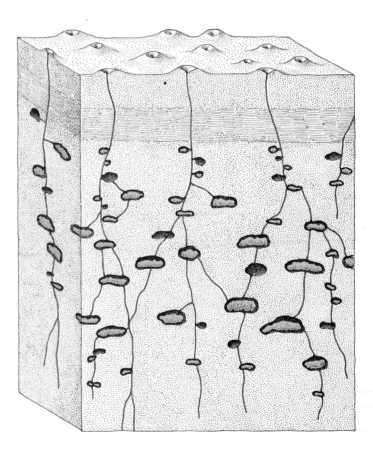

wasp larvae are made in wood infested with *Stereum* fungus, propagated by the insect (*c*). Fungus carried by an ambrosia beetle grows inside the insect's tunnels in timber (*d*). Mounds of earth

in which the termite nests contain fecal material permeated with fungus (*e*). *Atta texana* cultivates a garden of fungus in a huge underground nest (*f*). Here also the nests are not drawn to scale.

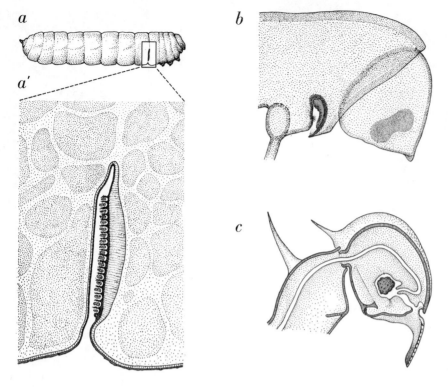

a

a'

b

c

FUNGUS CONTAINERS of three insects are depicted with the fungus indicated in color. Larvae of wood wasps that develop into females carry an inoculum of fungus behind the thorax (*a*). A section through the first two abdominal segments of the larva shows one of the fungus-filled organs (*a'*). The ambrosia beetle, shown here in longitudinal section, conveys spores of fungus in pockets located at the base of its front legs (*b*). A longitudinal section of the head of a fungus-growing ant reveals the pouch in which it transports fungus (*c*).

of fungus-impregnated wax that have fallen from the organs become lodged in the moist pouch at the base of the ovipositor. The flakes now give rise to a fungal mycelium, which develops the oidia that will coat the eggs. The transfer of the fungus from generation to generation of wood wasps is thereby assured.

Ambrosia beetles also carry fungi within their bodies. The numerous species of these wood-boring insects (families Scolytidae, Platypodidae and Lymexylonidae) cannot survive without ambrosia fungi (several genera of Ascomycetes and "imperfect" fungi). In their external skeleton are small pockets called mycangia (literally "fungus containers"); these pockets always contain a supply of viable fungus spores. When an ambrosia beetle tunnels into wood, spores are dislodged from the mycangia, and soon a mass of velvety fungus lines the interior of the tunnel. On this "ambrosia," which concentrates in its cells nutrients that have been extracted from the wood, the beetles feed.

Ambrosia beetles have been the subject of considerable research because they destroy much timber all over the

world. Their tunnels, sometimes called "shot holes," extend deep into the sapwood of trees and are surrounded by streaks of a stain manufactured by the enzymatic action of the fungus. The beetles most often attack hardwoods, preferring trees that have been weakened by drought, disease or fire, or fallen timber that is moist and filled with sap. Attracted by the odor of fermenting sap, the beetles fly upwind, usually at dusk; it is easy to collect them in the evening around a newly felled log. They are similarly attracted by the yeasty smell of beer and beer drinkers, and it is also convenient to collect them at a beer picnic! Some kinds bore into beer and wine kegs, which is why in Europe they are called "beer beetles."

The tunnels of ambrosia beetles can be distinguished from those of other wood-boring insects by a black or brown discoloration of the wood around the neat circular tunnel opening. There is, moreover, no wood dust or fecal matter inside the tunnel. When the beetles are excavating, fine wood particles, sometimes mixed with the insect's brown feces, accumulate outside the tunnel entrance. The beetle does not as a rule eat wood, and it rids its nest of wood

borings. The males of some species assist the females with tunnel excavation. Inside the ambrosia beetle's tunnel system one finds, depending on the species, either separate niches, each enclosing a single glistening larva or a pearl-like egg, or several larvae sharing an enlargement of the tunnel. In many species the adult insect, on emerging from the pupal skin and proceeding to feed on the mass of ambrosia fungus lining the tunnel, rocks back and forth in a curious manner. What this does is force fungus spores into the mycangia before the insect flies away to found its own nest.

Each species of ambrosia beetle is normally associated with only one species of ambrosia fungus. Ambrosia fungi are pleomorphic: they can readily change, when their growth medium is changed, from a fluffy moldlike form to a dense yeastlike form. In the mycangia and the tunnels of the ambrosia beetles the yeastlike form prevails. Recently we have discovered that ambrosia beetles can also change the form of other fungi from the moldlike form to the yeastlike one. This is a significant phenomenon, and we shall be returning to it.

The most conspicuous and most destructive of the fungus-growing insects are termites. The termites that cultivate fungi are native to the Tropics of Africa and Asia. In West Africa it is estimated that the yearly cost of repairing the damage done by these insects to buildings is equal to 10 percent of the buildings' value. In addition to wood the insects eat growing and harvested crops and objects made of rubber, leather and paper; they destroy documents, works of art, clothing and even underground cables. The enormous mounds that some termite species build for nests interfere with farming and hinder road construction. If they are incompletely destroyed, the insects rebuild them.

Many species in the genera *Macrotermes* and *Odontotermes* make their nests in spectacular steeple-like mounds of hardened earth, which in Africa reach a height of as much as 30 feet. Other species, in the genus *Microtermes*, are completely subterranean, and if it were not for their mating flights and the damage they do, they would be quite inconspicuous. Each nest contains a white, sausage-like queen and a king, usually enclosed together in a protective cell of earth; the much smaller workers, soldiers and young termites (nymphs) of various ages and both sexes are found throughout the nest. At certain seasons winged male and female reproductives (future kings and queens) are also present. In each nest are one or several fungus gardens, the number and shape depending on the species of termite. Material collected by the workers is chewed and swallowed, and the partly digested fecal material is deposited on a fungus garden when the workers return to the nest. In the nests of some species there is a single large mass of fungus garden; in one of the nests of *Odontotermes obesus* that we studied in India the mass was two feet in diameter and weighed 60 pounds. In other nests many fungus gardens one or two inches long are scattered along burrows throughout the nest. Each fungus garden is enclosed in a close-fitting cavity lined with a mixture of saliva and dirt. The chambers of some species are ventilated by an elaborate system of vertical conduits ex-

tending to the surface of the nest [see the article "Air-conditioned Termite Nests," by Martin Lüscher, beginning on page 271].

The fungus gardens look like a gray or brownish sponge or may be convoluted like a walnut meat. They are moist but usually firm and brittle, and are permeated by threadlike mycelium. Scattered over the surface and inside the pores of the gardens are numerous minute, glistening, pearly white spherules composed of masses of rounded fungus cells.

The role of the fungi in the nutrition of the fungus-growing termites is not clear. It is well known that many common Temperate Zone termites cannot digest the cellulose in the wood they eat but rely on certain cellulose-digesting protozoa that live in their intestines to do it for them. No protozoa live in the gut of the fungus-growing

termites; therefore it seems likely that the fungi growing in the gardens break down cellulose and may provide vitamins also. In fact, these termites soon die on a diet restricted to wood. The termites continually eat away the fungus gardens as they add fresh fecal material. There is thus a communal interchange of food, the fecal material being partly broken down by fungi in the garden, then eaten again and redeposited in the garden for further digestion by the fungi.

The white spherules are frequently picked up by the workers and moved to other parts of the fungus garden or are sometimes eaten. The king, queen, young nymphs and soldiers are apparently fed saliva by the workers; no trace of fungus or plant material can be found in their digestive tract. Some winged reproductive termites contain material from the fungus gardens, with which

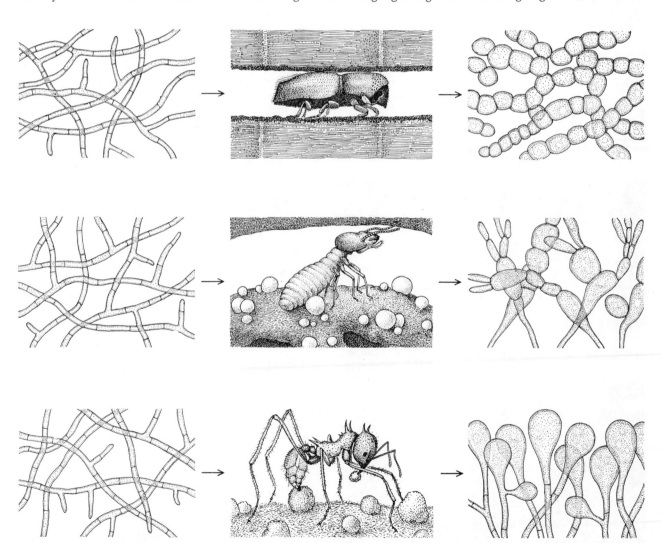

FUNGUS IS TRANSFORMED in being cultivated by insects. Under ordinary conditions in the laboratory fungus associated with the ambrosia beetle is threadlike (*top left*). In the beetle's tunnel, where it is continually grazed, the fungus is denser and more like a yeast (*top right*). The fungus-growing termites also modify their fungi (*middle*), which they fertilize, lick and enclose in mud. Under these conditions white spherules appear. The fungus of a fungus-growing ant (*bottom*) looks much like the others when grown in a culture; in association with the ant, which licks, manipulates and defecates on its garden, the fungus has thickened tips.

they may begin a new garden when they start a new nest.

Several genera of unrelated fungi grow in the fungus gardens of termites; the most abundant are species of the mushroom *Termitomyces*. The various species of *Termitomyces* are found only in nests of fungus-growing termites. Somehow the fruiting structure—the mushroom—of the fungi is not allowed to grow from fungus gardens while they are being actively tended by termites. If the termites are removed or die, however, some of the spherules grow into the mushrooms of *Termitomyces*.

In Africa and southern India termites in many nests simultaneously remove the outer layers of their fungus gardens and spread crumbs of them in a thin layer on the ground during the rainy season. Soon *Termitomyces* mushrooms appear, and after their spores have been disseminated by the wind the termites come to the surface to collect fungus that may have grown from a mixture of spores from many nests. It is believed that in this way the termites provide for the cross-fertilization of their fungi, as man does for corn and other crops.

Closely resembling the fungus-growing termites in behavior but only distantly related to them are the fungus-growing ants (tribe Attini). Here we have an example of convergent evolution, in which two nearly unrelated animals and their fungi occupy a very similar ecological niche. These ants are found only in the Western Hemisphere, and most of them are tropical. Some species are found in the deep South and the Southwest of the U.S.; a small species (*Trachymyrmex septentrionalis*) is found in sandy areas near the Atlantic coast as far north as Long Island.

Atta texana, which lives in eastern Texas and southern Louisiana, does considerable damage to citrus groves, gardens and plantations of young pine trees by cutting leaves from them for its fungus gardens. This ant is known locally as the "town ant," and it inhabits an ant metropolis that is sometimes 50 feet across and 20 feet deep. (One student of these ants, John C. Moser of the U.S. Forest Service, opens their nests with a bulldozer!) Other species of fungus-growing ants build smaller nests; some are so small that they are extremely difficult to find.

The fungus-growing ants probably represent the most advanced stage in the evolution of fungus gardening because they feed only on the fungus, and they actively cultivate it. The workers, depending on the species, collect cater-

pillar excrement, fallen flower anthers and other soft plant debris as well as leaves cut from trees. Rather than eating the material the ant cuts it into pieces and adds them to a fungus garden in the nest. The ants' gardens look somewhat like those of the termites: they are gray, flocculent masses of finely divided moist plant material loosely held together by threads of mycelium. In the underground chambers of the nest the fungus garden often is suspended from the roots of plants. Scattered over the surface of the older parts of the garden are white specks just visible to the unaided eye. These specks, called kohlrabi bodies, are clusters of bromatia, the swollen tips of the filaments forming the mycelium. The kohlrabi bodies look much like the white spherules found in the gardens of termites. When the ants are not feeding on the bromatia, they lick them.

The flying, nest-founding ant queen carries a small pellet of fungus in a pouch below her mouthparts, much as the ambrosia beetle carries fungus in its mycangia. In starting a new nest the young queen grows a small fungus garden on her excreta; with this she feeds the first worker larvae. When the workers are mature, they leave the nest to gather the material with which the garden is enlarged. They feed bits of bromatia to the larvae that nestle in the mycelium of the gardens.

As long as the ants actively tend the garden the fungus does not develop fruiting structures, but mushrooms of four genera have been found growing from abandoned nests of some species or have been cultured from fungus gardens in the laboratory. We do not know how the ants control the growth of their fungi so that they produce bromatia and nothing else; perhaps it is by constantly "pruning" away excess growth of the mycelium. It is also possible that the excreta and the saliva of the ants, which are deposited on the fungus garden, contain some substance that influences the growth of the mutualistic fungus and inhibits the development of the many spores that accidentally enter the nest.

With the fungus-growing ants our brief survey of the mutualistic associations between insects and fungi ends. It can be seen that there are two distinct kinds of relation. In the gardens of wood wasps, ambrosia beetles, termites, ants and probably those of midge galls the fungus extracts nourishment from a substrate and the insect feeds either on the fungus, the substrate predigested by the fungus or both. The fun-

BEETLE TUNNELS are marked by the dark fungus that lines the interior surface. The photograph above shows a cross section of excavations made in wood by ambrosia beetles. Dark circles are niches at right angles to the tunnel that hold larvae. The beetles have penetrated through the bark into the sapwood; in this way they destroy felled timber.

FUNGUS-GARDENING ANT *Mycetosoritis hartmani* is shown in its underground nest feeding on a "kohlrabi body." These bodies are made up of bromatia, particles that consist of the swollen tips of the filaments of the fungus and that form only in the presence of the insect. Surrounding the ant are the filaments themselves. Photograph was provided by John C. Moser of the U.S. Forest Service.

gus is prevented from producing sexual fruiting structures but is supplied by an insect partner with a suitable habitat and a means of dispersal. In the colonies of the fungus *Septobasidium* and scale insects the situation is reversed: the insect feeds on the substrate and nourishes the fungus, and the fungus provides shelter for its castrated insect partner.

Insects are unique among animals in having developed mutualistic relations with fungi. This may have come about because so many insects and fungi share the same tiny habitats. Moreover, most insects are equipped to carry living spores of fungi, either in their gut, in folds between their joints that contain waxy secretions or among their bristles.

The fungus-gardening insects convey into their nest the spores of many fungi other than the one on which they depend. If the insects are removed, the alien fungi will grow and soon overrun the nest; they do not grow in the nest, however, when the insects live there. Apparently the fungus-gardening insects either secrete or excrete antibiotic substances that prevent the growth of alien fungi. The substances may also act to transform the mutualistic fungi, causing either ambrosia, spherules or bromatia to appear rather than sexual fruiting structures.

In the case of the termite, which licks the spherules of its fungus and encloses the fungus garden in saliva-moistened mud, the saliva may contain the substances in question. We have tested the effect of adding saliva taken from termites to a culture of their fungus, which under ordinary growing conditions in the laboratory does not produce spherules. After saliva was added to the culture spherules grew; the saliva also

FUNGUS-GARDENING TERMITE of the genus *Odontotermes* is photographed crawling on the surface of its garden. The round white objects are spherules of the fungus, which arise only in gardens that are tended and fertilized by termites. The insect in the picture is a soldier defending the nest; it produces a copious supply of pungent saliva for this purpose.

inhibited the growth of alien fungi. We have performed other tests on the excreta that ants deposit on their nest gardens. Although we have found that the excreta inhibit the growth of certain bacteria, much experimental work remains to be done. The saliva of the ant, which also licks its fungus, may help to form bromatia.

Spores of the ambrosia beetle's fungus remain in the yeastlike form while they are carried by the insect, and it is possible that the waxy secretion might also affect the form of fungi in the tunnel, where the beetle and the fungus are in close contact. On the other hand, it has been shown that the mutualistic fungi of some species of the beetle can be modified to the yeastlike form by certain physical conditions and in the absence of the beetle. These physical conditions duplicate conditions in the beetle's tunnel, where the feeding insect steadily mows the tips of the fungus as they grow.

In nature the presence of a living insect partner is necessary to maintain ambrosia, spherules or bromatia, but these forms can be produced in the laboratory on special mediums in the absence of the insects. When the mutualistic fungi are grown on ordinary carbohydrate-rich laboratory mediums, fluffy mycelium and sometimes sexual fruiting bodies appear. If the same fungi are grown on acid mediums that are rich in amino acids, and are exposed to more than .5 percent carbon dioxide, then bromatia, spherules or ambrosia are formed. These cultural conditions apparently resemble conditions in the nests of the insects. The fungi of some ambrosia beetles also become ambrosial if they are repeatedly scraped or are grown at low temperatures. Clearly the problem of how insects control the growth of a fungus partner remains an intriguing one.

The Energetics of the Bumblebee

by Bernd Heinrich
April 1973

The bumblebee, like many other insects, evolved in interaction with the flowers it feeds on and pollinates. This evolutionary interaction is apparent in the energy budget of its activities

Charles Darwin discovered that when red clover was sequestered from visits by bumblebees, the plant failed to produce seed. This led two 19th-century contemporaries, the German biologists Karl Vogt and Ernst Haeckel, to observe that the British Empire owed its power and wealth largely to bumblebees, since its power resided mainly in the Navy, whose sailors subsisted on beef, which came from cattle that subsisted on clover, which, as the mother of the chain, depended for its propagation on pollination by bumblebees. The bumblebee's ecological puissance was demonstrated in a practical way by ranchers in New Zealand, who in 1885 imported the insect and found that it indeed brought about large increases in the production of clover seed.

Few members of the living world are linked together as intimately as bees and flowers. For bees the nectar of flowers is the sole source of food energy; for flowers bees serve essentially as copulatory organs, delivering pollen from one plant to another and thereby effecting fertilization. By mutual evolution bees and flowers have become exquisitely attuned to their mutual convenience. Many flowers have evolved features making them attractive to those bees that are efficient in pollinating them and making them unattractive or essentially inaccessible to other foragers. The flowers attract by signals such as scents and colors that identify them for their partners, and they minimize or avoid visits from other pollinators by blooming at times when the latter are not active or by holding their nectar in a long, tubular corolla where it can be reached only by the favored animals.

Some ecological effects of the evolutionary collaboration of bees and flowers have been investigated by Theodore Mosquin of the Canadian Department of Agriculture and by Herbert Baker of the University of California at Berkeley, working with Gordon W. Frankie at Texas A & M University and Paul Opler in Costa Rica. They have found that in each region the various plants requiring cross-pollination by bees bloom at different times spaced out over the growing season, so that they avoid excessive competition for the attentions of the available pollinators. This separation of blooming periods no doubt has been brought about by natural selection as influenced by the bees' season-long feeding needs.

The nature of the pollinating agent has determined the properties of flowers in another way. If the nectar-seeking insect could obtain a full meal at one sitting, there would be no need to flit from flower to flower and consequently no cross-pollination. Evolutionary selection has therefore dictated that the individual flower offer only a small part of the pollinator's requirement, thus compelling the forager to visit many blossoms to fill its needs. Each blossom must provide enough nectar to make a visit worthwhile but not enough to allow the pollinator to get its fill from just a few blossoms.

I have investigated the matter quantitatively by observing the feeding of a species of bumblebee (*Bombus vagans*) on the compound blossoms of hawkweed, which have only minute amounts of nectar at any one time and which are usually not very attractive to bumblebees. To test the bumblebee's capacity I placed a large deposit of nectar in a single blossom and found that 100 microliters or more was needed to sate a bee. Since a large fraction of the flowers on which bumblebees forage contain less than half a microliter of nectar, this indicated that a bumblebee in the field probably visits 200 or more such flowers during a foraging trip. I followed one bee during part of such a trip and observed that it visited 337 blossoms before I lost sight of it.

Bees of course are well known to be indefatigable workers. The nature of their interdependence with flowers therefore suggests interesting questions concerning the bee's energy budget and the balance sheet it shares with flowers. I had already been impressed by the remarkably high energy expenditure of the foraging sphinx moth and by its virtuosity in regulating its body temperature [see "Temperature Control in Flying Moths," by Bernd Heinrich and George A. Bartholomew; SCIENTIFIC AMERICAN Offprint 1252]. I was therefore drawn to a detailed study of the energetics of bumblebees.

The bumblebee is a particularly interesting subject because it can forage at temperatures as low as zero degrees Celsius, where all other insects are immobilized. Bumblebees are found not only in warm regions but also on high mountains and in arctic climates. As a cold-blooded animal ordinarily restricted in body temperature to the temperature of the environment, the bee must step up its generation of energy to heat its muscles to the temperature necessary for flight; it does this by exercising the muscles of its thorax (essentially shivering) before it takes off. Thanks to the bumblebee's ca-

CLINGING UPSIDE DOWN to a dangling groundsel blossom in a shady Maine bogland (*shown on p. 216*), a bumblebee of the species *Bombus ternarius* thrusts its proboscis (*left*) into the flower to gather nectar.

pability for generating enough heat to keep it active over a wide range of environmental temperatures, it is possible to obtain comparative information about its energy requirements at various ambient temperatures. Furthermore, since essentially its sole metabolic source of energy is the sugar in the nectar it collects from flowers, and since the extent of its foraging and the flowers it visits can be observed, one can estimate how much energy the bumblebee spends in its foraging trips.

I conducted my field studies of bum-blebee energetics at my family's farm in Maine and followed up with laboratory investigations at the University of California at Berkeley. The area in Maine (near Farmington) is a haven for a variety of flowers and many species of bees, among which bumblebees seem to be the

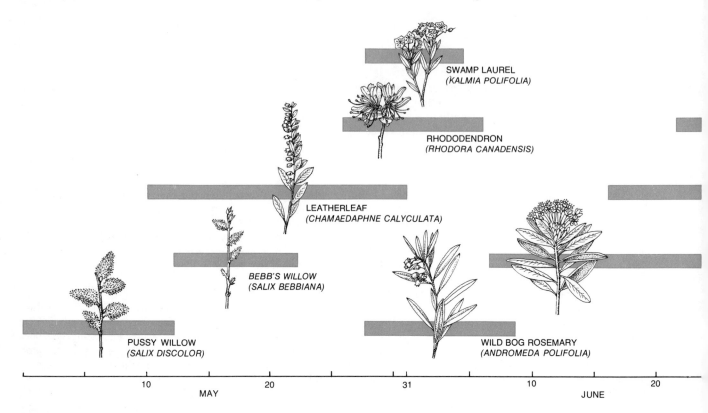

SEQUENCE OF BLOOMING among 10 common plants in a bog in Maine is staggered, beginning in late April (*far left*) with pussy willow and continuing without interruption into August (*far right*), when meadowsweet continues to bloom. At least one plant species

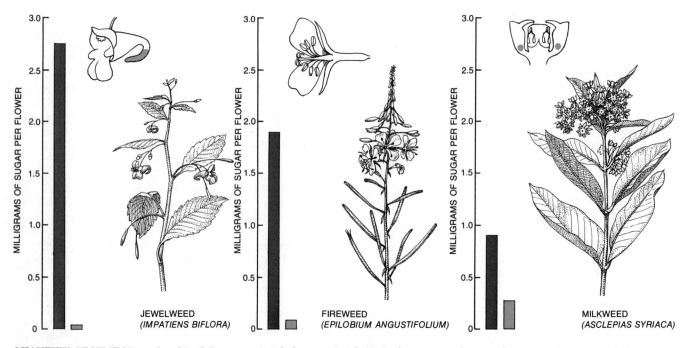

QUANTITY OF NECTAR produced by different species of plants is generally proportional to the size of the blossom. The 24-hour production of nectar per floret of five plants that were shielded from foragers is expressed here in milligrams of sugar (*gray*). A

most common flower-visitors. A bumblebee visits about twice as many blossoms per unit of time as other bees, and it works from dawn to dark. Active at all ambient temperatures, bumblebees serve as pollinators on nearly all days over the entire season, visiting the flowers that come into bloom one after the other.

Although bumblebees are potentially promiscuous, being attracted to many species of flowers, they do show definite preferences, presumably based on the comparative nectar reward of the favored flower. I came across an interesting case of individual taste: In a field where two almost identical species of hawkweed were blooming, the only apparent difference being that one was yellow and the other orange, one bumblebee I followed for 146 consecutive visits chose only the orange flowers, whereas another bee of the same species showed almost as definite a preference for the yellow, selecting during a foraging trip the yellow species 170 times and the orange only 14 times. Evidently each bee had developed its own preference on the basis of its foraging experiences. Whatever the reasons, most of the bumblebees I studied tended to be faithful to particular species of flowers. This was convenient for my research, because it enabled me to estimate how much sugar the bees collected in a foraging trip.

In order to investigate the bees' energy budget I had to find a means of measuring their rate of energy expenditure in the field. The usual method of obtaining this rate in an animal is to measure its oxygen consumption, a direct indication of its rate of metabolism. That method obviously would not be applicable to a bee engaged in complex behavior in the field. A good index to a bee's energy expenditure could, however, be obtained by measuring its temperature as it perched on a flower and timing the duration of its flights between flowers. The energy expended by a bumblebee in flight had been measured in the laboratory by observing the bee's rate of oxygen consumption. About 80 percent of the energy a bee expends goes into heat as a by-product of the heightened rate of metabolism. To get an indication of the bee's rate of energy expenditure when it was perched on a flower I therefore adopted a simpler technique: I would grasp it with a gloved hand between my thumb and forefinger and quickly thrust a tiny thermistor into its thorax, thus obtaining the temperature before the body could cool appreciably.

One striking finding that soon emerged was that whereas the thorax, where the muscles for the wings are located, shows a considerably elevated temperature, the abdomen (the rear part of the body) remains at just about ambient temperature. The bee does not waste energy on the body part that is not involved in powering flight, and thereby it saves itself half the metabolic cost of the energy it would have to produce if it heated its entire trunk.

Another interesting observation was that, regardless of the length of time the bumblebees perched on a flower and regardless of the proportion of time they

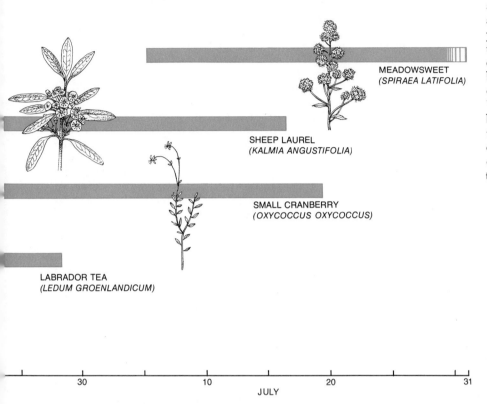

MEADOWSWEET
(SPIRAEA LATIFOLIA)

SHEEP LAUREL
(KALMIA ANGUSTIFOLIA)

SMALL CRANBERRY
(OXYCOCCUS OXYCOCCUS)

LABRADOR TEA
(LEDUM GROENLANDICUM)

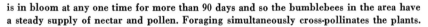

30   10   20   31
JULY

is in bloom at any one time for more than 90 days and so the bumblebees in the area have a steady supply of nectar and pollen. Foraging simultaneously cross-pollinates the plants.

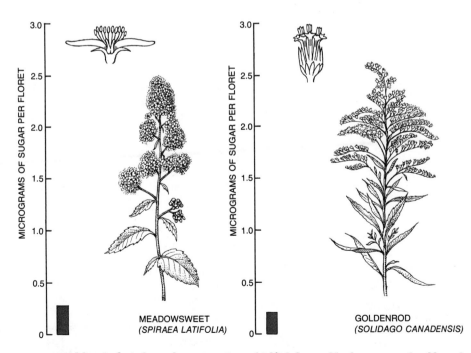

MEADOWSWEET
(SPIRAEA LATIFOLIA)

GOLDENROD
(SOLIDAGO CANADENSIS)

second bar (color) shows the amount in unshielded florets. Meadowsweet and goldenrod may seem low producers, but the one may have 45 florets per bloom and the other 1,300.

spent in flight during a foraging trip, they usually maintained their thoracic temperature at a high level: between 30 and 37 degrees C. (86 to 98.6 degrees Fahrenheit). This requires an exorbitant rate of heat production. A bumblebee may elevate its thoracic temperature by as much as 35 degrees C. when the ambient temperature is only about two degrees. For a bumblebee, only one or two tenths of a gram in weight, maintaining such an elevation of body temperature implies a prodigious rate of energy expenditure, in view of its high rate of heat loss to the atmosphere. This rate of loss from the bee's small body is unavoidably high even though it is covered with fur

(which serves to pick up pollen as well as to help to conserve heat in some measure).

One might suppose the bee cools off while it is perched on a flower. As a rule it does nothing of the sort. I found that in most cases bumblebees kept their body temperature at the level required for flight even during long periods of stationary feeding, which I would stretch out by filling blossoms with a large amount of sugar syrup. Why do they spend all that energy to regulate their temperature while they are not in flight? The answer seems obvious: the engine remains revved up so that the bee does not need to spend time warming up

in order to take off. In the field the bee usually keeps itself ready to take off at an instant's notice, whether for the purpose of flying on to another blossom or to escape some threat.

How much energy must a bumblebee spend to maintain an elevated temperature while it is not flying? On the basis of its passive rate of cooling when it is not foraging, I calculated that at an ambient temperature of five degrees C. a medium-size bumblebee must produce a little more than half a calorie of heat per minute to keep its thoracic temperature at 30 degrees, or 25 degrees higher than the air temperature. This rate of heat production is close to that required for flight itself. At high air temperatures, of course, the need for generating heat in the thoracic muscles is reduced. At ambient temperatures higher than 25 degrees C. the heat-regulation factor in perching bees is eliminated, and the total energy cost comes down to what is needed to power flight, with heat as an incidental product. My measurements of oxygen consumption in the laboratory show that in bumblebees, as in sphinx moths, the energy cost of flight is the same at all air temperatures.

Most other insects heat up their thorax only during and just before flight; the bees are almost unique in their ability to maintain an elevated thoracic temperature while remaining still. As the Danish physiologist August Krogh and other investigators showed many years ago, bees produce a considerable quantity of heat by activating their flight muscles in a shivering mode. Ann E. Kammer of Kansas State University and I have investigated the matter by electrophysiological methods and have confirmed that the activation of these muscles is in fact solely responsible for the heating of the thorax. Curiously, when the bee is stationary, this warm-up is not accompanied by any visible vibration of the wings, such as is seen in moths. We have not yet found out how the bumblebee uncouples its wings from the flight muscles during its warm-up. We think, however, that it does so by means of a mechanical clutch mechanism in the complex articulations at the base of its wings.

Armed with the foregoing background of theory and information and with a thermistor and a stopwatch, I was ready to investigate the bees' energy cost of foraging in the field. First I measured the energy income they would obtain from the flowers. I collected samples of the nectar from a given flower species, mea-

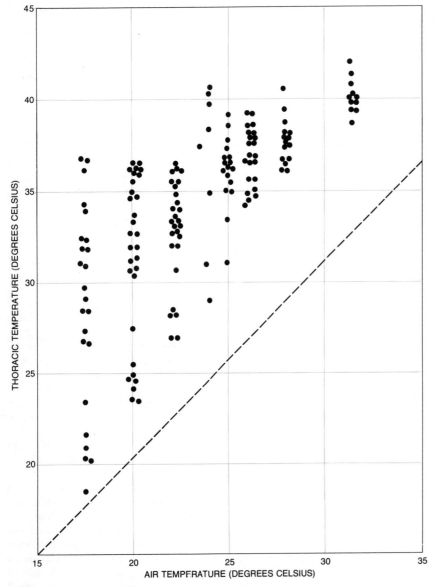

ENERGY IS CONSERVED when the foraging bumblebee can walk, rather than fly, from one nectar source to the next. The graph shows the thoracic temperature of bees that were foraging on meadowsweet. When the air temperature was below 24 degrees C., the thoracic temperature of the bees frequently fell below the 30-degree level required for flight as they crawled from floret to floret. Bees that had been most recently airborne were the warmest.

sured the sugar concentration in the nectar with a pocket refractometer and then computed the energy this represented in terms of calories. Such a measurement showed, for example, that on the average a fireweed blossom filled with nectar (having been shielded from feeders for 24 hours) contained enough sugar to support a bee's maximum metabolic rate (the rate required for continuous flight or for the maximum elevation of its body temperature when it is stationary) for about 13 minutes. Ordinarily, of course, a bee does not often come on such a bonanza in the field. I found that in field conditions the same blossom in the afternoon, having already fed a series of visitors, would on the average provide only enough nectar to supply a bee with energy for about a minute's flight. As a result to obtain a profit beyond the energy consumed in the foraging activity the bee would have to visit flowers at the rate of at least one or two per minute. Actually I observed that bumblebees commonly fed on fireweed blossoms at the rate of 20 to 30 per minute, which was more than sufficient to supply the bee's energy needs for flying and for keeping the engine revved up while it fed on the blossoms. Thus the flower amply repaid the bee's efforts, particularly since it might also provide a dividend of pollen that the bee would take back to its nest to feed its larvae.

This example only indicates a general picture. In practice there are several factors complicating the question of whether or not a given foraging expedition will be worthwhile for the bee. That depends not only on the amount of caloric reward offered by each flower but also on the distance between blossoms, on the air temperature at the time and on other factors.

In general, as we have seen, if a bumblebee must maintain the necessary body temperature by shivering continuously while it is resting on each blossom, it needs to obtain enough sugar to provide more than .54 calorie per minute throughout the duration of its foraging trip, regardless of how much of the time it spends in flight. If it does not spend energy for warming up while it is feeding but needs to spend more than 50 percent of the time flying from blossom to blossom, it requires an intake of at least .27 calorie per minute. If it can dispense with the stationary warm-ups and spend no more than 10 percent of the foraging time in flight, it can make an energy profit on an intake of only about

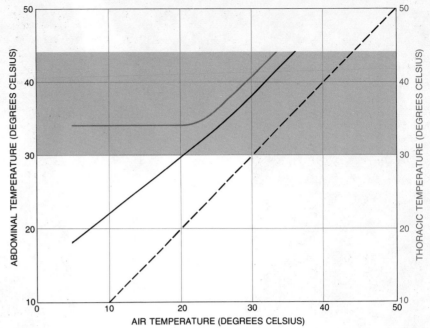

ENERGY INVESTMENT required to keep up the body temperature that enables a bumblebee to fly varies with the air temperature. The graph shows the temperature of the bumblebee's abdomen, averaged in both sunlight and shade, at various air temperatures (*black curve*) and the average temperature of the thorax, the site of the bee's flight muscles, which must not fall below 30 degrees Celsius or rise above 44 degrees (*colored curve*). The temperature of the abdomen, only a few degrees higher than the air temperature, is maintained by passive heat flow only. Until the air temperature approaches 25 degrees C., however, maintenance of the thoracic temperature at an average of 33 degrees requires an investment of energy far greater than the one required for intermittent flight from flower to flower.

.05 calorie per minute. Let us see how these requirements work out for the behavior of the bees and the pollination chances of various flowers.

In the spring, when the bumblebees are forming their colonies and the queens and workers presumably have their highest need for energy, the early-blooming flowers tend to be relatively rich in nectar. The foraging bees have ample energy for flying rapidly from flower to flower and keeping themselves well warmed up while feeding. Speed of foraging is at a premium at this time of year, and the bees are alert and difficult to capture even in the cool of dawn with the air temperature almost at the freezing point of water.

That is in sharp contrast to the situation in late summer, when the bee colonies are breaking up, the energy demands and the need to bring in a profit at a high rate are not so large and the sources of nectar tend to become less abundant. The foragers in our Maine area then have to depend on the nectar-poor blossoms of plants such as meadowsweet and goldenrod. Each floret has only a minute amount of nectar, but providentially the blossoms occur in

dense panicles, clusters consisting of hundreds or thousands of florets. The bee can crawl from blossom to blossom and may spend a long time on each cluster, using a significant amount of energy only when it flies from one panicle or plant to another. While feeding on such plants the bee does not trouble to keep itself warmed up. I found that in relatively cool air (20 degrees C. or less) the bees' thoracic temperature was generally below the threshold for flight. At such air temperatures many of the bees were so unready for flight while feeding that they could be shaken off the blossoms onto the ground. Bumblebees seldom ventured, however, to feed on meadowsweet or goldenrod unless the air temperature was above 20 degrees C. or they were warmed above this temperature by the sun. If passing clouds cut off the sunshine on a cool day, the bees lost flight readiness within minutes.

In short, these observations and similar ones on other plants showed that the bumblebee accommodates itself to a meager supply of nectar by practicing drastic economies in the use of energy. By means of these economies it is able to render the service of pollination to

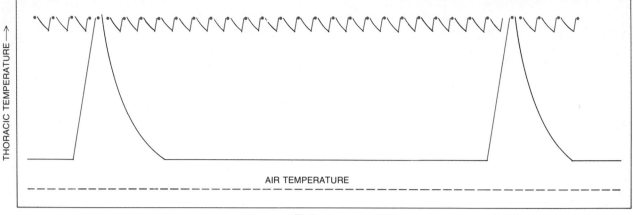

COMPARATIVE COST of foraging on plants with single or few blossoms and on plants with many florets per bloom is shown schematically. Given a low air temperature, a bumblebee that crawls around on the blooms of meadowsweet or goldenrod will only warm up its flight muscles (*color*) and take flight twice during a span of time when another bee, feeding on jewelweed or fireweed, will have warmed up and taken off many times. The second bee, however, will probably gather a larger amount of nectar.

plants offering only a spartan diet when richer sources are not available. In the case of the fireweed, a relatively rich provider (about .09 milligram of sugar in each floret), a bee can afford to spend 50 percent of its foraging time in flight from flower to flower and to keep itself warmed up in readiness for flying; in contrast, meadowsweet (offering only .005 milligram of sugar per floret) limits the bee to only a fifth as much flying and requires that the engine be cut to a low idling level during the stationary interval. The sphinx moth, lacking the adaptability and options of bees, cannot forage profitably on meadowsweet or goldenrod, because it hovers over a flower while feeding instead of settling on it and therefore must continuously produce heat even at high air temperatures.

The bumblebee may sometimes forage on some plants without taking nectar at all and instead collecting pollen to take to the nest. On meadowsweet, for example, the bee simply sweeps the entire panicle and flies rapidly from one to another; on bittersweet it shakes the pollen loose by flight-muscle vibrations that vibrate its body and the flower and make a buzzing sound. For such operations the bee must, of course, use a large amount of energy. If the plant from which the pollen is collected does not furnish enough nectar, the bee setting out on a pollen-foraging trip must either use honey from the nest for its energy supply or collect nectar from other plants before it visits the pollen suppliers.

We have seen enough to discern the outlines of an intricate web of interrelations among the bees and the flowers, governed by the energy needs and payoffs as its basic plan. The competition among plants for the pollinators' service, and among the pollinators for the plants' food rewards, decisively shapes the behavior and the structure and physiology of both the plants and the pollinators. The investigation of the energetics of the bumblebee therefore offers a beautiful case study for insight into the operations of evolution and the way a cooperative balance can be established in the ecology of a community.

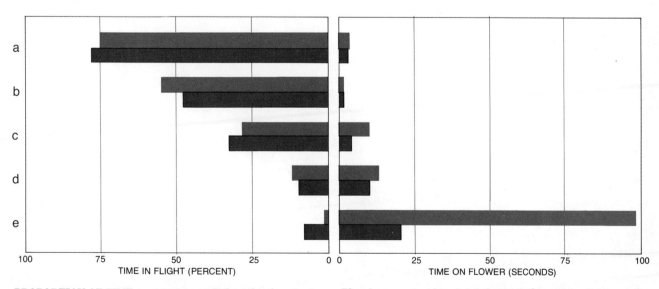

PROPORTION OF TIME spent by bees in flight and in foraging is more closely related to the kinds of bloom visited than it is to the air temperature. Black bars show both activities at an air temperature of 20 degrees C. in shade; colored bars, both at 30 degrees. The plants are jewelweed (*a*), fireweed (*b*), milkweed (*c*), meadowsweet (*d*) and goldenrod (*e*). The only significant increase in foraging time at low temperature occurred when bumblebees fed at length on the florets of goldenrod, which contain little nectar.

A DIVERSITY OF LIFE STYLES

IV

A DIVERSITY OF
LIFE STYLES

INTRODUCTION

The articles in this section have been selected to illustrate the natural history of some of the most specialized insect types. We begin with fleas and predatory wasps and then pass to three of the major groups of social insects: honeybees, ants, and termites. Note that the behavior of the two solitary insects is at least as complex as that of *individual* social insects. The more spectacular achievements of the social insects are made possible by the combination of many individual behavior patterns into still more complicated mass responses by colonies as a whole.

In "Fleas," Miriam Rothschild, the world authority on fleas, describes the peculiar adaptations that make these wingless descendants of flies some of the most efficient ectoparasites in the animal world. The rabbit flea is especially notable in the closeness of its adaptation to its host. The adults time their reproductive cycle to that of the host by responding to changes in the rabbit's hormone levels, which they are able to monitor directly in the blood they consume.

Howard Evans has devoted a lifetime to the biology and relationships of hunting wasps, with distinguished results. In his article "Predatory Wasps" he describes the specificity of the prey taken by different species and the behavioral adaptations they use to make their hunting expeditions more efficient. Both characteristics are genetically determined and can be used to reconstruct the evolutionary history of the hunting wasps as a whole.

Possibly the single most complex behavior pattern to be found in any insect is the famous waggle dance of the honeybee, by which a worker bee informs her nestmates of the direction and distance of a superior nest site or newly discovered source of nectar. The dance, performed on the vertical surface of a comb in the darkened hive, is actually a miniaturized, symbolic rehearsal of the journey to be undertaken. The straight-up direction on the comb surface represents the position of the sun; when the follower bees leave the hive afterward they use the sun itself to orient themselves (see Wehner's article, "Polarized-Light Navigation by Insects," in Section II). The distance in turn is symbolized by the length of time required to perform the central line in the figure-eight traced during the dance—the longer the journey, the longer the central line takes to dance. In "Dialects in the Language of Bees" Karl von Frisch, who shared the 1973 Nobel Prize in Physiology and Medicine, describes the basic dance and the differences or "dialects" in the coding of the direction information that distinguishes various geographical races of the honeybee.

An army ant colony marching through a tropical forest can be thought of as a kind of superorganism, traveling over the forest floor like a flowing blanket while snapping up insect prey with its million tiny mouths. The ultimate beneficiary of this activity is not the worker force that conducts the hunting, but rather the single mother queen who waits in a safe position back in the colony bivouac. It used to be thought that army ants repeat their expeditions in a simple response to hunger. But more recent research, reviewed here by Howard Topoff in "The Social Behavior of Army Ants," has revealed that the life of the colony is ruled by a remarkable pair of cycles, one timing the synchronous development of the immature ants and the other the intensity of the daily raids and the occurrence or avoidance of daily colony emigrations. The two cycles are interlocked in such a way as to adjust the activity of the colony to the stage of the development of the immature forms and hence to the overall food requirements of the colony.

In the north temperate zone a few ant species have adopted a special form of social parasitism with a superficial resemblance to human slavery. This phenomenon is discussed by E. O. Wilson in "Slavery in Ants." The slave-makers leave their nests in columns to attack the colonies of other, similar species in the neighborhood. Some species use powerful, sharp mandibles to destroy their opponents. Others scatter the defenders with "propaganda substances," glandular secretions that the defenders mistake for their own alarm substances. The slave-raiders then gather the pupae, take them home and allow them to transform into adult worker ants. Since the new "slaves" are unaware that they are captives in the nest of an alien species, they willingly join the labor force and treat the parasite queen as they would their own mother. The result is a larger, more vigorous colony that serves only the interests of the slave-makers.

Ant colonies are organized to a large degree by a small number of pheromones. One set is used to recognize adult nestmates, another to distinguish larvae from pupae and eggs, still another to mark trails, and so forth. This very simplicity provides opportunity for other insects to fool the ants and to exploit the social system to their own benefit. As described here by Bert Hölldobler, in "Communication Between Ants and Their Guests," such social parasites have "broken the code" of the ant colonies and penetrated colony life with varying degrees of success. In extreme instances they manage to be accepted as full members of the colony, after which they beg food from their hosts or even prey on them, yet without contributing labor in return.

The African savanna is dotted with the great mounds of the fungus-growing macrotermitine termites (see "The Fungus Gardens of Insects," by Suzanne and Lekh Batra, in Section III). These nests are not just piles of excavated earth. They contain an intricate internal architecture so precise in detail that termite specialists can distinguish some species entirely from maps of the nest plans. Martin Lüscher first discovered the significance of the structure, and discusses his findings in the article "Air-Conditioned Termite Nests." Each mound contains a colony of a million or more individuals, which in the aggregate weigh tens of kilograms. If all of that termite flesh simply crowded into a closed underground space, the colony would quickly die of anoxia or carbon dioxide narcosis. The structure of the mound permits a steady flow of air out of the central living area by means of convection, a freshening of this stale air in the outermost chambers of the mound, and finally a return flow of the air through the living space.

RELATED BOOKS

Askew, R. R. 1971. *Parasitic Insects*. Heinemann, London. An informative book on the many ways by which insects have come to meet the requirements of a highly specialized style of life.

Brues, Charles T. 1946. *Insect Dietary*. Harvard University Press, Cambridge, Massachusetts. An account of the food habits of insects. Compiles much useful information not summarized elsewhere.

Kirkpatrick, P. W. 1957. *Insect Life in the Tropics*. Longmans, Green, London. A general introduction to the stunningly diverse and frequently bizarre insects of the tropics.

Oldroyd, Harold. 1966. *The Natural History of Flies*. Norton, New York. An admirable account of a major order of insects, and of the adaptive specializations that led to their evolutionary success.

Pennak, Robert W. 1953. *Fresh-Water Invertebrates of the United States*. Ronald Press, New York. Devotes almost 200 pages to aquatic insects, serving as a useful first source of reference to this group.

Proctor, Michael, and Peter Yeo. 1972. *The Pollination of Flowers*. Taplinger, New York. A nicely written and well-illustrated book. Provides an excellent account of the reciprocal adaptations of flowers and flower-visiting insects.

Wilson, Edward O. 1971. *The Insect Societies*. Belknap Press of Harvard University Press, Cambridge, Massachusetts. A comprehensive review of the biology of social insects. Intended for both the specialist and the general reader.

Wilson, Edward O. 1975. *Sociobiology: The New Synthesis*. Belknap Press of Harvard University Press, Cambridge, Massachusetts. A monograph on the social phenomena in all animals, including insects, interpreted in the light of modern evolutionary concepts.

See also the books by Edmonds (1974) and Wickler (1968) listed in the introduction to Part III.

Fleas

by Miriam Rothschild
December 1965

*They have evolved some remarkable adaptations to
their hosts. Perhaps the most remarkable is found
in the European rabbit flea, the breeding cycle of
which is regulated by the reproductive hormones
of the rabbit*

Mammals have been available as possible hosts for parasitic insects for some 180 million years. There is little doubt that fleas became parasites of mammals comparatively early in the history of their hosts; a fossil flea, scarcely different from living species and displaying all the specialized features associated with them, has been found in Baltic amber dating from 50 million years ago.

It is not known how one animal first becomes parasitic on another, but it is fairly certain that all the principal groups of parasitic insects arose as free-living organisms. The genesis of parasitism is opportunity. The future parasite and its host must be brought together by circumstances intimately and frequently, and then sooner or later the smaller of the two exploits the situation. As an Edwardian wag said, familiarity breeds contempt, but you cannot breed without familiarity! This is not quite correct; certain starfish and more highly evolved animals consign their eggs and sperm to the water and as adults can dispense with even fleeting intimacy. It nonetheless applies in parasitic relationships.

Fleas probably arose as winged scavenging flies, feeding as larvae on the excrement in the homes of burrowing mammals. Almost countless generations of such pre-fleas may have eked out a sheltered life in prehistoric burrows before the first pioneer crept into the fur of a passing ratlike occupant. Possibly there is an even shorter step between piercing the dried outer layer of excrement to reach the semifluid matter below it and piercing a mammal's skin and imbibing the first drink of blood. Blood as food may confer such advantages that the insect is immediately started along the risky road to overdependence and overspecialization. Once fleas became parasites their fate was linked to the fate of their hosts; moreover, the 100-million-year running battle between host and parasite was joined, never to end unless one or the other should perish.

Although parasitic animals may well be more numerous than other animals, fleas do not constitute a notably successful group of organisms. Some 300,000 kinds of beetles have been described and named, but only 1,500 species of fleas are known. There are many more types of bird lice than there are types of birds, but mammalian species greatly outnumber the species of fleas, and one may deduce that many kinds of fleas have been exterminated in the past. This fact is advantageous for the investigator who studies fleas: he (or she) has to cope with only a relatively small literature and consequently can spend more time at the microscope and in the field and less in the library. A mere 1,000 works on fleas have been published during the past five years; a quarter of them are written in Russian.

The Hazards of Parasitism

The problems that beset parasites differ from those confronting nonparasitic animals. The rat flea, once it is on the rat, has at its disposal a virtually limitless supply of food. Provided that the flea can avoid the extremely efficient extermination tactics of the host—an end to which the flea's whole external anatomy has become highly modified—its difficulties as an individual are over. The nonparasitic animal must strive endlessly for its daily food and has highly developed sense organs to assist it. The flea's breakfast is permanently at its feet, but on the other hand the future of the species is always in jeopardy. Sometimes the interest of the individual parasite may even run counter to the interests of subsequent generations. For example, if too many fleas live on one rat, they may weaken their host and eventually kill it. Parasites must be modest in their demands and unobtrusive in their ways; they must attract the minimum of attention and yet somehow ensure that their offspring are always in a position to find a similar opportunity and continue their long and now essential intimacy with the host.

Occasionally some unforeseen circumstance arises that turns the well-adapted flea, in whose interest it is never to seriously harm the host on which it depends, into an instrument of self-destruction. Thus the rat flea, carrying the plague bacillus from one sick rat to its neighbor and then moving on to the next available host, was responsible for initiating pandemics that in the Middle Ages exterminated a quarter of the human population of Europe. The rat flea must therefore rank as one of the greatest killers of all time. Yet for every rat or man that died 10 times as many fleas must have perished.

Such hazards engendered by the intimate relation between parasite and host are even more dramatic if specialization has gone one step further and the parasite can feed on only one species of host. This situation has been studied recently in Britain as a result of the introduction of myxomatosis, a lethal virus disease of rabbits. In South America both the indigenous rabbits and their fleas have become reasonably adapted to the myxoma virus and recover from infections. In Britain the rabbit population was not immune and an ideal vector existed in the host-specific rabbit flea *Spilopsyllus cuniculi* Dale, one of the most successful of all known fleas. An epizootic swept the British rabbit population; perhaps as many as 100 million rabbits died during the first outbreak. It is estimated that each rabbit in Britain carried some 75 fleas; few, if any, of these parasites infesting rabbits dying of myxomatosis can have survived, since this particular species of flea is confined to a single host. (There is some evidence, however, that it is becoming adapted to the hare.) At a conservative estimate the epizootic must have killed off a billion fleas in Britain alone.

Thus added to the dangers of the parasite's own existence are the dangers to which the host is subjected. The successful parasite must adapt itself closely to the life of the host, and yet such adaptation inevitably involves dependence and a loss of potential versatility. When a cataclysm such as the advent of myxomatosis occurs, there are no alternative possibilities for a species such as the rabbit flea. The rat flea, which is not quite so highly specialized, can leave the dying host for a man or a mouse; without the rabbit the rabbit flea dies. Perhaps nowhere in the animal kingdom are the danger and cost of success more clearly illustrated. Blessed are the meek—that is, the not too successful—for they shall inherit the earth. One of the unpalatable truths about natural selection is that it imposes a certain mediocrity.

Easily the most interesting features of fleas are their adaptations, which they have been perfecting for perhaps 100 million years. They have adapted firstly to the general parasitic mode of life on a hairy or feathered warm-blooded host; secondly, they have achieved the extremely subtle specializations that enable them to survive on a particular type of mammal or bird. The European rabbit flea is an outstanding example of specialization: it has even surrendered to the host the control of its own breeding cycle! Of this I shall have more to say later.

Adaptations of the Flea

The early stages of a flea's life cycle are passed in the nest of the host or in refuse on the floors of caves or lairs. The larvae feed on debris, but the majority also require iron in order to form their hard external cuticle. This they obtain from blood that is squirted out of the anus of the adult flea and that frequently falls into the host's nest or cracks and crevices or onto the ground where the host sleeps.

Flea larvae are very susceptible to dryness and thrive best in a humid atmosphere, which is of course characteristic of burrows. They can be remarkably indifferent to cold. For example, it has recently been discovered that a bird flea parasitizes an Antarctic petrel; these fleas are found in the nest of the petrel, which is presumably buried for nine months of the year under several meters of ice and snow.

Even the adult rabbit flea is well adapted to survive cold spells, probably because it lives in a cool climate on a host that does not hibernate. Specimens can be kept in a refrigerator for nine months at about −1 degree centigrade (but not below −10 degrees C.), rattling about like pebbles in their glass container, and yet they appear quite unharmed and able to feed and jump only a few minutes after defrosting. Adaptations, particularly those of a physiological nature, that enable a living insect to cope with extreme cold have recently excited considerable attention. The storage of live animals (as well as live sperm) in a state of suspended animation for comparatively long periods of time has become a reality, and therefore such natural adaptations as those exhibited by the Antarctic flea and the rabbit flea are of general as well as scientific interest.

Other examples of refined adaptations in the flea have to do with finding the host and staying on it. Wings are clearly disadvantageous when the flea is living in fur: they impede progress. The permanent parasite must be elusive on

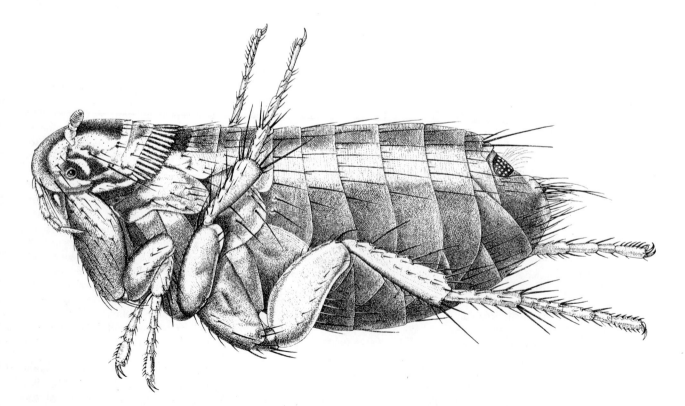

JUMPING FLEA, the common rat flea (*Nosopsyllus fasciatus*), is depicted on the basis of a rare photograph made during a jump and the results of an experimental procedure in which fleas were made to jump into a fixative. The flea frequently turns end over end several times during a jump, holding one or two pairs of legs aloft for use as grappling hooks when it lands on the fur of its host.

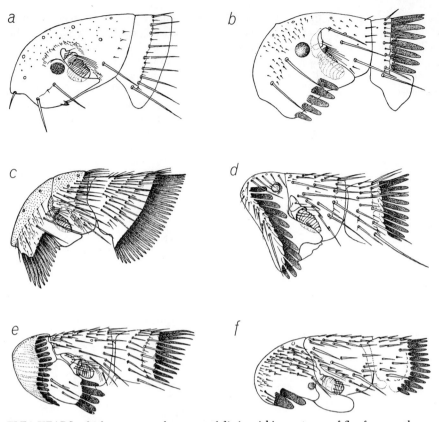

FLEA HEADS, which are among the means of distinguishing one type of flea from another, are depicted for several kinds of flea: (a) the human flea, (b) the European rabbit flea, (c) a mole flea, (d) a South African flea, which is found on small rodents, (e) a helmet flea, appearing on marsupials in Ecuador, and (f) a bat flea. The heads are not drawn to scale.

the host's body, and the loss of a more general mobility is the lesser of two evils. Only a few genuinely parasitic flies have wings, and these are often shed or bitten off when the flies have found a host. It is generally assumed that the majority of insects parasitic on mammals or birds had winged ancestors but lost their organs of flight during the course of evolution.

Fleas are presumably no exception (traces of wing rudiments have been reported in their pupal stage), but they have secondarily evolved powerful jumping legs to assist them in reaching a host. Such legs are unquestionably the most important of all their adaptations. Some species of fleas are better jumpers than others; it has been noted that there are differences in leaping ability even in various strains of the human flea. The jump is too rapid to follow with the human eye, but it has been supposed that the powerful thrust of the flea's leg is the result of the simultaneous extension of its two middle segments—the femur and the tibia.

A flea such as the rat flea that carries plague weighs between .15 and .40 milligram. Its average jump is about 18 centimeters—the record distance is 31 centimeters. It is not necessary to postu-

late some mysterious mechanism to account for these performances; the flea's powerful muscles are adequate for the job. There are, however, certain curious features in the flea's jump. First, the flea frequently lands facing in the direction from which it came, which suggests that the insect turns over in midair. Second, by making fleas jump into a fixative that "froze" them in their jumping attitudes it was found that during their leap they often hold one of their three pairs of legs (sometimes the second pair and sometimes the third) aloft, rotated upward at the trochanter and femoral joints through an angle of about 160 degrees.

This originally gave me the idea that possibly the large air sacs in the legs of fleas, first described by Sir Vincent Wigglesworth of the University of Cambridge, fulfilled some special function in jumping and did not merely provide buoyancy. It also occurred to me that perhaps the flea obtained some special advantage by turning cartwheels rather than somersaults, but after I had watched fleas jump onto rabbits a much simpler explanation presented itself. Such a standing jump for a flea is rather like a leap onto the side of a hairy, windswept cliff. It becomes obvious at

once that the legs held aloft, with their powerful claws directed forward, act as grappling irons. Under these circumstances all six legs provide a highly specialized and quite effective type of landing gear. In order to be sure that fleas do normally hold a pair of legs aloft while jumping, a camera was constructed by which the animal could take a photograph of itself in midair. The photograph showed that at that moment it was traveling through the air upside down with its second pair of legs held well and truly aloft [see illustration on preceding page].

It is in their host-finding abilities that fleas show their most impressive adaptability and versatility. One species of bird flea—the sand-martin flea—depends for its survival on a sensitive response to temperature and air currents and also possibly to shadows. These fleas, which spend the winter in the temporarily abandoned underground nests of sand martins, are so sensitive to the gradual onset of warmer spring weather in Britain that they may hatch from their cocoons on the very day the migrating sand martins return from Africa and arrive at their nesting sites. If an artificial sand martin with wings that are mechanically flapped is dangled on a string in front of the burrow nest, the expectant sand-martin fleas will jump onto it.

The cat flea, on the other hand, responds to the warm emanations of carbon dioxide exhaled by the cat, and the rat flea is attracted by the pungent odor of the rat. Fleas that are parasites of the large jird, a rodent that lives in the sandy soil along the Ili River of central Asia, congregate in the first bend of their host's burrow; it was observed that they became aware of the tread of a man within half a meter of the burrow and would emerge and pursue him for quite a distance. They can apparently distinguish the direction from which vibrations come and can also orient themselves to the direction of an air current. It seems that in their efforts to reach the right host, fleas are able to gain assistance from gravity, light, vibrations, noise, temperature gradients, atmospheric pressure, air currents, odors and other chemical stimuli.

Antony R. Mead-Briggs of the British Ministry of Agriculture has demonstrated the rabbit flea's talents in this regard. He liberated 270 marked specimens at intervals in an enclosed meadow with an area of 2,000 square yards. Into this enclosure he introduced three rabbits. Within a few days 45 percent of the marked fleas were recovered from them. The host-finding ability of the rabbit flea is therefore prodigious. It must be realized that a flea on the ground in a meadow is in the situation of a man in a forest where the trees are 600 feet high. (To be sure, the flea is much more mobile.)

The Rabbit Flea

The rabbit flea merits detailed discussion because it provides an example of a unique type of adaptation: dependence on the sex-hormone cycle of the vertebrate host. Once on the rabbit the fleas make their way to the ears, where they attach themselves to the skin with their serrated mouth parts. Being a semisedentary species, they usually remain with their piercing mandibles more or less continuously embedded in the rabbit's flesh for long periods of their lives.

The fleas that settle on the rabbit's ears can never breed unless their host becomes pregnant or they can transfer to a rabbit already expecting young or to newborn nestlings. In this way the breeding cycle of the flea has become geared to the sex hormones secreted by the host and concentrated in its blood. Ten days before the young rabbits are born the eggs of the female fleas begin to develop, and by the last day of the host's pregnancy they are ripe. A few hours after the rabbits are born the fleas detach themselves from the mother's ears and move to her face. While the mother is tending her young and eating

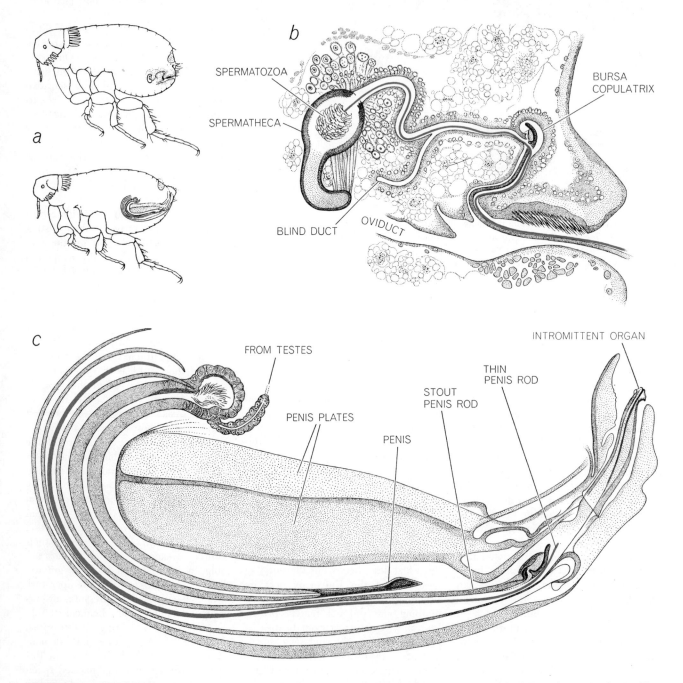

EUROPEAN RABBIT FLEA reproduces with the aid of an unusually complicated genital apparatus. At *a* the female (*top*) and male are depicted with their copulatory organs outlined, at *b* the female's organs are shown in detail and at *c* details of the male organ are depicted in part. The thin penis rod (*color*) runs through a slot in the spoonlike end of the stout penis rod, picking up sperm. The thick rod enters the female's *bursa copulatrix* and guides the thinner rod into the threadlike duct leading to the spermatheca, or sperm-storage organ of the female, as shown in *b*. The precise method by which the thin penis rod deposits the sperm is not known.

the placenta, the fleas pass on to the nestlings, on which they feed voraciously. There they mate and lay eggs. After about 12 days of egg-laying in the nest the fleas suddenly abandon the young rabbits and return to the mother. If she becomes pregnant again, they can begin a new breeding cycle.

The fleas come under the influence of physiological changes in the rabbit the moment the buck rabbit sets eyes on the doe. The temperature of pairing rabbits' ears rises precipitately—sometimes by as much as seven degrees centigrade —and the fleas as well as their hosts become excited and can be seen hopping about and moving from the buck to the doe and back again. In female rabbits ovulation follows coitus; within a few hours, perhaps sooner, the anterior lobe of the pituitary gland—the master gland controlling the sexual cycle of the rabbit—releases sex hormones into the blood. The sex hormones in turn stimulate target organs such as the ovaries and the adrenal glands to secrete other hormones.

One of the first noticeable effects on the fleas is to induce them to attach themselves more firmly to the skin of the doe. In spite of their semisedentary inclinations there is a considerable exchange of fleas between rabbits that come into contact with each other, but once a flea has moved onto a pregnant doe under the influence of the sex hormones it remains there. The future mother thus tends to amass a heavier load of fleas than her virgin companions or the bucks—to the great advantage of the fleas.

Ten days before the rabbit gives birth there is a rise of the level in its blood of another hormone from the anterior lobe of the pituitary: the adrenocorticotrophic hormone, which stimulates the adrenal glands to release corticosteroids. These are the principal hormones controlling maturation and egg-laying in the rabbit flea, although thyroxine and estradiol also play a significant role in these processes. The hormones known as progestins are responsible for checking the growth of the flea's ovaries and for initiating the regression and resorption of the yolk and developing eggs. It is worth mentioning that man-made progestins are used as human contraceptives—this is "the pill" that has recently attracted so much notice.

Apart from the development of the female reproductive organs both male and female fleas undergo profound changes under the influence of the maturation hormones. The salivary glands develop and more than double in size;

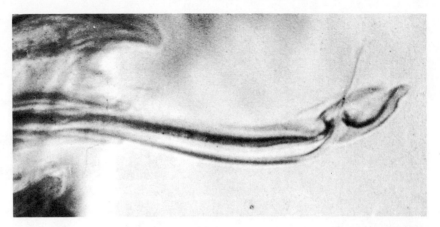

PENIS RODS of a flea appear in a photograph made by freezing two fleas during copulation and then gently separating them. These structures are shown in the illustration on the preceding page as they appear before protraction. The thinner rod is visible passing through the slot in the thicker rod like a rope over a pulley and then projecting upward. The faint fuzz at the end of the thinner rod is sperm, which is wound around the tip of the rod.

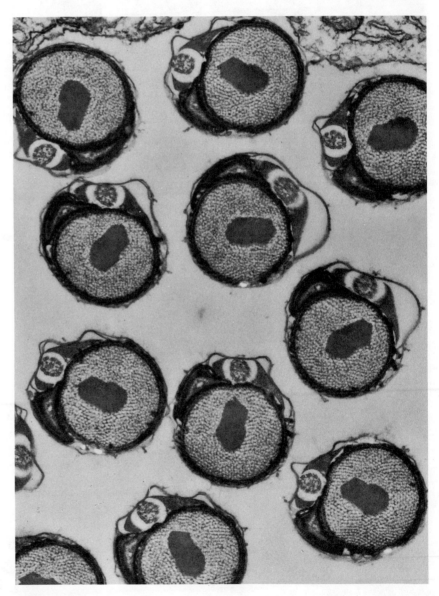

SPERM TAILS of the rat flea are shown in cross section at an enlargement of 58,000 diameters in this electron micrograph made by A. V. Grimstone of the University of Cambridge. The cross section is through the tails of a bundle of rat-flea sperm. A different view of such a bundle of sperm is shown in the illustration at top left on the following page.

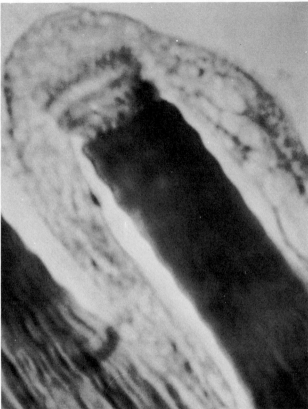

RAT-FLEA SPERM is shown enlarged 250 diameters. The partially developed heads (*center*) are held together in a gelatinous pointed cap. The tails of these sperm have short wave frequencies.

RABBIT-FLEA SPERM, enlarged 325 diameters, has a membranous envelope along the sides reminiscent of a bridal veil. The wave frequencies in the tails are longer than those in the rat-flea sperm.

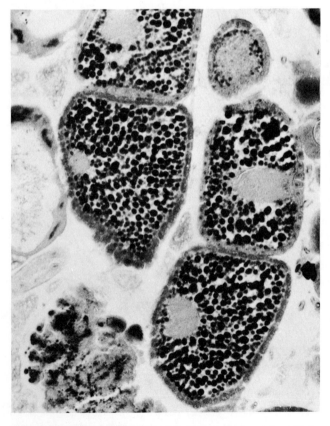

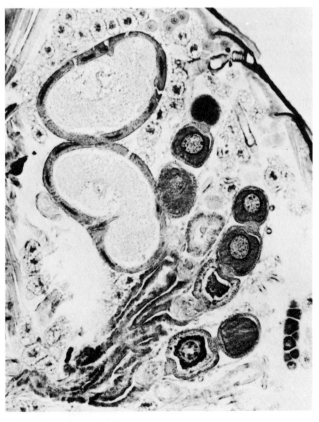

INFLUENCE OF HORMONES of the host on the eggs of a rabbit flea is depicted. At left the eggs are developing after the rabbit has been injected with hydrocortisone. At right the eggs, which are the dark circular structures to the right of the pale, dark-rimmed structures, are regressing after injections of a progestin hormone into the rabbit. The enlargement is approximately 40 diameters.

SPECIAL CAMERA constructed at a Royal Air Force experimental station to photograph the jump of a flea consisted of a bank of one-inch lenses with overlapping fields that covered all of a glass cell in which the flea jumped. The flea itself triggered the camera by interrupting a narrow beam of light as it jumped. The glass cell was nine inches long, seven inches in height and one inch thick.

there is an overall increase in the size of the gut, together with great enlargement and proliferation of the epithelial cells lining its middle portion, and the rate at which the fleas defecate increases steadily as the levels of corticosteroids rise. Normally a flea defecates about once every 20 minutes; immediately before the rabbit gives birth the female flea is squirting blood out of its anus once every one to four minutes and the male flea about once every four to six minutes. This blood, as I have previously noted, subsequently provides the flea larvae with an essential factor in their diet.

Whereas a slight increase in the level of hormones in the blood of the rabbit induces the fleas to attach themselves more firmly to the host—a fact easily demonstrated experimentally—a big rise reverses this effect: the fleas detach themselves and run onto the doe's face. A change in hormone levels is almost certainly the cause of their detachment immediately before they pass on to the young. By this extraordinary adaptation the fleas are assured of a suitable place in which to breed. The female rabbit generally builds her nest some distance from the main warren, in a "stop," or short tunnel. By gearing their own reproduction to that of the host the fleas are guided to the nest at precisely the right moment, and the eggs are ready for fertilization the very day the young rabbits are born. Moreover, the larvae are assured of enough dried blood on which to feed.

It has been possible to sort out which of the various pituitary hormones are involved in these processes by injecting the rabbits with each in turn, and in different combinations and at different levels; it has been particularly useful to employ castrated buck rabbits as the experimental hosts, since they have a minimum of their own sex hormones. It has also been found that the fleas react to steroid hormones sprayed on them, and that they respond differently to the different corticosteroid hormones. Thus the rabbit flea, used as a kind of biological indicator, suggested that the corticosteroids cortisol and corticosterone were both present in the pregnant female rabbit during the last 10 days of pregnancy and in the rabbit from one to seven days old, but that when the young were three to four weeks old the levels in their blood had fallen precipitately. These indications were subsequently confirmed by D. Exley of the University of Oxford, who examined the rabbit's blood by means of thin-layer chromatography and with the aid of radioactive tracers and fluorescent techniques.

Many bird fleas, if they are slightly warmed, copulate on emerging from their pupae, without a blood meal and before their ovaries mature. In the large majority of species, however, the female has to take a blood meal before she will mate. It has been noted that at least one species of male flea lacks the sexual drive if it is reared on an unusual host but recovers its keenness after a meal of blood from its normal host. The rabbit flea is quite an exceptional case; in nature it will mate only after the female has fed on rabbits one to seven days old. The two flea sexes can remain side by side for weeks or months on an adult rabbit, the females either immature or full of ripe eggs, and no attempt at mating is made. After a period of feeding on the young rabbits a transformation occurs in the female; she suddenly attracts the male and is herself willing to mate.

In this species neither maturation of the eggs nor maturation of the sperm is concerned with copulation. After feeding on a young rabbit a female flea with unripe eggs will mate with a male that lacks fully ripe sperm in its testes. What is the signal the female gives when she has imbibed the necessary copulation factor? Does she release a pheromone—a hormone secreted externally—that stimulates the male? The characteristic zigzag approach made by the male on these occasions suggests that it is following some airborne trail of scent.

In spite of the fact that the fleas do not mate on the pregnant doe there was considerable evidence to suggest that the factor was present in her blood but in weak concentrations. This clue was followed up; it was found during preliminary experiments that still another hormone secreted by the anterior lobe of the pituitary—somatotropin, the growth hormone—is one of the factors that can control the copulation of fleas. This hormone, unlike the corticosteroids, tends to be specific in its action. That is, the growth hormone of cattle or the human growth hormone can be expected to work effectively only if it is injected into the animal that normally secretes it. No rabbit growth hormone, which would be expected to activate the rabbit flea more effectively than any other growth hormone, is yet available for experiments. Nevertheless, injections of human growth hormone into the rabbit can sometimes stimulate the rabbit flea to copulate on the adult host and more frequently on young rabbits more than eight days old. (It is of interest that somatotropin is one of the hormones that have been used to increase fertility in women and that have attracted considerable attention following several multiple births to women so treated.) Other factors not fully understood also play a part in controlling the copulation of the European rabbit flea.

The Reproductive Process

Even though the male flea freshly emerged from its pupa already has a full complement of sperm in its testes, the sperm are by no means fully developed. They are gathered together in bundles; their heads, which are barely distinguishable at this stage, are held firmly in a pointed gelatinous capsule with a giant nucleus at its apex. Seen through the microscope, the bundles of sperm are enveloped in membranes that resemble gracefully flowing bridal veils [see illustration at top right on page 228]. Sometimes the individual sperm heads are already developed (their development may depend on the food supply of the larvae), but even so there is always plenty of space between the bundles of sperm in the testes. When the heads of the sperm are well developed, the tails are sufficiently free within their capsules to produce wonderfully synchronized wavelike undulations in the available space. After the male flea begins to feed on a host these spaces are gradually obliterated by the fact that the sperm increase in size, but it is only after the male flea has been feeding on the pregnant rabbit and her newborn young for a certain period that both the flea and its sperm reach their maximum size.

At this stage sections of the fleas' testes reveal a solid tangled mass; possibly the sperm are not capable of fertilizing the eggs until this stage of development is reached. It would require rather a long period of study with the aid of the electron microscope to clarify and work out the effect of the rabbit's sex hormones on the development of the sperm. The picture at the bottom of page 6 was made with such a microscope by A. V. Grimstone of the University of Cambridge. It is a transverse section, enlarged 58,000 diameters, through partly developed sperm from the testes of a flea feeding on a nonpregnant host. Each tail seen in the section has two fibers surrounded by a circular array of nine other fibers; this arrangement is characteristic of all cilia and flagella and is the basis for the swimming abilities of the sperm.

Even with the relatively low magnification of the light microscope it is pos-

sible to note differences between the sperm of different species of fleas. If the reader compares the micrographs of rat-flea and rabbit-flea sperm at the top of page 7, he will see that the wave frequency of the tails of the former is very much shorter than that of the latter; each tail of the rat-flea sperm at this stage of development has a kinky appearance. Rat-flea sperm are also much larger than rabbit-flea sperm. There appears to be a correlation between the size of the spermatheca, or sperm-storage organ of the female, and the size of the sperm. The mole flea (Hystrichopsylla talpae) belongs to a group of the largest fleas (between five and seven millimeters in length), but its sperm cell is relatively small and is stored in two correspondingly small spermatheca.

It would be interesting if an electron microscope study of the sperm confirmed the evolutionary relation of the order of fleas that was worked out by the late Karl Jordan of the Tring Museum in England. This classification is partly based on the organs that assist in conveying the sperm into the female. The copulatory apparatus of the male flea is the most elaborate genital organ in the animal kingdom. Recently the German entomologist Kurt Günther has described it for the mole flea and has clarified many obscure features. A glance at the illustration on page 5 will convey some idea of its complexity. Any engineer looking objectively at such a fantastically impractical apparatus would bet heavily against its operational success. The astonishing fact is that it works. Twenty-four hours after the rabbit fleas leave the doe for her young all the female fleas have been fertilized.

The various complicated steps in fertilization have not been observed in detail. The only part of the male flea's genitalia capable of extrusion are the two penis rods; these slide forward and uncurl like watch springs. Only in the rabbit flea has the conveyance of sperm actually been observed. The sperm is wound around the terminal portion of the thinner of the two penis rods rather like spaghetti on the end of a fork. This rod runs through a slot in the spoonlike end of the thicker penis rod like a rope running over a pulley. The thick rod enters the female's bursa copulatrix, into which it fits very snugly, and guides the thinner rod into the threadlike duct leading to the sperm-storage organ of the female. The photograph at the top of page 6 shows the end of the stouter rod with the thin rod running through the slot. The faint fuzz surrounding the tip is the mass of sperm. In order to

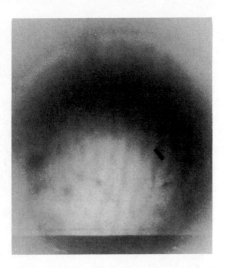

FLEA DURING JUMP was photographed with the apparatus shown on the preceding page. Base of cell is dark area at bottom.

take this photograph it was necessary to freeze two fleas during copulation, so that the penis rods remained erect when male and female were separated. Unfortunately the duct leading to the spermatheca is covered with heavy cuticle and therefore is not transparent. This makes direct observation by transmitted light impossible, and as a consequence the method by which the rod packs sperm into the spermatheca through this duct is not known.

George P. Holland, a Canadian entomologist who has greatly enlarged our understanding of copulation in various fleas, has described an odd membranous organ somewhat resembling a willow catkin with which the male strokes the female sensillum during the act of coitus. An analogous structure probably exists in many fleas but escapes attention because it is so transparent and diaphanous that it disappears entirely when specimens are prepared for permanent preservation. This is the case with the organ in the rabbit flea, which resembles a feather duster and is erected only during mating. Apparently it is also used for stroking the female, but on the lower surface. This is quite an astonishing fact; the clasping organs of the male flea are so elaborate and so encumbered with spines, struts and hooks that it would appear that only brute force is used to subdue the female. Furthermore, serious injuries are frequently inflicted on the female during impregnation, and it seems curious that she could notice the effect of this feather-like stimulator during the violent treatment she appears to be receiving simultaneously. Perhaps our interpretation of this organ is quite incorrect. Is it conceivable that it is the male who receives stimulation and with his feather duster sweeps up a pheromone released by the female?

Two particularly interesting questions are posed by the unraveling of the life cycle of the rabbit flea. First, how do these hormones act? Do they work by way of substances secreted by specialized cells in the flea's brain, which in turn act on the appropriate organ that releases the flea's own hormones, or do the corticosteroids, estrogens and progestins act directly on the various tissues of the flea? Second, what role do the host's hormones play in the lives of parasites in general? Is the hormonal dependence of the European rabbit flea unique?

Obviously the most promising species to investigate in this respect are the American rabbit fleas, which are fairly closely related to the European species. Unfortunately the cottontail rabbit is a difficult host to keep in captivity. It is quite certain, however, that the breeding of the plague-carrying Oriental rat flea (*Xenopsylla cheopis*) is not dependent on the hormones of the rat. This flea copulates and lays eggs even on a rat that has been castrated and in addition has had both its adrenal glands and its pituitary gland removed surgically, so that it is virtually deprived of all sex hormones. The fleas are probably less fertile than those laying eggs on a normal rat, and it is not yet known if their eggs produce offspring. It has been noted, however that the number of fleas on female bats increases noticeably in the spring just before the bats migrate to their summer breeding roosts. This suggests that in the case of bat fleas, as in that of the European rabbit flea, the hormones of the host may play an active role in the fleas' reproductive cycle.

Open Questions

It is characteristic of nature that some apparently unique feature displayed by a particular animal is only unique in degree. A careful examination of related species shows that the same tendencies are present but to a very modest extent and have consequently escaped notice. It seems reasonable to suppose that in the future many instances will be discovered in which the hormones of vertebrate animals play some unobtrusive but definite role in the development of their parasites, particularly those such as the parasitic worms that live in such naked intimacy with their hosts.

In the old literature it was repeatedly stated that women are attacked more frequently by fleas than men are. This has been generally attributed to the more delicate skin and more sensitive nature of the fair sex. In old books it is always women who are pictured wearing the latest flea trap [*see illustration at left.*] Perhaps this is faulty reasoning and the truth of the matter is that the human flea (*Pulex irritans*) also responds to the attraction of the ovarian hormones. This is food for reflection. Here we have a simple and fascinating line of research on which any one of us can embark tomorrow.

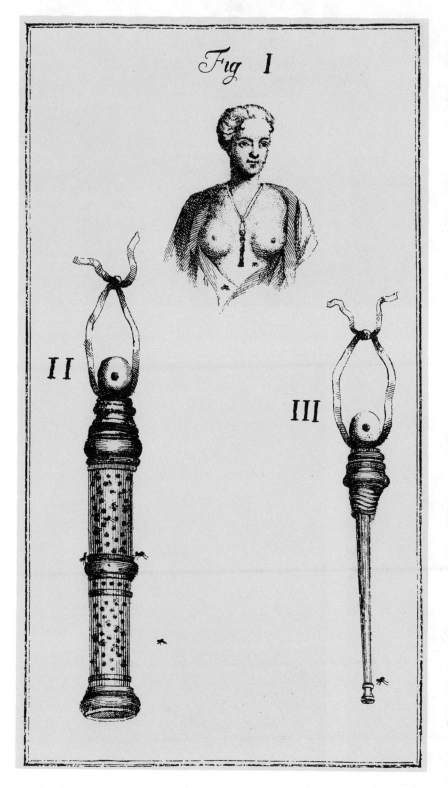

FLEA TRAP was depicted in a German book of 1739. Old books often show such traps being worn by women; it was often said that women were attacked by fleas more often than men were. The cause may conceivably have been a response by fleas to ovarian hormones.

SOLITARY WASPS take prey, which they paralyze by stinging, primarily as food for their larvae. This great golden digger wasp, *Sphex ichneumoneus,* has taken a large katydid, which it grasps with its mandibles. In flight the wasp carries its prey with its legs.

BEMBIX PRUINOSA, having prepared a nest in a sand dune, approaches the nest carrying a flower fly with its middle legs. *Bembix* is one of the few solitary wasps that bring their larvae fresh prey daily. The photographs on this page were made by the author.

APHILANTHOPS LATICINCTUS, a highly evolved wasp, preys only on one species of harvester ant, which it carries on specialized segments on its abdomen. This *Aphilanthops* is standing on its middle and hind legs and using its front legs to reopen its nest.

25

Predatory Wasps

by Howard E. Evans
April 1963

*Solitary wasps prey on spiders and insects to feed
their larvae. Their highly specific predatory behavior,
including choice of prey and manner of carrying it,
provides clues to the evolution of wasps*

The sting of bees, wasps and certain ants gives these insects a formidable defense against predators. In the solitary wasps, however, the sting still serves primarily the function for which it originally evolved: the taking of prey. The solitary wasps are hunters. Most familiar in the "digger" or "mud dauber" forms, they have diversified into hundreds of genera and thousands of species in pursuit of their fellow insects and other arthropods, such as the spiders. Each species tends to specialize, hunting down a particular prey and disregarding others of similar size and more ready availability. Some restrict their predation to a single species or genus and only a few claim victims from more than one order of arthropods. The affinity of predator to prey is, in each case, as characteristic of the wasp as the anatomical features that distinguish it from other wasps. Such specialization of behavior is not surprising in view of the difference in strategy and tactics required for capturing a caterpillar, for example, compared with a fly. The consequent diversity in the behavioral repertories of the solitary wasps has invited increasing attention in recent years, as zoologists have turned to the study of the decisive role of behavior in the origin of species.

Solitary wasps are predators of a rather special sort. Only a few take prey as food for themselves; for the most part the adults of all species feed on sugars in solution, which they find in the nectar of flowers, in ripe fruit or in the honeydew secreted by aphids and other plant-sucking insects. The male wasps, in fact, are not predators at all and feed exclusively on plant exudates. It is the females that take prey, and they do so primarily to feed their larvae. In this remarkable plan of behavior the solitary wasps foreshadow the still more elaborate larva-nurturing of the social Hymenoptera—

the ants, bees and social wasps—all of which apparently arose from certain long extinct groups of solitary wasps. (The termites arose from an entirely different stock, the cockroaches of the order Orthoptera.) The solitary wasps in turn have derived the elements of their behavior—their specificity as to prey, the restriction of the predatory habit to the female and the consignment of the prey to the nurture of the next generation—from their precursors in the Hymenoptera line.

The most primitive Hymenoptera, on the basis of many features of larval and adult structure, are the sawflies, and these first appear in the fossil record at the beginning of the Mesozoic era, some 200 million years ago. With its sawlike ovipositor the female deposits its eggs in plant tissue. Most species are highly host-specific. In the Jurassic, the second period of the Mesozoic, the parasitic Hymenoptera, including the ichneumon wasps, made their appearance. The female deposits its eggs on or in another arthropod (most commonly a plant feeder); the larvae feed on the host, causing its death only when they have completed their own development. These insects flourished almost immediately and even today form an enormous group of many thousands of species. Some are equipped with ovipositors twice the length of their bodies, with which they are able to plant their eggs on grubs burrowing deep in the trunks of trees.

For this unique form of parasitism O. M. Reuter of the University of Helsingfors many years ago coined the term "parasitoid." When the true wasps appeared toward the end of the Mesozoic, they inherited this manner of life; some living groups of primitive wasps still behave essentially like parasitoids. But most wasps paralyze their hosts (now called "prey") by stinging them,

then store them in the nest where the egg is laid and larval development takes place. The true wasps are no more predators in the usual sense than the ichneumon wasps are parasites. One might perhaps use the term "predatoid" to epitomize the origins and gross behavior of these insects.

The adapatation of a particular wasp to its prey presents one of the most intriguing problems in the study of behavior. In two widely separated localities, the digger wasp *Aphilanthops laticinctus* has been found to prey exclusively on one species: the prairie mound-building ant *Pogonomyrmex occidentalis*. A related species, *A. haigi*, seems to confine its predation to another ant, *P. barbatus rugosus*. I have seen *haigi* hunting in areas where a closely related ant, *P. maricopa*, was more abundant, and I have seen these wasps approach a worker *maricopa*, back away and proceed to hunt *barbatus rugosus* workers. *Maricopa* appears, however, to be the normal prey of another species of *Aphilanthops*, called *A. sculleni*. Reports of such narrow specialization should be further documented; sometimes a wasp that appears highly host-specific in one region is found to prey on another species, although usually a related species, elsewhere.

One *Aphilanthops*, *A. frigidus*, a common species in the eastern U.S., is known to prey on queen ants instead of workers; in museums there are many specimens pinned with their prey. Curiously, this wasp takes only winged queens at the time of their nuptial flight and ignores the queens that have lost their wings and are seen at times running in numbers over the ground. The wasp removes the wings from the ant, however, before placing it in the brood cell. Without exception the victims belong to the species

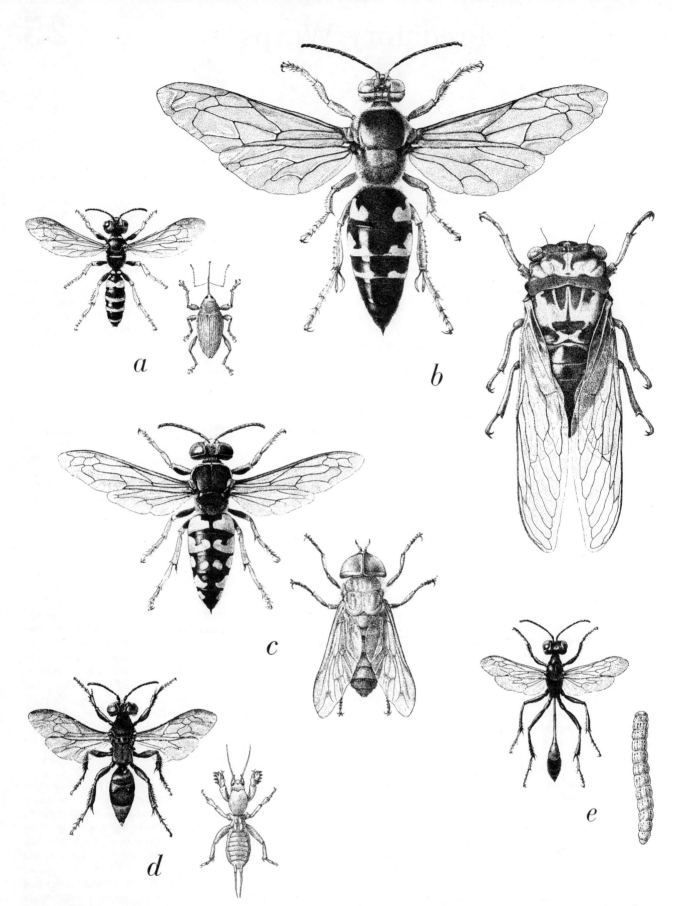

FEMALE WASPS, members of the family Sphecidae, are depicted with some of the insects they prey on (*prey are shown in color*): *Cerceris halone* with a weevil (*a*), *Sphecius speciosus* with a cica- da (*b*), *Stictia carolina* with a horsefly (*c*), *Larra analis* with an immature mole cricket (*d*) and *Ammophila arvensis* with a moth larva (*e*). The wasps and their prey are drawn about twice life size.

Formica fusca or one of two or three other closely related species of the genus *Formica*.

Wasps more commonly prey on several related species of a genus—*Cerceris halone*, for example, preys on the long-beaked weevils of the genus *Curculio*. Still more commonly, a given species of wasp will prey on several or even many genera of one family or several related families. The great golden digger, *Sphex ichneumoneus*, takes katydids and long-horned grasshoppers of several genera in at least two subfamilies; *Ochleroptera bipunctata*, a tiny wasp that sometimes nests in flowerpots, takes leaf hoppers and other plant-sucking insects (Homoptera) in five related families. Less commonly, a wasp may prey on a wide variety of insects of a given order. *Philanthus pacificus* has been found to take prey belonging to six different families of Hymenoptera, including bees, ichneumonids and even other wasps.

Such host-specificity is the more curious because the larvae of wasps can often be induced to develop normally on prey quite different from that provided by the mother. The French naturalist Jean Henri Fabre many years ago successfully reared *Bembix*, a predator of flies, on a diet of grasshoppers. Similar experiments have been performed by Fabre and other investigators on other species of wasps. The host must, of course, be paralyzed or freshly killed if it is to be acceptable.

For a wasp to take insects of more than one order is unusual, but several species are known to do so. *Crossocerus quadrimaculatus* preys on a wide variety of flies (Diptera) and also occasionally takes small moths (Lepidoptera) and caddis flies (Trichoptera). *Lindenius columbianus errans*, a minute wasp that happens to be quite common on a sandy road near my home in Lexington, Mass., fills its nest with a remarkable mixture of midges (Diptera), small parasitic wasps (Hymenoptera) and minute bugs (Hemiptera). Another unusual wasp is *Microbembex*, which is known to stock its brood cells with insects of 10 different orders as well as with spiders. The victims in this case, however, are picked up from the sand already dead or disabled; *Microbembex* is the only genus of digger wasps that has become a scavenger rather than a predator. If one wonders why this mode of life is not more prevalent among wasps, the answer may be that the scavenger's niche was amply filled at an earlier date by other Hymenoptera: the ants.

Many species of wasps take their prey in habitats quite different from and often distant from that in which the new adult emerges from the brood cell and where she eventually builds the brood cells of her offspring. Little is known about her initial hunting flights. These must often involve much random flying about before the wasp locates the source of prey appropriate to her species. Once she arrives in the proper habitat it is apparent that an assortment of cues direct her to her prey. In the case of the bee wolf, *Philanthus triangulum*, Nikolaas Tinbergen of the University of Oxford and his co-workers have observed that the wasp flies from one flower to another; when she sees a moving object on a flower about the size of a bee, she hovers a short distance downwind from it. At this point olfactory cues become important: if the object has the odor of a bee, the wasp pounces on it. But she does not actually sting it unless she finds it has the "feel" of a bee. Less thorough studies of a number of other digger wasps suggest that this succession of visual-olfactory-tactile cues may serve to guide wasps of many different species to their prey. The tendency to respond to appropriate cues in each of these sensory modalities is apparently part of the unlearned, genetically determined behavioral repertory of each

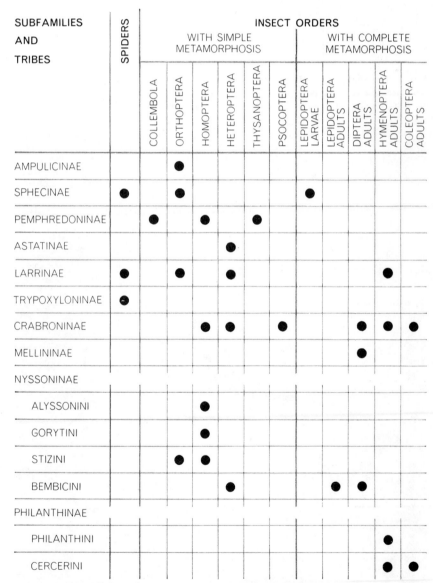

SUBFAMILIES AND TRIBES	SPIDERS	INSECT ORDERS WITH SIMPLE METAMORPHOSIS						INSECT ORDERS WITH COMPLETE METAMORPHOSIS				
		COLLEMBOLA	ORTHOPTERA	HOMOPTERA	HETEROPTERA	THYSANOPTERA	PSOCOPTERA	LEPIDOPTERA LARVAE	LEPIDOPTERA ADULTS	DIPTERA ADULTS	HYMENOPTERA ADULTS	COLEOPTERA ADULTS
AMPULICINAE			●									
SPHECINAE	●		●					●				
PEMPHREDONINAE		●		●			●					
ASTATINAE					●							
LARRINAE	●		●	●							●	
TRYPOXYLONINAE	●											
CRABRONINAE				●	●		●			●	●	●
MELLININAE										●		
NYSSONINAE												
ALYSSONINI				●								
GORYTINI				●								
STIZINI			●	●								
BEMBICINI					●				●	●		
PHILANTHINAE												
PHILANTHINI											●	
CERCERINI											●	●

SPECIFICITY of prey choice is illustrated in this chart. The major subfamilies (in some cases subdivided into tribes) of the Sphecidae, or digger wasps, are arranged at left in approximate evolutionary sequence (*top to bottom*). Their prey, indicated by the colored disks, include spiders and many orders of insects. Aside from some exceptional cases that are not illustrated here, each subfamily preys on remarkably few different orders of insects.

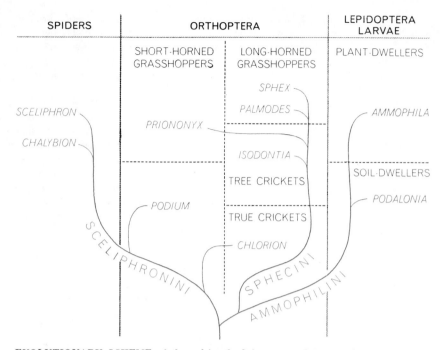

EVOLUTIONARY SCHEME of the subfamily Sphecinae is based on larval and adult structure. Changes in type of prey (*shown in black*) are correlated with the development of wasp tribes and genera (*color*). In general the advanced wasps prey on advanced insects.

PARASITIC HYMENOPTERA, which may have been the evolutionary precursors of the solitary wasps, lay their eggs on or inside the bodies of other insects or spiders. This parasitic ichneumon wasp, *Megarrhyssa macrura,* has inserted its extremely long ovipositor through the bark of a tree in order to lay its egg on the larva of a sawfly, the pigeon horntail.

species. William Morton Wheeler of Harvard University many years ago suggested that the olfactory system of the wasp is conditioned in the larval stage when it consumes the specimens of its future prey captured for it by its mother. This seems improbable in view of what has already been said about the diversity of prey taken by some species; in any case, it suggests no corresponding way in which the visual components in this behavior might be "conditioned."

Wasps do not normally "make mistakes" with respect to prey. I have accumulated thousands of prey records of various North American species of *Bembix*, and not a single one involves an insect other than a fly (Diptera). Yet in different parts of its range any one species of *Bembix* will hunt in quite different habitats and take quite a different array of flies. Wheeler found an Australian *Bembix* preying on damsel flies—slender insects of the entirely different four-winged order Odonata—and postulated that in this region the wasps had turned to damsel flies because true flies were scarce. It is quite possible, however, that damsel flies provide the usual prey of this Australian *Bembix* and that the species has come to respond innately to damsel flies and not to true flies. This would represent a comparatively recent development in evolution.

In nesting aggregations of *Bembix* I have often found the brood cells of one individual stocked with nothing but horseflies; in the nests of others I have found mostly flies captured on flowers; in the nests of still others, flies taken on carcasses or dung. Apparently once a given wasp has located a rich source of prey it returns again and again to the same place. I have also observed the prey taken by a single wasp change in character as she built a series of nests, indicating that one source of prey had become exhausted and another had been found.

Many Diptera-hunters take their prey mainly from mammals and in their hunting flights apparently seek out mammals likely to harbor biting flies. *Stictia carolina,* a cousin of *Bembix,* is known as the "horse guard" because it is so frequently seen hovering about the flanks of horses and cattle, whence it snatches horseflies. Joseph C. Bequaert of Harvard University has observed small wasps of the genus *Oxybelus* pouncing on, stinging and carrying away black flies from the skin of human beings in Guatemala.

Although one is most likely to see wasps hunting in broad daylight in the open air, this must not obscure the fact that important species do their hunting under entirely different circumstances. Wasps that prey on crickets and cockroaches do most of their hunting on the ground, creeping into crevices under stones and fallen timber and into holes in the ground. Diggers of the genus *Podalonia* unearth cutworms from the soil. One species of *Bembix* does all its hunting just at twilight, preying on Diptera that have come to rest for the night in vegetation. The members of the genus *Argogorytes* have a still stranger specialization: they extract immature spittle insects from their masses of supposedly protective froth on the stalks of plants.

The stinging of the prey that follows capture is a relatively stereotyped sequence of motions that differs from one major group of wasps to another in apparent adaptation to the anatomy and physiology of the prey. André Steiner of the University of Montpellier has observed that *Liris nigra* stings its cricket prey first in the vicinity of the nerve ganglion controlling the hind legs—the jumping legs—and then twice more in the vicinity of the ganglia controlling the

other two pairs of legs. As Fabre first pointed out, the hunters of caterpillars sting their prey not only on the thorax but also several times along the underside of the abdomen. In caterpillars the "prolegs" on the abdominal segments of the body are as important in locomotion as the thoracic legs, if not more so, and the nervous system is not highly concentrated in the thorax. On the other hand, there is much evidence that the predators of leaf hoppers, cicadas and other Homoptera, in which the nerve ganglia are concentrated in a single large mass in the thorax, administer a single, prolonged sting in the vicinity of this nerve center. Wasps that prey on other members of the order Hymenoptera also generally insert the sting only once.

The extensive literature that explains the stinging behavior of wasps in terms of the neural anatomy of the victim may have to undergo revision as the result of the recent work of Werner Rathmayer of the University of Munich. He observed that the bee wolf inserts its sting into the honeybee only once, in the membrane around the coxae, or anchor segments, of the front legs on the underside of the thorax, and that the stinging

lasts from 20 to 50 seconds. By careful dissection of the victims Rathmayer was able to show that the sting does not normally penetrate the ganglion. Instead the venom diffuses from the point of injection into the flight muscles and the muscles controlling the legs.

Rathmayer's finding that the venom does not act directly on or through the nervous system is well documented. It may be that the stings are inflicted through the underside of the thorax not because of the presence there of nerve ganglia but because "chinks in the armor" around the coxae give ready access to the muscles of locomotion. Rathmayer also found, incidentally, that a component in the blood of the bee wolf makes it immune to its own venom but that this does not protect it against injection of its venom directly into a ganglion. *Palarus variegatus*, a wasp that preys on other wasps, including the bee wolf, is also immune to wasp venom.

In the not yet completed task of classifying wasps, the study of behavior and particularly of prey selection has begun to shed light on difficult problems. Workers in our laboratory at Harvard University have recently divided one genus of

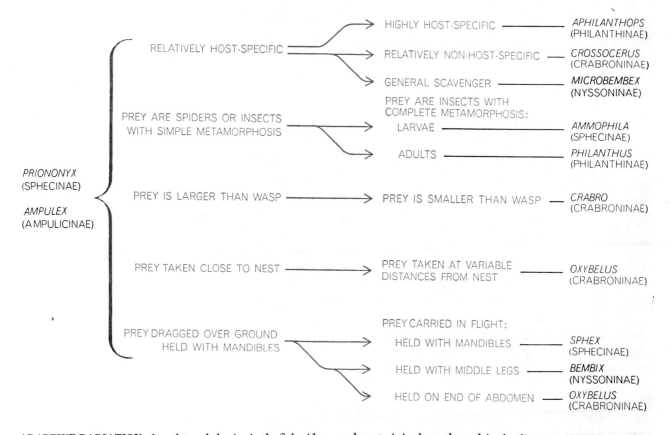

ADAPTIVE RADIATION of predatory behavior in the Sphecidae is illustrated in this chart. Characteristics of the behavior of the more primitive wasps are shown at the left with two examples (*black*) of wasps typical of this group. The arrows show how those

characteristics have changed in the direction of more specialization and more advanced predatory techniques. This more advanced behavior is exhibited by many wasps; those listed at the right (*black*) are merely genera of which each behavioral item is typical.

the tribe Bembicini into two: *Stictiella,* which has been found to provision its nests exclusively with moths and butterflies, and *Glenostictia,* which feeds its larvae from day to day on flies. Father Aloys Adriaanse of Tilburg in the Netherlands has carried this kind of discrimination of the species level, separating *Ammophila campestris,* which preys on the larvae of sawflies, from its sibling species *A. pubescens,* which preys on the larvae of moths.

The major steps in the evolution of wasps were taken millions of years ago. Many of the wasps found in Baltic amber look much like contemporary wasps, and it is probably safe to assume that many of them behaved much the way their relatives do today. Hence it is not surprising to find that those groups of wasps that are ranked as primitive on the basis of their structure and generally simpler behavior patterns prey largely on orders of insects considered low on the evolutionary scale. The Ampulicinae, for example, are an isolated and probably relict group of digger wasps; they limit their predation to cockroaches, dominant insects of earlier geologic time. Other roach-hunters turn up in the relatively primitive subfamilies Sphecinae and Larrinae, most of whose members are adapted to the now more dominant groups of Orthoptera, such as crickets and grasshoppers. Spiders, an arthropod order of ancient origin, also serve as prey for certain Sphecinae and Larrinae and do not attract predation by more advanced digger wasps. Correspondingly, the more advanced wasps take as their prey more advanced insects, such as flies, bees and beetles, that go through complete metamorphosis. The higher flies underwent most of their radiation during the Tertiary period, which began some 60 million years ago, and several groups of structurally advanced wasps quickly took advantage of them.

In the sequence of evolutionary development that begins to emerge from study of these relations, the size of the prey compared with the size of the wasp emerges as a significant factor. Once the prey has been immobilized it must be carried back to the nest. Obviously the size of the prey must strongly influence the mode in which the wasp transports it. Since primitive wasps generally install only a single victim in each brood cell, they must take prey as large as or larger than themselves if their larvae are to have enough food to reach full size. In this they betray their more immediate derivation from the parasitoid Hymenoptera, which are invariably smaller than their hosts. The more primitive wasps accordingly drag their prey over the ground, grasping the victim in their mandibles. Some beat their wings to facilitate their progress and some drag their prey up on a high object and glide off with it. As might be expected, they cannot cover much ground by these methods, and they nest correspondingly close to the habitat of their prey. Wasps of the genus *Priononyx,* for example, nest in bare spots on the prairie, where their grasshopper prey abounds.

Wasps of the related genus *Sphex* illustrate the first stage of progress beyond this simple pattern of behavior. They hunt green meadow grasshoppers

MUD DAUBER, *Sceliphron caementarium,* builds a substantial nest two or three inches across. The photographs on this page were made by William P. Nye and George E. Bohart.

NEST IS CUT OPEN, revealing parts of two separate cells stocked with paralyzed spiders to feed the larvae. The wasp's egg is the translucent ovoid object inside the white square.

in tall weeds and bushes, and yet they make their nests in bare sand and gravel. They are able to transport their victims considerable distances in flight because they take smaller prey. And because the grasshoppers are smaller the wasps must supply several of them to each larva. A species of the genus *Pemphredon* similarly may gather aphids in habitats far removed from the soft wood in which it constructs its galleries; this wasp flies back and forth between its hunting grounds and nest many times a day.

All of these species carry their prey in their mandibles. As a result they cannot dig while holding their prey, because it is held so far forward that it obstructs the use of their front legs. These wasps must leave their nests open or, if they close them, must put down the prey while they scrape open the entrance. Either of those actions exposes the prey or the contents of the nest to the attacks of a variety of parasites. The next breakthrough in the evolution of the digger wasps came, therefore, with the development of what I have called pedal prey-carrying mechanisms. Wasps that

have made this advance grasp their prey in their middle and hind legs or in their middle or hind legs only, thereby leaving their front legs and mandibles free. They close the nest entrance when they leave and they are able to open it readily when they return while still holding their prey. Since the prey is carried well back beneath the body close to the center of equilibrium in flight, the pedal mechanisms greatly enhance the carrying efficiency of these wasps. Four subfamilies have made this breakthrough, and some members of two of those subfamilies have made the further advance to what I have called abdominal mechanisms, carrying the prey on their sting and, in one genus, on special modifications of the segments at the end of their abdomen.

This significant trend in the evolution of more advanced wasps would not have been possible without a parallel adaptation toward smaller prey. The more advanced prey-carrying mechanisms thus emerge as part of the great adaptive radiation in behavior that distinguishes the numerous advanced types of digger wasps, a radiation that was influenced

not only by the availability of food niches but also by the pressure of parasites, by the independent evolution of complex nest-building behavior and by other factors that can be only dimly surmised.

A listing of the major groups of digger wasps in the probable order of their emergence as indicated by their morphology shows excellent concordance with changes in type of prey and in hunting and prey-carrying behavior. The crossing over of a line of wasps to a new type of prey clearly represents the invasion and occupation of a new adaptive zone. This has frequently resulted in diversification in the new zone and invasion of still further, previously inaccessible adaptive zones and subzones. Thus the emergence of new, successful groups of insects provided in the course of time a multitude of unoccupied or incompletely occupied niches into which most of the solitary wasps sooner or later moved.

What is remarkable about the solitary wasps is the thoroughness with which they pursued the evolutionary diversification of the arthropod phylum. Many of the arthropods preyed on are themselves predators; others exhibit protective coloration that appears to protect them from predators other than wasps; still others are mimics of stinging insects or are armed with chemical defense mechanisms that seem to hold other predators at bay. Preying mantids, those arch-predators of the insect world, are themselves the prey of at least two genera of wasps. The tree hoppers that look so remarkably like rose thorns and caterpillars that look like twigs are each preyed on by certain wasps. Diptera-hunters such as *Bembix* capture drone flies and other bee mimics, but bee-hunters such as *Philanthus* spurn bee mimics even under experimental conditions. The stink bugs, the defensive secretions of which are too well known to require comment, supply the brood cells of wasps of three separate and unrelated genera. Black widow spiders are frequently taken by blue mud daubers. Many formidable stingers, including worker harvester ants, bees of many kinds (not excluding bumblebees) and other wasps (not excluding social forms), are among the prey of solitary wasps. Evidently the various mechanisms of defense, deception and concealment elaborated by the insect world are primarily adapted to protect their possessors from predation by vertebrates, since they do not protect them from the solitary wasps.

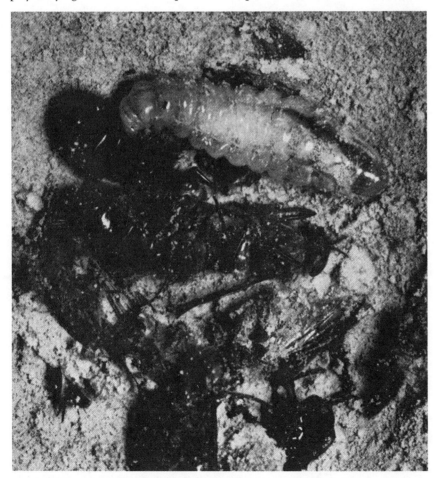

BEMBIX LARVA is seen in a rearing tin, feeding on flies of various kinds that have been supplied by the mother. A wasp of this genus stocks 20 to 40 flies in each cell of the nest.

AMMOPHILA URNARIA grasps a large leaf-eating caterpillar with its mandibles and front legs. The photograph, like most of those illustrating this article, was made by author.

The solitary wasps are esteemed by entomologists not only as subjects but also as colleagues of a sort. A small species of *Philanthus* nesting in my back yard a few years ago collected three new species of bees; these have since been described, one of them being named appropriately *philanthanus*. The prize example of this collaboration comes from the Congo. In 1915 Herbert Lang of the American Museum of Natural History trained several native assistants to collect flies being brought to their nests by *Bembix dira*. Among the nearly 1,000 flies brought in by the wasps there were more than 200 species belonging to 14 families. A great many thus collected were new to science, and several have not been rediscovered since!

26

Dialects in the Language of the Bees

by Karl von Frisch

August 1962

The dances that a honeybee does to direct its fellows to a source of nectar vary from one kind of bee to another. These variations clarify the evolution of this remarkable system of communication

For almost two decades my colleagues and I have been studying one of the most remarkable systems of communication that nature has evolved. This is the "language" of the bees: the dancing movements by which forager bees direct their hivemates, with great precision, to a source of food. In our earliest work we had to look for the means by which the insects communicate and, once we had found it, to learn to read the language [see "The Language of the Bees," by August Krogh; SCIENTIFIC AMERICAN Offprint 21]. Then we discovered that different varieties of the honeybee use the same basic patterns in slightly different ways; that they speak different dialects, as it were. This led us to examine the dances of other species in the hope of discovering the evolution of this marvelously complex behavior. Our investigation has thus taken us into the field of comparative linguistics.

Before beginning the story I should like to emphasize the limitations of the language metaphor. The true comparative linguist is concerned with one of the subtlest products of man's powerfully developed thought processes. The brain of a bee is the size of a grass seed and is not made for thinking. The actions of bees are mainly governed by instinct. Therefore the student of even so complicated and purposeful an activity as the communication dance must remember that he is dealing with innate patterns, impressed on the nervous system of the insects over the immense reaches of time of their phylogenetic development.

We made our initial observations on the black Austrian honeybee (*Apis mellifera carnica*). An extremely simple experiment suffices to demonstrate that these insects do communicate. If one puts a small dish of sugar water near a beehive, the dish may not be discovered for several days. But as soon as one bee has found the dish and returned to the hive, more foragers come from the same hive. In an hour hundreds may be there.

To discover how the message is passed on we conducted a large number of experiments, marking individual bees with colored dots so that we could recognize them in the milling crowds of their fellows and building a hive with glass walls through which we could watch what was happening inside. Briefly, this is what we learned. A bee that has discovered a rich source of food near the hive performs on her return a "round dance." (Like all the other work of the colony, food-foraging is carried out by females.) She turns in circles, alternately to the left and to the right [see top illustration on next page]. This dance excites the neighboring bees; they start to troop behind the dancer and soon fly off to look for the food. They seek the kind of flower whose scent they detected on the original forager.

The richer the source of food, the more vigorous and the longer the dance. And the livelier the dance, the more strongly it arouses the other bees. If several kinds of plants are in bloom at the same time, those with the most and the sweetest nectar cause the liveliest dances. Therefore the largest number of bees fly to the blossoms where collecting is currently most rewarding. When the newly recruited helpers get home, they dance too, and so the number of foragers increases until they have drained most of the nectar from the blossoms. Then the dances slow down or stop altogether. The stream of workers now turns to other blossoms for which the dancing is livelier. The scheme provides a simple and purposeful regulation of supply and demand.

The round dance works well for flowers close to the beehive. Bees collect their nourishment from a large circuit, however, and frequently fly several miles from the hive. To search at such distances in all directions from the hive for blossoms known only by scent would be a hopeless task. For sources farther away than about 275 feet the round dance is replaced by the "tail-wagging dance." Here again the scent of the dancer points to the specific blossoms to be sought, and the liveliness of the dance indicates the richness of the source. In addition the wagging dance transmits an exact description of the direction and distance of the goal. The amount and precision of the information far exceeds that carried by any other known communication system among animals other than man.

The bee starts the wagging dance by running a short distance in a straight line and wagging her abdomen from side to side. Then she returns in a semicircle to the starting point. Then she repeats the straight run and comes back in a semicircle on the opposite side. The cycle is repeated many times [see *middle illustration on next page*]. By altering the tempo of the dance the bee indicates the distance of the source. For example, an experimental feeding dish 1,000 feet away is indicated by 15 complete runs through the pattern in 30 seconds; when the dish is moved to 2,000 feet, the number drops to 11.

There is no doubt that the bees understand the message of the dance. When they fly out, they search only in the neighborhood of the indicated range, ignoring dishes set closer in or farther away. Not only that, they search only in the direction in which the original feeding dish is located.

The directional information contained in the wagging dance can be followed most easily by observing a forager's per-

ROUND DANCE, performed by moving in alternating circles to the left and to the right, is used by honeybees to indicate the presence of a nectar source near the hive.

WAGGING DANCE indicates distance and direction of a nectar source farther away. Bee moves in a straight line, wagging her abdomen, then returns to her starting point.

SICKLE DANCE is used by the Italian bee. She moves in a figure-eight-shaped pattern to show intermediate distance. A dancer is always followed by her hivemates.

formance when it takes place out in the open, on the small horizontal landing platform in front of the entrance to the hive. The bees dance there in hot weather, when many of them gather in front of the entrance. Under these conditions the straight portion of the dance points directly toward the goal. A variety of experiments have established that the pointing is done with respect to the sun. While flying to the feeding place, the bee observes the sun. During her dance she orients herself so that, on the straight run, she sees the sun on the same side and at the same angle. The bees trooping behind note the position of the sun during the straight run and position themselves at the same relative angle when they fly off.

The composite eye of the insect is an excellent compass for this purpose. Moreover, the bee is equipped with the second navigational requisite: a chronometer. It has a built-in time sense that enables it to compensate for the changes in the sun's position during long flights.

Usually the wagging dance is performed not on a horizontal, exposed platform but in the dark interior of the hive on the vertical surface of the honeycomb. Here the dancer uses a remarkable method of informing her mates of the correct angle with respect to the sun. She transposes from the ability to see the sun to the ability to sense gravity and thereby to recognize a vertical line. The direction to the sun is now represented by the straight upward direction along the wall. If the dancer runs straight up, this means that the feeding place is in the same direction as the sun. If the goal lies at an angle 40 degrees to the left of the sun, the wagging run points 40 degrees to the left of the vertical. The angle to the sun is represented by an equal angle with respect to the upright. The bees that follow the dancer watch her position with respect to the vertical, and when they fly off, they translate it back into orientation with respect to the light.

We have taken honeycombs from the hive and raised the young bees out of contact with older bees. Then we have brought the young bees back into the colony. They were immediately able to indicate the direction of a food source with respect to the position of the sun, to transpose directional information to the vertical and to interpret correctly the dances of the other bees. The language is genuinely innate.

When we extended our experiments to the Italian variety of honeybee (*Apis mellifera ligustica*), we found that its innate system had developed somewhat differently. The Italian bee restricts her round dance to representing distances of only 30 feet. For sources beyond this radius she begins to point, but in a new manner that we call the sickle dance. The pattern is roughly that of a flattened figure eight bent into a semicircle [*see bottom illustration at left*]. The opening of the "sickle" faces the source of food; the vigorousness of the dance, as usual, indicates the quality of the source.

At about 120 feet the Italian bee switches to the tail-wagging dance. Even then she does not use exactly the same language as the Austrian bee does. The Italian variety dances somewhat more slowly for a given distance. We have put the two varieties together in a colony, and they work together peacefully. But as might be expected, confusion arises when they communicate. An Austrian bee aroused by the wagging dance of an Italian bee will search for the feeding place too far away.

Since they are members of the same species, the Austrian and Italian bees can interbreed. Offspring that bear the Italian bee's yellow body markings often do the sickle dance. In one experiment 16 hybrids strongly resembling their Italian parent used the sickle dance to represent intermediate distances 65 out of 66 times, whereas 15 hybrids that resembled their Austrian parent used the round dance 47 out of 49 times. On the other two occasions they did a rather dubious sickle dance: they followed the pattern but did not orient it to indicate direction.

Other strains of honeybee also exhibited variations in dialect. On the other hand, members of the same variety have proved to understand each other perfectly no matter where they come from.

Our next step was to study the language of related species. The only three known species of *Apis* in addition to our honeybee live in the Indo-Malayan region, which is thought to be the cradle of the honeybee. The Asian species are the Indian honeybee *Apis indica*, the giant bee *Apis dorsata* and the dwarf bee *Apis florea*. Under a grant from the Rockefeller Foundation my associate Martin Lindauer was able to observe them in their native habitat.

The Indian honeybee, which is so closely related to ours that it was for a long time believed to be a member of the same species, has also been domesticated for honey production. Like the European bees, it builds its hive in a dark, protected place such as the hollow of a tree. Its language is also much like that of the European bees. It employs the round dance for distances up to 10 feet, then switches directly to the tail-wagging dance. Within its dark hive the Indian bee also transposes from the visual to the gravity sense. The rhythm of the dance, however, is much slower than that of the European bees.

The giant bee also exhibits considerable similarity to its European cousins and to the Indian species in its communications. It changes from the round dance to the wagging dance at 15 feet. In its rhythm it moves at about the same rate as the Italian bee does. The

hive of the giant bee, however, is built on tree branches or other light, exposed places. The inhabitants dance on the vertical surface of the comb, converting the angle with respect to the sun correctly into an angle from the vertical. But since the comb is out in the open, the dancers can always find a spot that commands a clear view of the sky. The fact that they do this indicates that the following bees can understand the instructions better when they have direct information about the position of the sun.

In the case of the dwarf bee, Lindauer found a clearly more primitive social organization and a correspondingly less

highly developed language. The dwarf bees, which are so small that a layman would probably mistake them for winged ants, build a single comb about the size of a man's palm. It dangles from an upper branch of a small tree. When the dwarf bees return from feeding, they always alight on the upper rim of the comb, where their mates are sitting in a closely packed mass that forms a horizontal landing place for the little flyers. Here they perform their dances. They too use a round dance for distances up to 15 feet, then a wagging dance. Their rhythm is slow, like that of the Indian bee.

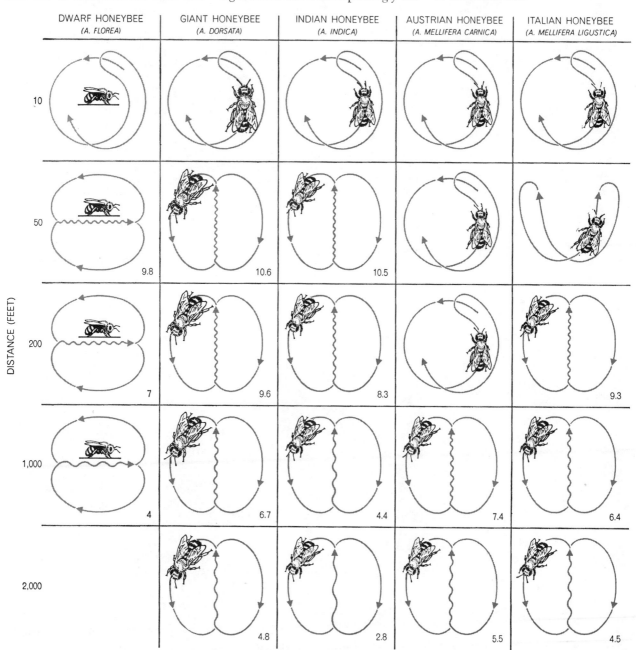

DIALECTS in the language of the bees are charted. The dwarf bee dances on a horizontal surface. All others dance on a vertical surface. The speed of the wagging dance carries distance instructions. The more rapidly the bee performs its wagging runs, the shorter is the distance. The figures in the squares represent the number of wagging runs in 15 seconds for each distance and kind of bee.

BEES ARE PAINTED with colored dots so that they can be identified during an experiment at the author's station near Munich. In this way the feeding station of a bee can be associated with its dance within the hive. The dish contains sugar water.

TWO VARIETIES OF BEE, the yellow Italian bee *Apis mellifera ligustica* and the black Austrian bee *A. mellifera carnica,* feed together. These two bees can live together in the same hive, but their dances do not have quite the same meaning. Accordingly one variety cannot accurately follow the feeding "instructions" of the other. Both of these photographs were made by Max Renner.

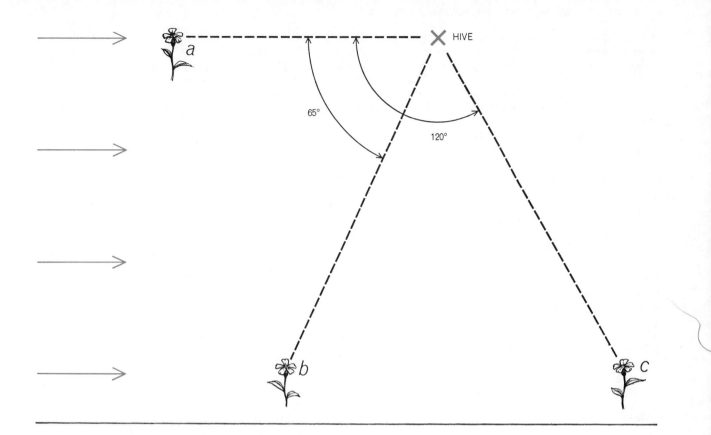

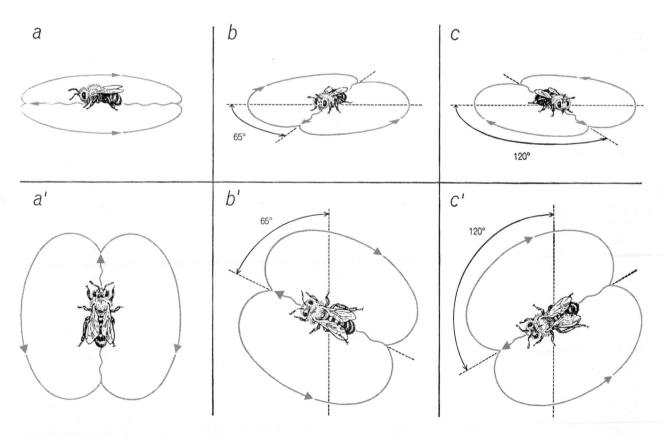

DIRECTION of a nectar source from the hive is shown by the direction in which a bee performs the straight portion of the wagging dance. The top section of the drawing shows flowers in three directions from the hive. The colored arrows represent the sun's rays. The middle section shows the dwarf bee, which dances on a horizontal surface. Her dance points directly to the goal: she orients herself to see the sun at the same angle as she saw it while flying to her food. The bottom section shows the bees that dance on a vertical surface. They transpose the visual to the gravitational sense. Movement straight up corresponds to movement toward the sun (a'). Movement at an angle to the vertical (b', c') signifies that the food lies at that same angle with respect to the sun.

The dwarf bee can dance only on a horizontal platform. Lindauer obtained striking proof of this on his field trip. When he cut off the branch to which a comb was attached and turned the comb so that the dancing platform was shifted to a vertical position, all the dancers stopped, ran up to the new top and tried to stamp out a dancing platform by running about through the mass of bees. When he left the hive in its normal position but placed an open notebook over its top, the foragers became confused and stopped dancing. In time, however, a few bees assembled on the upper surface of the notebook; then the foragers landed there and were able to perform their dances. Then, to remove every possible horizontal surface, Lindauer put a ridged, gable-shaped glass tile on top of the comb and closed the tile at both ends. In this situation the bees could not dance at all. After three days in this unnatural environment the urge to dance had become so great that a few bees tried to dance on the vertical surface. But they continued to depend on vision for their orientation and did not transpose the horizontal angle to a vertical one. Instead they looked for a dancing surface on which there was a line parallel to the direction of their flight. They tried to make a narrow horizontal path in the vertical curtain of bees, keeping their straight runs at the same angle to the sun as the angle at which they had flown when they found food. Under these circumstances only a very few bees were able to dance. Obviously the dwarf bee represents a far more primitive stage of evolution than the other species. She cannot transpose from light to gravity at all.

In trying to follow the dancing instinct farther back on the evolutionary scale, we must be satisfied with what hints we can get by observing more primitive living insects. Whereas a modern fossil record gives some of the physical development of insects, their mental past has left no trace in the petrified samples.

The use of sunlight as a means of orientation is common to many insects. It was first observed among desert ants about 50 years ago. When the ants creep out of the holes of their subterranean dwellings onto the sandy and barren desert surface, they cannot depend on landmarks for orientation because the wind constantly changes the markings of the desert sands. Yet they keep to a straight course, and when they turn around they find their way home along the same straight line. Even the changing position of the sun does not disturb them. Like the bee, the desert ant can take the shift into account and use the sun as a compass at any hour, compensating correctly for the movement of the sun in the sky.

Perhaps even more remarkable is the fact that many insects have developed an ability to transpose from sight to gravity. If a dung beetle in a dark room is placed on a horizontal surface illuminated from one side by a lamp, the beetle will creep along a straight line, maintaining the same angle to the light source for as long as it moves. If the light is turned off and the surface is tilted 90 degrees so that it is vertical, the beetle will continue to crawl along a straight line in the dark; it now maintains the same angle with respect to gravity that it earlier maintained with respect to light. This transposition is apparently an automatic process, determined by the arrangement of the nervous system. Some insects transpose less accurately, keeping the same angle but placing it sometimes to the right and sometimes to the left of the vertical without regard to the original direction with respect to the light. Some are also impartial as to up and down, so that an angle is transposed in any of four ways. Since the patterns do not transmit in-formation, their exact form makes no difference. Among the ancestors of the bees transposition behavior was probably once as meaningless as it is in the dung beetle and other insects today. In the course of evolution, however, the bee learned to make meaningful use of this central nervous mechanism in its communication system.

Both navigation by the sun and transposition, then, have evolved in a number of insects. Only the bees can use these abilities for their own orientation and for showing their mates the way to food. The straight run in the wagging dance, when performed on a horizontal surface, indicates the direction in which the bees will soon fly toward their goal. Birds do something like this; when a bird is ready to take off, it stretches its neck in the direction of its flight. Such intention movements, as they are called, sometimes influence other animals. In a flock of birds the movements can become infectious and spread until all the birds are making them. It is possible that among the honeybees the strict system of the wagging dance gradually developed out of such intention movements, performed by forager bees before they flew off toward their goal.

The most primitive communication system we have found among the bees does not contain information about distance or direction. It is used by the tiny stingless bee *Trigona iridipennis*, a distant relative of the honeybee. Lindauer observed this insect in its native Ceylon. Its colonies are less highly organized, resembling bumblebee colonies rather than those of honeybees.

When a foraging *Trigona* has found a rich source of nectar, she also communicates with her nestmates. But she does not dance. She simply runs about in great excitement on the comb, knocking against her mates, not by chance but intentionally. In this somewhat rude manner she attracts their attention to the fragrance of blossoms on her body. They fly out and search for the scent, first in the nearby surroundings, then farther away. Since they have learned neither the distance nor the direction of the goal, they make their way to the food source one by one and quite slowly.

We probably find ourselves here at the root of the language of the bees. Which way the development went in detail we do not know. But we have learned enough so that our imagination can fill in the evolutionary gaps in a general way.

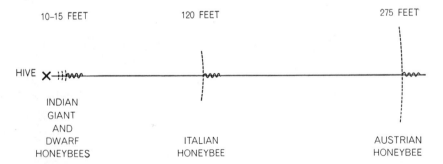

10–15 FEET   120 FEET   275 FEET

HIVE

INDIAN GIANT AND DWARF HONEYBEES   ITALIAN HONEYBEE   AUSTRIAN HONEYBEE

CHANGE FROM ROUND TO WAGGING DANCE occurs when nectar source lies beyond a certain radius of the hive. Change occurs at different distances among different bees. Because the wagging dance shows direction as well as distance, the Indian, giant and dwarf bees can give more precise information about a nearby source than the European bees can.

27

The Social Behavior
of Army Ants

by Howard R. Topoff
November 1972

*The complex and permanent social organization of
these insects is maintained by interactions among
a great many individuals. Each individual, however,
can alter its behavior only slightly*

Every living organism must at some time interact with other members of its species. As a result some degree of social behavior is the rule in the animal kingdom. The late T. C. Schneirla, for many years a curator in the department of animal behavior of the American Museum of Natural History, was greatly interested in the evolution and development of social behavior in species of animals representing many levels of evolutionary history. One of the groups of animals he selected for study was the army ants. These ants were already famous for their awesome marches in masses of hundreds of thousands of individuals. Their notoriety had given rise to an abundance of military metaphors, exemplified by the following description by A. Hyatt Verrill, a naturalist and explorer of animal life in South America: "In all the world, the army ants of the tropics are the most remarkable in many ways. Utterly blind, yet they move in vast armies across the land, overcoming every obstacle other than fire and water, maintaining perfect formation, moving with military precision and like a real army having their scouts, their engineering corps and their fighting soldiers."

In 1932 Schneirla proceeded to study army ants more objectively, and he discovered by close and long-continued observation of their habits that colonies of army ants show a degree of social organization every bit as impressive as the apocryphal stories of the early naturalists [see "The Army Ant," by T. C. Schneirla and Gerard Piel; SCIENTIFIC AMERICAN, June, 1948]. How were the ants' activities organized and coordinated? Schneirla's studies gave rise to various hypotheses, and the nature of the social bond in these insects continues to intrigue investigators of animal behavior.

During the past 10 years my colleagues and I have been continuing these investigations in an attempt to better understand the complex mechanisms that organize the remarkable social behavior of the army ants.

The army ants comprise one of the subfamilies of ants known as Dorylinae (so named from the Greek word meaning spear, because of their potent sting). There are some 150 species of army ants in the Western Hemisphere, most of them in Latin America, and about 100 other known species in Africa, Asia, Indo-Malaysia and Australia. The majority of species inhabit tropical regions, but many have adapted to temperate climates; some 20 species are found in the southern and mid-central U.S.

Practically all army ants are notable for four characteristics. The first is that they typically have very large colonies. Even small colonies, such as those of the Asian genus *Aenictus,* consist of at least 100,000 individuals. *Eciton burchelli* of Central and South America has colony sizes approaching a million individuals. In certain species of the African genus *Dorylus* colonies have been estimated to run to more than 20 million individuals. The second characteristic is the ants' periodic shifting of nesting sites. These colony movements, or emigrations, involve the entire colony: workers, brood and queen. At the end of each emigration the army ants settle down only in temporary bivouacs.

The third characteristic is that the army ants are almost exclusively carnivorous. They feed on other arthropods, particularly insects, and some species have been observed to eat small vertebrates such as lizards and snakes. The raiding parties of certain species are so huge that wherever they live the ants

rank as major predators in the ecological community. Edward Step, an observer of insect life, described the army ants' forays in these terms: "They march in such enormous numbers that everything which desires not to be eaten has to fly before them; from the cockroach to the mouse to the huge python, the elephant, the gorilla and the warlike native man, the story is the same." This is a gross exaggeration, but it is a well-authenticated fact that the ants' food consumption is tremendous; the workers of a colony of *Eciton burchelli,* for example, may bring in more than 100,000 other arthropods a day to feed the nest.

The last characteristic that typifies the behavior of doryline ants is their tight cohesiveness. Unlike many species of ants from other subfamilies, army ants do not forage for food individually. Instead all raiding and emigrations to new bivouacs are conducted by groups of individuals that closely follow a chemical trail deposited continuously by all the ants as they run along the ground.

To find an explanation of the social behavior of these animals we must look into their physiology and their means of communication, which, since they are essentially blind, is based mainly on chemical and tactual stimuli. Let us first examine the army ants' life-style. We shall consider specifically three species that are well known because they con-

MARAUDING COLUMN of army ants forms the diagonal ribbon in the photograph shown on page 250. These are ants of the genus *Dorylus,* native to Africa and famous for colonies that may number as many as 20 million ants. The photograph was made by William H. Gotwald, Jr., of Utica College.

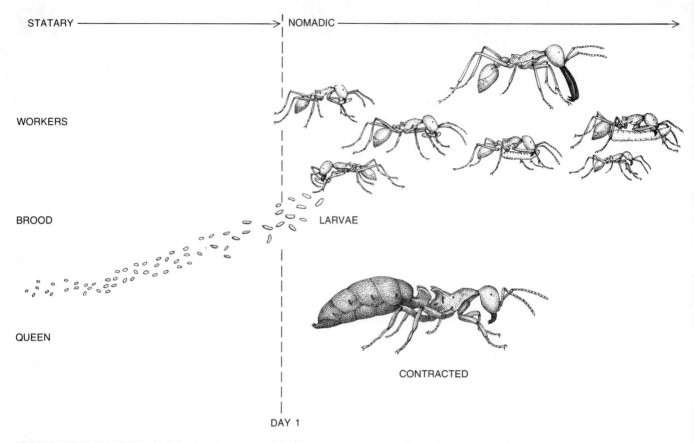

STATARY ──────────────────────→ NOMADIC ──────────────────────→

WORKERS

BROOD   LARVAE

QUEEN

                                          CONTRACTED

DAY 1

ALTERNATING PHASES in the behavior of army ants of the New World tropical genus *Eciton* are illustrated here, beginning with Day 1 of a nomadic phase (*left*). For 14 to 17 days after a new generation of workers emerges from the pupal stage a colony of army ants sends out large parties of raiders for food every day. Every night the colony shifts to a new bivouac, carrying the larvae that will become the next generation of workers. During the nomadic phase the queen's abdomen remains contracted. The phase

duct their activities principally aboveground: *Eciton hamatum* and *Eciton burchelli* of Central and South America and *Neivamyrmex nigrescens,* which ranges into temperate climates and is found in the U.S. The three species are closely related evolutionarily and are much alike in their life cycle and behavior.

Colonies of army ants typically consist of a single queen, a brood of developing young and a large population of adult workers. The queen is the colony's sole agent of reproduction, and she is responsible to a great extent for the colony's cohesion. The queen secretes certain substances that are attractive to the workers and therefore hold the colony together. More important, the chemical secretions of the queen actually enhance the survival of the workers (as has been shown by Julian F. Watkins II of Baylor University and Carl W. Rettenmeyer of the University of Connecticut). At regular intervals (about every five weeks) the queen's large abdomen swells with fatty tissue and eggs, and she may lay well over 100,000 eggs in the course of a week. The eggs then give rise to four successive stages of development:

embryo, larva, pupa and adult, which on emergence from the pupal stage is lightly pigmented and readily recognizable as a "callow," or young worker. The workers are all female but sterile, with underdeveloped ovaries.

In species of *Eciton* and *Neivamyrmex* the workers developing from a given batch of eggs vary in size and structure, a condition known as polymorphism. The developmental basis for polymorphism is not clear, although two possibilities exist. The first is that the developmental pathways leading to adult workers that differ in size and structure are determined by the amount and kind of food eaten by the larvae immediately after they hatch from the egg. This mode of development exists in honeybees. The second possibility is that the eggs laid by the queen are so different biochemically that the subsequent development of the larvae is unaltered by the quantity or quality of food consumed. (In some genera, such as *Aenictus,* the adults are not polymorphic.) Whatever the differentiating mechanisms may be, the adult ants that differ in size and structure also exhibit contrasting patterns of

behavior, with the result that there is a division of labor in the colony. Small workers (as little as three millimeters in length) spend most of their time in the nest feeding the larval broods; intermediate-sized workers constitute most of the population, going out on raids as well as doing other jobs. The largest workers (more than 14 millimeters in species of *Eciton*) have a huge head and long, powerful jaws. These individuals are what Verrill called soldiers; they carry no food but customarily run along the flanks of the raiding and emigration columns. An excited "soldier" is a formidable animal: it rears up on its hind legs, vibrates its antennae and rhythmically opens and closes its jaws. The tips of the mandibles are extremely sharp and are curved backward; if the ant bites a human being, they penetrate the skin and are difficult to remove.

In the colony's behavioral cycle there is a "nomadic" phase during which a large proportion of the adult workers go out on daily raids and collect food. In both species of *Eciton* the raids begin at dawn. The ants pour out of the bivouac and form several columns, each column later dividing into a network of

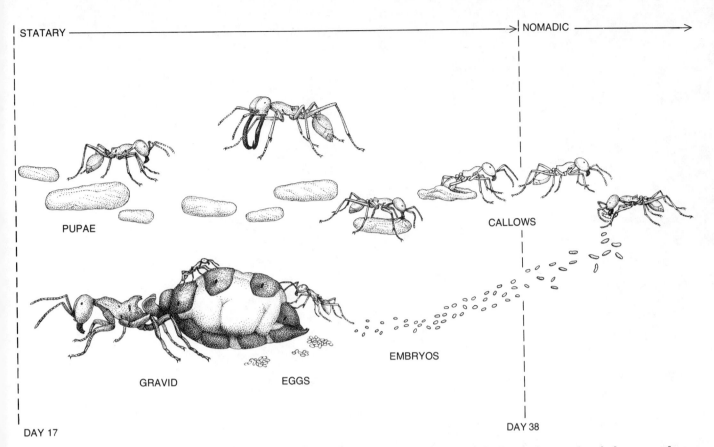

PUPAE

CALLOWS

GRAVID   EGGS   EMBRYOS

ends when the colony's larvae enter the pupal stage. The statary, or resting, phase then begins (*center*). The colony ceases to move nightly and the daily raiding parties are smaller. The statary phase continues for some 21 days. During the first week the queen's ab-

domen enlarges rapidly. During the second week she may produce as many as 100,000 eggs. By the end of the third week, as a new generation of worker ants completes the pupal stage, the queen's eggs hatch into larvae. This initiates a new nomadic phase (*right*).

branches. In running along these trails the ants seem not to depend much on vision. Species of *Eciton* and *Neivamyrmex* have vestigial eyes consisting of only a single facet; they can detect changes in the intensity of light but almost certainly cannot reproduce an image of an object. The raiding ants stay together by following a chemical trail laid on the ground by the other workers. Murray S. Blum of the University of Georgia and Watkins have determined that the substance deposited by the army ants originates in the hind intestine, but it is not yet established whether the substance consists of undigested food or a glandular secretion or a combination of both.

By midmorning the raiding columns have overrun an area extending a considerable distance from the nest, often more than 100 meters. At the front of the raiding columns the ants attack insects and other arthropods, biting and stinging the prey, pulling it apart and carrying the softer pieces back to the nest. Thus the column is actually a two-way stream, with some ants advancing and others returning with their prey.

At nightfall the entire colony moves

on to a new bivouac, typically emigrating along one of the principal raiding trails of that day. It may take the colony most of the night to complete the move to the new nesting site. This daily routine of massive raids and emigrations from bivouac to bivouac is followed for 14 to 17 days. Then, more or less abruptly, the colony settles down to a much quieter phase. Comparatively few of the workers go out on raids; their forays are much smaller and the colony stops emigrating and remains at the same nesting site. This "statary" phase lasts approximately three weeks. At the end of that time the cycle begins again; the colony resumes rushing out on great daily raids and making nightly emigrations.

The foregoing pattern is typical of the *Eciton* ants' behavior. The cycle in species of *Neivamyrmex* follows a similar pattern but differs in some aspects, depending on differences in the habitat; for example, in an area of high daytime temperature and low humidity the ants conduct both their raiding for food and their emigrations at night instead of during the day.

In 1932 Schneirla set out to learn what factors regulate the cycles of behavior

in *Eciton hamatum* and *Eciton burchelli*. At the time there were already two rival hypotheses. One suggested that the cycles of behavior were influenced by physical conditions of the environment, such as temperature, humidity, air pressure or the phases of the moon; the other suggested that the stimulus for emigrations might simply be depletion of the food supply in the area around the bivouac. Schneirla soon showed that both of these conjectures must be incorrect. He found that generally within a given environment some of the colonies were in the nomadic phase and some were in the statary phase; that ruled out environmental conditions as the determinant of whether or not a colony would make nightly emigrations. Schneirla disposed of the second hypothesis by observing that a colony of army ants would sometimes move into a nesting site that had just been vacated by another colony, and the newcomers would remain at this site even for a three-week statary period—clear evidence that the food supply around the bivouac had not been exhausted.

The actual regulator of the ants' nomadic and statary behavior, as Schneir-

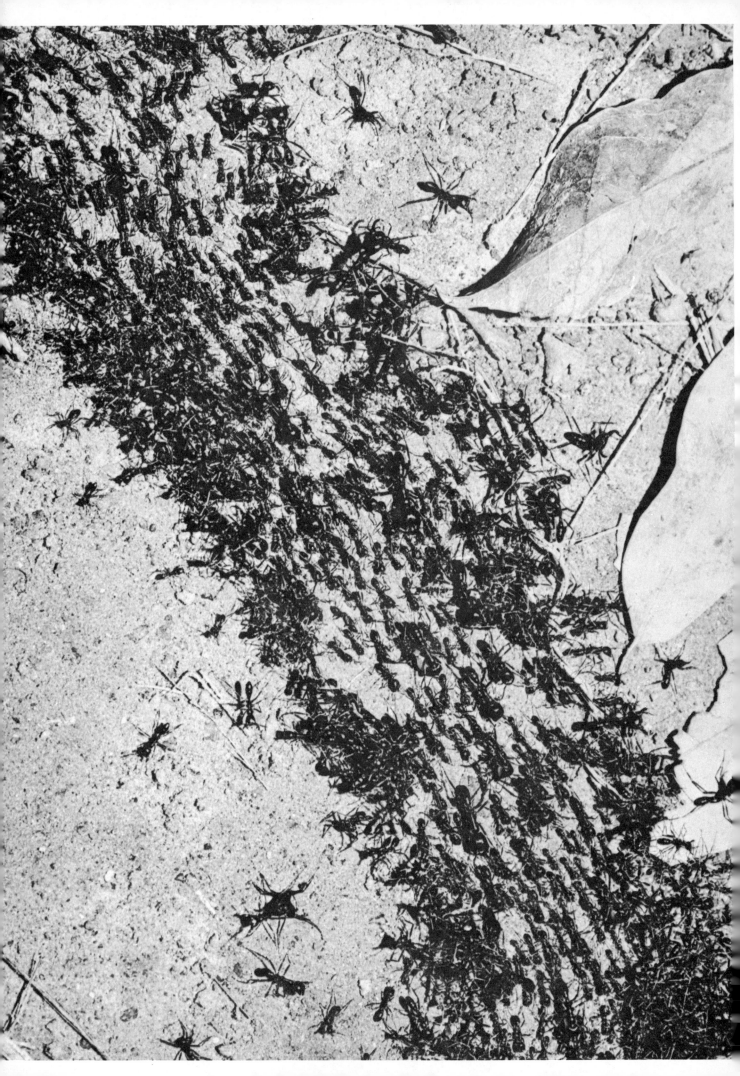

la eventually demonstrated, was not some external influence but the breeding cycle within the colony. He noted that the nomadic phase always coincided with the period when a larval brood was developing in the colony, and that the statary phase began when the larvae started to spin cocoons and went into the pupal stage of development.

When army ants emerge from the pupal cocoons as young workers, the nest is suddenly stirred to a high level of activity. The important stimuli for this excitation are probably substances secreted by these young callows; the older workers respond to the callows by stroking and licking them and by dropping pieces of food on them. This intense social stimulation, which originates with the interactions between the callows and the older workers, is subsequently transmitted throughout the bivouac by communication among the older adults. The result of this high level of mutual stimulation is that the nomadic phase of massive daily raids and emigrations from one bivouac site to another begins. As the callows mature, their chemical excitatory effects wear off but nomadic activities continue in the colony. These activities are maintained by comparable chemical and tactual stimulation imparted to the adult ants by a brood of developing larvae, which by this time have hatched from eggs laid by the queen during the previous statary phase. When the larvae have completed their development and progressed to the cocoon-wrapped pupal stage, the intensity of the mutual stimulation between them and the adult ants decreases abruptly. At this time the colony again lapses into the statary condition, which continues until the pupal brood once again emerges as callow workers.

Although the precise nature of the chemical interactions between adult workers and the brood is not yet known, the evidence supporting Schneirla's hypothesis is strong. For example, when he removed a larval brood from a colony during the nomadic phase, the colony stopped emigrating and the intensity of its daily raids diminished. By the same token, when he split a colony into two parts, only one of which contained the larval brood, the workers in the portion with the larvae continued to show considerable activity whereas those in the broodless portion became less active.

Schneirla's hypothesis predicts that the large differences in behavior exhibited by colonies of army ants during the nomadic and statary phases must result

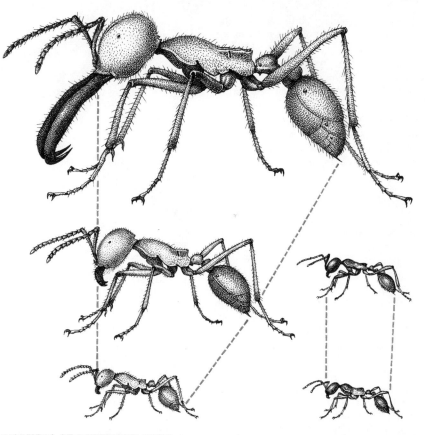

WORKERS OF DIFFERENT SIZES are common in some army ant species and virtually absent in others. Illustrated here are workers of the species *Eciton burchelli* (*left*) and of the Philippine species *Aenictus gracilis* (*right*), enlarged some seven diameters. Workers that differ in size also differ in patterns of behavior. The smallest *Eciton burchelli* workers do little more than feed and maintain larvae; the largest are the "soldiers" of the colony.

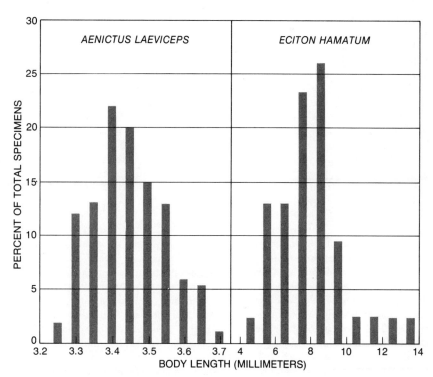

RANGES OF SIZE within two species of army ants are compared in this graph. In *Aenictus laeviceps* the body of the largest worker is scarcely half a millimeter longer than that of the smallest one. In *Eciton hamatum*, however, the body-length difference is nine millimeters.

from corresponding differences in the physiological condition and behavior of each individual ant during the two phases.' At the present time we are a long way from understanding the changes that take place in each ant's endocrine secretory activity, metabolic processes and sensitivity to physical and chemical stimuli. Nevertheless, several experiments have given us considerable insight into the kinds of factors involved.

Many of my own studies have been focused on the underground-nesting, nocturnal army ant species *Neivamyrmex nigrescens,* which I have observed in the field and in laboratory experiments at the Southwestern Research Station of the American Museum of Natural History in Arizona. I noticed that during the nomadic phase the ants not only spent most of the night raiding outside the nest but also frequently set out on their raids late in the afternoon when there was still considerable light on the ground. During the statary phase, in contrast, a smaller number of ants carried out weak and short raids, and they rarely emerged from the nest before dark. How could one account for this apparently slight but significant difference in behavior? One clue comes from studies of the relation between physiology and behavior in other species of animals. As an example, J. Goldsmid of Rhodes University in South Africa described a series of interesting behavioral changes in larvae of the blue tick *Boophilus decoloratus.* For a few days after hatching these larvae are strongly repelled by light and strongly attracted to one another by their common chemical secretions; the mutual attraction is so strong that the larvae come together even in an area under bright light. A week after the larvae have hatched, however, their behavior changes dramatically; they stop responding to one anothers' chemical secretions and do not withdraw from the light.

I was struck by the thought that the ticks' pattern of changing behavior might fit in with my observations of the army ants during the two behavioral phases. Suppose that during the statary phase the workers' negative response to light increases and at the same time their positive response to one another (as well as to the queen and brood) increases. This could account for the fact that during the colony's statary phase workers spend a greater amount of time inside the nest and the raids do not begin until dark. Conversely, if one supposes that during the nomadic phase the ants are less attracted to other individu-

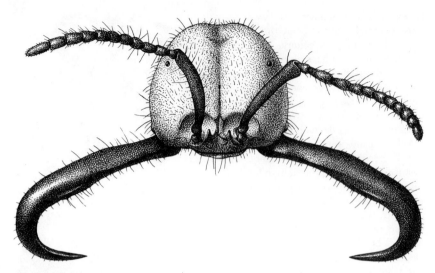

LARGE HEAD AND HUGE JAWS are characteristic of the soldiers in the genus *Eciton.* Once the sharp jaws have pierced an object their hooked tips make them difficult to remove.

als in the nest and less repelled by light, that might explain why most of them readily leave the nest for raiding and why they are not so deterred from starting their raids in daylight.

I designed a series of experiments to test whether or not these ants did indeed shift in their responses to light and to stimuli from other ants during the nomadic and statary phases. The experiments consisted in collecting ants in the field and placing them in an arena in the laboratory where they were able to enter into dimly lighted or brightly lighted areas. In order to minimize handling and artificial excitation of the ants I constructed a cylindrical cartridge in which they were picked up by suction. Without further disturbance of the insects the cartridge was then placed in the center of the arena, where through slits in the base of the cartridge the ants could move into dimly lighted quadrants or into quadrants where the light was 100 times more intense. To monitor the ants' movements we photographed their positions at five-second intervals for two minutes.

The results of this experiment showed that ants taken from colonies during the nomadic phase indeed behaved very differently from those taken from the colony during the statary phase. The nomadic ants traveled about indiscriminately in the bright and dim chambers of the arena, and they ran rapidly in columns with the individuals well spaced out. In contrast, ants in the statary-phase condition either entered into one of the dim areas immediately after the start of the test or else they tended to associate into tight clusters

near the edge of the brightly lighted central cartridge (as the newly hatched tick larvae did in Goldsmid's experiment). When these experiments were repeated with all the experimental areas kept totally dark, the results were just about the same. The record of the ants' movements (filmed by infrared photography) showed that the nomadic ants ran about freely and the statary ants again clustered tightly near the edge of the central cartridge. This supported the conclusion that the ants' attraction to one another changes significantly from the nomadic phase to the statary phase. Although the behavior of the ants in the field and in the laboratory still suggests that they also respond differently to light during the two phases, in the experimental tests their increased attraction to one another during the statary phase overrides their increased negative response to light.

Obviously these experiments are only a beginning in exploration of the interactions that take place among the individuals in an army ant colony during changes in the social behavior of the colony as a whole. Furthermore, we are still a long way from understanding the biological bases of these differences. For instance, does the excitatory stimulation that the adult workers receive from the callows and the larval brood influence their behavior through neural mechanisms alone, or does it also affect the secretory activity of their endocrine glands? Because every adult army ant continuously alternates from the nomadic phase to the statary phase and back again, these ants are excellent species for future studies of the relation between changes in physiological processes and corresponding changes in behavior.

I want to turn now to another interesting question we have been investigating. In primate societies, particularly those of humans, it is well known that newborn individuals do not become fully participating members of the society until they have matured and gained much experience within the family group, with their peers and with other members of the society. Many people believe animals such as insects emerge from the pupal stage of development with an immediate capacity to behave exactly like mature individuals. That is simply not so. With experimental procedures I devised in collaboration with Katherine Lawson, a graduate student at the City University of New York, we compared the behavior of callows and fully mature ants of the genus *Eciton* at the Smithsonian Institution's research station on Barro Colorado Island in the Panama Canal Zone.

The behavior of the callow members of a colony exhibits a puzzling inconsistency. During the first few days after the callows have emerged from their cocoons they do not join the mature adults in predatory raids. Furthermore, if a group of callows is taken from the nest and placed in the midst of a raiding column, they move only sluggishly and in a somewhat disoriented fashion, so that they interfere with the two-way traffic of the rapidly running mature ants in the columns. Yet surprisingly the callows have no hesitancy about going along with the entire colony in the emigration to a new bivouac after the day's raid.

Was the callows' failure to participate in raiding due to an inability to follow the trail deposited by the raiding ants? During the day's raid hundreds of thousands of foraging ants continually run from the bivouac to the raiding areas and then back again. As a result at the end of the raid the strength of the trail may be considerably higher than it is during the early hours of morning. That is a reasonable assumption on the basis of experiments conducted by Richard Torgerson of Wartburg College and Roger D. Akre of Washington State University, who demonstrated that the chemical trails of *Eciton* persist on the ground in the field for at least a week. Perhaps by the time a colony of army ants emigrates the trail is so strong that even the callows are able to follow it. To test this hypothesis we measured the comparative ability of callows and ma-

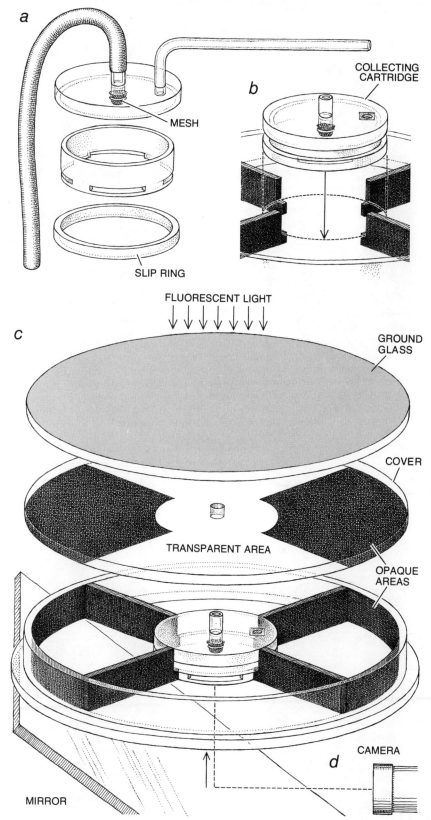

PLEXIGLASS ARENA (*c*) was constructed to study activity patterns of army ants in the nomadic and statary phases. *Neivamyrmex nigrescens*, a widely distributed New World species, was selected for the study. Ants from nomadic and statary colonies were drawn by suction, some 50 at a time, into collection cartridges (*a*). They then remained undisturbed until each cartridge was placed in the center of the arena; this raised the ring seal of the cartridge so that the ants were free to explore the arena (*b*). At first, to assess the ants' response to light, two of the arena quadrants were kept shaded while the other two and the central cartridge were lighted 100 times more brightly. Photographs made at five-second intervals (*d*) recorded changes in the ants' positions (*see illustrations on following page*).

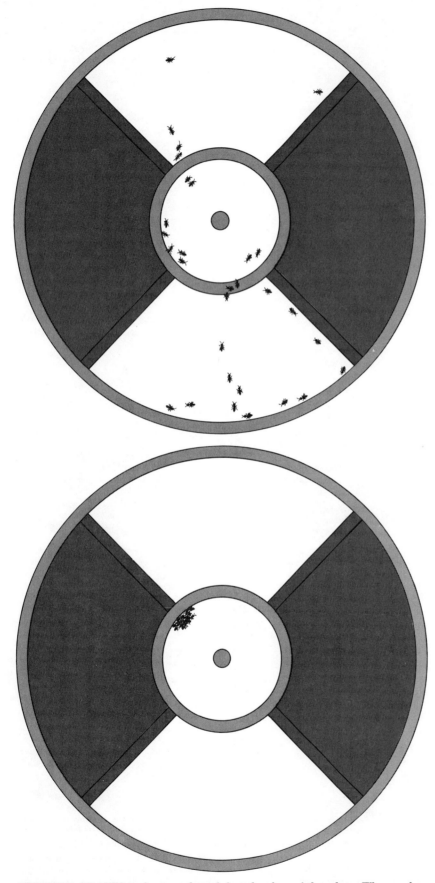

BEHAVIOR OF ANTS in the arena depended on the phase of the colony. When workers came from a colony in the early stage of a nomadic phase, they ran throughout the arena, spending equal time in light and dark areas (*top*). Statary workers usually went to one or both of the dark areas. In many tests, however, they remained in the cartridge (*bottom*).

ture adult ants to follow the trail substance of their colony.

To obtain the substance for the purposes of the experiment we washed ants from a colony in ether as a solvent. This procedure gave us an extremely potent solution of the substance that could be diluted to any desired strength by adding pure ether. An artificial trail was now deposited on a disk of chromatography paper that was rotated on a phonograph turntable as the solution flowed onto it from a microburette suspended above it. Within seconds after the circular trail had been deposited the solvent evaporated, leaving behind an invisible residue of the trail substance. The paper disk with the circular trail was removed from the turntable and placed on a template. The template had a black circle drawn on it that coincided exactly with the location of the invisible chemical trail on the disk of paper above it. Because the template circle was visible through the chromatography paper we could easily determine whether or not a test ant was indeed following the trail. Each ant was admitted to the circular trail through a tunnel, and its ability to detect and follow the trail was observed.

First we examined the ants' speed of running over the trail. As we had expected, callows taken from their colony soon after their emergence from the pupal cocoon were considerably slower than mature ants in following the trail. With each day of development in the nest the callows improved in speed on our test, and week-old callows were able to follow the chemical trail almost as rapidly as fully mature workers.

We then compared callows and mature adults on the basic ability to follow the trail, apart from the question of speed. Since the observations in the field and our speed tests had indicated that maturity was an important factor, we expected that the proportion of callows able to follow the trail without error would be considerably smaller than the proportion of adult workers able to do so. To our complete surprise it turned out that statistically the callows scored just about as high as the adults in the fundamental ability to follow the chemical trail of their colony. Evidently the callows were fully capable of recognizing the trail substance and their slowness must have been due to physical immaturity.

Thus we are still left with the question: Why do the young callows stay in the nest instead of going out on raids with other workers? There are several hypotheses to be considered. First, it has been noticed that much of the callows' time in the first few days is spent in intensive feeding on the nest's food supply. It is possible that this preoccupation with feeding could serve to keep them in the nest during the day. A second hypothesis, and one we plan to test, is that young callows are strongly attracted, probably more so than mature adults are, to stimuli of physical contact and chemical secretions that originate with other members of the colony. The intensity of both of these forms of stimulation is greatest inside the nest. A callow ant leaving the nest will experience a sudden reduction in the intensity of both classes of stimuli. Outside the nest the amount of tactual stimulation decreases as the adult ants fan out along the trail. In the outside air and on the narrow trails the colony's odors are also vastly diluted. As the mature adult workers depart on their massive daily raids, the tension of chemical and tactual attraction between the inside of the nest and the outside becomes less one-sided, but the concentration and pull of the inside might still be stronger. The direction of pull would be reversed only when the colony leaves the nest during an emigration to a new site. As the workers, the larval and pupal brood and the queen move out, the departing stimulation might attract the callows out of the nest. The decisive attractive force may be either the quantitative shift of the predominant mass of individuals or the departure of a source of stimulation that is particularly attractive to the callows, such as the queen, the developing brood, the total population of adult workers or the booty (the food supply).

We have recently made an interesting observation in the field that is consistent with the hypothesis that it is social stimuli that are responsible for keeping callow army ants in the nest. A colony of *Neivamyrmex nigrescens* was completing its statary phase in a bivouac located in the bank of a stream. One day there was a heavy rain followed by a flash flood that destroyed most of the colony; only a few hundred workers and fewer than 100 pupae were left. Under these conditions the callows ran along the entire route of the raiding column with the mature adult ants on the first night after their emergence from the pupal stage of development.

In many respects we have hardly scratched the surface in our attempts to understand how the social organiza-

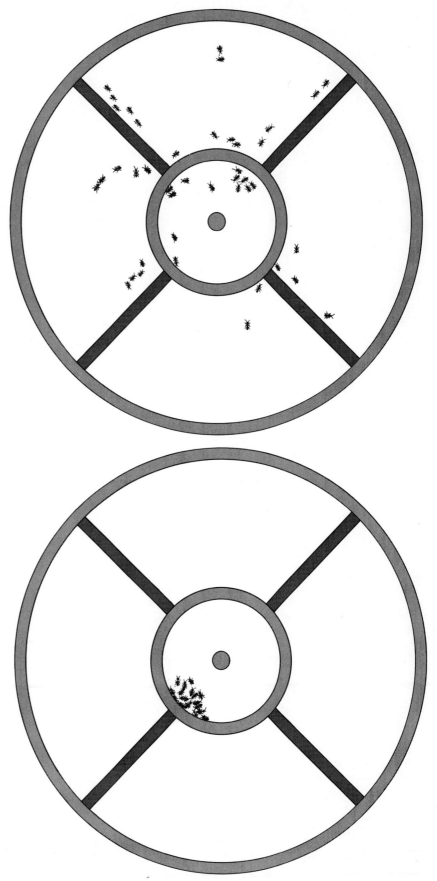

UNDER INFRARED ILLUMINATION the ants continued to behave as they had when they were exposed to visible light. Workers in the early nomadic phase ran rapidly through all the chambers of the arena (*top*) but statary workers often stayed in the cartridge (*bottom*).

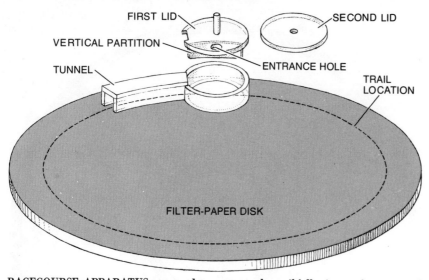

FIRST LID

SECOND LID

VERTICAL PARTITION

ENTRANCE HOLE

TUNNEL

TRAIL LOCATION

FILTER-PAPER DISK

RACECOURSE APPARATUS was used to compare the trail-following performances of newly emerged "callow" workers with older workers. A circular scent trail was deposited on a disk of filter paper (*broken line*). Each ant was then placed in a chamber with a partition that prevented any contact with the trail. When the partition was removed, the ant could run along a short segment of the trail enclosed by a tunnel. On emerging the ant was scored for its ability to complete the circular course and for its mean running speed. By diluting the scent the experimenters were able to simulate both "strong" and "weak" trails.

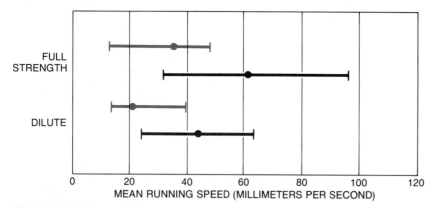

FULL STRENGTH

DILUTE

0   20   40   60   80   100   120
MEAN RUNNING SPEED (MILLIMETERS PER SECOND)

RUNNING SPEED of callow adults (*color*) of the species *Eciton burchelli* is compared with the speed of mature adults of the same species (*black*). Over a full-strength scent trail (*top bars*) the mature adult speed was better than 60 millimeters per second whereas the callow adult speed was little more than half that. Over a trail only a tenth as strong (*bottom bars*) the performance of both mature and callow ants was poorer but the gap was the same.

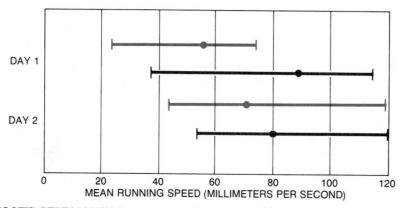

DAY 1

DAY 2

0   20   40   60   80   100   120
MEAN RUNNING SPEED (MILLIMETERS PER SECOND)

CALLOWS' PERFORMANCE improved as they matured. Graph compares the running speeds of callow (*color*) and mature adult (*black*) workers of the species *Eciton hamatum* on two consecutive days. On the first day the difference in mean speeds was some 30 millimeters per second (*top bars*). The next day the difference was less than 10 millimeters per second (*bottom bars*). Tests showed that the callows are virtually mature within seven days.

tion of army ants evolved, develops and is maintained by interactions among individuals, each of which has a limited capacity for behavioral adjustment. On the other hand, we have accumulated sufficient knowledge to enable us to compare processes that are important for the social organization of army ants with those that are important for the social organization of species representing other levels of evolutionary history. We know, for instance, that social organizations in all species of animals are maintained by physiological and behavioral interactions among the individuals that enable the group to function as an integrated unit. But each species of animal has an evolutionary and developmental history that is different from all others, and consequently each species has a unique morphology, physiology and behavior. This means that when the comparative animal behaviorist observes similar patterns of social behavior in two species of animals, he cannot automatically conclude that the mechanisms and processes underlying the behavior are the same for both.

For example, in both ant and human societies individuals exhibit different and specialized behavioral functions, giving rise to a division of labor within the group. But the role that any particular ant plays in its society is influenced directly by its biological organization, whereas human jobs are determined more by economic status, level of education, personal preferences and other cultural factors. Practically every behavior pattern that ants exhibit is based on their responses to a limited number of tactile and chemical stimuli; individuals in human societies interact by means of a much more complex form of communication based primarily on the use of symbolic language. Finally, although the behavior of every adult army ant is influenced by many social experiences it has during its development, the degree to which such developmental factors can modify adult behavior is certainly much smaller in ants than it is in humans. The goal of the comparative animal behaviorist is to study and clarify the bases for social behavior in species representing all levels of invertebrate and vertebrate evolutionary history. Only then shall we be able to judge how unique each species, including man, is. The study of the social behavior of army ants contributes to the attainment of this goal because it gives us a larger view of the diversity of social systems that are to be found within the animal kingdom.

28

Slavery in Ants

by Edward O. Wilson
June 1975

Certain species of ants raid the nests of other species for ants to work in their own nest. Some raiding species have become so specialized that they are no longer capable of feeding themselves

The institution of slavery is not unique to human societies. No fewer than 35 species of ants, constituting six independently evolved groups, depend at least to some extent on slave labor for their existence. The techniques by which they raid other ant colonies to strengthen their labor force rank among the most sophisticated behavior patterns found anywhere in the insect world. Most of the slave-making ant species are so specialized as raiders that they starve to death if they are deprived of their slaves. Together they display an evolutionary descent that begins with casual raiding by otherwise free-living colonies, passes through the development of full-blown warrior societies and ends with a degeneration so advanced that the workers can no longer even conduct raids.

Slavery in ants differs from slavery in human societies in one key respect: the ant slaves are always members of other completely free-living species that themselves do not take slaves. In this regard the ant slaves perhaps more closely resemble domestic animals—except that the slaves are not allowed to reproduce and they are equal or superior to their captors in social organization.

The famous Amazon ants of the genus *Polyergus* are excellent examples of advanced slave makers. The workers are strongly specialized for fighting. Their mandibles, which are shaped like miniature sabers, are ideally suited for puncturing the bodies of other ants but are poorly suited for any of the routine tasks that occupy ordinary ant workers. Indeed, when *Polyergus* ants are in their home nest their only activities are begging food from their slaves and cleaning themselves ("burnishing their ruddy armor," as the entomologist William Morton Wheeler once put it).

When *Polyergus* ants launch a raid, however, they are completely transformed. They swarm out of the nest in a solid phalanx and march swiftly and directly to a nest of the slave species. They destroy the resisting defenders by puncturing their bodies and then seize and carry off the cocoons containing the pupae of worker ants.

When the captured pupae hatch, the

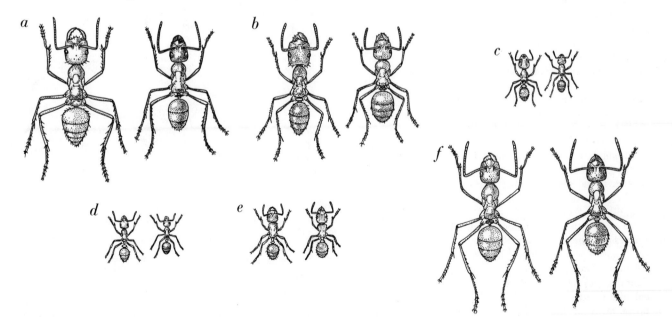

RESEMBLANCE of slave maker and slave was noted by an Italian myrmecologist, Carlo Emery, in 1909. In each pair of ants shown here the slave maker is on the left and the slave on the right. The species depicted are (a) *Polyergus rufescens* and *Formica fusca*, (b) *Rossomyrmex proformicarum* and *Proformica nasutum*, (c) *Harpagoxenus americanus* and *Leptothorax curvispinosus*, (d) *L. duloticus* and *L. curvispinosus*, (e) *Strongylognathus alpinus* and *Tetramorium caespitum* and (f) *F. subintegra* and *F. subsericea*.

workers that emerge accept their captors as sisters; they make no distinction between their genetic siblings and the *Polyergus* ants. The workers launch into the round of tasks for which they have been genetically programmed, with the slave makers being the incidental beneficiaries. Since the slaves are members of the worker caste, they cannot reproduce. In order to maintain an adequate labor force, the slave-making ants must periodically conduct additional raids.

It is a remarkable fact that ants of slave-making species are found only in cold climates. Although the vast majority of ants live in the Tropics and the warm Temperate zones, not a single species of those regions has been implicated in any activity remotely approaching slavery. Among the ants of the colder regions this form of parasitism is surprisingly common. The colonies of many slave-making species abound in the forests of the northern U.S., and ant-slave raids can be observed in such unlikely places as the campus of Harvard University.

The slave raiders obey what is often called Emery's rule. In 1909 Carlo Emery, an Italian myrmecologist, noted that each species of parasitic ant is genetically relatively close to the species it victimizes. This relation can be profitably explored for the clues it provides to the origin of slave making in the evolution of ants. Charles Darwin, who was fascinated by ant slavery, suggested that the first step was simple predation: the ancestral species began by raiding other kinds of ants for food, carrying away their immature forms in order to be able to devour them in the home nest. If a few pupae could escape that fate long enough to emerge as workers, they might be accepted as nestmates and thus join the labor force. In cases where the captives subsequently proved to be more valuable as workers than as food, the raiding species would tend to evolve into a slave maker.

Although Darwin's hypothesis is attractive, I recently obtained evidence that territorial defense rather than food is the evolutionary prime mover. I brought together in the Harvard Museum of Comparative Zoology different species of *Leptothorax* ants that normally do not depend on slave labor. When colonies were placed closer together than they are found in nature, the larger colonies attacked the smaller ones and drove away or killed the queens and workers. The attackers carried captured pupae back to their own nests. The pupae were then allowed by their captors to develop into workers. In the cases where the newly emerged workers belonged to the same species, they were allowed to remain as active members of the colony. When they belonged to a different *Leptothorax* species, however, they were executed in a matter of hours. One can easily imagine the origin of slave making by the simple extension of this territorial behavior to include tolerance of the workers of related species. The more closely related the raiders and their captives are, the more likely they are to be compatible. The result would be in agreement with Emery's rule.

One species that appears to have just crossed the threshold to slave making is *Leptothorax duloticus*, a rare ant that so far has been found only in certain localities in Ohio, Michigan and Ontario. The anatomy of the worker caste is only slightly modified for slave-making behavior, suggesting that in evolutionary terms the species may have taken up its parasitic way of life rather recently.

In experiments with laboratory colonies I was able to measure the degree of behavioral degeneration that has taken place in *L. duloticus*. Like the Amazon ants, the *duloticus* workers are highly efficient at raiding and fighting. When colonies of other *Leptothorax* species were placed near a *duloticus* nest, the workers launched intense attacks until all the pupae of the other species had been captured.

In the home nest the *duloticus* workers were inactive, leaving almost all the ordinary work to their captives. When the slaves were temporarily taken away from them, the workers displayed a dramatic expansion in activity, rapidly taking over most of the tasks formerly carried out by the slaves. The *duloticus* workers thus retain a latent capacity for working, a capacity that is totally lacking in more advanced species of slave-making ants.

The *duloticus* workers that had lost their slaves did not, however, perform their tasks well. Their larvae were fed at infrequent intervals and were not groomed properly, nest materials were carried about aimlessly and were never placed in the correct positions, and an inordinate amount of time was spent collecting and sharing diluted honey. More important, the slaveless ants lacked one behavior pattern that is essential for

RAID BY SLAVE-MAKING AMAZON ANTS of the species *Polyergus rufescens* (**light color**) against a colony of the slave species *Formica fusca* (**dark color**) is depicted. The *fusca* ants make their nest in dry soil under a stone. The raiding Amazon ants kill resisting

the survival of the colony: foraging for dead insects and other solid food. They even ignored food placed in their path. When the colony began to display signs of starvation and deterioration, I returned to them some slaves of the species *Leptothorax curvispinosus.* The bustling slave workers soon put the nest back in good order, and the slave makers just as quickly lapsed into their usual indolent ways.

Not all slave-making ants depend on brute force to overpower their victims. Quite by accident Fred E. Regnier of Purdue University and I discovered that some species have a subtler strategy. While surveying chemical substances used by ants to communicate alarm and to defend their nest, we encountered two slave-making species whose substances differ drastically from those of all other ants examined so far. These ants, *Formica subintegra* and *Formica pergandei,* produce remarkably large quantities of decyl, dodecyl and tetradecyl acetates. Further investigation of *F. subintegra* revealed that the substances are sprayed at resisting ants during slave-making raids. The acetates attract more invading slave makers, thereby serving to assemble these ants in places where fighting

breaks out. Simultaneously the sprayed acetates throw the resisting ants into a panic. Indeed, the acetates are exceptionally powerful and persistent alarm substances. They imitate the compound undecane and other scents found in slave species of *Formica,* which release these substances in order to alert their nestmates to danger. The acetates broadcast by the slave makers are so much stronger, however, that they have a long-lasting disruptive effect. For this reason Regnier and I named them "propaganda substances."

We believe we have explained an odd fact first noted by Pierre Huber 165 years ago in his pioneering study of the European slave-making ant *Formica sanguinea.* He found that when a colony was attacked by these slave makers, the survivors of the attacked colony were reluctant to stay in the same neighborhood even when suitable alternative nest sites were scarce. Huber observed that the "ants never return to their besieged capital, even when the oppressors have retired to their own garrison; perhaps they realize that they could never remain there in safety, being continually liable to the attacks of their unwelcome visitors."

Regnier and I were further able to gain a strong clue to the initial organization of slave-making raids. We had made a guess, based on knowledge of the foraging techniques of other kinds of ants, that scout workers direct their nestmates to newly discovered slave colonies by means of odor trails laid from the target back to the home nest. In order to test this hypothesis we made extracts of the bodies of *F. subintegra* and of *Formica rubicunda,* a second species that conducts frequent, well-organized raids through much of the summer. Then at the time of day when raids are normally made we laid artificial odor trails, using a narrow paintbrush dipped in the extracts we had obtained from the ants. The trails were traced from the entrances of the nest to arbitrarily selected points one or two meters away.

The results were dramatic. Many of the slave-making workers rushed forth, ran the length of the trails and then milled around in confusion at the end. When we placed portions of colonies of the slave species *Formica subsericea* at the end of some of the trails, the slave makers proceeded to conduct the raid in a manner that was apparently the same in every respect as the raids initiated by

fusca workers by piercing them with their saberlike mandibles. Most of the Amazon ants are transporting cocoons containing the pupae of *fusca* workers back to their own nest. When the workers emerge from the cocoons, they serve as slaves. Two dead *fusca* workers that resisted lie on the ground. Two other workers have retreated to upper surface of the rock over the nest's entrance.

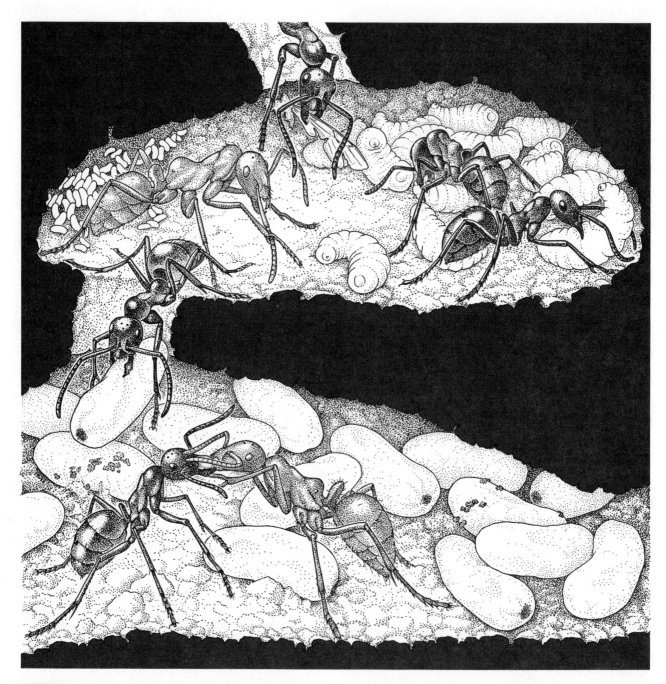

INTERIOR VIEW OF THE HOME NEST of a colony of Amazon ants shows *Formica fusca* slaves (*dark color*) performing all the housekeeping labor. At top center one of the slaves brings a fly wing into the nest for food. Other slave workers care for the small eggs, grublike larvae and cocoon-enclosed pupae of their captors. During the raiding season some of the pupae are likely to be those of *fusca* workers. The slave makers (*light color*) can do nothing more than groom themselves (*upper left*). In order to eat, the Amazon ants must beg slave workers to regurgitate liquid droplets for them (*lower left*). These ant species are found in Europe.

trails laid by their own scouts. Studies of the slave-making species *Polyergus lucidus* and *Harpagoxenus americanus* by Mary Talbot and her colleagues at Lindenwood College provide independent evidence that raids are organized by the laying of odor trails to target nests; indeed, this form of communication may be widespread among slave-making ants.

The evolution of social parasitism in ants works like a ratchet, allowing a species to slip further down in parasitic dependence but not back up toward its original free-living existence. An example of nearly complete behavioral degeneration is found in one species of the genus *Strongylognathus*, which is found in Asia and Europe. Most species in this genus conduct aggressive slave-making raids. They have characteristic saber-shaped mandibles for killing other ants. The species *Strongylognathus testaceus*, however, has lost its warrior habits. Although these ants still have the distinctive mandibles of their genus, they do not conduct slave-making raids. Instead an *S. testaceus* queen moves into the

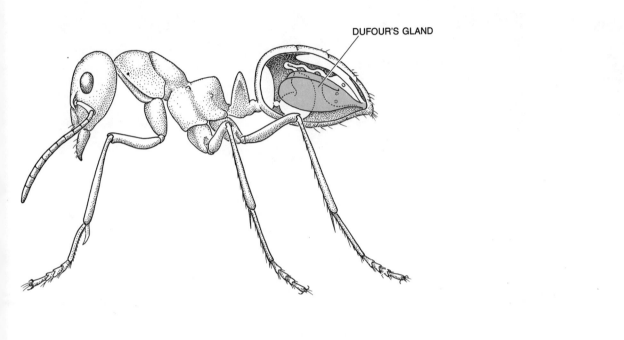

DUFOUR'S GLAND

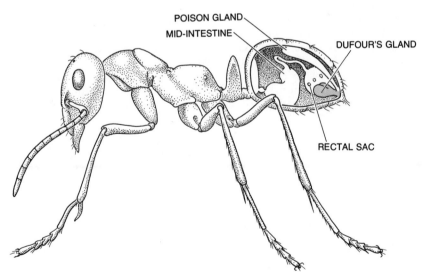

POISON GLAND
MID-INTESTINE
DUFOUR'S GLAND
RECTAL SAC

DUFOUR'S GLAND, which produces substances that serve as communication scents among ants, is much larger in the slave-making species *Formica subintegra* (*top*) than in the slave species *F. subsericea* (*bottom*). The *subsericea* ant releases its scent to alert its nestmates to the presence of danger. The *subintegra* sprays its secretions at resisting ants during slave raids. The secretions are so strong that they create panic in the colony being attacked.

COLONY OF ANTS housed in a glass tube consists of the rare species *Leptothorax duloticus* and a slave species, *L. curvispinosus*. The *duloticus* ant, found in Ohio, Michigan and Ontario, has only recently become a slave maker. One of the *duloticus* workers can be seen in the center of the photograph; below it are three slave workers. The white objects are immature forms of both species. When the slave workers are removed, the *duloticus* workers attempt to carry out necessary housekeeping tasks but do so poorly.

nest of a slave-ant species and lives alongside the queen of the slave species. Each queen lays eggs that develop into workers, but the *S. testaceus* offspring do no work. They are fed by workers of the slave species. We do not know how the union of the two queens is formed in the first place, but it is likely that the parasitic queen simply induces the host colony to adopt her after her solitary dispersal flight from the nest of her birth.

Thus *S. testaceus* is no longer a real slave maker. It has become an advanced social parasite of a kind that commonly infests other ant groups. For example, many species of ant play host to parasites such as beetles, wasps and flies, feeding and sheltering them (see "Communications between Ants and Their Guests," by Bert Hölldobler, beginning on page 263).

Does ant slavery hold any lesson for our own species? Probably not. Human slavery is an unstable social institution that runs strongly counter to the moral systems of the great majority of human societies. Ant slavery is a genetic adaptation found in particular species that cannot be judged to be more or less successful than their non-slave-making counterparts. The slave-making ants offer a clear and interesting case of behavioral evolution, but the analogies with human behavior are much too remote to allow us to find in them any moral or political lesson.

29

Communication between Ants and Their Guests

by Bert Hölldobler
March 1971

Ants feed and shelter many other species of arthropods. The key to this hospitality lies in the guests' ability to communicate in the same chemical and mechanical language used by their hosts

The world of the arthropods is marked by a curious phenomenon, discovered nearly a century ago, that has never ceased to intrigue investigators. Many species of insects and other arthropods live with ants and have developed a thriving parasitic relationship with them. A number of these myrmecophiles make their home in the ants' nests and enjoy all the benefits. Although the interlopers in some cases eat the host ants' young, the ants treat the guests with astonishing cordiality: they not only admit the invading species to the nest but feed, groom and rear the guest larvae as if they were the ants' own brood.

How do the myrmecophiles manage to gain this acceptance? Ants, as highly social animals, possess a complex system of internal communication that enables the colony to carry out its collaborative activities in nest-building, food-gathering, care of the young and defense against enemies. The fact that the ants do not treat their alien guests as strangers suggests that the guests must somehow have broken the ants' code, that is, attained the ability to "speak" the ants' language, which involves a diversity of visual, mechanical and chemical cues.

Studies of the social behavior and communication of ants over the past 10 years have produced information that now provides a basis for well-grounded investigation of the relations between myrmecophiles and their hosts. Among the thousands of myrmecophilous animals (which include not only such arachnids as mites but also collembolans, flies, wasps and many other insect groups) the staphylinid beetles, commonly known as the rove beetles, demonstrate the parasitic relationships in a particularly clear-cut fashion. Focusing mainly on this family of myrmecophiles, I have been looking into the details of their communication and relations with certain species of ants.

The relations vary considerably with the beetle species. Some species live along the ants' food-gathering trails, others at the garbage dumps outside the nest, others in outer chambers within the nest and still others all the way inside the brood chambers. Let us consider first the beetles that attain the brood chamber.

A well-known example of such a beetle is *Atemeles pubicollis,* a European species. During its larval stage it lives in the nest of the mound-making wood ant *Formica polyctena.* I found that the ant's adoption of the beetle larva depends in the first instance on chemical communication. The larva secretes from glandular cells in its integument a substance that apparently acts as an attractant for the ant. This substance may be an imitation of a pheromone that ant larvae themselves emit to release brood-keeping behavior in the adults [see the article "Pheromones," by Edward O. Wilson, beginning on page 92]. The brood-tending ants respond to the chemical signal from the *Atemeles* beetle larvae with intense grooming of the larvae. I was able to verify the existence of chemical communication by two kinds of experimental evidence. Experiments with radioactive tracers demonstrated that substances were transferred from the beetle larvae to the ants. When larvae coated with shellac to prevent liberation of their secretion were placed at the entrance to the nest, the ants either ignored the larvae or carried them off to the garbage dump. If at least one segment of a larva's body was left uncovered by shellac, however, the ants would take the larva into the nest and adopt it. They even carried in dummies of filter paper soaked with secretions extracted from the beetle larvae.

A different form of communication comes into play to elicit the ants' feeding of larvae. The beetle larvae imitate certain begging behavior of ant larvae involving mechanical stimulation of the brood-keeping adults. When a larva is touched by the adult ant's mouthparts or antennae, it promptly rears up and tries to make contact with the ant's head. If the larva succeeds in tapping the ant's lip with its own mouthparts, the ant regurgitates a droplet of food. The beetle larvae perform the begging behavior more intensely than the ant larvae do, and apparently for this reason they receive more food. In order to trace and measure the distribution of food to the larvae in a brood chamber I gave the ants food labeled with radioactive sodium phosphate. The experiment showed that in a mixed population of beetle and ant larvae the beetles obtained a disproportionately large share of the food. The presence of beetle larvae reduced the normal flow of food to the ant larvae; on the other hand, the presence of ant larvae did not affect the food flow to the beetle larvae.

The question arises: How does the ant colony manage to survive the beetle larvae's competition for the food and their intense predation on the ant larvae in the brood chamber? This turns out to have a simple answer. The beetle larvae are cannibalistic and unable to distinguish their fellow larvae from ant larvae by odor. They therefore cut down their

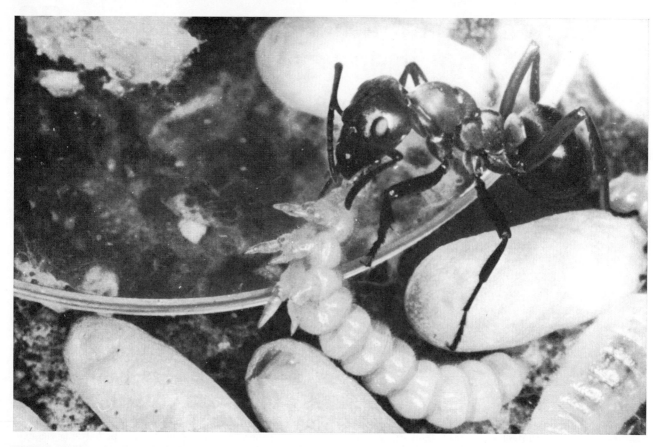

YOUNG GUEST, a beetle larva of the genus *Atemeles,* is given a droplet of liquid food by an ant attendant in the brood chamber of a nest of *Formica* ants. Not only beetles but also wasps, flies and many other arthropods are fed and sheltered by various ant hosts.

MATURING LARVA obtains added nourishment in the *Formica* brood chamber by eating the small ant larvae sheltered there. The beetle larvae also prey on one another. The nest in this photograph and the one at top of page is a man-made laboratory structure.

own population, whereas the ant larvae do not. Typically one finds that in a brood chamber the ant larvae are found in clusters but beetle larvae (particularly those belonging to the genus *Lomechusa*) show up as loners, having devoured their neighbors.

The *Atemeles* beetles have two homes with ants—one for the summer, the other for winter. After the larvae have pupated and hatched in a *Formica* nest, the adult beetles migrate in the fall to nests of dark brown, insect-eating ants of the genus *Myrmica*. The reason for the beetles' migration is that brood-keeping and the food supply are maintained in *Myrmica* colonies throughout the winter, whereas *Formica* ants suspend their raising of young. In the *Myrmica* nests the beetles, still sexually immature, can be fed and ripen to maturity by the spring, at which time they return to *Formica* nests for mating and the laying of eggs. Thus the life cycles and behavior of the *Atemeles* beetles and the *Formica* and *Myrmica* ants are so synchronized that the beetles can take maximum advantage of the social life of each of the two ant species that serve as hosts. In this respect *Atemeles* shows a remarkably advanced form of evolutionary adaptation. The *Lomechusa* beetles, also co-dwellers with *Formica* ants, do not change their environment for the winter; after hatching they simply move on to another *Formica* colony of the same species and share the food shortage. It appears that *Atemeles* evolved myrmecophilous relations with *Formica* to begin with and then "discovered" and adapted to a winter home with *Myrmica,* developing proficiency in a second language for that purpose.

Before leaving the *Formica* nest at the beginning of the fall the *Atemeles* beetle obtains a supply of food for its migration by begging from its *Formica* hosts. For this it employs a technique of tactile stimulation. The beetle first drums rapidly on an ant with its antennae to attract attention. It then induces the ant to regurgitate food by touching the ant's mouthparts with its maxillae and forelegs [*see bottom illustration on page 268*]. High-speed motion pictures show that ants themselves obtain food from one another by similar mechanical signals.

How does the migrating beetle find its way to a *Myrmica* nest? *Formica* nests are normally found in woodland, whereas *Myrmica* nests are found in the grassland beyond the woods. It can be shown experimentally that when *Atemeles* beetles leave the *Formica* nest, they generally move in the direction of

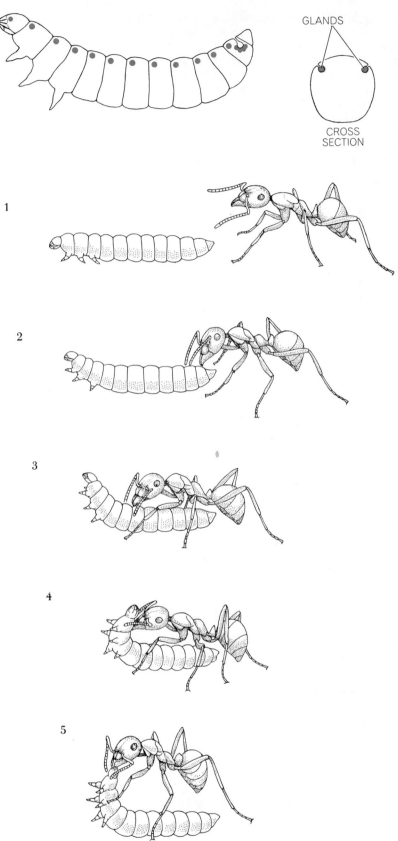

CHEMICAL ATTRACTANT secreted by a row of glands on each side of the beetle larva (*top*) causes the ant host to groom the larva intensively (*1–4*). Experiments with tracer substances indicate that the grooming process transfers secretions from larva to ant. Contact between ant and larva also makes the larva rear up. If the larva can make mouth-to-mouth contact with the ant (*5*), the stimulus causes the ant to regurgitate a droplet of liquid food. Except where noted, the representations of ant hosts and their guests, including the illustration on the cover, are based on a series of original illustrations by the author's wife.

increasing light. This may explain how the beetles manage to reach the relatively open grasslands where the *Myrmica* ants live. After reaching the open grassland the beetle has to use other cues to find a *Myrmica* nest. By means of laboratory experiments I have ascertained that it is guided to the nest by the odor of the host species of ant. The odor must be windborne; the beetle is not drawn to it in still air. Curiously, the beetle possesses only a temporary sensitivity to this

odor; it is limited to the two weeks after leaving the *Formica* nest. (In the spring the beetle locates a *Formica* nest in the same way, by its odor.)

On finding a *Myrmica* nest, the beetle obtains recognition and adoption with a ritual involving chemical communication. The beetle first taps the ant lightly with its antennae and raises the tip of its abdomen toward the host. The ant responds by licking secretions from glands on the abdomen's tip that I call "ap-

peasement glands," because their secretion apparently suppresses aggressive behavior in the ant. The ant is next attracted to a series of glands along the sides of the beetle's abdomen; I call these the "adoption glands," as the ant will not welcome or adopt the beetle unless it senses their secretion. Presumably the odor of this secretion mimics the odor of the ant species. Finally the beetle lowers its abdomen so that the ant can approach, and the ant then grasps

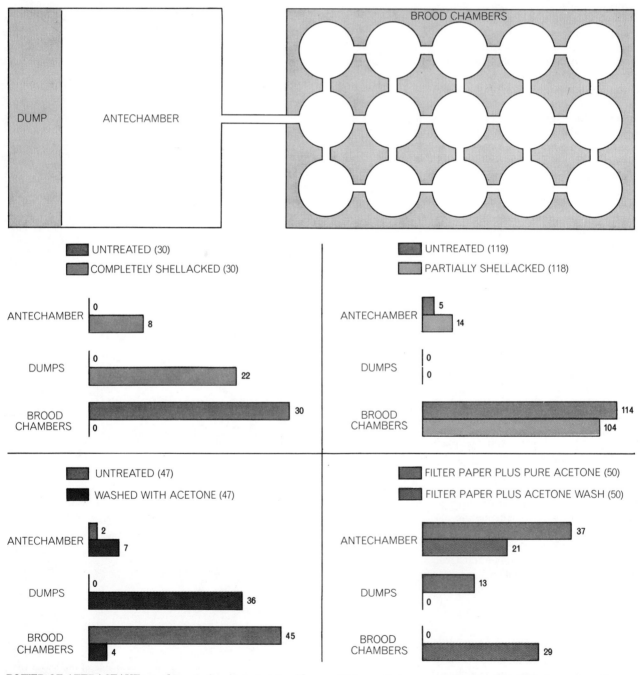

POWER OF ATTRACTANT was shown in four experiments with an artificial ant nest (*top*). The controls in three cases were normal beetle larvae. When normal larvae and others covered with shellac were placed in the antechamber, the ants moved all the normal larvae but none of the shellacked ones into the brood chambers. Most of the shellacked larvae were taken to a dump. Presented

with larvae that were coated except for one body segment, the ants accepted most of them. Faced with a choice between normal larvae and others whose attractant had been washed off in an acetone bath, the ants accepted most normal larvae but dumped most deodorized ones. In a choice between attractant-scented and unscented dummy larvae made of paper, the ants accepted only scented ones.

some bristles around the beetle's lateral glands and carries the guest into the brood chamber.

The *Atemeles* beetles are not the only myrmecophiles capable of making themselves at home with more than one kind of ant. More than 50 years ago the Harvard University entomologist William Morton Wheeler discovered that staphylinid beetles of the *Xenodusa* genus change their domicile with the seasons. The larvae live in *Formica* nests through the summer and the adults overwinter in nests of the carpenter ants of the genus *Camponotus*. It is interesting to note that the carpenter ants also maintain larvae throughout the winter. It may well be that the evolutionary history of the *Xenodusa* beetles parallels that of *Atemeles* in selecting and adapting to a winter home.

Unlike the *Atemeles*, *Lomechusa* and *Xenodusa* beetles, various other genera of staphylinid beetles do not possess the command of ant language that is required to gain entry into the brood chamber, the optimum niche for obtaining food. Staphylinids of the European genus *Dinarda*, for example, are limited to the peripheral chambers of the nests of their host (*Formica sanguinea*). *Dinarda* offers secretions from glands similar to *Atemeles*' appeasement glands, but these secretions only induce the ant to tolerate the beetle, not to adopt it and take it into the brood chamber. *Dinarda* is therefore reduced to living on such food as it can find or scrounge in the peripheral chambers. There it feeds on dead ants that have not yet been taken to the garbage dump and on food that it may steal or wheedle from the worker ants. Occasionally *Dinarda* snatches a food droplet from the mouth of a forager that is about to pass the food to another worker. Or the beetle may surreptitiously approach a food-laden forager and, by touching the forager's lip, induce the regurgitation of a small food droplet. The ant immediately recognizes the beetle as an alien, however, and starts to attack it. The beetle staves off the attack by raising its abdomen and offering the ant its appeasement secretion; while the ant is savoring the substance it has licked up, the beetle makes its escape.

Other groups of myrmecophilous staphylinid beetles (for example the genus *Myrmedonia*) have a bare minimum of communication with their ant hosts, sufficient only to allow the beetle to feed at the ants' garbage dumps. At the dump the foraging beetle can avert attack by an ant from the nest by offering it the appeasement secretion

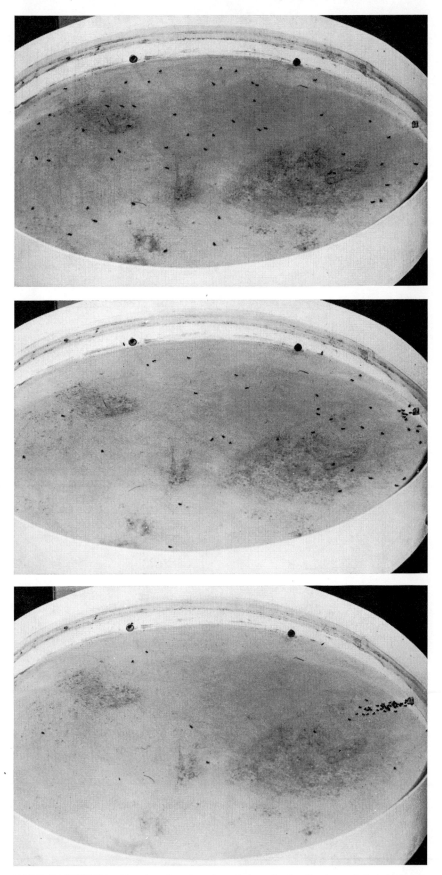

ROLE OF SCENT in directing the migration of *Atemeles* beetles from their initial residence in *Formica* nests to winter quarters in *Myrmica* nests is demonstrated in these laboratory photographs. At the start of the experiment (*top*) the beetles are distributed at random in a circular enclosure. Air scented with the odor of *Myrmica* ants is then blown into the enclosure through one of the eight holes around its rim (*center*). Ten minutes later (*bottom*) most of the beetles have collected in a cluster near the scent-emitting hole.

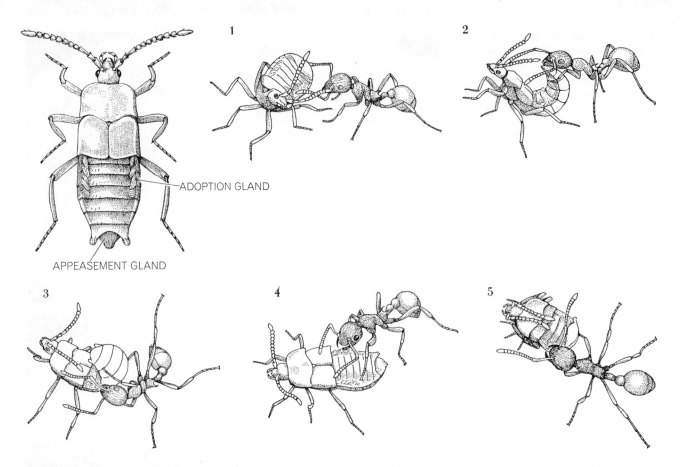

ADOPTION GLAND

APPEASEMENT GLAND

ADOPTION RITUAL, which gains entry for *Atemeles* beetles to nests of the ant genus *Myrmica*, depends on secretions from glands at the tip and along the sides of the beetle's abdomen (*top left*). On encountering a potential *Myrmica* host in the nest antechamber, the beetle attracts its attention (*1*) by tapping the ant lightly with its antennae and raising the tip of its abdomen. The response of the ant (*2*) is to taste the secretion from the glands there, known as "appeasement glands" because they apparently suppress the ant's aggressive behavior toward intruders. The next attractant is the secretion from the "adoption glands" (*3, 4*), so named because an ant will not welcome an intruder before it senses this secretion. The tightly curled beetle is then carried to a brood chamber (*5*).

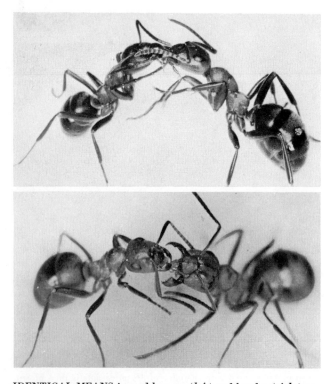

IDENTICAL MEANS is used by ants (*left*) and beetles (*right*) to make a food-laden forager regurgitate. A tapping of the forager's mouthparts with the food seeker's forelegs is the key stimulus (*top photographs*). Regurgitation is immediate (*bottom photographs*).

and thus winning time to escape. If the beetle is placed anywhere inside the nest, however, the appeasement does not avail; the ants promptly kill the beetle as an intruder.

There are myrmecophiles that possess only an elementary, one-way form of chemical communication with the ants they depend on for food. This is simply the ability to recognize the odor of the trail laid down between the nest and a food source by foragers of the particular ant species. For example, a small nitidulid beetle in Europe (*Amphotis marginata*) can thus identify the trails of a shiny black wood ant (*Lasius fuliginosus*), and in many localities these beetles abound along the trails. They act as begging highwaymen, intercepting food-laden ants on the trail and inducing them to regurgitate food droplets by tapping the ant's labium. The ant soon realizes it has been tricked and attacks the beetle. Although the beetle has no appeasement mechanism, it avoids injury by retracting its appendages and flattening itself on the ground.

Many myrmecophilous beetles closely resemble their ant hosts in appearance. This is particularly true of guests of the

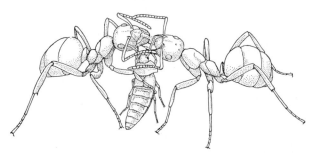

FOOD THIEVES, beetles of the genus *Dinarda*, are tolerated in the outer chambers but not the brood chambers of the *Formica* nest. By touching a forager ant's mouthparts (*left*) a *Dinarda* beetle may induce regurgitation of a food droplet. The beetle may also intercept a droplet (*right*) as it is being passed between two ants. If attacked, the beetle raises its abdomen, drawing attention to the glands that, like the *Atemeles* "appeasement glands," secrete a substance that the ants savor. While the ant tastes, the beetle flees.

HIGHWAYMAN BEETLES of the genus *Amphotis* locate foraging trails of the wood ant *Lasius* by the scent and ambush food-laden workers. By stimulating the ant's mouthparts (*top left*) the beetle causes it to regurgitate its cropful of food (*top right*). The robbed ant then reacts aggressively (*bottom left*), but passive defense (*bottom right*) enables the armored beetle to weather the attack.

BEETLE MIMICS that resemble their army-ant hosts include a seemingly headless species, *Mimanomma spectrum* (*top left*). Its host is the African driver ant *Dorylus nigricoms* (*top right*). Other army-ant mimics are *Crematoxenus aenigma* (*center left*) and *Mimeciton antennatum* (*bottom left*), shown with their respective New World hosts, *Neivamyrmex melanocephalum* and *Labidus praedator*. The drawings are based on original sketches by the late Charles H. Seevers of Roosevelt College. There is no evidence that mimicry affects guest-host relations. It may, however, protect the beetles from attack by other predators.

army ants, and some investigators concluded that the factor inducing the ants to accept beetles as their nestmates was the beetles' morphological resemblance to themselves. It was even thought to be the case with *Atemeles* and *Lomechusa*, although they do not particularly resemble their hosts. I have been able to show, by artificially altering the shape and color of these beetles, that morphological features do not contribute to the success of their relationship with their hosts. Instead it appears that communicative behavior remains the essential requirement for acceptance. I believe this is probably generally the case, even for the guests of the army ants. Very likely the guests' mimicry of their hosts' appearance has evolved as a protection against predation by birds. Predatory birds that follow army ants as they travel over open ground do not attack the ants themselves; they feed only on other insects that are stirred up by the ants' march. Presumably insects that resemble ants are ignored by the birds. With carefully designed experiments we should be able to resolve this question.

There remains for further exploration the fascinating question of how the extraordinarily effective system of communication between myrmecophiles and their hosts evolved. We can think of this evolution as a two-part process. First, viewing the myrmecophile as a signal-receiver, we can suppose the potential guest of a specific ant underwent gradual evolutionary modification of its receptor system that endowed it with the ability to recognize the ant's odor, the distinctions between the ant larva and the adult and other signals opening the way to a parasitic relationship. Second, regarding the myrmecophile as a transmitter of signals, we can see that through natural selection it must have evolved the set of secretions and behavioral acts that induces the ant to accept the guest in the nest and nurture it. Thus the development of the guest-host relationship would involve adaptive changes only in the guest, accommodating itself to the nature of the specific host. In all probability this is the way *Atemeles* and *Lomechusa* won their welcome and support in the homes of their respective species of ant hosts.

By careful analysis of various related species of beetles that enjoy differing degrees of intimacy with their hosts we can expect to learn more about the details of the evolution of the social associations between myrmecophiles and ants and their communication systems.

30

Air-Conditioned Termite Nests

by Martin Lüscher
July 1961

*Some African termites build nests that are brilliantly
designed to maintain the temperature and humidity
within the nest while permitting oxygen to flow into it
and carbon dioxide to flow out*

Termites live in critical dependence on the temperature and humidity of their immediate surroundings. An entire colony of the tree-dwelling termite of Africa (*Nasutitermes arboreus*) will perish in half a day's exposure to dry air; single individuals die in five hours. The few termite species that live in temperate regions are active only during the warm months of the year; in winter the termites stay motionless in their galleries unless the overheating of a building they inhabit encourages them to renewed activity. Not even in the tropics, where most termite species live, do these insects find high humidity and warm temperatures in the day-after-day constancy that their existence requires. Termites survive only because their elaborate social organization enables them to build nests in which they establish the microclimate suited to their needs. They live their entire existence in the closed environment of the nest and the tunnels that connect it to sources of food and water; only the reproductive forms of termite venture forth to found new colonies.

As air-conditioning engineers, termites maintain the warmth and humidity of their microclimates in various ways and with varying degrees of success, subject always to the satisfaction of a third and equally compelling need: termites, like other animals, must breathe. Their tissues take in oxygen from the atmosphere within the nest and give off carbon dioxide. The exchange of oxygen and carbon dioxide between the interior of the nest and the world outside must take place by diffusion through the wall of the nest. A thick wall that provides good insulation does not permit good ventilation; what is more, the nearly saturated air within the nest causes the pores in thick walls to fill with water, virtually cutting off

the movement of air. In general, temperature control can be achieved only at the expense of gas exchange and vice versa. The way in which these conflicting claims are compromised ultimately determines the size of termite colonies and limits the distribution of the various termite species.

A few advanced mound-building termites native to Africa have managed to obtain good ventilation through thick walls. These insects are able to establish their closely regulated microclimate in most of the habitats offered by the large continent of Africa and are the most widespread of all tropical termites. Only a few animals have achieved wider distribution; all of them (with the exception of the domesticated or parasitic animals that live with man) are social animals. Man is one of them; he long ago learned to clothe himself and heat his dwellings. Recently he has acquired more refined control over his microclimate, learning to cool it and regulate its humidity. Almost as ubiquitous as man is the honeybee *Apis mellifera* and its relatives. The honeybee makes its own microclimate and holds the temperature of the hive relatively constant in spite of variations in the environment. For the time being, at least, no termite species can rival the honeybee in geographic distribution.

In 1953, with the help of Urs Rahm, I conducted in the Ivory Coast of Africa a study of the microclimates in the nests of five termite species. We drilled holes in the nests with a special hollow borer that took gas samples the moment we breached a cavity wall. At the same locations we made measurements of the temperature and humidity over extended periods. These observations and careful study and dissection of the nest struc-

tures have given us a new appreciation of the technology of air conditioning as evolved by the termites long before man first evolved.

The humidity inside the nest usually ranged between 98 and 99 per cent; we never found it below 96.2 per cent. Part of the moisture that is so essential (apparently termites dry out easily, either because the outer layer of their waxy cuticle is poorly developed or because they constantly scrape it off in their tunnels) results from the metabolic processes of the members of the colony. In some nests additional moisture is furnished by fungi, which the termites cultivate in spherical combs of wood particles, thus rendering the wood more digestible for themselves. In addition, some termites make tunnels to water outside the nest. Pierre-Paul Grassé and Charles Noirot of the University of Paris have found that certain desert termites go as deep as 130 feet in the sandy soil to reach water, which they somehow carry back into the nest. With water soaking the nest, evaporation keeps the air close to the saturation point even when the temperature rises.

Temperature does not yield easily to such close regulation, and the temperature in the nests of most termite species tends to vary with that of the atmosphere. Some species build thin-walled nests in the open under the sun, where the temperature rises and falls throughout the day and night. Others construct mounds only deep in the shade of tropical forests, where the temperature normally remains fairly uniform. The mounds of a few species have walls of moderate thickness; within such mounds, and in those with thick walls, the temperature stays constant and considerably higher than the temperature outside. The metabolic heat of the ter-

NEST OF *THORACOTERMES*, one of the five termite species studied by the author in the Ivory Coast of Africa, is built like a column. It is always deep in the shade of the forest. Two devices for measuring temperature and humidity, installed by the author, are clearly visible after nest is cut open (*right*). Irregular compartments make up the interior. This nest is nearly five feet tall.

mites supplies the extra warmth. Where the termites cultivate fungi, the heat of fermentation in the fungus combs supplies still more warmth. It has been found that tropical termites do best at 30 degrees centigrade (86 degrees Fahrenheit); the corresponding temperature for Temperate Zone species is 26 degrees C. (79 degrees F.). At lower temperatures the growth and development of individuals and colonies slows down and eventually stops.

The third important variable in the microclimate of the nest—the supply of oxygen—not only varies inversely with improvement in insulation but also is limited by simple geometry. The larger the nest and the population inside, the smaller is the relative surface area available for exchange of respiratory gases. The occurrence of mounds more than three feet in height all over tropical Africa is a measure of the ingenuity of at least some species of termite.

The most primitive species we studied in the Ivory Coast, *Amitermes evuncifer* and *Thoracotermes macrothorax*, build thin-walled nests containing irregular cavities connected by narrow passages. The relatively soft building material consists of humus mixed with the saliva of the worker termites. *Amitermes* is the hardier of the two; it builds its more or less spherical mounds both in the shade and in the open. The nest we investigated lay on a slope directly exposed to the sun. *Thoracotermes* always builds its columnar nest in the shade of a forest. The temperature in the nests of these two species is only .1 to .5 degree C. above that of the surrounding atmosphere, and it fluctuates, with a short time lag, as the environmental temperature changes. Moreover, the nest of *Amitermes* does not efficiently exchange respiratory gases. The spherical shape of the nest gives it a small surface-to-volume ratio and, though the wall of the nest is thin, the atmosphere inside it contains a high concentration of carbon dioxide. The columnar mound of *Thoracotermes* provides a larger surface for gas exchange.

The species *Microcerotermes edentatus* builds a small, spherical, thin-walled nest in a tree. The nest consists of wood particles glued together with saliva and excrement to form a material rather like hard cardboard. Neat horizontal layers characterize the interior. The queen occupies a special compartment that is protected by being near the center of the nest. The nest we investigated had a volume of only four

CLOSE-UP OF INTERIOR of *Thoracotermes* nest shows details of structure and some soldier termites. Soft building material consists of humus mixed with saliva of termites.

NEST OF *MICROCEROTERMES* is arranged in horizontal compartments. The building material is wood particles glued together with saliva and excrement to make a hard board.

NEST OF *CEPHALOTERMES* is built of the same material as that of *Microcerotermes*. Its interior also consists of compartments arranged in numerous horizontal layers.

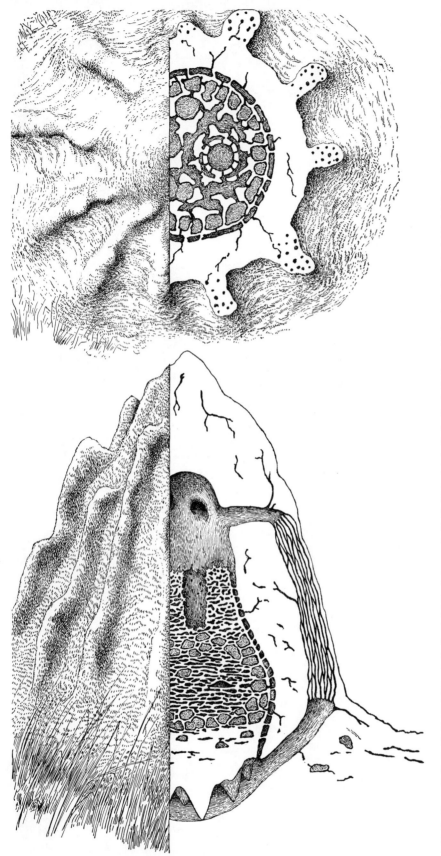

liters (a liter is approximately equal to a quart); it was too small for us to obtain a good gas sample. The temperature within rises and falls with the outside temperature but averages about 1.5 degrees above it. The thin walls and small size of the nest should ensure excellent ventilation.

Cephalotermes rectangularis constructs cone-shaped mounds that stand on the forest floor, often leaning against a tree. Like *Microcerotermes*, it manufactures a building material resembling hard cardboard, but the wall of the nest is two to three inches thick. Horizontal layers fill the interior; the queen lives in an enlarged compartment in the wall of the nest. The combination of a shady location and a thick wall keeps the inside temperature warmer and more stable than the surrounding air, but gas exchange is somewhat less efficient than in the mound of *Thoracotermes*.

By far the most advanced of the species we studied was *Macrotermes natalensis*. Its enormous pinnacled mounds, with curious ridges running like veins down their outer walls, are familiar to anyone who has traveled through equatorial Africa. The mounds sometimes reach a height of 16 feet and can have a diameter of 16 feet at the base. *Macrotermes* builds its mounds in the forest and in the open over much of the continent. The architecture of the mounds is far from uniform and can be quite different in various parts of Africa.

In the Ivory Coast the mounds of *Macrotermes* have walls 16 to 23 inches thick. The termites bring up particles of the African lateritic soil from below the humus layer and mix it with their saliva to make a hard cement. The nest proper stands within the mound on a firm foundation supported by pillars that rise from the floor of the "cellar," three feet below ground level. Above the nest is another hollow space—the "attic." Horizontal brood chambers surround the queen's cell in the center, and fungus combs form a spherical layer around the brood cells. Still another layer of small cells separates the combs from the wall of the mound.

The metabolism of the colony and of the fungi warms the air inside the nest and contributes moisture to its high humidity. Water brought up from the soil irrigates the interior of the nest and brings the air to the saturation point. The thick, dense wall of the mound securely insulates the microclimate from variations in the temperature and humidity of the atmosphere outside. But what about ventilation? Even in the dry

GIANT MOUND OF *MACROTERMES* is revealed in cross sections as a complex structure. Rising from the cellar are pillars that support the foundation of the nest proper. Large compartment in nest, just to right of center, is occupied by the queen. Brood chambers and fungus combs surround it. The hole visible in the back of the attic, above the nest, leads into an exterior ridge of the mound wall. Air channels in such a ridge are seen at right. At top is a partial horizontal cross section of the mound, made at the level of the queen cell.

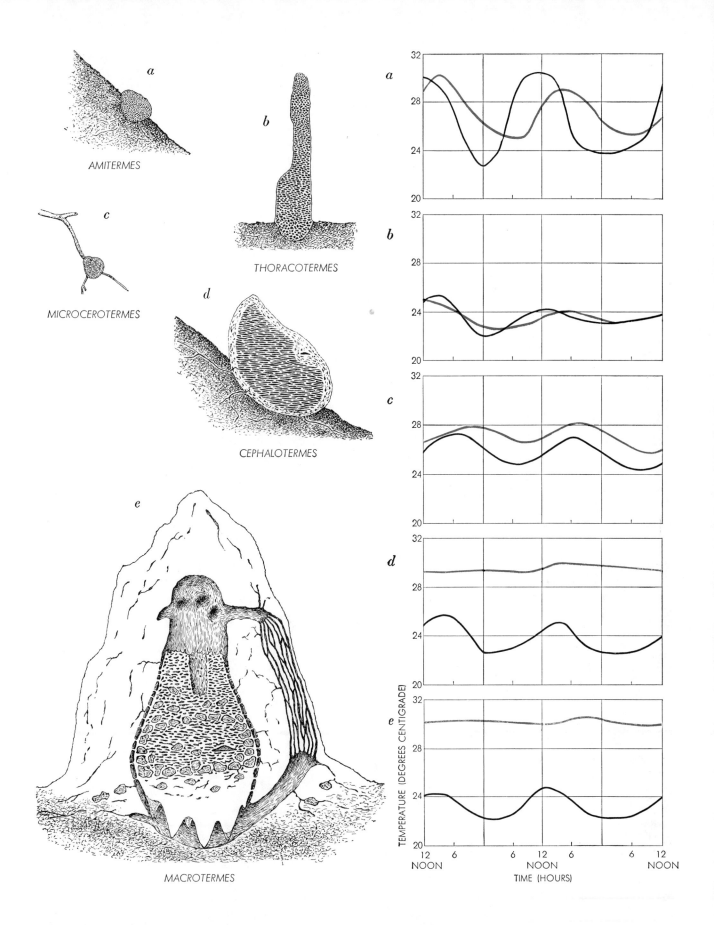

NESTS OF FIVE TERMITE SPECIES are drawn to scale in cross section. The *Macrotermes* mound is 10 feet high. Curves at right show temperature inside each mound (*color*) and outside the mound (*black*) over a period of two days. Temperature in mounds of *Macrotermes* and *Cephalotermes* hardly varies; in *Amitermes* nest it changes, after a delay, with the exterior temperature.

state the wall of the mound would be an effective barrier to the diffusion of air. The saturated air within the mound, however, fills the pores of the wall with water. Since the respiratory gases diffuse 10,000 times more slowly through water than through air, ventilation would appear to be shut off completely. Yet the mound of *Macrotermes* houses the largest termite city of all.

A medium-sized nest contains two million individuals that need at least 240 liters of oxygen, or 1,200 liters of air, a day. If the nest were hermetically sealed, the air in it would not last 12 hours. Nonetheless, our measurements showed a carbon dioxide content of only 2.7 per cent in the center of the nest, rather high compared with the other species but remarkably low under the circumstances. Study of the mound of *Macrotermes* revealed the function of

the ridges on the surface of the mound and disclosed the simple but ingenious mechanism that accomplishes the respiratory change.

Each ridge serves as a conduit carrying half a dozen or more narrow channels that link the air chambers in the cellar and the attic [*see illustration on next page*]. The mass of termites and the fungi in the nest proper keep the interior of the mound considerably warmer than the outside, where the ridges are. Our measurements of the temperature and analyses of the gas concentrations in various parts of the nest showed that convection currents circulate the air from the nest upward to the attic. There the air passes into the narrow channels in the external ridges and runs downward through the ridges to the cellar. The air flowing in the upper ends of the ridges contains more carbon dioxide than the air flowing in the lower ends, and a correspondingly

higher percentage of oxygen is found in the lower ends of the ridges than in the upper ends. By the time the air flows into the cellar it carries a new supply of oxygen. In good weather the ridges and the narrow air-circulation channels inside them stay completely dry. Gases diffuse easily across the ridge material because the diffusion distance is short, and the protrusion of the ridges from the mound wall greatly enlarges the surface available for gas exchange. The ridges can therefore be considered the lungs of the termite society.

When it rains, the ridges are soaked and their respiratory efficiency is impaired. Most of the water runs down between the ridges, however, and they always dry quickly. We do not know what happens when continuous rain keeps the ridges wet for prolonged periods. The termites may move the narrow channels in the ridges quite near the

EXPERIMENTAL EQUIPMENT attached to mound of *Macrotermes* measures and records temperature and humidity at differ-ent locations within the structure. The gas samples were taken through a hollow borer used to drill the necessary holes in wall.

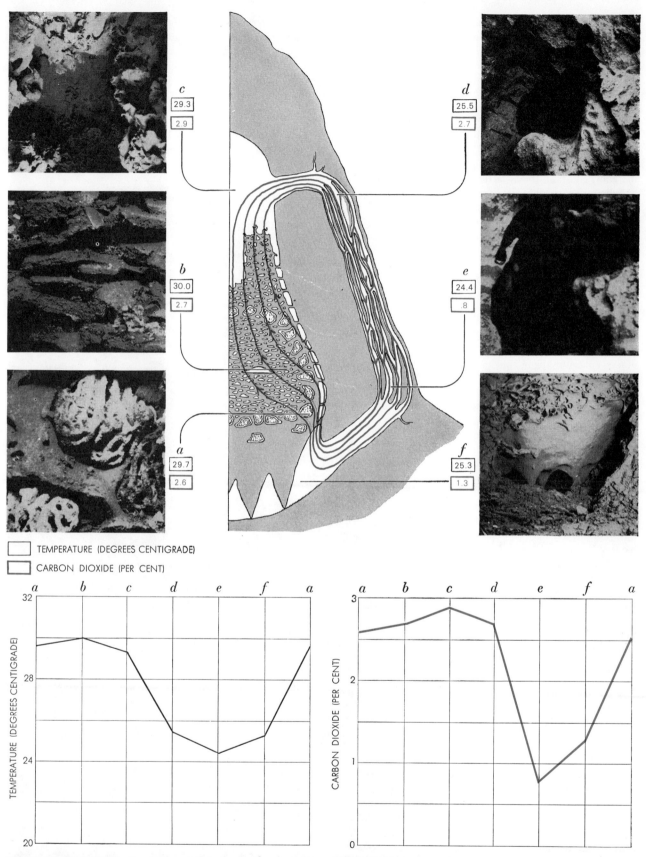

TEMPERATURE (DEGREES CENTIGRADE)

CARBON DIOXIDE (PER CENT)

c
29.3
2.9

d
25.5
2.7

b
30.0
2.7

e
24.4
.8

a
29.7
2.6

f
25.3
1.3

AIR IS CIRCULATED (*colored arrows*) ingeniously in mound of *Macrotermes*. This was shown by measurements of temperature and carbon dioxide at the following locations: (*a*) in fungus combs at bottom of nest proper, (*b*) in brood chambers, (*c*) in the attic, (*d*) in upper part of a ridge channel, (*e*) in lower part of a ridge channel and (*f*) in cellar. The locations are shown in the photo-graphs. Black figures in boxes are temperatures in degrees centi-grade; colored figures give percentage of carbon dioxide at each location. Curves at bottom of page show how temperature (*black*) and carbon dioxide content (*color*) of air changes during circu-lation. These changes take place due to diffusion of gases and the radiation of heat through the thin, dry walls of the ridges.

surface, thereby securing the necessary gas exchange, or they may even perforate the surface. It seems that no one has ever observed termite mounds closely during heavy rains, probably because most research workers, including the author, prefer to travel in Africa during the dry season.

The ridges may also hold the explanation of how *Macrotermes* keeps the interior temperature of its mounds so remarkably constant. It may be that colony members are steadily at work in the ridges, closing and opening the air-circulation channels and so regulating the flow of air through them. There would be nothing extraordinary in this; although the mound is an elaborate architectural masterpiece, it is not the finished, stable structure it seems to be when we open it. In reality we can see only a phase of a dynamic process, because the termites are always at work pulling down some parts, rebuilding others, enlarging the mound and remodeling every detail. The structure remains the same from day to day only in principle. With termites working all the time throughout the mound, some of them are no doubt at work in the channels of the ridges. They may close up some channels when the nest begins to cool and open new channels when the temperature rises. Unfortunately it is not possible to see exactly what is happening; invasion of the mound disturbs the termites and radically modifies their behavior.

In view of the fact that termites tend to be dried out by air currents, it was puzzling to learn that air circulates continuously in the mound. It can be shown, however, that the circulation is slow. Since the oxygen concentration increases about 10 per cent each time the air passes through the ridge channels, simple arithmetic indicates that the air must go through the channels about 10 times in 24 hours to supply the 240 liters of oxygen needed in a day. This circulation produces an air speed of about two millimeters per second in the ridges (approximately the speed of a moving snail) and only .15 millimeter per second in the nest cavities. Such an air speed is considerably slower than that experienced by a termite walking through still air; hence it is unlikely that the "breeze" disturbs the termites.

The feat of air conditioning has made *Macrotermes* and some other species remarkably independent of the outside temperature and humidity. It is no wonder, then, that *Macrotermes* has the wid-

est distribution of all African termites. Such independence is achieved, however, only after the nest has reached a certain size. New *Macrotermes* colonies pass through a "solitary" phase in which a king and queen go out alone to start a brood. For some time the colony is so small that it cannot build a nest large enough to control the temperature. Therefore new colonies must depend on

the tropical climate for heat, and this probably explains why these termites have not spread over North Africa and Europe. If evolution ever permits *Macrotermes* to form "worker swarms" as bees do, or bud large, complete colonies from the original mound as some species of termite already do, no climatic barrier will be strong enough to hold it back.

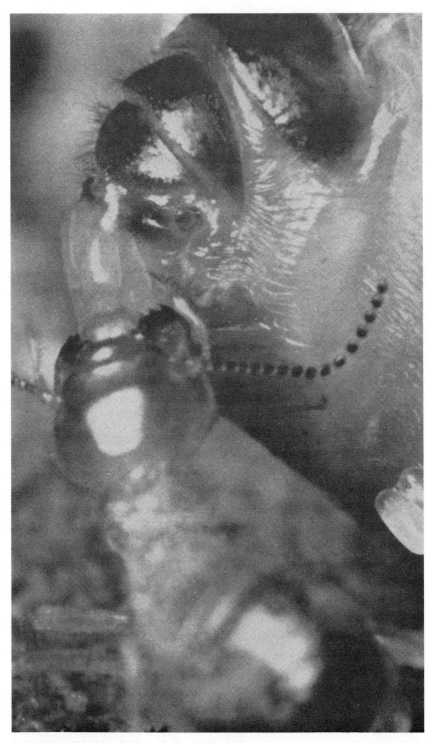

MACROTERMES WORKER, with "beaded" antennae, is seen in lower half of photograph taking an egg from its queen. All the photographs were made by the author in Africa.

V

INSECTS AND MANKIND

INSECTS AND MANKIND

V

INTRODUCTION

Thirty-five years ago applied entomology appeared to be on the threshold of its golden age. DDT was being widely used for the first time and other chlorinated hydrocarbons were on the way. For a while after their introduction the new insecticides appeared to be the equivalent of penicillin and the other broad-spectrum antibiotics. They could be broadcast to eliminate any insect pest we chose as a target—or so we thought. Rachel Carsons' *Silent Spring* and an embarrassingly frequent failure rate in control programs have made us wiser. In certain instances DDT and the other new chemicals, referred to by C. M. Williams as the second-generation pesticides, did live up to their promise. They have proved marvelously successful in controlling malaria and a few other insect-born diseases. In countries with a sufficiently advanced technology, widespread application of the pesticides have substantially increased crop yields. But two difficulties have appeared that limit their usefulness.

First, target insect species display a remarkable ability to develop new, pesticide-resistant genetic strains, requiring the use of larger and larger doses or even a change in the pesticide itself to maintain the same level of control. Second, and far more importantly, DDT and the other modern insecticides have proved too broadly effective. Insects other than the target pests are killed, with a resulting disruption of the surrounding ecosystems. The direct chemical control of the pest species can be more than offset l / an ecological disruption, because the other species destroyed by the chemicals often include the natural parasites and predators of the pests. With no help from these enemies, the burden falls entirely on the pesticides. Finally, fish, birds, and other vertebrates concentrate the chemicals in their own systems, sometimes with fatal effects. Human health itself is threatened.

This section begins with an early success story of medical entomology—the elucidation of the role of mosquitoes in the transmission of malaria. Knowledge of this role led to the partial control of the disease and even the prospect of its eradication worldwide. Subsequent articles describe some of the more sophisticated methods of control being developed by entomologists to circumvent the dangers of overuse of broad-spectrum pesticides. The implicit goal of the research they report is the discovery of "magic bullets" that can seek out and destroy particular species without significantly affecting the remainder of the ecosystem. Magic bullets include certain diseases, parasites, and predators that attack only one or a few species, or they can be concocted from substances that mimic hormones and pheromones. They even include males sterilized in the laboratory and released to frustrate the mating attempts of fertile males. All of these techniques, which have been used successfully in practice, have one important feature in common. They depend on a substantial knowledge not only of insect biology but also of the details of the natural history of the target species. For this reason, basic and applied entomology seem destined to become even more tightly connected in the future.

The discovery of the life cycle of the malarial parasite, with the identification of certain mosquitoes as the vectors, ranks as one of the great events in the history of medicine. Because malarial mosquitoes have a limited dispersal range and are particularly vulnerable to DDT, it has been possible to eradicate the disease in many parts of the world by employing relatively simple drainage and spraying techniques. As described by C. A. Alvarado and J. L. Bruce-Chwatt in their 1962 article "Malaria," total eradication of malaria was a goal of the World Health Organization 15 years ago. Its attainment now seems less probable than during the most optimistic years when chlorinated hydrocarbons were first being used.

Although written more than 20 years ago, "Insect Control and the Balance of Nature," by Ray F. Smith and William W. Allen, still presents a timely account of integrated control—the skillful manipulation of the ecosystem of a pest species to keep its numbers low with a minimum of expense and environmental disruption. This technique takes advantage of parasites and predators that are specialized on the target species, but it includes mechanical changes in the insect's environment and allows limited use of chemical pesticides at times when they can be shown to have maximum potential effectiveness.

Beyond DDT and the more sophisticated toxic chemicals that constitute the second generation of pesticides lies what C. M. Williams calls the third generation of control substances—the hormones of the insects themselves. Earlier research by V. B. Wigglesworth, Williams, and others revealed that topical applications of small quantities of juvenile hormone could delay growth and alter final adult development in ways that either kill or sterilize the insect. Williams was the first to conceive of utilizing this effect in control programs; he discusses the possibilities in the article "Third-Generation Pesticides." The special promise of the hormones is that insect pests are far less likely to develop resistance, since to do so would be to endanger their own normal development. Furthermore, the chemicals are not toxic to man and other vertebrates. But their broad effectiveness against insect species makes them less than perfect as magic bullets.

One of the most notable success stories of modern applied entomology is the control in the southeastern United States of the screwworm fly, a dangerous pest of livestock. Edward Knipling, who conceived and led the program, describes the history and methods of this major effort in "The Eradication of the Screwworm Fly." Kipling was convinced of its feasibility because of two weaknesses observed in the fly population. First, the population reached low levels and its range shrank to the Florida peninsula during the winter. Second, females of this species mate only once. Knipling and his co-workers exploited these biological features to mount a massive attempt at eradication. They reared large numbers of male flies in confinement, sterilized the adults with radiation from cobalt-60, and released them in the Florida peninsula during the winter. At the peak of the effort 50 million flies were liberated each week, so that Florida became populated with far more sterile than normal males. As a result, so many females were inseminated by the sterile males that the southeastern population was virtually eliminated within a year.

Since this article appeared in 1960, the sterile male technique has also been used in the southwestern United States, where the screwworm was also a serious pest. Initially, the results were spectacular, but beginning in 1972 the rate of infestation increased again. Prolonged factory raising of the flies had apparently resulted in selection for a strain of males no longer able to compete adequately with normal males for females in the wild (for details see Bush, G. L., R. W. Neck, and G. B. Kitto, *Science,* 193:491–493, 1976).

The dung of the kangaroo, the large, native herbivorous mammal of Australia, consists of dry pellets no larger than a golf ball. The dung pats dropped by cattle, horses, and sheep are much larger and moister, and are unattractive to the native dung beetles of Australia. The dung of these domestic animals is therefore left to disintegrate by weathering, a process requiring months or years to complete. As the populations of domestic animals increased following the European colonization of Australia, their dung accumulated to such levels that extensive pasturage was put out of service. The problem is now being solved by introducing dung beetles from other parts of the world where hoofed animals occur naturally. These insects have made spectacular progress in reducing dung heaps and returning pastures to full use, as D. F. Waterhouse describes in the article "The Biological Control of Dung." One economically attractive feature of this solution should not be overlooked: once established, the beetles are able to go about their good work indefinitely with no further assistance from entomologists.

RELATED BOOKS

Huffaker, C. B. (ed.). 1971. *Biological Control.* Plenum Press, New York. Articles by leading authorities on the theory and practicability of pest control using parasites, predators, and pathogens. Includes good accounts of instances in which biological control has proven effective in the past.

Jacobson, Martin (ed.). 1975. *Insecticides of the Future.* Marcel Dekker, New York. A useful collection of short essays on insect control by means other than pesticides (pheromones, morphogenetic agents, biological agents, sexual sterilization).

McKelvey, John J., Jr. 1973. *Man Against Tsetse.* Cornell University Press, Ithaca, New York. An excellent essay in medical entomology that traces the struggle against African sleeping sickness and its vector, the tsetse fly.

Metcalf, C. L., W. P. Flint, and R. L. Metcalf. 1962. *Destructive and Useful Insects,* fourth edition. McGraw-Hill, New York. A good first reference source for information on insect pests, including species that are harmful to humans.

Metcalf, R. L., and W. H. Luckmann. 1975. *Introduction to Insect Pest Management.* Wiley, New York. A good basic text on the principles, tactics, and strategies of pest control. Specific examples are treated in depth.

Metcalf, Robert L., and John J. McKelvey, Jr. (eds.). 1976. *The Future of Insecticides: Needs and Prospects.* Wiley-Interscience, New York. Deals with some of the problems presented by current uses of pesticides, e.g., resistance of target species, pollution, toxicity, and assesses the prospects for success of alternative approaches to control.

Wilkinson, C. F. (ed.). 1976. *Insecticide Biochemistry and Physiology.* Plenum Press, New York. An advanced up-to-date treatise dealing with insecticide penetration and distribution, metabolism, target site interactions, selectivity and resistance, and toxicology.

31 Malaria

by Carlos A. Alvarado and L. J. Bruce-Chwatt
May 1962

*It still disables more people than any other disease.
Many nations in which it is a major problem now
aim, with the aid of the World Health Organization, at
its total eradication*

Of all the ills that afflict mankind few have taken a higher toll than malaria. From earliest times it has laid a cruel burden on much of the earth's human population. Again and again it has erupted in epidemics as deadly as the plague of the Middle Ages. Today it still disables more people and exacts a higher material cost than any other disease.

Yet today the outlook is increasingly hopeful. Although many difficulties still lie ahead, the way to success has in principle been found. During the past 15 years modern methods have cut the number of cases of malaria from a worldwide total of 350 million to fewer than 100 million. Moreover, in several areas eradication has already been achieved. There now seems no reason to doubt that the same results could be attained in the remaining malarial regions of the globe. A continuing international campaign aims at nothing less than the complete eradication of malaria from the whole human population.

Of the antiquity of malaria there can be no doubt; that it antedates man himself is shown by the fact that the almost identical parasites that he shares with the anthropoid apes are survivals of a common heritage. As the earliest records from Assyria, Egypt and China attest, the disease was clearly recognized at the time of the most ancient civilizations. Hippocrates gave the first detailed clinical description of malaria, noting its cyclic character and its association with swamps. The Romans of a few hundred years later were well aware of this association and avoided marshy lands, particularly when they were building military camps and new settlements. During the whole of the Middle Ages and until the 19th century malaria was widespread throughout Europe, even in the northern latitudes. It is not known with any certainty whether malaria existed in pre-Columbian America. The Spanish conquerors of South America suffered from it, and it seems certain that the disease was widely spread by the slaves brought to America from Africa.

Malaria is essentially a chronic disease. It causes, apart from its classic fevers, high infant mortality, stillbirths and abortions; it produces anemia with enlargement of the spleen, and it predisposes those who suffer from it to other infections. In areas where agricultural production and levels of life are already low, its economic effects are obvious: food supplies are further reduced by the fact that large malarial areas are left untilled, and social and economic development are profoundly retarded.

The greatest epidemic of malaria in modern times struck the U.S.S.R. in the year following World War I. More than five million cases were reported in 1923, with at least 60,000 deaths. In Brazil the introduction of a foreign species of mosquito from Africa in 1938 produced 100,000 cases and killed 14,000 people. As recently as 1958 an epidemic in Ethiopia claimed thousands of lives.

The Parasite

Two thousand years ago in Rome, Columella and Varro surmised that diseases were caused by "minute animals," but until the 19th century malaria was ascribed to the effects of unwholesome emanations from damp, low-lying lands; hence the name *mal'aria*. As often happens, physicians found a way to treat the disease long before they understood its cause. In 1632, after the conquest of Peru, the bark of the cinchona tree was brought back to Europe and proved to be the first efficacious remedy. Some 200 years later quinine was extracted from cinchona. The availability of the preventive drug made it possible for men to enter the most malarial areas in comparative safety. On the west coast of Africa, where malaria had claimed hundreds of the early missionaries, explorers and traders, William Balfour Baikie's expedition up the Niger in 1854, supplied with quinine, lost not a single man. Yet 49 years earlier Mungo Park, on his last (and fatal) journey to discover the mouth of the Niger, lost 40 of his 45 men in five months.

Finally, in 1880, the French army physician Charles Louis Alphonse Laveran identified pigmented bodies in the blood of malarial patients as the organism responsible for the disease. There followed several years of intensive studies, and some confusion, before the development of the parasite in the red blood cell was traced and the different species of plasmodium were classified. By then it was established that four species infect man, *Plasmodium vivax*, the most widely distributed, causes benign tertian malaria (fever recurs every third day). *P. falciparum*, the second most common type, is responsible for the most dangerous infection, malignant tertian malaria, which is often fatal if not treated; this organism thrives best in hot climates and is mostly confined to the tropics. *P. malariae* causes quartan malaria, a relatively uncommon form that persists because it can remain in the blood for years. *P. ovale*, the rarest type, is confined to the west coast of Africa, where it produces a mild infection.

Once the parasite had been found, it became possible to study its transmission. The idea that mosquitoes might carry the infection is mentioned in a

INTENSIVE SPRAYING of an entire malarial region for several years is the key to eradication. Here a sprayman is working in an old caravansary near Kamaradi, Iran. The World Health Organization helped Iran start its eradication campaign in 1957.

Sanskrit work of the sixth century B.C. There was no serious investigation of the matter, however, until the 1890's, after mosquitoes had been proved to transmit filariasis. Then Ronald Ross, a British army surgeon in India, undertook to find out whether they play a similar role in malaria. At first he tried infecting *Culex* and *Aëdes* mosquitoes by allowing them to feed on malaria patients, but he discovered that the parasite failed to develop in these insects. Only when he began to work with the *Anopheles* mosquito did he find a host in which the plasmodia could complete their life cycle.

Unable to continue working with human volunteers, Ross transferred his experiments to the malaria of birds. He fed mosquitoes on infected birds, then laboriously traced the parasite in its different phases of development through the organs of the insect. After hundreds of dissections he at last found the answer he was seeking. The organism completes its cycle in the salivary gland of the mosquito, in the form of sickle-shaped bodies called sporozoites.

Ross's work (for which he won a Nobel prize in 1902), together with independent and slightly later studies of human malaria by Giovanni Battista Grassi in Italy, now provided a complete picture of the life cycle of *Plasmodium*, except for one gap. After a mosquito bites a human being, several days pass before the parasite appears in the blood. Where it goes in the meantime was not discovered until 1948. In a brilliant series of experiments H. E. Shortt and P. C. C. Garnham of the London School of Hygiene and Tropical Medicine traced the missing plasmodia to the liver.

The marvelously complicated life cycle of the malaria parasite now stood fully revealed [*see illustration on pages 288 and 289*]. When sporozoites are injected by a mosquito into the bloodstream of a human being, they migrate to the liver. There they remain for six to 12 days, developing into large bodies with many nuclei, called primary tissue schizonts. At the end of the period the bodies divide into a large number of small merozoites, which enter the bloodstream and invade the red blood cells. In some species of parasite, merozoites also lodge in the liver, producing secondary tissue schizonts. These mature periodically, releasing their crop of merozoites and causing relapses, often many months after the primary attack. In the red blood cell the merozoites grow first to trophozoites and then into small, pigmented erythrocytic schizonts. In a few days the infected cell ruptures, the schizonts release a new supply of merozoites into the circulating blood, and the red blood cell cycle starts over again. Some of the parasites in the blood develop into sexual forms called gametocytes, which are taken up by a mosquito with its blood meal.

In the mosquito's stomach the male gametocyte expels hairlike flagella that enter the female gametocyte and fertilize it. The fertilized gametocyte elongates, pierces the wall of the stomach and becomes encysted on its outer sur-

MALARIA HAS DISAPPEARED OR NEVER EXISTED

MALARIAL

IN CONSOLIDATION PHASE

MALARIA ERADICATED

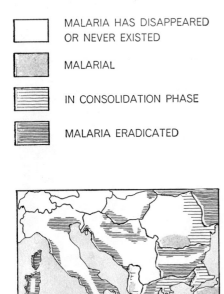

STATUS OF MALARIA throughout the world at the end of 1960 is shown on these maps. Eradication campaigns are being planned or are under way in many of the areas that are still malarial. On a map of this scale it is not possible to indicate the situation on smaller

face. Within this oöcyst thousands of sporozoites develop, to be released into the body cavity of the insect when the cyst bursts. The sporozoites migrate to the salivary glands, ready to continue their life cycle when the mosquito bites another human being.

The Control of *Anopheles*

Of some 2,000 known species of mosquito in the world, some 400 belong to the genus *Anopheles*. Females of about 100 species of the genus can harbor the malaria parasites of primates, including man. Only about 60 species, however, are sufficiently closely associated with man to rank as important vectors, or carriers of disease. Generally a continent or group of countries has no more than 10 different species of *Anopheles* that act as vectors, and often no more than one or two species are the main transmitters of malaria.

Once the role of the mosquito was recognized, malaria control became a practical possibility. Since Roman times swamps had been drained as an antimalaria measure. Now drainage was supplemented by the destruction of mosquito larvae on the surface of the water by means of poisonous substances. Shortly after the turn of the century campaigns in the Panama Canal Zone as well as in Malaya and India demonstrated that drainage and larvicides can exclude malaria from limited, intensively treated areas.

To apply these methods on a large scale, however, was prohibitively expensive and in many cases impossible. Drainage works are costly to undertake and require constant maintenance. Larvicides must be applied indefinitely and frequently. Many malarial areas contain no swamps or open waters and do not lend themselves to easy draining. Mosquitoes breed in puddles, gutters, holes in trees, wells, pools in rocks and forests, leaf axils, drains, furrows, hoofprints and other places that will hold water—many extremely difficult to locate, let alone drain or treat.

In 1935 G. A. Park-Ross and Botha de Meillon reported from South Africa that better and cheaper results could be obtained by attacking the adult mosquito with pyrethrum sprays in houses. Not only is the number of mosquitoes greatly reduced but also many die before the parasite can complete its development or before they can pass on the infection. Three years later the insecticidal effects of DDT were discovered; these effects, together with the fact that DDT sprayed on walls and ceilings retains

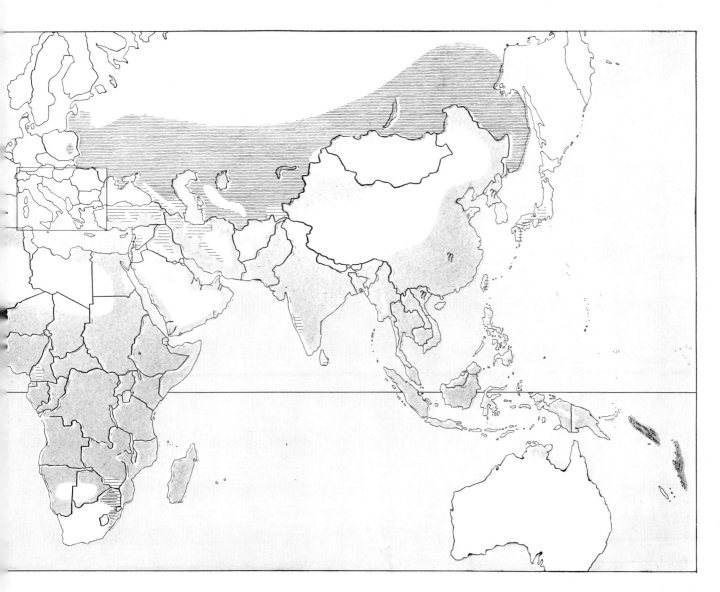

populous islands. Malaria has been eradicated on Puerto Rico and several other islands in the Caribbean; most of the remaining Caribbean islands have eradication programs. The status of malaria in mainland China, North Korea and North Vietnam is not known.

its potency for months, were to revolutionize antimalaria methods further. Female *Anopheles*, having fed on man, usually enter houses and settle there to rest and digest the blood meal that alone can ensure maturation of their eggs. On the treated surfaces they pick up a fatal dose of insecticide, from which they soon die. After the appearance of DDT other insecticides soon followed: benzene hexachloride, chlordane, dieldrin and malathion.

The Eradication of Malaria

It would be impossible to overesti-mate the importance of the change-over from the attempt to eliminate the larva to the attack on the adult mosquito. Houses, unlike potential breeding places, are easy to locate. Their area of wall surface can be closely estimated, and it is possible to forecast accurately requirements in materials, equipment, personnel and finance. Moreover, the residual effect of the insecticide reduces the number of applications to two or three a year. Thus for the first time the logistics of malaria control became relatively simple and campaigns became both operationally and economically possible.

After World War II many nations took up the new approach in earnest [see "The Eradication of Malaria," by Paul F. Russell; SCIENTIFIC AMERICAN, June, 1952]. The World Health Organization of the United Nations furnished leadership as well as technical and financial assistance. WHO inherited a long tradition of international co-operation in the fight against malaria, going back to the establishment of the Pan American Sanitary Bureau in 1902. In subsequent years the Rockefeller Foundation and the Malaria Commission of the League of Nations encouraged and helped the establishment of control schemes in many parts of the globe. The scope of their earlier

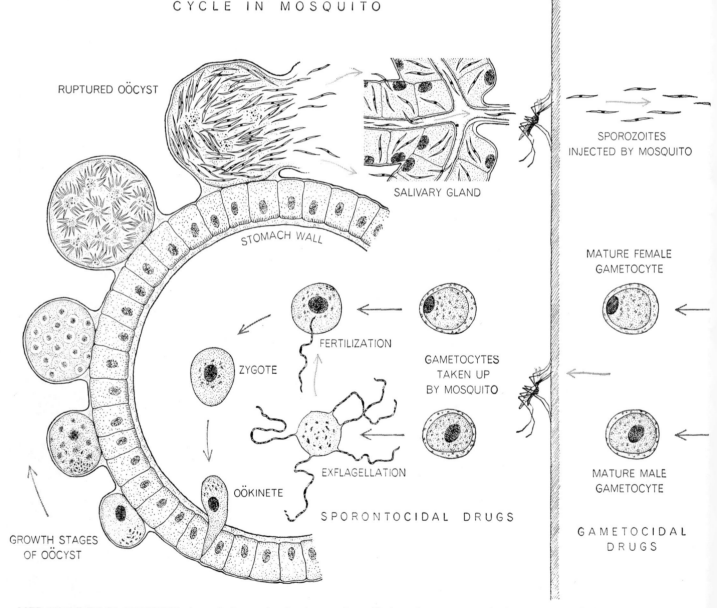

CYCLE IN MOSQUITO

RUPTURED OÖCYST

SALIVARY GLAND

SPOROZOITES INJECTED BY MOSQUITO

STOMACH WALL

MATURE FEMALE GAMETOCYTE

FERTILIZATION

ZYGOTE

GAMETOCYTES TAKEN UP BY MOSQUITO

EXFLAGELLATION

OÖKINETE

SPORONTOCIDAL DRUGS

MATURE MALE GAMETOCYTE

GROWTH STAGES OF OÖCYST

GAMETOCIDAL DRUGS

LIFE CYCLE OF *PLASMODIUM*, the malaria parasite, involves numerous changes of its form in both the mosquito and the human host. Various drugs can attack the parasite at different stages. Although most of the life cycle was known by the beginning of

efforts was set, however, by the limitations of the drainage and larvicide techniques.

Once the potentialities of large-scale spraying were demonstrated, the program expanded rapidly. The number of national malaria-control projects increased from 13 in 1949 to 29 in 1953. During the same period the number of people protected rose from 872,000 to 6.5 million. By 1955 the control of malaria had been widely extended and the idea of eradication was beginning to be considered as a real possibility. This was supported by four major considerations:

First, malaria control schemes as they then existed offered no hope of a final solution and postulated a permanent financial burden. Moreover, as soon as malaria ceased to be a problem of immediate urgency, interest flagged and it became more and more difficult to raise the funds necessary for the efficient maintenance of the control scheme. Eradication, although initially far more costly, held out hopes of a permanent solution and eventual release from heavy financial commitments.

Second, experience in Sardinia, Italy, Cyprus and British Guiana had shown that complete elimination of the *Anopheles* mosquito is not essential to eradicate malaria. One of the earliest and best-executed antimalaria programs proved this point on a large scale in Venezuela. Provided that the *Anopheles* population can be reduced below a certain critical level, transmission of the parasite is no longer maintained and the infection dies out.

Third, malaria infection in the two main forms found in man is not long lived, even in the absence of specific treatment. If, therefore, in a community, over a period of three years, all the old infections have been cured or have died out spontaneously, and if there is no importation of malaria from the out-

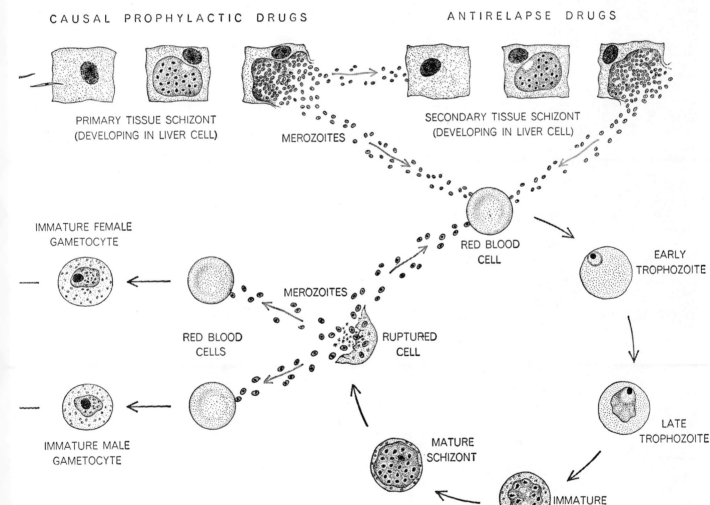

CYCLE IN MAN

CAUSAL PROPHYLACTIC DRUGS

ANTIRELAPSE DRUGS

PRIMARY TISSUE SCHIZONT
(DEVELOPING IN LIVER CELL)

MEROZOITES

SECONDARY TISSUE SCHIZONT
(DEVELOPING IN LIVER CELL)

IMMATURE FEMALE
GAMETOCYTE

RED BLOOD
CELL

EARLY
TROPHOZOITE

MEROZOITES

RED BLOOD
CELLS

RUPTURED
CELL

LATE
TROPHOZOITE

IMMATURE MALE
GAMETOCYTE

MATURE
SCHIZONT

IMMATURE
SCHIZONT

SCHIZONTOCIDAL DRUGS

this century, it was not until 1948 that the primary tissue stage in the liver was discovered. The light, wavy arrows here represent actual movement of the parasite from one place to another; the heavier arrows denote changes in the many stages of development.

SIR RONALD ROSS, who proved that mosquitoes transmit malaria, is shown with his wife, assistants and bird cages in Calcutta in 1898. He obtained the final proof in his monumental studies by infecting the mosquitoes with avian, not human, parasites.

side, no further infection should arise.

Fourth, the alarming reports of mosquito resistance to insecticides called for rapid and decisive action. Only by an intensification of effort, by the inclusion of all possible malarial areas and by the radical interruption of transmission in the shortest possible time could man hope to win his fight with malaria.

This last point was of particular significance. In 1951 the first reports of resistance of *Anopheles* to DDT had come from Greece. Even more disturbing were the later reports of higher degrees of resistance to some of the newer insecticides. In 1956 only five species of *Anopheles* were involved, but by the end of 1960 resistance had appeared in populations of 29 species, 16 of them important malaria vectors. At the present time most of the cases of resistance are to dieldrin or related compounds, some to DDT, and in a few cases resistance to both groups was reported. If the opportunity to eliminate malaria were not seized in time, the resistance of the mosquitoes might eventually put it out of reach. This explains why so much basic and applied research on the problem of resistance is now in progress.

The Eradication Campaign

The goal of the global eradication of malaria was formally adopted at the Eighth World Health Assembly in 1955. A resolution put the program under the supervision of WHO and the Pan American Health Organization. It also set up a special account for funds to be donated by UN member nations to help defray the additional cost of eradication campaigns.

These campaigns differ from control projects in the thoroughness with which they are planned and carried out. The time factor is a very important one; once spraying has started no delays can be tolerated. Careful preparation and accurate planning must cover all possible contingencies that might hold up the scheme. Spraying with a residual insecticide must cover the area completely in order to interrupt transmission as rapidly as possible. Thereafter all remaining cases of malaria must be detected and treated to prevent the reestablishment of transmission.

The campaign proper is preceded by a pre-eradication survey to delimit the malarial area of the country, to obtain data on the prevalence of malaria and to assess the effects of the disease on the population. In addition, an entomological investigation provides information on the local vectors and on their susceptibility to insecticides. Type, dosage and frequency of application of the insecticide are also determined at this stage. Existing facilities are examined and estimates made for supplies and equipment, transport and budget. On this basic information a plan of operations is drawn up that must be agreed on and signed by the government of the country concerned before the first phase of the campaign can be undertaken.

This preparatory phase consists of a geographical reconnaissance; that is, the enumeration of houses, the establishment of administrative boundaries and the arranging of itineraries. It also covers the setting up of laboratories and entomological units, the recruitment and training of spraying teams, technicians and administrative personnel and the organization of transport and supplies. During this period also comes the buildup of public relations and the health education of the population. If necessary legislation must be sought to ensure right of entry for the spraying teams and the enforcement of compulsory notification of malaria cases in the later stages. The preparatory phase must cover at least one year in order to take into account changing seasonal conditions.

Following the preparatory phase comes the attack phase: intensive, total-coverage spraying. At the same time infection rates and entomological findings are constantly reviewed to assess progress. Careful watch is kept for signs of resistance in the mosquito population. After a period of three to four years spraying may be stopped if it has been shown that transmission has been definitely interrupted and infection rates have been reduced to well below one per 2,000 of population.

Next is the phase of consolidation. All remaining pockets of transmission must be eliminated by small-scale spraying, and all people still infected must be cured. The main activity now consists in the detection of cases. This means checking every person with fever symptoms, by house-to-house visits and by screening fever patients in hospitals and clinics. All suspected cases are reported, and blood samples are promptly sent to the laboratory. Every person with confirmed malaria must undergo treatment at once.

These activities continue for at least three years. If at the end of that time no new infections are turning up, the program passes into its final phase of maintenance. A special organization is no longer required. The procedure now falls within the normal routine of the local health services. Reporting of malaria remains compulsory and all cases are treated by the local doctor or nurse. As far as possible the origin of each infection must be traced so that potential sources of disease can be dealt with.

The foregoing outline hardly suggests the magnitude of the effort and the difficulties that lie in its way. In 1959, for example, more than 100 million houses were sprayed. The campaign required 130,000 sprayers and consumed 60,000 tons of insecticide. On the medical side no fewer than 45 million blood smears are now being examined annually by 3,000 microscopists working full time. In some countries transport alone constitutes a herculean task. Elsewhere the chief problem may be the structure of the houses (which sometimes consist of no more than a roof and four posts), the habit of replastering or repainting houses at frequent intervals, or the nomadic life of the population and the impermanence of dwellings and settlements. Another difficulty is that some species of *Anopheles* tend to bite out of doors and do not settle on walls afterward.

Moreover, the efficiency of the spraying campaign—that is, the speed with which it interrupts transmission of malaria—depends on the type of malaria encountered. In intensely malarial areas transmission is high, a large proportion of the population is infected, the mosquito vector has a relatively long life and the climate favors rapid development of the parasite and repeated infection in the course of the year. Here the density and longevity of the vector must be reduced to a very low level to interrupt transmission. This requires a correspondingly long and intense effort.

As has been mentioned, a spraying campaign must go hand in hand with a continuous and accurate measurement of the amount of infection in the region. In the early stages this incidence can be determined by two classical methods: palpation of the spleen to detect its enlargement and examination of blood smears in random samples of the population. When the infection rate drops below 3 per cent, however, these methods are no longer sensitive enough. Then the only way to assess the amount of malaria remaining is to find and check every case of fever. In areas of endemic malaria even this may not be good enough. People who suffer frequent infection throughout life may develop a degree of tolerance to the parasite and show few, if any, clinical symptoms of their infection. Such carriers are the source of persistent infection in a community, and blood examination of the entire population is the only means of detecting them.

Antimalaria Drugs

Although total-coverage spraying is largely responsible for interrupting the transmission of malaria, the final clean-up can be accomplished only by using drugs to treat the remaining cases. The wide variety of synthetic antimalaria compounds now available is a legacy of World War II research, when the Japanese occupation of Indonesia cut off supplies of quinine. Some of the synthetic drugs—such as proguanil and pyrimethamine—are prophylactics; they prevent the establishment of the parasite in the liver, cutting the infection short before symptoms appear. Others —including quinine, mepacrine (atebrin), chloroquine and amodiaquin— attack the plasmodia in the red blood cells and are used for treatment. Pamaquine and the new primaquine also kill gametocytes, thereby interrupting transmission from man to mosquito. Anti-relapse drugs—such as primaquine—act on secondary tissue schizonts in the liver cells.

Mass drug administration has often been advocated as a means of eradicating malaria. Unfortunately all these drugs are rapidly excreted by the body and when used for prevention of malaria must be administered frequently and regularly. In military units and similar organized groups such mass administration of drugs has been most successful. On a country-wide scale, however, this approach, which would mean frequent and regular dosing of every man, woman and child in a large population, poses insoluble problems of organization, distribution and, above all, persuasion. Underdeveloped countries with inadequate health services are particularly unsuited to such an attempt.

Interestingly enough, the ingenious large-scale use of drugs has been introduced in certain parts of Brazil. Because one of the chief vectors in the area is an outdoor biter, and because most of the local houses have no walls, the spraying campaign met with little success. Chemotherapy seemed to be the only answer, but the vast territory involved, the inaccessibility of many villages and the shy and even hostile attitude of the more remote people made the direct distribution of drugs impossible. Mario Pinotti, the Brazilian Minister of Health, decided to add chloroquine to salt, much as iodine has been added in regions of endemic goiter. A government monopoly guaranteed that the whole population would get the medicated salt. It was expected that if everyone in the area received enough chloroquine to suppress malaria, this method would be completely effective. Pinotti's method is now undergoing field trials in several countries.

Meanwhile the plasmodium, like the mosquito, is developing resistance to some drugs. In certain parts of the world malaria parasites do not respond normally to the prophylactic drugs proguanil and pyrimethamine; in Colombia resistance to chloroquine and amodiaquin has been reported. The search for new antimalaria compounds continues, with the hope not only of keeping ahead of the developing resistance but also of some day finding a drug that will be ef-

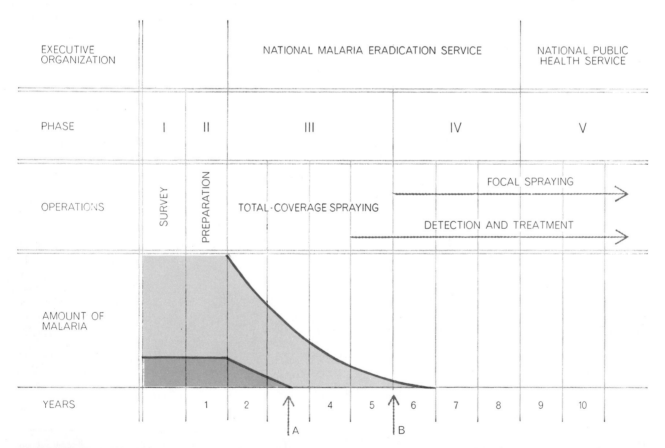

ERADICATION CAMPAIGN proceeds in well-defined phases taking about eight years. This chart shows a typical program: I, pre-eradication survey; II, preparatory phase; III, attack phase; IV, consolidation; V, maintenance. Lightly shaded area indicates decline in reservoir of old infections; deeper shading denotes rate of transmission or new infections. Arrow A marks interruption of transmission, B an infection rate of only one person in 2,000, at which point total-coverage spraying of the malarial region can end.

fective over a long period when given in a single dose.

In spite of all the practical problems, and of the growing resistance of mosquitoes and parasites, there is no doubt that well-planned eradication campaigns, unhindered by financial or administrative difficulties, can achieve complete success. Starting its campaign in 1952, the U.S.S.R. has eliminated malaria from the whole of its vast area. It was able to assign almost unlimited personnel to the task and to make use of its widespread network of public health units. Venezuela and Mexico have carried out their programs with outstanding drive and determination. In the latter country an imaginative educational effort enlisted the active support of all citizens, and the logistics of the program was planned and assisted by the Mexican army. At present India is conducting the biggest campaign, covering a population of 420 million. When it began in 1958, the Indian program ran into a number of difficulties, in large part because of its very size, but it is now progressing so satisfactorily that in the spring of 1962 areas inhabited by 140 million passed from the attack phase to the phase of consolidation. Mainland China, where mosquitoes are classed with flies, rats and sparrows as one of the four great

plagues, is known to be attacking malaria, but it has released little information on methods or results. On Taiwan a well-planned and well-executed malaria eradication program has met with outstanding success.

Two years ago an interesting incidental finding was considered by some to be a new threat to the goal of eradication. Some workers in a laboratory carrying out research on lower monkeys contracted an infection of *Plasmodium cynomolgi bastianellii*, which had previously been thought to be a purely simian parasite. Studies in the U.S. confirmed the ability of the parasite to infect man and also showed that it can be transmitted from man to monkey to man by an *Anopheles* mosquito. This remarkable discovery posed the problem of the feasibility of malaria eradication in areas where infected monkeys are numerous and live in comparatively close association with man.

It does not seem that these fears were justified. What is actually known is that two strains of malaria parasite of lower monkeys from Malaya can survive and develop in man and in lower monkeys, and that two species of North American *Anopheles* can transmit the infection under experimental conditions. That such transmission can occur in nature

is far from certain. It is not known whether other species of *Anopheles* mosquitoes, in Malaya or elsewhere, feed on monkeys in the wild, nor whether the insects become infected, nor whether they enter human dwellings and feed on man often enough to maintain the chain of transmission. The possible significance of simian malaria as a reservoir of infection for man will be clear only when human malaria comes close to the vanishing point in Malaya, Borneo, Indonesia, the Philippines, Brazil and Taiwan, where the monkeys may be infected.

The WHO Effort

A few figures will give an idea of the present extent of the international eradication effort. In 1961 the population living in malarial or previously malarial regions throughout the world amounted to 1,420 million. Of these, 317 million now live in malaria-free areas and 710 million more in places where eradication programs are now under way. Preliminary planning has begun in countries having a population of 170 million. This leaves some 223 million as yet totally unprotected.

Not all the programs are equally successful. Some have been disappointing

MALARIA CONVOY in Burma uses elephants. Tanks of spray guns can be seen on first two elephants. One of the most difficult aspects of an eradication campaign in countries without numerous roads is simply reaching the dwelling places in outlying areas.

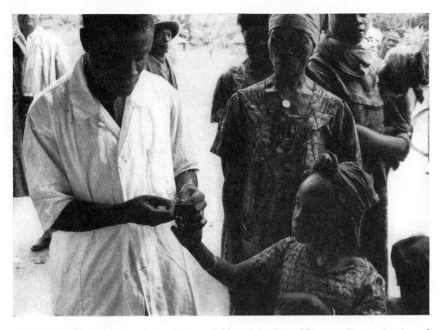

BLOOD SAMPLE is taken from African child in Cameroon. Microscopic examination of smear on slide will reveal any malaria parasites. Blood sampling is a key part of a campaign.

SALT CONTAINING CHLOROQUINE, an antimalaria drug, is distributed in Cambodia. The medicated salt helps eliminate malaria where spraying is not completely effective.

so far. Nevertheless, there is every reason for optimism. At the present rate of progress malaria should be eradicated from continental Europe by the end of 1962, and from the Americas, North Africa and a large part of Asia within the next 10 years. Progress in much of Africa is slower, however, and it would be difficult to make a forecast at this stage.

What is the cost of ridding the world of this burden? In 1959 WHO made a highly conjectural estimate of $1,691 million. For 1958 and 1959 an annual expenditure of $90 million can be definitely accounted for, and in 1960 $103 million. More than half of this amount came from the countries directly concerned. The rest was furnished by WHO, the United Nations International Children's Emergency Fund, the UN Technical Assistance Board, the Pan American Health Organization and U.S. bilateral funds. The sums mentioned do not include contributions from other sources, such as the Colombo Plan of the British Commonwealth, the French FIDES funds and other types of bilateral assistance.

Although the over-all contribution of the international agencies is much less than that of national governments, the international funds play an important catalyzing role. In many cases national funds would not have been forthcoming without the stimulus of international assistance. Until 1955 the financial requirements of the malaria campaign remained well within the regular budget of WHO. Thereafter they increased so rapidly that in 1955 the Malaria Eradication Special Account was created, the funds to be provided on a voluntary basis by member states of the UN. By the end of 1960 the total amount received or pledged amounted to $12,-772,000, of which $11 million came from the U.S. Unfortunately many countries that had never known malaria, or that had been free from the disease for a long time, gave little or nothing, and the contributions fell far short of actual needs. The World Health Assembly in New Delhi in 1961 therefore decided to finance malaria eradication programs out of the regular budget of WHO. As economic conditions improve and production rises in underdeveloped countries, they will be able to bear more of the costs. However, since most eradication schemes require at least eight years to reach the maintenance phase and since many areas are only in the planning stage, financial relief will not come soon.

In addition to helping to finance eradication programs, the funds disbursed by WHO support a massive program of research and training. Laboratories in many parts of the world are now carrying out a promising large-scale search for new insecticides. WHO has prepared and distributed special test kits for determining the susceptibility of different species of *Anopheles* to various insecticides. This information is useful not only in planning specific campaigns but also in fundamental studies of the biochemistry and genetics of resistance. Other entomological research is concerned with mosquito behavior, distribution, species differentiation and ecology; the chemistry of insecticides is also being studied. Parasitology, chemotherapy and epidemiology are the subjects of important research projects. To provide at least the cadres that can set up and operate eradication programs, WHO organizes courses for physicians, sanitarians, entomologists, laboratory technicians and administrative officers.

It is frequently said that antimalaria campaigns are adding to the world's woes by contributing to a population "explosion" in underdeveloped countries. There is no doubt that the malariologist's work invariably reduces death rates and increases longevity. To this he pleads guilty; but this indictment must be shared by the physicians who cure or prevent any disease, the engineers who build dams and pipe water supplies, the architects who convert slums into clean houses, and generally by all who in any way contribute to the improvement of health standards. But if some lives are saved and others prolonged, it is also true that regained health and energy are reflected in well-tended crops, more abundant harvests, reclamation of long neglected lands and regular attendance in workshop or factory.

This is not to deny that the rise in population has often outrun the rise in productivity and economic development. In countries where it has happened there is so much to do and there are so many problems to solve that progress cannot be uniform on all fronts. The best that the public health worker can do is to attempt to co-ordinate medical progress with progress in general and, where possible, to direct his efforts at those infections that play the most important part in the vicious circle of poverty, ignorance and disease. Healthy and educated populations are a prerequisite of rapid social and economic advance. In highly malarial countries no real progress in any field is possible until the burden of disease is lifted and men are free to give their full strength to the task of building a better life.

32

Insect Control and the Balance of Nature

by Ray F. Smith and William W. Allen
June 1954

The common alfalfa caterpillar provides a good example of how a pest may be controlled not only with insecticides but also by manipulating the ecological system of which it is a part

The activities of man are continually making changes in what has so inappropriately been called "the balance of nature." He has cleared the forest, plowed the plain, changed the courses of rivers, bred new plants and animals, introduced plants and animals into new areas, protected some from competition and provided others with new foods on which to flourish. For instance, the Colorado potato beetle, once an insignificant insect feeding on wild herbs in the Rocky Mountain region, has grown abundant on the cultivated potato.

Even in the absence of man, however, the balance of nature is a dynamic and ever-changing system. The relative numbers of the various kinds of plants and animals in the simplest natural community fluctuate constantly in accord with a complex web of interactions that ties them together. Under normal conditions the system as a whole tends to be self-regulating. Such factors as parasites, predators, disease, food supply and the competition for shelter keep any one organism from upsetting the balance. If man is to make a move that will shift the balance in his favor, he must understand all of the ramifications of the system.

Thus control of insect pests cannot be assured simply by inventing new and more potent insecticides. Our spectacular new chemical weapons have added immeasurably to the welfare of mankind. But they have also created new problems of their own; witness the phenomenal increase of destructive mites that has followed the slaughter of their insect enemies with DDT and other new insecticides, and the rise of new strains of insects resistant to the poisons. Chemical control is at best temporary. If we are to escape this ever tightening spiral of more complex problems and ever increasing costs of control, then we must integrate chemical control with the natural factors influencing populations.

For progress in this direction in recent years we are indebted to the science of ecology. This is the study of the interrelationships of organisms and their environment. We shall here recount such a study of an insect, carried out during the past 15 years in California, which will illustrate how complex these relationships can be. The insect is the orange alfalfa caterpillar, *Colias philodice eurytheme.*

In its adult form the insect is the common orange and yellow butterfly seen flitting about alfalfa and clover fields in summer. In alfalfa-growing sections of the country the butterflies often are so abundant that they clog the radiator

BUTTERFLIES of the alfalfa caterpillar are shown actual size. At the upper left is the female of the species from above; at the lower left, the same individual from the bottom. At the upper right is the male; at the lower right, the same individual from the bottom.

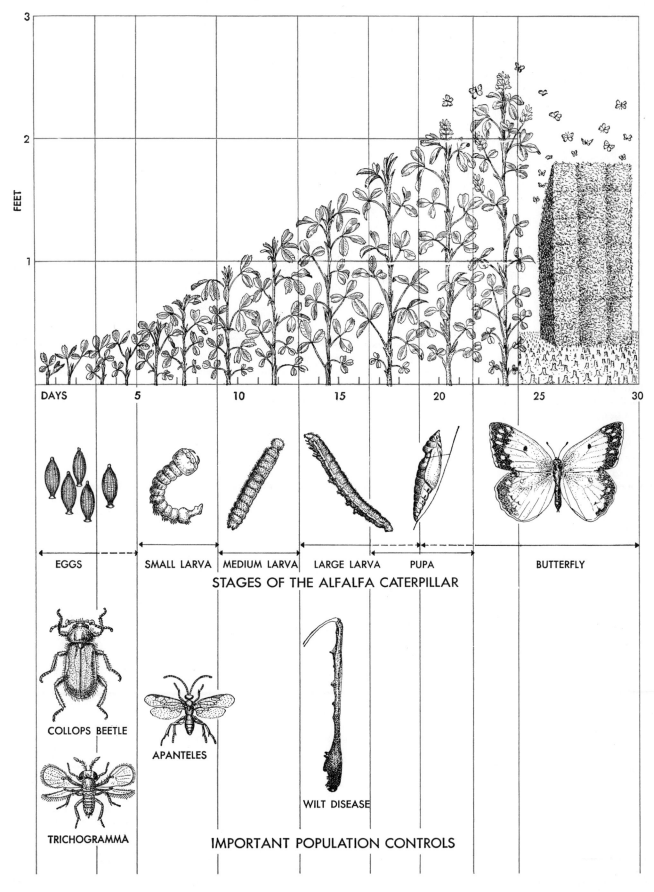

FEET

3

2

1

DAYS   5   10   15   20   25   30

EGGS   SMALL LARVA   MEDIUM LARVA   LARGE LARVA   PUPA   BUTTERFLY

STAGES OF THE ALFALFA CATERPILLAR

COLLOPS BEETLE

APANTELES

WILT DISEASE

TRICHOGRAMMA

IMPORTANT POPULATION CONTROLS

STAGES of the alfalfa caterpillar (*middle*) are geared to the growth and harvest of alfalfa (*top*). The important population controls of the caterpillar (*bottom*) are the *Collops* beetle and the wasp *Trichogramma minutum*, which eat its eggs; the wasp *Apanteles medicaginis*, which lays eggs in its small larvae; and wilt disease, which turns the large larvae into a semiliquid mass.

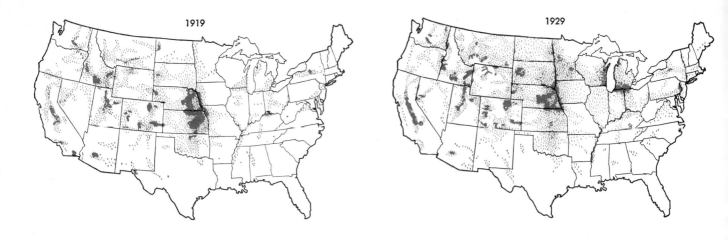

EASTWARD SPREAD of both alfalfa and the alfalfa caterpillar is indicated by these maps of the U. S. The map at the far left shows the pattern of alfalfa cultivation in 1919; the map second from the left, the pattern of cultivation in 1929; the map third from the left,

grills of automobiles. The female lays tiny, cigar-shaped eggs on the leaves of young alfalfa. In summer the eggs hatch in about three days; in cooler seasons they take up to 10 days or more. After hatching, the tiny caterpillar eats its eggshell and then begins to feed on young alfalfa leaves. Three days later it makes its first molt; it sheds its skin four times before it is fully grown. After each molt the caterpillar and its appetite increase in size. By the time it is full-grown it may consume more than a dozen leaves a day. After about 12 days (in hot weather) the caterpillar descends to the base of the plant to pupate. Five or six days later the beautiful butterfly emerges.

During the summer it has two peaks of activity each day. It spends the night near the base of the plant. After sunrise it crawls up the plant and turns its body to receive the maximum radiation from the sun. After its body temperature has warmed up to the necessary level, it takes off in flight. It feeds on flower nectar and stops from time to time to lay eggs. During the heat of midday it siestas in the cool alfalfa or on the moist soil. Then in the afternoon it goes forth again to flit about until the sun sinks.

The males spend most of their time seeking young females; the latter mate just after they have emerged from the pupal state. After mating, the female leaves the field in which it developed. To provide its young with proper food, it always lays its eggs on a young, succulent legume. This remarkable adaptation, originally evolved for survival on wild plants, stands the insect in excellent stead in alfalfa fields. Its eggs are laid only on very young alfalfa shoots; as a result the caterpillars can complete their development before the hay is cut.

Because females concentrate for egg-laying in recently cut fields where a new crop is beginning to leaf out, alfalfa fields can be classified according to the stage of development of their caterpillars. First is the egg-laying stage, when the alfalfa is short; the field is populated mainly by egg-laying females. In the second stage, when the alfalfa is less than a third grown, its population is mainly tiny larvae. In the third, when the alfalfa is about half grown and the larvae are bigger, it becomes possible to predict how much damage the population will do and to decide on preventive measures. In the fourth stage, the larvae do much damage to the maturing alfalfa. In the fifth, when the alfalfa is mature or nearly so, the field is full of pupae and butterflies, about three fourths of which are males. Any caterpillars that have not become butterflies when the field is mowed are out of luck—they die in the hot sun.

The critical requirements of the alfalfa caterpillar probably are: (1) a sufficient concentration of suitable legumes, (2) a period of warm weather long enough for the development of at least one generation, and (3) suitable places for survival during the unfavorable times of the year. These broad requirements can be met in many different ways, and the alfalfa caterpillar is therefore widespread in the U. S. [see map on the opposite page]. Its range changes with the seasons and the year-to-year fluctuations in the weather; for example, the butterflies migrate north in the spring and invade desert areas when rains produce legumes there. In the past few decades the alfalfa caterpillar has expanded tremendously in the Eastern U. S. since Eastern farmers began to lime the soil and grow alfalfa.

A single female butterfly can lay as many as 1,500 eggs. We would soon be smothered by alfalfa caterpillars but for a complex of natural control factors which we do not yet completely understand. The abundance of this insect, like that of any other organism, depends on natality and mortality. These in turn are determined by a complex system of ecological relationships which we call an ecosystem. The ecosystem includes the influences and relationships of all the living and non-living parts of the environment, among which must be counted food supply, weather, natural enemies and the caterpillar population itself. Because of its great complexity it is difficult, if not impossible, to study an ecosystem per se. However, we can study a particular kind of organism in its relationships to the ecosystem. Such a study has revealed some of the factors influencing the abundance of the alfalfa caterpillar.

When the alfalfa caterpillar was first discovered in California about 1850, its population level was much lower than today. It lived on scattered native legumes such as lupine, clover, lotus and locoweed, which are most abundant during the late spring. In summer it was restricted to streams and rivers or the mountains. Now not only its range but its population density has been increased enormously by the growing of alfalfa—today covering more than a million and a half acres in California. Alfalfa and certain cultivated clovers supply it with an abundance of food throughout the year. Furthermore, the concentrated cultivation of alfalfa in fields close together favors the reproduction of the caterpillars. Since the fields are not likely to be in the same stage of growth, the butterflies emerging from one field have a good chance of finding a nearby field which is

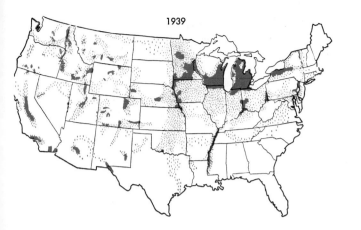

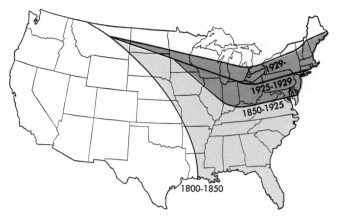

the pattern of cultivation in 1939. In the latter year the acreage of alfalfa cut for hay constituted about 20 per cent of the total acreage of hay. The fourth map shows the spread of the alfalfa caterpillar from 1850 (*lightest green area*) to the present (*darkest green area*).

in the proper stage for egg-laying. Thus a moderate outbreak in one field can result in a severe outbreak in another. This explains why some fields are hard hit while others nearby may be undamaged.

Within a given field the extent of the outbreak and the damage done will, of course, depend upon the growth pattern of the alfalfa, which in turn is influenced by the type of soil, drainage, irrigation methods, rainfall, topography and cultivation. Cool weather greatly affects the egg-laying of the females, since, as cold-blooded animals, they need warmth to become active. The alfalfa caterpillar passes the severest part of the winter as a small larva. In the short summer of the northern parts of its range only one generation can mature; in mild southern climates there may be as many as seven in a year. In the hot Imperial Valley the population peaks in the spring and fall. In the cool coastal areas of California, where it takes more than 40 days for a larva to develop into a butterfly, the insects do not thrive; the alfalfa is not retarded as much as the caterpillars, hence the hay is cut before the butterflies can emerge. If growers were to change to cutting the alfalfa later, the caterpillars probably would become more abundant.

California's San Joaquin Valley is highly favorable to caterpillars. But in that area the density of the caterpillar population itself provides a measure of control by bringing into play what the ecologist calls density-dependent factors. These are factors in which the intensity of effect increases as population density increases. Competition for food is such a factor, but it is not ordinarily important in the regulation of alfalfa caterpillar populations. Here the most important density-dependent factors are the insect's natural enemies. Among them are

beetles, dragonflies, viruses and parasitic wasps. The relationships of the alfalfa caterpillar to some of its enemies are summarized in the chart on the next page. The chart, however, does not show the indirect relationship of the alfalfa caterpillar to other organisms. For example, some of its enemies feed on a great many other hosts and are able to maintain their population levels even when the number of alfalfa caterpillars is low. Nor does the chart show the seasonal aspects of the picture. The parasitic wasp *Pterocormus instabilis* is of importance only during the spring months; the virus disease becomes important in late summer.

The tiny wasp *Apanteles medicaginis* is one of the most important parasites on the caterpillar population. The female wasp lays an egg in the caterpillar when it is a small larva. When the egg itself hatches into a larva, it feeds in the caterpillar's interior and retards its growth. After about a week the wasp larva emerges from its host and spins a bright yellow or white silken cocoon on the alfalfa leaves. The attacked caterpillar dies. The larvae of this little parasitic wasp are to be found in caterpillars throughout the year. They become more numerous, however, during the summer months when caterpillars are most abundant.

Each year *Apanteles* saves thousands of acres of alfalfa from damage. It has its own requirements, however, which must be met if it is to help farmers. It needs nectar or aphid honeydew as food. Since the wasp, like the caterpillar, must leave the alfalfa fields when they are cut, it can be fully effective only in areas where other food sources are plentiful. Weeds in fence rows and along irrigation ditches can provide it with nourishment.

If *Apanteles* fails to keep the caterpillar population at a low level, the population may be heavily attacked by a virus disease known to farmers as "wilt." The virus, harbored throughout the year in the soil and surface debris, infects the caterpillars only after it has contaminated the alfalfa. After the insects have fed on infected plants, they transmit the virus among themselves. An infected caterpillar soon stops feeding and dies. Then the body breaks down into a semi-liquid mass, which contaminates the surrounding leaves. In this way small foci of wilt develop, and soon the virus becomes widespread in the population. The wilt disease may completely destroy a large population in a few days.

Ordinarily an epizootic of this disease does not occur until the insects have badly damaged the alfalfa. However, one may be initiated artificially by spraying the alfalfa fields with virus when the caterpillars are small. Spraying with a certain bacillus which does not occur naturally in populations of the alfalfa caterpillar also is highly effective against the insect. In the application of these pathogens the proper timing is obviously important.

Let us turn now to the problem of the alfalfa farmer who must decide what to do about the insect situation in his field. It should be apparent from our brief description of some of the many interacting factors that every alfalfa field is a special problem, and the situation must be judged in the light of a complex ecological picture. Farmers know that the infestations vary from field to field and from time to time, and that by the time they have discovered an infestation it is usually too late to do much about it. Furthermore, it does not pay to do gen-

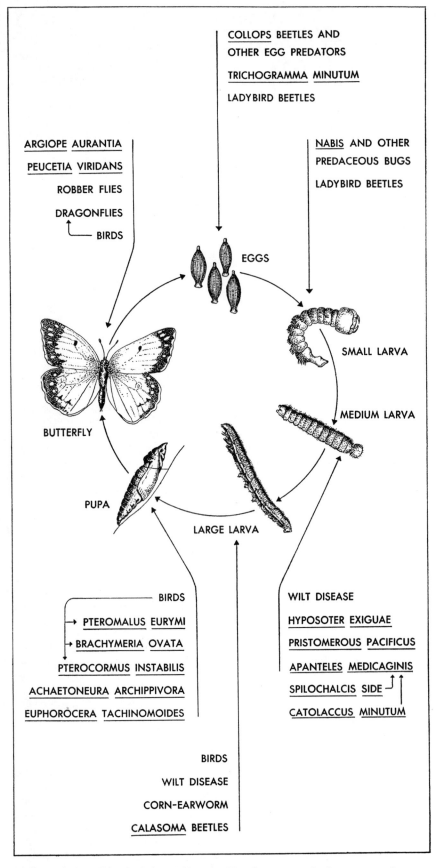

COLLOPS BEETLES AND
OTHER EGG PREDATORS
TRICHOGRAMMA MINUTUM
LADYBIRD BEETLES

ARGIOPE AURANTIA
PEUCETIA VIRIDANS
ROBBER FLIES
DRAGONFLIES
BIRDS

NABIS AND OTHER
PREDACEOUS BUGS
LADYBIRD BEETLES

EGGS

SMALL LARVA

MEDIUM LARVA

BUTTERFLY

PUPA

LARGE LARVA

BIRDS
PTEROMALUS EURYMI
BRACHYMERIA OVATA
PTEROCORMUS INSTABILIS
ACHAETONEURA ARCHIPPIVORA
EUPHOROCERA TACHINOMOIDES

WILT DISEASE
HYPOSOTER EXIGUAE
PRISTOMEROUS PACIFICUS
APANTELES MEDICAGINIS
SPILOCHALCIS SIDE
CATOLACCUS MINUTUM

BIRDS
WILT DISEASE
CORN-EARWORM
CALASOMA BEETLES

ECOLOGICAL SYSTEM of the alfalfa caterpillar shows not only the creatures that prey on it but also some of the creatures that control the predators. *Trichogramma, Hyposoter, Pristomerous, Apanteles, Spilochalcis, Catolaccus, Pteromalus, Brachymeria* and *Pterocormus* are wasps. *Achaetoneura* and *Euphorocera* are flies. *Argiope* and *Peucetia* are spiders.

eral preventive spraying of hay crops. The farmer needs a way of predicting what will happen in his fields so that he can apply control measures only where necessary.

As an answer to the farmer's dilemma a supervised control system has been developed in California. The farmer, or a group of farmers, hires an entomologist to follow the insect populations in the fields. On the basis of the conditions peculiar to each field and of his knowledge of the ecology of the alfalfa caterpillar, the entomologist makes a prediction early in the growth of the crop as to whether or not economic damage will occur. If the crop is threatened, he may suggest in some situations that the alfalfa be mowed a few days early to avoid damage. The caterpillars on the cut hay will be destroyed by the sun, and the ratio of parasites to caterpillars in the area will be shifted in favor of the parasites. In other cases he may recommend an application of the virus or the bacillus or a combination of the two. Since the timing is critical, they should be applied under supervised control. In still other cases he may prescribe chemical spraying. The insecticide should be one which will not leave any harmful residue on the hay, will not injure the plants, will cause minimum harm to the parasites, and will control the caterpillars economically. Thus far we have no such perfect insecticide; the closest to meeting the requirements are methoxychlor and perthane. Fortunately chemicals harmful to the parasite are not altogether excluded, because they may be used in fields where the caterpillar population is relatively high and the parasite population relatively low. Perhaps not the least of the benefits of the supervised control program to the farmer is the peace of mind he has through the assurance that his fields are under the constant supervision of qualified personnel.

This has been the story of the application of ecological research to the alfalfa caterpillar problem in California. Research is continuing on this problem and further benefits will accrue. The same approach is being made to insect problems in other parts of the world. We have a long way to go to unravel all the strands of this ecosystem of which man is a part. However, we are now in a position to take more intelligent steps toward an integrated control program which will utilize all the resources of ecology and give us the most permanent, satisfactory and economical insect control that is possible.

Third-Generation Pesticides

by Carroll M. Williams
July 1967

*The first generation is exemplified by arsenate of lead;
the second, by DDT. Now insect hormones promise to
provide insecticides that are not only more specific but
also proof against the evolution of resistance*

M an's efforts to control harmful insects with pesticides have encountered two intractable difficulties. The first is that the pesticides developed up to now have been too broad in their effect. They have been toxic not only to the pests at which they were aimed but also to other insects. Moreover, by persisting in the environment—and sometimes even increasing in concentration as they are passed along the food chain—they have presented a hazard to other organisms, including man. The second difficulty is that insects have shown a remarkable ability to develop resistance to pesticides.

Plainly the ideal approach would be to find agents that are highly specific in their effect, attacking only insects that are regarded as pests, and that remain effective because the insects cannot acquire resistance to them. Recent findings indicate that the possibility of achieving success along these lines is much more likely than it seemed a few years ago. The central idea embodied in these findings is that a harmful species of insect can be attacked with its own hormones.

Insects, according to the latest estimates, comprise about three million species—far more than all other animal and plant species combined. The number of individual insects alive at any one time is thought to be about a billion billion (10^{18}). Of this vast multitude 99.9 percent are from the human point of view either innocuous or downright helpful. A few are indispensable; one need think only of the role of bees in pollination.

The troublemakers are the other .1 percent, amounting to about 3,000 species. They are the agricultural pests and the vectors of human and animal disease. Those that transmit human disease are the most troublesome; they have joined with the bacteria, viruses and protozoa in what has sometimes seemed like a grand conspiracy to exterminate man, or at least to keep him in a state of perpetual ill health.

The fact that the human species is still here is an abiding mystery. Presumably the answer lies in changes in the genetic makeup of man. The example of sickle-cell anemia is instructive. The presence of sickle-shaped red blood cells in a person's blood can give rise to a serious form of anemia, but it also confers resistance to malaria. The sickle-cell trait (which does not necessarily lead to sickle-cell anemia) is appreciably more common in Negroes than in members of other populations. Investigations have suggested that the sickle cell is a genetic mutation that occurred long ago in malarial regions of Africa. Apparently attrition by malaria-carrying mosquitoes provoked countermeasures deep within the genes of primitive men.

The evolution of a genetic defense, however, takes many generations and entails many deaths. It was only in comparatively recent times that man found an alternative answer by learning to combat the insects with chemistry. He did so by inventing what can be called the first-generation pesticides: kerosene to coat the ponds, arsenate of lead to poison the pests that chew, nicotine and rotenone for the pests that suck.

Only 25 years ago did man devise the far more potent weapon that was the first of the second-generation pesticides. The weapon was dichlorodiphenyltrichloroethane, or DDT. It descended on the noxious insects like an avenging angel. On contact with it mosquitoes, flies, beetles—almost all the insects—were stricken with what might be called the "DDT's." They went into a tailspin, buzzed around upside down for an hour or so and then dropped dead.

The age-old battle with the insects appeared to have been won. We had the stuff to do them in—or so we thought. A few wise men warned that we were living in a fool's paradise and that the insects would soon become resistant to DDT, just as the bacteria had managed to develop a resistance to the challenge of sulfanilamide. That is just what happened. Within a few years the mosquitoes, lice, houseflies and other noxious insects were taking DDT in their stride. Soon they were metabolizing it, then they became addicted to it and were therefore in a position to try harder.

Fortunately the breach was plugged by the chemical industry, which had come to realize that killing insects was —in more ways than one—a formula for

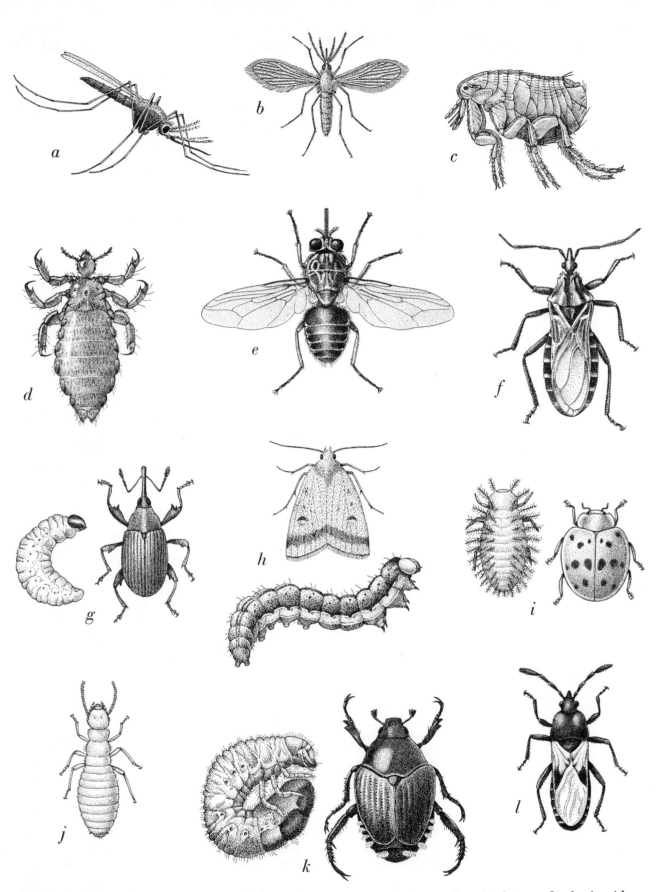

INSECT PESTS that might be controlled by third-generation pesticides include some 3,000 species, of which 12 important examples are shown here. Six (a–f) transmit diseases to human beings; the other six are agricultural pests. The disease-carriers, together with the major disease each transmits, are (a) the *Anopheles* mosquito, malaria; (b) the sand fly, leishmaniasis; (c) the rat flea, plague; (d) the body louse, typhus; (e) the tsetse fly, sleeping sickness, and (f) the kissing bug, Chagas' disease. The agricultural pests, four of which are depicted in both larval and adult form, are (g) the boll weevil; (h) the corn earworm; (i) the Mexican bean beetle; (j) the termite; (k) the Japanese beetle, and (l) the chinch bug. The species in the illustration are not drawn to the same scale.

getting along in the world. Organic chemists began a race with the insects. In most cases it was not a very long race, because the insects soon evolved an insensitivity to whatever the chemists had produced. The chemists, redoubling their efforts, synthesized a steady stream of second-generation pesticides. By 1966 the sales of such pesticides had risen to a level of $500 million a year in the U.S. alone.

Coincident with the steady rise in the output of pesticides has come a growing realization that their blunderbuss toxicity can be dangerous. The problem has attracted widespread public attention since the late Rachel Carson fervently described in *The Silent Spring* some actual and potential consequences of this toxicity. Although the attention thus aroused has resulted in a few attempts to exercise care in the application of pesticides, the problem cannot really be solved with the substances now in use.

The rapid evolution of resistance to pesticides is perhaps more critical. For example, the world's most serious disease in terms of the number of people afflicted continues to be malaria, which is transmitted by the *Anopheles* mosquito—an insect that has become completely resistant to DDT. (Meanwhile the protozoon that actually causes the disease is itself evolving strains resistant to antimalaria drugs.)

A second instance has been presented recently in Vietnam by an outbreak of plague, the dreaded disease that is conveyed from rat to man by fleas. In this case the fleas have become resistant to pesticides. Other resistant insects that are agricultural pests continue to take a heavy toll of the world's dwindling food supply from the moment the seed is planted until long after the crop is harvested. Here again we are confronted by an emergency situation that the old technology can scarcely handle.

The new approach that promises a way out of these difficulties has emerged during the past decade from basic studies of insect physiology. The prime candidate for developing third-generation pesticides is the juvenile hormone that all insects secrete at certain stages in their lives. It is one of the three internal secretions used by insects to regulate growth and metamorphosis from larva to pupa to adult. In the living insect the juvenile hormone is synthesized by the corpora allata, two tiny glands in the head. The corpora allata are also responsible for regulating the flow of the hormone into the blood.

At certain stages the hormone must be

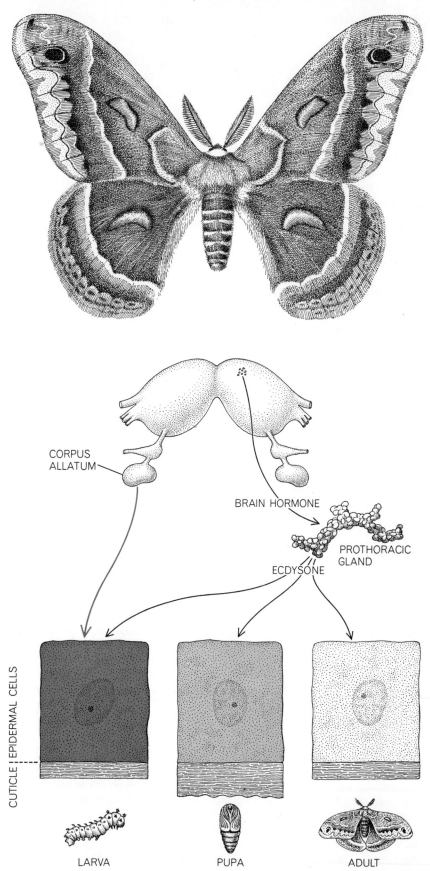

HORMONAL ACTIVITY in a Cecropia moth is outlined. Juvenile hormone (*color*) comes from the corpora allata, two small glands in the head; a second substance, brain hormone, stimulates the prothoracic glands to secrete ecdysone, which initiates the molts through which a larva passes. Juvenile hormone controls the larval forms and at later stages must be in low concentration or absent; if applied then, it deranges insect's normal development. The illustration is partly based on one by Howard A. Schneiderman and Lawrence I. Gilbert.

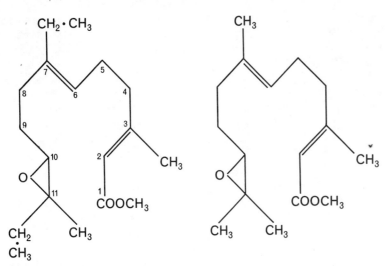

CHEMICAL STRUCTURES of the Cecropia juvenile hormone (*left*), isolated this year by Herbert Röller and his colleagues at the University of Wisconsin, and of a synthetic analogue (*right*) made in 1965 by W. S. Bowers and others in the U.S. Department of Agriculture show close similarity. Carbon atoms, joined to one or two hydrogen atoms, occupy each angle in the backbone of the molecules; letters show the structure at terminals and branches.

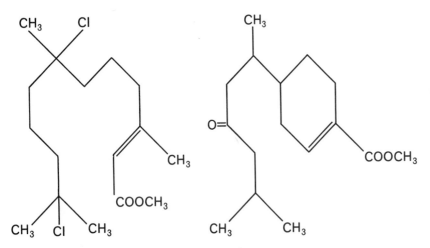

JUVENILE HORMONE ACTIVITY has been found in various substances not secreted by insects. One (*left*) is a material synthesized by M. Romanuk and his associates in Czechoslovakia. The other (*right*), isolated and identified by Bowers and his colleagues, is the "paper factor" found in the balsam fir. The paper factor has a strong juvenile hormone effect on only one family of insects, exemplified by the European bug *Pyrrhocoris apterus*.

secreted; at certain other stages it must be absent or the insect will develop abnormally [*see illustration on preceding page*]. For example, an immature larva has an absolute requirement for juvenile hormone if it is to progress through the usual larval stages. Then, in order for a mature larva to metamorphose into a sexually mature adult, the flow of hormone must stop. Still later, after the adult is fully formed, juvenile hormone must again be secreted.

The role of juvenile hormone in larval development has been established for several years. Recent studies at Harvard University by Lynn M. Riddiford and the Czechoslovakian biologist Karel Sláma have resulted in a surprising additional finding. It is that juvenile hormone must be absent from insect eggs for the eggs to undergo normal embryonic development.

The periods when the hormone must be absent are the Achilles' heel of insects. If the eggs or the insects come into contact with the hormone at these times, the hormone readily enters them and provokes a lethal derangement of further development. The result is that the eggs fail to hatch or the immature insects die without reproducing.

Juvenile hormone is an insect invention that, according to present knowledge, has no effect on other forms of life. Therefore the promise is that third-generation pesticides can zero in on in-

sects to the exclusion of other plants and animals. (Even for the insects juvenile hormone is not a toxic material in the usual sense of the word. Instead of killing, it derails the normal mechanisms of development and causes the insects to kill themselves.) A further advantage is self-evident: insects will not find it easy to evolve a resistance or an insensitivity to their own hormone without automatically committing suicide.

The potentialities of juvenile hormone as an insecticide were recognized 12 years ago in experiments performed on the first active preparation of the hormone: a golden oil extracted with ether from male Cecropia moths. Strange to say, the male Cecropia and the male of its close relative the Cynthia moth remain to this day the only insects from which one can extract the hormone. Therefore tens of thousands of the moths have been required for the experimental work with juvenile hormone; the need has been met by a small but thriving industry that rears the silkworms.

No one expected Cecropia moths to supply the tons of hormone that would be required for use as an insecticide. Obviously the hormone would have to be synthesized. That could not be done, however, until the hormone had been isolated from the golden oil and identified

Within the past few months the difficult goals of isolating and identifying the hormone have at last been attained by a team of workers headed by Herbert Röller of the University of Wisconsin. The juvenile hormone has the empirical formula $C_{18}H_{36}O_2$, corresponding to a molecular weight of 284. It proves to be the methyl ester of the epoxide of a previously unknown fatty-acid derivative [*see upper illustration on this page*]. The apparent simplicity of the molecule is deceptive. It has two double bonds and an oxirane ring (the small triangle at lower left in the molecular diagram), and it can exist in 16 different molecular configurations. Only one of these can be the authentic hormone. With two ethyl groups ($CH_2 \cdot CH_3$) attached to carbons No. 7 and 11, the synthesis of the hormone from any known terpenoid is impossible.

The pure hormone is extraordinarily active. Tests the Wisconsin investigators have carried out with mealworms suggest that one gram of the hormone would result in the death of about a billion of these insects.

A few years before Röller and his colleagues worked out the structure of the authentic hormone, investigators at several laboratories had synthesized a number of substances with impressive juvenile hormone activity. The most potent of the materials appears to be a crude mixture that John H. Law, now at the University of Chicago, prepared by a simple one-step process in which hydrogen chloride gas was bubbled through an alcoholic solution of farnesenic acid. Without any purification this mixture was 1,000 times more active than crude Cecropia oil and fully effective in killing all kinds of insects.

One of the six active components of Law's mixture has recently been identified and synthesized by a group of workers headed by M. Romaňuk of the Czechoslovak Academy of Sciences. Romaňuk and his associates estimate that from 10 to 100 grams of the material would clear all the insects from 2½ acres. Law's original mixture is of course even more potent, and so there is much interest in its other five components.

Another interesting development that preceded the isolation and identification of true juvenile hormone involved a team of investigators under W. S. Bowers of the U.S. Department of Agriculture's laboratory at Beltsville, Md. Bowers and his colleagues prepared an analogue of juvenile hormone that, as can be seen in the accompanying illustration [*top of opposite page*], differed by only two carbon atoms from the authentic Cecropia hormone (whose structure was then, of course, unknown). In terms of the dosage required it appears that the Beltsville compound is about 2 percent as active as Law's mixture and about .02 percent as active as the pure Cecropia hormone.

All the materials I have mentioned are selective in the sense of killing only insects. They leave unsolved, however, the problem of discriminating between the .1 percent of insects that qualify as pests and the 99.9 percent that are helpful or innocuous. Therefore any reckless use of the materials on a large scale could constitute an ecological disaster of the first rank.

The real need is for third-generation pesticides that are tailor-made to attack only certain predetermined pests. Can such pesticides be devised? Recent work that Sláma and I have carried out at Harvard suggests that this objective is by no means unattainable. The possibility arose rather fortuitously after Sláma arrived from Czechoslovakia, bringing with him some specimens of the European bug *Pyrrhocoris apterus*—a species that had been reared in his laboratory in Prague for 10 years.

To our considerable mystification the bugs invariably died without reaching sexual maturity when we attempted to rear them at Harvard. Instead of metamorphosing into normal adults they continued to grow as larvae or molted into adult-like forms retaining many larval characteristics. It was evident that the bugs had access to some unknown source of juvenile hormone.

Eventually we traced the source to the paper toweling that had been placed in the rearing jars. Then we discovered that almost any paper of American origin—including the paper on which *Scientific American* is printed—had the same effect. Paper of European or Japanese manufacture had no effect on the bugs. On further investigation we found that the juvenile hormone activity originated in the balsam fir, which is the principal source of pulp for paper in Canada and the northern U.S. The tree synthesizes what we named the "paper factor," and this substance accompanies the pulp all the way to the printed page.

Thanks again to Bowers and his associates at Beltsville, the active material of the paper factor has been isolated and characterized [*see lower illustration on opposite page*]. It proves to be the methyl ester of a certain unsaturated fatty-acid derivative. The factor's kinship with the other juvenile hormone analogues is evident from the illustrations.

Here, then, is an extractable juvenile hormone analogue with selective action against only one kind of insect. As it happens, the family Pyrrhocoridae includes some of the most destructive pests of the cotton plant. Why the balsam fir should have evolved a substance against only one family of insects is unexplained. The most intriguing possibility is that the paper factor is a biochemical memento of the juvenile hormone of a former natural enemy of the tree—a pyrrhocorid predator that, for obvious reasons, is either extinct or has learned to avoid the balsam fir.

In any event, the fact that the tree synthesizes the substance argues strongly that the juvenile hormone of other species of insects can be mimicked, and perhaps has been by trees or plants on which the insects preyed. Evidently during the 250 million years of insect evolution the detailed chemistry of juvenile hormone has evolved and diversified. The process would of necessity have gone hand in hand with a retuning of the hormonal receptor mechanisms in the cells and tissues of the insect, so that the use as pesticides of any analogues that are discovered seems certain to be effective.

The evergreen trees are an ancient lot. They were here before the insects; they are pollinated by the wind and thus, unlike many other plants, do not depend on the insects for anything. The paper factor is only one of thousands of terpenoid materials these trees synthesize for no apparent reason. What about the rest?

It seems altogether likely that many of these materials will also turn out to be analogues of the juvenile hormones of specific insect pests. Obviously this is the place to look for a whole battery of third-generation pesticides. Then man may be able to emulate the evergreen trees in their incredibly sophisticated self-defense against the insects.

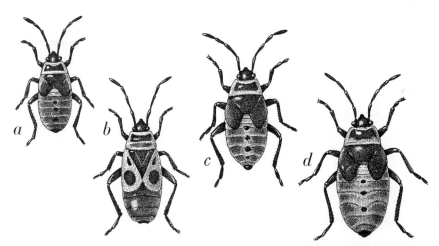

EFFECT OF PAPER FACTOR on *Pyrrhocoris apterus* is depicted. A larva of the fifth and normally final stage (*a*) turns into a winged adult (*b*). Contact with the paper factor causes the insect to turn into a sixth-stage larva (*c*) and sometimes into a giant seventh-stage larva (*d*). The abnormal larvae usually cannot shed their skin and die before reaching maturity.

34

The Eradication of the Screw-Worm Fly

by Edward F. Knipling
October 1960

This destructive parasite of livestock has been eliminated from the southeastern states by releasing large numbers of male flies that have been sterilized by ionizing radiation

A fundamentally new method for controlling animal populations— one that enlists the reproductive process of the species in its own extinction—has entirely eradicated a major agricultural insect pest throughout a large continental region. The pest is the screw-worm fly which infests livestock; not a single screw-worm fly has been seen in the southeastern U. S. for almost two years. This unprecedented achievement was effected within a few months the first time the self-eradication method was tried on such a large scale. The success of the method against the screw-worm fly suggests that it may be applied with the same results to other insect species and to rodents and other pests.

Entomologists and veterinarians of the Agricultural Research Service of the U. S. Department of Agriculture and the Florida Livestock Board reared millions of screw-worm flies in what was literally a screw-worm factory. The insects were made sexually sterile by exposure to high-energy radiation. They were then released in the infested area. The sterile males, mating with the females in the natural population, nullified their reproductive capacity. The result was the complete elimination of the natural population.

The new method offers obvious advantages over conventional techniques which are directed at killing the living generations of the pest. In the first place it is highly selective, involving only the single target species and leaving the rest of the ecological system completely undisturbed. Secondly, no species can acquire immunity to sterile matings as it can to the insecticides that have been used in the past. There is a third and not so apparent advantage. Killing agents tend to become progressively less efficient as the pest population declines, and so leave a few survivors to begin the cycle of geometric population-increase all over again. The sterile-male method has the theoretical and, as has been shown in the case of the screw-worm fly, practical capability of becoming increasingly efficient as the pest population reaches the vanishing point.

There are nonetheless disadvantages inherent in the method when it comes to planning campaigns against certain species and throughout large geographic regions. But eradication of the screw-worm fly surely urges the search for similar opportunities to bring the method to bear. The screw-worm fly itself remains a major objective. It continues to infest the livestock of the Southwest, where losses are estimated at $25 million each year.

The adult screw-worm fly has a metallic blue body, about 3/8 inch long. It lays a compact mass of 200 to 300 eggs in the wounds of warm-blooded animals. Any accidental or surgical wound, a tick bite or the navel of a newborn animal may become a site for screw-worm attack. The insect is especially damaging to newborn animals; in areas heavily populated with screw-worm flies few newborn calves, lambs, kids, pigs or young of the larger game species will escape attack.

Tiny maggots hatch from the eggs in 12 to 24 hours. They begin feeding on the flesh head-down and closely packed in the wound. The feeding larvae cause a straw-colored and often bloody discharge that attracts more flies, resulting in multiple infestation by hundreds to thousands of maggots of all sizes. Death is inevitable unless the animal is found and treated.

The maggots feeding in wounds become full grown in about five days, reaching a length of about 2/3 inch. Then they drop out of the wound, burrow into the ground and change to the pupal or resting stage in about one day. The adults emerge from the pupal case after about eight days during the summer months, live for two or three weeks and range for many miles, feeding on plant nectars, pollen, carrion, secretions of animal wounds and so on. They mate on about the third day after emergence, and the females are ready to lay eggs four days later, at which time they begin searching for suitable hosts on which to lay eggs and start the next generation. The generation period may thus be as short as three weeks and, in areas where the insect survives the year around, there may be from 10 to 12 generations during each year.

Fortunately the range in which the species may overwinter in the U. S. is limited. During years of average winter temperatures, the survival area for the insect is in the lower quarter of Texas and in smaller areas in the southern parts of New Mexico, Arizona and California —and, until recently, lower Florida. The population density of the insect in the overwintering areas is greatly reduced. During the spring and summer the insect increases in numbers and spreads northward from the overwintering area, greatly extending its range of destruction. Much of the spread is by its own flight, but the shipment of livestock infested with undetected eggs or larvae often spreads the screw-worm fly to distant areas in the spring, when it can cause considerable damage to livestock before cold weather arrives.

In 1937 it occurred to me that it might be economically feasible to rear and release screw-worm flies in sufficient numbers to exceed the natural population. The idea was suggested, in fact, by the observation of my colleague A. W. Lind-

quist, of the Uvalde, Tex., station of the Department of Agriculture, that the number of screw-worm flies trapped during the winter in that region is exceedingly small. If some method could be devised to cause the artificially reared and released insects to destroy those in the natural population, I thought, this might provide a means for annihilating the insect. The development of a genetic strain carrying a factor that would be lethal under natural conditions was one possibility. Development of a chemical that would induce sterility in the flies before release was another. However, the most promising approach seemed to be the sterilization of the flies by X- or gamma-rays. As long ago as 1916 G. A. Runner of the U. S. Department of Agriculture had shown that cigarette beetles produce infertile eggs after exposure to X-rays, and at the University of Texas in 1928 H. J. Muller had demonstrated similar effects in fruit flies. Significantly for my purpose, it had been found that

such exposure at the right stage in the insect's development had no other adverse effect.

The self-destruction approach to screw-worm control was discussed with a number of biologists during the next 12 years. The reaction was generally pessimistic. However, the possibilities, as determined by theoretical calculations, seemed too impressive to ignore. They indicated that, with the screw-worm population at a reasonably constant level, the sustained release of sterile males, initially outnumbering the natural population by two to one, could eradicate the population in four generations [see illustration on page 313]. Under favorable circumstances an insect population generally has a high potential for increasing in number from one generation to the next. But even under conditions that are favorable to a fivefold increase per generation, calculations showed that the release of sterile flies

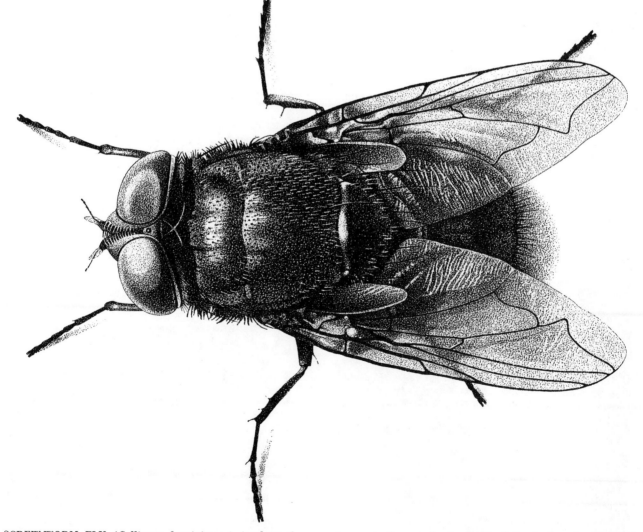

SCREW-WORM FLY (*Callitroga hominivorax*) is about three times larger than a housefly, and has a metallic blue color. It lays its eggs in the wounds of warm-blooded animals such as livestock and game. The larvae that hatch from the eggs feed on the wound.

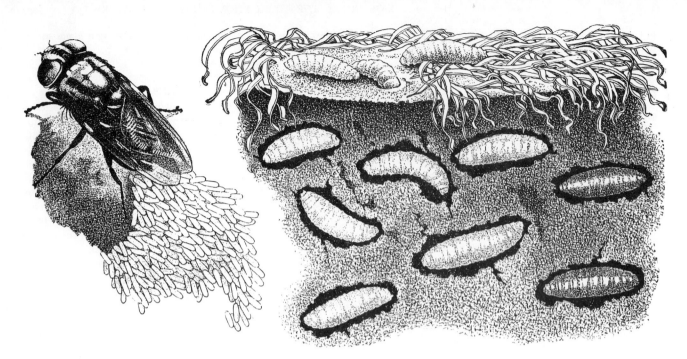

LIFE CYCLE OF SCREW-WORM FLY is depicted in these drawings. The female fly lays a compact mass of 200 to 300 eggs in the

wound of a warm-blooded animal (*left*). Within a day the eggs hatch into larvae, and five days later the larvae leave the wound,

in an initial nine-to-one ratio to the natural population could eliminate the fly in five generations.

In 1950 I sought the counsel of Muller, as an authority on radiation effects on genetic material. With his encouragement the Department of Agriculture initiated research at the Kerrville, Tex., station, under the direction of R. C. Bushland. In a series of well-executed experiments Bushland and his assistant D. E. Hopkins developed the promising information that exposure of screw-worm pupae to 2,500 roentgens or more of ionizing radiation caused sexual sterility in the males without serious side

effects. A dosage of 5,000 roentgens caused sexual sterility in the females.

Sexually sterile males were then placed in cages with normal males to test their ability to compete with normal males in mating with normal females. The results were extremely favorable. When the ratio of sterile to fertile males was one to one, about half the normal females produced sterile eggs. When the ratio was stepped up to nine to one, the sterility in the females was 83 per cent, sufficiently close to the theoretical expectancy of 90 per cent. The investigators showed that females of the screw-worm fly mate only once and do not

discriminate between irradiated sterile males and normal males. The presence of irradiated sterile females in the caged population did not alter the results, which meant that it would not be necessary to separate the sexes before releasing the flies in the field.

These findings clearly suggested that the sterile-male method was technically feasible. However, extensive field experiments would be required to demonstrate actual eradication.

In view of the long flight-range of the adult screw-worm fly it was not possible to conduct a valid experiment on a small scale within a large area infested with

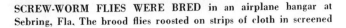

SCREW-WORM FLIES WERE BRED in an airplane hangar at Sebring, Fla. The brood flies roosted on strips of cloth in screeened

cages (*left*). After the flies had laid their eggs and the eggs had hatched into larvae, the larvae were fed in trays of ground meat,

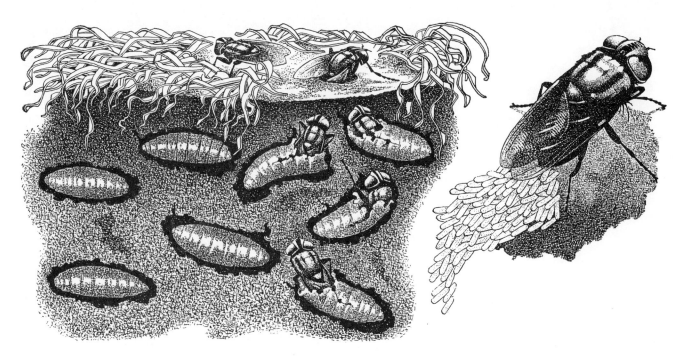

burrow into the ground and metamorphose into pupae (*second from left*). Some eight days later the pupae metamorphose into flies (*third from left*). About three days later the flies mate, and four days after that the female deposits her eggs (*fourth from left*).

the insect. It would be necessary to release millions of sterile flies to achieve results in an area of several thousand square miles. The only hope was to find a small infested island where the total population could be exposed to a less astronomical number of sterile males.

We chose Sanibel Island, off the west coast of Florida near Fort Myers, as the site for field studies. It has an area of only 15 square miles and was found to harbor a natural population of screwworm flies. Since it lies only two miles from the mainland, it did not afford the desired degree of isolation, but still it served our purpose.

Irradiated sexually sterile screw-worm males were released on the island at the rate of 100 per square mile per week for a period of three months. Goats that had wounds susceptible to screw-worm attack were placed in pens on the island to collect egg masses deposited by the female flies in the natural population. Sterile egg masses showed up about a week after sterile-male releases were started. Within two months 80 per cent of the egg masses were sterile. By the third month the natural population of the insect virtually vanished. It was not possible, however, to demonstrate eradication, because some already mated fertile females had migrated to the island from the mainland.

The next problem was to find a site where a valid eradication experiment could be conducted with the financial resources available. That problem was solved by a routine inquiry from B. A. Bitter, a veterinary officer on the island of Curacao in the Netherlands Antilles, who reported that the screw-worm fly was causing severe losses of goats on the island. A survey by A. H. Baumhover, who had supervised the Sanibel experiment, showed Curacao to be an ideal site; among other things it has an area

blood and water (*second from left*). Larvae were then permitted to burrow into sand, and after they had metamorphosed into pupae, the pupae were screened from the sand (*third from left*). Pupae were exposed to radiation from a cobalt-60 source (*fourth from left*).

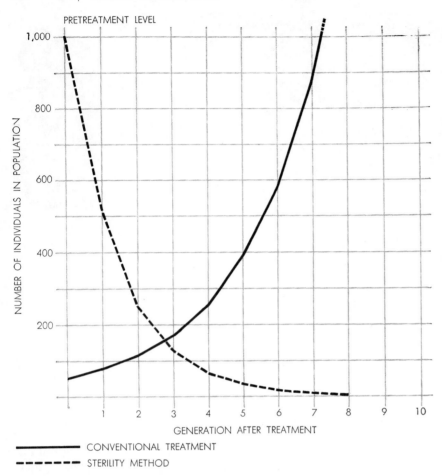

STERILITY METHOD of animal-pest control is compared with conventional treatment of merely killing the pest. The chart assumes a monogamous population of 1,000 with a rate of increase of 1.5 per cent per generation. If 95 per cent of the population are killed by conventional treatment, the remaining 5 per cent reproduce to equal or exceed the original population within eight generations (*solid curve*). If 95 per cent of the males in the population are sterilized, the population is eliminated within eight generations (*broken curve*).

of 170 square miles, and it is separated from other land areas by 40 miles. The Netherlands Antilles Government agreed to join in the experiment.

The insects were reared at Orlando, Fla., under the supervision of A. J. Graham. A cobalt-60 gamma-ray source loaned by the Oak Ridge National Laboratory irradiated the flies, and regular commercial airlines delivered them to Curacao, where crop-duster airplanes distributed them at the rate of 400 sterile males per square mile per week. In view of the large number of flies no attempt was made to segregate the males from the females. Since irradiated females are incapable of producing eggs, any sterility observed in the egg masses collected could be attributed to the sterile males only. As on Sanibel Island, daily collections of egg masses on penned goats provided a measure of the results accomplished. Before fly releases started, more than 99 per cent of egg masses were fertile.

The results on Curacao—100 per cent sterility of egg masses by the third generation and total eradication of the fly by the fourth—were more spectacular than any of the investigators had dared hope. The actual population trend completely confirmed the theoretical trends projected years before on paper.

When the success of the Curacao eradication experiment was announced in the press, the livestock industry virtually demanded that an eradication program be initiated in Florida. However, the Curacao experiment had required the production of only 170,000 screwworm flies per week (including brood flies). To achieve a similar saturation of the 50,000 square miles of the southeastern U. S. would require the production of about 50 million screw-worm flies per week. Insect-rearing on such a scale had never been undertaken.

Nonetheless the Department of Agriculture set the Sanibel-Curacao experimental group to work on projecting the

expansion of screw-worm fly production from pilot plant to full factory scale. In 1957 the Florida livestock industry obtained state appropriations to match Federal funds, and the project got under way. Construction of a screw-worm rearing plant in an airplane hangar at Sebring, Fla., was started by the Florida Livestock Board early in 1958, and was scheduled to go into operation in July of that year.

The winter of 1957 and 1958 proved, however, to be one of the coldest on record in Florida. Since the cold virtually destroyed all screw-worm flies as far south as central Florida, the pilot plant at Bithlo, Fla., which had been used for research purposes, started releasing sterile flies in January, 1958. Even though the initial capacity of the Bithlo plant was only two million flies per week, this was hopefully sufficient to establish a barrier north of the overwintering area. The opportunistic strategy proved decisive, because it prevented the usual northward movement of the pest in the spring and held its numbers down until the Sebring plant realized its capacity in August.

Production of the flies in the factory proceeded on an orderly schedule fixed by the life cycle of the species. The insects received the best of care in an air-conditioned, humidity-controlled room; thousands of flies roosted on cloth strips in each of a large number of screen cages. They were fed a diet of honey and extracts of ground meat, and after about eight days were induced to lay their eggs in a slurry of ground meat, blood and water in which pupae had previously been raised. The larvae generated factors in this medium that proved highly attractive to females ready to deposit their eggs, especially when the medium was heated to the body temperature of livestock (approximately 100 degrees Fahrenheit).

After hatching and five days of feeding, the larvae crawled out of the feeding vats into a large funnel, where they were collected in trays of moist sand. There they changed to pupae in about 24 hours. Screened from the sand into special screen baskets, the pupae were held at a controlled temperature of about 80 degrees. On the sixth day they were placed in cylindrical metal containers and exposed to 8,000 roentgens of gamma radiation from a cobalt-60 source, enough to assure the complete sterility of both male and female flies. The production line required six 500-curie cobalt-60 sources. After irradiation the pupae were packaged in small cardboard boxes in readiness for delivery to the field when they emerged as adults about two days later.

Air-conditioned trucks transported each day's output to the airstrips. The airplanes, provided with special equipment to break open each box as it was released, dropped from 100 to 3,000 flies per mile as they flew their courses.

When the Sebring plant reached full capacity, it was rearing, irradiating and releasing more than 50 million screw-worm flies each week. More than two billion flies were released over a period of about 18 months in Florida, and parts of Georgia and Alabama. The area in which flies were released totaled about 70,000 square miles. More than 40 tons of ground whale- and horse-meat were required to feed the larvae, and a fleet of 20 airplanes handled the task of distribution. Without doubt this was one of the most extraordinary programs ever undertaken in the field of applied biology.

By February 19, 1959, or approximately a year after initiation of the program and six months after all areas were

receiving sterile-fly releases, the insect appeared to be eradicated. Releases were continued, however, until November, 1959, when the screw-worm-fly rearing plant was at last shut down.

With the insect eradicated from its overwintering habitat in Florida, the entire Southeast is now free of the fly. The area between eastern Texas and northern Florida is unfavorable for screw-worm-fly survival throughout the winter and thus furnishes a barrier against natural re-establishment of the fly in Florida. To prevent the reintroduction of the insect into the Southeast by livestock shipped from the Southwest, the Department of Agriculture maintains animal inspection and treatment stations at all crossings on the Mississippi River.

Naturally livestock growers in the Southwest now want to see the same service performed for them. However, elimination of the insect from this region poses special problems that did not exist in the Southeast. In the Southwest continuous year-round survival areas for the insect extend from the southern part of Texas and parts of New Mexico, Arizona

and California deep into Mexico and possibly into Central and South America. It is probable that the insect could be eradicated in the Southwest—but only for a time. There is as yet no known way to prevent reinfestation from Mexico. It may be economically feasible to establish a barrier zone 100 miles or so deep by making continuous releases of relatively few sterile flies. An animal inspection and treatment program such as that along the Mississippi River would have to be set up to prevent reintroduction of the insect through the shipment of infested animals. The Department of Agriculture, in co-operation with officials in Mexico, is studying these possibilities.

The screw-worm-fly precedent has now inspired workers in various countries to investigate the possibility of using equivalent methods to control many other varieties of pest: the oriental, melon, Mediterranean and Mexican fruit flies, the pink bollworm and the boll weevil, the sugar-cane borer, the European corn-borer, the gypsy moth and the codling moth. The laboratory phase of

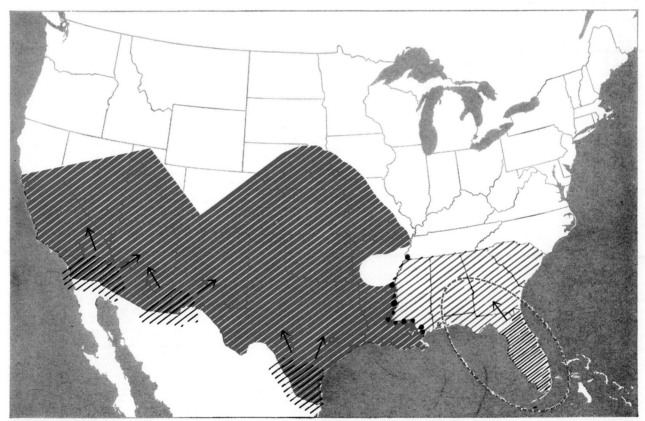

ERADICATION

AVERAGE OVERWINTERING

MIGRATION

------ FLY-RELEASE AREA

•   INSPECTION STATION

RANGE OF SCREW-WORM FLY originally included the entire southern part of the U. S. Release of sterile males in area indicated by broken line eliminated the fly from the southern states east of the Mississippi in 1958. The fly persists west of the Mississippi because it winters in areas adjoining vast areas of infestation in Mexico. Inspection stations along the Mississippi guard the southeastern states against reinfestation by cattle from the Southwest.

the fruit-fly effort has already been completed by the Hawaii Fruit Fly Laboratory of the Department of Agriculture. In co-operation with the U. S. Navy and the trust territories administration, the Department is now planning a pilot eradication campaign on the island of Rota in the southwestern Pacific. Of the insects that bother and menace man more directly, the mosquito is under study as a candidate for self-eradication in the Department of Agriculture center at Orlando, Fla., and the tsetse fly is being studied by the British and Dutch in Africa with this end in view.

In every case the same set of four criteria will determine the feasibility of the effort: Sexual sterility must be achieved without adverse effects on mating behavior, the insects must be rearable in large numbers, the sterile insects

must be readily dispersable in a manner that will bring them into effective competition with normal males, and the huge (even though temporary) increase in the population of the species must create no serious harm to crops, animals or man. The screw-worm fly was plainly an ideal subject. With respect to the last criterion, for example, the release of sterile males brings immediate diminution in the harm done by the insect, since sterile eggs are no bother to animals in which they are laid. Because the natural population of many species is so large, it may be necessary to reduce its size by conventional methods before attempting eradication by use of sterile males. Contrary to popular belief, monogamous mating by the female is not a requirement, providing the sterile sperm are fully competitive with normal sperm

when planted in the female genital tract.

Since the release of large numbers of certain organisms might be costly and also create damaging side effects, a more desirable way to utilize the sexual-sterility principle would be to induce sexual sterility in the natural population. A chemical agent that induced sterility in an insect species as readily as conventional insecticides destroy them would yield a very much greater return for the same effort. As the chart on this page shows, the conventional poison that kills 90 per cent of the population in each generation achieves a much slower population reduction from one generation to the next, and still leaves a significant breeding population in the fifth generation, the point at which the equivalent sexual-sterility agent would achieve eradication. The difference is easily explained. The sterilized insects do not themselves reproduce; this is the equivalent of death from the vantage of the survival of the population. But since the sterile males would nullify the reproductive capacity of 90 per cent of the females that escaped exposure to the sterilizing agent, the total effect would be a 99-per-cent population depression each generation instead of the 90 per cent produced by the killing agents.

The Entomology Research Division of the Department of Agriculture has initiated exploratory investigations in a search for sexual sterilants for insects. Norman Mitlin, insect physiologist, has shown that several compounds will prevent ovarian development in the housefly. Research workers at the fruit-fly laboratory in Mexico City have shown that certain compounds will produce sterility in the Mexican fruit fly. Similar effects have been produced in the housefly with certain compounds under investigation at the Orlando, Fla., laboratory. To achieve the bonus effect over killing agents, the chemicals must produce irreversible sexual sterility in both sexes, and the males so affected must be fully competitive with normal males in mating with normal females in the population.

The potential advantage of the sexual-sterility approach over killing agents for population control is not limited to insects. Theoretically it can be shown that the relative effect would be equally or more dramatic when applied to higher animals. Under certain circumstances it may be desirable to eliminate noxious animals, such as rodents, predators, destructive birds or aquatic animals from certain areas, or merely to regulate the population of desirable animal species,

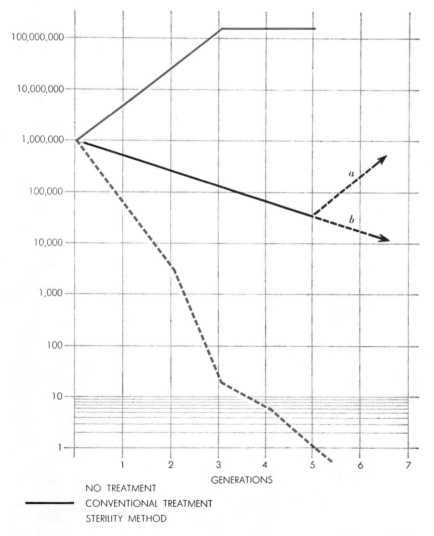

NO TREATMENT
CONVENTIONAL TREATMENT
STERILITY METHOD

CONTROLS AND NO CONTROLS on insect population that starts from low level and increases fivefold per generation result in trends depicted. Without controls, population would saturate environment and level off (*solid colored line*). Conventional controls (*black line*) which killed 90 per cent of each generation would require 20 generations to eliminate pest (*b*). Premature suspension of controls would lead to upsurge of population (*a*). Same effort with sterility method would eradicate pest by fifth generation (*broken colored line*).

such as certain large predators or large game species.

In the case of higher animals the assumptions applied to the reduction of insect populations need be modified only to take account of the relatively longer lifetime of the individual and the lower reproductive rate of mammals as compared to insects. A typical net increase for mammals may be taken as 50 per cent per generation. The contrast between the effects of the killing and of the sterility agents is drawn most sharply when it is assumed that the object is to eradicate the population. Assuming that the killing agent reduces the population by 95 per cent at the outset and that there are 1,000 animals in the initial population, then the 50 survivors and their descendants would restore the original number by the eighth generation. If the same population were exposed to an equally effective sterility agent, none would be killed, but 95 per cent would be deprived of their reproductive capacity. This 95 per cent would in turn nullify the reproductive capacity of those that escaped the effect of the agent. The cumulative impact on the population would be drastic. By the ninth generation the original 1,000 animals would have no survivors. Reproduction would have ceased by the sixth or seventh generation, and only a few sterile individuals would survive through the ninth [*see illustration on page 310*]. Theoretically the same relative effect could be achieved by trapping and removal if, instead of removing both males and females, the males were appropriately sterilized and returned to the environment. Such calculations do not require monogamous mating habits even in the higher animals; the sterilization procedure need only leave the sterilized male or his sperm fully competitive with the normal.

At present the basic information and experience are inadequate to determine the extent to which the self-eradication procedure can be developed and applied for controlling insect and other animal populations. It is a biological axiom, however, that the introduction of sexually sterile but otherwise sexually competitive individuals into the natural population of an animal species has a greater influence in reducing the biotic potential of the population than does the elimination of the same number of individuals by destruction or removal. That axiom has been amply demonstrated by the eradication of the destructive screw-worm fly from the southeastern states.

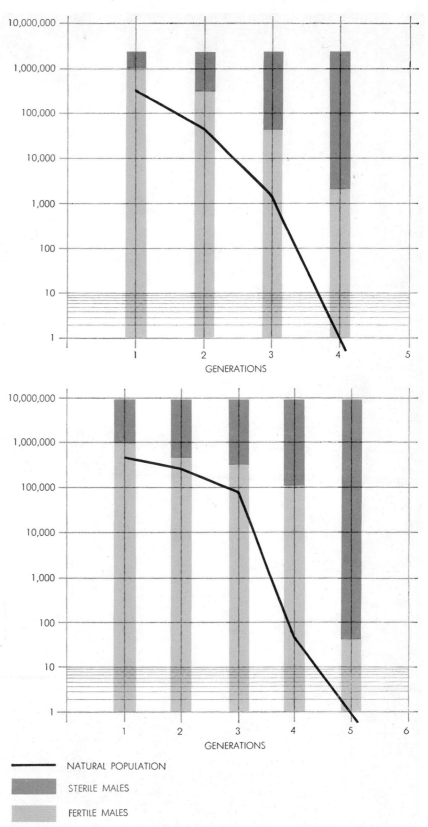

DECLINE OF INSECT POPULATIONS during sustained release of sterile males is projected. Graph at top applies to a normally stable population. Constant number of sterile males released (*solid colored bars*) exceeds the original number of fertile males (*shaded colored bars*) by a ratio of two to one. Result is an increasing ratio of sterile to fertile males, and the decline of the natural population (*black curve*). Graph at bottom applies to a population that normally increases fivefold per generation. Constant number of sterile males released in this case exceeds original fertile male population by a ratio of nine to one.

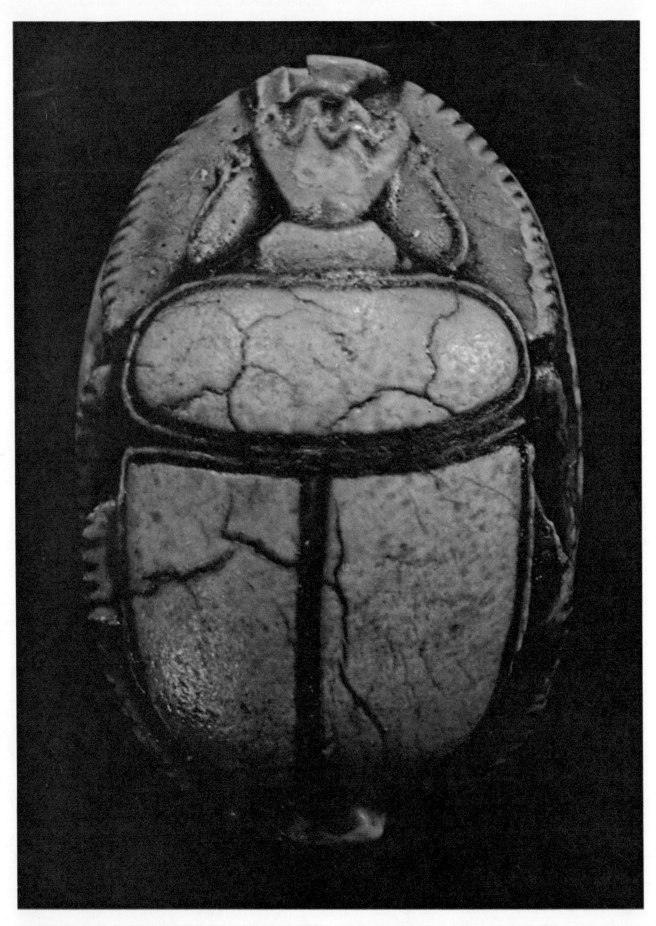

SACRED SCARAB OF ANCIENT EGYPT is a representation of the dung beetle *Scarabaeus sacer*, a species that populates the perimeter of the Mediterranean. This scarab, made of blue-glazed steatite and about an inch long, is from the Hyksos period of about 1650 to 1580 B.C. It is in the Carnarvon Collection (gift of Edward S. Harkness, 1926) of New York's Metropolitan Museum of Art.

The Biological Control
of Dung

by D. F. Waterhouse
April 1974

*When native Australian dung beetles cannot cope
with the large, moist dung pads of cattle, dung
covers pastureland and breeds insect pests. Now
foreign beetles are being imported to help out*

When the first English colonists arrived in Australia in January, 1788, they brought ashore with them five cows, two bulls, seven horses and 44 sheep, together with some uninvited fleas, lice and rats. Unfortunately certain important fellow travelers were missing from the company: bovine dung beetles. The omission created an ecological imbalance because dung beetles break down dung. For lack of dung beetles dung pads persist, obliterating pasturage and breeding insect pests. The results have become increasingly significant in the course of two centuries, as the number of bovines in Australia has increased from seven animals to 30 million. In the past 10 years our group in the Commonwealth Scientific and Industrial Research Organization (CSIRO) has undertaken to redress the imbalance between dung and beetles. In the process we have learned something about the nice interspecies adaptations that develop over millenniums, the trouble that can come when man upsets them and some ways man may be able to undo the damage.

The dung beetle and its works are well known to history. The scarab (*Scarabaeus sacer*), a beetle that populates the perimeter of the Mediterranean, was sacred to the early Egyptians. The ball of dung it forms and rolls along the ground was likened by them to the sun, and the beetle itself to the invisible power that daily propelled the sun across the sky. They went on to represent the sun god, their most important deity, as a scarab in both art and hieroglyphics. Later Aristophanes had Trygaeus, the hero of his comedy *The Peace*, mount to heaven on the back of a dung beetle. As for more scientific and practical references, there was useful investigation and writing concerning dung beetles a century ago, notably by the French

naturalist Jean Henri Fabre. Yet it was only in 1960 that G. F. Bornemissza of the CSIRO Division of Entomology pointed out what lack of the proper dung beetles meant in Australia.

Before the arrival of European colonists the largest herbivorous animals in Australia had been marsupials such as kangaroos, which produce comparatively dry, fibrous dung pellets no larger than a golf ball and generally less than half that size. Marsupial dung never accumulated excessively because it provided food and nesting material for a well-adapted group of native insects: some 250 kinds of scarab beetles of the subfamily Scarabaeinae, commonly known as "coprids." As Bornemissza recognized, the situation was completely different with regard to the larger, moister dung pads of imported cattle. These pads are unattractive to most native Australian beetles and so they are seldom more than partially utilized, and that only during limited periods of the year. Most cow pads soon dry out to a hard cake on the ground where they have fallen, often remaining substantially unchanged for months or even years until they are finally disintegrated by weathering, rotting, trampling by stock or attack by termites.

As long as the cattle were few and ranged over large areas, their dung pads were comparatively few and scattered and caused no problems. As their numbers increased, however, it became commonplace to see pastures littered with pads that ranged in age up to several years. These objects make their presence felt in a variety of ways. First of all, the area they cover is significant. On the average 12 dung pads are dropped by a single adult bovine every day. If they are not disposed of, the pads produced by each animal will blanket between 5 and 10 percent of an acre in a year.

Moreover, at the periphery of each dung pad there develops a zone of tall, rank herbage that cattle seldom eat and avoid for a year or more unless they are ravenous. The effective area of pasture is thereby reduced by each bovine by about 20 percent of an acre per year. A simple calculation indicates that the 30 million cattle in Australia, producing some 300 million or more dung pads a day, may be putting out of service as much as six million acres of pastureland each year. At least part of this effect may be cumulative, extending into subsequent years and constituting a truly enormous loss to the dairy and beef industries.

The situation is spectacularly different in areas of the world such as Africa, where many large herbivores evolved and still survive. Except when temperatures fall too low (below about 15 degrees Celsius) or when it is too dry for much insect activity, the dung in such regions is disintegrated by an almost bewildering variety of beetles. In Africa upward of 2,000 species of coprid beetles are known to utilize the dung of the many and diverse species of herbivorous animals. Some beetles are relatively undiscriminating and are attracted to dung from quite a range of herbivores. Others are specialists and avoid dung that does not have the size, special texture, composition, moisture content and other features characteristic of a particular herbivore species. Some beetles are adapted or even restricted to open pastures, whereas others prefer lightly timbered savanna woodland. Some coprids move from pad to pad only by night, whereas others are active during the day. There are also special adaptations to temperature, moisture, soil characteristics (sand, loam or clay), seasonal variations in the length of the day and other factors. These various adaptations, which have

COW DUNG ACCUMULATES in a pasture near Townsville, in the state of Queensland in northeastern Australia. Bovine dung beetles would break up the pads for food and nesting material; in their absence pads dry out and remain on the ground for many months.

DUNG PADS in another pasture, in New South Wales, stimulate the rank growth of undesirable herbage that cattle will not eat. This further reduces the amount of pasturage. Moreover, the dung pads serve as a breeding ground for the larvae of insect pests.

evolved over the millenniums, enable each species to occupy a particular ecological niche where it survives in spite of all competitors.

Dung beetles are powerfully attracted to fresh dung. In Africa the beetles are alerted as soon as a nearby buffalo lifts its tail to defecate and passes a little odorous fecal gas. By the time the steaming dung pad has hit the ground beetles are orienting to it. Minutes or even seconds later, before the buffalo has moved very far, many beetles have homed in on the dung and are already burrowing in it. Within a day, sometimes within only a few hours, nothing may remain of the pad except a few dry wisps of plant fiber on the surface of the fresh soil excavated by beetles tunneling under it. The numbers of beetles involved are huge. More than 7,000 have been counted in a single mass of fresh elephant dung in Kruger National Park in South Africa.

Different species of beetles utilize dung in different ways [*see illustration on next page*]. Most species excavate tunnels in the soil under or directly adjacent to the dung pad. They carry the dung down into the tunnels and fashion it into balls in which the females lay their eggs. In selecting the dung many species remove all irregularities from it, leaving material such as seeds behind on the surface. Seeds thus removed fall on ground that has been loosened by the tunneling, which makes it easier for them to become established when they germinate.

Beetles of another group carve a mass out of the dung and move it some distance from the pad before burying it. Some species simply butt the mass over the ground but others knead pieces of dung into smoothly rounded balls and roll them for many yards before they bury them. (Sometimes when the male is exerting prodigious energy pushing or pulling the ball, the female can be seen balancing on top of it as it rolls along.) Egg laying subsequently takes place in the soil chamber where the ball has been buried.

When feeding, adult beetles busily squeeze pellets of moist dung between their mouthparts and suck in the expressed juice. Their digestive tract is usually found to contain a dark fluid mixed with very fine particulate material, and so it appears that dung fluid and the soluble nutrients and microorganisms it contains provide their major food. It is supplemented to some extent by solids derived from dung particles, which are rubbed into a fine paste between specially adapted areas on the

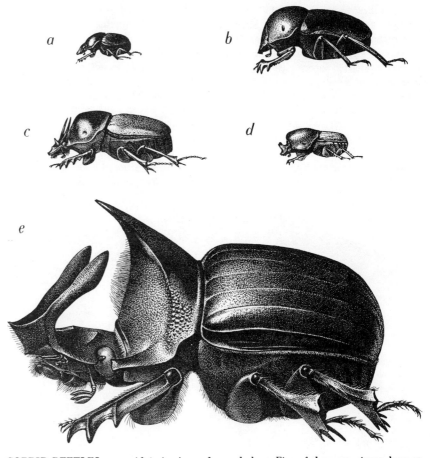

COPRID BEETLES vary widely in size and morphology. Five of them are shown here at the same scale, about twice natural size. *Onthophagus parvus* (a) is a native Australian beetle that does not utilize cattle dung. The others are bovine-dung beetles. *Garreta nitens* (b), recently introduced, is a ball-rolling species. *Onthophagus gazella* (c) and *Euoniticellus intermedius* (d) are the two tunneling species that have been most widely established. *Heliocopris gigas* (e) is a representative of a giant genus expected to resist attack by toads.

mandibles. The eggs of parasitic worms that were passed in the dung are seldom if ever found in the digestive tract of adult dung beetles, so that in spite of flying from pad to pad most species apparently play no part in dispersing the worms. On the contrary, the adult beetles are probably responsible for destroying many worm eggs as they grind their food to a paste.

In contrast to the adult food, the food of the beetle larvae consists of a paste of fine solids mixed with coarse particles. When a newly hatched larva begins to eat into the surrounding food ball, it enlarges the spherical space around itself, rotating as it consumes its food. Coprid larvae typically have a large hump, formed by the dilation of some of the abdominal segments, that encloses a coiled region of the digestive tract. This unusual adaptation makes it easier for the larva to move and feed within the confined space in which it is developing. The larvae are capable of sealing breaks in the wall of their dung balls with liquid feces. If they are removed from their

brood balls, they are unable to survive, and so they cannot attack plants or anything else of value to man.

One foreign dung beetle, *Onthophagus depressus* from South Africa, became established (apparently by accident) in Australia before 1900, but the first deliberate attempts to colonize coprids for man's benefit appear to have been made in Hawaii. A species from Mexico was introduced there in 1906 and a second from Germany in 1908, but they failed to become established. In 1923, however, three beetle species were successfully introduced into Hawaii from Mexico to aid in the control of the horn fly (*Haematobia irritans*), and success also attended the later introduction of an Afro-Asian species, *Onthophagus gazella*. Stockmen on the island of Hawaii say that the number of horn flies there has fallen markedly since dung beetles became abundant. In one experiment, when fresh pads were exposed to horn flies but protected against beetles, each pad produced hundreds of flies; pads not protected against beetles produced either a few stunted flies or none at all. The particular dung beetles concerned would colonize only pads dropped in open pastures, however, and not those dropped in the dense growth of mesquite, where the cattle sought shelter from the heat of the day. The flies that originate in the mesquite might yet be dealt with by beetles that are adapted to woodland and scrub.

Australia is plagued with the exceedingly abundant and pestiferous native

bush fly *Musca vetustissima* and the buffalo fly *Haematobia irritans exigua,* which was introduced from the Indonesian island of Timor. In experimental situations we have noted 80 to 100 percent reductions in bush-fly production when adult *O. gazella* beetles were allowed access to dung on which flies had deposited eggs. The beetles broke up and buried the cow pads within 30 to 40 hours, and a few surviving maggots matured as stunted flies that were in turn capable of laying very few eggs or

none at all. Neither fly eggs nor maggots were ever found in the dung balls; it is evident that they were discarded or destroyed by the beetles during the elaborate process of converting lumps of dung into brood balls. Almost complete control was also obtained in midsummer under natural field conditions near Pretoria in South Africa. It is relevant to note that *Musca vetustissima,* or at least a fly so similar that it produces fertile hybrids with its Australian relative, is found in South Africa. Whereas in Australia the

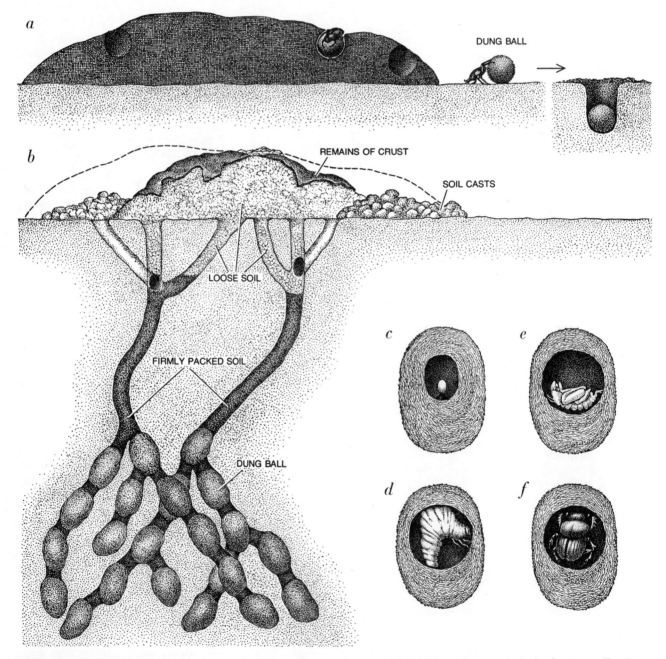

DUNG IS DISINTEGRATED in different ways by different dung beetles. One group, represented by such species as *Garreta nitens,* cuts bits of dung out of the pad, forms them into spherical balls and rolls the balls away to be buried in a shallow pit (*a*). Most species instead form their nests in a network of tunnels excavated below or adjacent to the pad (*b*). Working together, a male and female beetle dig a tunnel and carry dung down into it. The female

forms a ball (ovoid, in the case of *Onthophagus gazella,* shown here), lays an egg in it and closes the ball (*c*). As many as 40 balls are formed. The tunnels are backfilled with firmly packed soil; loose soil fills the upper parts of the tunnels and is left on the surface along with some remains of the dung pad. When the larva hatches (*d*), it feeds on the dung. After passing through the pupal stage (*e*) young adult (*f*) emerges and makes its way to surface.

abundant bush flies can make outdoor life in summer a misery for humans and domestic animals alike, in South Africa the flies are scarce and seldom a nuisance.

Flies are not the only pests affected. In both South Africa and Australia experiments on the transmission of common helminths, or intestinal worms, of cattle have shown that the activities of the beetles greatly reduce the number of infective larvae that reach the pasture from a dung pad. Pads attacked by beetles produced from 48 to 93 percent fewer worm larvae than intact pads.

Dramatic results have also been obtained in experiments designed to measure the effect of dung beetle activity on plant yield [*see bottom illustration on page 321*]. The coprids increase fertility primarily by dispersing the fertilizing dung through the soil. Other beneficial effects include an improvement in the permeability of soils to water. For example, five times as much water was required to produce waterlogging of a loamy soil worked by beetles as was required for undisturbed soil. There is also an improvement in soil structure, humus content and degree of aeration.

The decision was made in 1963 to begin establishing in Australia a range of beetles adequate to dispose of bovine dung pads in the most important locations and under the most prevalent conditions where cattle are raised. Two important questions had to be considered before the project could safely be undertaken. One was whether the candidate dung beetles themselves were likely to produce any adverse effects. What we knew about the feeding habits of both adults and larvae made it most unlikely that they would attack anything other than dung. Furthermore, there were no records indicating that the extremely abundant coprid fauna of Africa was causing any problems there.

The second problem was whether it would be possible to introduce a wide range of dung beetles without their being accompanied by any of the serious diseases of cattle, such as foot-and-mouth disease and rinderpest, that occur in Africa and some other places but not in Australia. Examination of the surfaces of adult beetles revealed that they do commonly carry many mites, that nematode worms shelter under the wing covers and that fungi and bacteria abound both on the cuticle, or tough outer surface, and in the excreta. The results of careful treatment with specific pesticides still did not give complete confidence that all fellow travelers could invariably

GARRETA NITENS is shown at work in these photographs made by John Green of the author's laboratory. First the beetle cuts a portion of dung out of a fresh cow pad (*top*). It shapes the dung into a ball (*middle*) and rolls ball away from pad to be buried (*bottom*).

be eliminated, and so an entirely different approach was adopted.

We found that we could transplant beetle eggs from the cavities in dung balls where they had been laid into "artificial" balls made of Australian dung, with a cavity simulating the one made by the female parent. The beetle eggs are removed from brood balls and carefully washed in a detergent solution to remove all adhering material. The clean eggs are then immersed for three minutes in a 3 percent solution of formalin, drained and thoroughly rinsed in sterile distilled water. This removes all reasonable doubts about security. Nevertheless, in our laboratory at Pretoria additional steps are taken to reduce the risk still further. The surface-sterilized eggs are transferred into moist, sterile peat moss in containers that have been sent in sealed packages from Australia. When the resealed packages are received in quarantine in Australia, artificial dung balls are prepared of a size, moisture content and consistency appropriate to the particular beetle species, an egg is transferred to each and the ball is sealed and then buried in moistened sandy soil. When one to three months later the resulting adults emerge (still in quarantine), they are allowed to mate and make their own dung balls. The eggs that subsequently hatch are surface-sterilized and are now considered clean enough to remove from the quarantine area so that mass rearing can be initiated. I have described this elaborate procedure in detail partly in the hope that it will discourage any enthusiast from attempting to import beetles without adequate precautions acceptable to quarantine authorities, a venture that might result in serious consequences for entire continents.

The first dung beetles were released in Australia in April, 1967. In the next three summers about 275,000 beetles of four species were liberated, mainly in tropical (northern) Australia. One species, *Onthophagus gazella,* has made spectacular progress [*see illustration below*]. Within two years it multiplied to countless millions and dispersed far and wide, colonizing 250 miles along the northern Queensland coast around Townsville, penetrating 50 miles inland and in the process closing the 50-mile gaps between the five individual release sites. During the first year it demonstrated its ability to make long-distance flights over water by colonizing Magnetic Island, four and a half miles off Townsville, and a year later it reached Palm Island, 18 miles off the coast.

In more recent years *O. gazella* has been distributed at many sites across the northern half of Australia and is reported to have built up into very large numbers in many places. In late 1973 it was found that colonizing had been successful on the east coast almost as far south as Newcastle.

In areas where *O. gazella* has become well established dung disposal is now almost complete for part of the year. Pads may disappear within 48 hours during a considerable portion of the wet summer period, which runs from January to April in the Townsville district, and partial disposal extends over another two months or so preceding and following this period. During the peak period of the beetle's activity the buffalo-fly nuisance was somewhat reduced for the first two seasons. There has not, however, been a prolonged, noticeable reduction in the number of flies in subsequent years. The buffalo fly becomes active early in the spring, before the temperature and soil moisture are high enough for *O. gazella* to begin disposing of pads; in the fall temperatures and moisture decrease enough to inhibit *O. gazella* activity several weeks before the flies cease to breed. Clearly additional species are required to complement *O. gazella* and provide more efficient dung burial over a wider range of seasonal conditions. This long-term need was recognized from the outset, since we had observed in Africa that many species colonize pads simultaneously and that the spectrum of species usually changes markedly with the season.

(The only complaint we have received about *O. gazella* has come from a cattle raiser who for years had used dried dung pads to level up the pipes he was using in the irrigation of his pastures. He complained that he now had to carry blocks of wood with him for the purpose!)

Two other African species, *Euoniticellus intermedius* and *E. africanus,* have increased spectacularly in northern New South Wales and southern Queensland little more than a year after their introduction. In irrigated pastures in the Narrabri district practically all dung pads are now eliminated rapidly and completely. *E. intermedius* has also increased to very large numbers in many areas where there is less rainfall, not only in central Queensland but also at places such as Broome and Wiluna in Western Australia. Already the economic returns, particularly in terms of the increased availability of pasture, must amount to hundreds of thousands of dollars a year.

In addition to the beetles I have mentioned, which are tunneling species, a number of ball-rolling species also hold great promise. One group of eight closely related species of the genus *Sisyphus* (aptly named for the miscreant in Greek mythology who was condemned to endlessly rolling a heavy stone uphill) has been studied closely in Zululand in South Africa, where all eight occur together. The fact that they are able to coexist indicates that each is adapted to

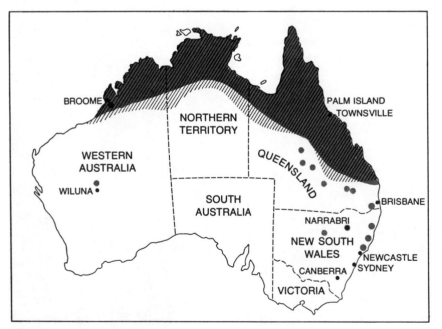

IMPORTED DUNG BEETLES were first released in Australia in 1967, primarily in the tropical northern regions afflicted by the buffalo fly (*hatching*). *Onthophagus gazella* has become particularly well established (*color*). *Euoniticellus intermedius,* released in generally cooler and drier regions (*gray*), has also increased to large numbers. Many more species are now being released that are adapted to varying climatic and other conditions.

EFFECT OF BEETLE ATTACK on a 1,000-milliliter dung pad (*left*) was observed near Pretoria in South Africa. After 24 hours less than 10 percent of the dung remained (*right*), mixed with loose soil excavated from tunnels in which dung had been buried.

EFFECT ON SOIL FERTILITY was demonstrated with Japanese millet. Six days before seed was sown a measured amount of dung and 20 pairs of dung beetles were put in the pot at left. The next pot had the same amount of dung but no beetles. Dung was placed in the third pot from left but removed before sowing. The control pot (*right*) received neither dung nor beetles. The plant with both dung and beetles took up much more nitrogen, phosphorus and sulfur than the others and its total yield was significantly greater.

utilizing either a different portion of the dung pad or pads found in particular situations in that environment. Since *Sisyphus* and other ball-rolling species obtain their dung preferentially from crevices in the pad or from around its base, they are likely to be of particular value in fly control, since these are the locations where pest flies most frequently lay their eggs.

A number of other countries where cattle are raised now but where there were no large native herbivores are also likely to benefit by the introduction of dung beetles. These include Papua New Guinea, New Zealand, various islands in the Pacific and the Atlantic, and perhaps North America, where both the horn fly and another dung-breeding cattle nuisance, the face fly, are prevalent. North America has a less diverse and less abundant dung-beetle fauna than might have been expected for the home of the bison and a region where many other large herbivores evolved. One hypothesis is that during the last ice age the herbivores that roamed the prairies were driven southward into regions where grasslands gave way to desert or jungle, and that many species became extinct along with their associated dung beetles. The precursor of the bison, according to this theory, later repopulated North America from Asia by means of a partially frozen land bridge across the Bering Strait—but left behind its associated beetles. Whether this sequence of events or some quite different one is responsible for the scarcity of North American coprids, the situation is now subject to change, and disease-free stocks of several dung-beetle species have already been supplied from Australia to the U.S.

Some attention has also been paid in Australia to another group of beetles that inhabit dung: the histerids. They do not eat dung, but both the adults and the larvae attack and voraciously consume fly maggots and pupae in the dung. Unfortunately the histerid species so far examined are not expert hunters, and only about 30 to 50 percent of the maggots in the cow pads are destroyed. Even this degree of destruction would be of value, however, and so five species have been introduced. Two of them, *Hister chinensis* and *H. nomas,* are known to be established.

The foregoing account may give the impression of a project that is complete except for the transfer of an adequate range of beetles to Australia. The ramifications of biological-control operations, however, are complex. Many new aspects are already known to require investigation and doubtless many more will emerge as the work proceeds.

One interesting question is whether or not it has been sensible to exclude from the consignments the mites that abound on the beetles in their native habitats. Carrion in the north of England is consumed competitively by blowfly maggots and carrion beetles of the genus *Necrophorus.* The beetles commonly provide transport for up to 30 mites, which appear to do the beetles no harm but which are known to attack and eat blowfly eggs and small maggots. When *Necrophorus* arrives at carrion, the mites immediately leave the beetles and move rapidly over the carcass in search of their blowfly food. If *Necrophorus* is deprived of its mites, it is unable to compete effectively with maggots for carrion. If the dung-burying activities of the introduced coprids do not reduce fly breeding to acceptable levels, it may be desirable to consider introducing some of the hundreds of species of predaceous mites that the beetles ordinarily carry with them.

A second problem requiring investigation relates to an apparent change in the behavior of the giant toad *Bufo marinus,* which was itself introduced via Hawaii in the 1930's to aid in the control of beetles that were damaging the roots of sugarcane in Queensland. (Opinion has been divided ever since on whether or not the toads provide any measure of control, although they appear to have reduced the abundance of many interesting and harmless native beetles. Certainly toads are often to be seen in summer sitting in a circle under streetlamps in coastal Queensland, waiting to consume insects attracted to the light.) Although these toads were not known to do so before, they are now observed to seek out the nearest fresh dung pad when they become active in the evening. With a flashlight one can spot them on or near a pad, swallowing *Onthophagus gazella* beetles as they land, and dissections show that a toad can consume as many as 80 beetles a night.

In order to deal with *B. marinus,* day-flying coprids are being sought, since such beetles should largely escape attack by the toads. Another possible countermeasure is the introduction of certain giant, heavily armored and immensely powerful dung beetles of the genus *Heliocopris.* Some are almost the size of a golf ball and cannot be retained in the closed hand, so powerful are the digging motions of their legs [see the illustration on this page]. They fly principally at dusk or dawn, when toads are active, and it seems likely that if a toad swallows one of these beetles whole (as is the toad's habit), the beetle would be strong enough to break out through the toad's body wall. (This has been observed to happen with a small Australian frog that swallowed the native *Onthophagus cuniculus.*) Even apart from their toad-proof potential, the 50-odd species of *Heliocopris* beetles in Africa are worth serious consideration. A single pair are capable of burying a dung pad overnight, fashioning from it brood balls as big as croquet balls.

I shall close with a sobering and yet somehow inspirational indication of the formidable disposal task that faces our growing force of dung-devouring immigrant beetles. During the 30 minutes you may have taken to read this article more than six million cattle dung pads have been deposited on the surface of Australia!

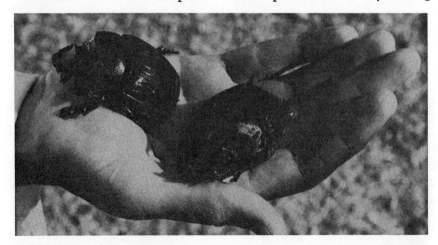

GIANT HELIOCOPRIS beetles are so large and strong that they cannot be retained in the closed hand. These are a male and a female *Heliocopris dilloni.* Such species are to be introduced from Africa into Australia in an effort to counter the effects of the toad *Bufo marinus,* which has begun to prey on the smaller imported beetles such as *Onthophagus gazella.*

BIBLIOGRAPHIES

I THE KEYS TO SUCCESS: ANATOMY AND PHYSIOLOGY

1. Insect Eggshells

THE STRUCTURE AND FUNCTION OF THE RESPIRATORY HORNS OF THE EGGS OF SOME FLIES. H. E. Hinton. In *Philosophical Transactions of the Royal Society of London: Series B*, Vol. 243, No. 699, pages 45–73; June 16, 1960.

PLASTRON RESPIRATION IN AQUATIC INSECTS. W. H. Thorpe. In *Biological Reviews of the Cambridge Philosophical Society*, Vol. 25, No. 3, pages 344–390; July, 1960.

RESPIRATORY SYSTEMS OF INSECT EGG SHELLS. H. E. Hinton. In *Annual Review of Entomology: Vol. XIV*, edited by Ray F. Smith and Thomas E. Mittler. Annual Reviews, 1969.

2. Insect Breathing

THE PRINCIPLES OF INSECT PHYSIOLOGY. V. B. Wigglesworth. Dutton, 1950.

3. The Flight of Locusts

FAT COMBUSTION AND METABOLIC RATE OF FLYING LOCUSTS. T. Weis-Fogh. In *Philosophical Transactions of the Royal Society of London: Series B*, Vol. 237, No. 640, pages 11–36; August 14, 1952.

THE HEAT OF ACTIVATION AND THE HEAT OF SHORTENING IN A MUSCLE TWITCH. A. V. Hill. In *Proceedings of the Royal Society, Series B:* Vol. 136, No. 883, pages 195–211; June 23, 1949.

THE INTRINSIC RANGE AND SPEED OF FLIGHT OF INSECTS. B. Hocking. In *Transactions of the Royal Entomological Society of London*, Vol. 104, Part 8, pages 223–345; October 23, 1953.

THE PHYSIOLOGICAL COST OF NEGATIVE WORK. B. C. Abbott, Brenda Bigland and J. M. Ritchie. In *Journal of Physiology*, Vol. 117, No. 3, pages 380–390; July 28, 1952.

4. The Flight Muscles of Insects

LOCOMOTION: FLIGHT. J. W. S. Pringle. In *The Physiology of Insecta: Vol. II*, edited by Morris Rockstein. Academic Press, 1965.

THE ORGANIZATION OF THE FLIGHT MUSCLE IN A DRAGONFLY, AESHNA SP. (ODONATA). David S. Smith. In *The Journal of Biophysical and Biochemical Cytology*, Vol. 11, No. 1, pages 119–145; October, 1961.

THE SARCOPLASMIC RETICULUM. Keith R. Porter and Clara Franzini-Armstrong. In *Scientific American*, Vol. 212, No. 3, pages 72–80; March, 1965.

5. Metamorphosis and Differentiation

THE PHYSIOLOGY OF INSECT METAMORPHOSIS. V. B. Wigglesworth. Cambridge University Press, 1954.

6. The Juvenile Hormone

INSECT METAMORPHOSIS. R. E. Snodgrass. Smithsonian Miscellaneous Collections, Vol. 122, No. 9; April, 1954.

THE JUVENILE HORMONE OF INSECTS. Carroll M. Williams. In *Nature*, Vol. 178, No. 4,526, pages 212–213; July 28, 1956.

Morphogenesis and the Metamorphosis of Insects. Carroll M. Williams. In *The Harvey Lectures,* Vol. 47, pages 126–155; 1953.

The Physiology of Insect Metamorphosis. V. B. Wigglesworth. Cambridge University Press, 1954.

7. The Biological Clock of Insects

Photoperiodism and Seasonal Development of Insects. A. S. Danilevskii. Oliver & Boyd, 1965.

The Physiological Clock: Endogenous Diurnal Rhythms and Biological Chronometry. Erwin Bünning. Springer Verlag, 1973.

The Photoperiodic Clock in the Flesh-fly, Sarcophaga argyrostoma. D. S. Saunders. In *Journal of Insect Physiology,* Vol. 19, No. 10, pages 1941–1954; October, 1973.

Circadian Oscillations in Cells and the Circadian Organization of Multicellular Systems. Colin S. Pittendrigh. In *The Neurosciences: Third Study Program,* edited by Francis O. Schmitt and Frederic G. Worden. MIT Press, 1974.

Evidence for 'Dawn' and 'Dusk' Oscillators in the Nasonia Photoperiodic Clock. D. S. Saunders. In *Journal of Insect Physiology,* Vol. 20, No. 1, pages 77–88; January, 1974.

Insect Clocks. D. S. Saunders. Pergamon Press, 1976.

8. The Sexual Life of a Mosquito

A Study of Mosquito Behavior. Louis M. Roth. In *The American Midland Naturalist,* Vol. 40, No. 2, pages 265–352; September, 1948.

A Study of Oviposition Activity of Mosquitoes. Robert Charles Wallis. In *American Journal of Hygiene,* Vol. 60, No. 2, pages 135–168; September, 1954.

II   THE KEYS TO SUCCESS: NEUROBIOLOGY AND BEHAVIOR

9. The Sex-Attractant Receptor of Moths

Chemicals Controlling Insect Behavior: Symposium of the American Chemical Society. Edited by M. Beroza. Academic Press, 1970.

Olfactory Receptors for the Sexual Attractant (Bombykol) of the Silk Moth. D. Schneider. In *The Neurosciences: Second Study Program,* edited by F. O. Schmitt. Rockefeller University Press, 1970.

Insect Olfaction. Karl-Ernst Kaissling. In *Handbook of Sensory Physiology: Vol. IV/1,* edited by L. M. Beidler. Springer Verlag, 1971.

Insect Sex Pheromones. M. Jacobson. Academic Press, 1972.

Gypsy Moth Control with the Sex Attractant Pheromone. M. Beroza and E. F. Knipling. In *Science,* Vol. 177, No. 4043, pages 19–27; July 7, 1972.

10. Pheromones

Olfactory Stimuli in Mammalian Reproduction. A. S. Parkes and H. M. Bruce. In *Science,* Vol. 134, No. 3485, pages 1049–1054; October, 1961.

Pheromones (Ectohormones) in Insects. Peter Karlson and Adolf Butenandt. In *Annual Review of Entomology,* Vol. 4, pages 39–58; 1959.

The Social Biology of Ants. Edward O. Wilson. In *Annual Review of Entomology,* Vol. 8, pages 345–368; 1963.

11. The Neurobiology of Cricket Song

The Role of the Central Nervous System in Orthoptera during the Coordination and Control of Stridulation. Franz Huber. In *Acoustic Behavior of Animals,* edited by R. G. Busnel. American Elsevier, 1964.

Intracellular Activity in Cricket Neurons during the Generation of Song Patterns. David Bentley. In *Zeitschrift für vergleichende Physiologie,* Vol. 62, pages 267–283; 1969.

Neuromuskulare Aktivitat bei Verschiedenen Verhaltensweisen von Drei Grillenarten. Wolfram Kutsch. In *Zeitschrift für vergleichende Physiologie,* Vol. 63, pages 335–378; 1969.

Postembryonic Development of Adult Motor Patterns in Crickets: A Neural Analysis. David R. Bentley and Ronald R. Hoy. In *Science,* Vol. 170, No. 3965, pages 1409–1411; December 25, 1970.

Genetic Control of an Insect Neuronal Network. David R. Bentley. In *Science,* Vol. 174, No. 4014, pages 1139–1141; December 10, 1971.

12. Brains and Cocoons

Cocoon Construction by the Cecropia Silkworm. William G. Van der Kloot and C. M. Williams. In *Behaviour,* Vol. 5, Parts 2 and 3, pages 141–174; and Vol. 6, Part 4, pages 233–255; 1953 and 1954.

13. Genetic Dissection of Behavior

BIOLOGY OF DROSOPHILA. Edited by M. Demerec. Hafner, 1965.

BEHAVIORAL MUTANTS OF DROSOPHILA ISOLATED BY COUNTERCURRENT DISTRIBUTION. Seymour Benzer. In *Proceedings of the National Academy of Sciences of the United States of America,* Vol. 58, No. 3, pages 1112–1119; September, 1967.

CLOCK MUTANTS OF DROSOPHILA MELANOGASTER. Ronald J. Konopka and Seymour Benzer. In *Proceedings of the National Academy of Sciences of the United States of America,* Vol. 68, No. 9, pages 2112–2116; September, 1971.

MAPPING OF BEHAVIOR IN DROSOPHILA MOSAICS. Yoshiki Hotta and Seymour Benzer. In *Nature,* Vol. 240, pages 527–535; December 29, 1972.

14. The Flight-Control System of the Locust

THE CENTRAL NERVOUS CONTROL OF FLIGHT IN A LOCUST. Donald M. Wilson. In *The Journal of Experimental Biology,* Vol. 38, No. 2, pages 471–490; June, 1961.

EXPLORATION OF NEURONAL MECHANISMS UNDERLYING BEHAVIOR IN INSECTS. Graham Hoyle. In *Neural Theory and Modeling: Proceedings of the 1962 Ojai Symposium,* edited by Richard F. Reiss. Stanford University Press, 1964.

15. Polarized-Light Navigation by Insects

THE DANCE LANGUAGE AND ORIENTATION OF BEES. Karl von Frisch, translated by Leigh E. Chadwick. Harvard University Press, 1967.

POLARIZATION SENSITIVITY IN INSECT EYES WITH FUSED RHABDOMS. R. Menzel. In *Photoreceptor Optics,* edited by A. W. Snyder and R. Menzel. Springer Verlag, 1975.

A FOVEA FOR E-VECTOR ORIENTATION IN THE EYE. P. Duelli. In *Journal of Comparative Physiology,* Vol. 102, No. 1, pages 43–56; 1975.

TWISTED AND NON-TWISTED RHABDOMS AND THEIR SIGNIFICANCE FOR POLARIZATION DETECTION IN THE BEE. R. Wehner, G. D. Bernard, and E. Geiger. In *Journal of Comparative Physiology,* Vol. 104, No. 3, pages 225–245; 1975.

16. Moths and Ultrasound

THE DETECTION AND EVASION OF BATS BY MOTHS. Kenneth D. Roeder and Asher E. Treat. In *American Scientist,* Vol. 49, No. 2, pages 135–148; June, 1961.

MOTH SOUNDS AND THE INSECT-CATCHING BEHAVIOR OF BATS. Dorothy C. Dunning and Kenneth D. Roeder. In *Science,* Vol. 147, No. 3654, pages 173–174; January 8, 1965.

NERVE CELLS AND INSECT BEHAVIOR. Kenneth D. Roeder. Harvard University Press, 1963.

III PROCESSES OF EVOLUTION AND ECOLOGY

17. Moths, Melanism, and Clean Air

ECOLOGICAL GENETICS. E. B. Ford. Wiley, 1964.

AN EXPERIMENTAL STUDY OF THE CLINE OF INDUSTRIAL MELANISM IN BISTON BETULARIA (L.) (LEPIDOPTERA) BETWEEN URBAN LIVERPOOL AND RURAL NORTH WALES. J. A. Bishop. In *Journal of Animal Ecology,* Vol. 41, pages 209–243; February, 1972.

THE EVOLUTION OF MELANISMS THE STUDY OF A RECURRING NECESSITY WITH SPECIAL INDUSTRIAL MELANISM IN THE LEPIDOPTERA. Bernard Kettlewell. Oxford University Press, 1973.

18. Defense by Color

ADAPTIVE COLORATION IN ANIMALS. Hugh B. Cott. Methuen, 1940.

SOCIAL BEHAVIOUR IN ANIMALS: WITH SPECIAL REFERENCE TO VERTEBRATES. N. Tinbergen. Wiley, 1953.

SOME EXPERIMENTS ON THE CAMOUFLAGE OF STICK CATERPILLARS. L. de Ruiter. In *Behaviour,* Vol. 4, Part 3, pages 222–232; 1952.

19. The Love Song of the Fruit Fly

STIMULI PROVIDED BY COURTSHIP OF MALE DROSOPHILA MELANOGASTER. H. C. Bennet-Clark and A. W. Ewing. In *Nature,* Vol. 215, No. 5101, pages 669–671; August 5, 1967.

THE WING MECHANISM INVOLVED IN THE COURTSHIP OF DROSOPHILA. H. C. Bennet-Clark and A. W. Ewing. In *The Journal of Experimental Biology,* Vol. 49, No. 1, pages 117–128; August, 1968.

THE COURTSHIP SONGS OF DROSOPHILA. Arthur W. Ewing and H. C. Bennet-Clark. In *Behaviour,* Vol. 31, Parts 2 and 3, pages 288–301; 1968.

20. The Aerial Migration of Insects

THE DISTRIBUTION OF INSECTS IN THE AIR AND THE EMPIRICAL RELATION OF DENSITY TO HEIGHT. C. G. Johnson. In *The Journal of Animal Ecology*, Vol. 26, pages 479–494; 1957.

INSECT MIGRATION. C. B. Williams. Collins, 1958.

PHYSIOLOGICAL FACTORS IN INSECT MIGRATION BY FLIGHT. C. G. Johnson. In *Nature*, Vol. 198, No. 4879, pages 423–427; May 4, 1963.

WEATHER AND THE MOVEMENTS OF LOCUST SWARMS: A NEW HYPOTHESIS. R. C. Rainey. In *Nature*, Vol. 168, No. 4286, pages 1057–1060; December 22, 1951.

21. Butterflies and Plants

BIRDS, BUTTERFLIES, AND PLANT POISONS: A STUDY IN ECOLOGICAL CHEMISTRY. Lincoln Pierson Brower and Jane Van Zandt Brower. In *Zoologica*, Vol. 49, No. 3, pages 137–159; 1964.

BUTTERFLIES AND PLANTS: A STUDY IN COEVOLUTION. Paul R. Ehrlich and Peter H. Raven. In *Evolution*, Vol. 18, No. 4, pages 586–608; January 28, 1965.

COEVOLUTION OF MUTUALISM BETWEEN ANTS AND ACACIAS IN CENTRAL AMERICA. Daniel H. Janzen. In *Evolution*, Vol. 20, No. 3, pages 249–275; 1966.

22. The Fungus Gardens of Insects

AMBROSIA FUNGI: EXTENT OF SPECIFICITY TO AMBROSIA BEETLES. Lekh R. Batra. In *Science*, Vol. 153, No. 3732, pages 193–195; July 8, 1966.

FUNGUS-GROWING ANTS. Neal A. Weber. In *Science*, Vol. 153, No. 3736, pages 587–604; August 5, 1966.

SYMBOISIS AND SIRICID WOODWASPS. E. A. Parkin. In *Annals of Applied Biology*, Vol. 29, No. 4, pages 268–274; August, 1942.

TERMITES: THEIR RECOGNITION AND CONTROL. W. Victor Harris. Longmans, Green, 1961.

TRAILS OF THE LEAFCUTTERS. John C. Moser. In *Natural History*, Vol. 76, No. 1, pages 32–35; January, 1967.

23. The Energetics of the Bumblebee

THE FERTILIZATION OF FLOWERS. Verne Grant. In *Scientific American*, Vol. 184, No. 6, pages 52–56; June, 1951.

BUMBLEBEES. John B. Free and Colin G. Butler. Macmillan, 1959.

TEMPERATURE REGULATION IN THE BUMBLEBEE BOMBUS VAGANS: A FIELD STUDY. Bernd Heinrich. In *Science*, Vol. 175, No. 4018, pages 185–187; January 14, 1972.

ENERGETICS OF TEMPERATURE REGULATION AND FORAGING IN A BUMBLEBEE, BOMBUS TERRICOLA KIRBY. Bernd Heinrich. In *Journal of Comparative Physiology*, Vol. 77, No. 1, pages 49–64; 1972.

ENERGETICS AND POLLINATION ECOLOGY. Bernd Heinrich and Peter H. Raven. In *Science*, Vol. 176, No. 4035, pages 597–602; May 12, 1972.

IV A DIVERSITY OF LIFE-STYLES

24. Fleas

FLEAS, FLUKES, AND CUCKOOS: A STUDY OF BIRD PARASITES. Miriam Rothschild and Theresa Clay. Collins, London, 1952.

PLAGUE. R. Pollitzer. World Health Organization, 1954.

THE RABBIT FLEA AND HORMONES. Miriam Rothschild. In *Endeavour*, Vol. 24, No. 93, pages 162–168; September, 1965.

25. Predatory Wasps

COMPARATIVE ETHOLOGY OF DIGGER WASPS OF THE GENUS BEMBIX. Howard E. Evans. Cornell University Press, 1957.

DAS VERHALTEN DER SOLITÄREN WESPEN MITTELEUROPAS: VESPIDAE, POMPILIDAE, SPHECIDAE. Günter Olberg. Deutcher Verlag der Wissenschaften, 1959.

WASP FARM. Howard E. Evans. The Natural History Press. In press.

26. Dialects in the Language of Bees

COMMUNICATION AMONG SOCIAL BEES. Martin Lindauer. Harvard University Press, 1961.

THE DANCING BEES. Karl von Frisch. Harcourt, Brace, 1955.

"SPRACHE" UND ORIENTIERUNG DER BIENEN. Karl von Frisch. Verlag Hans Huber, 1960.

27. The Social Behavior of Army Ants

BEHAVIORAL STUDIES OF ARMY ANTS. Carl W. Rettenmeyer. In *University of Kansas Science Bulletin*, Vol. 44, pages 281–465; September, 1963.

ARMY ANTS: A STUDY IN SOCIAL ORGANIZATION. T. C. Schneirla, edited by Howard Topoff. W. H. Freeman, 1971.

POLYMORPHISM IN ARMY ANTS RELATED TO DIVISION OF LABOR AND COLONY CYCLIC BEHAVIOR. Howard Topoff. In *The American Naturalist*, Vol. 105, No. 946, pages 529–548; November–December, 1971.

28. Slavery in Ants

SLAVE-RAIDS OF THE ANT POLYERGUS LUCIDUS MAYR. Mary Talbot. In *Psyche, Cambridge,* Vol. 74, No. 4, pages 299–313; 1967.

THE INSECT SOCIETIES. Edward O. Wilson. Belknap Press of Harvard University Press, 1971.

CHEMICAL COMMUNICATION AND "PROPAGANDA" IN SLAVE-MAKER ANTS. F. E. Regnier and E. O. Wilson. In *Science,* Vol. 172, No. 3980, pages 267–269; April 16, 1971.

LEPTOTHORAX DULOTICUS AND THE BEGINNINGS OF SLAVERY IN ANTS. E. O. Wilson. In *Evolution,* in press.

29. Communication Between Ants and Their Guests

THE SYSTEMATICS, EVOLUTION AND ZOOGEOGRAPHY OF STAPHYLINID BEETLES ASSOCIATED WITH ARMY ANTS (COLEOPTERA, STAPHYLINIDAE). Charles H. Seevers. In *Fieldiana: Zoology,* Vol. 47, No. 2, pages 139–351; March 22, 1965.

BEHAVIOR OF STAPHYLINIDAE ASSOCIATED WITH ARMY ANTS (FORMICIDAE: ECITONINI). Roger D. Akre and Carl W. Rettenmeyer. In *Journal of the Kansas Entomological Society,* Vol. 39, No. 4, pages 745–782; October, 1966.

CONTRIBUTION TO THE PHYSIOLOGY OF GUEST-HOST RELATIONS (MYRMECOPHILY) IN ANTS, II: THE RELATION BETWEEN THE IMAGOS OF ATEMELIES PUBICOLLIS AND FORMICA AND MYRMICA. B. Hölldobler. In *Zeitschrift für Vergleichende Physiologie,* Vol. 66, pages 215–250; 1970.

30. Air-Conditioned Termite Nests

DWELLERS IN DARKNESS. S. H. Skaife. Longmans, Green, 1956.

OUR ENEMY THE TERMITE. Thomas Elliott Snyder. Comstock, 1948.

TERMITES: THEIR RECOGNITION AND CONTROL. W. V. Harris. Longmans, Green, 1961.

V INSECTS AND MANKIND

31. Malaria

CHEMOTHERAPY OF MALARIA. Sir Gordon Covell, G. Robert Coatney, John W. Field and Jaswant Singh. World Health Organization.

EXPERT COMMITTEE ON MALARIA, SIXTH REPORT. WHO Technical Report Series, No. 123, 1957.

EXPERT COMMITTEE ON MALARIA, SEVENTH REPORT. WHO Technical Report Series, No. 162, 1959.

EXPERT COMMITTEE ON MALARIA, EIGHTH REPORT. WHO Technical Report Series, No. 205, 1961.

INSECTICIDE RESISTANCE IN ARTHROPODS. A. W. A. Brown. WHO Monograph Series, No. 38, 1958.

MAN'S MASTERY OF MALARIA. Paul F. Russell. Oxford University Press, 1955.

32. Insect Control and the Balance of Nature

THE RELATION OF FLIGHTS OF COLIAS TO LARVAL POPULATION DENSITY. Ray F. Smith, D. E. Bryan, and W. W. Allen. In *Ecology,* Vol. 30, No. 3, pages 288–297; July, 1949.

SOME NATURAL FACTORS LIMITING THE ABUNDANCE OF THE ALFALFA BUTTERFLY. A. E. Michelbacher and Ray F. Smith. In *Hilgardia,* Vol. 15, No. 4, pages 269–396; October, 1943.

33. Third-Generation Pesticides

THE EFFECTS OF JUVENILE HORMONE ANALOGUES ON THE EMBRYONIC DEVELOPMENT OF SILKWORMS. Lynn M. Riddiford and Carroll M. Williams. In *Proceedings of the National Academy of Sciences of the U.S.A.,* Vol. 57, No. 3, pages 595–601; March, 1967.

THE HORMONAL REGULATION OF GROWTH AND REPRODUCTION IN INSECTS. V. B. Wigglesworth. In *Advances in Insect Physiology: Vol. II,* edited by J. W. L. Bement, J. E. Treherne, and V. B. Wigglesworth. Academic Press, 1964.

SYNTHESIS OF A MATERIAL WITH HIGH JUVENILE HORMONE ACTIVITY. John H. Law, Ching Yuan, and Carroll M. Williams. In *Proceedings of the National Academy of Sciences of the U.S.A.,* Vol. 55, No. 3, pages 576–578; March, 1966.

34. The Eradication of the Screwworm Fly

A METHOD OF REARING COCHLIOMYIA AMERICANA C. AND P. ON ARTIFICIAL MEDIA. Roy Melvin and R. C. Bushland. U.S. Bureau of Entomology and Plant Quarantine, ET-88, 1933.

POSSIBILITIES OF INSECT CONTROL OR ERADICATION THROUGH THE USE OF SEXUALLY STERILE MALES.

E. F. Knipling. In *Journal of Economic Entomology*, Vol. 48, No. 4, pages 459–462; August, 1955.

SCREW-WORM CONTROL THROUGH RELEASE OF STERIL-IZED FLIES. A. H. Baumhover *et al.* In *Journal of Economic Entomology*, Vol. 48, No. 4, pages 462–466; August, 1955.

STERILE-MALE METHOD OF POPULATION CONTROL. E. F. Knipling. In *Science*, Vol. 130, No. 3,380, pages 902–204; October 9, 1959.

STERILIZATION OF SCREW-WORM FLIES WITH X-RAYS AND GAMMA RAYS. R. C. Bushland and D. E. Hopkins. In *Journal of Economic Entomology*, Vol. 46, No. 4, pages 648–656; August, 1953.

35. The Biological Control of Dung

COULD DUNG EATING INSECTS IMPROVE OUR PASTURES? G. F. Bornemissza. In *Journal of the Australian Institute of Agricultural Science*, Vol. 26, No. 1, pages 54–56; March, 1960.

THE NATURAL HISTORY OF DUNG BEETLES OF THE SUB-FAMILY SCARABAEINAE (COLEOPTERA, SCARABAE-IDAE). G. Halffter and E. G. Matthews. In *Folia Entomologica Mexicana*, Vol. 12; 1966.

BIOLOGICAL CONTROL OF PESTS AND WEEDS. D. F. Waterhouse and Frank Wilson. In *Science Journal*, Vol. 4, No. 12, pages 31–37; December, 1968.

A NEW TYPE OF BROOD CARE OBSERVED IN THE DUNG BEETLE ONITICELLUS CINCTUS (SCARABAEIDAE). G. F. Bornemissza. In *Pedobiologia*, Vol. 9, pages 223–225; 1969.

MYCETOPHAGOUS BREEDING IN THE AUSTRALIAN DUNG BEETLE, ONTHOPHAGUS DUNNINGI. G. F. Bornemissza. In *Pedobiologia*, Vol. 11, pages 133–142; 1971.

INDEX

Adam, Gerold, 88
Adaptation
    slave and master ant, 258–259
    survival by, 224–225, 229
    wasp to prey, 233
Adaptive Coloration in Animals, 173
Adenosine triphosphate (ATP), 44,
    45, 48
Adoption glands, 266
Adriaanse, Father Aloys, 238
Aedeagus, 10–11
Aedes, 286
Aenictus, 247, 251
Aerophyles, 22–29
Air, and water, 22–29
Air bubble, and egg respiration, 29
Airfoil, wings as, 35, 37–39
Akre, Roger D., 253
Alarm system of insects, 95, 97, 101
Alexander, Richard D., 110
Alkaloids, 197
All-or-nothing principle, 113–114
Amazon ants (*Polyergus*), 257
Ambrosia beetle, and fungi, 206
American cockroach sex attractant, 81
Amitermes evuncifer, 273, 275
Ammophila arremsis prey, 234
Amphotis marginata, 269
Anderson, J. R., 78
Anderson, T. F., 33
Anopheles, 286, 287
    DDT resistance of, 303
Ants, 263–270
    army, 249, 253–254
    colony odor, 267
    communication, 96–98
    fungus growing, 208
    glandular system 94–95, 97, 100
    larvae feeding, 263
    migratory, 190
    parasites of, 262
    social behavior, 247–256
    trail scent, 95, 96, 101, 249, 253–254
Aphid (*Apis fabre*) migration, 188,
    190–191, 192, 193
Aphilanthops frigidus, and queen ant,
    233–235
Aphilanthops haigi prey, 233

Aphilanthops sculleni prey, 233
Appeasement glands, 266–269
Aquatic insect respiration, 33–34
Arctiid clicks, 158
Aristophanes, 315
Aristotle, 34, 50
Army ants, 247–256
    chemical trails, 249, 253–254
Arthropoda, orders, 14
Askew, R. R., 164
Asphondylia cystisii, 203
Asteromyia, 203
Atemeles pubicollis, 263–270
Attractant, chemical, 81, 84–91, 93,
    94, 99
Auditory discrimination,
    echolocation, 157
Australian bushfly (*Musca vetustissima*)
    egg, 25
Autrum, Hansjochem, 146

Baikie, William Balfour, 284
Baker, Herbert, 211
Balsa-fir paper factor, 305
Bastock, Margaret, 118
Bat, and moth, 150–158
Baumover, A. H., 309
Beckman, Carolyn, 118
Bee
    dance, 96, 98–99, 241–246
    flight orientation, 140, 242, 246
    navigation, 148–149 (*see also*
        Honeybee)
Beetle, 4, 189–190, 315–322
    and ants, 263–270
    Collops, and alfalfa caterpillar, 297
    mimic, 270
Bee wolf wasp, (*Philanthus triangulum*)
    235, 237
Behavior
    communication, 92–101, 241–245
    and heredity, 80, 114–116, 118
    and neuronal network growth,
        105–107
    mating, 131
    mutant, 118–122
    and nerve cell, 114, 139
    and pheromones, 92–101

physiological control, 132
    ritualized, 266, 268
    social, 247–256, 263, 271–278
    sophisticated ant, 257
    survival, 150
    weaving, 114–116
Behavioral foci, 126–127
Bembex larvae, 239
Bembex pruinosa prey, 232, 236
Bequaert, Joseph C., 236
Bernard, Gary D., 146
Beroza, Morton, 90, 93, 94
Bilateral–submissive focus
    hypothesis, 128
Biller, B. A., 309
Biological control, 322
Biological indicator, 229
Bird flea, 225, 229
Bird memory, 176, 179
Blakers, Margaret, 147
Blastoderm genes, 124–128, 131
Blest, A. D., 176–177, 179
Blest, David, 158
Blindness, and genes, 122
Blood, and active respiration, 32
Blowfly (*Calliphora erythrocephala*)
    egg, 24
    tracheae and tracheoles, 31
Blum, Murray S., 249
Boettiger, Edward G., 41
Bohart, George, E., 238
Bombyx mori, 58–59, 84–91, 113–117
Bombykol, 84–91, 93, 94, 95, 99
Boophilus decoloratus, 252
Boot, L. M., 93
Bornemissza, G. F., 315
Bossert, William H., 94
Bounhiol, Jean, 58
Bowers, W. S., 305
Brain, 115, 116–117
Breathing, 6, 30 (*see also* Respiration)
Breeding techniques, fleas, 227,
    229–230
Brower, Lincoln P., 199
Bruce, Helen, 93
Bünning, Erwin, 64, 67, 70
Buffalo fly (*Haematobia irritans
    exigua*), 318

Bulldog ant, 147
Bumblebee (*Bombus vagans*), 211–217
  energy budget, 211
  individual color preferences, 213
Burkhalter, Res, 144
Bush fly (*Musca vetusissima*), 318
Bushland, R. C., 308
Butterfly
  Ascia monuste migration, 190, 193
  defenses, 198–199, 201
  egg respiration, 29
  families, 197
  food preferences, 197–198
Butenandt, Adolf F. J., 84, 93

Cactus moth, and prickly pear, 195
Camouflage, 173–179
Carbon dioxide
  respiration of, 32
  and termites, 273
Carpenter, Frank M., 4
Carson, Rachel, 281, 303
Caterpillar, 113
  Cossus, and oxygen, 32
  defenses, 174, 176, 179
  metamorphosis, 50–51
Cat flea, 225
Cecropia, 113–117, 304
Cell function, 113
Central-control hypothesis, 134
Central nervous system circuitry, 114
Cephalotermes rectangularis, 274, 275
Cerceris halone prey, 234, 235
Chambliss, O. L., 201
Chandrasekhar, S., 140
Chappell, J., 166
Chemical adaptability, 201
Chemical attractants, 81, 84–91
Chemical communication, 92–101, 247
  ant beetle, 263–270
  army ant trails, 247, 249, 253–254
  moth, 84–91
Chemopsychological warfare, 195, 196, 197
Chemoreceptors, 85–88, 94
Chlorinated hydrocarbons, and ecology, 281
Chromosomes
  cricket, 108–109
  fruit fly, 123–124
Cinchona, and malaria, 284
Circadian clocks, 63–70
Circadian rhythm
  fruit fly, 121–122
  mutant, 131
Civetone, 93, 99
Clarke, C. A., 169, 170, 171
Clock, internal, 104, 242
Clover, bumblebee and, 211
Clouded sulphur butterfly (*Colius philodice*) eggs, 200
Clidemia, and thrips, 195
Cockburn, A. J., 192
Cockroach (Blattodea) evolution, 4
Cockroach sex attractant, 81, 94, 99
Coitus interruptus, 118
Coleoptera evolution, 4
Collops, 297
Colorado potato beetle, proliferation, 296

Columella, 284
Communication
  army ant chemical trails, 247, 249, 253–254
  bee dance, 96, 98–99, 241–246
  and behavior, 92–101, 241–245
  chemical, 84–91, 92–101, 247, 249, 253–254, 259, 263–270
  social animal, 263
  songs, 101, 180–187
Command interneurons, 105, 110
Coordination patterns, 137, 139
Concealment, and color, 173–179
Copulation, flea, 229–230
Corpora pedunculata, 117
Corpus allatum, and metamorphosis, 53–55, 58
Cott, Hugh B., 173
Couch, John N., 203
Courtship, 131, 180–187
Creed, E. R., 167
Crematoxenus aenigma, 270
Cricket, 101–111
Crisp, D. J., 25
Crossocerus quadrimaculatus prey, 235
Culex, 286
Cuticle, exoskeleton advantages, 5–6

Dale, C. E. M., 171
Damselfly (*Enallagma*) flight muscle, 41–42, 43, 45–46
Dance, honeybee, 96, 98–99, 241–246
Darwin, Charles, 211, 258
Defense mechanisms, 10
Delbrück, Max, 88
Dendrite, silk moth antennae, 86
Deoxyribonucleic acid (DNA), 118
Desert ant (*Cataglyphis bicolor*), navigation, 143–144
Dethier, Vincent G., 197
Diamond back moth (*Plutella maculipennis*) migration, 189, 191
Diapause, 63, 64
Differentiation, 50–56
Digger wasp (*Aphilanthops laticinctus*) prey, 232, 233
DDT, 296, 301
  deficiencies, 301–302
  and ecology, 281
  malaria control, 287, 288
Discrimination, auditory, 157
Disease carriers, 71, 302, 314
Disparlure (gyplure), 81, 90, 91, 93–94, 95, 99
Displodia, 203
Diversity, 2, 219–220
Diving bell insect, 34
Dobzhansky, Theodosius, 186
Dorylus, 247
Dorylus nigricoms, 270
Dragonfly, 4, 8
Dragonfly (*Libellula pulchella*) migration, 189, 190, 193
Drosophila, 25–26, 118–131, 180–187, 312
Drosophila melanogaster, 118–122, 125–126, 129–130, 131
Drugs, anti-malaria, 284, 292
Dubowitz, V., 129
Duckett, J. G., 167

Duelli, Peter, 144
Dufour's gland, 95, 97, 100–101, 261
Dujardin, Felix, 117
Dung, 315–316, 319–322
  eggs in, 26, 28, 317
Dung beetle, 315–322

Ears, moth, 150, 152
Echolocation, 150–158
Eciton chemical trail, 253
Eciton burchelli, 247, 249, 251
Eciton hamatum, 248, 249, 251
Ecology, 2, 315
  dung beetle, 315–322
  insect control, 296–301
  malaria, 284
Ectohormones, 92
Edleston, R. S., 166
Edrich, Wolfgang, 144
Edwards, John, 111
Ege, Richard, 34
Eggs, 22–29
  army ant, 248
  clouded sulphur butterfly, 200
  desert locust, 193
  mosquito delivery system, 78
  mud dauber, 238
Electroantennogram, 87
Elm bark beetle, 189, 190
Emery, Carlo, 257, 258
Emery's rule, 258
Endocrine gland of insects, 92–93, 100
Energy
  bumblebee requirement, 211–217
  flight energetics, 35, 37–40
  migration needs, 192
Entomology, pest control and, 300
Environment and organisms, 92 (see also Ecology)
Ernst, K. D., 88
Escherichia coli, nervous system, 118
Euoniticellus africanus, 320
Euoniticellus intermedius, 317, 320
European water scorpion (*Nepa rubra*) horned egg, 28
Evolution, 2–5, 263–270
  bee, 246
  bumblebee, 211–217
  cyclic AMP, 264
  fleas, 223–225
  flight, 41
  prey-carrying wasp, 239
Exaltolide, 101
Exley, D., 229
Exocrine glands of ant, 95
Exoskeleton, 5–6
Experience, extraproprioceptive feedback, 139
Eye
  Drosophila melanogaster, 129–130
  and polarized light, 144–149
Eye spot display, 176–177

Fabre, Jean Henri, 84, 94, 235, 237, 315
Fate map, 126–130
Feedback, silkworm loop, 117
Feeding, mouthpart diversity and, 12
Filariasis, and mosquito, 286
Flatt, Immanuel, 144

Flea, 224–231
  host-finding by, 225–226
  jumping technique, 224, 225
Flight, 8–10, 37
  damselfly muscle, 41–42, 43, 45–46
  energetics, 35, 37–40
  fuel, 36, 39–40
  honeybee orientation, 242, 246
  mechanism, 41, 49
Flower, bee and, 211
Fly (Fannia armata), 25, 27
Food
  army ant, 247, 249
  dung beetle, 317, 319, 322
Forel, August, 84
Formica, 259, 261
Formica fusca, 257, 258–259, 260
  wasp and queen, 233, 235
Fossil flea, 223
Fraenkel, Gottfried, 32–33
Frankie, Gordon W., 211
French, R. A., 192
Frisch, Karl von, 140, 162
Frit fly (Oscinella frit), 189, 193
Fruit fly (Drosophila)
  clock, internal, 121–122
  courtship, 180–187
  egg respiration, 25–26
  learning, 131
  sterility control program, 312
Fruit fly (Geotaxis), 118–119
Fungus gardens, 203–210, 271, 273–274

Galls, and fungi, 203
Gallup, Belinda, 129
Garcia-Bellido, Antonio, 126
Garnham, P. C. C., 286
Garreta nitens, 317, 318–319
Gaskell, Elizabeth, 165, 166
Geiger, Esther, 146
Genetics, 122, 124–128, 131
  cricket song, 101, 109
  defense, 301
  hybrid cricket, 107–110
  isolation mechanism, 181–187
  mutations, 127–129, 131
  selective pressures, 51–56
Genital, flea, 230
Giant toad (Bufo marinus), 322
Gilbert, Lawrence I., 54, 61, 303
Gill, Kulbir, 118
Gillett, J. D., 78
Gills, 34
Gland secretion
  ant trail scent, 97–98
  bombykol, 86
  honeybee, 99
Goldsmid, J., 252
Goldsmith, Timothy H., 142
Goro, F. W., 119
Gotwald, William H., 247
Gouras, Peter, 122
Graham, A. J., 310
Grasshopper
  air movement in, 32–33
  metamorphosis, 52
Grassé, Pierre-Paul, 271
Grassi, Giovanni Battista, 286
Green, John, 319
Gribakin, F. G., 146

Griffin, Donald R., 157
Grimstone, A. V., 227, 230
Growth, and juvenile hormone, 57–62
Growth processes, 50–56
Günther, Kurt, 230
Gyplure (disparlure), 81, 93–94, 95, 99

Haddon, A. J., 78
Haeckel, Ernst, 211
Haeger, James S., 190
Haldane, J. B. S., 2, 96
Hall, Jeffry C., 118, 130–131
Hall, Linda, 130–131
Hansen, Thomas E., 129
Hanson, Jean, 44
Harkness, Edward S., 314
Harpagoxenus americanus, 261
Harper, P., 164
Harris, William A., 131
Harvey, William, 50, 51
Hearing, moth, 150, 152
Heisenberg, Martin, 122
Heliocopris gigas, 317, 322
Helversen, Otto von, 144
Herrling, Paul L., 147
Hippocrates, 284
Hirsch, Jerry, 118
Hister chinensis, 322
Hister nomas, 322
Holland, George P., 230
Holst, Erich von, 176
"Homunculi", 51
Honeybee (Apis mellifera)
  dance, 96, 98–99, 241–245
  flight orientation, 140, 242, 246
  microclimates, 271
  pheromones, 99, 100
  sting, 99
Hopkins, D. E., 308
Hormones, 226–231, 304
  adrenocorticotrophic, 227
  analogues, 305
  diapause, 64
  insect control, 301–305
  juvenile, 303–304
  progestins, 227
  somatropin, 229–230
Horn fly (Haematobia irritans), 317, 322
"Horse guard" wasp, 236
Horsfall, William R., 78
Hotta, Yushiki, 122, 125–127, 130
Housefly
  metamorphosis, 51
  sterility studies, 312
Hoy, Ronald, 131
Hoyle, Graham, 137, 139
Huber, Franz, 102
Huber, Pierre, 259
Human flea (Pulex iriitans), 321
Humidity termite nest, 271
Hummingbird hawk moth (Macroglossa stellaterum) migration, 189
Huxley, H. E., 44, 47
Huxley, Julian, 84
Hybrid, 107–110, 118–131
Hydrostatic pressure, and eggs, 25–26
Hymenoptera, 233
Hyperkinetic fruit fly, 118, 125–126

Image, sonic, 157

Indian water bug (Lethocerus indicus)
  egg, 23
Information processing, bee, 241–245
Insecticides, 281, 296, 301–303
  control of malaria, 287–289
  resistance to, 291
  and tracheal systems, 30
Ionized radiation, sterilization by, 307–311

Jacobson, Martin, 93, 94
Jensen, Martin, 35, 38–39
Jewell, B. R., 49
Jones, C. M., 201
Jones, William, 93
Jordan, Karl, 230
Judd, Burke H., 121
Judson, Charles L., 78
Juvenile hormone
  and corpus allatum, 53–55, 58
  Cecropia moth, 304
  and metamorphosis, 57–62

Kafka, W. A., 85
Kaissling, K.-E., 85
Kammer, Ann E., 214
Kankel, Douglas R., 130–131
Kaplan, William D., 118, 126
Kasang, K., 85
Kazuo, Okeda, 126
Kennedy, J. D., 188
Kennedy, J. S., 192
Kettlewell, H. B. D., 164, 169
Kirshfeld, Kuno, 146
Kölliker, Anton, 43–44
Kolb, Gertrud, 146
Konopka, Ronald, 121, 131
Kramer, E., 85
Krogh, August, 32, 35, 214
Kutsch, Wolfram, 102

Labidus praedator, 270
Ladybird beetle (Adalia bipunctata), melanics of, 172
Ladybird beetle (Hypodamia convergens) migration, 189, 193
Lang, Herbert, 240
Lange, R., 91
Larra analis prey, 234
Larvae
  army ant, 248, 249
  cannibal beetle, 263–265
  dung beetle, 317–319, 322
  flea, 224, 229
  puss moth, 173
  wasp, 233, 239
Laveran, Charles, 284
Law, John H., 305
Lawson, Katherine, 253
Learning, Drosophila, 131
Lee, S. van der, 93
Lee–Boot effect, 93
Lees, D. R., 167
Le Magnen, J., 101
Leptothorax curvispinosus, 257, 259, 262
Leptothorax duloticus, 257, 258, 262
Lesser, F. Ch., 84
Lewis, Edward B., 122
Lewis, Trevor, 192
Light, polarized, 140–149

Lindauer, Martin, 148, 242, 246
Lindenius columbianus errans, 235
Lindquist, A. W., 307
Liris nigra sting technique, 237
Locust, 35–40, 132–139
    pheromones, 92–93, 98
    Schistocerca gragaria migration, 188,
        189, 190, 191, 192, 193
Lomechusa, 265, 267
Long-horned grasshopper (*Plagiostira
    gilletti*) egg, 24
Lorenz, Konrad, 162

Macrotermes natalensis, 274, 275, 278
Malaria
    Anophiles, 287
    control, 284–295, 303
    historical extent, 284
    simian, 293
    total eradication program, 291–292
Malpighi, Marcello, 30
Manning, A. W. G., 181
Marine insects, 12, 33
Mating
    behavior, 131
    cricket song, 107–108
Mead-Briggs, Antony R., 225
Medical entomology, 281–282
Megarrhyssa macrura, ovipositor, 236
Meillon, Botha de, 287
Melanism, and natural selection,
    164–172
Menzel, Randolf, 146, 147
Merriam, John R., 121, 126
Metabolism, 30, 32
    humidity control, 271, 274
    locust, 40
    mitochondria, 45–46
Metamorphosis, 6–8, 50–56
    cockroach wing, 4
    juvenile hormone, 57–62
Microcerotermes edentalus, 206–207,
    273, 274
Microclimate maintainance, 271–278
Midge (*Itonididae*), 203
Migration, 188–194
    army ant cycle, 249, 251
    myrmecophiles, 265–267
Mimanomma spectrum, 270
Mimeciton antennotum, 270
Mimetic beetle, 270
Mimetic butterfly, 201
Mites
    carriers, 322
    increased population, 296
Mitochondia, and metabolic demand,
    45–46
Mosaic fruit fly, 123–125
Mole flea (*Hystrichopsylla talpae*), 230
Molting, 6–8
Monarch butterfly (*Danaus plezipus*),
    192, 193, 194
Morphogenetic fields, and
    differentiation, 55–56
Möss, Dieter, 102
Moser, John C., 208, 209
Mosquin, Theodore, 211
Mosquito
    Aedes taeniorhynchus migration, 189,
        190, 192

breeding places, 287
and disease, 71, 284
respiration, 33, 34
sex life, 71–78
sterility control studies, 312
Mostler, Georg, 176
Moth
    Bombyx mori, 58–59, 84–91, 113–117
    Cecropia, 113–117, 304
    ear, 150
    egg, 23
    evasion tactic, 150–158
    flight pattern, 156–157
    noise maker, 158
    pheromones, 84–91, 93–94, 95, 99
    Semiothisa signaria, 23
    sonic image, 157
Motor system, pattern generators,
    137–139
Mound-building ant (*Pogonomyrmex
    occidentalis*), and wasp, 233
Mouth part, diversity, 12
Mühlman, Hans, 176
Muggleton, J., 164
Muller, H. J., 307, 308
Murphey, Rodney K., 110, 112
Muscle
    ATP energy in, 44, 48
    flight, 35, 39–40, 41–49
Muscular dystrophy, 129
Muskone, 93, 99
Mutalism, 203–210
Mutant
    behavior, 118–122
    brain deterioration, 128
    cricket, 110–111
    genetic, 127–128, 131
Mutual excitation, 137
Myrmedonia, 267
Myrmecophile, 263–270
Myxomatosis, flea and, 223–224

Natural selection
    and atmospheric pollution, 164–172
    mechanics, 211
    and pesticides, 281
    and protective pattern, 179
Navigation, and polarized light,
    140–149
Nectar availability, 212–213
Neivamyrmex melanocephalum, 270
Neivamyrmex nigresians, 248, 249, 255
Nemotode worms, and dung beetle, 319
Nervous system
    and behavior, 105–107, 114, 139
    cells, 101, 113, 139
    cricket, 101–103
    Drosophila melanogaster, 118, 125–126
    firing patterns, 113–114
    respiration center, 33
    silkworm, 116
Nest
    fungus in, 204
    mud dauber, 238
    Priomonyx, 238
    termite, 271–278
Neurons, 103–104, 110
Nicholson, A. J., 34
Nielsen, E. T., 190
Noirot, Charles, 271

Nutrients, and genetics, 51–56
Nye, William P., 238

Oak silkworm (*Anthera perryi*) egg, 23
Ochleroptera bipunctata prey, 235
Odor
    attractant, 84–85
    human physiology, 101
    insect behavior, 93, 94, 95–96, 99
    molecule, 90
    silk moth, 84–91
Ommatidum, role in navigation,
    144–147
Onthophagus depressus, 317
Onthophagus gazella, 317, 318, 320, 322
Onthophagus parvus, 317
Opler, Paul, 311
Orange alfalfa caterpillar butterfly
    (*Colias philodice eurytheme*), 296
Orientation
    honeybee, 242, 246
    sun, 148–149, 242, 246
Otto, Ditmar, 102
Oxygen
    availability, termite nest, 273
    diffusion, 32
    and eggs, 22–29

Palarus variegatus, 237
Pale brindled beauty moth (*Phigalia
    pilosaria*), melanics of, 169–170
Palka, John M., 111
Pak, William L., 122
Paper factor, 305
Parasite
    genesis, 223
    hazards, 223–224
    host-finding, 225–226
    relationship, 263–270
    slavery, 257–262
Park, Mungo, 284
Park-Ross, G. A., 287
Pathogen, 299
Paul, Robert, 109
Payne, Roger, 155, 158
Peace, The, 315
Peppered moth (*Biston betularia*),
    164–172, 178
Peripheral-control hypothesis, 132–134
Pest control
    and juvenile hormone, 57–62
    sex lure for, 91
Pesticides, 301–305
    ecology, 281
    resistance to, 301, 303
Pheromones, 92–101, 229, 231
    chemistry, 84
    mice, 93, 98
    receptor antennae, 84–91
Philanthus pacificus prey, 235
Photoperiodic clock, and metabolism,
    63–70
Physiological change, and behavior,
    252–255
Physiological inhibitors, 92
Picture, sonic, 157
Piezodorus lituratus egg, 23
Pittendrigh, Colin S., 67, 68, 121
Plague, insect borne, 303
Plant chemicals, and herbivores, 195

Plasmodium, 284
  Cynomolgi bastianellii, and
      Anopheles, 293
  life cycle, 286, 288–289
Plastron, 22–29
Pogonomyrmex, 233
Poisson curve, 86–87, 91
Pollution, and natural selection,
      164–172
Polyergus rufescens, 257, 258–259
Polymorphism
  army ant, 248
  external influence, 53
  melanic, 164–172
  and migration, 194
Population
  density, 2
  pheromone control, 93
  termite mound, 276
Posture, and proprioceptive
      feedback, 134
Poulson, Donald F., 126
"Predatoid" wasp, 233
Predator wasp, 233–240
Prey-carrying wasp, 238–239
Preying mantid as prey, 239
Priesner, E., 85
Pringle, J. S., 41, 49
Prolactin, 93
Propeller, wing as, 35, 37
Proprioceptive
  feedback, 133–135
  reflexes, 137, 139
Protective marking, 173–179
Provost, Maurice W., 190
Pulex irritans, 231
Pupae
  caterpillar, 113
  juvenile hormone, 57
  slave ant, 257–258
Puss moth (Cerura vinula), egg
      respiration, 26
Puss moth (Dicranure binula),
      larva, 173
Pye, David, 158
Pyrethrum, and malaria control, 287
Pyrrhocoris apterus, and paper factor,
      304–305

Queen ant
  army ant, 248
  and fungi, 208
  and wasp, 233, 235
Queen termite, 206–207, 273, 274
Quinine, and malaria, 284
Quinn, William G., Jr., 131

Rabbit flea (Spilopsyllus scuniculi
      Dale), 223–231
Rahm, Urs, 271
Rainey, R. C., 188
Ramskou, Thorkild, 141
Rat flea, 224–225, 231
Rathmayer, Werner, 237
Rat-tailed maggot snorkel, 34
Rayleigh, Lord, 140
Ready, Donald F., 129, 130
Réaumur, René, 84
Reflexes, 132–137
Regnier, Fred E., 259

Releaser effect of pheromone, 92–93, 94
Remington, Charles L., 202
Renner, Max, 244
Reproduction, 10–11
  alfalfa caterpillar, cycle, 298
  army ant, 248
  and chemical order, 92, 93
  flea, 226–231
  yellow-fever mosquito, 71–78
Research techniques
  cricket song, 103, 109–110
  fruit fly, 122–125
  locust flight, 132–139
  silk moth olfactory system, 85–87
Respiration
  egg, 22–29
  marine insect, 33
  muscle requirement, 45–46
  passive, 32
  tracheal system, 30
Research, chimera problem, 111
Resonant system and wing beat, 136
Rettenmeyer, Carl W., 248
Reuter, O. M., 233
Rhabdomes, twisted, 146–147
Rhodopsin, and polarized light,
      142–143
Richards, A. G., 33
Riddiford, Lynn M., 304
Roeder, Kenneth D., 41
Röller, Herbert, 304
Roelofs, Wendell L., 91
Romanuk, M., 305
Rosenhof, August, 84
Ross, Ronald, 286, 290
Rossel, Samuel, 148
Roth, Louis M., 74
Rüegg, J. C., 49
Ruiter, Leen de, 174, 179
Runner, G. A., 307

Sacculi laterales, in Bombyx, 86
Sarcoplasmic reticulum, 47–49
Scalloped hazel moth (Gonodonlis
      bidentia), melanics of, 168–170
Scarab beetle (Scarabaeus sacer),
      314, 315
Scavenger wasp (Microbembex), 235
Schistocerca gregaria, 35
Schneiderman, Howard A., 54, 61, 303
Schneirla, T. C., 247, 249, 251
Schönherr, H., 91
Schwarz, F., 91
Schwinck, Ilse, 94
Sclerotium asteris, 203
Scolytus multistiatus, 189, 190
Scorpion fly (Panorapa amomala) egg
      respiration, 25
Screwworm fly
  controlled, 306–313
  life cycle, 306–307
Seevers, Charles H., 270
Sekera, Zdenek, 140
Sense organ, moth ear, 150, 152
Sensillum, 88
Sensory system, feedback loops, 137
Septo basidium, and coccidae, 203, 204
Sex attractant, 94, 96, 97
  bombykol, 84–91, 93–95, 99
  chemistry, 81, 99, 100

Shelter, fungus-supplied, 204
Sheppard, P. M., 169, 170, 171
Shivering, 214
Shorey, H. H., 91
Shortt, H. E., 286
Sickle cell anemia, 301
Sickle dance, Italian bee, 242
Siddiqi, Obaid, 121
Signal
  discrimination, 115, 116–117
  insect chemical, 95–98, 101
  moth, 84
  sonic, 150–158
Silent Spring, 281, 303
Silkworm (Bombyx mori), 84–91
Silkworm (Cecropia), 57, 60–62,
      113–117
Silverfish (Thysanura), 4
Simian malaria, and man, 293
Sisyphus, 320, 322
Size, ecologic advantage of, 4
Skertchly, S. B. J., 192
Sláma, Karel, 304
Slave ants and masters, 257–262
Snyder, Allen W., 146
Social behavior, army ant, 247–256
Socialization, 263
Soil fertility, and dung beetle, 319, 321
Solavalta, O., 41
Soldier ant, 248
Sonar, 150–158
Southwood, T. R. E., 193
Souvenirs Entomologiques, 84
Species integrity, 11–12
Sphecidae, 234
Sphecius speciosus prey, 234
Sphex ichneumones prey, 235
Spider walking patterns, 137, 139
Spielman, Andrew, 75
Spilopsyllus cuniculi Dale, 223
Sporozoites of malaria, life cycle,
      286–287
Steinbrecht, R. A., 85
Steiner, André, 237
Step, Edward, 247
Sterilization
  control by, 306–313
  ionized radiation, 307–311
Stick insect proprioceptors, 134
Stimuli, chemical, 98, 101
Sting technique, predator wasp, 237
Stone fly (Pteronarcys dorsata) egg,
      28–29
Stout, John, 109
Strictia carolina prey, 234, 236
Strongylognathus testaceus queen,
      261–262
Stuck mutant, 118
Sturtevant, A. H., 126
Sturt unit, 126–127
Sun orientation, 242, 246
Sunstone, 140–141
Survival mechanisms, 158
Suzuki, David, 121, 130–131
Swammerdam, Jan, 50, 51
Symbiosis, 203–210

Talbot, Mary, 261
Tarantula locomotion, 137, 139
Teleogryllus commodus, 106–108

Teleogryllus oceanicus, 105, 107–108
Temperature cycles, and diapause, 65,
  67–68
Termites
  and fungi, 206–208
  migratory, 190, 192
  pheromones, 92, 94
Territoriality, and pheromones, 93,
  96, 97
Thoracotermes macrothorax nest, 272,
  273, 275
Thorpe, W. H., 25
Thorsteinson, A. J., 198
Tinbergen, Nikolaas, 235
Torgerson, Richard, 253
Tracheae, 6, 34
Tracheaters, 30
Tracheolar system, 48
Trap, flea, 231
Treat, Asher E., 150
Tribolite eye, 141
Trigonia bee dance, 246
Tritium isotope, 85
Tsetse fly, sterility-control studies, 312
Twig caterpillar, 174–175, 179
Tympanic nerve of moth, 152–153
Tyshchenko, V. P., 67

Ultra sound, 150–158
Ultraviolet receptors, 144–148

Varro, 284
Ventilation, termite nest, 276–278
Verrill, A. Hyatt, 247

Verschaeffelt, E., 198
Vertebrates, muscle reflex, 134
Viking navigation, 140–141
Vision
  army ant, 249
  trichromatic bee, 149
Visual-cell orientation, 144
Vogt, Karl, 211

Waggle dance of bee, 96, 98–99, 241
Walker, Thomas J., 109
Wallis, Robert C., 78
Wallman, Joshua, 155, 157
Waloff, Z. V., 188
Warfare, chemical, 259
Wasp, 8, 9–10
  and alfalfa caterpillar, 297, 299
  habitats, 235–236
  Polistes flight muscle, 43
  prey specialization, 237
  Pterocormus instatilis, 299
  Trichogramma minutum, 297
Waste, 8
Water
  and air, 22–29
  and eggs, 22–29
  mosquito preferences, 78
Waterman, Talbot H., 141–142
Watkins, Julian F., II, 248, 249
Webster, Frederic, 151, 157
Weiler, Reto, 144
Weis-Fogh, Torkel, 82, 134
Wendler, Gernot, 134

Wheeler, William Morton, 236,
  257, 267
White, J. H., 192
Whitten, W. K., 93
Wigglesworth, Vincent, 34, 57, 64,
  225, 282
Williams, C. B., 2
Williams, Carroll M., 114, 202,
  281, 282
Wilson, Donald M., 102
Wilt disease, and alfalfa caterpillar, 297
Windecker, Wilhelm, 176
Wind tunnel, and locusts, 35–39
Wing, 8–10
  evolution, 4, 41
  movement, 35, 37
Wingbeat, 41
  Drosophila, 182–183
  locust, 37
  moth and bat, 156
Wood ant (*Formica polyctena*), 263–265
Wood ant (*Lasius fuliginosus*), 269
World Health Organization (WHO)
  malaria program, 293–295

Xenopsylla cheopis, 231

Yamamoto, Robert T., 94
Yellow-fever mosquito (*Aedes
  aegypti*), 71
Yellow underwing moth, melanic, 171

Zaretsky, Malcom, 109
Zeve, Victor H., 73